Information Assurance

The Morgan Kaufmann Series in Networking
Series Editor, David Clark, M.I.T.

Information Assurance: Dependability and Security in Networked Systems
Yi Qian, James Joshi, David Tipper, and Prashant Krishnamurthy

Network Analysis, Architecture, and Design, Third Edition
James D. McCabe

Wireless Communications & Networking: An Introduction
Vijay K. Garg

Ethernet Networking for the Small Office and Professional Home Office
Jan L. Harrington

IPv6 Advanced Protocols Implementation
Qing Li, Tatuya Jinmei, and Keiichi Shima

Computer Networks: A Systems Approach, Fourth Edition
Larry L. Peterson and Bruce S. Davie

Network Routing: Algorithms, Protocols, and Architectures
Deepankar Medhi and Karthikeyan Ramaswami

Deploying IP and MPLS QoS for Multiservice Networks: Theory and Practice
John Evans and Clarence Filsfils

Traffic Engineering and QoS Optimization of Integrated Voice & Data Networks
Gerald R. Ash

IPv6 Core Protocols Implementation
Qing Li, Tatuya Jinmei, and Keiichi Shima

Smart Phone and Next-Generation Mobile Computing
Pei Zheng and Lionel Ni

GMPLS: Architecture and Applications
Adrian Farrel and Igor Bryskin

Network Security: A Practical Approach
Jan L. Harrington

Content Networking: Architecture, Protocols, and Practice
Markus Hofmann and Leland R. Beaumont

Network Algorithmics: An Interdisciplinary Approach to Designing Fast Networked Devices
George Varghese

Network Recovery: Protection and Restoration of Optical, SONET-SDH, IP, and MPLS
Jean Philippe Vasseur, Mario Pickavet, and Piet Demeester

Routing, Flow, and Capacity Design in Communication and Computer Networks
Michal Pióro and Deepankar Medhi

Wireless Sensor Networks: An Information Processing Approach
Feng Zhao and Leonidas Guibas

Communication Networking: An Analytical Approach
Anurag Kumar, D. Manjunath, and Joy Kuri

The Internet and Its Protocols: A Comparative Approach
Adrian Farrel

Modern Cable Television Technology: Video, Voice, and Data Communications, Second Edition
Walter Ciciora, James Farmer, David Large, and Michael Adams

Bluetooth Application Programming with the Java APIs
C. Bala Kumar, Paul J. Kline, and Timothy J. Thompson

Policy-Based Network Management: Solutions for the Next Generation
John Strassner

MPLS Network Management: MIBs, Tools, and Techniques
Thomas D. Nadeau

Developing IP-Based Services: Solutions for Service Providers and Vendors
Monique Morrow and Kateel Vijayananda

Telecommunications Law in the Internet Age
Sharon K. Black

Optical Networks: A Practical Perspective, Second Edition
Rajiv Ramaswami and Kumar N. Sivarajan

Internet QoS: Architectures and Mechanisms
Zheng Wang

TCP/IP Sockets in Java: Practical Guide for Programmers
Michael J. Donahoo and Kenneth L. Calvert

TCP/IP Sockets in C: Practical Guide for Programmers
Kenneth L. Calvert and Michael J. Donahoo

Multicast Communication: Protocols, Programming, and Applications
Ralph Wittmann and Martina Zitterbart

MPLS: Technology and Applications
Bruce Davie and Yakov Rekhter

High-Performance Communication Networks, Second Edition
Jean Walrand and Pravin Varaiya

Internetworking Multimedia
Jon Crowcroft, Mark Handley, and Ian Wakeman

Understanding Networked Applications: A First Course
David G. Messerschmitt

Integrated Management of Networked Systems: Concepts, Architectures, and their Operational Application
Heinz-Gerd Hegering, Sebastian Abeck, and Bernhard Neumair

Virtual Private Networks: Making the Right Connection
Dennis Fowler

Networked Applications: A Guide to the New Computing Infrastructure
David G. Messerschmitt

Wide Area Network Design: Concepts and Tools for Optimization
Robert S. Cahn

For further information on these books and for a list of forthcoming titles, please visit our Web site at http://www.mkp.com.

The Morgan Kaufmann Series in Computer Security

Information Assurance: Dependability and Security in Networked Systems
Yi Qian, James Joshi, David Tipper, and Prashant Krishnamurthy

Digital Watermarking and Steganography, Second Edition
Ingemar Cox, Matthew Miller, Jeffrey Bloom, Jessica Fridrich, and Ton Kalker

Network Recovery: Protection and Restoration of Optical, SONET-SDH, IP, and MPLS
Jean-Philippe Vasseur, Mario Pickavet, and Piet Demeester

For further information on these books and for a list of forthcoming titles, please visit our Web site at http://www.mkp.com.

Information Assurance

Dependability and Security in Networked Systems

Yi Qian

James Joshi

David Tipper

Prashant Krishnamurthy

AMSTERDAM • BOSTON • HEIDELBERG • LONDON
NEW YORK • OXFORD • PARIS • SAN DIEGO
SAN FRANCISCO • SINGAPORE • SYDNEY • TOKYO

Morgan Kaufmann is an imprint of Elsevier

Acquisitions Editor   Rick Adams
Publishing Services Manager   George Morrison
Project Manager   Mónica González de Mendoza
Assistant Editor   Gregory Chalson
Production Assistant   Lianne Hong
Cover Design   Eric Decicco
Composition   diacriTech
Interior printer   Sheridan Books, Inc.
Cover printer   Phoenix Color Corporation

Morgan Kaufmann Publishers is an imprint of Elsevier.
30 Corporate Drive, Suite 400, Burlington, MA 01803, USA

This book is printed on acid-free paper.

Library of Congress Cataloging-in-Publication Data
Information assurance : dependability and security in networked systems / Yi Qian ... [et al.].
    p. cm. – (The Morgan Kaufmann series in networking)
Includes bibliographical references and index.
ISBN 978-0-12-373566-9 (pbk. : alk. paper) 1. Computer networks–Security measures. 2. Computer networks–Reliability. 3. Computer security. I. Qian, Yi, 1962–
TK5105.59.I5247 2007
005.8–dc22

                                                                                    2007033726

ISBN: 978-0-12-373566-9

For information on all Morgan Kaufmann publications,
visit our Web site at *www.mkp.com* or *www.books.elsevier.com*

Printed and bound by CPI Group (UK) Ltd, Croydon, CR0 4YY

To my wife Melodee, son Joshua and daughter Michelle
—*Yi Qian*

To my wife Tripti, daughter Jaimee, and parents Hem and Prava
—*James Joshi*

In memory of my father, C.E. Tipper who encouraged and enabled my education
—*David Tipper*

To my parents, Krishnamurthy and Shantha whose blessings
I count as my fortune every day
—*Prashant Krishnamurthy*

Contents

Preface   xxiii

Contributors   xxvii

1   **Information Assurance**   1

by Yi Qian, University of Puerto Rico at Mayaguez, Puerto Rico, and James Joshi, David Tipper, and Prashant Krishnamurthy, University of Pittsburgh, USA

1.1   **Introduction**   1

1.2   **Information Assurance: Dependability and Security of Networked Information Systems**   3

1.3   **Book Organization**   7

    1.3.1   The Three Parts of the Book   7

    1.3.2   Chapter 2: Network Security   8

    1.3.3   Chapter 3: Security for Distributed Systems: Foundations of Access Control   8

    1.3.4   Chapter 4: Network Survivability   9

    1.3.5   Chapter 5: System Survivability   9

    1.3.6   Chapter 6: Taxonomy and Framework for Integrating Dependability and Security   9

    1.3.7   Chapter 7: Stochastic Models/Techniques for Secure and Survivable Systems   10

    1.3.8   Chapter 8: Integrated Dependability and Security Evaluation Using Game Theory and Markov Models   10

    1.3.9   Chapter 9: Scenario Graphs Applied to Network Security   11

    1.3.10   Chapter 10: Vulnerability-Centric Alert Correlation   11

       1.3.11 Chapter 11: Monitoring and Detecting Attacks in All-Optical
               Networks   11
       1.3.12 Chapter 12: Robustness Evaluation of Operating Systems   12
       1.3.13 Chapter 13: Intrusion Response Systems: A Survey   12
       1.3.14 Chapter 14: Secure and Resilient Routing: A Framework for Resilient
               Network Architectures   13
       1.3.15 Chapter 15: Wireless Systems Security and Survivability   13
       1.3.16 Chapter 16: Integrated Fault and Security Management   14
   1.4   Conclusion   14
       References   14

Part I: Foundational Background on Security and Dependability
            Techniques   17

2   **Network Security**   19
       by James Joshi and Prashant Krishnamurthy, University of Pittsburgh, USA
   2.1   **Introduction**   19
   2.2   **Network Attacks and Security Issues**   19
       2.2.1   Network Communications   20
       2.2.2   Some Example Security Attacks   23
       2.2.3   Security Attacks, Services, and Architecture   26
   2.3   **Protection and Prevention**   27
       2.3.1   Firewalls and Perimeter Security   27
       2.3.2   Cryptographic Protocols   30
   2.4   **Detection**   34
   2.5   **Assessment and Response**   36
   2.6   **Conclusion**   37
       References   37

3   **Security for Distributed Systems: Foundations of Access Control** 39
       by Elisa Bertino, Purdue University, USA, and Jason Crampton, University of London, UK
   3.1   **Introduction**   39

3.2   Identification and Authentication   40

   3.2.1   Password-Based Authentication   41
   3.2.2   Insecure Communication Channels   42
   3.2.3   Challenge-Response Systems   42
   3.2.4   Authentication in Distributed Systems   43

3.3   Access Control   46

   3.3.1   Access Control Based on Subject–Object
            Relationships   48
   3.3.2   Protection Matrix Model   48
   3.3.3   An Information Flow Policy for Confidentiality   53
   3.3.4   Bell-LaPadula Model   55
   3.3.5   Clark-Wilson Model   56
   3.3.6   Role-Based Access Control   59

3.4   Access Control in Distributed Systems   60

   3.4.1   Overview of Relevant Standards   61
   3.4.2   Advanced Approaches   65

3.5   Digital Identity Management   72

   3.5.1   Shibboleth   73
   3.5.2   CardSpace   74
   3.5.3   Higgins Trust Framework   75
   3.5.4   Research Approaches   75

3.6   Conclusion   76

   References   77

4   Network Survivability   81

*by Bjorn Jager, Molde University, Norway, John Doucette,
University of Alberta Edmonton, Canada, and David Tipper
University of Pittsburgh, USA*

4.1   Introduction   81

4.2   Prevention Techniques   83

4.3   Survivable Network Design and Traffic Restoration Concepts   84

   4.3.1   Typical Network Architecture   84
   4.3.2   Basic Survivability Concepts   86
   4.3.3   Basic Network Management Concepts   87

    4.3.4 Protection versus Restoration   88
    4.3.5 Other Issues   89

4.4 **Transport Network Recovery Techniques**   91
    4.4.1 Automatic Protection Switching   91
    4.4.2 Ring-Based Survivability   93
    4.4.3 Span Restoration   95
    4.4.4 Shared Path Protection   96
    4.4.5 Shared Path Restoration   97
    4.4.6 *p*-Cycles   98

4.5 **Survivable Network Design Techniques**   101

4.6 **Multilayer Issues**   104

4.7 **Conclusion and Future Research Areas**   107
    References   108

5   System Survivability   113
           by Axel Krings, University of Idaho, USA

5.1 **Introduction and Background**   113

5.2 **Survivability and the Impact of Fault Models**   115
    5.2.1 Dependability Considerations   116
    5.2.2 Survivability Considerations   118

5.3 **Design for Survivability**   119
    5.3.1 Identification of Essential Functionalities   121
    5.3.2 Tolerating Faults   123
    5.3.3 Dealing with Common-Mode Faults   124
    5.3.4 Applying the Notion of Optimality   125

5.4 **Decentralized Storage**   126

5.5 **Survivability of Large Distributed Systems**   128

5.6 **Borrowing from Well-established Fields**   133
    5.6.1 Problem Transformation   133
    5.6.2 Scheduling Problems   136
    5.6.3 Case Study: Autonomous Mobile Agents   139

5.7 **Conclusion**   141
    References   142

Part II: Modeling the Interaction between Dependability and Security 147

6 Taxonomy and Framework for Integrating Dependability and Security 149

by Jiankun Hu, Peter Bertok, and Zahir Tari, RMIT University, Australia

6.1 Introduction 149

6.2 Basic Concepts and Related Work 150

6.2.1 Dependability 150

6.2.2 Integration of Dependability and Security 152

6.3 Proposed Taxonomy and Framework 154

6.3.1 Key Notations of the Feedback Control System Model 154

6.3.2 Definitions of Basic Concepts of Dependability and Security within the Proposed Framework 155

6.4 Dependability, Security, and their Attributes 155

6.4.1 Taxonomy of Faults 157

6.5 The Means to Attain Dependability and Security 164

6.5.1 Fault Prevention 164

6.5.2 Fault Tolerance 166

6.5.3 Fault Removal 166

6.6 Conclusion 168

References 168

7 Stochastic Modeling Techniques for Secure and Survivable Systems 171

by Kishor S. Trivedi, Duke University, USA, and Vaneeta Jindal and Selvamuthu Dharmaraja, Indian Institute of Technology, India

7.1 Introduction 171

7.1.1 Survivability and Security 172

7.2 Analytical Modeling Techniques 173

7.2.1 Markov Models 174

7.2.2   Semi-Markov Process   176

7.2.3   Higher-Level Model Formalisms   177

7.3   Security Modeling   179

7.3.1   Intrusion-Tolerant Systems [3]   180

7.3.2   Security Modeling of SITAR Security System [4]   188

7.4   Survivability Modeling   190

7.4.1   System Description [31]   192

7.5   Conclusion   205

References   205

8   Integrated Dependability and Security Evaluation Using Game Theory and Markov Models   209

by Bjarne E. Helvik, Karin Sallhammar, and Svein J. Knapskog, University of Science and Technology, Norway

8.1   Introduction   209

8.1.1   Previous Work   212

8.1.2   Outline   213

8.2   Stochastic Modeling   213

8.2.1   Failure Process   215

8.2.2   Modeling Intrusion as Transitions   216

8.2.3   Modeling the System   217

8.2.4   Obtaining System Measures   218

8.2.5   Model Parametrization   220

8.3   Predicting Attacker Behavior   221

8.3.1   Reward and Cost Concept   222

8.3.2   Modeling Interactions as a Game   223

8.3.3   Stochastic Game Model   224

8.4   Defining and Solving the Game   225

8.5   Tuning the Game Parameters   230

8.5.1   One Possible Attack Action   231

8.5.2   Two Possible Attack Actions   233

8.5.3   Attacker Profiling   235

8.6   Case Study: DNS Service   236

8.6.1   Stochastic Model   237

8.6.2   Stochastic Game   237

8.6.3   Four Scenarios   238
8.6.4   Comparing the Scenarios   239
8.7   **Conclusion**   240
      References   243

9   **Scenario Graphs Applied to Network Security**   247
      by Jeannette M. Wing, Carnegie Mellon University, USA

9.1   **Introduction**   247
9.2   **Algorithms for Generating Scenario Graphs**   248
      9.2.1   Symbolic Algorithm   248
      9.2.2   Explicit-State Algorithm   250
9.3   **Attack Graphs are Scenario Graphs**   251
9.4   **Network Attack Graphs**   253
      9.4.1   Network Attack Model   253
      9.4.2   Network Components   254
9.5   **Example Network**   257
      9.5.1   Example Network Components   259
      9.5.2   Sample Attack Graphs   264
9.6   **Attack Graph Analysis**   266
      9.6.1   Single Action Removal   267
      9.6.2   Critical Action Set Minimization   267
9.7   **Practical Experience**   269
      9.7.1   Performance   269
      9.7.2   Toolkit   271
9.8   **Related Work**   272
9.9   **Future Work and Conclusion**   274
      References   276

10   **Vulnerability-Centric Alert Correlation**   279
      by Lingyu Wang, Concordia University, Canada, and Sushil Jajodia, George Mason University, USA

10.1 **Introduction**   279
10.2 **Review of Alert Correlation and Related Techniques**   282
10.3 **Attack Graph**   284

10.4 **Alert Correlation, Hypothesis, Prediction, and Aggregation**   287

    10.4.1 Alert Correlation in Offline Applications   287
    10.4.2 Vulnerability-Centric Alert Correlation   289
    10.4.3 Alert Hypothesis and Prediction   292
    10.4.4 Alert Aggregation   296
    10.4.5 Empirical Results   298

10.5 **Conclusion**   300

10.6 **Acknowledgments**   300

    References   301

Part III: Design and Architectural Issues for Secure and Dependable Systems   305

11   Monitoring and Detecting Attacks in All-Optical Networks   307

by Arun K. Somani and Tao Wu, Iowa State University, USA

11.1 **Introduction**   307

    11.1.1 Security Problems in All-Optical Networks   308
    11.1.2 Possible Attacks   308
    11.1.3 All-Optical Network Attack Types   309
    11.1.4 Issues in Crosstalk Attack Diagnostic Algorithms   310

11.2 **Crosstalk Attack Features and Monitoring Techniques**   311

    11.2.1 Crosstalk Attack Features   311
    11.2.2 Security Consideration   312
    11.2.3 Overview of Current Monitoring Methods   313

11.3 **Node, Attack, and Monitor Models**   315

    11.3.1 Node Model   315
    11.3.2 Crosstalk Attack Model   315
    11.3.3 Monitor Node Model   318

11.4 **Necessary and Sufficient Conditions for Crosstalk Attack Detection**   320

    11.4.1 Single Crosstalk Attack in a Network   320
    11.4.2 Monitoring Relationship   320

11.5 **One-crosstalk Attack Diagnosable Conditions**   325

    11.5.1 Detecting the Status of a Connection under One–Original Attack Flow Conditions   327
    11.5.2 Computational Complexity   329

11.6 *k*-Crosstalk Attacks in the Network   329

11.6.1 *k*-Crosstalk Attack Diagnosable Condition   330

11.6.2 Detecting Global Status of Connections   334

11.6.3 Computational Complexity   335

11.7 **Sparse Monitoring and Routing Algorithms   336**

11.7.1 Sparse Monitoring, Test Connection, and Routing for a Single Original Attack Flow Policy I   336

11.7.2 Examples   337

11.7.3 Sparse Monitoring, Test Connection, and Routing Policy II   338

11.7.4 Connection Routing Algorithm in One–Original Attack Flow Networks   340

11.7.5 Example   341

11.8 **Sparse Monitoring, Test Connection, and Routing for More than One Original Attack Flow   342**

11.8.1 Examples   343

11.9 **Conclusion   345**

References   345

12   **Robustness Evaluation of Operating Systems   349**

by Andréas Johansson and Neeraj Suri, Technische Universität of Darmstadt, Germany

12.1 **Introduction   349**

12.1.1 Case Study   351

12.2 **Evaluation Goals   352**

12.2.1 Case Study   353

12.3 **Target System   353**

12.3.1 Case Study   354

12.4 **Error Model and Workload Selection   355**

12.4.1 Error Type   356

12.4.2 Error Location   358

12.4.3 Error Timing   358

12.4.4 Workload Selection   358

12.4.5 Case Study   359

12.5 **Robustness Metrics   361**

12.5.1 Case Study   362

12.6 Presentation and Interpretation of Results   365

12.7 Conclusion   369

References   370

13   Intrusion Response Systems: A Survey   377

by Bingrui Foo, Matthew W. Glause, Gaspar M. Howard, Yu-Sung Wu,
Saurabh Bagchi, and Eugene H. Spafford, Purdue University, USA

13.1 Introduction   377

13.2 Static Decision-making Systems   381

13.2.1 Generic Authorization and Access Control—Application Programming
Interface   381

13.2.2 Snort Inline   384

13.2.3 McAfee Internet Security Suite   385

13.2.4 Other Systems   386

13.3 Dynamic Decision-making Systems   387

13.3.1 Broad Research Issues   387

13.3.2 Adepts   388

13.3.3 ALPHATECH Light Autonomic Defense System   390

13.3.4 Cooperating Security Managers and Adaptive, Agent-Based
Intrusion Response Systems   392

13.3.5 Emerald   394

13.3.6 Other Dynamic Intrusion Response Systems   396

13.4 Intrusion Tolerance through Diverse Replicas   397

13.4.1 Broad Research Issues   398

13.4.2 Building Survivable Services Using Redundancy and Adaptation   398

13.4.3 Scalable Intrusion-Tolerant Architecture   399

13.4.4 Survival by Defense Enabling   400

13.4.5 Implementing Trustworthy Services Using Replicated State
Machines   401

13.4.6 Distributing Trust on the Internet   402

13.5 Responses to Specific Kinds of Attacks   403

13.5.1 Primitives for Responding to DDoS   404

13.5.2 CITRA   404

13.5.3 Cooperative Counter-DDoS Entity   406

13.6 Benchmarking Intrusion Response Systems   407

13.7 Thoughts on Evolution of IRS Technology   410

13.8 Conclusion   412

References   412

14   Secure and Resilient Routing: Building Blocks for Resilient
         Network Architectures   417

*by Deep Medhi, University of Missouri–Kansas City, USA, and Dijiang
Huang, Arizona State University, USA*

14.1 Introduction   417

14.2 Traffic Engineering Perspective and its Relation to Network
     Robustness   419

    14.2.1 An Illustrative Example   421

14.3 Components of a Resilient Network Architecture   423

14.4 Threats and Countermeasures in Link-State Routing   424

    14.4.1 Link-State Routing Model and Threat Model   424
    14.4.2 Preventive Cryptographic Countermeasures against Attacks   428

14.5 Resilient Architecture: Virtualization and Routing   435

    14.5.1 An Enabling Framework for Adaptive and Secure Virtualized
           Networking   435
    14.5.2 Routing Protocol Extension: OSPF-E   440
    14.5.3 Network Analysis: Preliminary Results   444

14.6 Conclusion   446

References   446

14.A Secure Group Communication   449

    14.A.1 Using One-Way Function Chain to Build Key Chain   449
    14.A.2 Key Distribution   451
    14.A.3 Key Agreement Protocol   454
    14.A.4 Assessment   456

15   Security and Survivability of Wireless Systems   459

*by Yi Qian, University of Puerto Rico at Mayaguez, Puerto Rico, and
Prashant Krishnamurthy and David Tipper, University of Pittsburgh, USA*

15.1 Introduction   459

15.2 Background   460

15.3 Current Security Approaches in Wireless Networks   463

15.4 Current Survivability Approaches in Wireless Networks   465

15.5 Framework for Wireless Network Survivability and Security   467

15.6 Interaction between Survivability and Security in Wireless Networks   470

   15.6.1 Extending the Framework to Include Interactions between Security and Survivability   472
   15.6.2 Case Study I: Idle Handoffs   475
   15.6.3 Case Study II: Key Management in Heterogeneous Sensor Networks   476

15.7 Conclusion   484

   References   485

16   Integrated Fault and Security Management   489

   by Ehab Al-Shaer, DePaul University, USA, and Yan Chen, Northwestern University, USA

16.1 Introduction   489

16.2 Active Integrated Fault Identification Framework   490

   16.2.1 Background   490
   16.2.2 Related Work   491
   16.2.3 Challenges and Problem Formalization   492
   16.2.4 Integrated Fault Intrusion Reasoning   495
   16.2.5 Simulation Study   502

16.3 Fault and Security Management on High-speed Networks   506

   16.3.1 Background   506
   16.3.2 Related Work   508
   16.3.3 Architecture of the HiFIND System   511
   16.3.4 Evaluation   515

16.4 Conclusion   520

   References   520

Index   523

Preface

About five years back, we initiated an information assurance program at the University of Pittsburgh under the flagship of Laboratory of Education and Research in Information Assurance Education (LERSAIS), which was created for that purpose. We had to often explore and discuss issues related to security, dependability, survivability, etc., with respect to what could be accommodated within the area of IA, while planning for (a) the curricular content that aligns with the National Security Agency's center of excellence in information assurance education (CAEIAE) program and it's Committee on National Security Systems (CNSS) information assurance (IA) standards (now considered the US national IA education standards), and (b) the long term research agenda for LERRSAIS. Coming from different research background including that of security, dependability and others, we often found it difficult to reconcile the different perspectives related to the notion of IA and more specifically that of *assurance* which roughly appears to have brought together the notion of integrating *security* and *dependability* aspects of networked information systems. We realized that there is no well established definition of *assurance*, and more importantly, there is a lack of interaction between the security and the dependability communities. At the same time, our interest in research related to integrated approach to addressing security and dependability aspects grew and we were convinced that such an approach would help generate more wholesome solutions to trustworthy and high assurance systems.

With the rapid developments in information technologies (IT) over last several years, our global society has embarked in a path where we are critically dependent on IT infrastructures. Infrastructural failures, cyber attacks and cyberwars are now looming realities that can have catastrophic effects on the global society and each individual's life. With the growing complexity and interconnectedness of information systems, even simple disruptive event can have dire consequences.

Securing and ensuring the dependability of such IT environment is a growing challenge and there is a critical need for pragmatic solutions that can accommodate known and unknown disruptive events and enable systems to adopt and survive any type of disruptions. We are convinced that only through the involvement of both the dependability and security communities can such a singular goal of developing highly assured, survivable information systems can be achieved. While there have been some efforts towards this direction, it has not been very successful. We planned this book with a hope to generate the needed momentum that matches the criticality of this need.

APPROACH

Both security and dependability areas are rich and well-developed enough to have several books on their topics and trying to bring all issues together is going to be simply futile. Our attempt here, therefore, has been to bring together issues that emphasize the interaction and integration between the technologies available within the security and dependability areas with the hope to convince the readers about the importance of and the critical need for combined, more holistic approaches. Towards this, we have included chapters that provide overviews of the various issues in a concise manner as well as more technically detailed chapters that focus on some significant issues. We have also tried to accommodate the diversity of issues by incorporating chapters that focus on different systems and architectural components such as operating platforms, wired and wireless networks, applications, etc.

ACKNOWLEDGMENTS

We are sincerely indebted to the contributors of this book for their support and diligent work, without which this book would not have been possible. We express our deep appreciation for their understanding and bearing with our organizational weaknesses. We would like to thank the reviewers of proposal for this book for their comments and suggestions. In particular, we were highly motivated by their support for the view that "interaction" aspect of our goal for the book is a crucial component; their "cautionary note" with regards to the challenge of appropriately hitting the "interaction" note helped us take extra measure to ensure that we achieve that goal. We hope that we have done that.

We express our thanks to the staff of Elsevier Inc. for their support for this undertaking. In particular, we would like to thank Rick Adams, Senior Acquisitions Editor at Elsevier, for all the support and guidance, as well as for providing the needed extra push to keep us in schedule. We thank Gregory Chalson, Assistant Editor at Elsevier, and Monica Gonzalez de Mendoza, Project Manager at Elsevier, for their patience in dealing with electronic transfer of manuscripts and handling publication issues.

We thank Prof. Michael Spring, one of the co-founders of LERSAIS for his wisdom, input and efforts leading to the successful establishment of LERSAIS.

Lastly, we thank our families (Yi thanks his wife Melodee; James thanks his wife Tripti, David thanks his wife Cindy and daughters Meredith and Evelyn; Prashant thanks his wife Deepika) for their support and patience while we worked on this book.

We believe that we (the authors and the editors) have given our best to ensure the readability, completeness and accuracy of each chapter. However, it is possible that some errors and omissions may still have remained undetected. We appreciate any feedback intended to correct such errors. And finally, we believe many more chapters could have been relevant for our book, however, we had to remain within the constraints of the publication process.

Yi Qian
Email: yqian@ece.uprm.edu

James Joshi
Email: jjoshi@mail.sis.pitt.edu

David Tipper
Email: dtipper@mail.sis.pitt.edu

Prashant Krishnamurthy
Email: prashant@mail.sis.pitt.edu

November, 2007

Contributors

Ehab Al-Shaer is an associate professor and the director of the Multimedia Networking Research Lab (MNLAB) in the School of Computer Science, Telecommunications, and Information Systems at DePaul University, Chicago, IL since 1998. His primary research areas are network security, Internet monitoring, fault management, and multimedia protocols. He is coeditor of a number of books in the area of multimedia management and end-to-end monitoring. Professor Al-Shaer was also the program cochair for IEEE Integrated Management (IM), 2007, Management of Multimedia Networks and Services (MMNS), 2001, and End-to-End Monitoring (E2EMON), 2003–2005. Professor Al-Shaer was a guest editor for number of journals, including *Journal of High-Speed Networking* and *Journal of Computer Communications*. He has served as TPC member, workshop chair, session chair, and tutorial presenter for many IEEE/ACM/IFIP conferences, including INFOCOM, ICNP, IM, NOMS, DOSM, MMNS, and others. He received Best Paper Awards in IM'03 and MMNS'04, and fellowship awards from NASA and USENIX in 1997 and 1992, respectively.

Saurabh Bagchi is an assistant professor in the School of Electrical and Computer Engineering at Purdue University, West Lafayette, IN. He is a faculty fellow of the Cyber Center and has a courtesy appointment in the Department of Computer Science at Purdue University.

He received his M.S. and Ph.D. degrees from the University of Illinois at Urbana–Champaign in 1998 and 2001, respectively. At Purdue, he leads the Dependable Computing Systems Lab (DCSL) where he and a set of wildly enthusiastic students try to make and break distributed systems for the good of the world. His work is supported by NSF, Indiana 21st Century Research and Technology Fund, Avaya, and Purdue Research Foundation, with equipment grants from Intel and Motorola. His papers have been runner up for the best paper in HPDC (2006), DSN (2005), and MTTS (2005). He has been an Organizing Committee member and Program Committee member for the Dependable Systems and Networks Conference (DSN) and the Symposium on Reliable Distributed Systems (SRDS).

Elisa Bertino is professor of Computer Sciences and Electrical and Computer Engineering at Purdue University, West Lafayette, IN, and serves as research director of the Center for Education and Research in Information Assurance and Security (CERIAS). Previously, she was a faculty member at the Department of Computer Science and Communication of the University of Milan where she directed the DB&SEC laboratory. She has been a visiting researcher at the IBM Research Laboratory (now Almaden) in San Jose, CA, Microelectronics and Computer Technology Corporation at Rutgers University, and Telcordia Technologies. Her main research interests include security, privacy, digital identity management systems, database systems, distributed systems, and multimedia systems. In those areas, Professor Bertino has published more than 250 papers in all major refereed journals and in proceedings of international conferences and symposia. She is coauthor of the books *Object-Oriented Database Systems: Concepts and Architectures* (Boston: Addison-Wesley International, 1993), *Indexing Techniques for Advanced Database Systems* (New York: Kluwer Academic Publishers, 1997), *Intelligent Database Systems* (Boston: Addison-Wesley International, 2001), and *Security for Web Services and Service Oriented Architectures* (New York: Springer, 2007, in press). She is a coeditor-in-chief of the *Very Large Database Systems* (VLDB) journal. She serves also on the editorial boards of several scientific journals, including *IEEE Internet Computing, IEEE Security & Privacy, ACM Transactions on Information and System Security, ACM Transactions on Web, Acta Informatica, Parallel and Distributed Database Journal, Journal of Computer Security, Data & Knowledge Engineering,* and *Science of Computer Programming.* She has been consultant to several companies on data management systems and applications and has given several courses to industries. She has served as A Program Committee member of several international conferences, such as ACM SIGMOD, VLDB, ACM OOPSLA, as program cochair of the 1998 IEEE International Conference on Data Engineering (ICDE), and as program chair of the 2000 European Conference on Object-Oriented Programming (ECOOP 2000), the 7th ACM Symposium of Access Control Models and Technologies (SACMAT 2002), the EDBT 2004 Conference, and the IEEE Policy 2007 Workshop. Her research has been sponsored by several organizations and companies, including the USA National Science Foundation, the U.S. Air Force Office for Sponsored Research, the I3P Consortium, the European Union (under the fifth and sixth IST research programs), IBM, Microsoft, and the Italian Telecom. She is a fellow member of IEEE and ACM and has been named a Golden Core Member for her service to the IEEE Computer Society. She received the 2002 IEEE Computer Society Technical Achievement Award "for outstanding contributions to database systems and database security and advanced data management systems," and the 2005 IEEE Computer Society Tsutomu Kanai Award "for pioneering and innovative research contributions to secure distributed systems."

Peter Bertok is an academic staff member at the School of Computer Science, Royal Melbourne Institute of Technology, Australia. He received his Ph.D. from the University of Tokyo, Japan, and master's degree from the Technical University of Budapest, Hungary. He has authored more than 80 refereed publications. His main research areas are networked and distributed computing, web services, and computer security.

Yan Chen is an assistant professor and the director of the Lab for Internet and Security Technology (LIST) in the Department of Electrical Engineering and Computer

Science at Northwestern University, Evanston, IL. He got his Ph.D. in computer science at the University of California at Berkeley in 2003. His research interests include network security, network measurement and monitoring, and wireless networks. Professor Chen is the organization and TPC cochair for the 15th IEEE International Workshop on Quality of Service (IWQoS), 2007. He also served on the Technical Program Committee of several major networking conferences, including ACM MobiCom, IEEE INFOCOM, IEEE ICNP, IEEE ICDCS, etc. Professor Chen won the Department of Energy Early CAREER award in 2005, the U.S. Air Force of Scientific Research (AFOSR) Young Investigator Award in 2007, and the Microsoft Trustworthy Computing Awards in 2004 and 2005 with his colleagues.

Jason Crampton is a reader in information security in the Information Security Group at Royal Holloway, University of London, U.K. His primary research interests are in role-based access control, particularly focusing on the use of mathematical formalisms to study administration and separation of duty. He is also interested in the use of cryptographic mechanisms for access control. He has served on a number of program committees, including the ACM Symposium on Access Control Models and Technologies in 2006 and 2007, the European Symposium on Research in Computer Security in 2006, and the 21st Annual IFIP WG 11.3 Working Conference on Data and Applications Security. He has recently received grants from the Engineering and Physical Sciences Research Council (U.K.) and Microsoft Research. He is also a research associate at Birkbeck, University of London.

S. Dharmaraja received Ph.D. in mathematics from Indian Institute of Technology Madras, India, in 1999 and is currently working at the Indian Institute of Technology Delhi, India. Before joining this institute, he was a postdoctoral fellow at the Department of Electrical and Computer Engineering, Duke University, Durham, NC, and then was a research associate at TRLabs, Winnipeg, Canada. His current research interests include queuing theory, Markov modeling, and performance issues of wireless networks and dependability analysis of communication systems. His work has been published in several international journals and conference proceedings.

John Doucette completed a B.Sc. in mathematics from Dalhousie University, Halifax, Nova Scotia, in 1992, a B.Eng. in industrial engineering from the Technical University of Nova Scotia (TUNS, now Dalhousie University), Halifax, in 1996, and a Ph.D. in electrical and computer Engineering from the University of Alberta, Edmonton, Canada, in 2004. He is currently an assistant professor of engineering management in the Department of Mechanical Engineering at the University of Alberta, where he conducts research in network restoration and protection, network reliability and availability, network design and optimization, and eHealth networks. He also holds an Adjunct Scientist appointment at TRLabs, Edmonton, Alberta, where he conducts part of his research program. Prior to his current positions, he held staff research scientist and research engineer positions at TRLabs from 2000–2005, was an instructor in the Department of Electrical and Computer Engineering at the University of Alberta from 1998–2001, and was an industrial engineer at Syncrude Canada Ltd., Fort McMurray, Alberta, from 1996–1997. In 2000 and in 2001, he was one of three finalists for the Alberta Science and Technology (ASTech) Leaders of Tomorrow Award. He has authored or coauthored over 20 peer-reviewed journal and conference publications and approximately 20 technical reports, and is coinventor of four patents granted or pending.

Bingrui Foo is a Ph.D. student in the School of Electrical and Computer Engineering at Purdue University in West Lafayette, IN. Presently, he is involved in two research projects. The first is in the field of network security, specifically the design of intrusion-tolerant systems and automated response mechanisms. The second is in the field of statistical modeling, consisting of extending mixture models by adding hierarchal structure to images and videos. His papers have appeared in DSN and ACSAC.

Matthew W. Glause
Center for Education and Research in Information Assurance and Security (CERIAS)
Dependable Computing Systems Laboratory
School of Electrical and Computer Engineering
Purdue University

Bjarne E. Helvik received his Siv.ing. degree (M.Sc. in technology) from the Norwegian Institute of Technology (NTH), Trondheim, Norway in 1975. He was awarded the degree Dr. Techn. from NTH in 1982. Since 1997, he has been professor in the Department of Telematics at the Norwegian University of Science and Technology (NTNU). He is principal academic at the Norwegian Centre of Excellence (CoE) for Quantifiable Quality of Service in Communication Systems (Q2S). He has previously held various positions at ELAB and SINTEF Telecom and Informatics. In the period of 1988–1997 he was appointed as adjunct professor at the Department of Computer Engineering and Telematics at NTH. His field of interests includes QoS, dependability modeling, measurements, analysis and simulation, fault-tolerant computing systems and survivable networks, as well as related communication system architectural issues. His current research focus is on distributed, autonomous, and adaptive fault management in telecommunication systems, networks, and services. Professor Helvik has been active in RACE, ACTS, IST, and EURESCOM collaborations, and in a number of program committees, among them committees for the International Symposium on Fault-Tolerant Computing (FTCS), the European Dependable Computing Conferences (EDCC), the ITC Specialist Seminars, the International Teletraffic Congress (ITC), GlobeCom, and the International Conference on Dependable Systems and Networks (DSN), and recently co-chaired the EURO-NGI 2007 conference on Next-Generation Internet Networks. He has authored/coauthored a number of research papers and textbooks.

Jianku Hu is a senior lecturer at the School of Computer Science and IT, RMIT University, Australia. He has obtained his bachelor's degree in industrial automation in 1983 from Hunan University P.R. China; Ph.D. degree in engineering in 1993 from the Harbin Institute of Technology, P.R. China; and a master's degree of research in computer science and software engineering from Monash University, Australia, in 2000. He was a research fellow of the Alexander von Humboldt Foundation at the Department of Electrical and Electronic Engineering, Ruhr University, Germany, during 1995–1997. He worked as a research fellow in the Department of Electrical and Electronic Engineering, Delft University of Technology, The Netherlands, in 1997. Before he moved to the RMIT University, Australia, he was a research fellow in the Department of Electrical and

Electronic Engineering, the University of Melbourne, Australia. His major research interest is in computer networking and computer security. Dr. Hu has about 80 referred publications, including top IEEE transactions. Dr. Hu has been listed in *MARQUIS Who's Who in Science and Engineering*. More details can be found at http://goanna.cs.rmit.edu.au/~jiankun/.

Dijang Huang is an assistant professor at the Department of Computer Science and Engineering in the School of Computing Informatics, Arizona State University, Tempe, AZ since 2005. His primary research areas are computer networking, network protocols and mobility simulation, security and privacy, key management, authentication protocol, attack analysis, privacy preserving, and attack-resilient network design.

Bjorn Jager is an associate professor in informatics in the Department of Economics, Informatics, and Social Science at Molde University College in Norway. Prior to joining Molde University in 1993 he was a group leader in Department of Telecommunication Management Networks at ABB Nera, Norway. He received an M.S. degree in nuclear physics, and a Ph.D. degree in informatics from the University of Bergen, Norway. He was the head of the Department of Informatics, Molde University College, from 2004–2005. His current research interests are traffic restoration, reliable distributed systems, and virtualization in value chains and clusters. He was a visiting researcher at the Centre of Excellence: Centre of Quantifiable and Quality of Service in Communication Systems, Trondheim, Norway, in summer 2004. Professor Jager's research has been supported by several grants from the Norwegian Research Council, the University of Bergen, the Norwegian Centre for International Cooperation in Higher Education, and other government and corporate sources.

Sushil Jajodia is university professor, BDM International Professor of Information Technology, and the director of Center for Secure Information Systems at the George Mason University, Fairfax, VA. His research interests include information security, temporal databases, and replicated databases. He has authored 6 books, edited 27 books and conference proceedings, and published more than 300 technical papers in the refereed journals and conference proceedings. He received the 1996 Kristian Beckman award from IFIP TC 11 for his contributions to the discipline of information security, and the 2000 Outstanding Research Faculty Award from GMU's School of Information Technology and Engineering. He has served in different capacities for various journals and conferences. He is the founding editor-in-chief of the *Journal of Computer Security* and is on the editorial boards of *IEE Proceedings on Information Security*, *International Journal of Cooperative Information Systems*, and *International Journal of Information and Computer Security*. More information can be found at http://csis.gmu.edu/faculty/jajodia.html.

Vaneeta Jindal received her M.Sc. in mathematics from the Indian Institute of Technology Delhi, India, in 2003. She is currently a Ph.D. student in the Department of Mathematics at the Indian Institute of Technology Delhi, India. Her research interests include queuing theory, Markov modeling, and performance issues of wireless networks and dependability analysis of communication systems.

Andréas Johansson received his M.Sc. in Computer Engineering from Chalmers, Gothenburg, Sweden. He is currently a Ph.D. student at the Technical University in Darmstadt, Germany. His research primarily targets issues of error propagation and impact in Operating Systems. This entails development of quantifiable and repeatable experimental fault injection technologies, focusing on errors in device drivers. Other research interests include software fault tolerance, failure analysis, dependability benchmarking and threat modeling.

James Joshi is an assistant professor in the School of Information Sciences at the University of Pittsburgh, PA. He is a cofounder and the director of the Laboratory of Education and Research on Security Assured Information Systems (LERSAIS). At Pitt, he teaches several information assurance (IA) courses and coordinates the IA program. His research interests include access control models, security and privacy of distributed multimedia systems, trust management, and information survivability. His research has been supported by the National Science Foundation and he is a recipient of the NSF-CAREER award in 2006. He received his M.S. degree in computer science and a Ph.D. degree in electrical and computer engineering from Purdue University, West Lafayette, IN, in 1998 and 2003, respectively.

Svein J. Knapskog received his Siv.ing. degree (M.S.E.E.) from the Norwegian Institute of Technology (NTH), Trondheim, Norway, in 1972. Since 2001, he has been professor in the Department of Telematics at the Norwegian University of Science and Technology (NTNU). He is presently principal academic at the Norwegian Centre of Excellence (CoE) for Quantifiable Quality of Service in Communication Systems (Q2S). He has previously held various positions in the Norwegian public sector, SIN-TEF, and industry. From 1982–2000, he was associate professor in the Department of Computer Science and Telematics at NTH (later NTNU), where he also served a three-year term as head of the department. In the academic year 2005–2006 he has been acting head of the Department of Telematics. His field of interests include information security and QoS as well as related communication system architectural issues. His current research focus is on information security primitives, protocols, and services in distributed autonomous telecommunication systems and networks, and security evaluation thereof.

Professor Knapskog has been active in a number of conference program committees and has authored/coauthored a number of technical reports, research papers, and a textbook (in Norwegian).

Axel Krings is a professor of computer science at the University of Idaho, Moscow, ID. He received his Ph.D. (1993) and M.S. (1991) degrees in computer science from the University of Nebraska–Lincoln, and his M.S. (1982) in electrical engineering from the FH-Aachen, Germany. Dr. Krings has published extensively in the area of computer and network survivability, security, fault tolerance, and real-time scheduling. He has organized and chaired conference tracks in the area of system survivability and has been on numerous conference program committees. In 2004/2005 he was a visiting professor at the Institut d'Informatique et Mathématiques Appliquées de Grenoble, at the Institut National Polytechnique de Grenoble, France. His work has been funded by DoE/INL, DoT/NIATT, DoD/OST, and NIST. His current research in survivability of ad hoc networks is funded by the Idaho National Laboratory.

Prashant Krishnamurthy is an associate professor with the Graduate Program in Telecommunications and Networking at the University of Pittsburgh, PA. At Pitt, he regularly teaches courses on wireless communication systems and networks, cryptography, and network security. His research interests are wireless network security, wireless data networks, position location in indoor wireless networks, and radio channel modeling for indoor wireless networks. He has had funding for his research from the National Science Foundation and the National Institute of Standards and Technology. He is the coauthor of the books *Principles of Wireless Networks: A Unified Approach* and *Physical Layer of Communication Systems* (Prentice Hall; 1st edition, December 11, 2001). He served as the chair of the IEEE Communications Society, Pittsburgh Chapter, from 2000–2005. He obtained his Ph.D. in 1999 from Worcester Polytechnic Institute, Worcester, MA.

Deep Medhi is professor of computer networking in the Computer Science and Electrical Engineering Department at the University of Missouri–Kansas City. Prior to joining UMKC in 1989, he was a member of the technical staff in the traffic network routing and design department at the AT&T Bell Laboratories. He was an invited visiting professor at the Technical University of Denmark and a visiting research fellow at the Lund University, Sweden. He is currently a Fulbright Senior Specialist. He serves as a senior technical editor of the *Journal of Network & Systems Management*, and is on the editorial board of *Computer Networks, Telecommunication Systems*, and *IEEE Communications Magazine*. He has served on the technical program committees of numerous conferences including IEEE INFOCOM, IEEE NOMS, IEEE IM, ITC, and DRCN. His research interests are resilient multilayer networks architecture and design; dynamic quality-of-service routing; Internet routing protocols; network design, optimization, management, performance, and security; and next-generation Internet architecture. His research grants have been funded by DARPA, NSF, Doris Duke Charitable Foundation, and various industries. He has published more than 70 peer-reviewed papers, and is coauthor of the books *Routing, Flow, and Capacity Design in Communication and Computer Networks* (San Francisco: Morgan Kaufmann, 2004) and *Network Routing: Algorithms, Protocols, and Architectures* (San Francisco: Morgan Kaufmann, 2007). He received a B.Sc. (Hons.) in mathematics from Cotton College, Gauhati University, India, an M.Sc. in Mathematics from the University of Delhi, India, and an M.S. and Ph.D. in computer sciences from the University of Wisconsin–Madison.

Gaspar Modelo-Howard is a Ph.D. student in the Department of Electrical and Computer Engineering and a member of the Center for Education and Research in Information Assurance and Security (CERIAS) at Purdue University, West Lafayette, IN. He came to Purdue after spending seven years as an information security officer for the Panama Canal Authority and five years as a college professor for network security courses. His current research interests include machine-learning techniques for intrusion response and the convergence between security and dependability. He has an M.S. in information security from Royal Holloway, University of London, and a B.S. in electrical engineering from Universidad Tecnológica de Panamá.

Yi Qian is an assistant professor in the Department of Electrical and Computer Engineering, University of Puerto Rico at Mayaguez. At UPRM, Dr. Qian regularly teaches courses on wireless networks, network design, network management, and network performance analysis. Prior to joining UPRM in July 2003, he worked as a technical advisor and senior consultant for several start-up companies and consulting firms in the areas of voiceover IP, fiber-optical switching, Internet packet video, network optimizations, and network planning. He has also worked as a senior member of scientific staff and a technical advisor for the Wireless Systems Engineering Department, Nortel Networks in Richardson, TX. Professor Qian received a Ph.D. degree in electrical engineering with a concentration in telecommunication networks from Clemson University, Clemson, South Carolina. His current research interests include information assurance, network security, network design, network modeling, simulations and performance analysis for next-generation wireless networks, wireless sensor networks, broadband satellite networks, optical networks, high-speed networks, and the Internet. He has publications and patents in all these areas. He has been on numerous conference technical committees, including serving as the general chair of the International Symposium on Wireless Pervasive Computing, 2007, the technical program cochair of the IEEE GLOBECOM 2006 Symposium on Wireless Communications and Networking, and the technical program cochair of the Workshop on Information Assurance, 2006 and 2007. Dr. Qian is a member of Sigma Xi, ACM, IEICE, and a senior member of IEEE.

Karin Sallhammar received her Civ.ing. degree (M.S.) in media technology and engineering from the Linköping University, Sweden, in 2003. She is currently a Ph.D. candidate in the Department of Telematics at the Norwegian University of Science and Technology (NTNU), and is associated with the Norwegian Centre of Excellence (CoE) for Quantifiable Quality of Service in Communication Systems (Q2S). Her field of interests include information security primitives and protocols, network monitoring and intrusion detection, as well as dependability modeling and analysis. Her current research focus is on stochastic models for security and dependability evaluation.

Arun K. Somani is currently the Anson Marston Distinguished Professor at Iowa State University, Jerry R. Junkins Endowed Chair Professor, and chair of electrical and computer engineering. He earned his M.S.E.E. and Ph.D. degrees in electrical engineering from the McGill University, Montreal, Canada, in 1983 and 1985, respectively. He worked as scientific officer for the government of India, New Delhi, from 1974–1982 and as a faculty member in the electrical engineering and computer science and engineering departments at the University of Washington, Seattle, from 1985–1997. Professor Somani's research interests are in the area of fault-tolerant computing, computer interconnection networks, WDM-based optical networking, and reconfigurable and parallel computer system architecture. He has taught courses in these areas and published more than 250 technical papers, several book chapters, and has supervised more than 60 master's and more than 25 Ph.D. students. He is the chief architect of an anti-submarine warfare system (developed for the Indian navy), Meshkin fault-tolerant computer system architecture (developed for the Boeing Company), and architected, designed, and implemented a 46-node multicomputer cluster-based system, Proteus, using a large grain message-passing model with separate data (fiber-optic) and control (electronic) planes during 1990–1992. His current research is in developing scalable architectures and algorithms to manage, control, and deliver dependable service efficiently for network employing optical fiber technology, wavelength division multiplexing, wavelength conversion, wavelength sharing, traffic grooming, access network design, and fault and attack management (FAM) in optical networking. He has served on several leadership roles in IEEE conference organizations, as IEEE distinguished visitor, and as IEEE distinguished tutorial speaker. He has delivered several keynote speeches, tutorials, and distinguished and invited talks all over the world. He has been elected a fellow of IEEE for his contributions to theory and applications of computer networks. He was awarded the Distinguished Scientist member grade of ACM in 2006.

Eugene H. Spafford is one of the most senior and recognized leaders in the field of computing. He has an on-going record of accomplishments as a senior advisor and consultant on issues of security, education, cyber crime, and computing policy to a number of major companies, law enforcement organizations, and academic and government agencies, including Microsoft, Intel, Unisys, the U.S. Air Force, the National Security Agency, the GAO, the Federal Bureau of Investigation, the National Science Foundation, the Department of Energy, and for two presidents of the United States. With nearly three decades of experience as a researcher and instructor, Dr. Spafford has worked in software engineering, reliable distributed computing, host and network security, digital forensics, computing policy, and computing curriculum design. He is responsible for a number of "firsts" in several of these areas. Dr. Spafford is a professor with a joint appointment in computer science and electrical and computer engineering at Purdue University, West Lafayette, IN, where he has served on the faculty since 1987. He is also a professor of philosophy (courtesy) and a professor of communication (courtesy). He is the executive director of the Purdue University Center for Education and Research in Information Assurance and Security (CERIAS). As of 2007, Dr. Spafford is also an adjunct professor of computer science at the University of Texas at San Antonio, and is executive director of the Advisory Board of the new Institute for Information Assurance there. Dr. Spafford serves on a number of advisory and editorial boards, and has been honored several times for his writing, research, and teaching on issues of security and ethics.

Neeraj Suri received his Ph.D. from the University of Massachusetts at Amherst. He currently holds the TU Darmstadt Chair Professorship in "Dependable Embedded Systems and Software" at TU Darmstadt, Germany. His earlier academic appointments include the Saab Endowed Professorship and faculty at Boston University. His research interests span design, analysis and assessment of dependable and secure systems/software. His group's research activities have garnered support from DARPA, NSF, ONR, EC, NASA, Boeing, Microsoft, Intel, Saab among others. He is also a recipient of the NSF CAREER award. He serves as an editor for IEEE Trans. on Dependable and Secure Computing, IEEE Trans. on Software Engineering, ACM Computing Surveys, Intl. Journal on Security & Networks, and has been an editor for IEEE Trans. on Parallel and Distributed Systems. He is a member of IFIP WG 10.4 on Dependability, and a member of Microsoft's Trustworthy Computing Academic Advisory Board. More professional and publication details are available at: http://www.deeds.informatik.tu-darmstadt.de/suri

Zahir Tari is a full professor at RMIT University, Australia. He is the director of the DSN (Distributed Systems and Networking) discipline at the School of Computer Science and IT at RMIT. His main areas of expertise are on performance, reliability, and mobility. Professor Tari has published in reputable conferences and journals, such as *ACM/IEEE Transactions*. He also acted as the program committee chair as well as general chair of more than 20 international conferences (e.g., DOA, CoopIS, ODBASE, GADA, and IFIP DS 11.3 on Database Security). Professor Tari is the coauthor of a few books. More details about him and his team can be found at http://www.cs.rmit.edu.au/eCDS.

David Tipper is an associate professor of telecommunications, with a secondary appointment in electrical engineering, at the University of Pittsburgh, PA. Prior to joining Pitt in 1994, he was an associate professor of electrical and computer engineering at Clemson University. He is a graduate of the University of Arizona and Virginia Tech. His current research interests are network design and traffic restoration procedures for survivable networks, infrastructure protection, network control techniques, and performance analysis. Professor Tipper's research has been supported by grants from various government and corporate sources, such as NSF, DARPA, NIST, AT&T, and IBM. He is a senior member of IEEE. He served as the coguest editor of the special issue on "Designing and Managing Optical Networks and Services for High Reliability," *Journal of Network and Systems Management*, March 2005, and the special issue on "Fault Management in Communication Networks," *Journal of Network and Systems Management*, June 1997. He was technical program chair of the Fourth International IEEE Design of Reliable Communication Networks Workshop. He is the coauthor of the textbook *The Physical Layer of Communication Systems* (Artech House, 2006). He can be reached at tipper@mail.sis.pitt.edu.

Kishor Trivedi holds the Hudson Chair in the Department of Electrical and Computer Engineering at Duke University, Durham, NC. He has been on the Duke faculty since 1975. He is the author of the well-known text *Probability and Statistics with Reliability, Queuing and Computer Science Applications* (Englewood Cliffs, NJ: Prentice-Hall), this text was reprinted as an Indian edition, and a thoroughly revised second edition (including its Indian edition) was published by John Wiley, New York. He has also published two other books entitled *Performance and Reliability Analysis of Computer Systems* (New York: Kluwer Academic Publishers,) and *Queuing Networks and Markov Chains* (New York: John Wiley). He is a fellow of the Institute of Electrical and Electronics Engineers and a Golden Core Member of IEEE Computer Society. During a sabbatical year 2002–2003, he was the Poonam and Prabhu Goel Professor in the Department of Computer Science and Engineering at IIT Kanpur while at the same time he was a Fulbright Visiting Lecturer to India. He has published over 350 articles and has supervised 39 Ph.D. dissertations. He is on the editorial boards of *IEEE Transactions on Dependable and Secure Computing, Journal of Risk and Reliability, International Journal of Performability Engineering,* and *International Journal of Quality and Safety Engineering*.

Lingyu Wang joined the Concordia Institute for Information Systems Engineering as an assistant professor in 2006. He received a Ph.D. in 2006 in information technology from George Mason University, Fairfax, VA. From 2000–2006, he worked as a research assistant in the Center for Secure Information Systems at George Mason University. His specific area of research interest is in information security and electronic privacy. His areas of expertise include database security, data privacy, access control, network security, intrusion detection, and vulnerability analysis. Dr. Wang has published in top journals, conferences, and workshops in these areas.

Jeannette M. Wing is the President's professor of computer science and the head of the Computer Science Department at Carnegie Mellon University, Pittsburgh, PA. Starting July 1, 2007, she will head the Computer and Information Science and Engineering Directorate at the National Science Foundation. Professor Wing's general research interests are in the areas of specification and verification, concurrent and distributed systems, and programming languages. Her current focus is on the foundations of trustworthy computing. Professor Wing has been a member of many advisory boards, including the Networking and Information Technology (NITRD) Technical Advisory Group to the President's Council of Advisors on Science and Technology (PCAST), the National Academies of Sciences' Computer Science and Telecommunications Board, the ACM Council, the DARPA Information Science and Technology (ISAT) Board, NSF's CISE Advisory Board, Microsoft's Trustworthy Computing Academic Advisory Board, and the Intel Research Pittsburgh's Advisory Board. She was or is on the editorial board of ten journals. She is a member of AAAS, ACM, IEEE, Sigma Xi, Phi Beta Kappa, Tau Beta Pi, and Eta Kappa Nu. Professor Wing is an ACM fellow and an IEEE fellow.

Tao Wu

Dependable Computing and Networking Lab
Department of Electrical and Computer Engineering
Iowa State University

Yu-Sung Wu is a Ph.D. student in the School of Electrical and Computer Engineering at Purdue University, West Lafayette, IN, since 2004. His primary research areas are information security and fault tolerance in computer systems. He is a member of the Dependable Computing Systems Laboratory at Purdue, where he participates in the research projects for ADEPTS (an intrusion response system) and CIDS (a correlation framework for intrusion detection). Yu-Sung also has been working closely with researchers at Avaya Labs on building the IDS/IPS solutions for voiceover IP systems.

1 Information Assurance

Yi Qian University of Puerto Rico at Mayaguez, Puerto Rico
James Joshi University of Pittsburgh, USA
David Tipper University of Pittsburgh, USA
Prashant Krishnamurthy University of Pittsburgh, USA

1.1 INTRODUCTION

Recent advances in computer networks and information technology (IT) and the advent and growth of the Internet have created unprecedented levels of opportunities for the connectivity and interaction of information systems at a global level. This has provided significant new possibilities for advancing knowledge and societal interactions across the spectrum of human endeavors, including fundamental scientific research, education, engineering design and manufacturing, environmental systems, health care, business, entertainment, and government operations. As a result, our society has already become intrinsically dependent on IT. In fact, networked information systems have been recognized as one of the basic critical infrastructures of society [1]. A consequence of the increasing dependence on networked information systems has been the significantly heightened concerns regarding their *security* and *dependability*. In particular, the interconnections, interactions, and dependencies among networked information systems and other critical infrastructure systems (e.g., electric power grids) can dramatically magnify the consequence of damages resulting from even simple security violations and/or faults. Hence, there is an urgent need to ensure that we have in place a solid foundation to help us justify the trust that we place on these information technologies and infrastructures.

Research and development activities focused on ensuring that a networked information system (a) functions correctly in various operational environments, and (b) provides the protection of critical information and resources associated with them, have been pursued within both the security and dependability communities. Although the security and dependability communities appear to focus on significantly overlapping concerns (e.g., *availability*), the efforts to converge their approaches and accumulated knowledge to generate innovative solutions have not been forthcoming or has been very slow at best. At the same time, the threats to the emerging networks and infrastructures, as well as the sophistication level of automated attack tools and malicious agents to easily inflict serious damages, are growing rapidly. It is a common belief now that ensuring *absolute security* is an unachievable practical goal. Hence, a growing concern is that of ensuring that networks and systems provide an assured level of functionalities even in the presence of disruptive events that attempt to violate their security and dependability goals. The capability of a system has been described by various terms, such as, *survivability, resilience, disruption tolerance,* and so on. A plethora of solutions has also been generated within these communities to address their respective, albeit overlapping, concerns related to increasing the trustworthiness of the overall system. We believe that efforts should be directed toward exploiting the synergies that exist among various piecemeal solutions from both security and dependability areas to seek out integrated, holistic solutions that allow us to provide assurances about the trustworthiness of the networks and systems that we use. It is worth noting that similar sentiments have recently been expressed in the research community [2–5].

We have conceived of this book as an effort toward the key goal of exploring the issues related to the *integration of* and *interaction between* approaches, models, architectures, and so on, prevalent in the security and dependability areas. In particular, we view *information assurance* (IA) as a growing area that can form an umbrella to bring together the efforts in security and dependability areas, mainly because their primary goal is to provide an adequate level of assurance that the networked information systems and infrastructures can be relied upon and trusted. Furthermore, the interaction between dependability and security is only beginning to be addressed in the research literature but is a crucial topic for successfully building IA into IT systems.

To the best of our knowledge, there is currently no comprehensive book that focuses on such an integrated view of IA. This book is an initial attempt to fill this gap. The goal of this book is to present a sample of the state-of-the-art survey of *dependability* and *security* techniques followed by an in-depth look at how these two components interact in providing IA and what the challenges are for the assurance of emerging systems. Our hope here is that by bringing both areas together, we will make a start toward integrating the approaches.

1.2   INFORMATION ASSURANCE: DEPENDABILITY AND SECURITY OF NETWORKED INFORMATION SYSTEMS

As mentioned earlier, we view IA as encompassing both dependability and security areas. In this section, we briefly introduce key terminologies from these areas and present our view on the need for such an integrated view.

Information or computer security primarily focuses on the issues related to *confidentiality, integrity,* and *availability* (CIA) of information [7]. *Confidentiality* refers to ensuring that highly sensitive information remains unknown to certain users. *Integrity* refers to the authenticity of information or its source. *Availability* refers to ensuring that information or computer resources are available to authorized users in a timely manner. Other key security issues often added include *accountability, non-repudiation,* and *security assurance* [7]. *Accountability* ensures that an entity's action is traceable uniquely to that entity; *non-repudiation* refers to ensuring that an entity cannot deny its actions; and *security assurance* refers to the confidence that the security requirements are met by an information system. Policy models, mechanisms, and architectural solutions have been extensively investigated by the security community to address issues related to specification and enforcement of the security requirements of networked information systems. In addition to proactive, preventive techniques, reactive techniques that involve detection followed by response and recovery continue to be developed to address the overall protection issues. Cryptographic techniques are widely used as mechanisms to achieve the above mentioned security goals.

The *dependability* area, on the other hand, has primarily focused on how to quantitatively express the ability of a system to provide its specified services in the presence of failures, through the measures of *reliability, availability, safety,* and *performability* [6]. *Reliability* refers to the probability that a system provides its service throughout the specified period of time. *Availability,* a key goal of security also, more specifically refers to the fraction of time that a system can be used for its intended purpose within a specified period of time. *Safety* refers to the probability that a system does not fail in such a way as to cause a major damage. *Performability* quantitatively measures the performance level of a system in the presence of failures. An important observation that can be made here is that of the richness of the quantitative techniques within the dependability area in contrast to the scarcity of such techniques in the security area. One reason for this is the difficulty in applying quantitative techniques for *confidentiality* and *integrity* issues, as well as the cryptographic techniques. Confidentiality and integrity issues were the primary security concerns for the security community for a considerable period of time and several "formal" approaches focused on these were developed to address the issues of verification and qualitative validation of security properties. Interestingly, both *confidentiality* and *integrity* issues are also sometimes considered as relevant dependability goals [8].

A related notion that attempts to capture both the security and dependability concerns is that of *survivability*. *Survivability* has been defined in various ways by different researchers and no consensus yet exists on its standard definition. One way to define survivability is as the capability of a system to fulfill its mission, in a timely manner, in presence of attacks, failures, or accidents [6]. A key goal here is to provide a quantitative basis for indicating that a system meets its security and dependability goals. A key motivation towards this direction is provided by the fact that absolute security is an unachievable goal, as indicated by the undecidability of the *safety problem* related to security shown by Harrison, Ruzzo, and Ullman in their seminal paper [9]. It is also virtually impossible to completely identify all the vulnerabilities in a networked information environment that is characterized by ever increasing heterogeneity of its components. In the face of such an insurmountable challenge, a key alternative is to set *provisioning of an acceptable level of services in presence of disruptive events* as a practical goal; in other words, a more realistic goal is that of ensuring a desired level of assurance that the required security and dependability goals are met by a system throughout its life cycle.

While there is an urgent need for solutions that integrate dependability and security, the two communities have largely remained separated, although efforts can be seen towards desirable interactions between them. A simple and often cited difference between the two areas is that dependability focuses primarily on faults and errors in the systems that are typically non-malicious in nature (primarily from the fault tolerance design area), while security focuses mainly on protection against malicious attempts to violate the security goals. However, such a difference is not accurate and can be seen in the various taxonomies developed within each community. For instance, the taxonomies for security vulnerabilities developed by Landwehr et al. [10] and later by Avizienis et al. [11] incorporate both *intentional* and *unintentional* sources of security vulnerabilities. The growing realization of the overlapping nature of the two areas can be seen among researchers in their efforts towards cross-pollinating the two areas in order to synthesize integrated frameworks.

This book first aims to highlight the overlapping aspect of the dependability and security areas (Figure 1.1), an understanding which we believe is fundamental to exploiting the synergies within the two communities. An integrated taxonomy that congregates the attributes of dependability and security is an important goal and some efforts towards this direction can be seen (e.g., Chapter 6). A natural outcome of the overlapping concerns of the two areas is that of using the well developed techniques in one area to address issues in the other or of

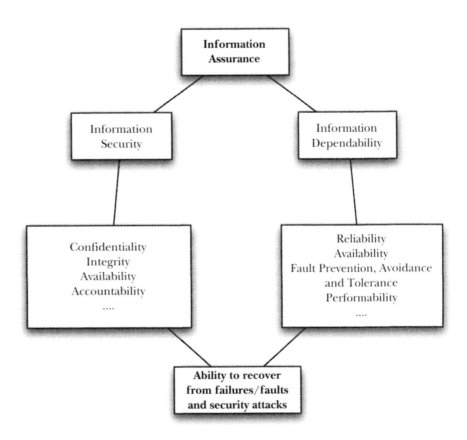

Information assurance: interaction between security and dependability.

synthesizing similar techniques from the two areas to create more effective, integrated solutions. One such area of cross-pollination can be seen in the use of fault-diagnosis techniques using fault trees in the fault tolerance community that parallels the use of attack trees/graphs to characterize security intrusions. Furthermore, correlating alerts and symptoms to more accurately identify the source of a problem and/or its consequences are important diagnostic activities related to both dependability and security. This commonality provides prospects for integrated diagnostic frameworks that can capture disruption scenarios related to malicious activities or non-malicious events. Such integrated fault and attack diagnosis and alert correlation approaches have already emerged as active research foci. An important observation related to security is the non-predictability of security threats and attacks; it makes modeling attackers significantly challenging. Furthermore, as mentioned earlier, the security area currently lacks viable quantitative techniques. These deficiencies add newer research challenges to generating integrated, holistic solutions to modeling, analysis, and evaluation of security and dependability of a networked information system to establish assurance of its quality (e.g., lack of vulnerability, or appropriate measures against possible threats) and eventually its trustworthiness. Sophisticated stochastic techniques, such as Markov models, which have been widely used for dependability analysis, are currently being adopted and extended to additionally address security issues as discussed in Chapter 7. Such quantitative techniques, as well as newer game-theory based approaches (e.g., Chapter 8), are also currently being pursued to address the challenges related to the coincident effect of all types of disruptive events. Furthermore, it is important to note that the security and dependability concerns related to different system or architectural layers/components, such as operating systems, applications, networks, wireless infrastructures, and so on, bring forth their unique challenges. In addition to developing solutions for these different types of IT environments, there is also a crucial need to synthesize these solutions to ensure the survivability of huge infrastructures against large scale cyber attacks, which could become a catastrophe for a society that now relies so much on the technology.

In summary, we characterize IA to encompass dependability and security concerns and emphasize that combined IA approaches that address security and dependability together is the needed direction because:

+ Many threats to dependability and security are common or similar. Combined modeling of failures and security threats will help provide more accurate understanding of the underlying problems.

+ There is a need for both qualitative and quantitative base when establishing the overall assurance that a system maintains a desired level of trustworthiness. Quantitative and qualitative techniques that are abundant in dependability and security areas, respectively, complement each other and will help create more effective IA solutions.

+ In reality, all types of disruptive events (faults and attacks) may coexist within a single networked information system. Hence, all types of disruptive events should be modeled together so that any coincident effect of different disruptive events and their emergent characteristics can be more accurately understood.

+ Different techniques developed within each area may be useful in the other area. For instance, design diversity and redundancy, which were typically employed in fault-tolerance community, have been beneficial for security. At the same time, a combined approach will avoid duplication of effort.

1.3   BOOK ORGANIZATION

In this section, we briefly overview the organization of the book, which has been divided into three parts, each containing several chapters.

1.3.1   The Three Parts of the Book

One of our key goals for this edited book has been to emphasize the need to bring together the communities and rich research results from the areas of security and dependability to exploit the synergies that exist between them, so that the growing issue of survivable and resilient networked information systems can be addressed in a holistic manner. Toward this goal, our key efforts have been to focus on the interaction and integration of tools and techniques from the security and dependability areas. Figure 1.2 illustrates the generic organization of the book into three parts.

Part I focuses on the foundational concepts from both security and dependability areas and sets the stage for looking at the issues related to their integration and interaction. A key goal of these chapters is to provide the overview of the various concepts and terminologies needed to understand the later chapters so that the book is self-contained.

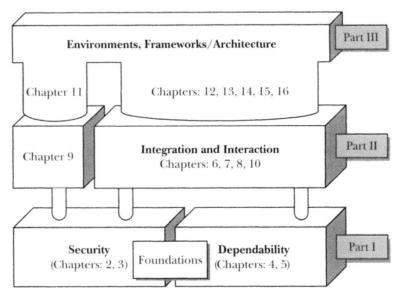

FIGURE   Organization of the book into three parts, each containing multiple chapters.

1.2

Part II focuses on the interaction and integration of mechanisms and approaches from the areas of security and dependability. Chapter 9, which stands separate from the other four chapters in this part, focuses more on security, although its approach is generically applicable to the integrated environment. Also, the content of Chapter 9, generating attack trees and capturing attack scenarios, is a crucial step in building a resilient system and can potentially be integrated with fault tree concepts from the dependability community.

In Part III, which further builds on interaction and integration of security and dependability approaches, we have grouped the chapters that address related issues in specific types of environments (e.g., operating systems in Chapter 12 and wireless systems in Chapter 15) or the design of frameworks/architecture (e.g., integrated fault and security management framework in Chapter 16). Chapter 13 focuses on intrusion response systems that we believe are crucial for building survivable systems. We have included Chapter 11 in Part III, although it primarily focuses on security vulnerabilities, because it addresses a specialized environment (i.e., optical network environments) and monitoring and detection issues that are key components for survivable systems.

An overview of each chapter is provided in the following sections.

1.3.2   Chapter 2: Network Security

This chapter introduces key concepts related to *network security*. In particular, the chapter focuses on issues related to the assessment of networks' current state of security, mechanisms to prevent and detect security violations, and policies, procedures, and techniques to respond to security intrusions. The chapter overviews various security services currently available and introduces cryptographic techniques and security protocols that are commonly used for securing a networked environment. The chapter also briefly overviews network security threats and attacks and how they can be addressed by using various security services and architectural configurations.

1.3.3   Chapter 3: Security for Distributed Systems: Foundations of Access Control

This chapter provides a comprehensive overview of key concepts underlying the foundations of access control and a discussion of key issues and trends in *access control for distributed systems*. The chapter introduces the notions of identification, authentication, and access control for distributed systems. It touches on various access control models, such as the *role-based access control* (RBAC) and *Bell-LaPadula* models, and surveys the main techniques for their implementation. The chapter also presents newly emerging access control-related standards such as *Security Assertion Markup Language* (SAML) and *EXtensible Access Control Markup Language* (XACML). Newer security issues within the context of distributed systems, such as *trust negotiation, secure interoperation, location-based security,* and *federated digital identity management* are also discussed.

1.3.4   Chapter 4: Network Survivability

This chapter explores *network survivability* and dependability mechanisms used to construct fault-tolerant communication networks. Basic network survivable design and traffic restoration concepts are reviewed. Research issues in the current literature are discussed along with potential avenues for integration with security techniques.

1.3.5   Chapter 5: System Survivability

This chapter introduces several topics that are at the core of *systems survivability*. It first introduces the notion of survivability and discusses its relation to fault models to establish a bridge between survivability and fault tolerance. It analyzes the limitations of standard fault-tolerance techniques to environments subjected to malicious acts. The chapter introduces the concept of *design for survivability* and discusses various design approaches for survivability. The author introduces *decentralization* as a basic concept in overcoming the impact of faults and security compromises, and discusses it as a mechanism to achieve survivability. The chapter finally presents a transformation model that can be used to relate survivability problems to problems from other well-established theoretical fields, followed by a discussion on how this will enable us to find solutions to survivability issues in new solution spaces, and allow for complexity analysis and comparison of solutions.

1.3.6   Chapter 6: Taxonomy and Framework for Integrating Dependability and Security

This chapter surveys various taxonomies and frameworks for integrating *dependability* and *security*. It emphasizes that security issues have not been comprehensively treated in existing taxonomies and frameworks. For instance, the security issues of authenticity and nonrepudiation have not been well integrated into the existing taxonomies and frameworks. In addition, many elements of existing taxonomies appear loosely integrated without generic relationships that capture interactions among different elements. Based on this observation, the authors present a novel integrated generic taxonomy and framework by using a feedback control system as a model to integrate concepts and attributes of both dependability and security. The chapter further expands the framework to cover lower-level techniques related to security and survivability.

1.3.7   Chapter 7: Stochastic Models/Techniques for Secure and Survivable Systems

This chapter focuses on the need for the quantitative analysis of dependability attributes, in particular, security and survivability. In this chapter, the authors explain *stochastic modeling techniques* based on Markovian and non-Markovian models for evaluating the system security and survivability. In particular, efforts toward capturing the details of real architectures for the systems often result in large stochastic models that are difficult to solve. The chapter emphasizes the use of higher-level formalisms based on stochastic Petri nets and their extensions for this purpose. The chapter presents these formalisms and illustrates them in the context of security and survivability modeling of the networked systems.

1.3.8   Chapter 8: Integrated Dependability and Security Evaluation Using Game Theory and Markov Models

This chapter attempts to interpret and assess the trustworthiness of networked information systems by combining security and dependability approaches. In particular, the chapter emphasizes the need for a combined approach in order to more accurately model reality. The chapter discusses the security of a system in a probabilistic manner with a goal to supplement assessment techniques from both security and dependability domains. The chapter extends a continuous-time Markov chain (CTMC) to include security attacks modeled using *game theory techniques* and categorized as intentional faults. It shows how dependability modeling and analysis can be further used to obtain quantitative metrics of system security as well as system trustworthiness.

1.3.9   Chapter 9: Scenario Graphs Applied to Network Security

This chapter deals with the complex problem of generating attack graphs. While the traditional model-checking approach produces one counterexample to illustrate a violation of a property by a model of a system, this chapter adopts the model-checking approach to generate all counterexamples that violate a given property. The chapter presents algorithms to create a set of *all* the counterexamples, called a *scenario graph*, for a networked system. The chapter explains how a scenario graph can be used to study what attacks are possible on a particular configuration of a networked system. Using a detailed example, the chapter illustrates how one can model a computer network and automatically generate and analyze attack graphs. The attack graph produced by the algorithms presented shows all ways in which an intruder can violate a given desired security property.

1.3.10   Chapter 10: Vulnerability-Centric Alert Correlation

This chapter discusses issues related to survivability of systems under multistep network intrusions. Defending a network against such intrusions is particularly challenging because experienced attackers can circumvent security controls and detections by gradually elevating their privileges on the intermediate hosts before reaching the final goal. This chapter describes recent advances in correlating intrusion alerts for the defense against such multistep network intrusions. Alert correlation techniques aim to reassemble correlated intrusion detection system (IDS) alerts into more meaningful attack scenarios. The chapter presents a *vulnerability-centric* approach to alert correlation that benefits from the advantages of topological vulnerability analysis and those of alert correlation. The chapter discusses how this method can effectively filter out irrelevant alerts, defeat the so-called *slow attacks*, and add to alert correlation the capabilities of hypothesizing missing alerts, predicting possible future alerts, and aggregating repetitive alerts. Empirical results presented show that these tasks can be fulfilled faster than the IDSs can report alerts under intensive attacks.

1.3.11   Chapter 11: Monitoring and Detecting Attacks in All-Optical Networks

This chapter focuses on the security attacks related to an all-optical network (AON). An AON is essentially a network in which data does not undergo optical-to-electrical (O-E) or electrical-to-optical (E-O) conversion within the network.

Although AONs are a viable technology for future telecommunication and data networks, little attention has been devoted to the intrinsic differences between AONs and existing electro-optic/electronic networks in issues of security management. AON features like transparency and nonregeneration make attack detection and localization difficult. However, it is important to detect and localize an attack quickly in a transparent AON. The chapter specifically focuses on the diagnosis of crosstalk attacks as crosstalk attacks have the potential to create the widespread damage in AONs. The chapter provides a crosstalk attack model and a monitoring model, and then shows that it is possible to effectively reduce the number of monitors while still retaining all diagnostic capabilities. In particular, the chapter presents necessary and sufficient conditions for diagnosis of both single as well as multiple (i.e., k-crosstalk) attacks. The key ideas used for this include employing the status of existing connections along with that of test connections for diagnosis. The chapter also develops efficient monitor placement policies, test connection setup policies, and routing policies for such a network.

1.3.12   Chapter 12: Robustness Evaluation of Operating Systems

This chapter focuses on the *robustness* of the operating system (OS). Because it is a key component in all computer systems, it is imperative that the OS has an ability to correctly support the applications running on it even in the presence of operational perturbations. The chapter introduces *OS robustness* as the degree to which an OS can handle the perturbations and maintain its correct functionality. Among various perturbations that an OS may have to withstand include hardware malfunction, buggy software, invalid inputs, and stress generated by applications running on it. In essence, OSs are highly complex functional entities with countless environment interaction scenarios that limit the use of static analytical approaches. This chapter emphasizes experimental evaluations of *OS robustness* as a preferred approach and discusses various experimental methods. The chapter places key emphasis on *target system definition, choice of evaluation strategy, the metrics to use,* and *interpretation of the results.* Using a case study, the chapter illustrates these various aspects of the robustness evaluation methods.

1.3.13   Chapter 13: Intrusion Response Systems: A Survey

Protecting networks from security attacks is an important concern. While the *intrusion prevention* and *intrusion detection* systems have been the subject of much study, the actions that need to follow the steps of prevention and detection, namely *response*, have received less attention from researchers or practitioners. It was traditionally thought of as an offline process with humans in the loop, such as system administrators performing forensics by going through the system logs and determining which services or components need to be recovered. This chapter lays out the design challenges in building an autonomous intrusion response systems and provides a classification of existing work on the topic in four categories: *response through static decision tables*, *response through dynamic decision process*, *intrusion tolerance through diverse replicas*, and *intrusion response for specific classes of attacks*. The existing intrusion response systems are analyzed by using the classification schemes presented in this chapter. The chapter also presents methods for benchmarking the intrusion response systems.

1.3.14 Chapter 14: Secure and Resilient Routing: A Framework for Resilient Network Architectures

This chapter presents a generic framework for a secure and *resilient network routing architecture*. Such an architecture provides different services with different priorities to coexist in a virtualized environment. A key issue here is to provide robustness to the routing architecture to protect against network overloads and security attacks. The chapter discusses building blocks for the proposed framework, which is shown to be conducive to providing secure traffic engineering as well as network resiliency. The approach taken in this chapter starts with the identification of the need for the service requirement for security and resiliency in a prioritized environment and works backwards to identify the desirable architectural components to support this service paradigm.

1.3.15 Chapter 15: Security and Survivability of Wireless Systems

Information assurance techniques employed in wired networks have limited direct applicability in *wireless networks* because of the unique aspects of wireless networks (e.g., user mobility, wireless communication channel, power conservation, limited computational power in mobile nodes, security at the link layer, and so on). The interaction between the components of information assurance, namely availability and security, in a wireless network environment poses new challenges. In this chapter, recent research on understanding survivability and security in wireless networks and their interaction is presented.

1.3.16 Chapter 16: Integrated Fault and Security Management

This chapter focuses on an integrated framework for managing *faults* and *security intrusions*. The chapter emphasizes the need to be careful while identifying symptoms related to faults and security attacks, which may be similar, and classifying faults or security attacks based on such symptoms. Integration of fault and intrusion management is, however, a natural result of the similarity in the techniques used to analyze and identify them (i.e., based on symptom collection, correlation, and evaluation). The chapter presents an active problem diagnosis framework that analyzes faults and security alarms using the same engine. A key challenge is to ensure that incomplete symptom information is handled to properly identify faults and intrusions. The chapter then presents an architecture for network-based intrusion detection systems that analyzes traffic collected from different sensors, identifies faults and intrusions, and initiates actions to mitigate the intrusions/faults and their effects.

1.4 CONCLUSION

As noted above, the goal of the book is to provide the reader with an appreciation of the need for integrating security and dependability techniques to address information assurance problems. Note that the chapters included in this book represent some pressing issues and they are not in anyway exhaustive in considering the integration of the security and dependability areas; for example, discrete event simulation has been used for both security and dependability analysis [6], but currently we have no chapter addressing the discrete event simulation approach.

Lastly, the editors wish to thank the authors for their contributions to the book and help in its publication.

References

[1] T. Lewis, *Critical Infrastructure Protection in Homeland Security: Defending a Networked Nation* (Wiley-Interscience, 2006).

[2] E. Jonsson, "An Integrated Framework for Security and Dependability," *Proceedings of 1998 ACM Workshop on New Security Paradigms*, Charlottesville, Virginia, United States 1998.

[3] J. McDermott, A. Kim, and J. Froscher, "Merging Paradigms of Survivability and Security: Stochastic Fault and Designed Faults," *Proceedings of ACM New Security Paradigms Workshop*, Ascona, Switzerland 2003.

[4] National Science and Technology Council, "Federal Plan for Cyber Security and Information Assurance Research and Development," April 2006, at http://www.nitrd.gov/.

[5] Secure IST Advisory Board, "Recommendations for a Security and Dependability Research Framework," Issue 3.0, January 2007, at http://ftp.cordis.europa.eu /pub/ist /docs/trust-security/securist-ab-recommendations-issue-v3-0_en.pdf.

[6] D. Nicol, W. Sanders, and K. Trivedi, "Model-Based Evaluation: From Dependability to Security," *IEEE Transcript on Dependable and Secure Computing* 1, No. 1 (January–March 2004). pp. 48–65

[7] M. Bishop, "Computer Security: Art and Science," Addison-Wesley (ISBN: 0-201-44099-7), 2002.

[8] B. E. Helvik, "Perspectives on the dependability of networks and services," Telektronikk (100th Anniversary Issue: Perspectives in telecommunications), Vol. 3, 2004, pp. 27–44.

[9] Michael A. Harrison, Walter L. Ruzzo and Jeffrey D. Ullman, "Protection in Operating Systems", Communications of the ACM, Vol. 19, No. 8, August 1976, pp. 461–471.

[10] Carl E. Landwehr, Alan R. Bull, John P. McDermott, William S. Choi, "A taxonomy of computer program security flaws" ACM Computing Surveys (CSUR), Vol. 26 , Issue 3 (September 1994) pp. 211–254.

[11] Avizienis, A., J. C. Laprie, B. Randell and C. Landwhehr, "Basic Concepts and Taxonomy of Dependable and Secure Computing," IEEE Transactions on Dependable and Secure Computing, Vol. 1, No. 1, Jan–March 2004, pp. 11–33.

PART I

FOUNDATIONAL BACKGROUND ON SECURITY AND DEPENDABILITY TECHNIQUES

CHAPTER 2 Network Security
(James Joshi and Prashant Krishnamurthy, University of Pittsburgh, USA)

CHAPTER 3 Security for Distributed Systems: Foundations of Access Control
(Elisa Bertino, Purdue University, USA, and Jason Crampton, University of London, UK)

CHAPTER 4 Network Survivability
(Bjorn Jager, Molde University, Norway, John Doucette, University of Alberta Edmonton, Canada, and David Tipper, University of Pittsburgh, USA)

CHAPTER 5 System Survivability
(Axel Krings, University of Idaho, USA)

2 Network Security

CHAPTER

James Joshi   University of Pittsburgh, USA
Prashant Krishnamurthy   University of Pittsburgh, USA

2.1   INTRODUCTION

Information assurance (IA) deals with security and dependability of systems and networks. In this chapter, we provide an overview of issues, terminology, and techniques related to the security of the *network*. Network security comprises of ongoing activities that (a) assess the network for its current state of security, (b) have in place protection and prevention mechanisms against security threats, (c) implement detection mechanisms to rapidly identify security attacks that may have been successful, and (d) have policies, procedures, and techniques in place to respond to attacks. We discuss these aspects in a succinct manner in this chapter. In Section 2.2, we describe the network communications and how they are vulnerable to security attacks and provide a brief overview of security services. Section 2.3 is devoted to mechanisms that are used to protect networks from security threats or prevent successful attacks and here we discuss firewalls and cryptographic protocols. Intrusion detection is examined in Section 2.4 and response mechanisms are considered in Section 2.5.

2.2   NETWORK ATTACKS AND SECURITY ISSUES

In this section, we provide a very brief overview of communications across networks and discuss some specific attacks that illustrate how security is impacted in networks.

2.2.1   Network Communications

It is instructive to examine, at a very high level, how two hosts on the Internet usually make connections to one another to understand how attacks occur over the network. However, our goal here is not to explain protocols from a communications perspective (such as performance, reliability, and so on) or explore their details. Please note that what is described below corresponds only to a typical scenario and there are exceptions and many different possible variations for communications across the Internet.

Let us suppose that a client application on host A on network P wishes to connect to a server application on host B on network Q. The client and server applications run as processes on the respective hosts. The client application creates data that is sent down the protocol stack to the transport layer. The transport layer adds information to this data in a structured manner creating a *segment* that is passed down to the network layer. The transmission control protocol (TCP) and the user datagram protocol (UDP) are two common transport layer protocols. The transport layer segment forms the payload of a network layer *packet* or *datagram* usually carried by the Internet protocol (IP). The IP datagram is further carried by a link or medium access control (MAC) layer protocol in a *frame* on each link between host A and host B (examples are Ethernet and WiFi). Each link may have its own physical layer-dependent transmission mechanisms.

At the transport layer, a *port number* will identify the process in host A; let us denote this port number as P_A. Host A will have an IP address that belongs to network P; let us denote this as IP_A. The tuple $< P_A, IP_A >$, which is sometimes called a *socket*, is a globally unique identifier of the client process that intends to communicate with the server process. Similarly, the server process will be associated with a port number P_B and an IP address IP_B. A connection between the client and server can thus be uniquely identified through the tuple $< P_A, IP_A, P_B, IP_B >$. The transport layer segment consists of a header containing the source port P_A and the destination port P_B. The IP datagram has a header that contains the source IP address IP_A and the destination IP address IP_B.

Network interface cards only recognize the MAC address. When the network interface card in host A creates a MAC frame on the physical medium of network P, it typically uses a 48-bit source MAC address and a 48-bit destination MAC address. Obviously, host B is on a different network, possibly using a different link and physical layer. Thus, the destination MAC address does not belong to host B, but instead to a gateway or router that connects network P to other networks or the Internet. The IP address of the gateway is either manually installed in host A or host A finds this information using a *dynamic host configuration protocol* (DHCP). DHCP is also used to dynamically assign IP addresses to hosts in a network. However, knowledge of simply the IP address of the gateway does not suffice since the MAC address is necessary for the frame to be received by the gateway. A mapping of the IP address to the MAC address can be obtained using the *address resolution protocol* (ARP). Similarly, when a frame arrives at the gateway from the Internet to the host on the network Q, the gateway will have to use the ARP to determine the MAC address of the destination host. The gateway is responsible for routing the IP datagram in the received MAC frame to another router in the Internet, which forms a node on one of the available paths to the destination network Q. Such paths are determined using routing information through routing protocols like the routing information protocol (RIP), open shortest path first (OSPF), and border gateway protocol (BGP).

How does the application process on host A know the IP address of host B? Usually, the IP address is not known, instead a domain name such as "www.cnn.com" that is human friendly is used in the application. It is necessary for host A to use the *domain name service* (DNS) to determine the IP address of host B. This has to happen *prior* to the actual data being sent in an IP packet to host B. Each network has a local name server that is known to every host in that network (possibly through DHCP). Host A contacts the local name server when the application process in host A desires to send a packet to host B with information about host B (say "www.cnn.com"). If the local name server has cached information about the IP address of host B, it provides that information to host A immediately. If not, it contacts a root name server (there are only 13 of these worldwide). The root name servers have information about authoritative name servers that in turn have information related to hosts on their networks. In the above example, the root name server may provide the local name server of network P, the IP address of the authoritative name server for network Q. The local name server of network P then contacts the authoritative name server of network Q to obtain the IP address of host B. Then the IP address is forwarded to host A.

Now suppose that host A was successful in finding the IP address of host B using DNS. The application process in host A with port number P_A sends data to a process in host B with port number P_B. How did the process in host A know the port number P_B? Standard applications have standard port numbers. For example, a web server usually employs the port number 80, a telnet server uses 23, a web server running the secure sockets layer (SSL) uses 443, the simple mail transport protocol (SMTP) uses 25, and so on. Port numbers may also be changed after initial contact as in the case of protocols like the file transfer protocol (FTP) or applications like Skype. Although port numbers for standard services are well known, this does not automatically imply that such services are not available at other port numbers. For instance, it is quite possible to run a web server at a port number other than 80.

Services on servers "listen" for initial contact from clients at the standard port numbers. These are what we call "open" ports. When a packet from host A arrives at host B, it is sent up the protocol stack to the transport layer where the server that is listening at port number P_B receives the application data in the transport layer segment. The server processes the data appropriately and responds to the client at port number P_A, which is known because of the initial received packet.

Figure 2.1 shows a very simplified view of some of the many protocols and applications that are common in networked communications today. It is to be noted that this is just a very small fraction of the protocols and applications in use today. Each of these protocols could perhaps create security problems because they are capable of being abused by malicious entities in ways in which they were not anticipated to be used.

Security problems occur for a variety of reasons, but one common reason is that servers listening at known ports have bugs in their implementation (e.g., buffer overflows). For example, it is possible for a malicious entity (we will refer to a malicious entity—a human, a criminal organization, or software—as Oscar in this chapter) to craft packets that can be sent to buggy services. When a service is compromised, it can enable Oscar to take control over the host. This means Oscar can perhaps install malicious software on the host, use the host to launch other malicious packets, steal files that are stored on the host or on other hosts

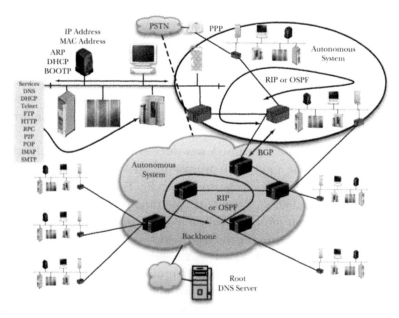

FIGURE   Simplified view of the many protocols that impact network communications.

2.1

on the network that trust the compromised host, and so on as described in the following examples.

2.2.2   Some Example Security Attacks

The emergence of very large cyber-crime operations has moved network security attacks from the realm of hobbyists to criminal organizations, making them more dangerous with potential for great economic harm. In this section, we discuss some specific security attacks that will lead us to a general discussion of security attacks and security services in the next section. We do not provide an exhaustive list of attacks but have picked a few for illustration. The web site of US-CERT (United States Computer Emergency Readiness Team) [1] is a good source for past and recent vulnerabilities and security incidents.

TCP SYN Flood Attack

As mentioned earlier, TCP is the most common transport layer protocol. It is used by many application layer protocols like the HyperText Transfer Protocol (HTTP) and FTP. TCP was designed to provide reliable service on top of the unreliable network layer provided by IP. So among other things, TCP is connection oriented and it carefully maintains buffers, windows, and other resources to count segments and track lost segments. When host A wants to connect to host B, a "three-way" handshake occurs to set up the connection. First, host A sends a TCP segment with a SYN flag set (this is one of six flags used for synchronization—bits—in TCP for indicating information). Host B acknowledges the SYN segment with its own TCP segment with the SYN flag and ACK flag (used to acknowledge the receipt of the SYN packet) set. Host A completes the handshake with a TCP segment with the ACK flag set. Then data transfer begins. Whenever a server receives a SYN segment from a client, it sets aside some resources (e.g., memory) anticipating a completed handshake and subsequent data transfer. As there are limited resources at a server, only a set number of connections can be accepted. Other requests are dropped. Oscar can make use of this "feature" to deny services to legitimate hosts by sending a flood of crafted SYN segments to a server with possibly spoofed source IP addresses. The server responds with SYN-ACK segments and waits for completion of the handshake, which never happens. Meanwhile, legitimate requests for connection are dropped. Such an attack is called a SYN flood attack and has been the cause of denial of service to popular web servers in recent years. Note that Oscar primarily makes use of a feature in a communications protocol to launch denial of service (DoS). The absence of authentication of the source IP address makes it difficult to block such attacks since it is hard to separate legitimate requests from malicious requests. Similarly, Internet

Control Message Protocol (ICMP) and other protocols can be used to launch floods that result in DoS. Distributed DoS (DDoS) attacks have recently made headlines by bringing down several popular web sites in recent years as well as launching attacks on root DNS servers. A taxonomy of DDoS attacks is available in Mirkovic and Reiher [2].

Address Spoofing and Sequence Number Guessing Attacks

Several services use the IP address or host name to provide access to the service. As discussed previously, it is very easy for Oscar to craft packets. Spoofing IP addresses is as trivial as spoofing host names. There have been instances of attacks where root access to certain hosts have been obtained by sending crafted packets with spoofed IP addresses. In many of the attacks, it is not sufficient to spoof IP addresses; it is also necessary to guess sequence numbers (of other protocols carried in the IP packet as payload such as TCP or DNS). For example, we previously discussed the TCP three-way handshake. As part of the handshake, both the client and the server use initial sequence numbers that are incremented in the corresponding acknowledgments. If the IP address is spoofed and Oscar wishes to fool the server into believing that a legitimate client has connected with it, Oscar needs to "guess" the sequence number generated by the server. This is because the server's SYN-ACK segment is delivered to an IP address that does not belong to Oscar (and hence Oscar may not receive the response from the server). The server sequence number is supposed to be random and difficult to guess. However, poor implementations of TCP have allowed malicious entities to easily guess the sequence number generated by the server. Similarly, spoofed DNS responses that can poison the DNS cache (see the section below on pharming) can be generated if the sequence numbers associated with DNS requests can be guessed.

Worm Attacks

Worms are self-replicating, malicious software programs that can crash hosts or services, open trapdoors for installing keyboard sniffers, or perform other malicious activity. Once a worm is installed on a host, it probes other networked hosts for bugs or vulnerabilities in services that can be exploited. This essentially means that the worm sends crafted packets to certain port numbers at IP addresses. If the services listening to such port numbers are vulnerable, the worm can exploit such vulnerabilities to install itself on such hosts. For example, in July 2001, web servers running Microsoft's Internet Information Server (IIS) software were discovered to have a buffer overflow bug. Although a patch was issued for this bug, not every host running IIS was patched. The Code Red (two versions) and Code Red II worms exploited this bug and spread it rapidly across the Internet [3]. It is estimated that Code Red infected at least 350,000 hosts.

The speed with which a worm spreads depends on the design of the worm (e.g., the rate at which it scans for other vulnerable hosts), whether patches exist for the vulnerability exploited by the worm, the number of hosts running the vulnerable software, and the clean-up rate [4]. The way worms find other hosts to exploit can also influence their spread. Many early worms would randomly pick IP addresses to probe for vulnerabilities. This, however, meant that many IP addresses would either not belong to hosts that existed or to hosts that did not run the vulnerable service or operating system, thereby limiting the spread of the worm. Others had a hard-coded sequence of IP addresses that would be probed. This meant that infected hosts would likely probe other infected hosts first.

Recent worms are intelligent—they look for "neighboring" IP addresses first. Some worms use Internet search engines to discover vulnerable hosts. However, most search engines present the same set of results for a query, thereby reducing the set of hosts scanned for vulnerabilities. The most rapidly spreading worms use email and entries in the address books of infected hosts to reach a variety of legitimate and potentially vulnerable hosts. In the past, exploits for vulnerabilities would not appear quickly, but it is common to see so-called "zero-day" exploits today. A zero-day exploit, for instance, can result in a worm that can be released on the same day that a vulnerability is discovered in a service. This makes it almost impossible to patch the exploit in time, enabling the worm to spread extremely rapidly.

Phishing, Evil Twins, and Pharming

Phishing is an example of a social engineering security attack where legitimate users are fooled into revealing information such as logins, passwords, credit card numbers, and so on by making them visit web sites that look like legitimate sites, but are actually fake ones run by criminal organizations. Legitimate users can visit such sites, for instance, by clicking on links that appear in emails that look legitimate. Most phishing attacks target financial organizations like banks or e-commerce sites like Paypal or eBay.

Recently, a special form of phishing attacks, called "evil twins," has appeared whereby WiFi access points are placed in areas (e.g., hot spots like coffee shops or hotels) close to where legitimate service is being provided by some service provider. When a legitimate user tries to connect to such access points placed by Oscar, a web page, similar to ones displayed by legitimate service providers, is displayed. It is common for subscribers to enter credit card and other sensitive information on these web pages, enabling Oscar to steal such information.

Pharming is a more dangerous security attack. As described previously, DNS is used to discover IP addresses associated with domain names. In the case of pharming, DNS caches can be poisoned with fake entries so that a user sees a fake web site even if a legitimate URL is typed in the browser. DNS cache poisoning is possible when name servers use vulnerable versions of software that can be exploited with unsolicited DNS responses. Once again, the impact is similar to phishing attacks where a legitimate user will reveal sensitive information to the criminals.

2.2.3   Security Attacks, Services, and Architecture

In the previous section, we have seen some examples of security attacks, such as denial of service, session hijacking, worms, and social engineering. One way of classifying security attacks is to consider their nature—whether they are passive or active. In the case of passive attacks, Oscar does not interfere with the information flow or storage (e.g., eavesdropping), making such attacks hard to discover. It is important to prevent such attacks. Active attacks (such as masquerading) involve interference and participation by Oscar. As they are hard to prevent, they must be detected and stopped as rapidly as possible.

Security attacks can be of many types: eavesdropping (interception) on information and reveling such information; interrupting the flow or availability of information; masquerading as a legitimate entity to access services, information, or resources; and fabricating information with the aim of causing damage are all different security attacks. Security attacks usually do not occur in one shot. Oscar typically first engages in mapping out the victim's network, resources, IP addresses, open services, and so on. This is sometimes called reconnaissance, and Oscar may try to get information that appears to be harmless if revealed, but may impact security later. This is followed up by exploitation of vulnerabilities, theft of information, taking over of hosts, and so on. An excellent treatment of the security attack process is available in Bejtlich [5].

The common security services to protect against security attacks as defined in the literature are *confidentiality, authentication, integrity, nonrepudiation,* and availability [6]. *Confidentiality* implies that information or data is kept secret from unauthorized entities, specifically Oscar. In the case of *authentication*, it is necessary for communicating parties to (a) ensure at the start of communications that they are communicating with who they think they are communicating with, that is, Oscar should not fool an honest Alice into thinking that she is communicating with an honest Bob, and (b) ensure that after communications have been established and verified to be between legitimate parties, that Oscar does not hijack the communications session and interpose himself as one of the legitimate parties. The second part of authentication is often called *message authentication* and it is combined with *integrity*. In such a case, once legitimate communications have been established, it is necessary to ensure that any messages exchanged have not been modified, fabricated, reordered, replayed, or deleted. *Nonrepudiation* refers to a security service where once a person has sent a message, he or she cannot deny having created the message. *Availability* refers to a security service that ensures that services are made available to an authorsized person in a timely manner

Note that all security services may not be present all the time, and different protocols and applications support different subsets of security services. Sometimes architectural methods (using firewalls, screened subnets, and demilitarized zones) are necessary for ensuring some of the security services (e.g., *confidentiality* or *availability*).

2.3   PROTECTION AND PREVENTION

In this section, we consider security mechanisms for protection against and prevention of security attacks. We consider firewalls and perimeter security in Section 2.3.1 and cryptographic protocols in Section 2.3.2. The interested reader is referred to Northcutt et al. [7] and Cheswick et al. [8] for more details on firewalls. A good reference that considers cryptography and cryptographic protocols is Stinson [9].

2.3.1   Firewalls and Perimeter Security

To block malicious packets from entering a network, it is common to employ firewalls. Firewalls in olden days referred to thick walls of brick constructed especially for preventing the spread of fires from one building to another. Firewalls today refer to hardware, software, and policies to prevent the spread of security attacks into an organization's (or individual's) network or host. As discussed previously in Section 2.2, attacks of many kinds occur due to maliciously crafted packets that arrive at the target network. If such packets can be identified and discarded, they will no longer be a threat to the security of the network. This is in essence the idea behind firewalls. However, it is not trivial to efficiently identify such packets correctly all the time. As shown in Figure 2.2, the firewall sits between the "inside" and the "outside." The inside is usually what needs to be protected. The term *firewall* can mean many things today, from a simple packet filter to a complex intrusion prevention system that is capable of examining a series of packets and reconstructing sessions for comparison with known attack signatures.

A *packet filter* is the simplest type of firewall. It filters incoming or outgoing packets based on *rules* created manually by the administrator of a network. Packet filters usually have a default "drop" policy. This means that if a packet does not satisfy any of the rules that allow it into the inside, it is dropped. Each packet

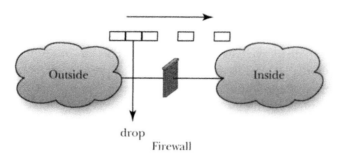

Schematic of a firewall.

is considered independently without consideration of previous or future packets, making packet filters fast and capable of handling high data rates. The simpler the rules are, the faster the filtering and the smaller the performance hit. Cisco's standard access control lists (ACLs) filter packets based solely on source IP addresses. In this case, it is easy to filter packets with source IP addresses that are obviously spoofed or other packets from sources that are not expected to communicate with the inside. Examples are IP packets that arrive from the outside with nonroutable source IP addresses, loopback IP addresses, or IP addresses that belong to hosts on the inside. However, standard ACLs cannot block packets to specific hosts on the inside or packets that correspond to specific protocols. The extended ACL from Cisco allows a packet filter to look at source and destination IP addresses, TCP or UDP port numbers, and TCP flags and make decisions on whether or not a packet should be allowed into the inside. Other firewall software (e.g., IPTables in Linux) and hardware have equivalent access control lists for filtering packets.

The rules in the packet filter are considered in strict order creating potential for configuration errors as the list of rules grows in size. One way of overcoming this problem is to use so-called dynamic packet filters or stateful firewalls. Dynamic packet filters build rules on the fly. The assumption is that hosts on the inside are to be trusted. When they send packets to open connections with hosts on the outside, a stateful firewall builds a rule on the fly that allows packets from the specific external host (and port number at that host) to the specific internal host (and the port number at this host). The rule is deleted when the connection is terminated. This reduces the number of hard-coded rules and makes it difficult for Oscar to guess what packets may make it through a firewall.

Packet filters can still be fooled through a variety of loopholes that exist (e.g., by sending fragmented packets). In order to determine whether or not packets are legitimate, it is often necessary to look at the application payload. Sometimes it is even necessary to reconstruct the application data. This is possible if proxy firewalls are used. Proxy firewalls consist of hardened hosts (usually dual-homed) that run reduced modules of certain applications. When an internal host makes a connection to the outside, it really makes a connection (say TCP) with the proxy firewall. The proxy then makes a connection to the external host. Thus, there are two connections that exist. External hosts only see the proxy firewall. They are not even aware of the existence of other internal hosts. When packets are returned, they make their way up the protocol stack where the application (with reduced features) reconstructs the data. If the data is legitimate, it is forwarded to the internal host. Moreover, Oscar can gain very little knowledge during reconnaissance because internal hosts are not visible to the outside world. However, proxy firewalls create performance bottlenecks. They also do not support a variety of applications, often frustrating legitimate network communications.

Architectural approaches can approximate the benefits of proxy firewalls, and yet keep performance levels reasonable. One common approach is to screen the inside from the outside by using one or more packet filters. In Figure 2.3, for example, packet filter A allows packets (from most legitimate hosts on the outside) through interface p to reach either the web server or the mail server. As almost anyone can reach these servers, this is called a *demilitarized zone* (DMZ). If it is also a router, it does not advertise the existence of the inside network to the outside world. Similarly, packet filter B allows packets from either the web server or the mail server to the inside through interface r. Thus, the inside network is screened from the outside.

Note that packet filters can also be used to stop packets from the inside from going out (e.g., through interfaces s and q in Figure 2.3). This may be necessary

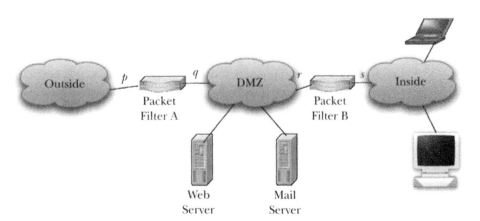

FIGURE   Schematic of a screened subnet and demilitarized zone.

2.3

if hosts on the inside have been compromised and are launching attacks, or hosts are trying to access services not allowed by corporate policy.

Nowadays, firewalls are more than simple packet filters. They can maintain state, do load balancing (if multiple firewalls are used), do some inspection of application payloads, detect attacks based on known signatures, maintain logs useful for forensics or analysis, and also act as endpoints for connectivity to mobile users who need to connect to the inside from the outside. For example, firewalls can now be the terminating points for virtual private network (VPN) connections using IPSec or SSL, which make use of cryptography to prevent outsiders from connecting to the inside or monitoring connections made by mobile employees. We discuss cryptographic protocols next.

2.3.2   Cryptographic Protocols

Security services such as confidentiality and integrity can be provided to communication protocols using cryptography. In this section, we provide a brief overview of the important topics in cryptography and cryptographic protocols. More details can be found in Stallings [6], Cheswick et al. [8], and Kaufmann [10].

Cryptographic protocols make use of cryptographic *primitives* that are used to provide the required security services. A classification of such primitives is shown in Figure 2.4. Cryptology is the broad discipline that includes the science of designing ciphers (cryptography) and that of breaking ciphers (cryptanalysis). Data that is encrypted is called "plaintext" and the result of encryption is called "ciphertext." Ciphers or encryption algorithms can be classified into secret key and public key categories.

In the case of secret key encryption, two honest parties, say Alice and Bob, share a secret key k that is used with an encryption algorithm. Both encryption and decryption make use of the same key k and both parties have knowledge of the key. Secret key algorithms can further be classified into block ciphers and stream ciphers. Block ciphers encrypt "blocks" of data (e.g., 64, 128, or 256 bits) at a time. Each block is encrypted with the same key. Common block ciphers include the Advanced Encryption Standard (AES), Blowfish, and CAST. Stream ciphers use the key k to generate a key stream. The key stream is XORed with the data stream to create the ciphertext. At the receiver, the same key stream is generated and XORed with the ciphertext to obtain the data. Block ciphers can be used to create key streams through standard modes of operation [6, 9]. RC-4 is a common stream cipher that is not derived from a block cipher. It is recommended that the key size for good security with block or stream ciphers should be at least 128 bits today. It is common to assume that everyone, including Oscar, knows the encryption algorithms, but the key is secret and known only to honest communicating parties, in this case, Alice and Bob.

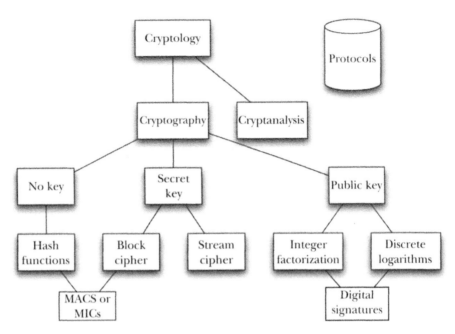

FIGURE   Classification of cryptographic primitives.

2.4

Public key encryption is based on the property that given a pair of related information, one part of the information can be revealed. However, the other part of the information cannot be discovered even with knowledge of the first part. For example, if some large prime numbers are randomly selected and multiplied, revealing the product does not enable others to guess or calculate the prime numbers that are factors of the product. This property is used in RSA. The information that is revealed is called the "public key" and the information kept secret is called the "private key." To encrypt information, the public key is used. To decrypt information, the private key is used. Another mathematical technique used for public key encryption is based on discrete logarithms. Because of the mathematical nature of public key encryption, key sizes are typically longer for good security—around 1,024 bits for RSA.

Public key encryption is also computationally expensive. Consequently, it is common to use public key encryption for key establishment and digital signatures. Confidentiality and integrity of bulk data are achieved using secret key schemes. Although the public key of an honest party like Alice can be made public, its authenticity needs to be verified since Oscar can claim to be Alice and publish his key as hers. It is common to use digital certificates signed by one of a few trusted certification authorities to verify the authenticity of the public key (see below for more on digital signatures). This approach is used in modern web browsers for e-commerce applications.

We also include hash functions in the classification in Figure 2.4. They are not strictly encryption schemes. They map any sized data to a fixed-size digest. Given the digest, it is considered infeasible to obtain any data that maps to the digest if the size of the digest is at least 160 bits. Popular hash functions in use today are MD-5 and SHA.

Block ciphers and hash functions can be used to create *message authentication codes* (MACs) or *message integrity checks* (MICs). These are checksums on data created using block ciphers or hash functions with a shared secret key between the communicating parties. MACs or MICs provide message authentication and integrity. If Oscar were to fabricate a message or modify a legitimate message, the checksum would always fail, alerting the receiver of a problem with the received data. The Cipher Block Chaining MAC (CBC-MAC) that uses block ciphers and keyed-hash MAC (HMAC) that employs hash functions are popular standard implementations of MACs.

Digital signatures are like physical signatures. They attest some information and are bound to that information. Typically this involves encrypting the hash value of some information with the private key of a public key/private key pair. Suppose Alice generated some data and created a digital signature of the data. Anyone can verify the signature because decrypting the signature requires the public key, which is available to everyone. No one except Alice can generate the signature because she is the only one in possession of the private key. Recall that knowledge of the public key does not help Oscar or others deduce the private key.

The cryptographic primitives discussed above are used in cryptographic protocols, which are designed with specific security objectives in mind. Cryptographic protocols are notoriously hard to design since they will likely have pitfalls that are hard to detect [10]. A good example of a cryptographic protocol that fails to meet most of its security objectives is the *Wired Equivalent Privacy* (WEP) protocol used in legacy IEEE 802.11 wireless local area networks [11]. Moreover, cryptographic primitives make use of keys shared between communicating parties. Establishing secret keys between legitimate parties interested in communicating, such that Oscar does not obtain any knowledge of the keys, is not trivial and requires cryptographic protocols. Key establishment is usually based on master keys established with trusted third parties or public key cryptography.

Most well-designed cryptographic protocols have three phases. In the first phase, the communicating entities *identify* or *authenticate* themselves to one another. In some cases the entity authentication is unilateral (i.e., Alice authenticates herself to Bob, but not vice versa). Entity authentication makes use of passwords, PIN, pass phrases, biometrics, security tokens, and the like. Challenge-response protocols that do not require an entity to reveal the password, but only demonstrate knowledge of the password, are commonly used for entity authentication. In the second phase, or as part of the first phase, the communicating entities also establish keys for security services to be provided next. Establishment of keys can be in two ways: key transport or distribution, where one party generates the keys (or a master key) and transports them securely to the other party, or key agreement, where both parties exchange information used in the secure creation of the same key at both ends. It is common for both parties to exchange random numbers, sequence numbers, or time stamps (called nonces, or numbers used once) that are used as input in key generation. In the third phase, the established keys are used to provide confidentiality (through encryption with a block or stream cipher) and integrity (through MACs or MICs). We briefly describe some examples in the following sections.

Kerberos

Kerberos is used for authenticating users when they access services from workstations, typically on a local area network. An authentication server shares a password with all users and a key with a ticket-granting server. When a user logs on to a workstation, the workstation contacts the authentication server. The authentication server issues a ticket to the user and also sends a key that the user will share with the ticket-granting server. This key is encrypted with the user's password. The workstation will not be able to retrieve the key if the user is not legitimate. Thus, recovery of the key to be shared with the ticket-granting server indirectly authenticates the user. Note that in this phase, a key has been transported to the user as well. Of course, this assumes that a password has been manually shared between the user and the authentication server. The ticket itself is encrypted with a key shared between the authentication server and the ticket-granting server. It includes, among other things, the key that has been transported to the user. When the user desires to access a service, the workstation presents the ticket to the ticket-granting server and a message authentication code created using the key that was initially received from the authentication server. This verifies the user's legitimacy to the ticket-granting server, which then issues a key and a ticket to the workstation for use with the requested service. A similar authentication mechanism is used with the server providing the service. Kerberos is more complicated than what has been described here. More details are available in Stallings [6] and Kaufmann et al. [10]

IPSec

IPSec encrypts all IP traffic between two hosts, or two networks, or combinations of hosts with possibly different terminating points for different security services.

Keys may be manually established or a very complex protocol called *Internet Key Exchange* (IKE) can be used for authenticating entities to one another and establishing keys. Keys are established as part of a unidirectional "security association" that specifies the destination IP address, keys, encryption algorithms, and "protocol" to be used. "Protocol" here corresponds to one of two specific security services provided by IPSec: *Authentication Header* (AH) and *Encapsulated Security Payload* (ESP). In AH, a MAC is created on the entire IP packet minus the fields in the IP header that change in transit. This enables the receiver to detect spoofed or modified IP packets. However, the payload is in plaintext and visible to anyone who may be capable of capturing the IP packet. ESP provides confidentiality and integrity to the payload of the IP packet but not the header. Use of the two protocols in the above manner is called "transport mode." It is also possible to use a "tunnel mode" where the original IP packet is tunneled in another IP packet. This makes the original IP packet the payload, thereby protecting it completely.

SSL

The secure sockets layer (the latest version is called transport layer security or TLS) is used in web browsers to secure data transfer, especially for e-commerce applications, banking, and other confidential transactions. At a high level, the browser is not required to be authenticated by the server (although this is possible and optional in SSL). The user employing the web browser is authenticated using passwords or other techniques proprietary to the organization using the server. The server, however, is authenticated by the browser through its digital certificate. This provides the user some assurance that the transaction is taking place with a legitimate bank or e-commerce site. Note that the use of SSL is not the assurance of authenticity of the server since any site or any server could use SSL. It is the information contained in the digital certificate that authenticates the server. The digital certificate contains the public key of the server, signed by a certification authority. The browser creates a random secret, encrypts it with the server's public key, and sends it to the server. This random secret, along with previously exchanged nonces, are used to generate keys (at both the server and the browser) that are used for encryption with block or stream ciphers (RC-4 is commonly used) and integrity with message authentication codes.

2.4   DETECTION

Irrespective of the protection and prevention mechanisms in place, it is possible that security attacks succeed and proceed in an organization's network. It is extremely important to detect such attacks at the earliest onslaught so that action can be taken to stop further damage. More details of detection mechanisms and processes can be found in Bejtlich [5], Northcutt and Novak [12], and Amoroso [13].

Intrusion detection is the broad term used to describe the process for identifying the fact that a security attack has occurred (or is occurring). There is no single method for identifying attacks; typically, three methods are used. In host-based intrusion detection, audit trails, logs, deployment of suspicious code, logins, and so on are monitored to detect the occurrence of a security attack. In network-based intrusion detection, the packets entering the network are examined to see if they correspond to signatures of known security attacks. Anomaly-based intrusion detection looks for abnormal usage of network or system resources and flags potential problems.

Audit trail processing, used with host-based intrusion detection, is usually done offline. Care has to be taken to ensure that logs in hosts have not been tampered with. Logs from many hosts and systems may have to be correlated to detect attacks. Network-based intrusion detection is in real time as packets are captured. This can be problematic if the amount of data flowing into the network is extremely large, as the buffering capacity may be limited and packets may be dropped by an intrusion detection system (IDS). Using signatures of known attacks is a common technique used for intrusion detection. However, this may miss new and unidentified attacks. If signatures are made too specific, security attacks may be missed resulting in false negatives. If signatures are made too general, it is likely that some normal traffic and activity is flagged as a security attack resulting in false positives. Thus, careful tuning is often necessary to detect intrusions with low false positives or negatives. The algorithms used for intrusion detection can be fairly complex, making use of data mining, pattern matching, decision making, and so on.

Often, IDSs deploy *sensors* to probe or monitor the network or systems in question. It is necessary to deploy sensors on either side of a firewall to get an idea of the attacks that are being blocked. Multiple redundant sensors may be necessary depending on the network topology. Sensors themselves may have to be networked to correlate the collected data. Such a network may or may not be sepa- rate from the network that is being monitored. The Internet Engineering Task Force is working on formats for exchange of intrusion detection information.

It is possible that IDSs may themselves be subject to security attacks. There are techniques that Oscar may employ to thwart detection by IDSs (such as fragmentation, flooding, unrelated attacks). Recent trends in intrusion detection include *distributed intrusion detection* where system administrators from all over the world submit their monitored information to a service that then performs correlations to detect and identify attacks.

There are several kinds of intrusion detection systems available today including specialized appliances from vendors. SNORT is an open-source intrusion detection system that is available for free. While evaluating an IDS, it is necessary to consider the types of attacks that an IDS can detect, the operating systems it supports, whether it can handle huge amounts of traffic, if it is capable of displaying large amounts of data in an easily understandable manner, the management framework that it provides, and its complexity.

Today, combinations of IDSs and firewalls, called intrusion prevention systems (IPSs), are also available. Rate-based IPSs block traffic flows if they are seen to exceed normal rates. Signature-based IPSs block traffic when signatures of known security attacks are detected. Such systems are part of the intrusion response systems discussed in detail in Chapter 13.

Honeypots or Internet traps are systems used to detect and divert security attacks. Such systems look like real resources, perhaps with vulnerabilities. Their value lies in the fact that Oscar may probe them, launch attacks against them, and perhaps compromise some of the systems. Monitoring Oscar's activities using honeypots can help detect other attacks against real systems or design methods of prevention.

2.5   ASSESSMENT AND RESPONSE

It is important to periodically *assess* the security of the network and systems in an organization. Additionally, assessment becomes important after a security incident has been detected and a *response* to the attack has been put in place. In this section, we briefly consider elements of assessment and response. See Northcutt et al. [7], Whitacker and Newman [14], and McNab [15] for more details.

Assessment of a network can be done using external auditors who can perform penetration tests (act essentially like Oscar, but not damage systems), enumerate the entities in the network, discover potential vulnerabilities, and verify if the protection and prevention mechanisms (like firewalls, access control schemes, password management) are working as they are expected. Vulnerability assessment tries to identify the presence of known vulnerabilities that can be and must be patched if patches are available. Since vulnerabilities are often operating system specific, vulnerability scanners may not pick up all vulnerabilities present on hosts in a network. Nessus is a popular open-source vulnerability scanner. Commercial options also exist.

Responding to security attacks when detected is also an important aspect of security. The person in charge of a network needs to be immediately notified if an attack is detected (possibly through redundant means of communication). The security incident must be documented clearly. There must be processes in place to contact vendors and other external help if necessary. Actions to mitigate the impact of the security attack must be taken, followed by eradication of the vulnerability that caused the attack. An assessment of reasons as to why the attack was successful and steps to prevent recurrence must be taken.

2.6   CONCLUSION

In this chapter, a high-level overview of network security was provided. The way network communications take place was discussed. Example security attacks were described. Terminology associated with security services was introduced. Protection against attacks using firewalls and prevention mechanisms that make use of cryptography were considered with examples of Kerberos, IPSec, and SSL. Detection of security attacks, security assessment of networks and systems, and response to security incidents were briefly discussed.

References

[1] The United States Computer Emergency Readiness Team, at http://www.us-cert.gov.

[2] J. Mirkovic and P. Reiher, "A Taxonomy of DDoS Attack and DDoS Defense Mechanisms," *ACM Computer Communications Review* 34, No. 2 (April 2004), pp. 39–53.

[3] D. Moore, C. Shannon, and K. Claffy, "Code Red: A Case Study on the Spread and Victims of an Internet Worm," *Proceedings of the 2nd ACM SIGCOMM Workshop on Internet Measurement (IMW)*, Marseille, France, 2002, pp. 273–284.

[4] Z. Chen, L. Gao, and K. Kwiat, "Modeling the Spread of Active Worms," *Proceedings of IEEE Infocom*, San Franciso, CA, April 2003.

[5] Richard Bejtlich, *The Tao of Network Security Monitoring* (Boston: Addison-Wesley, 2004).

[6] W. Stallings, *Network Security Essentials*, 2nd ed. (Englewood Cliffs, NJ: Prentice Hall, 2003).

[7] S. Z. Northcutt, L. Winters, S. Frederick, and K. K. Ritchey, *Inside Network Perimeter Security* (Indianapolis: New Riders, 2005).

[8] W. R. Cheswick, S. M. Bellovin, and A. D. Rubin, *Firewalls and Internet Security* (Boston: Addison-Wesley, 2003).

[9] D. Stinson, *Cryptography: Theory and Practice*, 3rd ed. (Boca Raton, FL: Chapman & Hall/CRC Press, 2006).

[10] C. Kaufmann, R. Perlman, and M. Speciner, *Network Security: Private Communication in a Public World* (Englewood Cliffs, NJ: Prentice Hall PTR, 2002).

[11] J. Edney and W. A. Arbaugh, *Real 802.11 Security: Wi-Fi Protected Access and 802.11i* (Englewood Cliffs, NJ: Prentice Hall, 2004).

[12] S. Northcutt and J. Novak, *Network Intrusion Detection: An Analyst's Handbook* (Indianapolis: New Riders, 2001).

[13] E. G. Amoroso, *Intrusion Detection: An Introduction to Internet Surveillance, Correlation, Trace Back, Traps, and Response* (.Sparta, N.J.:Intrusion.net Books, 1999).

[14] A. Whitaker and D. Newman, *Penetration Testing and Network Defense* (Indianapolis, IN: Cisco Press, 2005).

[15] C. McNab, *Network Security Assessment: Know Your Network* (Sebastopol, CA: O'Reilly Books, 2004).

3 CHAPTER

Security for Distributed Systems: Foundations of Access Control

Elisa Bertino   Purdue University, USA
Jason Crampton   University of London, UK

3.1   INTRODUCTION

A computer system is typically used to store information and run programs that manipulate data. Users interact with the system by reading from and writing to files containing data, or by executing programs that perform computations with that data. The basic goals of computer security are to prevent unauthorized disclosure and unauthorized modification of data [1]. In other words, computer security mechanisms seek to preserve the *confidentiality* and *integrity* of the data stored in a computer system. Additionally, computer systems must guarantee the availability of information to authorized users. The focus of this chapter is on the part that access control has to play in preserving confidentiality and integrity.

Access control is concerned with protecting resources from unauthorized access. In particular, confidentiality is addressed by limiting the files that users can read, while integrity is addressed by limiting the files that users can modify. In its most general sense, access control may be concerned with physical objects, such as physical memory addresses or even buildings, as well as with logical objects, such as computer files. Physical memory locations are typically protected using mechanisms built into the hardware. In this chapter we do not consider the protection of physical objects. Instead, we focus on the underlying principles that are used to design access control mechanisms that are implemented in software for the protection of logical objects.

In order to implement access control, it is necessary to have an access control policy that specifies which users are authorized to access which resources.

This implies that users can be identified and that their identity can be confirmed through some authentication process. Until recently, identification and authentication has been a relatively straightforward process because a "closed-world" assumption was made, that is, all users of the system are known, and any unknown user is assumed to be unauthorized. This meant that a centralized database or file of user names and authentication information could be maintained. However, the closed-world assumption is not appropriate for many modern computer systems: The users of web services and resources in a grid computing environment, for example, will not necessarily be known to the mechanisms that must protect those services and resources. In short, authentication, and hence access control, in open distributed systems becomes far more challenging.

In this chapter, we begin with a brief overview of identification and authentication techniques in both closed and open systems. We then discuss the access control policies and models that have been developed over the past 30 years for closed systems. While these models, being based on user identities, are not necessarily directly applicable to open distributed systems, much can be learned from the principles embodied in these approaches. Indeed, modern access control frameworks such as XACML employ many of the abstractions introduced up to 30 years ago. We then go on to discuss SAML and XACML, emerging standards for exchanging authentication and authorization information and for specifying and enforcing access control policies, respectively. We also discuss state-of-the-art models for access control in distributed systems such as trust negotiation and multidomain role-based access control.

3.2   IDENTIFICATION AND AUTHENTICATION

In order to control access to resources and to make users of a computer system accountable for their actions, it is necessary that the computer system has some way of associating actions with users. This means that the computer system must have some way of identifying and distinguishing users. The standard way of doing this is to provide each user with an account. This account provides a way of linking human users with the actions they perform while interacting with the computer.[1]

Having successfully logged on to a computer system, the user is provided with an interactive environment from which he or she can execute programs. This environment is usually in the form of a command line interface (often known as a *shell*) or a graphical user interface (often known as a *desktop*). In the former

---

[1] In networked systems, each machine usually has an account, so that, for example, a client machine can request actions on a remote server and have those actions linked to the client.

case, the user types the name of a program that he or she wishes to execute; in the latter, the user clicks on the appropriate icon. In both cases, the interface is provided by the execution of a computer program that is executed following a successful log-in.

The process associated with that program is identified with the account of the authenticated user. Any new programs that are executed by the user from this interface will also be associated with that user account. Hence, the actions of any programs executed by the user can be accounted for. Moreover, we can enforce security policy requirements of the form "Jason can read file.txt but Mick cannot." Any program that is associated with Jason's user account will be permitted to access file.txt, and any program associated with Mick's user account will not.

Each user account is bound to security information for the corresponding user. In the simplest case, this is just the user's *security identifier* (SID). Many access control policies specify the access rights for which an SID (and therefore the user) is authorized. Typically, the security information will also include one or more of the following types of security attribute: *group identifiers* (GIDs), *roles*, and *security levels*.

3.2.1 Password-Based Authentication

Everyone is familiar with the process of entering a password into a computerized device in order to gain access. Everyday examples include the PINs we enter to use ATM machines and unlock mobile phones, and the password we enter to log on to our computer at work. Nevertheless, passwords are a poor method of authenticating users: Passwords are reused for each authentication event, and passwords are generally easy for an attacker to obtain, either through social engineering, the carelessness of users, or by exploiting the fact that passwords are generally easy to guess or brute-force.

Ideally, passwords should be easy to remember and hard to guess. Of course, these are conflicting requirements, and users often choose weak passwords that are easy for attackers to guess. This means that passwords are a particularly poor method of authentication in distributed systems, in which the password may have to travel over a network; even if the password is encrypted, an attacker may capture the password in transit and mount an offline brute-force or dictionary attack to recover the password.

Password-based authentication is still the most widely used method of authentication in computer systems. As we have already noted, password information must be readable by the log-in process, so it must be stored within the computer system. This suggests that either the password file containing this information must be very well protected or the information itself must be protected in some way.

There are two obvious possibilities: deploy very strong access controls for the file containing passwords or encrypt the passwords. In practice, both strategies are employed in modern operating systems. It is instructive to consider the authentication method used in early Unix systems to demonstrate why both types of controls are required.

In earlier versions of Unix, the /etc/passwd file contained user information such as user and group identifiers, as well as a ciphertext derived from each user's password. The /etc/passwd file was readable by all users because other Unix services needed access to some of this user information (but not the passwords). This meant that any user of the system could create a copy of the file and try to "crack" the passwords in his or her own time.

3.2.2 Insecure Communication Channels

In order to authenticate to a computer system, the user must communicate with the system. If an attacker can position him- or herself in some way between the user and the computer system, then he or she can intercept the password. In the past, a common way of doing this was to spoof the authentication process. This problem arises because the user does not confirm that he or she is communicating with (i.e., authenticate) the genuine log-in process. The standard technique for preventing so-called man-in-the-middle attacks is for the communicating parties to mutually authenticate. In many distributed systems, the authentication process is mutual: The (client) user is authenticated by the (server) computer system and the server is also authenticated by the client.

Trusted path functionality (a requirement for B classifications in TCSEC[2]) is used to provide a lightweight method of ensuring that a user is communicating with the genuine authentication process. The user invokes the authentication process through some special key combination. This combination can only be trapped by the operating system kernel and therefore cannot be detected by third-party programs (including malicious programs that attempt to spoof the authentication process). Perhaps the best known example of trusted path functionality is the Ctrl+Del+Enter *secure attention sequence* (SAS) provided by Windows 2000.

3.2.3 Challenge-Response Systems

One of the problems with using passwords is that they are generally reused. One-time passwords are one solution to this problem [2]. An alternative is to

---

[2] See www.radium.ncsc.mil/tpep/library/rainbow/5200.28-STD.html.

use a *challenge-response mechanism*. Whenever a user wishes to authenticate, the authentication service issues a challenge to the user. The user is only authenticated if he or she responds in an appropriate way. Like one-time passwords, an intercepted challenge is useless to the attacker, because it will be different for each authentication event.

The challenge-response mechanism may be based on the ability to correctly compute some function of a value provided by the authentication process. The user could share a secret key k with the authentication service. The authentication service sends a random value m to the user, which the user encrypts and returns the ciphertext c to the authentication service. The authentication service also encrypts m to produce a ciphertext c'. The authentication service compares c and c', and the user is authenticated if the two values are identical. Of course, the authentication process must be assumed to be completely compromised if k is lost or stolen.

If we assume the existence of a public key infrastructure, the user could sign a challenge m with his or her (private) signature key. The authentication service authenticates the user if the signature can be verified using the corresponding (authenticated) public key of the user (since no other user could have produced such a signature).[3]

3.2.4   Authentication in Distributed Systems

Networks of computers are now commonplace, and the client-server model adopted by many distributed applications means that user authentication is performed by an application running on a different machine from the one at which the user is working. Users authenticating to a Windows 2000 domain, for example, are authenticated by a domain controller, not the workstation at which they log in. Let us assume that we have a client C and a server S. Generally, we want S to authenticate C and to establish a secure communication channel between C and S. We can establish a secure channel by creating a shared session key that is used to encrypt data transmitted between C and S (using a symmetric encryption algorithm). As noted above, C may also wish to authenticate S.

Let us assume that the client has chosen a password and the server knows this password. Authenticating a user over a potentially insecure network is considerably harder than authenticating a user locally. If a password-based authentication mechanism is used, we obviously cannot allow passwords to be transmitted over the network in the clear. Ideally, we should not even allow encrypted passwords to

---

[3] The authenticity of the public key is guaranteed by a certificate signed by some certification authority trusted by the authentication service.

be transmitted over the network, because an attacker may intercept the encrypted password and crack the password using a brute-force or dictionary attack. Hence, it is commonplace for authentication mechanisms in distributed applications to include a challenge-response component.

In a distributed system, there may be many different servers, each running services that require client (user) authentication. Clearly it is inconvenient for a client to be authenticated by each of these servers or services, not least because this will require the existence of some prior "trust relationship" between the client and server. In practice, it is far simpler to have an *authentication server* that is used to authenticate users. This authentication server will have a trust relationship with each server and will therefore be able to provide some kind of assurances about client identities to those servers. Instead of having trust relationships defined between every pair of entities in the system, there exists a trust relationship between every client and the authentication server and between every server and the authentication server. The precise nature of the trust relationship will vary: It may be that every entity (client and server) shares a distinct secret key with the authentication server; alternatively, each entity may have a public and private key and the authentication server is a certification authority that authenticates the binding between entities and their respective public keys (typically by signing digital certificates).

Using Shared Keys

Kerberos is the most widely used protocol for authenticating users in a distributed system using shared keys [3]. It is based on the Needham-Schroeder protocol and uses an authentication server, which acts as a trusted third party. The authentication server enables two parties A and B to be mutually authenticated and to establish a shared session key. In the context of distributed computer systems, A might represent a client and B might be a service on a remote machine that requires client authentication.

If A wants to communicate with B, A first sends a message to the authentication server S, including A and B's identities. S responds by sending two messages to A: The first is encrypted using the key shared by S and A, and includes the session key and a lifetime for which that key is valid; the second message is encrypted using the key shared by S and B, and also contains the session key and the lifetime, in addition to A's identity. The second message is sometimes called a *ticket*. A forwards the ticket to B and a second message encrypted using the session key, which contains A's identity and a timestamp to ensure freshness. Finally, B returns a message to A in which the timestamp is encrypted using the shared session key. The ticket serves to authenticate A to B, and the fact that B can correctly encrypt the timestamp authenticates B to A.

Using Public Key Cryptography

In the simplest case, A can authenticate B if A simply sends a nonce to B and B signs the nonce using his private key. A then verifies that signature using B's public key. In fact, A has only confirmed that a valid private–public key pair has been used to sign and verify a signature. In order for B to be properly authenticated, A needs to be assured that the key used to sign the nonce is actually associated with B. A can satisfy herself of the authenticity of a public key if a third party trusted by A has signed a digital certificate binding B's identity to his public key. (Of course, this requires methods for creating and managing public–private key pairs and for binding public keys to identities using digital certificates. Collectively, these methods form part of a *public key infrastructure.*)

As we noted before, authentication protocols in distributed systems often exchange a symmetric key that is used to encrypt subsequent communication between the two parties. A can exchange a session key with B (again provided A can be assured of the authenticity of B's public key) by encrypting the session key using B's public key and sending it to B. Only B will be able to recover the session key, assuming that B is uniquely associated with that public key and B's secret (private) key has not been compromised.

Single Sign-On

In the shared symmetric key setting, the authentication server can issue a ticket encrypted using a key shared by the authentication server and a *ticket-granting server* (TGS). (This ticket is usually called a *ticket-granting ticket.*) The TGS issues further tickets for network services requiring user authentication, based on the prior authentication of the user by the authentication server (implied by the ticket encrypted with the key shared by the TGS and the authentication server). In this way, Kerberos, for example, can be used to provide single sign-on within a domain in which the servers have a trust relationship with the TGS.

In the public key setting, the authentication server issues "tickets" or "assertions" confirming that A has been authenticated. These tickets will be signed using the authentication server's private key. All servers that trust the authentication server will accept such tickets and permit the subject of the ticket to use their respective services. This type of model was used by Digital Equipment Corporation in their Distributed System Security Architecture [4].

The Security Assertion Markup Language (SAML), a recent standards-based initiative, is an "XML-based framework for creating and exchanging security information between online partners" [5] that we review in more detail in Section 3.4. One of SAML's main applications is to support single sign-on. The standard defines a number of different types of assertions, including *authentication assertions,* which are made by *SAML authorities.*[4] Of course, this still requires relying parties to trust the SAML authorities and hence for there to be some kind of trust relationship between them. As usual, these trust relationships may be defined explicitly using shared symmetric encryption keys or using some kind of public key infrastructure.

3.3   ACCESS CONTROL

In a computer system, users typically wish to read and write files, browse directories, and execute programs. In multi-user systems, different users will be authorized to access different resources. In other words, there generally will be a security policy that determines the resources to which each user has access.

An *authorization service* (also known as a *reference monitor* or *access control mechanism*) is a computer program that enforces an *authorization policy* (or *access control policy*). Any computer system that offers any level of protection will ensure that the authorization service intercepts all user requests to access resources in order to ensure that all user requests are properly authorized before a user gains access to the requested resource. Most authorization policies directly or indirectly specify the set of authorized requests. The standard implementation of an authorization service denies any request that is not authorized by the policy. (There are other possible approaches, such as to explicitly prohibit certain requests, with the default response to grant a request unless it is denied.)

Figure 3.1 illustrates a generic architecture for an authorization service. A *policy enforcement point* (PEP) intercepts all access requests and forwards them to the *policy decision point* (PDP). The PDP consults the access control policy, decides whether the request is authorized, and returns its decision to the PEP. If the decision is to deny the request, the PEP may generate a suitable message for the user. If the decision is to permit the request, the PEP will make the object available to the user.

Typically, the PDP will require certain information to make a decision. In particular, the PDP will need to know *who* is requesting access to *what*. In many systems, the PEP is responsible for gathering this information and forwarding it to the PDP with the request, although this is not the only possibility. Generally the "who" question is answered by authenticating each user of the system and associating each process that a user runs with his or her identity. The "what" question is answered by consulting information maintained by the operating system about

---

[4] Obviously, the authenticity of such assertions needs to be established. The XML encryption and XML Digital Signature standards provide mechanisms for providing the relevant security services.

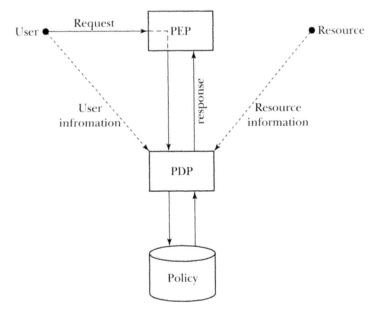

FIGURE

3.1
A generic access control architecture.

the resources it protects. It is customary to refer to the user as the *subject* and the resource as the *protected object* or *object*.

Generally, the PDP will also need to know *how* the subject wishes to interact with the object. The more common interactions between subject and object include read, write, and execute. The exact operational meaning of these generic interactions will be dependent on the type of object and other contextual information.

An *access control model* provides a method for encoding an access control policy and states the conditions that must be satisfied for an access request to be granted. In other words, it provides a blueprint for an access control mechanism. The conditions that determine whether a request is authorized may be expressed as security properties. One way to express the conditions that determine whether a request is authorized is to specify the *state* (more accurately the *protection state*) of the system following the request. The state of the system is a snapshot of security-relevant features in the system. Usually, it is sufficient to consider the state to be the set of access requests that have been granted by the access control mechanism.

In this section, we will examine some of the important theoretical models for access control. Such models are used as the framework for the development of authorization services in operating systems and applications such as relational database management systems.

3.3.1   Access Control Based on Subject–Object Relationships

Perhaps the simplest type of access control mechanism is one based on the relationship that exists between the object and the subject. The Unix and VMS operating systems are perhaps the best known examples of this type of approach.

Every resource, including printers and disc drives as well as files and directories, is treated as an object and every object is associated with an owner and a group. A subject may belong to one or more groups. Every subject has a subject identifier (SID) and every group has a group identifier (GID). When a subject requests access to an object, the operating system determines the relationship that exists between the object and the subject by comparing the SID and the GIDs associated with the subject to the owner SID and GID associated with the object. Unix identifies three possibilities: the subject is the owner of the object, the subject belongs to the group associated with the object, or the subject is not the owner and does not belong to the group associated with the object. For convenience, we usually refer to these relationships as "owner," "group," and "world," respectively.

Unix uses three generic access rights: read (r), write (w), and execute (x). Therefore, each object is associated with nine access rights; three for each of the three relationships that exist between subject and object. The access rights associated with an object are called an *access mask* or *permission mask*.

Internally, a permission mask consists of 9 bits; if a bit is set, the corresponding access right is granted. The permission mask is logically divided into three groups of 3 bits, where each group of 3 bits indicates read, write, and execute access, respectively. The three groups correspond to the owner, group, and world relationships, respectively. Unix programs (such as ls) display the permission mask symbolically, for example, rwx r-x r-x is used to denote the access mask 111 101 101.

3.3.2   Protection Matrix Model

A *protection matrix* is an abstract representation of an access control policy. The matrix represents those access requests that are authorized by the system. A protection matrix is arranged as a two-dimensional array, with each row labeled by a subject and each column labeled by an object. A matrix entry in the row labeled *s* and column labeled *o* determines the authorized actions for *s* with respect to *o*.

Hence, if the matrix entry for *s* and *o* contains read, a request from *s* to read object *o* is authorized. In other words, the protection matrix encodes triples of the form subject–object–action; object–action pairs are often referred to as *permissions* or *capabilities*. The protection matrix has proved to be a powerful and abiding abstraction for the design of protection mechanisms in operating systems and application software. Many authorization services, such as the security reference monitor in Windows 2000 and the security policies in Java, are based on the protection matrix.

Implementing an Authorization Service

We may use a protection matrix in order to implement an authorization service. This service will receive access requests and make a decision as to whether the request should be granted. The request will only be granted if it is authorized by the protection matrix. In order to use a protection matrix, it is necessary to know the following: the identity of the subject making the request, the identity of the object that the subject wishes to access, and the type of interaction that the subject wishes to have with the object.

The identity of the subject is determined by examining the security information associated with the subject (the process that generated the access request). This information will typically be a user account associated with the authenticated user that caused the process to be created. When making the request, the identity of the object will be specified by the subject and will refer to some resource protected by the operating system. Finally, the type of interaction requested is usually represented as an *access mask*, which is a binary string of *n* bits, where *n* is the number of access rights supported by the system. If a particular bit is set in the access mask, then the corresponding access right is being requested.

Given a user account identifier *s*, an object identifier *o*, and an access mask, the authorization service finds the matrix entry corresponding to *s* and *o* and compares the access mask in the request with the one in the matrix entry. If every bit that is set in the requested mask is also set in the matrix entry, then every access right that has been requested is authorized by the matrix and the request may be granted.

However, an authorization service rarely uses a protection matrix to store authorization information. This is because in a large computer system with many subjects and objects, the memory requirements for such a data structure would be prohibitively large. Moreover, many entries in the matrix may be empty, meaning that large amounts of memory allocated for the storage of the protection matrix would remain unused. Clearly this represents a poor use of such a vital computing resource.

Access Control Lists

It is more usual to implement the matrix as a set of *access control lists* (ACLs) or *capability lists*. These structures have the feature that only relevant matrix entries are stored, with empty matrix entries being ignored. An access control list is associated with an object and consists of a number of entries defining the rights assigned to each subject for that object. Conceptually, an access control list is a list of access control entries. Each entry in the list identifies a subject and a set of access rights. In other words, each access control entry in an access control list for object o specifies how the subject identified in the entry can interact with o.

In order to implement an authorization service using access control lists, the same information is required as for a protection matrix implementation. In order to check whether a request should be granted, the authorization service first finds the access control list for the requested object. It then checks each access control entry to see if it refers to the requesting subject. If it does, the requested rights are compared with the rights in the access control entry. Access is granted if every requested right is in the access control entry and denied otherwise.

Capability Lists

In contrast to ACLs, a capability list is associated with a subject. Conceptually, a capability list is a list of permissions, each identifying an object and the right that has been assigned to the subject for that object. In other words, each permission in a capability list for a subject specifies how that subject may interact with the object specified in the permission.

Security Groups

In a large user population, many users will share certain characteristics. In a commercial setting, perhaps the most obvious characteristic would be job description or function. All users with the same job description are likely to have similar access to certain objects; clearly, it would be laborious to create the same matrix entries (or access control entries) to these objects for each of these users. Hence, many authorization systems include the ability to specify *security groups*. The idea is that certain access rights to certain objects can be assigned as one block to a group subject.

However a user may be associated with a number of different groups. When a user typically logs on to a computer system, he or she is associated with identifiers both for his or her own user account as well as for any group to which he or she belongs. Strictly speaking, user identifiers and group identifiers are used to label the rows of a protection matrix or the entries in an access control list. That is to say, the rows of a protection matrix actually represent the authorizations for a particular *principal*.[5]

Access Control Lists and Multiple Principals

A number of different options exist for authorization systems based on access control lists when a subject may be associated with a number of different principals. Some systems only permit each object to be associated with a fixed number of subjects. In other words, each object has a fixed-length access control list. Unix is an example of such a system, in which each object has an access control list with three entries: one for the object owner, one for the group associated with the object, and one for every other user (sometimes referred to as "the world"). Windows 2000, in contrast, permits access control lists of arbitrary length.

We can also decide whether the authorizations of a subject are represented by the most relevant principal or by the aggregation of the authorizations for each principal associated with that subject. Unix chooses the first option: If the subject is the owner of the requested resource, only the authorizations of the owner principal are considered when deciding whether to allow the request. If the subject is not the owner but belongs to the group, then only the authorizations of the group principal are considered. If the subject is neither the owner nor belongs to the group, then the authorizations of the world principal are considered. This means that an owner could have less access than a member of the group, although the owner can always change the access control list so that he or she has all access rights. In contrast, Windows will check every entry in an access control list in deciding whether an access request should be granted.

Negative Authorization

In recent years, we have seen the emergence of authorization mechanisms that support negative authorization policies, in which certain actions are explicitly prohibited. Such authorization policies are particularly useful for enforcing exceptions to a more general policy. For example, we may wish to grant access to a particular set of objects to many different subjects; clearly, the most convenient way of doing this is to create a group for those subjects and then authorize the group to access those objects. However, if there is one member s of the group g who should not be allowed access to one particular object o, it is rather cumbersome to enforce this requirement without negative authorizations. The only option in this case is to remove s from g and then grant s access to all the objects

---

[5]   Saltzer and Schroeder define a principal to be the entity to which authorizations are granted.

to which members of g have except o. A less burdensome way of implementing this requirement is to keep s in the group and simply prohibit access by s to o. Windows 2000 permits the inclusion of negative access control entries in access control lists. XACML, the recent standard for XML-based authorization policy specification and enforcement [6], also supports negative authorizations.

Nevertheless, negative authorizations are not without their problems. In particular, it becomes extremely difficult to reason about the overall security policy. Another problem is that negative authorizations give rise to policies that may have conflicting authorizations. That is, a positive and negative authorization may exist for the same request. In the example just given, s will have a positive authorization to access o from his or her membership of g, but also a negative authorization explicitly denying him or her access to o. The intention in this case is that access should be denied, but how is the authorization service to know this?

In order to address these types of issues, *policy conflict resolution mechanisms* are defined. The most obvious and widely used mechanism is to insist that a negative authorization always take precedence over a positive one. This is known, naturally, as the "deny-overrides" algorithm in XACML. There are other possibilities, such as "permit-overrides" and "first-applicable." The latter assumes that authorization rules are processed in a particular order and that the first relevant authorization is to be used. Windows 2000 has a hybrid approach that groups access control entries in a particular order and implements what might be called a "deny-overrides-if-first-applicable" algorithm. This ordering of access control entries is first determined by the creator of the access control entry, with entries created by the creator of the object (rather than ones inherited from the object's container) taking precedence. Within each such group of entries, negative entries precede positive entries.

Windows 2000: An Illustrative Example

Windows 2000 (and its successor Windows XP) is perhaps the most widely used operating system in the world. A Windows 2000 installation will include one or more domains, each of which contains users, machines, and resources. A user is authenticated to a domain using Kerberos. Each domain has at least one Kerberos authentication server that also acts as a ticket-granting server. A user logged on to a domain account benefits from single sign-on: Whenever he or she requests a network service, any further authentication is performed without any additional input from the user (based on the domain's prior authentication of the user).

When a user logs on and authenticates successfully to a Windows 2000 domain, the *local security authority* (LSA) obtains SIDs (via the messages exchanged in the Kerberos protocol) for the user and for each security group to which the user belongs. This information is obtained from a network directory service,

Active Directory, which stores information about all entities in the system. The SIDs form part of the *access token*, which contains all security information related to the authenticated user.

When the user executes a program, a process is created that inherits a copy of the access token. The *security reference monitor* (SRM) uses this token and an object's security descriptor to determine whether an access request should be granted. The security descriptor contains a *discretionary access control list* (DACL), which comprises zero or more *access control entries* (ACEs). Each entry includes an SID (called a *trustee* in Windows 2000 literature) and a set of access rights. ACEs can be used to deny access rights as well as grant access rights. In other words, Windows 2000 supports negative authorizations.

When a user makes an access request, the object manager, which acts as the PEP, constructs a requested access mask indicating which access rights have been requested by the user, obtains the user's access token and the requested object's DACL, and forwards the request to the SRM, which acts as the PDP. The SRM traverses the DACL, matching SIDs in the access token to trustees in the DACL's ACEs. During this traversal, the SRM constructs a granted access mask indicating the access rights for which the user is authorized. After inspecting each ACE, the SRM compares the requested access mask and the granted access mask: If they match, access is granted and the SRM returns a positive decision to the object manager. If the SRM reaches the end of the DACL and the two access masks do not match, the SRM returns a negative decision to the object manager.[6] The traversal of the DACL will terminate prematurely and a negative decision is returned to the object manager if any requested access right is contained in a matching negative ACE.

3.3.3 An Information Flow Policy for Confidentiality

We now consider a very different approach to authorization policies, in which access to resources is determined by the respective attributes of the subject and object. Much of the early research on secure computer systems was funded by the U.S. military. The prime concern of this research was to ensure the confidentiality of sensitive electronic resources. The research sought ways to mimic paper-based systems in which documents are stamped with labels such as "Confidential" and

---

[6] In fact, the algorithm for deciding whether an access request is considerably more complicated. Windows 2000 includes the notions of *restricted SIDs* and *impersonation access tokens*, which affect the algorithm. The reader is referred to Microsoft's Distributed Security Guide (http://www.microsoft.com/technet/prodtechnol/windows2000ser v/reskit/distrib/dsce_ctl_ajfg.mspx?mfr=true) for further details.

"Top Secret" and are filed securely according to their classification. A user is only allowed access to a document if his or her security clearance is as high as that of the document. In the late 1960s, the military began to fund research on implementing such an access control policy in computerized systems. Two important models from this period include the lattice-based model for information flow [7] and the Bell-LaPadula model [8].

The act of accessing an object can be regarded as initiating an information flow. In particular, reading an object causes information to flow from the object to the subject, while the flow is in the opposite direction if the subject writes to the object. An information flow policy specifies which information flows are authorized. As we might expect, an information flow policy for confidentiality requires that high-level information cannot flow to a lower level, for example, an unclassified user cannot read classified material.

In order to describe an information flow policy in formal terms, it is necessary to define a set of security labels L and a security function λ. The set of security labels is ordered, meaning that it is possible to compare two different security labels. A widely used set of security labels in military circles is {unclassified, classified, secret, top_secret}, where the ordering is defined to be unclassified < classified < secret < top_secret.

The security function λ is used to associate a security label with each subject and each object.[7] The information flow policy states that information may only flow from an entity e to another entity f if $\lambda(e) \leq \lambda(f)$. In other words, information flow between two entities obeys the ordering on the entities' respective security labels. Hence, it is not allowed, for example, for information to flow from a top_secret source to a less secure entity. In contrast, information may always flow from an unclassified source.

When we consider different interactions between subjects and objects we derive the following rules:

♦ A subject s is authorized to read an object o only if the security label of s is at least as high as that of o. This is sometimes referred to as the *no-read-up rule* or *simple security property* [8].

♦ A subject s is authorized to write to an object o only if the security label of o is at least as high as that of s. This is sometimes referred to as the *no-write-down rule* or **-property* [8].

A word of explanation is required regarding write access. It is possible that a subject with top_secret clearance may (inadvertently) run a Trojan horse program

---

[7] Formally, $\lambda : S \cup O \rightarrow L$; that is, λ is a function from the set comprising all subjects and objects to the set of security labels.

that has been installed by an attacker. Such a program might attempt to write top_secret information to a less secure file. The no-write-down rule prevents the Trojan horse program from performing this action, limiting the damage that an attacker can inflict by installing such a program. (Of course, if the attacker can obtain top_secret access, then he or she can obtain the top_secret information anyway.) Another security compromise that the no-write-down rule prevents is that of a subject mistakenly writing sensitive information to an object with a lower security level. The classic example of this is printing top_secret documents on a printer that has an unclassified security label. (A request to print a document is usually interpreted as a request to write to a printer object.)

3.3.4 Bell-LaPadula Model

Clearly, it is unlikely that an information flow policy will be able to define all the authorization requirements of a computer system. Notice that an information flow policy authorizes access purely on the basis of labeling of the subject and object, and is independent of any ownership considerations. This is sometimes referred to as a *mandatory* access control policy. In practically all cases, no user should actually be authorized to write to a file with a higher security label, but the information flow policy does not prevent this from happening. Therefore, it is necessary to augment the mandatory information flow policy with a *discretionary* access control policy, defined by the object owners and implemented using a protection matrix.

The Bell-LaPadula model is perhaps the most famous of all access control models and has had a significant influence on the development of research into access control. It allows for the definition of a mandatory information flow policy and a discretionary access control policy. The first contribution of the Bell-LaPadula model was to formally define what it meant for a computer system to be in a *secure state*. A second contribution was to prove that it is possible to construct computer systems that only exist in secure states. That is, it is possible to build a computer system and define a security policy such that for all future points in time, the system is in a secure state.

The Bell-LaPadula model implements an information policy for confidentiality, and includes a protection matrix to further refine the information flow policy. The *protection state*, or simply *state*, of a computer system is a snapshot of all security-relevant information that is subject to change. The Bell-LaPadula model defines the state of the system to be (V, M), where V denotes the set of *active triples*.[8] V models those requests that have been granted and represents the set of

---

[8] For ease of exposition, we assume that λ is fixed. In the most general form of the model, this is not the case, and λ is included as part of the state.

objects that are in main memory currently in use by subjects. For example, if a request from *s* to read *o* is granted then the object is brought into main memory, which is modeled by adding the triple (*s, o,* read). It will become apparent that this is an important consideration in checking access requests.

The Bell-LaPadula model defines three security properties. All triples in *V* must satisfy the simple security property and *-property. In addition, every triple in *V* must satisfy the *discretionary security property*, which requires that every granted request has been authorized by the protection matrix.

A state is said to be *secure* if it satisfies the discretionary, simple, and *-properties. In order to maintain the system in a secure state, it must not be possible to grant a request that would violate any of the three security properties. Hence, when a user makes an access request, the system must check both the access matrix to see that the request is authorized by the matrix and compare the security labels of the subject and object to determine whether the simple security property and *-property are satisfied.

The operating system is responsible for all state transitions and must ensure that each command that causes a state transition moves the system from a secure state to another secure state. Therefore, the operating system will contain a number of functions that implement security checks to ensure that the state transition results in a state that conforms to the security policy of the system.

3.3.5   Clark-Wilson Model

The Bell-LaPadula model was inspired by security requirements for military computer systems. In contrast, the Clark-Wilson model is concerned with commercial computer systems. Typically, the business processes of a commercial organization will have certain consistency constraints that must be satisfied. A banking application, for example, might include a process that transfers money from one account to another account. A consistency constraint in this case would be that the total amount deposited in the two accounts is the same before and after the transfer. It is vital that business processes ensure that all consistency constraints are satisfied.

A computerized business process is often called a *transaction* and comprises a sequence of operations that transform one state of a computer system to another.[9] Transactions are a central concept in data processing applications such as relational database management systems. A transaction is *well formed* if it transforms

---

[9]   The state of a computer system is a rather broad and informal concept compared to that introduced in the description of the Bell-LaPadula model. It refers as much to the data and business objects in the system as the actual objects in main memory.

a consistent state into another consistent state. The Clark-Wilson model is concerned with ensuring that a commercial system is consistent with the business rules (or security policy) of the organization running that system.

The model introduces the following concepts: *constrained data items* (CDIs), *unconstrained data items* (UDIs), and *transformation procedures*. A CDI can be thought of as a protected object. Clark and Wilson propose a model for protecting the integrity of CDIs and for ensuring that the transformation of a CDI is consistent with the related security policy. In contrast, UDIs are not protected. However, if a UDI is used as an input to a business process, it must first be transformed into a CDI in order to ensure that it cannot subsequently violate the integrity of the system.

In order to ensure the integrity of CDIs, users can only interact with CDIs through well-defined interfaces called *transformation procedures* (TPs). A TP can be thought of as a complex access operation, which changes the CDI in some way or into a different type of CDI. A TP may only interact with certain CDIs: It would make no sense for a TP that transfers money between two accounts to operate on CDIs that are not bank accounts, for example. Associating TPs with particular CDIs ensures that only well-formed transactions may be executed.

Moreover, only certain users are allowed to perform particular TPs. A bank clerk, for example, might be allowed to perform a TP that effects a transfer of funds from one account to another, but would not be allowed to perform a transformation procedure that authorized an overdraft. In other words, subjects are associated with TPs that determine what interaction they may have with CDIs. This enables an authorization policy to be specified. Clark and Wilson suggest that this can be achieved by defining relationships of the form (t, o) and (s, t, o), where t is a transformation procedure, o is a constrained data item, and s is a subject.

Certification Rules

The Clark-Wilson model proposes a number of certification and enforcement rules. The certification rules basically express a high-level generic security policy. The certification rules are:

C1. *Integrity verification procedures (IVPs) must ensure that all CDIs are in a valid state.* An IVP is used to check that a CDI is in a valid state. Since it is assumed that a TP will only transform a valid CDI into another valid CDI (see C2 rule), and that an IVP can check that CDIs are in a valid state initially, we can guarantee the validity of all CDIs at every point in time.

C2. *Each TP must be certified to be valid* (i.e., valid CDIs must be transformed into valid CDIs by the TP). *Each TP is certified to access a specific set of CDIs.* In other words, the correctness of each TP must be guaranteed and the correctness of each association between a TP and CDI must be guaranteed.

C3. *The access rules must satisfy any separation of duty requirements.* In other words, any associations between users and TPs must be guaranteed to satisfy the separation of duty requirements.

C4. *All TPs must write to an append-only log.* In other words, there must be a complete audit trail and entries in that trail cannot be modified after their creation.

C5. *Any TP that takes a UDI as input must either convert it into a CDI or fail.* In other words, the TPs must be designed in such a way as to ensure that for any unconstrained input, the resulting state is valid. This may be because the TP rejects the input and does not change the state, or transforms the UDI into a valid CDI. This is a particularly important point in general for computer security. Many vulnerabilities in computer systems arise because inadequate checks are performed when handling input from untrusted sources.

Enforcement Rules

The certification rules are implemented by the enforcement rules. The enforcement rules are:

E1. *The system must maintain and protect the list of constrained data items that a transformation procedure is certified to access.* In other words, if rule C2 says that TP1 is certified to access CDI1 and CDI2 (and no other CDIs), then we must create a list [CDI1, CDI2] and associate it with TP1. This list and association must be protected by the operating system to prevent tampering.

E2. *The system must maintain and protect the list of transformation procedures that a user can execute.* In other words, we must create an association between each user and a set of TPs, or put another way, the system must maintain a set of capability lists, where each list contains the TPs that the associated user can perform. The association of TPs with CDIs means that users are indirectly associated with the CDIs they are authorized to access.

E3. *The system must authenticate each user requesting the use of a transformation procedure.* Interestingly, the Clark-Wilson model does not insist that a user has to be authenticated when using a computer system, rather only when trying to execute a transformation procedure. In principle, this is correct, as the execution of a TP provides access to a protected object, and hence, it is necessary to ensure that the user is associated with that TP. However, in a practical system, it would be more realistic to authenticate the user once at logon time, rather than before each execution of a TP.

E4. *Only a certifier of a transformation procedure can change the certification. The certifier must not be allowed to execute the transformation procedure.* This is an example of separation of duty. Each access list in rules E2 and E3 must be created by a subject. This rule ensures that a malicious subject cannot create a TP, assign himself to that TP, and thereby execute that TP.

The Clark-Wilson model is not really an access control model in any formal sense. It more closely resembles a set of evaluation criteria. We can imagine assigning a security rating to a system based on the degree to which certification and enforcement rules were implemented. The model also provides a useful checklist when designing and developing secure applications.

3.3.6 Role-Based Access Control

A long-standing problem in practical security systems is the administrative burden of maintaining access control lists or other similar access control data structures. In a system with 1,000 users, 100,000 objects, and 10 access rights (a relatively small system by today's standards), there are $10 \times 1,000 \times 100,000 = 10^9$ possible authorization triples. Role-based access control (RBAC) is a relatively recent attempt to alleviate this burden. It achieves this by introducing the concept of a *role*, which acts as a bridge between users and permissions. The idea is that there will be far fewer roles than either users or permissions. Typically, roles are associated with job descriptions, although this is not the only possibility.

The basic concepts of RBAC are illustrated in Figure 3.2. The ANSI RBAC standard was released in 2004 [9]. It is based on earlier work by researchers at George Mason University and NIST, notably Ravi Sandhu [10]. The two main components are the *core* component, which does not include role hierarchies, and the *hierarchical* component, which does.

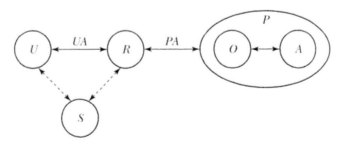

FIGURE   Core RBAC. From Sandhu et al. [10].

3.2

There is a set of users U, a set of permissions P, and a set of roles R. A permission is usually assumed to be an object–action pair, where an action is synonymous with an access right. Users are associated with roles using a user–role assignment relation UA. This relation is a set of pairs of the form (u, r), meaning that user u is assigned to role r. Permissions are similarly associated with roles using a permission-role assignment relation PA.

Users interact with an RBAC system by activating a *session*. Typically, the user authenticates to the system and chooses to act in one or more of the roles to which he or she is assigned. If s makes an access request for permission p during the session, the permissions of the session roles and their junior roles are considered. If the requested permission is among them, the access request is granted.

In a sense, RBAC can be thought of as an extension of the Clark-Wilson model. Permissions represent an association between a CDI and TP. Roles introduce an extra level between users and TPs, and are used to reduce the number of associations that need to be maintained.

RBAC further reduces the administrative burden by introducing the idea of a *role hierarchy*, which is modeled as a directed acyclic graph in which the roles are nodes. In other words, the role hierarchy is represented as a binary relation RH on R. The transitive, reflexive closure of this relation defines a partial ordering on the set of roles.

The basic idea is that a role high up in the hierarchy will inherit the permissions of lower roles, without having to be explicitly assigned to those permissions. Clearly, this significantly reduces the number of permissions that need to be assigned to more senior roles, thereby reducing the administrative overheads in an RBAC system. Of course, this introduces an overhead into the access-checking algorithm, because it is necessary to consider the permissions of all junior roles when making a decision.

RBAC is now widely supported in commercial systems, such as Oracle, Sybase, Windows 2003, and Solaris. An RBAC profile exists for XACML and it is widely used in workflow management systems. The interested reader is directed to the recent book by Ferraiolo et al. [11], which provides an excellent overview of RBAC and its applications.

3.4   ACCESS CONTROL IN DISTRIBUTED SYSTEMS

Access control mechanisms are particularly critical for today's distributed systems, in which applications and users need to interact across different administrative domains. Moreover, several new applications are emerging, such as collaborative applications, workflows, and grid computing, for which different access control policies may need to be combined. Some important requirements for suitable access control systems in such context are:

* Authorizations should be expressed in terms of the qualifications and characteristics (i.e., *attributes*) of subjects, rather than being expressed in terms of user log-in names. In many cases, users of web applications do not have local log-in names, because in practice managing log-in accounts for a dynamically changing population of users is not feasible. Recent approaches to access control for distributed systems are based on the notion of attribute-based access control (ABAC); this is the case of the XACML standard and of more advanced models, like Author-X [12]. When adopting ABAC, however, there is the issue of how to exchange assertions about values for these attributes and whether these assertions can be trusted. SAML, briefly described in the following subsection, addresses the first of such issues. We discuss issues related to trust also in the context of the discussion about SAML.

* *Contextual information* should be taken into account in access control decisions. In several applications characterized by mobile users, it is crucial, for example, that access to sensitive resources is only performed when the user is located in specific locations. A model supporting this requirement is GEO-RBAC, which is briefly discussed in Section 3.4.2.

In the remainder of this section, we elaborate on some of the relevant standards, and then we discuss advanced solutions and research issues.

3.4.1   Overview of Relevant Standards

The standard world has been very active in developing standards related to XML and more recently to web services technology. Those standards cover many security components and techniques, ranging from encryption to digital signature techniques and access control. Here, we briefly review the standards that are more relevant in the context of access control, namely SAML and XACML.

SAML

The Security Assertions Mark-up Language (SAML) [5] is an XML-based framework, developed by OASIS, to support the exchange of security information, also called trust assertions, between parties in a distributed system. The applications and environments that can use SAML range from simple browser-based applications to more complex n-tiered architecture web services. Security information takes the form of security assertions, where an assertion states certain facts (characteristics and attributes) about a subject. The current SAML framework supports three kinds of security assertions: authentication, attribute, and authorization decisions. Specifically:

+ An authentication assertion states that the subject S has been authenticated by means of an authentication method M at a certain time. It is issued by the party that successfully authenticated the subject.

+ An attribute assertion states that the subject S is associated with the set of attributes A with values B (e.g., that Alice is associated with attribute "Company" with value "Hertz").

+ An authorization decision assertion states that a subject S has been authorized to execute an action on resource R (e.g., that a user has been authorized to use a given service).

Assertions are issued by SAML authorities, namely authentication authorities, attribute authorities, or policy decision points. In order to support the exchange of security assertions between involved parties, SAML provides a request and response protocol that consists of XML-based messages; a client uses this protocol to request a specific assertion or to make authentication, attribute, and authorization decisions queries to an SAML authority. These messages can be bound to many different underlying communication and transport protocols.

SAML also defines several profiles. Generally, a profile of SAML defines constraints and/or extensions of the core protocols and assertions in support of the usage of SAML for a particular application by specifying how particular statements are communicated using appropriate protocol messages over specified bindings. For example, the Web Browser SSO Profile specifies how SAML authentication assertions are communicated using the Authentication Query and Response messages over a number of different bindings in order to enable single sign-on for a browser user. SAML assumes that the two or more endpoints of an SAML transaction are uncompromised, but the attacker has complete control over the communications channel.

SAML has been successfully used in a number of systems, such as those for federated digital identity management, that are discussed in a later section. However, it is important to emphasize that SAML does not address the problem of the use of assertions once they are received by a party, nor whether these assertions can be actually trusted. In particular, trust in such context consists of two different requirements: being able to trust the keys used to sign the assertions and being able to trust the actual content of the assertion. The first requirement can be easily addressed by the use of key infrastructures. The second requirement is much more difficult to assess, in that an assertion may convey information that is not correct because of errors made by the issuing party or because the issuing party did not adequately verify the information. Addressing such requirements is much more challenging, and it requires adopting organizational measures in addition to technical techniques. Research in the area of data quality, which aims at developing techniques to improve the quality of digital data, may be very relevant to address such requirements.

XACML

XACML [6] provides an extensible, XML-encoded language for managing authorization decisions. To this end, XACML language allows one to express access control policies and access requests/responses. XACML was conceived as one component of a distributed and interoperable authorization framework, with the following underlying rationales:

1. Access control policies do not have to be embedded or tightly linked to the system they govern.

2. XACML policies can be applied to different heterogeneous resources such as XML documents, relational databases, application servers, web services, and so on.

3. A standard policy exchange format allows different parties to exchange or share authorization policies, as well as to deploy the same policy to heterogeneous systems.

It is worth noting that XACML also includes a non-normative data flow model (see [6], Section 3.1, Data Flow Model), reported in Figure 3.3, that describes the major components involved in processing of access requests. This model, which can be considered as an evolution of the ISO 10181-3 model [13], can be used as a reference model for the implementation of an XACML engine. The components of such a model are:

✦ The Policy Administration Point (PAP) supports authorization policy authoring and stores the authored policies in the appropriate repository.

✦ The policy enforcement point (PEP) performs access control by making decision requests and enforcing authorization decisions.

✦ The policy information point (PIP) serves as the source of attribute values or the data required for policy evaluation.

✦ The policy decision point (PDP) evaluates the applicable policy and renders a response to the PEP containing the authorization decision. The possible response values are: Permit, Deny, Indeterminate (in case an error occurred or some required value was missing, so a decision cannot be made), or Not Applicable (the request cannot be answered by this service).

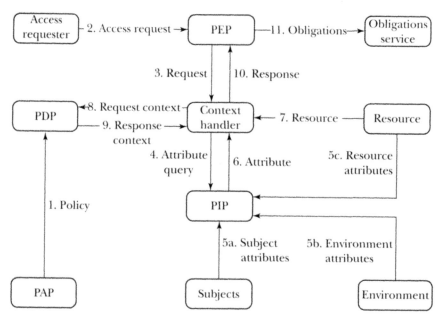

FIGURE   Data flow model for XACML. From OASIS [6].

3.3

The PEP and PDP both might be colocated within the same application, or might be distributed across different servers. In XACML, the access request is represented by the Request schema that specifies the requesting Subject, the requested Object, and the specific Action requested on the Object. The XACML policy language was designed to be general enough so as to describe general access control requirements. It is also extensible, by means of standard extension points, in order to accommodate the definition of new functions, data types, combining logic, and so forth.

In XACML, a policy is the smallest element that the PDP can evaluate. A policy represents a single access control policy, expressed through a set of Rules. A Rule specifies the Target that it applies to and the effect of the Rule, such as Permit or Deny. The Target basically models the access request by means of a set of simplified conditions for the Subject, Resource, and Action that must be met (i.e., evaluate to true) for the Rule to apply to a given request. Any number of Rule elements may be used, each of which generates a true or false outcome. Combining these outcomes yields a single decision for the Policy, which may be "Permit," "Deny," "Indeterminate," or a "Not Applicable" decision. As a policy example, consider the following: "MPEG movie for adults cannot be accessed by users with age less than 18 years." The movie is the resource that the access to must be controlled; it will be modeled by an element having an attribute "category." Similarly, the subject will have an attribute "age." In this case, the policy is composed by a single Rule that specifies the condition—"age less than 18 years"—for the subject; the condition— category = "adult only"—for the resource; the condition—"download"—for the action: and the effect—"Deny." More than one Rule (or policy) may be applicable to a given access request; XACML defines a set of Combining Algorithms to reconcile multiple outcomes into a single decision, namely, Deny-overrides, Permit-overrides, First-applicable, or Only-one-applicable. Recently, an OASIS XACML Profile for Web-Services, hereafter referred to as XACML2, has been developed in order to support access control for web services.

Even though XACML has contributed to make widely known important research notions developed by academia, such as attribute-based and credential-based access control [12], it also has some drawbacks. It has been designed to be used in applications in which there is a centralized administration; it is also very complex and thus analysis of XACML policies is quite difficult. A recent paper [14] provides preliminary results concerning the integration of XACML policies for independently administered domains. However, such an approach is very preliminary and more research is needed on this topic.

3.4.2 Advanced Approaches

Recent advanced approaches to access control in distributed systems have mainly focused on the problem of how a system can control access when users are not previously known to the system. Most such approaches rely on the use of credentials that users wishing to access resources management by a party have to provide. In what follows, we describe first an approach in which access is given based on a credential exchange process; we refer to such a process as trust negotiation. We then discuss the case in which the resource to which access has to be controlled is a set of roles; therefore, the issue is how to automatically verify that users, from an administrative domain, have the right to log-in under a role in another administrative domain. Another important issue that has been recently investigated is related to mobile users that need to access certain resources; user location is thus an important contextual parameter that should be taken into account when deciding whether a user can access a given resource. This is a critical issue for many applications that require that access to critical resources be only possible when the user is in a secure location. In this section we discuss Geo-RBAC [15], the first comprehensive approach addressing such a requirement.

Trust and Trust Negotiation

The notion of trust is a key notion in distributed systems, in which very often parties unknown to each other need to communicate in order to exchange information and share resources. Trust is a complex notion about which no consensus exists in the computer and information science literature, although its importance has been widely recognized. Different definitions are possible depending on the adopted perspective. For example, Kini and Choobineh [16] define trust from the perspectives of personality theorists, sociologists, economists, and social psychologists. Their definition of trust is: "A belief that is influenced by the individual's opinion about certain critical system features." A different definition is based on the notion of competence and predictability. The Trust-EC project (http://dsa-isis.jrc.it/TrustEC/) of the European Commission Joint Research Centre (ECJRC) defines trust as: "The property of a business relationship, such that reliance can be placed on the business partners and the business transactions developed with them." Such a definition emphasizes the identification and reliability of business partners, the confidentiality and integrity of sensitive information, the guaranteed quality of digital goods, the availability of critical information, and the dependability of computer services and systems. Another relevant definition is by Grandison and Sloman [17] who define trust as: "The firm belief in the competence of an entity to act dependably, securely, and reliably within a specified context." They argue that trust is a composition of many different attributes—reliability, dependability, honesty, truthfulness, security, competence, and timeliness—that may have to be considered depending on the environment in which trust is being specified.

A main difficulty of all these definitions, as well as others, is that they provide a notion of trust for which establishing metrics and developing evaluation methodologies is quite difficult. A more restricted notion of trust, which is the one underlying trust negotiation systems, was initially proposed by Blaze et al. [18] according to whom, "Trust management problems include formulating security policies and security credentials, determining whether particular sets of credentials satisfy the relevant policies, and deferring trust to third parties." Such a definition of trust basically refers to security policies regulating accesses to resources and credentials that are required to satisfy such policies, and it is thus very relevant in the context of access control for distributed systems.

Trust negotiation refers to the process of credential exchanges that allows a party requiring a service or a resource from another party to provide the necessary credentials in order to obtain the service or the resource [19]. Access control policies are expressed in terms of conditions against the possession of specific credentials and properties. Notice that, because credentials may contain sensitive information, the party requiring the service or the resource may ask to verify the other party's credentials before releasing its own credentials. Trust negotiation is a peer-to-peer interaction and consists of the iterative disclosure of digital credentials, representing statements certified by given entities, for verifying properties of their holders in order to establish mutual trust. In such an approach, access to resources (data and/or services) is possible only after a successful trust negotiation is completed.

A trust negotiation system typically exploits digital identity information for the purpose of providing a fine-grained access control to protected resources. However, unlike conventional access control models, trust negotiation assumes that the interacting parties are peers and that each peer needs to be adequately protected. For instance, with respect to the peer owning the resource to be accessed, assets that need to be protected are, in addition to the resource, the access control policies, as they may contain sensitive information, and the credentials of the resource owner. With respect to the peer requiring access to the resource, the assets to be protected are the credentials, as they often contain private information about the individual on behalf of whom the peer is negotiating.

We now briefly describe how negotiations are generally intended and identify the main phases and functional components of negotiations as given in Bertino et al. [19]. Trust negotiation typically involves two entities, namely a *client*, that is, the entity asking for a certain resource, and a *server*, that is, the entity owning (or more generally, managing access to) the requested resource. The model is peer-to-peer: Both entities may possess sensitive resources to be protected and thus must be equipped with a compliant negotiation system. The notion of *resource* comprises both sensitive information and services, whereas the notion of entity includes users, processes, roles, and servers. The term *resource* is intentionally left generic to emphasize the fact that the negotiations we refer to are general purpose, that is, a *resource* is any sensitive object (e.g., financial information, health records, and credit card numbers) whose disclosure is protected by a set of *policies*.

Figure 3.4 illustrates a typical negotiation process. During the negotiation, trust is incrementally built by iteratively disclosing *digital credentials* in order to verify properties of the negotiating parties. Credentials are typically collected by each party in appropriate repositories, called *subject profiles*. Another key component is the set of access control policies, referred to as *disclosure policies*, governing access to protected resources through the specification of the credential combinations that must be submitted to obtain access to the resources. To carry out a trust negotiation, parties usually adopt a strategy, which is implemented by an algorithm determining which credentials to disclose, when to disclose them, and whether to succeed or fail the negotiation. Several trust negotiation strategies can be devised, each with different properties with respect to speed of negotiations and caution in releasing credentials and policies [20].

Because of the relevance of trust negotiation for web-based applications, several systems and research prototypes have been developed. Well-known systems include Keynote [18] and Trust-X [19].

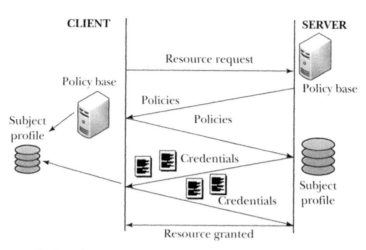

Organization of trust negotiation process. From Bertino et al. [19].

Keynote has been developed to work for large- and small-scale Internet-based applications. It provides a single, unified language for both local policies and credentials. Keynote credentials, called *assertions*, contain predicates that describe the trusted actions permitted by the holders of a specific public key. As a result, Keynote policies do not handle credentials as a means of establishing trust, mainly because the language was intended for delegation authority; also, Keynote does not support optimization strategies and does not address the problem of privacy.

Trust-X is a more advanced system that supports all aspects of negotiation; it supports an XML-based language, known as X-TNL, for specifying Trust-X certificates and policies. Trust-X has a typing credential system and addresses the issue of vocabulary agreement using XML namespaces. The use of namespaces combined with the certificate-type system helps the trust negotiation engine in correctly interpreting different credentials' schema, even when issued by different entities not sharing a common ontology.

A novel aspect of X-TNL is its support for special certificates, called *trust tickets*. Trust tickets are issued upon successfully completing a negotiation and can speed up subsequent negotiations for the same resource. X-TNL provides a flexible language for specifying policies and a mechanism for policy protection, based on the notion of policy preconditions. A Trust-X negotiation consists of a set of phases that are sequentially executed. In particular, Trust-X enforces a strict separation between policy exchange and resource disclosure. This distinction results in an effective protection of all the resources involved in negotiations.

Trust-X also provides various trust negotiation strategies that allow one to trade-off between efficiency and protection requirements. In particular, Trust-X supports three different negotiation modes. The first, based on trust tickets, can be adopted when the parties have already successfully completed a negotiation for the same resource. The second mode, based on using specific abstract data structures called *negotiation trees*, performs a runtime evaluation of the negotiation's feasibility by determining a sequence of certificate disclosures that can successfully end the negotiation. The last mode exploits a notion of similarity between negotiations, and is based on the observation that a service provider usually handles many similar negotiations. Recent investigation carried out in the framework of Trust-X includes support for privacy [21], anonymity [22], the development of a recovery protocol [23], and the integration with federated identity management [24].

Multidomain RBAC

The Web has made possible a large variety of collaborative applications, in areas such as e-learning, healthcare, and e-government. Most of these applications require different organizations, or even different units within the same organization, to be able to establish dynamic coalitions in which users of one domain can seamlessly access resources from other domains. Approaches in which users are explicitly and directly given access to all resources they need to access across the coalition domains are not practical and do not scale. Moreover, they make authorization revocation cumbersome and error prone. Different approaches are required to keep the administration costs at a reasonable level and supporting a manageable authorization revocation.

One such approach has been recently proposed based on the X-GTRBAC model [25], an XML-based RBAC model supporting a large variety of temporal constraints on the use of roles by users. The key idea underlying such an approach is to associate with each role a set of preconditions for the use of roles. Each user verifying such preconditions is given permission to use the role; there is no need to grant these users an explicit permission for the role, thus simplifying the management of the UA relation (see Figure 3.2).

In X-GTRBAC, such preconditions are expressed against user credentials, which are encoded in SAML. In particular, by using the precondition language supported by X-GTRBAC, it is possible to condition the use of a role in a domain, referred to as the *target domain*, to the authorization of using the same role or even another role in another domain, referred to as the *source domain*. A user authorized to use a role r in the source domain can thus use a role r' in the target domain, provided that the authorization to use r is a precondition for the use of r'. Assertions concerning the fact that a user can use a role r in a given domain are encoded by the source domain using SAML. In addition to accepting SAML assertions as input, X-GTRBAC also generates SAML assertions as a result of access control; therefore, whenever the X-GTRBAC instance at the target domain determines that a user can access a role, it generates an SAML assertion stating this fact. Such an assertion can then be used for accessing a role in another domain.

This type of role interoperability enhances decentralization and autonomy. Each domain can independently decide the preconditions that the users of another domain need to verify for gaining access to the local roles. Such preconditions can be different for users from different domains. Revoking the authorizations to use a local role from remote users is very easy, in that one only has to drop the preconditions concerning such users.

Even though X-GTRBAC represents an important approach to the problem of multidomain access control, several issues still need to be investigated, including anonymous accesses and delegation.

GEO-RBAC

The widespread deployment of location-based services and mobile applications, as well as the increased concern for the management and sharing of geographical information in strategic applications like environmental protection and homeland security, have resulted in a strong demand for spatially-aware access control systems. These application domains pose interesting requirements against access control systems. In particular, the permissions assigned to users depend on their position in a reference space. Users often belong to well-defined categories, and objects to which permissions must be granted are located in that space. Access control policies must grant permissions based on object locations and user positions.

As an example, consider a mobile application for the personnel and patients of a health care organization. Individuals are given a location-aware terminal with which they can request information services provided by an application server. The organization consists of individuals who have different functional roles (e.g., nurse, doctor, and patient). We can notice that, depending on the organizational context, the services available to users may differ based on the functional roles of users. For example, the services available to nurses may be different from those available to doctors, not simply because of the individual preferences but mainly because of organizational and functional reasons. Further, the availability of services may depend on the position of the requester. For example, a nurse may be allowed to request the record of a patient only when located in the department he or she has been assigned to. To deal with the requirements listed above, an access control model with spatial capabilities is needed. Since in location-aware applications users are often grouped in distinct categories, like nurse and doctor, RBAC represents a reasonable choice. However, conventional RBAC does not suffice to support such applications and needs to be extended with suitable constraints specifying location constraints, that is, constraints concerning the locations in which a given role can be accessed by a user. It is important to notice that locations can be physical, that is, expressed as coordinates in the reference space, or logical, that is, expressed in terms of spatial objects (such as the city of Milan, the West Valley Hospital) that have a semantics that are relevant to the specific application domains. When dealing with location-based applications it is also important to take into account relevant standards for the representation of spatial objects; one such standard is the one by the Open Geospatial Consortium [26].

GEO-RBAC is a recently developed model that directly supports such types of location constraints. It is based on the notion of *spatial role* that is a geographically-bounded organizational function. The boundary of a role is defined as a geographical feature, such as a road, city, or hospital, and specifies the spatial extent in which the user has to be located in order to use the role. Besides a physical position, obtained from a given mobile terminal such as a global positioning system–based vehicle tracking device or a cellular phone, users are also assigned a logical and device-independent position representing the feature in which the user is located. *Logical* positions can be computed from *real* positions by using specific mapping functions and can be represented at different granularities, depending on the spatial role played by the user. If the user is located inside the spatial boundary of the role that has been selected (*activated*) during the session, the role is said to be *enabled*. To specify the type of spatial boundary of the role and the granularity of the logical position, GEO-RBAC has introduced the concept of *spatial role schema*. Spatial roles are specified as instances of role schemas.

As RBAC, GEO-RBAC encompasses a family of models:

+ Core GEO-RBAC includes the basic concepts of the model, thus the notion of spatial role, role schema, real/logical position, and activated/enabled role.

+ Hierarchical GEO-RBAC extends the conventional hierarchical RBAC by introducing two distinct hierarchies: one over role schemas and one over role instances.

+ Constrained GEO-RBAC supports the specification of separation of duty (SoD) constraints for spatial roles and role schemas. Since exclusive role constraints are important to support the definition and maintenance of access control policies in mobile contexts, SoD constraints are extended to account for different granularities (schema/instance level), dimension (spatial/nonspatial), and different verification time (static, dynamic at activation time, dynamic at enabling time). The resulting set of constraints developed for GEO-RBAC represents the first comprehensive class of constraints for spatially-aware applications.

Even though GEO-RBAC provides a comprehensive model for location-based access control, many issues still need to be investigated, such as architectural issues and session management.

3.5   DIGITAL IDENTITY MANAGEMENT

Digital identity can be defined as the digital representation of the information known about a specific individual or organization. Such a notion encompasses not only log-in names (often referred to as *nyms*), but many additional pieces of information, referred to as *identity attributes* or *identifiers*. Digital identity management is the set of processes, tools, social contracts, and a supporting infrastructure for creating, maintaining, utilizing, and terminating a digital identity. Identity management has strong links with security, privacy, and trust. Traditionally, identity management has been a core component, in some limited form, of system security environments in which it is used for maintaining account information used to control log-in accesses to a system. Therefore, control is the primary focus for such digital identity management systems.

More recently, however, identity management is viewed as a key enabler for electronic business. As the richness of individuals' electronic lives begin to mirror the interactions taking place in the physical world, activities such as shopping, collaborations, health care management, and entertainment are conducted as readily in the cyber world as in person. As a result, users require more convenience from electronic systems; they expect their personal preferences and profiles to be readily available. In such context, identity management (IdM) systems are increasingly playing a crucial role in underpinning accountability in business relationships, protecting individual privacy, and complying with regulatory controls.

Because of the relevance of identity management in an increasing number of applications and organizations, several initiatives are currently ongoing, some of which we describe here. In general, all these initiatives define architectural frameworks for the management of digital identity and protocols supporting sharing of identity information across different domains. Most such frameworks identify three main logical entities involved in the management of digital identity: *identity providers*, which are entities in charge of provisioning and managing identity information; *service providers*, also referred to as *relying parties*, which are entities providing some services for which they need identity attributes about the requesting parties; and *users*, which are entities about which identity information is issued and managed and that require services by the service providers. Most of these initiatives are also targeted toward the notion of identity management *federations*.

These are sets of identity providers and service providers that have some preexisting agreement about sharing identity information and that usually adopt the same policies concerning the management of this information.

An important distinction to make among the various proposals of IdM frameworks is between identity provider–centric frameworks and user-centric frameworks. In the first class of framework, an example of which is Shibboleth [27], identity attributes are directly exchanged between the identity provider and the service provider, with very little intervention from the user. In the second class of framework, an example of which is CardSpace, all interactions between the identity provider and the service provider are mediated by a client running on behalf of the user. We briefly describe some of those initiatives and outline research efforts.

3.5.1   Shibboleth

Shibboleth is a project of Internet2/MACE with the goal of developing architectures, policy languages, and an open-source implementation to support interinstitutional sharing of web resources subject to access control. It supports Web single sign-on (SSO) across or within organizational boundaries. Thus, whenever a user wants to connect to an institution I federated with his or her home institution, the Shibboleth system at I requires from the user information about the home institution and then redirects the user to this institution for authentication. Once the user has been authenticated at the home institution, the Shibboleth system at the home institution generates an opaque user ID, referred to as a *handle*, which is then the identifier under which the user is known at I; the handle does not contain any information about the actual user log-in information at the home institution, thus keeping this information private. The home institution and I may further carry some exchanges in case I needs to know some identity attributes of a user in order to provide him or her with access to the requested resource.

In Shibboleth, as in many other frameworks, identity attributes among federation entities are exchanged according to the SAML protocols. Shibboleth is an example of federated management of identity attributes in which the identity providers, that is, the home institution of the user, provide attribute assertions expressed in SAML about that user to the service provider, that is, the target institution. A trust fabric exists among institutions that allows each institution to identify any other institution in the federation and assign to it a trust level. Identity providers are responsible for authenticating users and they can use any authentication means to do so. Access control in Shibboleth is based on identity attributes, which may encompass a large variety of information, such as the project the user is working on or whether the user is taking a particular course.

Shibboleth has defined an initial standard set of such attributes, based on the eduPerson object class that includes individual attributes widely used in higher education institutions.

An interesting notion supported by Shibboleth is the notion of identity attribute import policy and attribute export policy. The first policy refers to which identity attributes an institution is willing to accept from another institution, whereas the second policy refers to which identity attributes an institution is willing to provide to another institution. Even though this notion is quite simple, several issues related to it need to be investigated, such as negotiation protocols that the institutions need to carry on in order to decide about attributes to be imported or exported. Also suitably rich languages for expressing such policies need to be developed.

3.5.2   CardSpace

CardSpace is a technology developed by Microsoft for securely managing users' identity attributes and credentials, as well as for providing an interface that allows a user to select specified identity attributes and credentials, encoding them in order to carry out a transaction with a service provider. CardSpace supports the management of identity attributes through the use of *virtual cards*. Virtual cards are the analog of the real-world forms of identity, such as business cards, driver licenses, and passports. When a service provider requires some identity attributes from the user, the CardSpace system at the client presents the user with all the virtual cards. Each card is issued by an identity provider and records some identity attributes. The same user will typically have multiple cards, possibly issued by different identity providers, such as government agencies, financial institutions, and educational institutions; also the same identity attribute, for example the birth date, may be recorded on several cards. Users may also create their own identity cards. The CardSpace interface allows a user to select the card that has to be submitted to the service provider in order to provide the required identity attributes. Once a card is selected by the user, the CardSpace system issues a request to the identity provider to verify the identity attributes encoded in the selected card. The identity provider returns a signed and encrypted security token that contains the required information. At this point, the user decides whether the information should be sent to the service provider. If the user decides to send the information, the CardSpace system will forward the information to the service provider; otherwise, the token is not sent.

CardSpace is an interesting system that mirrors, through the notion of a virtual card, the way people manage identity in the real world. An interesting issue is whether the CardSpace approach can be extended with strategies that do not require an online exchange with the identity provider in order to obtain the token during the transaction execution. This is important for performance and for minimizing the frequency of the interactions between the client system and the various identity providers.

3.5.3 Higgins Trust Framework

The Higgins trust framework is a recent important initiative, the goal of which is to ensure interoperability among different IdM systems [28]. Higgins aims at providing a framework for user-centric identity and personal information management applications. It also aims at simplifying the management of identity attributes, profiles, and reputation information across different domains. In order to reduce the cost of application development and maintenance, Higgins provides a unified API on top of which applications can be developed; such unified API interfaces all major IdM systems and protocols, such as CardSpace [29], and OpenID [30].

The Higgins framework also introduces a new application layer, referred to as *context*. Applications that link the context layer have the potential to link identity information across different IdM systems. Each IdM system will have an adapter that links the context layer to the system. The interoperability features of the Higgins trust framework make possible the support of new applications. Applications will be able to manage users' profiles, identity attributes, and reputation information across different domains, while at the same time assuring user privacy.

3.5.4 Research Approaches

Issues related with identity management to date have not been really investigated by the research community. Past work has mainly focused on the problem of credential management, and approaches have been developed specifically dealing with anonymous credentials. In anonymous credential systems, organizations know the users only by pseudonyms. Different pseudonyms of the same user cannot be linked. Yet, an organization can issue a credential to a pseudonym. The corresponding user can prove possession of this credential to another organization (which knows this user by a different pseudonym) without revealing anything more than the fact that the user owns such a credential.

Idemix [31] is the first system supporting anonymous credentials in a federated identity management system. Idemix provides a flexible scheme for issuing and revoking anonymous credentials. It also provides a mechanism for all-or-nothing sharing and a Public Key Infrastructure (PKI) based nontransferability. A major drawback of credential-based approaches, however, is that anonymous credentials may not be useful in real e-commerce applications and web services requiring strong identifiers.

A different approach that does not have such shortcomings is the one developed in the context of the VeryIDX project [32]. Such an approach specifically addresses the problem of misuse of identity attributes through the use of multi-factor verification of attributes. This approach requires that whenever a service provider requires an identity attribute from a client, it has to verify the identity by requiring additional identity attributes. To ensure privacy, the approach adopts a novel zero-knowledge proof protocol that allows the client to prove the knowledge of the additional attributes without disclosing their actual values. Such protocol is also flexible in that it allows each service provider to require any combinations of identity attributes, and moreover different service providers may require different combinations. The protocol is efficient and allows one to prove the knowledge of any combination of attributes in constant time.

3.6   CONCLUSION

In this chapter, we have discussed the main notions and models for access control and presented extensions that are relevant in the context of distributed systems. It is important to emphasize that in addition to what has been discussed in this chapter, the research field is very active in the area of access control for distributed systems, and many relevant research directions are being investigated. A relevant direction is represented by access control for grid computing systems and virtualized environments. Those systems and environments are quite challenging because of the very large number of users and distributed administration of resources. In particular, they are characterized by the fact that there is no single authority controlling all resources that may be required by a user to perform certain tasks. In such a case, the user must be able to obtain multiple authorizations from independent administrative authorities; this approach, however, entails the issue of conflicting authorizations. The management of identity attributes is also an important requirement for those systems and environments; however, it is not yet clear whether current IdM solution would scale well to support dynamic, very large user populations and resource providers. Another important area is represented by the web service security and workflow systems. Despite the several initiatives ongoing in the industry community, and in particular the definition of an XACML profile for web services, the problem of access control is still largely unexplored. Research is needed to address the problem of conversational web services and the development of access control system suitable for business processes expressed according to workflow models.

References

[1] J. P. Anderson, "Information Security in a Multi-user Computer Environment", *Advances in Computers*, Vol. 12 (1972): 1–35. (New York: Academic Press, 1973).

[2] L. Lamport, "Password Authentication with Insecure Communications," *Communications of the ACM* 24 (1981): 770–771.

[3] B. C. Neuman and T. Ts'o, "Kerberos: An Authentication Service for Computer Networks," *IEEE Communications* 32(9) (1994): 33–38.

[4] M. Gasser, A. Goldstein, C. Kaufman, and B. Lampson, "The Digital Distributed System Security Architecture," *Proceedings of the 12th National Security Conference*, Baltimore, MD, 1989, pp. 305–319.

[5] OASIS, "Assertions and Protocol for the OASIS Security Assertion Mark-up Language (SAML)," OASIS Standard V1.1 (oasis-sstc-saml-core-1.1), Sept. 2, 2003.

[6] OASIS, "OASIS eXtensible Access Control Mark-up Language 2 (XACML)," OASIS Standard Version 2.0, Feb. 1, 2005.

[7] D. Denning, "A Lattice Model of Secure Information Flow," *Communications of the ACM* 19(5) (1976): 236–243.

[8] D. E. Bell and L. LaPadula, "Secure Computer Systems: Unified Exposition and Multics Interpretation," Mitre Corporation, Technical Report MTR-2997, Bedford, MA, 1976.

[9] American National Standards Institute, "ANSI INCITS 359-2004 for Role Based Access Control," American National Standards Institute, New York, NY, 2004.

[10] R. S. Sandhu, E. J. Coyne, H. L. Feinstein, and C. E. Youman, "Role-Based Access Control Models," *IEEE Computer* 29(2) (1996): 38–47.

[11] D. Ferraiolo, D. R. Kuhn, and R. Chandramouli, *Role-Based Access Control*, 2nd ed. (Boston: Artech House, 2007).

[12] E. Bertino, S. Castano, and E. Ferrari, "Securing XML Documents with Author-X," *IEEE Internet Computing* 5(3) (2001): 21–31.

[13] International Organization for Standardization and International Electrotechnical Commission, "Information Technology—Open Systems Interconnection—Security Frameworks for Open Systems: Part 3: Access Control Framework," Geneva, Switzerland: ISO/IEC, 1996.

[14] P. Mazzoleni, E. Bertino, B. Crispo, and S. Sivasubramanian, "XACML Policy Integration Algorithms: Not to be Confused with XACML Policy Combination Algorithms!," *11th ACM Symposium on Access Control Models and Technologies*, Lake Tahoe, CA 2006, pp. 219–227.

[15] E. Bertino, B. Catania, M. L. Damiani, and P. Persasca, "GEO-RBAC: A Spatially Aware RBAC," *Proceedings of 10th Symposium on Access Control Models and Technologies*, Stockholm, Sweden 2005, pp. 29–37.

[16] A. Kini and J. Choobineh, "Trust in Electronic Commerce: Definition and Theoretical Considerations," *Proceedings of Thirty-first Annual Hawaii International Conference on System Sciences*, Kohala Coast, HI 1998, pp. 51–61.

[17] T. Grandison and M. Sloman, "A Survey of Trust in Internet Applications," *IEEE Communications Surveys and Tutorials* 3(4) (2000), pp. 2–16

[18] M. Blaze, J. Feigenbaum, and J. Lacy, "Decentralized Trust Management," *Proceedings of IEEE Symposium on Security and Privacy*, Oakland, CA, 1996, pp. 164–173.

[19] E. Bertino, E. Ferrari, and A. C. Squicciarini, "Trust-X: A Peer-to-Peer Framework for Trust Establishment," *IEEE Transactions on Knowledge and Data Engineering* 16(7) (2004): 827–842.

[20] A. C. Squicciarini, E. Bertino, E. Ferrari, F. Paci, and B. Thuraisingham, "PP-Trust-X: A System for Privacy Preserving Trust Negotiations," *ACM Transactions on Information and Systems Security* 10(3) (2007) to appear.

[21] A. C. Squicciarini, E. Bertino, E. Ferrari, and I. Ray, "Achieving Privacy in Trust Negotiations with an Ontology-Based Approach," *IEEE Transactions on Dependable and Secure Computing* 3(1) (2006): 13–30.

[22] A. C. Squicciarini, A. Trombetta, and E. Bertino, "K-Anonymity-Based Trust Negotiations," Submitted to 9th International Conference on Information and Communications Security, Zhengzhou, China, 12–15 December, 2007.

[23] A. C. Squicciarini, A. Trombetta, and E. Bertino, "Supporting Robust and Secure Interactions in Open Domains through Recovery of Trust Negotiations," in *27th IEEE International Conference on Distributed Computing Systems (ICDCS 2007)*, Toronto, Canada, 2007, p. 57.

[24] A. Bhargav-Spantzel, A. C. Squicciarini, and E. Bertino, "Integrating Federated Digital Identity Management and Trust Negotiation," *IEEE Security & Privacy* 5(2) (2007): 55–64.

[25] R. Bhatti, A. Ghafoor, E. Bertino, and J.B.D. Joshi, "X-GTRBAC: An XML-Based Policy Specification Framework and Architecture for Enterprise-Wide Access Control," *ACM Transactions on Information and Systems Security* 8(2) (2005): 187–227.

[26] Open GIS Consortium, "Open GIS Simple Features Specification for SQL," Open GIS Consortium Revision 1.1, 1999.

[27] Internet2/MACE, "Shibboleth Project Homepage," at http://www.shibboleth.internet2.edu.

[28] Eclipse Foundation, "Higgins Trust Framework Project Homepage," at http://www.eclipse.org/higgins.

[29] K. Cameron, "Windows CardSpace Design Rational," at http://www.identityblog.com.

[30] OpenID Community, "OpenID Project Wiki," at http://www.openid.net/wiki/index.php/MainPage.

[31] J. Camenisch and E. V. Herreweghen, "Design and Implementation of the Idemix Anonymous Credential System," *Proceedings of the 9th ACM Conference on Computer and Communications Security* (Washington, DC: ACM Press, 2002), 21–30.

[32] R. Xue, A. Bhargav-Spantzel, A. C. Squicciarini, and E. Bertino, "Efficient Identity Theft Prevention Using Aggregated Proof of Knowledge," *ACM Transactions on Information and System Security*, (in press).

4 Network Survivability

Bjorn Jager   Molde University, Norway
John Doucette   University of Alberta Edmonton, Canada
David Tipper   University of Pittsburgh, USA

4.1   INTRODUCTION

Due to the widespread use of communication networks, society is increasingly dependent on the exchange of information for basic societal functions. Several widely publicized network outages illustrated that disruption of communications services can be very expensive to businesses and critical services, for example, loss of emergency services, air traffic control systems, and financial services. In fact, existing communication networks, such as the Internet, circuit-switched telephone networks, and cellular networks, are considered part of the critical national infrastructure (CNI) of various nations [1–3]. The United States President's Commission on Critical Infrastructure Protection (PCCIP) noted that "our security, economy, way of life, and perhaps even survival, are now dependent on the interrelated trio of electrical energy, communications, and computers" [4]. Furthermore, traditional critical infrastructures like health, banking, transportation, defence and public administration all heavily depend upon data communication networks through their dependence of supervisory control and data acquisition (SCADA) systems causing the network infrastructure to be considered one of the key critical infrastructures [1, 2].

A network failure is typically defined as a situation when the network fails to deliver the committed *quality of service* (QoS). A network failure can be a degradation of service or service disruptions ranging in length from seconds to weeks. It can occur due to a variety of reasons: Typical events are cable cuts, hardware malfunctions, software errors, natural disasters; earthquakes, floods, hurricanes for example, human errors; typically incorrect maintenance, and malicious physical and electronic attacks [5, 6]. The growing vulnerability of the public-switched network has been addressed by the U.S. National Research Council, which noted,

"As we become more dependent on networks, the consequences of network failure become greater and the need to reduce network vulnerabilities increases commensurately." Thus, it is imperative to minimize service degradation, disruption and destruction and communication networks need to be designed to adequately respond to failures. This has led to an increasing interest in design of survivable networks.

A number of definitions of *network survivability* have appeared in the literature [7–20], including "the capability of a network where a certain percentage of the traffic can still be carried immediately after a failure" [8]; "the ability to provide service continuity upon network failure" [9]; or "the set of capabilities that allows a network to restore affected traffic in the event of a failure" [10]. In effect the survivability of a network is its ability to support the committed QoS continuously in the presence of various failure scenarios. Techniques to improve a network's survivability can be classified into three categories:

1. Prevention.
2. Network design.
3. Traffic management.

Prevention or avoidance techniques focus primarily on improving component and system reliability and security in order to reduce the occurrence of faults. This contributes to the survivability of the network by making the number of surviving elements larger, thereby increasing the ability of the techniques in category two and three to handle failures that do occur. This is particularly so because at present the category two and three techniques mainly handles single network failures while multiple failures are usually not guaranteed to be survivable. Perhaps the most obvious prevention techniques are physical security measures, such as housing equipment in highly secure and sound structures, providing backup power systems, implementing "call-before-you-dig" practices, and so on. Prevention also includes electronic security techniques to protect network resources like routers and user data from unauthorized access, as well as improving software reliability.

Survivable network design techniques try to mitigate the effects of system-level failures, such as link or node failures, by placing sufficient diversity and capacity in the network topology. A typical example is multihoming nodes by making each node two or more connected so that a single link failure cannot isolate a node from the remainder of the network. The basic survivable network design technique is to add redundancy to the network, with the critical issues being where and how much redundancy to add.

Traffic management procedures seek to quickly detect a failure or degraded QoS and direct the network load such that the committed QoS is maintained, thus making the network inherently fault-tolerant and self-healing [7]. The traffic management procedures essentially seek to take advantage of preplanned redundancy and any available capacity in the network after a failure. A typical example is the use of preconfigured backup label–switched paths in *multiprotocol label switched* (MPLS) networks.

Thus, the combined goal of the three categories of survivability techniques is to make a network failure imperceptible to network users by providing the desired QoS. However, cost and complexity are always an issue. The key challenge is to provide the minimum required QoS at a minimum cost and in the simplest fashion. This chapter provides background information and surveys the existing literature in network survivability. The focus is on survivable network design and traffic management procedures. Section 4.2 briefly discusses prevention techniques. In Section 4.3, basic survivable network design and traffic restoration concepts are surveyed. Section 4.4 presents typical survivable network design models and mechanisms. Section 4.5 discusses the survivable network design techniques, and includes an example ILP formulation. Section 4.6 discusses the survivability challenges presented by multilayer networks. Lastly, Section 4.7 concludes the chapter and presents areas for future network survivability research.

4.2 PREVENTION TECHNIQUES

Prevention techniques focus primarily on improving component and system reliability in order to reduce the occurrence of faults. Prevention techniques can be technical or nontechnical in nature. Examples of technical prevention techniques are the use of fault-tolerant hardware architectures in switch/router designs, provisioning backup power supplies at network equipment, and predeployment stress testing of software to name a few. Examples of nontechnical prevention techniques [20] are providing physical and electronic security for networking infrastructure, call-before-you-dig regulations to reduce the likelihood of cable cuts, formal training for network maintenance personnel, and regular scheduled maintenance.

The major survivability techniques described in this chapter focus on network design, traffic management and restoration, which are primarily targeted at protecting the network from random failures and accidents like cable cuts and other human errors. However, network resources are vulnerable to malicious attacks and acts of terror by people who are knowledgeable of the network architecture and operational mechanisms. Therefore, any network resource, including routers, software, databases, and traffic along a path should be protected by security measures. For each network resource, the main goals of security are ensuring confidentiality, integrity, availability, non-repudiation and authentication

(C-I-A-N-A). Confidentiality means that network resource information is accessible only to those authorized to have access, while integrity means that data can not be created, changed, or deleted without authorization. Here availability express that the network resource information, the resource itself and the other security controls of C-I-A-N-A are all available and functioning correctly when the information is needed. Non-repudiation ensures that a transferred message has been sent and received by the parties claiming to have sent and received the message, and lastly authentication is the verification of the identity of a person, process or element. For example whenever routing updates are exchanged, authentication ensures that a router receives reliable routing information from a trusted source. Actions that can cause the network security to be compromised include attacks on control and management systems, sniffing of data traffic, and denial-of-service (DoS) attacks. In a DoS attack, an attacker tries to make a network resource unavailable by resource exhaustion for example by allocating all link bandwidth and sending more requests to network management and control systems than they can handle. Some examples of techniques to prevent security to be compromised are separation of control and traffic planes, encryption, firewalls, intrusion detection, and intrusion prevention. Chapter 2 gives a detailed discussion on network security.

4.3   SURVIVABLE NETWORK DESIGN AND TRAFFIC RESTORATION CONCEPTS

4.3.1   Typical Network Architecture

In terms of studying the survivability of communication networks, it is useful to examine the basic structure of a typical network architecture. Here, we consider the Internet and the technologies used. Note that as traditional telephone and private data services migrate to the shared Internet, the survivability of the architecture becomes more important. Broadly speaking, the Internet consists of a set of interconnected networks that can be categorized based on their geographic size and function as either *access networks, metropolitan area networks* (MANs), or *wide area networks* (WANs), as shown in Figure 4.1.

Access networks provide the end communication path to and from the users. A wide variety of technologies are utilized in access networks, including cellular networks, wireless LANs, cable modems, DSL, fiber to the home or office, and Ethernet. Access networks typically have a tree or hub-and-spoke type of topology with little or no redundancy provided due to cost constraints, though customers willing to pay for it (generally medium to large commercial customers) can often be provided with dual-homed premises.

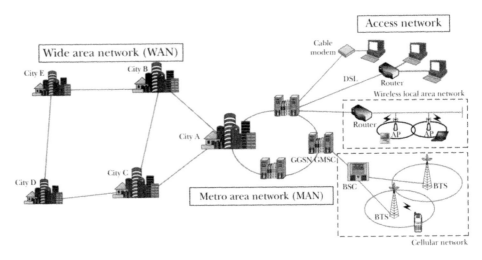

FIGURE   Typical network architecture.

4.1

MANs provide a local backbone network spanning a city or metro area. Technologies used here include wavelength division multiplexing (WDM) optical fiber, SONET, Ethernet, WiMAX, point-to-point microwave, free space optical, and so on.

WANs, also known as core backbone or long-haul networks, are the most uniform technology with almost all now using optical communication links with WDM or dense WDM (DWDM) technology.

Note that the Internet component networks are multilayer in nature, accommodating a wide variety of users and applications. Broadly speaking, each network consists of a top layer where services such as voice, video, data, and multicast and broadcast video are provided. These services are provided over a middle or switched layer (e.g., IP packet switching, MPLS label switching). Lastly, the middle layer is provided over a transport layer technology such as DWDM light paths on optical fibers. Note that the transport layer may contain several sublayers (e.g., SONET and DWDM). In the future, each layer is expected to be reconfigurable (e.g., rearrangeable light paths, LSPs. Lastly, it is worth noting that virtualization is a growing trend in all three types of networks with virtual private networks (VPNs) being deployed within a network (e.g., within an individual MAN or even backbone ISP WAN), across multiple networks, or end-to-end at the application layer. However, virtualization can often lead to poor resilience if the virtual network is not carefully designed to avoid failure propagation, as discussed in Section 4.6.

Network survivability research originated with telecommunications network operators and has been a subject of study for decades [21, 22]. Additionally, some research on survivability in an unfriendly environment was part of the early work on the Internet [23]. In recent years, however, there has been increasing interest in network resilience and survivability. Various journals have dedicated special issues to the survivability of networks and their components (e.g., [24]). There are now specialized conferences focused on the topic (e.g., IEEE Design of Reliable Communication Networks (DRCN) and IEEE Dependable Systems and Networks (DSN)) and several excellent books have been published [7, 9, 12–17, 20]. The current literature tends to focus on providing survivability in a particular technology at a specific layer, such as the application overlay layer [25], switched layer (IP [26], ATM [15], MPLS [27]), or transport layer [16], or in a specific part of the network architecture (e.g., MAN or WAN). Examples include development of techniques for implementation of light path restoration in core DWDM optical backbone sections of the Internet (e.g., a Tier 1 ISP network) [17] or survivable SONET ring techniques to overcome link failures in MANs [14]. While the implementation of survivability in a particular technology or protocol in a component network involves many details particular to the application, the basic techniques and principles used are largely the same in each case. Here, we present a technology-independent discussion of survivable network design concepts and principles, beginning with a discussion of the basic concepts.

4.3.2   Basic Network Survivability Concepts

While a variety of survivability techniques (e.g., multiple homing, trunk diversity, self-healing rings, preplanned backup routes, *p*-cycles) have been proposed for a range of network technologies, they all work on the concept of *redundancy* and *diversity*. First, consider how diversity is utilized in a mesh network where traffic is routed on fixed end-to-end paths (e.g., light paths in a WDM network). An active path (AP), also sometimes called the working path, is the route taken by the traffic under normal operating conditions. For the network to be survivable to failures in the active path, one must be able to find a suitable backup path (BP) (i.e., an alternate path around the failure) in the topology. Obviously, the backup path and the active path must be *physically diverse* or *disjoint* so that both paths are not lost at the same time.

Diversity can be achieved in the active and backup paths in several ways. For example, they may be link disjoint, as shown in Figure 4.2a or node disjoint, as shown in Figure 4.2b. As shown in the figure, the link disjoint BP can potentially recover from any link failure in the AP, whereas the node disjoint BP can potentially recover from any link or relay node failure in the AP. Note that for diverse

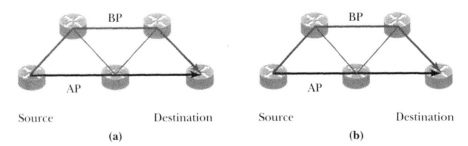

FIGURE
4.2 Survivable network concepts: (a) link disjoint and (b) node disjoint.

AP and BP paths to exist, the physical network topology must allow at least two disjoint end-to-end paths from every source destination pair. However, even though a BP may exist for an AP, restoration cannot proceed unless there are enough spare resources on the BP to carry the AP traffic at the required QoS level. This requires the allocation of *redundant* resources on the BP, which are typically not used except in the case of failure. The focus of survivable network design is to plan the allocation of diversity and redundancy in the network to support resilience to a set of failure scenarios (e.g., any single link failure). In order to take advantage of the redundancy and diversity in the network, appropriate fault management and traffic restoration procedures need to be in place.

4.3.3 Basic Network Management Concepts

When studying the survivability of communication networks, it is also useful to look at the general framework in which traffic management is implemented. Network management has become an indispensable tool of communication networks since it is responsible for ensuring continuous and secure functioning of a network. Generally, network management is divided into several functional areas: *performance management, configuration management,* and *fault management.* These key areas are implemented by control modules that operate in an integrated way to manage the network, including functions that support traffic management and restoration survivability techniques.

As an example, we can look at how fault management fulfills its goals. The key functions of fault management, RRRR [28], in prioritized order are:

1. Restore services.

2. Root cause identification of failures.

3. Repair failed components.

4. Report the incidences.

To implement the highest priority task, that is, *restore services*, fault management uses the functionality provided by configuration management and performance management. Upon detection of a network failure by the fault management system or detection of QoS degradation by the performance management system, the failed traffic connections are identified by the configuration management system, new paths are searched for if needed, the best path i.e., the one with the lowest cost, is selected for each failed connection, and the traffic is rerouted by establishing new connections along the selected paths. In parallel with the service restoration process, a repair process should begin with the network manager performing root cause identification followed by the detailed repair or replacement of the failed components. Once the failed components have been repaired, they can be put back in service and a normalization or reversion process might occur that consists of moving the traffic from their current routes to their original prefailure routes. Furthermore, all incidents in the process are monitored and reported for billing and management purposes.

The steps in the service recovery process are sometimes denoted as DeNISSE(RN) [29], which is derived from the restoration process' major steps:

1. Detection of the failure.

2. Notification of the failure to the entities responsible for restoration.

3. Identification of failed connections.

4. Search for new paths.

5. Selection of least-cost paths for the failed connections.

6. Establishment of the new paths by signaling and rerouting.

7. Report for billing and management.

8. Normalization.

These steps are summarized in Figure 4.3.

4.3.4   Protection versus Restoration

A quick scan of the literature will reveal the use of the terms *protection* and *restoration*, in many cases interchangeably and/or with little differentiation between the two. We define each separately here, but the reader should note that the differentiation we provide is not strictly adhered to by everyone in the industry.

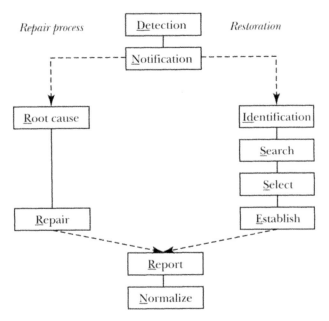

FIGURE

4.3

Major steps in traffic management during restoration of service.

In transport network survivability, *protection* usually refers to mechanisms where any postfailure switching actions are predefined and utilize spare capacity that is dedicated for a specific set of failure scenarios. In its purest form, the signal is either already duplicated on a backup path, such as in $1+1$ automatic protection switching, or at the very least the backup path is preconfigured into a pretested and ready-to-use state, such as in *p*-cycles. Protection also often refers to survivability methods where a protection route is predefined but is not preconfigured, such as in shared backup path protection. In that case, capacity seizure and cross-connection is accomplished postfailure in real time.

Restoration usually refers to survivability mechanisms where backup paths are neither predefined nor preconfigured, and where spare capacity is not dedicated for any specific sets of failure scenarios, but rather is available and configured as needed when failures arise. In its purest form, backup path determination, spare-capacity seizure, and cross-connection are all accomplished postfailure in real time either through a centralized or distributed protocol. This is often how span or link restoration and shared path restoration are envisioned to occur. In accordance with this, restoration falls within the traffic management category defined in 4.1, and protection falls within the network design category. However, depending on the specific implementation, many such restoration mechanisms actually perform route-finding and preplanning exercises, and in some cases, even limited preconfiguration.

As such, most survivability mechanisms are actually not strictly pure protection or pure restoration as we just defined. Rather, they inhabit the space between the two and are only referred to as one or the other depending on historical considerations, convention, and so on.

4.3.5   Other Issues

Other important factors to consider in determining which mechanisms to use in assuring survivability are; which of the network layers that will be responsible for restoration, where the rerouting will take place, and what rerouting algorithm will be used (e.g., minimum cost, lowest latency).

The Layer Responsible for Restoration

Internet component networks are multilayer in nature, where lower layers are said to provide services to the layers immediately above them, and the inner workings of each layer is hidden by general interfaces to the layer. Thus, in order to deliver the services in a more reliable way, each layer could implement their own survivability techniques. The *end-to-end principle* [30] has been used as a guiding principle for allocating responsibility for overall network survivability among various layers in a network. In short, the principle says that one should let the end nodes of a connection (i.e., the higher layer) take care of reliability issues since functions placed at lower layers may be redundant or too costly in terms of performance. However, as demand shifted to high-speed, multiservice networks with strict QoS requirements, the argument does not hold anymore. In order to provide guaranteed QoS, each layer should deliver its services according to the QoS committed. Thus, each layer typically includes survivability functions as described further in Section 4.6 on multilayer issues.

The Location of Rerouting

Each step in the restoration process (DeNISSE(RN)) can take place in a node close to the failure or by a network node or management node more distant to the failure. Consider the essential step of rerouting a connection, that is, the establishment of a new connection along a new path. There are two major schemes based on how far upstream from the failure the rerouting is performed, namely, path

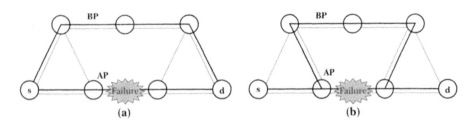

FIGURE

4.4
(a) Path-based and (b) link-based survivability schemes.

and link (span) restoration. In path restoration, the *source nodes* of the active path connections that are affected by the failure perform the rerouting (Figure 4.4a). In link restoration, the nodes adjacent to the failure are responsible for rerouting *all* affected traffic demands around the failed link (Figure 4.4b). The main advantages of path restoration are capacity efficiency, the possibility of rerouting each connection individually, and the ability to respond to a wider range of failure scenarios. For link restoration, the main advantages are speed and simplicity of implementation.

Rerouting Algorithms

For dynamic restoration schemes, be they path or link based, the node responsible for restoration typically will have many failed connections that need to be restored simultaneously. Some of the connections may carry traffic that requires retransmission of lost packets. Retransmission introduces a burst not seen under normal operation that may cause transient network congestion. It has been shown that selection of an appropriate rerouting algorithm can control this congestion to some extent and improve the QoS provided. In particular, for lightly loaded networks, algorithms that distribute the load over a large area should be selected. For heavily loaded networks, minimum-delay algorithms should be used possibly in combination with preemption of some connections to ensure an acceptable QoS for the surviving connections [31–33].

4.4   TRANSPORT NETWORK RECOVERY TECHNIQUES

We now discuss some of the more common basic methods for performing traffic recovery after a failure.

4.4.1   Automatic Protection Switching

One particular survivability method that can be thought of strictly as a protection mechanism is $1 + 1$ *automatic protection switching* ($1 + 1$ APS) [12]. In $1 + 1$ APS, a primary end-to-end working channel is duplicated via *head-end bridging* on a dedicated physically diverse backup channel and both channels are monitored by the receiver. Upon failure of equipment along the path of the primary channel (or simple degradation of its signal), the receiver performs a *tail-end transfer* to select the backup channel. This is the only widely used survivability mechanism where there is no sharing of spare capacity among multiple working channels, failure scenarios, and so on. Therefore, it generally requires significantly greater amounts of spare-capacity resources relative to other mechanisms where spare-capacity sharing occurs. As a result of the lack of sharing, $1 + 1$ APS requires a *minimum* commitment of at least 100 percent redundancy, and usually considerably higher redundancy. While this may seem to be excessively inefficient, $1 + 1$ APS has found widespread use with simpler point-to-point terminals and single-hop channels, as well as in cases where simplicity and restoration speed are crucial and/or when capacity efficiency is not particularly important.

Similar methods that allow sharing of backup channels are 1:1 APS and 1:N APS. The former is nearly identical to $1 + 1$ APS, with the key difference being that in 1:1 APS, the backup channel does not carry a live copy of the signal. Rather, in 1:1 APS, the backup channel either remains unused (though regularly tested and exercised) or in some cases allowed to carry a low-priority preemptible and unprotected signal. In either case, the entire backup path is fully preconnected in advance. When an outage (or degradation) of the working signal is detected by the receiver, it notifies the transmitter, which establishes a head-end bridge of the working signal onto the backup, and the receiver then performs a tail-end transfer. This means that 1:1 APS will be somewhat slower than $1 + 1$ APS, but it still provides reasonably rapid protection. Depending on the circumstance, the ability to use the backup path to carry low-priority (but still revenue-generating) traffic can more than balance the slower recovery.

1:N APS is a very similar mechanism that is used to provide protection of typically single-hop working channels, where rather than working and backup channels corresponding one-for-one, a single backup channel is used to protect multiple working channels (N of them). Like in 1:1 APS, the receiver detects a failure or signal degradation on one of the working channels, verifies availability of the backup channel, signals the transmitter to establish a head-end bridge of the failed working channel onto the backup channel, and then performs its own tail-end transfer to access the backup channel in place of the working channel in question. 1:N APS is illustrated in Figure 4.5. The multihop transport network equivalent of 1:N APS is called *generalized trunk diversity* in the public switched

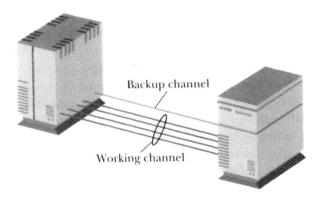

Backup channel

Working channel

FIGURE

4.5

Illustration of 1:N automatic protection switching. Used with permission from
Doucette [29].

telephone network (PSTN) [8, 14] and *demand-wise shared protection* (DSP) in
optical networks [34, 35]. In an even more general case of automatic protection switching, M:N APS, N disjoint working channels with a common pair of
end nodes can be protected by M backup channels. Ordinarily, $N \geq M$, but some
high-availability networks might have more than one backup channel per working
channel to protect against multiple simultaneous failures [36].

4.4.2   Ring-Based Survivability

Another very simple network survivability mechanism is a survivable ring [7, 13,
37, 38]. While there are several different varieties, in general, a survivable ring is a
cyclic structure (i.e., closed loop) of preconfigured transmission systems typically
using add-drop multiplexing (ADM) nodal devices that allow signals to be added
or dropped from the main line signals within the ring. The transmission capacity between an adjacent pair of ADMs is divided into two halves, one of which
is used to carry payload-bearing traffic signals and the other is reserved for use
in rerouting a failed signal in the event of failure of some span within the ring.
Because of the cyclic nature of the ring, it provides two disjoint routes between
any pair of ADMs within it, and so any traffic utilizing the ring will use one route
for its primary working channel and a disjoint route as a redundant backup.
Since protection is performed locally within the ring and the entire structure is
preconfigured (and in the case of spare capacity, ready and waiting on standby),
the only postfailure action generally required is for the ADMs on either side of the
failure to switch a failed working channel onto its associated backup channel.

A ring network consists of a number of individual rings that are interconnected at predefined locations, and a typical end-to-end working signal would transit multiple rings along its route.

There are two primary types of survivable rings. The first type is the *unidirectional path-switched ring* (UPSR), or the WDM-equivalent *optical path protection ring* (OPPR) [37]. A UPSR can be thought of as a collection of logical $1+1$ APS systems adhering to a closed-loop configuration, as shown in Figure 4.6. A UPSR is composed of a system of working channels that transmit working traffic in just a single direction around the ring and a system of protection channels that transmit a backup copy in the opposite direction. Just like in $1+1$ APS, receivers simply select the backup signal on a protection channel via tail-end transfer when a failure arises. Survival of the backup signal is assured because the working and backup signals do not occupy channels on a common span anywhere along their routes. In terms of spare-capacity requirements, UPSRs are no more efficient than standalone $1+1$ APS systems, and in general are even worse, since the latter could use any pair of disjoint routes through the network while UPSRs require signals to respect individual ring structures and their interconnections. If we assume that all signals are bidirectional, then the working capacity on any span within a UPSR is the sum of the bandwidths of all signals routed through the ring; the same is true of the spare capacity on any span within the ring. In spite of this, UPSR networks are very common because their closed-form nature, simple implementation and operation, very high speed (in the order of 50 ms [38]), and use of inexpensive nodal devices make them particularly attractive to network operators.

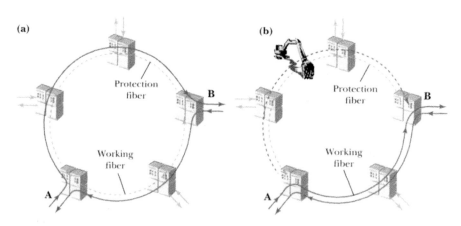

Basic operation of a UPSR: (a) prefailure and (b) postfailure. Used with permission from Doucette [29].

The second primary type of survivable ring is the *bidirectional line-switched ring* (BLSR), or the WDM-equivalent *optical shared protection ring* (OSPR) [37]. BLSRs are significantly more capacity-efficient than UPSRs, though somewhat more complex in implementation and operation. The source of BLSRs' improved capacity efficiency is from the loop-back mechanism they utilize, which allows spare capacity to be shared among a number of working signals within the ring. Recall in the UPSR that a bidirectional signal will be routed on working channels on both sides of the same ring (Figure 4.6b) and a corresponding pair of protection channels will be required as well to route the duplicate backup signals. However, in a BLSR, both directions of a bidirectional signal are routed on the same side of the ring and the backup signals are not permanently bridged to the protection channels. When a failure occurs along the working path, the two ADMs adjacent to the failure perform a loop-back operation to switch the failed signals onto the protection channels transmitting in opposite directions, as illustrated in Figure 4.7. Since the working signals are only routed on one side of the BLSR, all of the corresponding working channels (i.e., occupying the same wavelengths if we're dealing with a WDM network) on the other side of the ring are still available for use by other working signals; similarly with the protection channels. A BLSR, therefore, is capable of carrying a greater amount of traffic than a UPSR with the same capacity. However, a BLSR can still never achieve better than 100 percent redundancy, because protection capacity around the entire ring must at least meet the largest cross-section of working capacity anywhere within the ring. And since signaling and protection switching must be coordinated between the two ADMs adjacent to the failure, BLSR operation is somewhat slower than that in UPSRs.

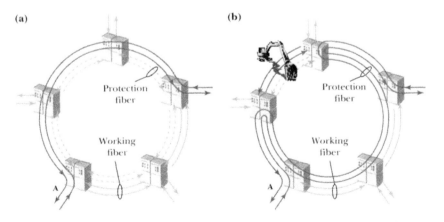

FIGURE

4.7

Basic operation of a BLSR: (a) prefailure, and (b) postfailure. Used with permission from Doucette [29].

4.4.3 Mesh Survivability: Span Restoration

The simplest form of mesh survivability is perhaps *span restoration*, also referred to as *link restoration* [39]. Span restoration is a localized mechanism where a collectively coordinated set of replacement paths is formed between the end nodes of a failed span, as shown in Figure 4.8, with one replacement path required for each working channel on the failed span. It is often the case that the restoration paths follow relatively few and short localized routes. However, there is generally no restriction on the length or number of distinct routes they can follow, and in extreme cases, each working channel could be rerouted along a different route that could extend to the far reaches of the network. While these restoration paths may have been preplanned prior to failure, spare-capacity seizure and cross-connection occurs strictly postfailure. Spare capacity is shared and available for any number of individual failure scenarios, and in some networks can also be used to carry low-priority, preemptable, and unprotected traffic. Since restoration paths are formed between the end nodes of the failure itself, there is typically no consideration for the ultimate origins and destinations of any constituent working channels on the failed span. As such, it is not uncommon for a repaired signal's complete end-to-end route to loop back on itself on one or both sides of the failure.

4.4.4 Mesh Survivability: Shared Backup Path Protection

Shared backup path protection (SBPP), also called *shared path protection* (SPP) or *failure-independent path protection* (FIPP), is a more recent transport network survivability mechanism that also finds uses in IP/MPLS networks [40,41]. Like in

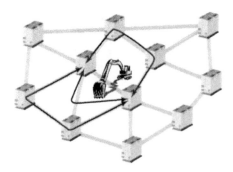

FIGURE   An example of span restoration. Used with permission from Doucette [29].

4.8

1 + 1 APS, each working path in an SBPP network has a single preplanned disjoint end-to-end backup path. However, the difference is that spare capacity can be shared among multiple working signals' backup paths if those working signals are themselves routed over mutually disjoint working routes. As long as that condition is met, no two backup paths will simultaneously require use of the same spare capacity in the event of a single failure. This greatly reduces spare-capacity redundancy as compared to 1 + 1 APS, and in fact, SBPP is one of the most capacity-efficient survivability mechanisms known (in most networks only shared path restoration, described in Section 4.4.5, can be more capacity-efficient).

If we further require that working paths are node disjoint from their backup paths rather than simply span disjoint, and likewise that a set of working paths are mutually node disjoint if their respective backup paths share any spare capacity, then SBPP will also provide protection against node failures. This is in contrast to span restoration that, by its very nature, is incapable of providing node failure protection. We illustrate SBPP in Figure 4.9, where two node pairs each route a working path (solid lines) through the network. Since the two working paths are disjoint, there is no single span failure that will fail both working paths simultaneously, and so their associated backup paths (dotted lines) can safely share capacity on a common span (in this case span X-Y) without risk of spare-capacity contention. In other words, when one of the backup routes is required to restore service on its working path, the other will not also be required.

While SBPP does have its advantages as discussed, it also has some disadvantages as well. The primary issue is that each node in the network requires an up-to-date network state database detailing all spare channel-sharing arrangements, topology, and capacity usage information. Every time there is a change in network state (e.g., a new connection has arrived, an existing connection is

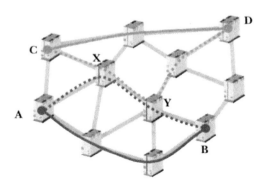

FIGURE
4.9

An illustration of shared backup path protection. Used with permission from Doucette [29].

released), all node databases must be updated. A further disadvantage is that upon failure of just a single span, there is potential for a large number of individual working paths to simultaneously fail as a result. This could require very many nodes to perform cross-connections at the same time, which means the associated signaling for spare-capacity seizure, activation of concatenated backup paths, etc. could become an issue.

4.4.5   Mesh Survivability: Shared Path Restoration

A related mechanism called *shared path restoration* (SPR) can also be considered to be the end-to-end equivalent of span restoration. SPR is also commonly called *failure-dependent path protection* (FDPP), or more simply, just *path restoration* [41]. The primary difference between path restoration and SBPP is that in path restoration, there is no single predetermined restoration route for each working path. Instead, all failed working paths are simultaneously rerouted end-to-end using restoration routes that are collectively optimized in the presence of that specific failure. So any individual working path could make use of a different restoration route for every possible failure that affects it. Furthermore, path restoration makes use of a mechanism called *stub release* through which the surviving ends or stubs of a failed working path are released and made available as spare capacity. These two features guarantee that path restoration is at least as efficient as SBPP (in fact, an SBPP solution can be exactly duplicated with path restoration by simply foregoing use of stub-released capacity and using a single disjoint backup path for each working path), but in general it is even more capacity efficient than SBPP.

We illustrate path restoration in Figure 4.10, where three node pairs each route their demands through working paths, shown in Figure 4.10a. When a failure occurs, as shown in Figure 4.10b, end-to-end restoration routes are formed for

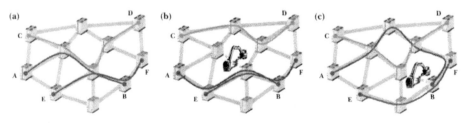

FIGURE

4.10

An illustration of path restoration with stub release. Used with permission from Doucette [29].

each working path affected by the failure, and because of stub release, restoration routes are allowed to reuse spare capacity on the surviving stub portions of the affected working paths. If a different failure occurs, as shown in Figure 4.10c, a similar end-to-end reroute is performed for the affected working paths, but we can note that working route A-B can now use a different restoration route than the one it used in response to the failure in Figure 4.10b. Obviously, path restoration is operationally more complex than span restoration or SBPP as it requires identification of the specific failure in the working path before restoration can begin. Hence path restoration typically has a slower restoration speed than span or SBPP, but it is more capacity-efficient than either, and like SBPP, path restoration is capable of protecting against node failures.

4.4.6   Mesh Survivability: *p*-Cycles

One final survivability mechanism we will discuss is *p*-cycles [36, 42, 43]. *p*-Cycles are usually considered to be a form of mesh network restoration, though using the definition above, they are more properly classed as a shared preplanned (and preconfigured) protection mechanism. Like rings, *p*-cycles are cyclic structures of preconfigured capacity that can be used to provide a fast switchover of failed working channels onto standby spare channels. When a failure occurs on a protected span, the *p*-cycle mechanism inserts the failed working channel onto the corresponding protection channel allowing the signal to bypass the failure around the other surviving portion of the *p*-cycle. This is illustrated in Figure 4.11. When the *p*-cycle shown in Figure 4.11a suffers a failure of an on-cycle span in Figure 4.11b, the working channels on the span can be restored the long way around the *p*-cycle.

However, *p*-cycles have several key differences that set them apart from rings. The principal difference is that in addition to protecting working channels on

FIGURE
4.11
An illustration of *p*-cycle restoration: (a) a prefailure *p*-cycle, (b) protection response for on-cycle failure, and (c) protection response for straddling span failure. Used with permission from Doucette [29].

spans crossed by the *p*-cycle (so-called *on-cycle* spans), it is also capable of protecting *straddling spans*, which are spans whose end nodes are on the cycle but that are not themselves a part of the *p*-cycle. More importantly, a single unit-size *p*-cycle can actually protect two working channels on each straddling span; if it is a straddling span that has failed, then the entire *p*-cycle remains intact, essentially providing two disjoint paths around the *p*-cycle between the end nodes of the failed span. As shown in Figure 4.11c, if a failure arises on a straddling span, the mechanism can use either direction of the *p*-cycle to restore a working channel on the failed straddling span. If the failed straddling span has two working channels on it, then both sides of the *p*-cycle can be used, with each restoring one of the failed working channels. The process is the same no matter which straddling span fails.

Figure 4.11 assumes only a single unit-size *p*-cycle, but in reality the entire network will be protected by a number of overlapping and/or stacked *p*-cycles so that there are enough protection paths available to restore all of the failed working channels on any span. For instance, a failed span with 15 working channels might be an on-cycle span for five unit-size copies of one *p*-cycle and four unit-size copies of another, as well as a straddling span for three unit-size copies of another distinct *p*-cycle, which would provide protection for six of that span's working channels. Like span restoration, there is no consideration made for the original end-to-end working path of the failed working channels. Rather, they are simply restored between the end nodes of the failure itself. So it is possible, for instance, that a restored working path may loop back on itself on either side of the failure, though this source of inefficiency is no worse than what would be observed in span restoration itself.

Another important difference relative to rings is that *p*-cycles are protection structures only, meaning that they are composed purely of spare capacity (recall that in rings, half of the capacity of the ring is for working channels and the other half is for spare channels). The implication is that working paths need not be constrained by the *p*-cycle systems that will ultimately protect them, as is the case with rings. This allows working paths to be routed via shortest paths or any other route desired through the network. Also, because straddling spans are protected by *p*-cycles that explicitly do not cross over them, it is not unheard of for some spans in a *p*-cycle network to carry working channels only. Design and implementation is further simplified as a consequence, since the spare-only nature of *p*-cycles means that there is no need for any cycle interconnection the way we have in rings, and protection relationships can be considered on an individual span basis.

p-Cycles also provide very fast protection. As with rings, it is only the end nodes of the failed span that need to act in order to provoke a restoration response. In advance of failure, *p*-cycles are formed in the network by simply forming cross-connections between spare channels on adjacent spans, ensuring that the cross-connections form a closed structure. Then when a failure arises (say on an on-cycle span), the end nodes of the failed span detect the failure and cross-connect each end of a working channel into the spare channels of the *p*-cycle. There is no need to search for available connections, notify any other nodes, and so on, as the entire response of assignment of working channels to specific *p*-cycles is preplanned, requiring only a local cross-connection into the protection structure (the response is virtually identical to that of a BLSR). Since all of the other cross-connections are preconfigured, any signal inserted into the *p*-cycle by one end node will automatically transit the *p*-cycle until it emerges at the failed span's other end node, which has cross-connected the working channel's other end into the same *p*-cycle. For this reason, and because of *p*-cycles' meshlike capacity efficiency, *p*-cycles are often referred to as combining the speed of rings with the efficiency of mesh [7].

The significant capacity-efficiency advantage *p*-cycles enjoy over rings is easily demonstrated in Figure 4.12. If we consider a single unit-size copy of the 8-hop ring indicated by the solid dark spans shown in Figure 4.12a, that ring can only protect the 8 spans it crosses. However, a single unit-size copy of a *p*-cycle that crosses the same spans can protect working channels on 13 spans, as shown in Figure 4.12b. In addition, since five of the spans are straddling spans, the unit-size *p*-cycle can actually protect two working channels on those spans, meaning the 8-hop *p*-cycle can protect 18 individual working channels, whereas the ring could only protect eight working channels. If we define a system's redundancy as the sum of the spare capacity divided by the sum of the working capacity, then the ring in Figure 4.12a will have a minimum of 100 percent redundancy (if all working channels are signal-bearing) while the equivalent *p*-cycle will have a redundancy of only $8/18 = 44.4$ percent. *p*-Cycle network redundancies as low as 35 percent have been reported in a real network [44], and if Hamiltonians

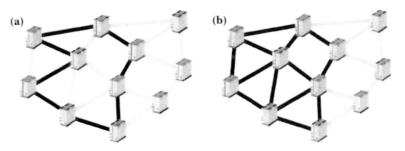

FIGURE

4.12

Spans protected by (a) a unit-capacity ring and (b) an equivalent *p*-cycle. Used with permission from Doucette [29].

[45] are used, p-cycle network redundancy can theoretically achieve the $1/(\bar{d}-1)$ lower bound on span-restorable redundancy [46]. The drawbacks of p-cycles are that they are not as capacity efficient as path restoration and the recovery path after a failure may be too long as compared to the working path, thereby violating QoS requirements.

4.5   SURVIVABLE NETWORK DESIGN TECHNIQUES

Given a specific traffic restoration scheme (e.g., p-cycles), the survivable network design problem is to determine the network topology or virtual topology to survive a set of failure scenarios. Survivable network design typically makes use of graph theoretic or optimization-based formulations [7, 9, 12, 39]. While there are a number of different approaches used, one differentiating characteristic is whether working routing is optimized jointly with restoration/protection routing and spare capacity, or if working routing is performed separately (e.g., often through shortest-path or minimum-cost routing). The former is usually referred to as *joint-capacity allocation* (JCA), while the latter is called *spare-capacity allocation* (SCA).

The goal of many survivable network design problems is to place sufficient capacity to fully protect against all single-span failure scenarios at minimal cost, though other design problems seek to reduce blocking probabilities, maximize single or dual-failure restorability, maximize network availability, and so on. Most of the various minimum-cost network design formulations used can also be divided into two main classes of optimization problem: *arc-path* approaches and *transshipment* approaches. In the arc-path approaches, the network graph topology is preprocessed to enumerate all or at least a subset of all distinct logical routes that can be used for restoration/protection routes, and an optimization problem formulated to select among them to provide full survivability (usually at minimum cost) [39]. The transhipment approaches formulate a series of conservation-of-flow type of constraint equations, where each working demand has a source and sink node, and all other nodes act as transhipment or intermediary nodes where any flow of a particular demand *into* the intermediary node must subsequently flow *out* of that node.

For illustration purposes, we now provide the arc-path formulation of the span restoration SCA and JCA problems [29, 39]. We first define the network topology as consisting of a set of spans S, a set of nodes N, and a set of demand relations D. In the transhipment approach, we also need to pass node and span adjacency information to the design optimization problem (i.e., the design problem needs to know which spans are adjacent to which nodes, and so on, in order to deal with the conservation of flow constraints), but in the arc-path approach, such information is only used in preprocessing to identify eligible route sets. Any method desired can be used to enumerate eligible routes, so long as we have a set of such routes to provide to the solver. Typically, custom-designed preprocessing software is used, often using a depth-first search algorithm that crawls through the network topology identifying eligible routes. The set of eligible routes could be the complete set of all distinct possible routes that can be drawn in the network's topology, but generally this set can be quite large (negatively impacting on the design problem's runtime). So we often restrict the eligible set to a subset of all distinct routes in the network such that, say, only the shortest 25 routes between each span's end nodes are included, or alternately all the paths satisfying a hop count limit are included. In any case, through preprocessing of the network's topology, we enumerate a set P_i of all distinct eligible routes that are available to act as restoration routes for working channels on failed span $i \in S$, and a set Q_r of all distinct eligible routes that are available to carry working path traffic for demand relation $r \in D$.

Eligible routes can be represented in a number of different ways, including as an ordered or unordered list of spans crossed, a list of nodes crossed, or, in our example here, through binary parameters. We encode restoration routes using the parameter $\delta_{i,j}^{p} \in \{0,1\}$, where $\delta_{i,j}^{p} = 1$ if restoration route p for working channels on failed span j crosses span i, and $\delta_{i,j}^{p} = 0$ otherwise. Similarly, we encode working routes using the parameter $\zeta_{j}^{r,q} \in \{0,1\}$, where $\zeta_{j}^{r,q} = 1$ if working route q, that can be used to carry working path routing for demand relation r crosses span j, and $\zeta_{j}^{r,q} = 0$ otherwise. The number of unit-size working paths needed by demand relation r is denoted by parameter d^r, and the cost of placing a single unit of working or spare capacity on span j is c_j. This latter parameter is usually equated with the Euclidean distance between the end nodes of the span in order to represent costs that are roughly proportional to a span's length (e.g., fiber itself, rights of way, amplifiers), though any other value(s) desired could be used. We then define a number of decision variables for the optimization problem to determine, namely: $w_i \geq 0$ and $s_i \geq 0$ are the amount of working capacity and spare capacity, respectively, that are placed on span i in the final solution. $g^{r,q} \geq 0$ is the number of working channels assigned by the solver to working route q that can be used to carry working path routing for demand relation r, and $f_{i,p} \geq 0$ is the number of spare channels assigned to restoration route p that can be used for restoration of working channels on failed span i.

Strictly speaking, since all four decision variables are usually required to take integer values only (say, corresponding to a WDM optical network where a unit of capacity would represent an individual wavelength), the optimization design problem is called an *integer linear programming* (ILP) problem. However, we often solve the ILP as a *mixed integer linear programming* (MIP) problem, where we allow working and restoration routing variables to take on fractional (i.e., noninteger) values. It has been shown that as long as the working and spare-capacity variables are forced to take on integer values, the integrality requirement of the underlying $g^{r,q}$ and $f_{i,p}$ variables can be relaxed without affecting optimality [47, 48]. We would solve the problem in this manner because a greater number of integer variables generally increases, often quite considerably, the complexity (and runtime) of an MIP/ILP problem. Using the notation just discussed, we can then express the span-restorable JCA network design problem as follows:

$$\text{Minimize:} \quad \sum_{\forall j \in S} c_j \times (s_j + w_j) \tag{4.1}$$

$$\text{Subject to:} \quad \sum_{\forall q \in Q^r} g^{r,q} = d^r \quad \forall r \in D \tag{4.2}$$

$$\sum_{\forall r \in D} \sum_{\forall q \in Q^r} \zeta_j^{r,q} \times g^{r,q} = w_j \quad \forall j \in S \tag{4.3}$$

$$\sum_{\forall p \in P_i} f_{i,p} = w_i \quad \forall i \in S \tag{4.4}$$

$$\sum_{\forall p \in P_i} \delta_{i,j}^p \times f_{i,p} \leq s_j \quad \forall i,j \in S \,|\, i \neq j \tag{4.5}$$

The objective function in Eq. 4.1 seeks to minimize the total cost of working and spare capacity assigned to the various spans in the network. Eq. 4.2 represents a set of constraints (one for each $r \in D$) that ensure the total number of working channels assigned to all eligible working routes for demand relation r are sufficient to fully route its entire demand, d^r. The constraints in Eq. 4.3 then place enough working capacity on each span to accommodate all working channels routed over it. Eq. 4.4 represents a similar set of constraints as those in Eq. 4.2, except that it ensures that the total number of spare channels assigned to all eligible restoration routes for failed span i are sufficient to fully restore all working channels, w_i, on that failed span. Finally, the constraints in Eq. 4.5 place enough spare capacity on each span j to accommodate all restoration paths that will be simultaneously routed over it for any single span failure scenario (i.e., failure of span i).

As already mentioned, the above ILP design model is the JCA version of the problem. It can easily be modified into the SCA version by changing Eq. 4.1 into $\sum_{\forall j \in S} c_j \times s_j$, removing Eqs. 4.2 and 4.3, performing working routing offline in advance, and then converting the w_i decision variables into input parameters. Alternatively, one could leave the model exactly as presented and simply provide only a single eligible working route for each demand relation, thereby forcing working routing to take a specified configuration. This problem also assumes there is no limit on the capacity of each span. We can easily implement span-capacity limits by adding a new set of constraints that enforce $s_j + w_j \leq T_j$, for instance, where T_j is the capacity limit on span j. In a similar fashion, many useful variations on this basic survivable network design problem embedding it in a particular technology can be formulated by modifying/adding constraints and the objective function. The interested reader is encourage to consult [7, 9, 12–17, 20] and the recent literature.

4.6   MULTILAYER ISSUES

As noted above, the networks composing the Internet are multilayer in nature and survivability and restoration can be addressed at multiple layers with different techniques at each layer. However, the majority of the literature focuses on providing survivability for various network technology (WDM, SONET, MPLS, ATM, IP, Overlay/Application) layers independently and multilayer issues are an area of ongoing research [49] that present several challenges.

Consider, for example, a two-layer backbone network such as an MPLS/WDM network. Survivability techniques in two-layer networks can be classified as survivability at the bottom layer, survivability at the top layer, and survivability at both layers, depending on the layer in which the survivability technique is deployed [13]. In the bottom-layer approach, recovery from a failure is performed only at the bottom layer (e.g., recovering failed light paths in the WDM network). This scheme has the benefits that it is simple and provides fast recovery of aggregate traffic. However, the major drawback of this scheme is that it cannot recover from failures that occur in the top layer, such as the failure of a top-layer router or its interfaces. With survivability at the top-layer, failure recovery is performed *only* at the top layer e.g., by recovering failed label-switched paths (LSPs) in an MPLS network using fast reroute. The advantage of this scheme is that it can recover from failures that occur in both layers. It also allows a service differentiation among top-layer flows by recovering each individual flow in the top layer, which is difficult in the bottom-layer survivability scheme where an aggregate of top-layer flows is recovered. Among the drawbacks of the top-layer approach are its complexity and slower speed of fault recovery.

One of the major problems in the survivability of multilayer networks is *fault propagation*, which occurs when the failure of a bottom-layer link or node results in the simultaneous failure of multiple higher-layer links. For example, consider Figure 4.13, which shows an MPLS over WDM network. At the MPLS layer, the

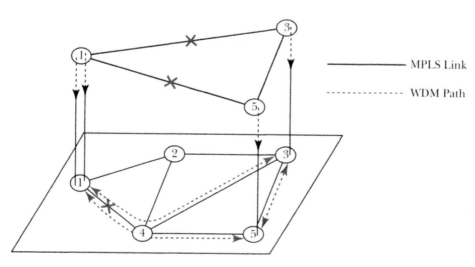

——————— MPLS Link
················· WDM Path

FIGURE   Fault propagation example.

4.13

three nodes are connected into a ring topology that can be provisioned with enough capacity for any single MPLS layer link (i.e., an LSP) to be fault tolerant. However, suppose in the lower WDM layer, the MPLS link 1-3 is routed on the WDM path 1-4-3, the MPLS link 1-5 is routed on the WDM path 1-4-5, and the MPLS link 5-3 is routed on the WDM path 5-3. We can immediately see that the MPLS links 1-3 and 1-5 are not diverse at the lower WDM level. Thus, if the WDM link 1-4 fails at the lower layer, both the upper-layer MPLS links 1-3 and 1-5 will be affected. Note, that fault propagation is essentially a correlated failure at the higher layers. An additional cause of fault propagation is *shared-risk link groups* (SRLGs), which are defined by a set of links that *fail together* due to *physical placement* of cabling in conduits or a common infrastructure [50] (e.g., separate cables crossing a bridge).

If failure propagation is not considered appropriately in multilayer networks, the survivability at the top-layer technique may fail to recover the communication services after a failure. This is an especially important point that has been ignored in much of the higher-layer survivability schemes in the literature. In part due to failure propagation, each layer of a network will typically employ self-healing capabilities to address faults occurring in their own layer. In such a multilayer scheme, coordination between layers is required to provide an efficient recovery process upon a failure. This coordination is called an escalation strategy, which determines which layer will perform a recovery first in response to a particular failure, and when and how responsibility will be transferred to another layer if the current layer fails to recover from the failure [13].

The design of survivable multilayer networks has been considered in the literature [13, 49]. The common theme in the current literature involves an exchange of interlayer topology information. For example, in Liu et al. [51], we consider the problem of provisioning spare capacity in two-layer backbone networks using a shared backup path protection approach in order to meet survivability requirements. First, two SCA optimization problems are formulated as ILP models for protection in the top layer against failures in the bottom layer. Both problems use overlay mapping information between the two layers to determine the location and the amount of spare capacity as well as the backup routes to protect a set of given working routes. The first model captures failure propagation across network layers, so the backup paths meet diversity requirements correctly. The second model improves bandwidth efficiency by moving the spare-capacity sharing from the top layer to the bottom layer. It requires the top-layer backup route be able to reserve bottom-layer spare capacity. This exposes a trade-off between bandwidth efficiency and extra cross-layer operation. In addition, the SCA model for shared path protection at both layers is developed. This approach is also called *common pool protection*. It allows spare capacity to be shared across layers to further reduce the network redundancy with significant savings possible. However, the implementation of such approaches requires cross-layer signaling and fault management coordination.

While the current literature provides a foundation for general survivable multilayer networks, there are still major open research issues, such as determining what type of survivability mechanism should be implemented at each layer to meet speed and availability requirements, coordination of alarms and resilience mechanisms at the layers, prioritization of traffic for fault recovery within and among the layers, techniques for collection and dissemination of cross-layer topology information, and understanding the overall system behavior to avoid instability when multilayer restoration schemes operate concurrently.

4.7   CONCLUSION AND FUTURE RESEARCH AREAS

In this chapter, we have provided basic background on network survivability techniques, which are a critical component to providing information assurance in networked systems. We conclude with our opinions of future research areas for network survivability.

In addition to the multilayer survivability issues raised above in Section 4.6, several problems are receiving attention from the networking research community. There has been very little research on a systematic approach to end-to-end Internet resiliency. A specific issue that needs to be addressed is cost-effective access network survivability. In many cases, there are actually overlapping competing access network technologies serving a geographic location. For example, a small office could have several options for Internet access, such as DSL, cable modem, wireless ISP based on IEEE 802.11 or IEEE 802.16 (WiMAX), and advanced 3G cellular services like HSDPA/HSUPA in UMTS systems. From a redundancy point of view, it is ironic that the technology and policies for seamlessly switching from one access network to another after a failure are currently not available. Other end-to-end issues include inter-autonomous systems resilience techniques across multiple ISPs.

An additional weakness in the literature is an emphasis on combating single isolated failure conditions; mechanisms for providing resilience in the face of multiple failures and widespread outages have received little attention. Note, that even for the random single failure case, the literature does not adequately differentiate between the risks of different threats. For example, the risk of cable cuts varies greatly (i.e., two orders of magnitude) with geographic location (e.g., dense urban versus rural environments). How to include the variable levels of fault risk into resilience mechanisms is an open issue with some preliminary work using fault trees discussed in Vajanapoom and Tipper [52]. Integration of risk-based analysis using fault trees with risk-based security analysis using attack trees as discussed in Chapter 9 would appear to be a possible technique for considering both security and fault risks in survivable network design.

We note that very high levels of resilience are required for certain societal critical services (e.g., VoIP emergency services, SCADA for the power grid), which are expected to be only a fraction of total network traffic. Thus, future network architectures should support various "resilience traffic classes" with varying levels of availability/survivability. While this concept has been discussed in the current literature in a qualitative fashion, schemes for providing classes of protection in an end-to-end fashion over multitechnology layer networks with dynamic provisioning has not been addressed. Note that current survivability mechanisms typically provide either full protection to a set of preplanned failure scenarios or no protection; the ability to have an application tune its resilience is not provided.

We note that performance evaluation techniques have been used in a variety of network survivability studies [32, 53–56] to evaluate the detection and restoration times, determine network congestion after a failure, evaluate dynamic restoration schemes, examine postfailure protocol behavior, determine actual spare-capacity requirements, evaluate the time-varying QoS after a failure, and evaluate the impact of various failure scenarios. While analytical-based approaches have occasionally appeared in the literature [54], this work has largely been conducted by simulation. Hence, there is a need for analytical techniques to facilitate such work and to support the integration with security in order to provide information assurance. Chapters 7 and 8 discuss analytical techniques for this integration.

References

[1] T. Lewis, *Critical Infrastructure Protection in Homeland Security: Defending a Networked Nation* (New York: Wiley-Interscience, 2006).

[2] The National Strategy for the Physical Protection of Critical Infrastructure and Key Assets, Whitehouse, Feb. 2003, at http://www.whitehouse.gov/pcipb/physical.html.

[3] Public Safety Canada, "Cyber Security and Protecting Canada's Critical Infrastructure," Feb. 2, 2005, at http://www.publicsafety.gc.ca/media/bk/2005/bg20050202-2-en.asp.

[4] The President's Commission on Critical Infrastructure Protection (PCCIP) Report, Sept. 1997, at http://www/pccip.org/.

[5] R. Kuhn, "Sources of Failure in the Public Switched Telephone Network," *IEEE Computer* 30, No. 4 (April 1997): 31–36.

[6] G. Iannaccone, C.-N. Chuah, R. Mortier, S. Bhattacharyya, and C. Diot, "Analysis of Link Failures in an IP Backbone," *Proceedings of ACM Sigcomm Internet Measurement Workshop*, Marseille, France, Nov. 2002.

[7] W. D. Grover, *Mesh-Based Survivable Networks: Options and Strategies for Optical, MPLS, and ATM Networking* (Upper Saddle River, NJ: Prentice Hall, 2003).

[8] W. E. Falconer, "Service Assurance in Modern Telecommunications Networks," *IEEE Communications Magazine* 28, No. 6 (June 1990): 32–39.

[9] M. Pioro and D. Medhi, *Routing, Flow, and Capacity Design in Communication and Computer Networks* (San Francisco: Morgan Kauffman Publishers, 2004).

[10] E. Mannie and D. Papadimitriou (Eds.), "Recovery (Protection and Restoration) Terminology for Generalized Multi-Protocol Label Switching (GMPLS)," IETF RFC 4427, March 2006.

[11] W. Grover, J. Doucette, M. Clouqueur, D. Leung, and D. Stamatelakis, "New Options and Insights for Survivable Transport Networks," *IEEE Communications Magazine* 40, No. 1 (Jan. 2002): 34–41.

[12] R. Bhandari, *Survivable Networks: Algorithms for Diverse Routing* (Boston: Kluwer Academic Publishers, 1999).

[13] J.-P. Vasseur, M. Pickavet, and P. Demeester, *Network Recovery: Protection and Restoration of Optical, SONETSDH, IP, and MPLS* (San Francisco: Morgan Kaufmann Publishers, 2004).

[14] T.-H. Wu, *Fiber Network Service Survivability* (Boston: Artech House, 1992).

[15] T.-H. Wu and N. Yoshikai, *ATM Transport and Network Integrity* (New York: Academic Press, 1997).

[16] H. Mouftah and P.-H. Ho, *Optical Networks: Architecture and Survivability* (Norwell, MA: Kluwer Academic Publishers, 2003).

[17] A. Somani, *Survivability and Traffic Grooming in WDM Optical Networks* (Cambridge: Cambridge University Press, 2006).

[18] D. Medhi, "A Unified Approach to Network Survivability for Teletraffic Networks: Models, Algorithms and Analysis," *IEEE Transactions on Communications* 42 (Feb.–April 1994): 534–548.

[19] K. Murakami and H. S. Kim, "Virtual Path Routing for Survivable ATM Networks," *IEEE/ACM Transactions on Networking* 4, No. 1 (Feb. 1996): 22–39.

[20] A. Hines, *Planning for Survivable Networks* (New York: John Wiley, 2002).

[21] K. Steiglitz, P. Weiner, and D. J. Kleitman, "The Design of Minimum-Cost Survivable Networks," *IEEE Trans. Circuit Theory* 16, No. 4 (Nov. 1969): 455–460.

[22] H. A. Malec, "Communications Reliability: A Historical Perspective," *IEEE Transactions on Reliability* 47, No. 3 (1998): 333–345.

[23] P. Baran, *On Distributed Communications*, twelve volumes, Rand Report Series, 1964.

[24] W. Grover and D. Tipper (Guest Eds.), "Special Issue on Designing and Managing Optical Networks and Services for High Reliability," *Journal of Network and Systems Management* 13, No. 1 (March 2005).

[25] D. Andersen, H. Balakrishnan, M. F. Kaashoek, and R. Morris, "Resilient Overlay Networks," *Proceedings of the 18th ACM SOSP*, Banff, Canada, Oct. 2001.

[26] S. Rai, B. Murkherjee, and O. Deshpande, "IP Resilience within an Autonomous System: Current Approaches, Challenges, and Future Directions," *IEEE Communications Magazine* 43, No. 10 (Oct. 2005): 142–149.

[27] G. Agrawal, D. Huang, and D. Medhi, "Network Protection Design for MPLS Networks," *Proceedings of IEEE International Workshop on the Design of Reliable Communication Networks (DRCN 2005)*, Naples, Italy, Oct. 2005.

[28] R. Glitho and S. Hayes (Eds.), "Special Issue Enter the World of TMN," *IEEE Communications Magazine* 33, No. 3 (March 1995).

[29] J. Doucette, *Advances on Design and Analysis of Mesh-Restorable Networks*, Ph.D. Dissertation, University of Alberta, Edmonton, Alberta, Canada, Dec. 2004.

[30] J. H. Saltzer, D. P. Reed, and D. D. Clark, "End-to-End Arguments in System Design," *The Second International Conference on Distributed Computing Systems*, Paris, April 8–10, 1981, pp. 509–512.

[31] B. Jager and D. Tipper, "Prioritized Traffic Restoration in Connection Oriented QoS Based Networks," *Computer Communications* 26, No. 18 (Dec. 2003): 2025–2036.

[32] A. Srikitja and D. Tipper, "On Providing Survivable QoS Services in the

Next Generation Internet," *Proceedings of the IEEE Military Communications Conference 1999*, Atlantic City, NJ, Oct. 1999.

[33] B. Jager and K. Danielsen, "On Rerouting in MPLS Based Networks," *WSEAS Transactions on Communications* 5, No. 9 (Sept. 2006): 2024–2030.

[34] A.M.C.A. Koster, A. Zymolka, M. Jäger, R. Hulsermann, and C. Gerlach, "Demand-Wise Shared Protection for Meshed Optical Networks," *Design of Reliable Communication Networks (DRCN 2003)*, Banff, Alberta, Canada, Oct. 19–22, 2003, pp. 85–92.

[35] C. Gruber, A. Koster, A. Zymolka, R. Wessäly, and S. Orlowski, "A Computational Study for Demand-Wise Shared Protection," *Design of Reliable Communication Networks (DRCN 2005)*, Island of Ischia (Naples), Italy, Oct. 2005.

[36] L. Guo, L. Li, H. Yu, and J. Cao, "Heuristic of Differentiated Path-Shared Protection for Dual Failures in Restorable Optical Networks," *Optical Engineering* 46, No. 2, 025009 (Feb. 2007).

[37] M. W. Maeda, "Management and Control of Transparent Optical Networks," *IEEE Journal on Selected Areas in Communications (JSAC)* 16, No. 7 (Sept. 1998): 1005–1023.

[38] R. Ramaswami and K. N. Sivarajan, *Optical Networks: A Practical Perspective*, 2nd ed. (San Francisco: Morgan Kaufmann Publishers, 2002).

[39] M. Herzberg, S. J. Bye, and A. Utano, "The Hop-Limit Approach for Spare-Capacity Assignment in Survivable Networks," *IEEE/ACM Transactions on Networking* 3, No. 6 (Dec. 1995): 775–784.

[40] S. Sengupta and R. Ramamurthy, "Capacity Efficient Distributed Routing of Mesh-Restored Light Paths in Optical Networks," *IEEE Global Telecommunications Conference (GlobeCom 2001)*, San Antonio, TX, Nov. 2001, pp. 2129–2133.

[41] Y. Liu, D. Tipper, and P. Siripongwutikorn, "Approximating Optimal Spare Capacity Allocation by Successive Survivable Routing," *ACM/IEEE Transactions on Networking* 13, No. 1 (Feb. 2005): 198–211.

[42] W. D. Grover and D. Stamatelakis, "Cycle-Oriented Distributed Preconfiguration: Ring-like Speed with Mesh-like Capacity for Self-Planning Network Restoration," *IEEE International Conference on Communications (ICC 1998)*, Atlanta, June 1998, pp. 537–543.

[43] D. A. Schupke, C. G. Gruber, and A. Autenrieth, "Optimal Configuration of *p*-Cycles in WDM Networks," *International Conference on Communications (ICC 2002)*, New York, April-May 2002, pp. 2761–2765.

[44] W. D. Grover, J. Doucette, A. Kodian, D. Leung, A. Sack, M. Clouqueur, and G. Shen, "Design of Survivable Networks Based on *p*-Cycles," in *Handbook of Optimization in Telecommunications*, edited by M. G. C. Resende and P. M. Pardalos (New York: Springer-Verlag, 2006).

[45] A. Sack and W. D. Grover, "Hamiltonian *p*-Cycles for Fiber-Level Protection in Homogeneous and Semi-Homogeneous Optical Networks," *IEEE Network* 18, No. 2 (March/April 2004): 49–56.

[46] W. D. Grover and J. Doucette, "Advances in Optical Network Design with *p*-Cycles: Joint Optimization and Pre-Selection of Candidate *p*-Cycles," *IEEE Lasers & Electro-Optics Society (LEOS) Summer Topicals 2002*, Mont Tremblant, Canada, July 2002, pp. 49–50.

[47] R. Ahuja, T. Magnanti, and J. Orlin, *Network Flows: Theory, Algorithms, and Applications* (Englewood Cliffs, NJ: Prentice Hall, 1993).

[48] Y. Wang, "Modeling and Solving Single and Multiple Facility Restoration Problems," Ph.D. dissertation, Sloan School of Management, MIT, Boston, June 1998, pp. 32–33.

[49] A. Jajszczyk, B. Mukherjee, R. Sabella, and X. Xiao (Eds.), "Traffic Engineering for Multi-Layer Networks," *IEEE Journal on Selected Areas in Communications (JSAC)* 25, No. 5 (June 2007): 865–867.

[50] J. Doucette and W. D. Grover, "Shared-Risk Logical Span Groups in Span-Restorable Optical Networks: Analysis and Capacity Planning Model," *Photonic Network Communications* 9, No. 1 (Jan. 2005): 35–53.

[51] Y. Liu, D. Tipper, and K. Vajanapoom, "Spare Capacity Allocation in Two-Layer Networks," *IEEE Journal on Selected Areas in Communications (JSAC)* 25, No. 5 (June 2007): 974–986.

[52] K. Vajanapoom and D. Tipper, "Risk Reduction Based Survivable WDM Network Design," *Proceedings of IEEE IPCCC Workshop on Information Assurance*, Phoenix, AZ, April 2006.

[53] T. Grubesic, M. O'Kelly, and A. Murray, "A Geographic Perspective on Commercial Internet Survivability," *Telematics and Informatics* 20 (2003): 51–69.

[54] D. Tipper, J. Hammond, S. Sharma, A. Khetan, K. Balakrishnan, and S. Menon, "An Analysis of the Congestion Effects of Link Failures in Wide Area Networks," *IEEE Journal on Selected Areas in Communications* 12, No. 1 (Jan. 1994): 179–192.

[55] W. P. Wang, D. Tipper, B. Jaeger, and D. Medhi, "Fault Recovery Routing in Wide Area Packet Networks," *Proceedings of 15th International Teletraffic Congress (ITC)*, Washington, DC, June 1997.

[56] P. McGregor, R. Kaczmarek, V. Mosley, D. Dease, and P. Adams, "National Security/Emergency Preparedness and the Next-Generation Network," *IEEE Communications Magazine* 44, No. 5 (May 2006).

5 System Survivability

Axel Krings   University of Idaho, USA

5.1   INTRODUCTION AND BACKGROUND

There is no single agreed-upon definition for system survivability. Instead, one may use as a starting point the vague notion that a system has to be able to tolerate diverse faults. This includes those faults typically considered in the area of fault-tolerant system design, such as faults resulting from component failure as a consequence of aging, fatigue or breakdown of materials. These faults may exhibit very predictable behavior and frequency. However, in the last decade there has been much attention on humanly-induced malicious faults (e.g., hacking, denial of service, virus, Trojan horses, spoofing). These kind of faults may be totally unpredictable. Before elaborating on the predictability of faults, or lack thereof, let us investigate some definitions of system survivability.

Definitions of system survivability can be partitioned into qualitative and quantitative definitions [1]. Survivability definitions vary even within the same application domain. For example, the American Institute of Aeronautics and Astronautics (www.aiaa.org) defines aircraft combat survivability as "the capability of an aircraft to avoid or withstand a man-made hostile environment." Whereas this definition is qualitative, its measurement is quantitative, that is, it can be measured by the probability the aircraft survives an encounter (combat) with the environment. A more general definition of aircraft survivability is the capability of an aircraft to avoid or withstand hostile environments, including both man-made and naturally occurring environments, such as lightning strikes, mid-air collisions, and crashes. A qualitative definition that has been used extensively was introduced by Ellison et al. [2], defining "survivability as the capability of a system to fulfill its mission, in a timely manner, in the presence of attacks, failure, or accidents." This definition of survivability is refining the mission-oriented notion of survivability that dates back to the 1960s in the context of mission reliability as seen in MIL-STD-721 or DOD-D 5000.3. The Ellison definition has been the basis for several procedural approaches to enhance survivability based on the concept of Survivability Network Analysis (SNA), introduced by Mead et al. [3]. Similarly, Neumann [4] states: "survivability is the ability of a computer-communication system-based application to satisfy and to continue to satisfy certain critical requirements (e.g., specific requirements for security, reliability, real-time responsiveness, and correctness) in the face of adverse conditions. Survivability must be defined with respect to the set of adversities that are supposed to be withstood." Survivability of software systems has been defined by Deutsch [5] as "the degree to which essential functions are still available although some part of the system is down."

Qualitative definitions of survivability, such as those indicated above, have been identified as useful in conveying the general notion of survivability, however, they are less suitable to measure survivability, compare the survivability of different systems, or measure the impact of efforts to increase survivability. For example, the SNA shown by Mead [3] helps to identify which parts of a system are deemed essential and results in recommended actions to increase survivability; but there is no direct way to measure the benefits of individual recommendations. This suggests the need for quantitative definitions.

A formal definition of system survivability was given by Knight [6, 7] where "a system is survivable if it complies with its survivability specification." The survivability specification is then defined as an n-tuple. Specifically, in [6]:

The survivability specification is given in a four-tuple (E, R, P, M), where:

+ Environment E is a definition of the environment in which the survivable system has to operate. It includes details of the various hazards to which the system might be exposed together with all of the external operating parameters. To the extent possible, it must include any anticipated changes that might occur in the environment.

+ Specification set R is the set of specifications of tolerable forms of service for the system. This set will include one distinguished element that is the normal or preferred specification, i.e., the specification that provides the greatest value to the user and with which the system is expected to comply most of the time. It is worth noting that at the other extreme, a completely inert system, i.e., no functionality at all, might be a tolerable member of this set.

+ Probability Distribution P; A probability is associated with each member of the set R with the sum of these probabilities being one. The probability associated with the preferred specification defines the fraction of operating time during which the preferred specification must be operational. The probabilities associated with the other specifications are upper bounds and define the maximum fractions of operating time that the associated specifications can be operational.

✦ A finite-state machine M denoted by the four-tuple (S, s_0, V, T), where S is a finite set of states, each of which has a unique label, which is one of the specifications in R, s_0 is the initial (or preferred) state of the machine, V is the finite set of customer values, and T is the state transition matrix.

In this definition, probabilities are assumed with each state and system survivability is defined by the probability of being in a preferred state. The reader is referred to the articles by Knight [6, 7] for more details and examples.

A definition that focuses on what happens after a fault occurs is given by the T1A1.2 group and is stated by Liu and Trivedi [1]: "Suppose a measure of interest *M* has the value m_0 just before a failure occurs. The survivability behavior can be depicted by the following attributes: m_a is the value of *M* just after the failure occurs, m_u is the maximum difference between the value of *M* and m_a after the failure, m_r is the restored value of *M* after some time t_r, and t_R is the time for the system to restore the value of m_0." The interesting aspect of this definition is that the actual time of the fault is of no importance. Thus, the definition addresses the state of a system just before a fault and captures the impact of the fault (i.e., the behavior of the system after the fault occurred).

Whereas it is important to understand the differences and expressive powers of the individual definitions above, we shall not be too pedantic about definitions and rather focus on general strategies to understand the impact of faults (i.e., fault models and the implications of these models on recovery and thus survivability).

5.2 SURVIVABILITY AND THE IMPACT OF FAULT MODELS

Before analyzing the survivability of a system, one has to understand the notion of faults. There are many kinds of faults and the literature in fault-tolerant system design has addressed this diversity in the context of fault models. However, the causes of the faults considered in the dependability community have been attributed mainly to failing components, for example, material fatigue, breakdown of physical or electronic components, accidents, or environmental influences. The impact of malicious behavior as the result of hacking, whether it be from external sources or even insiders; viruses or Trojan horses; denial of service; and so on have traditionally not been addressed. It was only later in research work, such as presented by Laprie [8] and Avizienis [9], that accidental and intentional faults were discussed side by side. Thus, when considering survivability, one may take the approach of using the standard notions from fault tolerance and extending the definition of a fault to include those attributable to malicious acts. Alternatively, one may view faults based on their very nature and attempt to classify faults that have been traditionally addressed in fault tolerance and those that have a computer or network security flavor. Which approach is better is probably more a philosophical question and there are good reasons for justifying both. As a result, we want to look at faults first from the viewpoint of fault-tolerant system design and then extend this view to consider malicious acts.

5.2.1 Dependability Considerations

In fault-tolerant system design, the easiest assumptions about faults are that they exhibit fail-stop behavior. In the context of a processor, this implies that the faulty processor simply ceases operation and alerts other processors of this fault, leaving open a way to access its system state (e.g., its memory). Whereas fail-stop behavior is very desirable, it does not always coincide with most of our personal experiences to say the least. Theoretically, building a fail-safe system is very expensive. For example, Schneider [10] addressed the complexity of building a k-fault fail-stop processor (i.e., a processor that obeys fail-stop behavior if no more than k of its components fail). Based on the enormous cost, it is probably safe to say that realistic efforts attempt to approximate fail-safe behavior rather than provably achieve it.

There are more realistic definitions of faults. For example, crash faults assume that a system fails and loses all of its internal state (e.g., the processor is simply down). One speaks of omission faults when values are not delivered or sent (e.g., due to a communication problem). If outputs are produced in an untimely fashion, then one speaks of a timing fault. Transient faults imply temporary faults (e.g., glitches) with fault-free behavior thereafter. If transient faults occur frequently, one speaks of intermittent faults. The list goes on and this discussion is making no attempt to derive a comprehensive taxonomy of faults. Interested readers are referred to the literature describing the fundamental concepts of dependability, such as Avizienis [9], as well as Chapter 6 of this book.

The diversity of faults and their consequences on a system have been the primary motivator for the definition of fault models. Fault models have played a major role in reliability analysis, agreement, and consensus algorithms. A fault model addresses the behavior of the faults, that is, the fault assumptions and the redundancy level required to tolerate a single fault type or perhaps a mix of fault types. Many different fault models have been proposed over the years ranging from the simple model by Lamport [11], which makes no assumptions about fault behavior, to hybrid fault models [12, 13], which consider multiple fault behavior.

In an attempt to get away from specific fault definitions, fault models attempt to capture the impact of diverse faults with respect to replication and agreement algorithms. Specifically, fault models have been considered who express three main fault behaviors, i.e., benign, symmetric, and asymmetric, as was demonstrated by the three-fault hybrid fault model of Thambidurai and Park [13]. *Benign* faults are considered globally diagnosable, meaning that every node is aware of the fault. This makes fault treatment simple. *Symmetric* faults assume that faulty values are seen equal by all nonfault processes, and *asymmetric* faults (often called Byzantine faults) make no assumptions on fault behavior. Asymmetric faults have also been called *malicious faults* [13, 14]. However, we will not use this term in order to avoid confusion with malicious acts (i.e., intentional faults). The fault model of Lamport [11] considered all faults to be asymmetric. Perhaps the most flexible fault model is the five-fault hybrid fault model by Azadmanesh et al. [12], which extended the three-fault model of Thambidurai of benign, symmetric, and asymmetric faults by considering transmissive and omissive versions of symmetric and asymmetric faults. Specifically, the fault types are:

+ *Benign.* A benign fault is self-evident to all nodes.

+ *Transmissive symmetric.* A single, erroneous message is delivered to all receiving nodes. The messages, which are faulty, are all identical. This kind of fault captures the meaning of symmetric faults of Thambidurai and Park [13].

+ *Omissive symmetric.* No message is delivered to any receiving node. As before, all nodes are affected in the same way. However, the omissive behavior results in the destination nodes to most likely take different action as if the message had been received.

+ *Transmissive asymmetric.* This fault can exhibit any form of arbitrary asymmetric behavior capable of delivering different erroneous messages to different receivers. This interpretation captures the meaning of asymmetric (Byzantine) faults in the three-fault model.

+ *Strictly omissive asymmetric.* A correct message is delivered to some nodes and no message is received by other nodes. Here, the omissions have the capability of affecting a system in an asymmetric way, since those nodes that have not received the message will most likely react differently from those that have received the message (e.g., selecting a default action).

The discussion so far still assumed that faults are independent. When there are no assumptions about the behavior of a fault, including the possibility of common-mode faults, then one speaks of *arbitrary* faults. Arbitrary faults are the most difficult to deal with since the independence-of-fault assumption no longer applies. For example, simple redundancy using identical components is of little use since the same input will produce the same output for each component. Thus, if a component induces a fault on a specific input, it will do so on all the replicas.

5.2.2   Survivability Considerations

Whereas the fault types and models of the previous section are well understood in the context of dependability, they are not obvious or questionable in malicious environments in the context of system survivability. For example, in Avizienis et al. [9] a broader discussion of faults is presented addressing the specific implications of survivable systems. There are many questions that arise from attempting to map malicious acts to traditional fault descriptions and models. For example, where does sophisticated hacking fit in? It cannot possibly be equated with an asymmetric fault of the three-fault model, which is considered by Thambidurai and Park [13] to be the unlikely result of pathologically failing hardware. What about a Trojan horse? If a system has a Trojan, but it has not been triggered, does this constitute a fault since nothing has happened yet? Clearly, with respect to the standard definition of reliability, which is the probability that a system performs as specified for the entire time interval of consideration, the untriggered Trojan seems to have no impact.

This brings us closer to the real dilemma. In the dependability models, the faults were clearly defined and statistically predictable. For example, the probability of failure or fail rate of a disc drive can be directly extracted from product information such as the mean time to (or between) failure (MTTF, MTBF). This constant fail rate is derived from the approximately constant bottom part of the so-called bathtub curve [15]. The curve (resembling the shape of a bathtub) partitions the lifetime of a component into three phases: the infant mortality phase, the useful lifetime, and the wear-out phase. The fail rate λ of the useful lifetime, which is the inverse of the MTTF, is the basis for determining the reliability $R(t)$ of a system as $R(t) = e^{-\lambda t}$. However, statistical predictability of fail rates in systems subject to malicious acts is arguably difficult. What is the fail rate when we are discussing root attacks? The fail rate, which was considered constant in the reliability analysis used in fault tolerance, suddenly may have little meaning. For example, assume you have a computer with a known vulnerability and nobody knows about it. Then the probability of a hacking attack may be considered small. Now assume someone posts a message in a hacker newsgroup indicating your IP address and the nature of the vulnerability. It is probably safe to say that the probability that the computer gets hacked approaches one. Even if one considers a general hazard function (i.e., a fail-rate function dependent on time) and perhaps other parameters rather than a constant fail rate, the function itself may not be predictable, not even mentioning the computational implications of dealing with such a function.

The evolution of hybrid fault models was driven by the observation that some fault types were more likely to occur than others. As the complexity of the models increased, so did the reliability of the systems they were applied to. The main reason was that the level of redundancy to mask different types of faults increases with the complexity of the fault. For example, to mask b benign faults, one only needs $N = b + 1$ components, whereas for a asymmetric faults, one needs at least $N = 3a + 1$ components [11] to mask their effects. And this still assumes independence of faults. The general argument that complex fault types were much less likely than simpler types could be made. For example, a benign fault was argued to be much more likely to occur than a symmetric fault, which in turn was much more likely than an asymmetric fault. As a result, given a fixed number of components, more faults could be tolerated (e.g., for $N = 4$), one can tolerate three benign faults but only one asymmetric fault. Now, however, we are operating in an environment in which fail rates cannot be considered constant anymore. Furthermore, with respect to intentional faults, it is perhaps more likely that a fault is more sophisticated than benign. This is the inverse to the evolution of hybrid fault models. In essence, when it comes to security concerns we may be back where we started from, that is, back to the model of Lamport [11] where every single fault should be considered malicious. Even under this pessimistic assumption, one still has to find ways of ensuring that the independence of faults is preserved.

Modeling survivability is difficult, unless one finds ways to eliminate the impact of fail rates, as was shown in the approaches by Liu and Trivedi [1]. Otherwise, one is back to a nonconstant fail rate (i.e., a hazard function with possibly multiple variables such as time, threat levels, or other environmental inputs). This renders entire methods that were traditionally used to aid in assessing objectives questionable. For example, risk assessment is difficult if not impossible. How can the risk associated with an event be determined if there is no reliable way to predict the probability of that event? Unlike application domains where there is a wealth of historic data, the past may not say much about the present or future. Even expert opinion may be subjective or misguiding. Thus, even deviations from usual behavior or usage cannot necessarily be approximated by informed or intended approaches, as was applicable in Thambidurai and Park [13]. This leads to a notion where a system should be designed with survivability concerns as a main design objective.

5.3   DESIGN FOR SURVIVABILITY

When addressing certain aspects of a problem that become too difficult to handle in an add-on fashion, an integrated approach is advised. *Design for testability* is a perfect example. By the 1980s, integrated circuits had become so large that exhaustive testing became infeasible. To test a circuit, an input vector (or sequence of vectors) is applied that will produce different outputs in the presence and absence of a fault [16]. The problem is termed the *test vector problem*, and the determination of vectors that reveal faults are known as the *test vector generation problem*. There are algorithms for testing combinational circuits [17], however, the problem of generating test vectors for given faults has been shown to be NP complete by Cheng [18] even for combinational circuits. In the presence of sequential circuits, the number of vectors increases exponentially and becomes infeasibly large even for relatively small circuits. This presents problems not only for testing chips, but also carries over to other areas (e.g., it puts limitations on modern approaches to evolving digital circuits, as was shown by Imamura et al. [19]). The approach to overcoming the test vector problem was to design circuits using the *design for testability* paradigm. Extra hardware was added to allow for more effective testing or the tolerance of faults in the absence of testing certain functionalities.

Design for survivability takes the similar approach to utilizing survivability mechanisms as an integral part of system design, rather than as an add-on feature. The result can be design strategies that avoid certain kinds of faults. For example, in the Boeing 777 design, extra efforts were taken to eliminate the potential for asymmetric faults in the primary flight computer system [20]. Thus, asymmetric faults were not attempted to be treated but avoided by design. Another example is the use of broadcast communication to eliminate the impact of asymmetric faults. Examples include the so-called R-redundant broadcast network shown by Babaoglu and Drummond [21] and cross-monitoring of ad hoc network communication described by Krings and Ma [22].

When considering design for system survivability, the first question coming to mind is what definition of survivability should be used? A logical approach is to first use a definition based on essential services or functionalities and then attempt to quantify the survivability. This way one can take advantage of reducing the complexity of the overall system to different degrees of essentiality without losing the capability of quantifying the result. Quantification can then be a motivator for system adaptation. This quantification can be the result of offline or real-time monitoring [7]. Alternatively, analysis can be used to derive deterministic primitives that are building blocks of survivable systems as demonstrated by Krings and Ma [22]. In dealing with a system that may be subjected to a malicious act, one has to realize that the advantage is on the side of the attacker. The attacker only has to succeed in finding *one* of a possibly large number of attack scenarios to cause system failure. The exact universe of attack scenarios may be impossible to enumerate and may be constantly evolving. Thus, an attack strategy is *depth first*. A defense strategy to a nonpredictable attack is, however, *breath first* if no information about the attack is available. The strategies may be motivated by predictions or risk analysis, but, if the attacker knows the strategy, then the attack can be optimized to take advantage of this knowledge. Therefore, having a non-breath-first strategy may benefit the attacker. Thus, one should find ways to eliminate such advantage and make no assumptions about attack scenarios. Such approach was taken in Germain and Playez [23] and Krings et al. [24, 25], and will be described in Section 5.5, where large distributed computations were certified against accidental or malicious corruption (i.e., massive attacks) with no assumptions about the attack strategies and distributions. Other applications lend themselves to game-theoretical considerations in attempting to optimize defense strategies in rounds. This is difficult even if the rules are precise (e.g., as in the game of chess), but if a game has no rules and "anything goes," then how does one determine strategic moves?

When designing systems and strategies that consider survivability, the fields of fault tolerance and computer and network security are obvious candidates for finding solutions. However, the mechanisms of fault tolerance are not yet necessarily well suited to malicious environments, as we have seen in the discussions above. On the other hand, according to Maxion [26], the lack of success in securing networked computer systems using solutions from the field of computer and network security may be attributable to the missing theoretical groundwork and mathematical models. Most approaches to security and survivability are ad hoc. In the absence of standardized security test procedures, claims can often not be verified. For example, comparing the effectiveness of intrusion detection systems has been shown to be a sobering exercise by Allen [27]. The source of the problems lies in part in the lack of formal descriptions of the detection methods or the fact that the detection algorithms may not be described at all as they are considered proprietary. Furthermore, it may be difficult or not possible to compare relative results; as such, comparisons would require a common basis. This problem is addressed in Section 5.6.

Design Approach: If one thinks of a system as a collection of functionalities that must perform specific tasks, then the design of a survivable system can be thought of as a multistage process. It should be noted that, in a malicious environment, each stage has its limitations. It is important to know and understand these limitations.

5.3.1 Identification of Essential Functionalities

To find essential functionalities, the SNA method of Mead et al. [3] can be used. This limits the focus of survivability to those components that are deemed essential, rather than considering an entire system, which may be very large, unbounded, and complex. An example of such a system is the power grid. The four-step SNA starts with the *System Definition*, exposing the mission objectives, system requirements, architecture, and risks in the operational environment. In step two, *Essential Capability Definition*, essential services, assets, and system components are identified. Next, in step three, *Compromisable Capability Definition*, intrusion scenarios are selected based on certain selection criteria and these scenarios are then traced through a system to identify those components that are compromisable. At this point the essential functionalities of a system have been identified. The actions performed to actually increase survivability of a system are then addressed in step four, *Survivability Analysis*. The readers unfamiliar with the SNA concept are referred to the work by Mead et al. [3]. Rather than discussing the details of their SNA approach, we want to focus on the general issues surrounding the trade-off space when choices have to be made. Specifically, in the SNA it is assumed that selected intrusion scenarios are used to address survivability of essential functionalities. However, the selection itself may not be as simple as it may seem. Furthermore, the quality and comprehensiveness of the set of intrusion scenarios depend on the skills of the analysts conducting the SNA.

The first SNA step, *System Definition*, helps identify the functionalities or services that a system needs to provide. This may be interpreted in different ways and the system specifications have to resolve any ambiguity. Thus, during the specification phase of product design, the survivability requirements have to be defined. Let us consider several possible scenarios. A system may have services that *cannot* (under no circumstance) be lost or interrupted. Alternatively, it may suffice that the service continues in a degraded fashion, perhaps performing the functionality correctly but slower. The term *graceful degradation* usually describes this mode of operation. There may be multiple levels of essentiality. However, this leads to interesting questions like "Assuming that choices have to be made, is it better to survive two lower-level or one high-level event?" This simple question actually gets to the core deficiency of risk-assessment-based approaches in hostile environments. The survivability specifications would actually need to address this trade-off space, which is especially difficult if the solution space is affected by resource constraints. For example, given the reality of a limited budget, which functionalities can one afford to design for survivability? The answer to this very question already gives an opponent an advantage. In a simplistic view of a system, where every functionality has an associated known cost and penalty, the problem of selecting functionalities given a resource constraint, such as a limited budget, is equivalent to the knapsack problem. In this well-known problem, objects of different sizes and values are to be included into a knapsack of a given size (e.g., our limited budget) in order to maximize its value. However, in a complex system the determination of sizes and values, which of course correspond to a functionality's cost of implementing survivability and the cost associated with failure, are difficult, to say the least. For the rest of the discussion, we assume that one can find consensus on a set of essential services.

5.3.2 Tolerating Faults

In the last step of the SNA, survivability measures are applied. For each intrusion scenario selected, existing approaches to resist against, recognize, and recover from attacks are identified. Then strategies to increase the resistance, recognition, and recovery are suggested. One may argue about the specific suggestions. For example, how much more survivable is the specific functionality after the implementation of the suggestion? This assumes that survivability can be measured and brings up the same issues that were discussed earlier, with respect to the cost-benefit ratio: Which suggestions should be taken and how does that affect survivability if the attacker knows the selection strategy? In the end, any strategy adopted aims to present a hurdle with a certain threshold that should not be exceeded. In other words, one attempts to raise the bar with respect to how many faults and what fault types can be tolerated. We could simplify this view and just say that in the end we are attempting to eliminate a single point of failure, even if this single point represents, in general, a threshold function whose value should not be exceeded. The resulting strategy boils down to designing a functionality that can tolerate k compromised components.

In traditional fault tolerance, tolerating faults is typically achieved utilizing the *principle of redundancy*. Information redundancy usually considers the inclusion of additional information as the basis for fault recovery. A typical example is an error correction code. Time redundancy relies on multiple executions skewed in time on the same node and is often used to mask omissions. Lastly, spatial redundancy uses multiple components, each computing a value, and the final value is derived from a convergence function (e.g., majority voting). The resulting N-modular redundant (NMR) system implements a k-of-N system, which implies that the system functions as long as k or more components are fault free. A typical configuration is a triple-redundant redundancy (TMR), which is a 2-of-3 system.

Many different schemes have been proposed that implement spatial redundancy with more or less sophisticated redundancy management strategies and any text on fault-tolerant system design can be used as a reference. The application environment has been typically described in the standard literature on agreement and consensus algorithms. In other words, given a fault model, for example, those by Thambidurai and Park [3] or Azadmanesh [12], and the mix of faults one attempts to tolerate, determine the number of components needed and identify a suitable agreement strategy.

5.3.3   Dealing with Common-Mode Faults

In tolerating different faults, any of the solutions in the literature on fault models and agreement and consensus algorithms can be used. However, the models largely assume the independence of faults. In fact, it can be easily argued that common-mode faults cannot be tolerated in general, since by their very definition, all modules subjected to this type of fault are affected the same. In this case, redundancy has no benefit and the solution to the problem lies in finding ways to avoid common-mode behavior or using design strategies that have the maximization of independence as a key objective.

Let's consider the following scenario. Assume that a system has centralized administrative control and a person with full understanding of how the system works attempts an insider attack. If the attacker has sufficient privileges, he or she may tip the fault model toward common-mode behavior. For example, redundant functionalities may be disabled simultaneously. Thus, the faults, which in this case are induced by the insider, are not independent anymore. This leads us to the notion of decentralization as an approach to reducing common-mode behavior. If control is decentralized so that no single person or process has control over all its components, then this strategy can be used to implement redundant control. This view is not new; as a matter of fact, it was introduced with the elimination of single voters in modular redundant systems. Multiple voters were used to address the concern of "Who guards the guards?"

Experience with achieving decentralization in an add-on fashion has proven to be possible, but difficult. The principles of hardware and software redundancy were applied by Krings and McQueen [28] to decentralize essential functionalities within the Linux operating system. Rather than replicating entire systems, only certain operating system or network functionalities were decentralized. For example, Domain Name Servers (DNSs), which resolve network addresses, are one common target of attack. Rather than the usual single DNS executing on one specific server, assume that DNS is replicated on several network nodes. Upon receiving a DNS resolution request, the DNSs initiate a voting process to reach agreement on proper DNS resolution, thus masking and possibly identifying any compromised DNS. This approach, of course, assumes that enough servers have been unaffected by an attack. The main challenge in eliminating central control of functionalities was found to be the implementation of the support infrastructure. For example, the communication primitives associated with exchange of data (to be voted upon) are themselves possible targets of attacks (e.g., spoofing attacks). Thus, an implementation of a distributed agreement algorithm needs to consider the full spectrum of network attacks.

Decentralization as a strategy to eliminate the effects of common-mode behavior may be a natural for unbounded systems. On one hand, unbounded systems have the noted concern of a lack of centralized control, for example, managing user permissions and access to resources can be difficult across different administrative domains. But on the other hand, it is exactly the lack of centralized control that may be part of the solution to problems with common-mode concerns. Thus, from a design point of view, the question should be "How can one take advantage of the decentralized control?" This brings us back to the solution space of standard approaches in fault-tolerant system design utilizing redundancy.

Dissimilarity or diversity can be an alternative to decentralization. Rather than ensuring that common-mode behavior is minimized by assuring that no outside influence can "reach" multiple functionalities, the functionalities themselves may be designed to maximize the independence of faults. One such approach, N-version software, dates back to the mid-1980s and is discussed by Avizienis in [29, 30]. Essentially, N-versions of the same functionality are produced in independent environments in the hope that by developing them in isolation, different approaches and implementations are used. This in turn is expected to maximize the independence of faults. It should be noted that achieving true independence of faults using N-version software has been also disputed by Knight and Leveson [31] using the arguments that it is practically impossible to truly provide the conditions that ensure the creation of true dissimilarity. Nevertheless, dissimilarity in hardware and software has been a successful key strategy in many ultrareliable systems. For example, Airbus' fly-by-wire aircraft use dissimilar processors and dissimilar software. Similarly, the Boeing 777 uses different types of processors and dissimilar compilers for the same Ada code [20]. Dissimilarity is often applied to general applications and we frequently resolve everyday problems applying this concept, perhaps not even noticing it. For example, we commonly experience that one web browser succeeds when another one seems to fail to perform certain functionalities. In general, this strategy implies that a failed functionality is replaced by another that is equivalent or sufficiently similar. This, however, implies that a mechanism is in place that indicates when such a switch should occur.

5.3.4 Applying the Notion of Optimality

Any mechanism or strategy that attempts to provide survivability should be guided by the *principle of optimization*. Any suboptimal strategy could potentially be circumvented or outperformed by a counterattack that is better (or optimal). In general, there is no benefit in not addressing this point. In fact, applying the principle of optimization may lead to better design strategies or shed information about the space or time complexity of the problem.

Optimization of reliability has been the driving force in the development of hybrid fault models. Specifically, reliability of a system is optimized by determining a suitable fault model, which in turn identifies the appropriate redundancy level and management strategy. Risk assessment–based approaches attempt to identify system components based on some risk metrics. Then, optimization typically consists of applying mediation to the high-risk components. Applications that lend themselves to game-theoretical approaches attempt to bias their defense or attack strategies to use those moves that optimize the chances of success. If critical population densities are a concern (e.g., sensor placement), percolation theory may be used. The list of mathematical tools is long. It is, therefore, a natural consequence to consider specific survivability problems and investigate how they map (or are related) to problems in other domains. We will consider such strategies in Section 5.6.

5.4   DECENTRALIZED STORAGE

Decentralization as a means to improve survivability of data storage systems has been described in the context of the PASIS project at Carnegie Mellon University (CMU). Essentially, the trade-off space of security, availability, and performance was investigated with respect to data storage across distributed storage units. Survivability is addressed by decentralizing storage, in other words, spreading information among independent storage nodes. Much research has been conducted on issues of distributed or virtual storage and the CMU PASIS project's publication list contains many references. Our interest in survivable storage is more focused on the different data distribution schemes as they can be adapted for different application domains.

Wylie et al. [32] introduced a *p-m-n* threshold scheme where data is encoded into n shares. Any m of the n shares can be used to reconstruct the data and less than p shares reveal no information about the data. This scheme is, of course, very interesting in many survivability and security applications. For example, a scheme with $m < n$ is interesting if the loss of shares has to be tolerated (i.e., up to $l = n - m$ shares may be lost or damaged). If confidentiality is of concern, then parameter p is critical, since it indicates the minimum number of shares that, if captured, would expose partial or all information. Different schemes can be derived:

- *Decimation or Striping* $(1, n, n)$. In this scheme, a large block of data is partitioned into n equally sized shares. All n shares are needed to retrieve the data. Each share reveals some information.

- *Splitting* (n, n, n). This is a scheme where $n - 1$ shares contain random values. The values in the $n - 1$ shares are EXORed with the values of the nth share in order to retrieve the original data. Thus, all shares are needed to extract the data and, hence, $p = m = n$. Whereas this scheme maximizes confidentiality, it carries the highest cost.

- *Secret Sharing* (m, m, n). Only m of the n shares are required to reassemble the data and the theft of less than m shares reveals no information. In Blakley's scheme, a value is determined as the intersection of nonparallel planes in n-space. For example, if a data point is derived by the intersection of three planes, then any two planes only give a line. If one chooses nonparallel lines, then any two of three lines intersect at the same data point.

- *Ramp Scheme* (p, m, n). This scheme can be implemented using polynomial-based math (i.e., $p - 1$ random values and $m - (p - 1)$) secret values). For $p = 1$, this is equivalent to information dispersal, and $p = m$ is equivalent to secret sharing.

Obviously, any of the distribution schemes can be modified to combine replication with encryption. The question for survivable systems then becomes one of balancing the parameters under consideration of the intended fault model. For example, the threshold schemes as described above only consider benign faults. If more elaborate fault models are required then the appropriate modifications need to be made. For instance, one way to address value faults (e.g., symmetric faults) is to use signatures based on hash functions such as MD5 or SHA. Thus, the signatures can expose when shares have been modified. However, one has to be aware of the fact that a particular scheme is only as good as the underlying technology. In Wylie et al. [32], the level of effort required for an adversary to compromise the security of a system is considered. For example, if one considers compromising confidentiality in an (n, n, n) scheme, then the effort required is the minimum of (1) compromising the authentication system, or (2) breaking into all n systems. Wylie et al. [32] then extend the level-of-effort approach to consider encryption, which requires the additional effort of either stealing the key or doing crypto-analysis.

Whereas the threshold schemes were discussed with respect to survivable storage, the principle can be adopted by many applications. The mobile agent application in subsection 5.6.3 is an example in which the principle, in that case secret sharing, was applied to the code to be executed, that is, the "storage data shares" were assembled at the destination to derive the executable payload of the agent.

5.5 SURVIVABILITY OF LARGE DISTRIBUTED SYSTEMS

The purpose of decentralization in the previous discussion was to increase security and performance in the context of data storage systems. The usage of shares to decentralize data was used to increase security. The second property of the distribution schemes was the potential for increased performance, which for data storage means larger data bandwidth.

In this section, we want to address decentralization to increase performance in the context of distributed computing. In distributed computing, a large degree of distribution, or parallelism, is utilized to deal with large computational problems. For example, global computing systems like GRID or peer-to-environments use thousands of resources for computationally intensive applications. However, since the computational nodes operate in an unbounded environment, they are subjected to a wide range of attacks. It is, in general, not realistic to assume that mechanisms (e.g., IDS) are in place to identify faults and intrusions at all nodes. This is especially true for voluntary computing, which is used in the SETI@home project, in which participating nodes volunteer their resources to verify the significance and validity of possible signals of alien life.

As the number of nodes in a distributed computation increases, so does the probability for failure. As a matter of fact, in large applications, one of the main problems is that the duration of the computation often exceeds the MTBF of the underlying infrastructure. This has been the driving factor for the development of log-based and checkpoint-based recovery approaches such as those described by Mootaz et al. [33] and Jafar et al. [34]. For example, a popular checkpointing library used in systems like CoCheck [35], MPICH-V2, and MPICH-CL [36] is the Condor checkpointing library [37].

Survivability considerations of large distributed computations are driven by two factors. The first addresses the fact that global computations are expected to tolerate certain low rates of faults. Thus, it is required to use algorithms that can tolerate a certain number of compromised nodes. The thresholds on the number of node faults that can be tolerated depend on the applications and underlying infrastructure. The second consideration is that of detecting attacks that surpass the built-in resilience of the fault-tolerant algorithms. Such *massive attacks* are especially of concern due to the potential of common-mode faults, might they be the result of virus or Trojan attacks or orchestrated attacks against widespread vulnerabilities of specific operating systems. There are different approaches that have been used in the past to address these two considerations, as outlined in the following:

Voting. Approaches based on voting assume that the values that are at the basis for voting have been derived from redundant computations. This makes voting an expensive approach since it increases the complexity of the computations by the level of redundancy required for the voting scheme. For example, to tolerate m value faults (i.e., a symmetric fault), one needs a redundancy level of $N = 2m + 1$. Thus, the work to be performed is N-fold. Alternatively, a more efficient strategy is an m-first voting scheme in which one stops collecting results after receiving m matching results.

Spot-checking. It may suffice to perform some sort of result checking. In spot-checking, a node to be tested is assigned a computation for which the result is already known or can be easily verified by the testing node. If the tested node returns a correct result, then it has passed the check. The effectiveness of such a strategy depends on how many checks are performed and the way in which the checks are performed. The node should not know when it is being checked or have information about the actual check. Otherwise, the node can elect to perform correctly during the time of the expected test or in response to a suspected test. Thus, the essential parameters of this method are the number of checks to be performed, the selection criteria, and lastly the test. Failing the spot-check may result in blacklisting the node that failed to produce the correct results. However, blacklisting may be difficult or impossible since malicious nodes may reenter the system using new identities.

Credibility-based approaches. Here, the credibility threshold principle is applied, which implies that a result from a node is only accepted if the node has a certain credibility, that is, if the conditional probability of the result being correct is above some threshold value. The credibility of the node reflects the credibility of the result. A node's credibility can be based on the number of spot-checks passed. Past credibility can be rewarded and new nodes may enter the system at a lower credibility rating. Of importance are the algorithms used to determine the credibility for schemes with and without blacklisting and how the credibility of a node affects the credibility and, thus weight, of the result.

Partial execution on reliable resources. This approach partitions the workload into those computations that are to be executed on reliable resources and those that execute on unreliable resources with given error probability, in order to maximize the expected number of correct results [38]. The advantage of having reliable resources is that critical computations can be executed on these nodes. However, the general question is how and whether one can actually partition the application in a meaningful way to take advantage of the scheme. From a practical point of view, a guaranteed reliable resource is only an approximation of the theme.

Reexecution on reliable resources. Rather than executing portions of the work on reliable resources, here the entire workload is executed on unreliable nodes and only some (randomly selected) computations are reexecuted on reliable resources to verify the results. This is different from spot-checking, where the result is known in advance or easily verifiable by the checking node. The number of randomly selected computations determines the certainty with which the computation is assumed to be determined as correct.

Performance issues of voting, spot-checking, and credibility-based approaches have been addressed by Sarmenta [39] and those of partial execution on reliable resource by Gao and Malewicz [38]. All approaches above are affected to some extent by different assumptions associated with the expected malicious behavior, the authentication mechanism, and encryption support. Whereas authentication and encryption are well understood, the possible behavior of an adversary may be impossible to predict. Therefore, let us consider an approach where there are no assumptions about faults and the capabilities or effects of malicious acts. Specifically, we want to look at the probabilistic certification of large-scale applications of Krings [24, 25], which is based on reexecution on reliable resources.

The goal is to certify the computations of a large application. Thus, we want to detect if the threshold of faults that can be tolerated by the fault-tolerant algorithm executing the workload has been surpassed as the result of a massive attack. If a massive attack is detected then recovery needs to be initiated. Let us consider the environment that allows for such approach.

The basis for the execution of an application is the global computing platform (GCP) shown in Figure 5.1. The GCP consists of computers or a cluster of workstations, checkpoint server(s), and reliable resources. The global computation is initiated by a user and unfolds in a direct acyclic graph describing

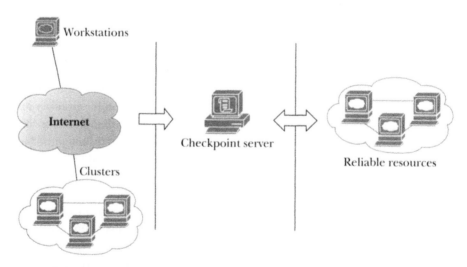

FIGURE

5.1

Global computing platform.

the data flow between all elementary tasks. The GCP includes two types of resources: *workers* and *verifiers*. The workers are unreliable resources that compute tasks in a nonsecure environment. The verifiers are reliable resources that verify the correctness of selected tasks by reexecuting them. Communications between workers and verifiers are only performed through a (possibly distributed) checkpoint server, containing computations submitted by workers, as described by Jafar [34]. Whereas any attack can occur on a worker or between a worker and the checkpoint server, the checkpoint server and verifiers are considered secure (i.e., reliable).

A principal concept allowing certification of results based on partial reexecution is a macro data-flow graph G that is maintained by the checkpoint server as the result of checkpoints reflecting task creations and terminations as well as the creation and deletion of shared data objects. The dynamic data-flow graph G represents a global checkpoint of the application and contains the results to be certified. The checkpoint of a process itself consists of the entries of the process' state (e.g., its stack). As such, it constitutes its tasks and their associated inputs, and not the task execution state on the processor itself. Understanding this difference between the two concepts is crucial. Checkpointing the tasks and their inputs simply requires storing the tasks (their identifiers) and their input data in the data-flow graph. On the other hand, checkpointing the execution of a task usually consists of storing the execution state of the processor as defined by the processor context, that is, the processor registers such as program counters and stack pointers as well as data. In the first case, it is possible to move tasks and their inputs, assuming that both are represented in a platform-independent fashion. In the latter case, the fact that the process context is platform dependent requires a homogeneous system in order to perform a restore operation or a virtualization of this state, as shown by Strumpen [40].

An important fact is that the data-flow graph G represents a global (platform-independent) state of the computation. Thus, it can be the basis for certification at any time. For example, if one waits until the computation is completed, then it can be used to certify the entire computation. If, however, one is interested in certifying partial computations, then the snapshot of G at a particular time can be the basis for certification.

Probabilistic certification is a probabilistic algorithm that uses randomization in order to state if a computation, denoted by E, has failed or not. Note that E is completely described by the data-flow graph G on the checkpoint server. Given E, a Monte Carlo certification is defined as a randomized algorithm that takes as input an arbitrary ε, $0 < \varepsilon \leq 1$, and delivers either (1) CORRECT or (2) FAILED, together with a proof that E has failed. The probabilistic certification is to be with error ε, if the probability of the answer CORRECT, when E has actually failed, is less than or equal to ε.

An example of how such an algorithm can be used for certification of a workload with independent computations is given by Krings et al. [25] where Monte Carlo Test (MCT) is defined as follows:

1. Uniformly choose one task T in workload G. The input and output of T and E are denoted by $i(T, E)$ and $o(T, E)$, respectively, and are available on the checkpoint server at the end of the execution of T.

2. Reexecute T on a verifier (a reliable resource) using the same input $i(T, E)$ to get the correct output, denoted by $\hat{o}(T, E)$. If $o(T, E)$ and $\hat{o}(T, E)$ differ, then return FAILED.

3. Return CORRECT.

A certification of an execution consists of repeatedly invoking the MCT. It can be shown that after N consecutive invocations of MCT, each of which returning CORRECT, the execution is certified to be correct with probability of error less than or equal to ε. Specifically, after N independent applications of MCT, the error is $\varepsilon \leq (1 - q)^N$, where q is the attack ratio, which is the threshold for the fraction of tasks that are expected to be failed. Note that this is exactly the threshold of the fault-tolerant algorithm executing the application. Thus, if the application can tolerate an attack ratio of up to q, then the certification detects if the application correctly executed in the presence of a massive attack (one which surpasses the fault tolerance of the application), with a possible error in that assessment of ε. This error can be selected to be as small as desired. Furthermore, the number N of invocations of the MCT necessary to guarantee ε grows only logarithmically in ε, specifically $N \geq \left\lceil \frac{\log \varepsilon}{\log(1-q)} \right\rceil$.

Applications executing only independent tasks have the nice property that the inputs of the tasks available on the checkpoint server are always the original (correct) inputs. Thus, a reexecution of independent tasks on a reliable resource will always produce the correct outputs. For workloads containing task dependencies, this is not necessarily true anymore. Now one has to deal with the issue of fault propagation. This complicates matters and one has to account for the fact that a reexecution of a task on a reliable resource using faulty input may not produce a difference in results. Thus, both results $o(T, E)$ and $\hat{o}(T, E)$ may be the same but incorrect. In Krings et al. [24, 25], extended MCTs are presented that deal with this problem. This results in a larger number of reexecutions N as now it is not the attack ratio q, but the probability of randomly selecting those tasks for reexecution that will expose faulty values. Now the ratio of so-called *effective initiators* determines the convergence of ε rather than the attack ratio q alone. The performance of certification depends on the graph structures and is shown for common graphs in the literature.

Using certification of large applications, survivability can be achieved by means of rolling back the application upon failing to certify the full or partial results. This allows the designer to derive an application that can tolerate a certain threshold of wrong results, and upon exceeding this threshold, to take recovery measures (e.g., initiate a roll back).

5.6   BORROWING FROM WELL-ESTABLISHED FIELDS

When considering the derivation of solutions to survivability problems we will subscribe to the notion of optimality. In an attempt to find solutions and increase rigor in certain critical cyber problem domains, we will investigate transformations of security and survivability problems to other well-established disciplines, utilizing their mathematical models.

Using problem transformation in order to solve hard problems is not a new strategy; it has been used extensively in mathematics and engineering. Well-known examples include exponentiation or Laplace transformation. The general strategy is to transform the original problem into a different problem space in which known solutions exist, or solutions can be found at lesser cost. After a solution has been derived in the new problem space, a reverse transformation is used to translate the solution found back to the original problem space.

The general interest in transformation is two-fold. First, we are interested in practical solutions to the original survivability problem. This includes potential algorithms and heuristics. Second, we want to use the transformation domain as a source for information that helps us understand the time and space complexity of the original problem. This will give us valuable information about computational feasibility and scalability. Furthermore, it can potentially be the basis for comparing different solutions to the original problem in the transformation domain.

5.6.1   Problem Transformation

Many survivability applications can be addressed by utilizing the five-stage transformation model introduced by Krings [41]. The basic philosophy of the model, shown in Figure 5.2, will be explained using a simple example of a networked computer system (e.g., a cluster of workstations or a grid). The transformation domain will be assumed to be that of scheduling theory. Any other suitable domain could be used as well, for example, graph theory, game theory, Markov models, Monte Carlo approaches, or economic modeling.

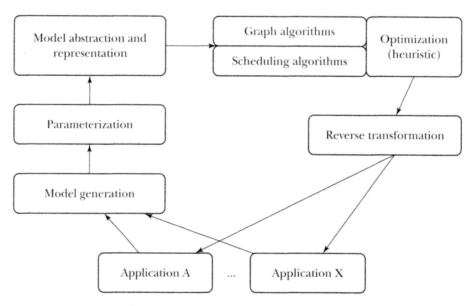

FIGURE   Transformation model.

5.2

Application

Let us assume that the application is a general networked computer system. One can envision the system as a collection of workstations connected via local area networks (LANs) and wide area networks (WANs), consisting of typical components like switches, routers, bridges, or gateways. The components themselves are connected via diverse technologies and protocols.

Model Generation

The application is transformed into a task graph together with the task model specification, if applicable. Given the infrastructure graph of the system in our example, the graph view comes natural. Thus, the general model is based on a directed graph $G = (V, E)$, where V is a finite set of vertices v_i, and E is a set of edges e_{ij}, $i \neq j$, representing precedence relations between v_i and v_j in V. In our example, vertices are the workstations and network components like routers or bridges. The edges are the interconnections.

Parameterization

Now that the application is mapped to vertices and edges of G, a mapping of application specific parameters to generic parameters is needed. Examples of parameters for vertices are computational power of workstations, and those for network components and connections are quality of service (QoS) parameters such as network throughput, propagation delay, communication cost, or priority. The vertices and/or edges of the graph need to be assigned weights representing their characteristics. The results can be generalized by integer or real valued weights. Thus, for each vertex in V and edge in E, vertex and edge weights are defined respectively. Let w_i^v denote the vertex weight of vertex v_i and w_{ij}^e denote the weight of edge e_{ij}.

Model Abstraction and Representation

The weighted graph G can now be considered in the context of a problem in the target domain (e.g., a graph or scheduling problem). For example, a graph theoretical formulation could follow directly from G together with a suitable manipulative objective (e.g., finding the least-cost path between two vertices). Similarly, a scheduling theoretical formulation would imply the specification of a suitable scheduling model S, specifying the task and processing environment as well as the optimization criteria.

Algorithmic Solutions

Assume that we consider a transformation to scheduling theoretical formulations. The scheduling model S is now subjected to scheduling algorithms. The goal is to find optimal or suboptimal solutions for the specific survivability criteria, applying the best suitable algorithm(s). A wealth of algorithms and heuristics of varying space and time complexity exist. Appropriate algorithms need to be identified that suit the optimization criteria. In addition, useful information about the time or space complexity may be inherited from the algorithms. This may provide valuable information about the solution space. After the application of the scheduling algorithms or heuristics, optimal or suboptimal solutions will be available. It should be pointed out that the focus of this discussion is not on scheduling algorithms, but on the identification of an appropriate scheduling model. Once the model is specified, a literature review for potential algorithms is required. However, given the semi-standardized formulations of scheduling models, this process can be very efficient. Of course, one can hand the problem over to experts in the transformation field. But, given the elegance of the formulations of scheduling problems, which are outlined below, one does not necessarily have to be a scheduling theorist to find the problems in the literature.

Reverse Transformation

The solutions of the graph or scheduling algorithms must now be translated back to the application. This requires a reverse transformation analogous to the transformation used in the model generation section above. This step represents the transformation from the solution space back to the application space.

Before giving some examples of how the transformation model can be used to solve security or survivability problems, some basic explanations of our transformation domain, in this case scheduling theory, are needed.

5.6.2   Scheduling Problems

The key to the model transformation is to understand how to derive an appropriate transformation. Our target domain is scheduling (i.e., a scheduling model S) and its interpretation in the context of the specific survivability application. This burden cannot be taken over by a scheduling expert, unless he or she has insight into security or survivability research. In order to avoid lengthy descriptions of scheduling models S, a compact classification description of the form $S = (\alpha|\beta|\gamma)$ is widely used in the literature [42–44]. The fields α, β, and γ indicate the processor environment, the task and resource characteristics, and the optimization criteria, respectively. Each field will be briefly introduced next, together with some standard notation indicated in parenthesis.

The first field of S (i.e., α) specifies the assumptions placed on the processor environment. There are many different attributes associated with processors. For example, processors may be identical, uniform, unrelated, or dedicated. Identical processors (P) refer to a homogeneous processor environment. Uniform processors (Q) assume different speeds b_i for each processor. In scheduling, uniformity implies that processor speeds differ but the processor's speed is constant over time (i.e., it does not depend on the task it executes). If the speed is dependent on the task performed, processors are called unrelated. In the transformation model, unrelated processors, denoted by (R), can be a convenient model to describe computers subjected to denial of service (DoS) attacks, which may be distributed denial of service (DDoS). Lastly, some problems require dedicated processors that are assumed to be specialized for the execution of certain tasks. Other applications execute tasks in stages at different processors or clusters. In scheduling theory, such problems are described in open shop, flow shop, and job shop systems.

The second field of S (i.e., β) specifies the task and resource characteristics. Tasks may be nonpreemptive (Φ) or preemptive (*pmtn*). Once a nonpreemptive task is started, its execution can *not* be interrupted. If preemption is allowed, task execution can be interrupted. If the tasks are subjected to precedence constraints, the specific constraints are indicated, for example, (Φ) indicates independent tasks and (*chain*) indicates task chains.

The last field of S (i.e., γ) indicates the optimization criteria. Optimization is often defined based on task completion times, flow times, lateness, tardiness, or earliness. The completion time C_j of the last task T_j of the schedule is called the *makespan*. Thus, the *makespan* indicates the overall length of the schedule. *Makespan* optimization is denoted by (C_{max}). Another interesting criterion is the flow time F_j, which is the sum of the waiting time and processing time of a task, and optimization of average flow time or weighted flow time is denoted by (ΣF_j) and ($\Sigma w_j F_j$), respectively. Other optimization criteria include minimization of lateness $L_j = C_j - d_j$ (i.e., the completion time minus the task's deadline); tardiness $D_j = \max\{C_j - d_j, 0\}$, which considers only the contribution of late tasks; or earliness $E_j = \max\{d_j - C_j, 0\}$.

Many security or survivability problems can be mapped to scheduling problems. One key observation is that security personnel or mechanisms can be viewed as the processor environment. There are many ways to map the security problem examples described below to a scheduling problem $S = (\alpha|\beta|\gamma)$. The formulations shown are only examples. Especially in the task and resource characteristics (i.e., β), many interpretations and formulations are possible. This vagueness should be seen as a strength, not a weakness, as it introduces flexibility in generating a solution space.

1. Response management: $P||C_{max}$: Each of the P identical processors represents a security specialist.

2. Response management: $P|r_j|C_{max}$ or $P|r_j,d_j|\Sigma w_j D_j$: These are variations of the previous case, where release times r_j, due dates d_j, and tardiness D_j are considered. Schedule the security tasks as they arrive (perhaps with dynamic arrival times) under considerations of deadlines.

3. Response management: $Q|r_j|C_{max}$ or $Q|r_j,d_j|\Sigma w_j D_j$: In this variant, the realistic assumption is taken that the security personnel have different levels of expertise (e.g., junior versus senior security officer). Thus, uniform processors Q represent personnel.

4. Response management: $J||C_{max}$: If the assumption is that different personnel have different qualifications (e.g., specialization with respect to specific operating systems), then processors might be considered to be *dedicated*. In this case, the problem might be treated as a job shop (J).

5. Response management: $Pm|r_j|C_{max}$ or $Pm|r_j,d_j|\Sigma w_j D_j$: Given a specific task to be performed in a time-critical application, determine the suitable number m of specialists needed for a given objective.

6. Response management: $P|pmtn|C_{max}$ or $P|pmtn, r_j, d_j|\Sigma w_j D_j$: Preemptive scheduling (*pmtn*) considers context switching time and the number of preemptions. This could include minimizing the number of preemptions. Members of technical support staff of most customer response centers subject their technicians to multiple cases at a time.

7. Physical security: $P|prec, group, |r_j, d_j||\Sigma w_j D_j$ or $P|chain, group, r_j, d_j||\Sigma w_j D_j$: A facility is monitored by security cameras and observation personnel. Different locations to be observed are represented by task groups G_i, where G_i consists of n_i tasks, $T_{i1}, T_{i2}, \ldots, T_{in_i}$. Each task T_{ij} represents an observation window of processing length p_{ij}. The processors are the observation monitor(s) or observation person(s). Groups are to be scheduled with deadlines less than the times required by a skilled adversary to infiltrate the facility. Solutions would be based on group scheduling or scheduling with *strong precedence* under consideration of precedence (prec).

8. Physical security: $F||C_{max}$ or $J|d_j|\Sigma w_j D_j$: The previous physical security application can also be formulated as a flow-shop problem, capturing the requirement that T_{ij-1} needs to be executed before T_{ij}, or as a job-shop problem.

9. Agent security: $1|r_j|C_{max}$ or $Pm|d_j|\Sigma w_j D_j$: In systems facilitating migratory autonomous agents to perform security-related operations (e.g., version tracking, diagnostics), the agent might have a set of critical tasks to perform on specific systems [45]. In the case of DDoS attacks, timing might be crucial when implementing survivability measures using the agent, as the defensive measures race in time against the increasing affects of the DDoS attack. The agent is represented by a processor, and the systems to be traversed are the tasks.

10. Agent security: $R|r_j|C_{max}$ or $Rm|d_j|\Sigma w_j D_j$: The previous case can be viewed with respect to the affects of the DDoS attack. In this case, it might be valid to consider unrelated processors. Recall that the speed of an unrelated processor depends on the particular task processed.

11. Agent security: $1|r_j, p_j|C_{max}$ or $Pm|d_j|\Sigma w_j D_j$: Similarly, if agents are used for patch management, installing patches has to be coordinated with the usage of the system in order to avoid conflicts with the tasks executing on the system. This is very obvious in operating systems that require applications to be terminated before installing the patches or rebooting after installation.

12. Intrusion detection systems: $P|r_j, p_j|C_{max}$ or $Pm|p_j, d_j|\Sigma w_j D_j$: Many intrusion detection systems (IDSs) rely on centralized computers to collect data

from log files and audit traces of different clients in order to check for coordinated attacks. The individual log files can be large in size and need to be downloaded in LANs or WANs.

13. Attack recognition systems: $1|p_j, \tau|C_{\max}$: Certain low-level attack recognition systems [45] need to be scheduled with end-to-end and real-time requirements, guaranteeing that they are instantiated at regular intervals τ. The periodic tasks are (1) sensor data collection and (2) attack signature evaluation.

5.6.3   Case Study: Autonomous Mobile Agents

When an application executes code that it receives from the outside, then the obvious question is how does one know that the code has not been corrupted or is hostile? For example, executing an executable file attached to an email is like taking a leap of faith, as it constitutes a significant risk (e.g., a virus may be part of the code). We will use migratory mobile agents as an example of traversing code that may be subject to attacks or may attack itself. There are no points made about pros or cons of agent-based systems, but every security researcher will agree that this paradigm, by its very nature, constitutes real security challenges.

In order to address security concerns and system survivability, let us suggest that the agent systems use redundancy with a specific focus on secret sharing [32, 46] rather then pure spatial or information redundancy [47–50]. In secret sharing, the information is divided into k shares and one has to have all shares to use the information. If each agent carries a single share, secret sharing using k shares can be extended to achieve survivability by adopting an m-of-k scheme, in which the information of m out of k uncorrupted agents is needed to perform an action [46]. We now apply the transformation process described above.

Assume we want to investigate the feasibility or wisdom of using a multi-agent system to implement critical functionalities on a set of networked computer systems. The relative importance of each computer of the system is prioritized (e.g., indicated by an indexed priority scheme). Next, assume that a secret sharing scheme is implemented requiring k_i shares for a specific processing element (i.e., the computer PE_i). Thus, all k_i agents must be present at computer PE_i to perform their specific function. Given this secret sharing agent scheme, it is important to find efficient agent traversal paths, for example, paths that maximize the efficiency of agents assembling at computers to perform the intended task, such as response to malicious acts. In other words, how does one direct the individual agents, carrying their shares, to congregate at different computers efficiently?

The application is translated into a task graph $G = (V, E)$ consisting of K job chains C_k each representing a group of computers. Each computer to be traversed by the agents is shown as a vertex (i.e., job $J_{k,i} \in C_k$, for $1 \leq k \leq K$). The position of $J_{k,i}$ in C_k (i.e., the chain position) indicates the relative computer priority.

The parameters reflecting the functionality executed by the agents during job $J_{k,i}$ need to be specified. The job priorities are implicitly defined by the position of $J_{k,i}$ in chain C_k, and the processing and release times of $J_{k,i}$ are determined by $p_{k,i}$ and $r_{k,i}$, respectively. Potential cost or liabilities due to malicious acts can be modeled by weight $w_{k,i}$.

Suitable scheduling models for this description can be found in Dror et al. [51], where "Strong"—"Weak" chain constrained scheduling is discussed. The specific model considered is:

$$Pm|fix_j, chain, p_j = 1|C_{max}$$

where m is the number of machines (represented by agents) in the system. The number of machines necessary to process a job is indicated by fix_j and $chain$ indicating chain precedence. It should be noted that fix_j indicates the degree of secret sharing. To show how this model suits the application an example from Dror et al. [51] is given. Let J denote a partition of all jobs $J_{k,j}$. Furthermore, let J^{expr} denote the set of jobs that require all machines with indices indicated in $expr$ for execution. Now jobs can be partitioned by their resource requirements. If one assumes $m = 3$, then jobs can be partitioned as:

$$J = \{J^{123}, J^{12}, J^{13}, J^{23}, J^1, J^2, J^3\}. \tag{5.1}$$

The superscripts indicate the machines required, for example, J^{123} comprises all jobs that need machines $M1$, $M2$, and $M3$ to execute, whereas jobs in J^{12} only require $M1$ and $M2$. The number of indices listed in the superscripts indicates the degree of secret sharing required by each of the jobs of the associated set. For example, each job in J^{123} requires that in the application domain three agents be present before their respective functionality can be executed. Similarly, each job in J^{12}, J^{13}, and J^{23} requires two agents; however, each set has its specific set of associated agents. The problem

$$P3|fix_j, chain, p_j = 1|C_{max}$$

captures the notion of scheduling the tasks in J.

It is shown in Dror et al. [51] that the problem $Pm|fix_j, weakchain, p_j = 1|C_{max}$ can be solved in $O(n)$ time if all jobs of chain k belong to the same partition in Eq. 5.1. The last constraint is called *agreeable machine configuration*. The *weak chain* constrained implies that scheduling two jobs of a chain, under consideration of the chain precedence constraint, may be interleaved with other jobs. This interleaving is not allowed in *strong chain* constrained scheduling. The problem $Pm|fix_j, strong$ *chain*, $p_j = 1|C_{max}$, for $m > 1$ has been shown to be NP-hard in the strong sense [46]. Similarly, problem $P3|fix_j, strongchain, p_j = 1|C_{max}$ with agreeable machine configuration is NP-hard in the strong sense [52, 53].

The reverse transformation is quite trivial. A valid schedule produced by any scheduling algorithm directly reflects the agent traversal path.

In conclusion to this example, we want to point out that the point made in this discussion on problem transformation is not to insist on using a specific approach to solve a problem, but to identify a methodology that allows us to analyze and perhaps derive direct solutions from other fields, thereby taking advantage of all benefits inherited by using their mathematical models. This may allow us to analyze the space and time complexity, shedding light on scalability and even feasibility. The previous example is not trivial, but neither is the survivability application. Understanding the scheduling model exposes the inherited limitations or expense of using secret sharing in such an application. However, given the application domain (i.e., migratory agents), the security challenges may leave little choice if one wants to guarantee survivability.

5.7   CONLUSION

This chapter considered the interdependencies of fault models and survivability approaches. It was shown that fault models have to be considered in any survivability approach since recovery depends on the types of faults assumed. The design for the survivability paradigm gives some useful suggestions for possible approaches and limitations or trade-off spaces. One of the great challenges of any approach is that of overcoming the problem of single points of failure, which leads us to take a closer look at the issues associated with decentralization. Whereas intentional decentralization was argued to potentially improve survivability, it has its own problems, especially if the application is largely decentralized to begin with. Finally, a model was presented that may allow technology transfer from other well-established fields. Besides opening up survivability applications to possible solutions adapted from those fields, it may serve as a platform for complexity analysis and comparison.

References

[1] Y. Liu and K.S. Trivedi, "Survivability Quantification: The Analytical Modeling Approach," *International Journal of Performability Engineering* 2, No. 1 (Jan. 2006): 29–44.

[2] R. J. Ellison, D. A. Fisher, R. C. Linger, H. F. Lipson, T. Longstaff, and N. R. Mead, "Survivable Network Systems: An Emerging Discipline," *Technical Report CMU/SEI-97-TR-013*, Nov. 1997, Revised May 1999.

[3] N. R. Mead, R. J. Ellison, R. C. Linger, T. Longstaff, and J. McHugh, "Survivable Network Analysis Method," *Technical Report CMU/SEI-2000-TR-013*, Software Engineering Institute, Carnegie Mellon University, Pittsburgh, PA, 2000.

[4] P. G. Neumann, "Practical Architectures for Survivable Systems and Networks (Phase-Two Final Report)," SRI International, June 2000, at http://www.csl.sri.com/users/neumann/arl-one.html.

[5] M. S. Deutsch and R. R. Willis *Software Quality Engineering: A Total Technical and Management Approach* (Englewood Cliffs, NJ: Prentice Hall, 1988).

[6] J. C. Knight, E. A. Strunk, and K. J. Sullivan, "Towards a Rigorous Definition of Information System Survivability," *DISCEX 2003*, Washington, DC, April 2003, pp. 78–89.

[7] J. C. Knight and K. J. Sullivan, "On the Definition of Survivability," *Technical Report CS-TR-33-00*, Dept. of Computer Science, University of Virginia, Charlottesville, 2000.

[8] J. C. Laprie (Ed.), *Dependability: Basic Concepts and Terminology* (New York: Springer-Verlag, 1992).

[9] A. Avizienis, J. Laprie, and B. Randell, "Fundamental Concepts of Dependability," *Information Survivability Workshop (ISW2000)*, Boston, Oct. 24–26, 2000.

[10] F. B. Schneider, "Byzantine Generals in Action: Implementing Fail-Stop Processors," *ACM Transactions on Computer Systems* 2, No. 2 (May 1984): 145–154.

[11] L. Lamport, M. Pease, R. Shostak, "The Byzantine Generals Problem," *ACM Transactions on Programming Languages and Systems* 4, No. 3 (July 1982): 382–401.

[12] M. H. Azadmanesh and R.M. Kieckhafer, "Exploiting Omissive Faults in Synchronous Approximate Agreement," *IEEE Trans. Computers* 49, No. 10 (Oct. 2000): 1031–1042.

[13] P. Thambidurai and Y.-K. Park, "Interactive Consistency with Multiple Failure Modes," *Proceedings of the 7th Symposium on Reliable Distributed Systems*, Columbus, OH, Oct. 1988, pp. 93–100.

[14] F. J. Meyer and D. K. Pradhan, "Consensus with Dual Failure Modes," *IEEE Transactions on Parallel and Distributed Systems* 2, No. 2 (April 1991): 214–222.

[15] B. W. Johnson, *Design and Analysis of Fault-Tolerant Systems* (Reading, MA: Addison Wesley, 1989).

[16] V. D. Agraval and S. C. Seth (Eds.), *Tutorial: Test Generation for VLSI Chips* (IEEE Computer Society Press, Los Alamitos, CA, Sept. 1988).

[17] H. Fujiwara, *Logic Testing and Design for Testability* (Boston: MIT Press, 1985).

[18] K.-T. Cheng and V. D. Agrawal, *Unified Methods for VLSI Simulation and Test Generation* (Kluwer Academic Publishers, Norwell, MA, 1989).

[19] K. Imamura, J. Foster, and A. Krings, "The Test Vector Problem and Limitations to Evolving Digital Circuits," *Proceedings of the 2nd NASA/DoD Workshop on Evolvable Hardware*, (IEEE Press, Palo Alto, CA, July 13–15, 2000, pp. 75–80).

[20] Y. C. Yeh, "Triple-Triple Redundant 777 Primary Flight Computer," *1996 IEEE Aerospace Applications Conference*, Aspen, CO, 3–10 Feb. 1996, pp. 293–307.

[21] O. Babaoglu and R. Drummond, "Streets of Byzantium: Network Architectures for Fast Reliable Broadcasts," *IEEE Transactions on Software Engineering* SE-11, No. 6 (June 1985): 546–554.

[22] A. Krings and Z. Ma, "Fault-Models in Wireless Communication: Towards Survivable Ad Hoc Networks," *MILCOM 2006, Military Communications Conference*, Washington, D.C., Oct. 23–25, 2006.

[23] C. Germain and N. Playez, "Result Checking in Global Computing Systems," *Proceedings of the 17th Annual ACM International Conference on Supercomputing (ICS 03)*, San Francisco, CA, June 23–26, 2003.

[24] A. Krings, J.-L. Roch, and S. Jafar, "Certification of Large Distributed Computations with Task Dependencies in Hostile Environments," *IEEE Electro/Information Technology Conference, (EIT 2005)*, Lincoln, NE, May 22–25, 2005.

[25] A. Krings, J.-L. Roch, S. Jafar, and S. Varrette, "A Probabilistic Approach for Task and Result Certification of Large-Scale Distributed Applications in Hostile Environments," *Proceedings of the European Grid Conference (EGC2005)*, in LNCS 3470 (Amsterdam: Springer Verlag, Feb. 14–16, 2005).

[26] R. Maxion, "CMU," Keynote Speech of the Information Survivability Workshop, International Conference on Dependable Systems and Networks, DSN-2001, Goteborg, Sweden, 2001.

[27] J. Allen, A. Christie, W. Fithen, J. McHugh, J. Pickel and E. Stoner, "State of the Practice of Intrusion Detection Technologies," *Technical Report, CMU/SEI-99-TR-028, ESC-99-028*, Jan. 2000.

[28] A. Krings and M. McQueen, "A Byzantine Resilient Approach to Network Security," *Proceedings of the 29th International Symposium on Fault-Tolerant*

Computing, Digest of FastAbstracts: FTCS-29, Madison, WI, June 15–18, 1999, pp. 13–14.

[29] A. Avizienis, "The N-Version Approach to Fault-Tolerant Software," *IEEE Transactions of Software Engineering* SE-11, No. 12 (Dec. 1985): 1491–1501.

[30] M. R. Lyu (Ed.), *Software Fault Tolerance* (Chichester, England: John Wiley and Sons, Inc., 1995).

[31] J. C. Knight and N. G. Leveson, "An Experimental Evaluation of the Assumption of Independence in Multi-version Programming," *IEEE Transactions on Software Engineering* SE-12, No. 1 (Jan. 1986): 96–109.

[32] J. J. Wylie, M. Bakkaloglu, V. Pandurangan, M. W. Bigrigg, S. Oguz, K. Tew, C. Williams, G. R. Ganger and P. K. Khosla, "Selecting the Right Data Distribution Scheme for a Survivable Storage System," *Technical Report, CMU-CS-01-120*, Carnegie Mellon University, Pittsburgh, PA, May 2001.

[33] E. N. (Mootaz) Elnozahy, L. Alvisi, Y.-M. Wang and D. B. Johnson, "A Survey of Rollback-Recovery Protocols in Message-Passing Systems," *ACM Computing Survey* 34, No. 3 (2002): 375–408.

[34] S. Jafar, A. Krings, T. Gautier, and J.-L. Roch, "Theft-Induced Checkpointing for Reconfigurable Dataflow Applications," *IEEE Electro/Information Technology Conference (EIT 2005)*, Lincoln, NE, May 22–25, 2005.

[35] G. Stellner, "CoCheck: Checkpointing and Process Migration for MPI," *Proceedings of the 10th International Parallel Processing Symposium (IPPS'96)*, 15–19 April, Honolulu, HI, April 15–19,. 1996, pp. 526–531.

[36] A. Bouteiller, P. Lemarinier, K. Krawezik, and F. Capello, "Coordinated Checkpoint versus Message Log for Fault Tolerant MPI," *Proceedings of the 2003 IEEE International Conference on Cluster Computing*, Honk Hong, 2003, p. 242.

[37] M. Litzkow, T. Tannenbaum, J. Basney, and M. Livny, "Checkpoint and Migration of UNIX Processes in the Condor Distributed Processing System," *Tech. Report CS-TR-97-1346*, University of Wisconsin, Madison, 1997.

[38] L. Gao and G. Malewicz, "Internet Computing of Tasks with Dependencies Using Unreliable Workers," *8th International Conference on Principles of Distributed Systems (OPODIS'04)*, in LNCS 2004 (Amsterdam: Springer Verlag, Dec. 15–17, 2004).

[39] L. F. G. Sarmenta, "Sabotage-Tolerance Mechanisms for Volunteer Computing Systems," *Future Generation Computer Systems* 4, No. 18 (2002).

[40] V. Strumpen, "Portable and Fault-Tolerant Software Systems," *IEEE Micro* 18, No. 5 (Sept. 1998): 22–32.

[41] A. Krings, "Agent Survivability: An Application for Strong and Weak Chain Constrained Scheduling," *37th Hawaii International Conference on System Sciences, (HICSS-37)*, Minitrack on Security and Survivability in Mobile Agent Based Distributed Systems, paper STSSM01, Jan. 2004.

[42] J. Blazewicz, K. H. Ecker, E. Pesch, G. Schmidt, and J. Weglarz, *Scheduling Computer and Manufacturing Processes* (Berlin; New York: Springer-Verlag, 1996).

[43] P. Brucker, *Scheduling Algorithms*, 4th ed. (Berlin; New York: Springer-Verlag, 2004).

[44] E. L. Lawler, J. K. Lenstra, A. H. G. Rinnooy Kan, and D. B. Shmoys, *Sequencing and Scheduling: Algorithms and complexity*, Vol. 4 of Handbook in Operations Research and Management Science (Amsterdam: North-Holland, 1993).

[45] A. Krings, W. S. Harrison, N. Hanebutte, C. Taylor, and M. McQueen, "A Two-Layer Approach to Survivability of Networked Computing Systems," *Proceedings of the International Conference on Advances in Infrastructure for Electronic Business, Science, and Education on the Internet*, L'Aquila, Italy, Aug. 6–12, 2001, pp. 1–12.

[46] F. B. Schneider, "Towards Fault-Tolerant and Secure Agentry," *Proceedings of the 11th International Workshop on Distributed Algorithms*, Saarbrücken, Germany, Sept. 1997.

[47] D. Johansen, R. van Renesse and F. B. Schneider, "Operating System Support for Mobile Agents," *Proceedings of the 5th IEEE Workshop on Hot Topics in Operating Systems*, Washington, DC, May 4–5, 1995, pp. 42–45.

[48] D. Johansen, K. Marzullo, F. B. Schneider, K. Jacobsen, and D. Zagorodnov, "NAP: Practical Fault-Tolerance for Itinerant Computations," *Technical Report TR98-1716*, Department of Computer Science, Cornell University, Ithaca, NY, Nov. 1998.

[49] K. Rothermel and M. Strasser, "A Fault-Tolerant Protocol for Providing the Exactly-Once Property of Mobile Agents," *Proceedings of the IEEE Symposium on Reliable Distributed Systems (SRDS'98)*, West Lafayette, Indiana, Oct. 1998, pp. 100–108.

[50] F.M.A. Silva, "A Transaction Model Based on Mobile Agents," Ph.D. Thesis, Technical University, Berlin, Germany, 1999.

[51] M. Dror, W. Kubiak, and P. Dell'Olmo, "'Strong'–'Weak' Chain Constrained Scheduling," *Ricerca Operativa* 27 (1998): 35–49.

[52] J. Blazewicz, P. W. Dell'Olmo, M. Drozdowski, and M. G. Speranza, "Scheduling Multiprocessor Tasks on Three Dedicated Processors: Corrigendum," *Information Processing Letters* 49 (1994): 269–270.

[53] J. Blazewicz, P. W. Dell'Olmo, M. Drozdowski, and M. G. Speranza, "Scheduling Multiprocessor Tasks on Three Dedicated Processors," *Information Processing Letters* 41 (1992): 275–280.

PART II

MODELING THE INTERACTION BETWEEN DEPENDABILITY AND SECURITY

CHAPTER   6   Taxonomy and Framework for Integrating Dependability and Security
(Jianku Hu, Peter Bertok, Zahir Tari, RMIT University, Australia)

CHAPTER   7   Stochastic Modeling Techniques for Secure and Survivable Systems
(Kishor Trivedi, Duke University, USA, and Vaneeta Jindal and S. Dharmaraja,
Indian Institute of Technology, India)

CHAPTER   8   Integrated Dependability and Security Evaluation Using Game Theory and
Markov Models
(Bjarne E. Helvik, Karin Sallhammar, and Svein J. Knapskog,
University of Science and Technology, Norway)

CHAPTER   9   Scenario Graphs Applied to Network Security
(Jeannette M. Wing, Carnegie Mellon University, USA)

CHAPTER   10   Vulnerability-Centric Alert Correlation
(Lingyu Wang, Concordia University, Canada, and Sushil Jajodia,
George Mason University, USA)

6 CHAPTER

Taxonomy and Framework for Integrating Dependability and Security[1]

Jiankun Hu   RMIT University, Australia
Peter Bertok   RMIT University, Australia
Zahir Tari   RMIT University, Australia

6.1   INTRODUCTION

With rapidly developed network technologies and computing technologies, network-centric computing has become the core information platform in our private, social, and professional lives. This information platform is dependent on a computing and network infrastructure, which is increasingly homogeneous and open. The backbone of this infrastructure is the Internet, which is inherently insecure and unreliable. With an ever-accelerating trend of integrating mobile and wireless network infrastructure, things become worse. This is because wireless radio links tend to have much higher bit error rates, and mobility also increases the difficulty of service quality management and security control. The increased complexity of the platform and its easy access has made it more vulnerable to failures and attacks, which in turn has become a major concern for society. Traditionally there are two different communities separately working on the issues of dependability and security. One is the community of dependability that is more concerned with nonmalicious faults [1–4], to name one of just a few.

---

[1] This work is supported by ARC Linkage Projects LP0455324, LP0455234 and LP0667600. For further information, please email the authors at: { jiankun, pbertok, zahirt}@cs.rmit.edu.au.

The other is the security community that is more concerned with malicious attacks or faults [5, 6].

Dependability is first introduced as a general concept covering the attributes of reliability, availability, safety, integrity, maintainability, and so on. With ever-increasing malicious catastrophic Internet attacks, Internet providers have realized a need to incorporate security issues. Effort has been made to provide basic concepts and taxonomy to reflect this convergence [7–9]. The original integration effort was to form a joint committee on "Fundamental Concepts and Terminology" by the Technical Committee (TC) on Fault-Tolerant Computing of the IEEE CS, and the IFIP WG 10.4, "Dependable Computing and Fault Tolerance" [7, 10]. Security has been added as an attribute of the class of intentional malicious faults in the taxonomy of faults [10]. Avizienis et al. [7] has provided a very comprehensive set of basic concepts and taxonomy of dependable and secure computing. Jonsson [9] has proposed a system model that views environmental influence as the system input, and system behavior as the system output.

Measures for security and dependability have also been discussed. Based on the work by Avizienis et al. [7] and Jonsson [9], we propose a framework that can generically integrate dependability and security. This chapter does not intend to cover every detail of dependability and security. It places major relevant concepts and attributes in a unified feedback control system framework and illustrates the interaction via well-established control system domain knowledge. Furthermore, the framework has included discussions on lower-level security techniques, such as techniques for confidentiality, authenticity, and so on, which have not been addressed in depth in prior work [7, 9]. In this chapter, Section 6.2 provides basic concepts and related work, proposed framework is given in Section 6.3, taxonomy and illustration of the major concepts and attributes under the proposed framework are provided in Section 6.4, and Section 6.5 provides a discussion on the means to attain dependability and security.

6.2   BASIC CONCEPTS AND RELATED WORK

In this section, we present basic concepts relevant to the discussion of dependable and secure computing. We also present relevant work in this field.

6.2.1   Dependability

Traditionally, dependability is defined as the user's justifiably trustworthiness on the ability of a system delivering the service to the users [7, 11, 12]. An alternate definition of the dependability of a system is a system's ability to avoid service failures that are more frequent and more severe than is acceptable [7]. Although there exist many different ways describing dependability, a consensus view is to describe dependability via threats, attributes, and means. A typical top-level ontology of the dependability is shown in Figure 6.1 [12].

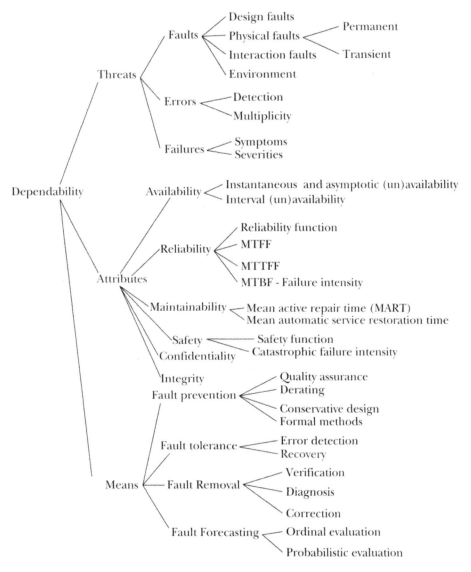

FIGURE

6.1

Dependability ontology based on concepts and terms from IFIP WG 10.4. From Helvik [12].

Under this ontology, faults, errors, and failures are causes of producing threats to dependability that may arise from physical imperfections in a system, external disturbance, mistakes made during specifications, designs, development, operational activities, and so on. Threats can also be intentional and hostile. Means are mechanisms to avoid and reduce threats plus recovery from the consequence of threats. Attributes refer to characteristics with respect to dependability, which include [12]:

1. *Availability:* Readiness to provide a set of services at a given time.

2. *Reliability:* Ability to provide uninterrupted service.

3. *Safety:* Ability to provide services without the occurrence of catastrophic failures.

4. *Maintainability:* Ability of a system to support fault removal and service restoration and undergo change.

5. *Confidentiality:* Ability to prevent unauthorized access to and/or handling of information.

6. *Integrity:* The absence of improper alterations of information.

This framework has made a major step in classifying dependability issues and also made an attempt of integration of security and dependability. However, security issues are still treated as a rather standalone component and have not been adequately addressed.

6.2.2   Integration of Dependability and Security

In order to integrate dependability and security, one needs to understand essential security issues. Security is a very broad issue even under the context of a networked environment, which is the focus in this chapter. Normally, security has been described via attributes of confidentiality, integrity, and availability [7]. Confidentiality refers to the absence of unauthorized disclosure of information. Integrity refers to the absence of unauthorized alteration of systems or information. Availability refers to readiness for service. Security issues involve many concepts and technologies including cryptography, networking, and intrusion detection. For more background on security techniques, interested readers are referred to Chapter 2 of this book and Stallings [13]. This chapter focuses more on the framework that integrates dependability and security.

Due to the enormous complexity and vast broad areas of dependability and security as well as the rapidly evolving technologies, integrating dependability and security is a challenging and ongoing effort. Avizienis et al. [7] and Jonsson [9] have proposed a system view to integrate dependability and security that uses system function and behavior to form a framework. A schema of the taxonomy of dependable and secure computing is proposed, as shown in Figure 6.2 [7].

Although this taxonomy and framework are discussed under the context of a system interacting with its environment, there seems to be a lack of a cohesive and generic integration. Jonsson [9] has made an attempt to provide a more generic integration framework by using an input-output system model. In this scheme, faults are introduced as inputs to a system and delivery of service and denial of service are considered as system outputs. However, it is still difficult to illustrate the interactions among many other components. Overall, both system models proposed by Avizienis et al. [7] and Jonsson [9] are open-loop systems that are unable to provide a comprehensive description of the interaction relationship. For instance, there is no mechanism showing the relationship between fault detection and fault elimination in a system. In Section 6.3, we propose a new framework to address these issues.

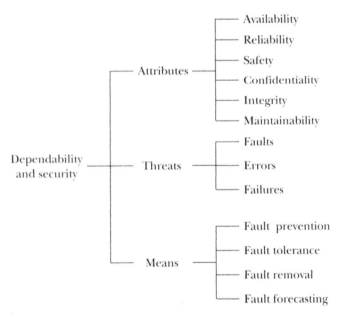

FIGURE   The dependability and security tree. From Avizienis et al. [7].

6.2

6.3   PROPOSED TAXONOMY AND FRAMEWORK

In this section, we propose a feedback control system (Figure 6.3) as a framework that can generically integrate dependability and security. Key notations and concepts for the illustration of this framework are also provided.

6.3.1   Key Notations of the Feedback Control System Model

The following are conventional notations of feedback control systems. They are tailored whenever needed for our framework.

Control system: A system that is under control, normally under regulators' control, to achieve the desired objectives.

Desired trajectory: Desired objectives normally specified by the user.

Disturbance: Anything that tends to push system behavior off the track is considered a disturbance. A disturbance can occur within a system or from the external environment.

Feedback: Use of the information observed from a system's behavior to readjust/regulate the corrective action/control so that the system can achieve the desired objectives.

Feedback control system: A control system that deploys a feedback mechanism. This is also called a closed-loop control system.

Filter: A mechanism retrieving a system's state to deliver output perceived by the user.

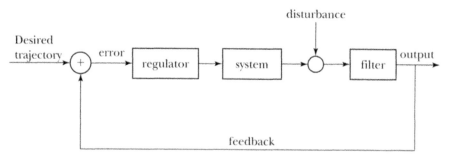

FIGURE   Feedback control system.

6.3

Open-loop control system: A control system without a feedback mechanism.

Regulator: A mechanism that can combine the input/users' instructions and feedback information to take corrective control actions to make a system's behavior achieve its desired objectives.

System: A composite constructed from functional components. The interaction of these components may exhibit new features/functions that none of the composite components possess individually.

System output: System behavior perceived by the user.

6.3.2   Definitions of Basic Concepts of Dependability and Security within the Proposed Framework

Correct service: Delivered system behavior is within the error tolerance boundary.

Desired service: Delivered system behavior is at or close to the desired trajectory.

Error: Deviation of system behavior/output from the desired trajectory.

Error tolerance boundary: A range within which the error is considered acceptable by a system or user. This boundary is normally specified by the user.

Fault: Normally the hypothesized cause of an error is called fault [7]. It can be internal or external to a system. An error is defined as the part of the total state of a system that may lead to subsequent service failure. Observing that many errors do not reach a system's external state and cause a failure, Avizienis et al. [7] have defined active faults that lead to error and dormant faults that are not manifested externally.

Service failure or failure: An event that occurs when system output deviates from the desired service and is beyond the error tolerance boundary.

6.4   DEPENDABILITY, SECURITY, AND THEIR ATTRIBUTES

The original definition of dependability refers to the ability to deliver a service that can be justifiably trusted. The alternative definition is the ability to avoid service failures that are more frequent and severe than is acceptable. The concept of trust can be defined as accepted dependence, and dependability encompasses the following attributes [7]:

+ *Availability:* Readiness for correct service. The correct service is defined as what is delivered when the service implements a system function.

+ *Reliability:* Continuity of correct service.

+ *Safety:* Absence of catastrophic consequences on the users and environment.

+ *Integrity:* Absence of improper system alterations.

+ *Maintainability:* Ability to undergo modifications and repairs.

Security has attributes of confidentiality, integrity, and availability. In this chapter, it is assumed that a system does have concern about the security and has reasonable security mechanisms in place. Confidentiality, however, is absent from the above interpretation of dependability. Interestingly, other attributes, such as authenticity and nonrepudiation, are not considered in the previous work. Avizienis et al. [7] merged the attributes of dependability and security together, as shown in Figure 6.2. Similarly, the above attributes can be reframed as follows under the proposed framework that is shown in Figure 6.3:

+ *Availability:* Readiness for correct service. The correct service is defined as delivered system behavior that is within the error tolerance boundary.

+ *Reliability:* Continuity of correct service. This is the same as the conventional definition.

+ *Safety:* Absence of catastrophic consequences on the users and the environment. This is the same as the conventional definition.

+ *Integrity:* Absence of malicious external disturbance that makes a system output off its desired service.

+ *Maintainability:* Ability to undergo modifications and repairs. This is the same as the conventional definition.

+ *Confidentiality:* Property that data or information are not made available to unauthorized persons or processes. In the proposed framework, it refers to the property that unauthorized persons or processes will not get system output or be blocked by the filter.

+ *Authenticity:* Ability to provide services with provable origin. In other words, the output can be verifiably linked to a system.

+ *Nonrepudiation:* Services provided cannot be disclaimed later. In our model, once the system provided an output, there is no way to deny it.

Note that authenticity and nonrepudiation have not been addressed before in the security and dependability framework [7, 11, 12]. These two attributes do not fit into conventional attributes of availability, confidentiality, and integrity (ACI) of security. It seems difficult to include authenticity as a part of ACI. However, we observe that the authenticity issue connects to any of the availability, confidentiality, and integrity problems. Hence, it is more appropriate to express authenticity as an intermediate event toward security faults and also a means to achieving security and dependability. Similarly, it is difficult to include the nonrepudiation as part of ACI. However, unlike the authenticity issue, nonrepudiation problems do not necessarily lead to any of problems of availability, confidentiality, and integrity. Therefore, it seems appropriate to classify nonrepudiation as an independent attribute. An expanded security and dependability tree is given in Figure 6.4.

6.4.1   Taxonomy of Faults

In the conventional framework, a fault is defined as a cause of an error. Under the proposed approach, a failure is linked to the error that is outside of the

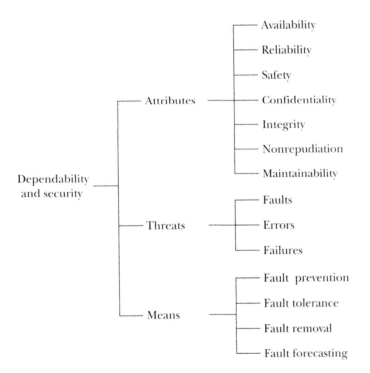

FIGURE   Expanded dependability and security tree.

6.4

error tolerance boundary and is caused by a fault. As for the classification of faults, the most popular method is to categorize them as either malicious or nonmalicious [7].

According to the conventional definition, malicious faults have the objective of altering the functioning of a system during use [7, 9]. Hence "exploit" is classified as operational, external, human-made, software, and malicious interaction fault. Intrusion attempts are also considered as faults. This approach has several flaws. For instance, people often exploit their own system security vulnerability in order to identify security loopholes that do not represent a "malicious objective." Exploit events are not always faults. Some harmless intrusions that are just designed for fun do not damage a system and do not have malicious objective to interfere with the normal operation of the system. Even if we consider such a fun exercise as malicious, it does not affect the correct service or cause a service error. A fault claim does not fit the definition of faults.

Avizienis et al. [7] has also proposed eight elementary fault classes. However, the combination of these elementary fault classes can generate nonexisting faults. To address this problem, three major partially overlapping groupings, namely, development faults, physical faults, and interaction faults, are introduced in Avizienis et al. [7]. The framework suffers from the problem of classifying nonmalicious activities or error-free activities as malicious faults. We attempt to provide a set of elementary fault classes with minimum overlapping. An intuitive choice is to start with classes that have minimum overlap. We start with two classes, namely, human-made faults (HMF) and nonhuman-made faults (NHMF).

HMF

Human-made faults result from human actions. They include absence of actions when actions should be performed (i.e., omission faults). Performing wrong actions leads to commission faults. Avizienis et al. [7] have categorized human-made faults into two basic classes: malicious faults and nonmalicious faults. They are distinguished by the objective of a developer or of the humans interacting with a system during its use. An exploit activity is classified as malicious fault. As mentioned above, this classification originated from the fault-analysing community and does not integrate well with security. We propose the following new definitions and classifications. HMFs are categorized into two basic classes: faults with unauthorized access (FUA), and other faults (NFUA).

Faults with unauthorized access (FUA).   This class attempts to cover traditional security issues. We investigate FUA from the perspective of availability, integrity, and confidentiality. Nonrepudiation events normally have the authorized access and hence do not fit in the FUA category.

FUA and confidentiality.   Confidentiality refers to the property that information or data are not available to unauthorized persons or processes, or that unauthorized access to a system's output will be blocked by the system's filter. Apparently, confidentiality faults fit FUA nicely and can be regarded as a subclass of FUA. Confidentiality faults are mainly caused by access control problems originating in cryptographic faults, security policy faults, hardware faults, and software faults. Cryptographic faults can originate from encryption algorithm faults, decryption algorithm faults, and key distribution methods. Security policy faults are normally management problems and can appear in different forms (e.g., as contradicting security policy statements).

FUA, integrity, and authenticity.   Integrity is referred to as the absence of malicious external disturbance that causes a system to produce incorrect output. This deviated output can be the result of component failure, but can also be linked to unauthorized access. An integrity problem can arise if, for instance, internal data are tampered with and the produced output relies on the correctness of the data. Integrity problems are related to but different from authenticity problems, as in the latter case where output produced somewhere else is attributed to the system regardless of correctness. As an example, a person-in-the-middle attack can produce integrity and authenticity faults by altering a message or by producing a totally new one. A confidentiality fault can also occur, if the person-in-the-middle attack gains access to confidential information. This example illustrates that one incident can result in different types of faults.

FUA and availability.   Availability refers to a system's readiness to provide correct service. Availability faults can be human-made or nonhuman-made. A typical cause of such faults is some sort of denial of service (DoS) attack that can, for example, use some type of flooding (SYN, ICMP, UDP) to prevent a system from producing correct output. The perpetrator in this case has gained access to a system, albeit a very limited one, and this access is sufficient to introduce a fault. Most viruses and worms also interfere with availability when executing. Some malware that is activated remotely might turn a system into a zombie or sleeping agent. System availability is reduced, sometimes to zero, when these zombies are activated by a perpetrator, when at other times the system is normally available. While availability is affected only temporarily, the fault (i.e., the malware), is continuously present in the system.

Many FUA faults aim at making system output deviate from its desired trajectory and beyond tolerance. At other times, the fault is unintentional (e.g., the result of an operator error). To make a clear distinction between these two cases, we introduce a new concept not discussed elsewhere: malicious attempt fault.

Malicious attempt fault has the objective of damaging a system. A fault is produced when this attempt is combined with other system faults. From the perspective of elementary security attributes—availability, confidentiality, integrity, and nonrepudiation—we classify malicious attempt faults according to their aims as:

1. Intention to disrupt service (e.g., DoS attack).

2. Attempt to access confidential information.

3. Intention to improperly modify a system.

4. Having gained services.

Note that a malicious attempt fault is not a real fault unless it is combined with other faults.

NFUA.   There are human-made faults that do not belong to FUA. Most of such faults are introduced by error, such as configuration problems, incompetence issues, accidents, and so on. Fault detection activity, including penetration testing, is not considered to be a fault itself, as it does not cause system output to deviate from its desired trajectory. Nonrepudiation fault also belongs to the NFUA category, as it normally has an authorized access.

Nonhuman-made faults (NHMF).   NHMF refers to faults caused by natural phenomena without human participation. These are physical faults caused by a system's internal natural processes (e.g., physical deterioration of cables or circuitry), or by external natural processes. The latter ones originate outside a system but cross system boundaries and affect the hardware either directly, such as radiation, or via user interfaces, such as input noise [7]. Communication faults are an important part of the picture. They can also be caused by natural phenomena. For example, in communication systems, a radio transmission message can be destroyed by an outer space radiation burst, which results in system faults, but has nothing to do with system hardware or software faults. Such faults have not been discussed before in the existing literature.

From above discussions, we propose the following elementary fault classes, as shown in Figure 6.5. From these elementary fault classes, we can construct a tree representation of various faults, as shown in Figure 6.6.

Figure 6.7 shows different types of availability faults. The Boolean operation block performs either "Or" or "And" operations or both on the inputs. We provide several examples to explain the above structure. We consider the case when the Boolean operation box is performing "Or" operations. F1.1 (a malicious attempt fault with intent to availability damage) combined with

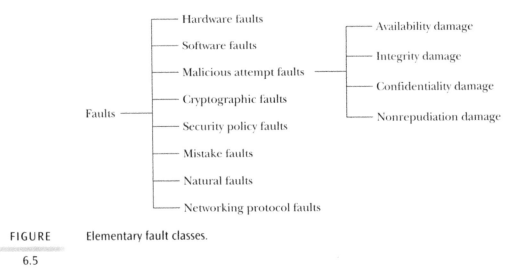

Faults
- Hardware faults
- Software faults
- Malicious attempt faults
  - Availability damage
  - Integrity damage
  - Confidentiality damage
  - Nonrepudiation damage
- Cryptographic faults
- Security policy faults
- Mistake faults
- Natural faults
- Networking protocol faults

FIGURE 6.5   Elementary fault classes.

software faults will cause an availability fault. A typical example is the Zotob virus that can lead to shutting down the Windows operation system. It gains access to the system via a software fault (buffer overflow) in Microsoft's plug-and-play software, and attempts to establish permanent access to the system (back door). F1.1 in combination with hardware faults can also cause an availability fault. F7 (natural faults) can cause an availability fault. F1.1 and F8 (networking protocol) can cause a denial of service fault. Figure 6.8 shows the types of integrity faults.

The interpretation of S2 is similar to that of S1. The combination of F1.2 and F2 can alter the function of the software and generate an integrity fault. Combining F1.2 and F4 can generate a person-in-the-middle attack and so on. Figure 6.9 shows types of confidentiality faults.

The interpretation of S3 is very similar to those of S1 and S2. Combination of F1.3 and F2 can generate a spying type of virus that steals users' logins and passwords. It is easy to deduce other combinations.

Now let us look at the complex case of a Trojan horse. The Trojan horse may remain quiet for a long time or even forever, and so it will not cause service failure during the quiet period. This is hard to model by conventional frameworks. Within our framework, we need to observe two factors first for the classification. The first factor is the consequence of introducing the Trojan horse, that is, whether it causes a fault or combination of faults, such as availability, integrity, and confidentiality faults. If there is no consequence (i.e., no service deviation error) after introducing it then it is not considered as a fault. This conforms to the basic definition of faults. The second factor is whether the intrusion belongs to

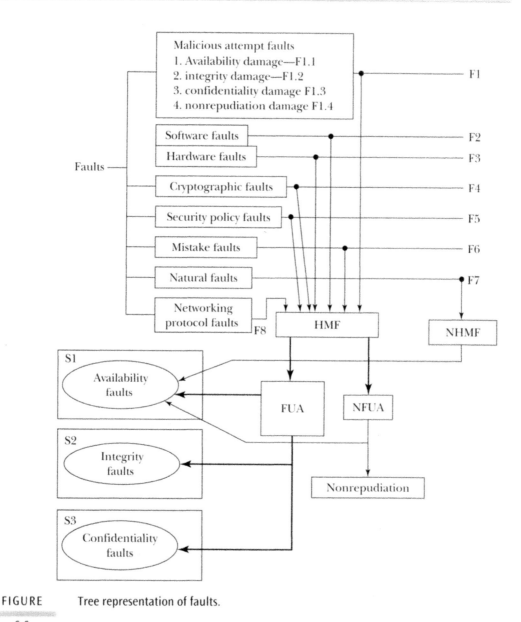

FIGURE   Tree representation of faults.

6.6

a malicious attempt. Apparently, a network scan by the system administrator is not considered as a fault. When the objective of a Trojan horse is not malicious and it never affects system service, it is not considered as a fault in our framework. Such scenarios have not been addressed properly in many other frameworks where

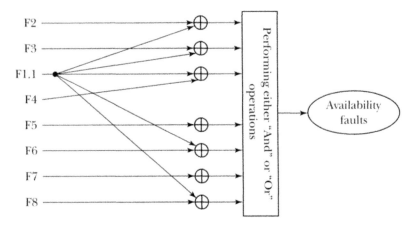

FIGURE Detailed structure of S1.

6.7

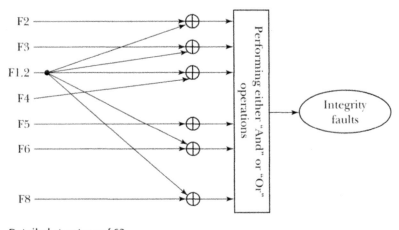

FIGURE Detailed structure of S2.

6.8

exploit-type activities are characterized as faults even though they may never cause service deviation. If, however, a Trojan horse has a malicious attempt fault and does cause service deviation, then it is considered as a fault classified by S1, S2, and S3 components.

Because a service failure is mainly due to faults, we concentrate our discussion on faults and means to attain fault prevention, fault tolerance, fault detection, and fault removal in this chapter.

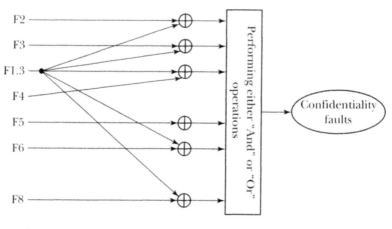

FIGURE   Detailed structure of S3.

6.9

6.5   THE MEANS TO ATTAIN DEPENDABILITY AND SECURITY

6.5.1   Fault Prevention

Fault prevention is a general engineering practice and encompasses broad areas
including software, hardware, and so on. A comprehensive discussion of this issue
is beyond the scope of this chapter. Prevention is better than "curing," which is also
true here. In security-related faults, prevention is paramount. In reducing confidentiality faults and integrity faults, fault prevention is a must and perhaps the
only effective mechanism as it faces an unknown proactive effort to create confidentiality and integrity faults. This effort may be made by the most knowledgeable
people with enormous resources (e.g., the National Security Agency). The most
effective fault prevention mechanism to reduce confidentiality and integrity faults
is the deployment of powerful cryptographic schemes. This refers to minimizing
cryptographic faults F4. It is also important to manage cryptographic schemes
(F5) to further reduce the faults. Cryptographic schemes can provide encryption,
that is, a mathematical transformation of the information into an unintelligible
form. Only legitimate users with a decryption key can decrypt the encrypted information, which provides confidentiality. As shown in Figure 6.3, it is equivalent to
blocking the system output by using the filter. Only users with authorized access
to the filter can get access to the information needed.

Although an encryption/decryption mechanism is most powerful and also a
required component in providing confidentiality, encryption alone is not enough

to provide integrity faults prevention. This is because in a network environment, people can still cause integrity faults even though they do not have the cryptographic key. A typical case is a replay attack, in which previous legitimate messages are replayed to cause integrity faults even though the attackers do not have the cryptographic key. Authentication and related digital signatures are very effective schemes addressing these issues.

Authentication is a technique used to verify the communicating party for who it claims to be. Digital signature is based on authentication techniques and mainly used for nonrepudiation purposes. Similar to handwritten signatures, a digitally signed message is expected to meet the following requirements [13]:

1. The recipient can verify the claimed identity of the sender.

2. The sender cannot later repudiate the contents of the message.

3. The recipient cannot possibly have concocted the message him- or herself.

For more details of cryptography, network security, access control and their latest development, see Chapters 2 and 3.

In general, cryptographic-based authentication techniques have a built-in weakness. They are all based on the possession of a certain cryptographic key. This will lead to several security issues. First, the protocol can only verify that the communicating party is the one who has possessed the right key. However, it cannot verify that the communicating party is the genuine user. Secondly, this key is hard to maintain without any risk of leakage and also can be lost. When human beings are involved, biometric authentication seems to be an excellent solution. Biometrics refers to the automatic identification of a living person based on physiological (fingerprint, face, hand geometry, iris) and/or behavioral (voice, signature, keystroke dynamics) characteristics. Biometric identification is preferred over traditional methods involving passwords and PINs (personal identification numbers) for various reasons, mainly that biometric information cannot be used by anyone other than the individual, it cannot be lost or forgotten, it can be used by an illiterate person, and, in conjunction with smart cards, biometrics can provide strong security.

Various types of biometric systems are being used for real-time identification [14–18]. Of all the biometric techniques, fingerprint-based authentication is one of the most mature and proven [14]. Most of biometric authentication protocols are virtually matching issues in the sense that they care about whether the input biometrics match the template biometrics, which does not address other problems such as replay attacks, and so on. Han et al. [17] have proposed a hybrid crypto-biometric protocol that can be used in the network environment. This scheme still needs to transfer the key for the recovery of the fingerprint image, which can be a weak point. The ideal case is to use biometric features directly as cryptographic keys. However, this is still an unresolved challenging issue as biometric features tend to not be precise while conventional cryptography requires accuracy on the cryptographic keys [18]. New security protocols are continuously being developed, and new methods to ensure confidentiality and authenticity under different circumstances are published regularly.

6.5.2　Fault Tolerance

A fault will generate a service error. Hence, fault tolerance aims to maintain error within the error tolerance boundary when faults occur, which is also called failure avoidance. Referring to our proposed framework shown in Figure 6.3, fault tolerance means that a system tries to regulate system output so that it keeps track of the desired trajectory even when internal and/or external disturbances are present. It is observed that the fault tolerance in our framework needs a regulator to control system output. The operation of a regulator relies on the error information generated from the feedback. This clearly indicates that fault tolerance needs both error detection and regulation. Although it is not new to consider fault tolerance being composed by both error detection and recovery [7], a generic integration of them as illustrated in this chapter is new. In our framework, error detection and recovery (regulation) are no longer two independent components as proposed in the existing literature [7]. Instead, a regulator needs the error as its input. Our proposed framework provides a better integration of these notions in a generic and seamless way. One common fault tolerance example is router malfunction. When a router error is detected, the system will use the backup router to regulate/recover the system back to the normal operation.

6.5.3　Fault Removal

Fault removal and fault forecasting are normally considered separately [7]. Fault removal is considered during system development and system use. During the development phase, fault removal consists of three steps: verification, diagnosis, and correction. During the system use phase, fault removal is considered as corrective or preventive maintenance. Corrective maintenance aims to remove faults that have produced one or more errors that have been reported. Preventive maintenance aims to uncover and remove faults before they might cause errors during normal operation. Fault forecasting is done by evaluating the system behavior with respect to fault occurrence or activation. In this chapter, we do not treat them separately as such. We attempt to integrate them under the proposed unified framework.

We consider that verification, diagnosis, and correction are ongoing and can happen during normal system use. In real-life applications, it is always a good practice to periodically perform verification, diagnosis, and correction. A typical example is the frequent use of "ping" to diagnose network faults during system use. In the proposed framework, sending a "ping" can be interpreted as the input, and the error observed is used to identify faults. For instance, a "not alive" ping reply from a certain, supposedly active server may indicate faults with the server.

System behavior evaluation is also an ongoing process. The evaluation is performed either in passive ways or in proactive ways. In passive ways, system behavior may be evaluated unconsciously by what users perceive. Testing is a typical proactive way of system behavior evaluation. Intrusion (including virus, worms) detection systems (IDS) always evaluate system behavior to identify intrusions, and may directly block and eliminate the intrusions, or alert the system administrator to do so. Generally, intrusion detection techniques can be classified into two categories: misuse-based intrusion detection and anomaly-based intrusion detection.

Misuse-Based Intrusion Detection

This technology retrieves intrusions' features/signatures and establishes a library for the collection of such intrusions. When a particular signature is detected, it is interpreted as an intrusion and is removed from the system. We consider this as evaluating system behavior against a list of predefined system behavior. This can also be called deterministic evaluation. This technique is very effective in detecting known intrusions, but poor in detecting unknown intrusions.

Anomaly-Based Intrusion Detection

This technique first builds a profile for a system's normal behavior and then compares operational system behavior with this nominal profile. If a significant deviation is found, an intrusion is announced. This technique is ideal for detecting unknown intrusions but current methods still have a high false rate. The fundamental principle behind such techniques is probabilistic evaluation. Much research effort has been concentrated on the hard-to-detect and malicious intrusions that modify an existing program [19–23]. It involves many PC viruses such as zotob and zombies.

It is interesting to observe that anomaly-based intrusion fault removal is quite similar to fault tolerance, as anomaly-based intrusion detection also needs to detect an error and then use this error to regulate the system output. However, misuse-based intrusion detection is different. It is not confined to detecting an error that has already happened; it can remove faults that have not caused errors yet.

6.6   CONCLUSION

In this chapter, a framework has been proposed for the integration of dependability and security. The major contribution of this chapter is to introduce a feedback system to link various concepts and attributes of dependability and security. The framework can help generate relevant taxonomies in a generic and seamless way. Many important concepts and attributes of dependability and security have been illustrated via this framework. Unlike conventional malicious fault classification, we proposed a new concept of malicious attempt fault. This malicious fault is not considered as a real fault unless it combines with other faults that lead to downgrading a system's performance. Such classification provides a more accurate description of dependability and security. Authenticity and nonrepudiation have also been included into the framework. Extensive coverage of low-level techniques has been given under the context of means of achieving fault prevention. Biometric authentication techniques have also been introduced as the latest development in this field. Various intrusion detection techniques have also been addressed as a means of achieving fault removal.

References

[1] A. Birolini, *Reliability Engineering, Theory and Practice* (New York: Springer Verlag, 2003).

[2] G. Buja and R. Menis, "Conceptual Frameworks for Dependability and Safety of a System," *International Symposium on Power, Electronics, Electrical Drives, Automation and Motion*, Taormina (Sicily)-Italy May 23–26, 2006, pp. 44–49.

[3] J. C. Laprie, "Dependable Computing and Fault Tolerance: Concepts and Terminology," *Proceedings of the 15th IEEE International Symposium on Fault-Tolerant Computing (FTCS-15)*, Ann Arbor, MI June 1985, pp. 2–11.

[4] J. C. Laprie, "Dependability—Its Attributes, Impairments and Means," in *Predicting Dependable Computing Systems*, edited by B. Randell, (Berlin; New York: Springer: 1995), pp. 3–24.

[5] W. Molisz, "Survivability Function—A Measure of Disaster-Based Routing Performance," *IEEE Journal on Selected Areas in Communications* 22, No. 9 (Nov. 2004): 1876–1883.

[6] D. Medhi and D. Tipper, "Multi-Layered Network Survivability—Models, Analysis, Architecture, Framework and Implementation," *Proceedings of DARPA Information Survivability Conference and Exposition, DISCEX'00*, Hilton Head, SC, Jan. 25–27, 2000, pp. 173–186.

[7] A. Avizienis, J. C. Laprie, B. Randell, and C. Landwhehr, "Basic Concepts and Taxonomy of Dependable and Secure Computing," *IEEE Transactions on Dependable and Secure Computing* 1, No. 1 (Jan.–March 2004): 11–33.

[8] J. J. Clark and W. M. Fitzgerald, "SecurIST: Coordinating the Development of a Strategic Research Agenda for Security and Dpendability R&D," *39th Annual International Carnahan Conference on Security Technologies, CCST'05*, Las Palmas de Gran Canaria, Spain. Oct. 11–14, 2005, pp. 295–299.

[9] E. Jonsson, "An Integrated Framework for Security and Dependability," *Proceedings of the 1998 Workshop on New Security Paradigms,*, (Charlottesville, Virginia: ACM Press, 1998), pp. 22–29.

[10] Special Session, "Fundamental Concepts of Fault Tolerance," *Proceedings of the 12th IEEE International Symposium on Fault-Tolerance Computing (FTCS-12)*, Santa Monica, USA June 1982, pp. 3–38.

[11] K. Kyamakya, K. Jobmann, and M. Meincke, "Security and Survivability of Distributed Systems: An Overview," *Proceedings of IEEE Milcom*, Los Angeles, CA, May 2000, pp. 449–454.

[12] B. E. Helvik, "Perspectives on the Dependability of Networks and Services," *Telektronikk* 3 (2004): 27–44.

[13] W. Stallings, *Cryptography and Network Security: Principles and Practices*, 3rd ed., (Englewood Cliffs, NJ: Prentice Hall, 2003).

[14] Y. Wang, J. Hu, and D. Philip, "A Fingerprint Orientation Model Based on 2D Fourier Expansion (FOMFE) and Its Application to Singular-Point Detection and Fingerprint Indexing." *IEEE Transactions on Pattern Analysis and Machine Intelligence* 29, No. 4, pp. 573–585 (April 2007).

[15] Y. Wang, J. Hu, and F. Han, "Enhanced Gradient-Based Algorithm for the Estimation of Fingerprint Orientation Field," in *Applied Mathematics and Computation*, Vol. 185, No. 2, pp. 823–833, Feb. 2007, (Boston: Elsevier, 2007).

[16] A. K. Jain, S. Prabhakar, L. Hong, S. and Pankanti, "Filterbank-Based Fingerprint Matching, " *IEEE Transactions on Image Processing* 9, No. 5 (2000): 846–859.

[17] F. Han, J. Hu, X.Yu, Y. Feng, and J. Zhou, "A Novel Hybrid Crypto-Biometric Authentication Scheme for ATM Based Banking Applications," *IAPR International Conference on Biometrics (ICB2006)*, Hong Kong, Jan. 5–7, 2006. Published in *Lecture Notes in Computer Science* 3832 (New York: Springer-Verlag, 2005), pp. 675–681.

[18] F. Han, J. Hu, and X. Yu, "A Biometric Encryption Approach Incorporating Fingerprint Indexing in Key Generation," *International Conference on Intelligence Computing (ICIC06)*, Kunming, China, 2006. Published in *Computational Intelligence and Bioinformatics, Lecture Notes in Computer Science* 4115 (New York: Springer-Verlag, 2006), pp. 342–351.

[19] D. Song, M. I. Heywood, and A. N. Zincir-Heywood, "Training Genetic Programming on Half a Million Patterns: An Example from Anomaly Detection," *IEEE Transactions on Evolutionary Computation* 9, No. 3 (June 2005): 225–239.

[20] F. Valeur, G. Vigna, C. Kruegel, and R. A. Kemmerer, "A Comprehensive Approach to Intrusion Detection Alert Correlation," *IEEE Transactions on Dependable and Secure Computing* 1, No. 3 (July–Sept. 2004): 146–168.

[21] X. D. Hoang, J. Hu, and P. Bertok, "Intrusion Detection Based on Data Mining," *The 15th International Conference on Enterprise Information Systems*, Vol. 3, Angers, France, 2003, pp. 341–346.

[22] X. D. Hoang, J. Hu, and P. Bertok, "A Multi-Layer Model for Anomaly Intrusion Detection," *Proceedings of IEEE International Conference on Networks*, vol. 1, Atlanta, Georgia, Sept. 2003, pp. 531–536.

[23] X. D. Hoang and J. Hu, "An Efficient Hidden Markov Model Training Scheme for Anomaly Intrusion Detection of Sever Applications Based on System Calls," *Proceedings of IEEE International Conference on Networks*, Vol. 1, Singapore, 2004, pp. 470–474.

Stochastic Modeling Techniques for Secure and Survivable Systems

Kishor S. Trivedi   Duke University, USA
Vaneeta Jindal   Indian Institute of Technology, India
Selvamuthu Dharmaraja   Indian Institute of Technology, India

7.1   INTRODUCTION

Our societal infrastructure, such as defense, emergency services, and telecommunications, has become dependent on distributed networking systems. These systems typically consist of components of varying quality and are integrated to provide essential services for the end users. This pervasive societal dependency on networks magnifies the consequences of failures and amplifies the vital importance of ensuring their survivability. As a result, methods for achieving system survivability are receiving increasing attention [1, 2]. At the same time, public awareness of security is growing with the implications of computer systems and their applications operating in the unbounded environment of the global information grid. Thus, network security is also an issue of increasing practical concern and research attention [3].

Most of the work in computer security has focussed on the methods of detection of intrusions. More recent work is on intrusion tolerance [4]. Most of the work on survivability relates to the different phases of system development such as architecture planning, network design, and software/hardware implementation. In particular, survivability issues have been analyzed for wired networks such as Asynchronous Transfer Mode (ATM) networks and Public Switched Telephone Network (PSTN). With the increasing deployment of wireless access networks for information exchange, survivability analysis for these networks is receiving attention. We study the models and techniques that are helpful in the validation of the security and survivability attributes of networked systems [5].

7.1.1   Survivability and Security

Dependability of networked systems is quantified by several attributes such as reliability, availability, performability, security, and survivability. In this chapter, we concentrate on two of these attributes: security and survivability. Survivability of a system is the capability of a system to fulfill its mission in a timely manner in the presence of attacks, failures, or accidents. The term *mission* refers to a set of very high-level requirements or goals. Missions are not limited to military settings, since any successful organization or project has a vision of its objectives expressed as a mission statement. The terms *attack*, *failure*, and *accident* are meant to include potentially damaging events. Attacks are the damaging events that include probes and denial of service (DoS). Moreover, the threat of an attack may have a severe impact on a system since the system assumes the defensive position and may reduce its functionality and also divert additional resources to monitor the environment and protect its assets. Failures may be due to software design errors, hardware degradation, human errors, and corrupted data. Accidents describe the broad range of randomly occurring and damaging events such as natural disasters [6, 7]. We can say that accidents are externally generated events and failures are internally generated events.

Security is informally defined as the resilience of a computer system or network to malicious attacks. These systems and networks are accessible through public networks (e.g., the Internet), and hence are easily prone to the security intrusions. The range of security intrusions may vary from minor mischief, to DoS, to criminal intent for stealing or destroying assets controlled by such systems. This has brought increasing attention to security attributes, which include availability, data integrity, and confidentiality. Data integrity means that a system does not allow the protected data to be modified in an unauthorized fashion, while confidentiality means that a system does not allow protected data to be read in an unauthorized fashion. Associating integrity and availability with respect to authorized actions, together with confidentiality, leads to security. A distinguishing feature of security vulnerabilities is that some external agent can deliberately exercise the vulnerability and comprise security, for example, inducing faults in a system in order for failures to occur.

It is important to recognize the relationship between survivability and security. Security is defined as the combination of availability, confidentiality, and integrity and focuses on *recognition and resistance to attacks*. On the other hand, the concept of survivability is broader than security and focuses on the *adaptation and evolution to attacks.* A survivable application must be able to survive malicious attacks (e.g., intrusions, probes, DoS), in addition to failures (e.g., software design errors, hardware degradation, human errors, corrupted data) and accidents (e.g., disasters). Thus, we can conclude that while security primarily concerns itself with attacks, survivability deals with system failures, accidents, and attacks. In other words, we say that survivability includes the security issues. Further, survivability is concerned with system transient behavior (performance) just after the occurrence of a failure (attack or natural disaster) until the system stabilizes (gets repaired or recovers).

This chapter explains the concepts and approaches for evaluating network survivability and security. The techniques differ from most other treatments of system survivability and security in that we use stochastic modeling. We make stochastic assumptions about system vulnerabilities, attacker behavior, system intrusion detection/tolerance behavior, and system recovery behavior subsequent to a disaster/failure. We then solve the models for various survivability and security measures.

7.2   ANALYTICAL MODELING TECHNIQUES

Survivability and security attributes of a system can be predicted in several ways: build prototypes and takes measurements, use discrete event simulation to model a system, or construct an analytical model for evaluating the attributes of a system.

Measurement is the direct method for assessing an existing system, but it is not a feasible option during system design and implementation phases. Discrete event simulation techniques are a commonly used modeling approach. Simulation can capture system characteristics to a high degree of fidelity. Many software packages are available to facilitate the construction and solution of discrete event simulation models. However, these models tend to be too expensive since it takes a long time to run them, particularly when highly accurate results are required.

Analytical modeling has proven to be a cost-effective and accurate approach for system analysis. A model is an abstraction of a system that includes sufficient details to facilitate the understanding of system behavior. Due to the recent developments in model generation and solution techniques, and the availability of software packages, large and realistic models can be developed and studied. An analyst can choose from different types of analytical models based on the accessibility, construction, efficiency, and accuracy of solution algorithms, and the availability of suitable software packages.

Analytical models can be broadly classified into nonstate space and state space models. Nonstate space models, also known as combinatorial models, do not enumerate all possible system states to solve for the required attributes.

Some of the commonly used combinatorial models are reliability block diagrams, reliability graphs, fault trees, and attack trees [5]. However, system features, such as dependent behavior, imperfect coverage, and nonzero reconfiguration delays, are not easily captured by these models. These limitations can be overcome by state space models, since they enable us to model the complicated interactions between the components and the trade-offs between different measures of interest.

State space models are much more comprehensive. They allow explicit modeling of complex relationships and their transition structure can encode important sequencing information. The most commonly used state space models are Markov chains. They provide great flexibility for modeling performance, reliability, availability, survivability, and security. But the size of state space of Markov chains grows much faster than the number of system components, thereby making the model specification difficult and an error-prone process. Some of the techniques that have been used extensively to reduce the size of the models include state truncation methods, fixed-point iteration, and hierarchical models. Another state space modeling formalism is stochastic Petri nets and their extensions that allow for concise specification and automated generation of an underlying Markov chain [8]. Models in this chapter are analyzed by a software package like SHARPE, which was developed by the researchers at Duke University, Durham, NC.

In this section, we define Markov chains and Markov reward models. Later, we see how the Markovian constraints are relaxed by using semi-Markov processes. Finally, stochastic Petri net, a high-level formalism for solving underlying model types, is discussed.

7.2.1   Markov Models

Let $\{X(t), t \geq 0\}$ be a stochastic process with state space $S = \{1, 2, \ldots, n\}$ that characterizes the dynamics of a system, where the random variable $X(t)$ represents a structure state of the system at time t. With the assumption that the sojourn time in each state is exponentially distributed, the stochastic process $\{X(t), t \geq 0\}$ is a continuous-time Markov chain (CTMC). In a CTMC, the past history of the process is completely summarized in the current state for all time t, that is, for any $t_0 < t_1 < t_2 < \cdots < t_n < t$,

$$P[X(t) \leq x | X(t_n) = x_n, \ldots, X(t_0) = x_0] = P[X(t) \leq x | X(t_n) = x_n]$$

This is known as the Markov property. A CTMC is said to be irreducible if every state is reachable from every other state.

Let $Q = [q_{ij}]$ be the infinitesimal generator matrix of the CTMC $\{X(t), t \geq 0\}$, where $q_{ii} = -\sum_{\substack{j=0 \\ i \neq j}}^{n} q_{ij}$. Let $P_i(t) = P\{X(t) = i\}$ denote the unconditional probability of the CTMC being in the state i at time t. The row vector $\mathbf{P}(t) = [P_1(t), P_2(t), \ldots, P_n(t)]$ of the time-dependent state probabilities is computed by solving the Kolmogorov forward equation [9]:

$$\frac{d}{dt}\mathbf{P}(t) = \mathbf{P}(t)Q \tag{7.1}$$

given $\mathbf{P}(0)$, the initial state probability vector (at time $t = 0$). For an irreducible, aperiodic CTMC with all states non-null recurrent, the limit $\pi_j = \lim_{t \to \infty} P_j(t)$, $j \in S$ always exists and the steady-state probability vector π, defined as $\pi = [\pi_0, \pi_1, \ldots]$, satisfies Eq. 7.2 [9]:

$$\pi Q = \mathbf{0}, \quad \sum_{i \in S} \pi_i = 1. \tag{7.2}$$

At times, the cumulative probabilities are also of interest. Define $L_i(t) = \int_0^t P_i(u)du$; then, $L_i(t)$ denotes the expected cumulative time spent by the CTMC in state i during the interval $[0, t)$. Let the vector $\mathbf{L}(t) = [L_i(t)]$. Then, by integration of Eq. 7.1, we get [9]:

$$\frac{d}{dt}\mathbf{L}(t) = \mathbf{L}(t)Q + \mathbf{P}(0), \quad \mathbf{L}(0) = \mathbf{0}$$

Once state probabilities $P_i(t)$ and π_i have been computed, measures of interest are usually obtained as the weighted averages of these quantities. Assigning reward rates to the states of the CTMC defines a Markov reward model (MRM). Assume a weight or reward rate r_i is assigned to state i. Reward rate assignment is made based on the desired measures of security and survivability. Let $Z(t) = r_{X(t)}$ be the instantaneous reward rate of the MRM at time t. Then the expected instantaneous reward rate at time t is:

$$E[Z(t)] = \sum_{i \in S} r_i P_i(t)$$

The expected reward rate in steady state is:

$$E[Z] = \sum_{i \in S} r_i \pi_i$$

Let the accumulated reward over the interval $[0, t)$ be given by [10]:

$$Y(t) = \int_0^t Z(u)du = \int_0^t r_{X(u)}du$$

Then the expected accumulated reward in the interval $[0, t)$ is given by:

$$E[Y(t)] = \sum_i r_i L_i(t)$$

Based on the definitions of $X(t)$, $Y(t)$, $Z(t)$, which are nonindependent random variables, various measures can be defined. In general, it is difficult to compute the distribution $P\{Y(t) \le y\}$, $y \in \mathbb{R}$ of the accumulated reward over time $[0, t)$ for complex reward structures [11]. The problem is simplified if we restrict our interest to the expectations and other moments of the random variables.

The essential requirement for a stochastic process to be a Markov chain is that the sojourn time in each state must be exponentially distributed. However, in modeling practical situations, the restrictions of exponential distribution for sojourn times in each state may not hold. A semi-Markov process (SMP) is a generalization of the Markov chain where the distribution of the time the process spends in a given state is allowed to be nonexponentially (generally) distributed. Many problems in queueing theory, reliability, and security have been approached through semi-Markov processes. Further, generalization is provided by Markov regenerative processes. We discuss SMP in detail in this chapter.

7.2.2   Semi-Markov Process

Consider a system with state space $E = \{0, 1, \dots\}$. Suppose that the initial state of the system at time t_0 is X_0. It stays there for a non-negative random amount of time (which is generally distributed), and then, the next transition takes place at time t_1 to state X_1 (which could be the same as X_0). It stays there for a non-negative amount of time and then jumps to state X_2 at time t_2, and continues this way forever. Thus, t_n is the time instant of the nth transition and X_n is the nth state visited by the system. Let $Y(t)$ be the state of the system at time t. Then, $Y(t_n) = X_n$ for $n = 0, 1, \dots$

A stochastic process $\{Y(t), t \ge 0\}$ described above is called an SMP if it satisfies the Markov property at the time of transitions. That is, the evolution of the process from time $t = t_n$ onwards depend only on the history of the process up to time t_n. In other words, if $\{Y(t), t \ge 0\}$ is an SMP, the process $\{Y(t + t_n), t \ge 0\}$ given the entire history $\{Y(t), 0 \le t \le t_n\}$ and $X_n = i$, $i \in E$, is independent of $\{Y(t), 0 \le t \le t_n\}$ and is probabilistically identical to $\{Y(t), t \ge 0\}$ given $X_0 = i$.

The process $\{Y(t),\ t \geq 0\}$ is called an SMP since the Markov property is satisfied at the transition epochs $\{t_n\}$ and not at all times. Also, note that the future from time t_n does not depend on n either. This implies that the SMP $\{Y(t), t \geq 0\}$ is time-homogeneous. The Markov property of $\{Y(t), t \geq 0\}$ at each of the transition epochs $\{t_n\}, n = 0, 1, \ldots$, implies that the Markov property holds for $\{X_n, n = 0, 1, \ldots\}$. Thus, $\{X_n, n = 0, 1, \ldots\}$ is a time-homogeneous embedded discrete-time Markov Chain (DTMC) with state space E.

An SMP is embedded by a two-stage method. In the first stage, the SMP stays in a state $i, i \in E$ for an amount of time $H_i(t)$, the sojourn time distribution in state i. In the second stage, the SMP moves from state i to state j with probability $p_{i,j}$ (i.e., $p_{i,j} = P\{X_{n+1} = j | X_n = i\}$, $i, j \in E$). Thus, the SMP is described by a transition probability matrix $P = [p_{i,j}]$ and the vector of sojourn time distributions $\mathbf{H}_i(t)$. To compute the steady-state probability vector $\pi = [\pi_0, \pi_1, \ldots]$ for the SMP, we first calculate the mean sojourn time $h_i = \int_0^\infty (1 - H_i(t)) dt$ in each state i. Next, we find the steady-state probability vector $\pi^d = [\pi_0^d, \pi_1^d, \ldots]$ for the embedded Markov chain by solving the system of equations given by $\pi^d = \pi^d \times P$; $\pi^d \times \mathbf{e} = 1$, where $\mathbf{e}$ is a column vector with all entries 1s. Finally, compute the steady-state probabilities for the SMP as follows [9]:

$$\pi_i = \frac{\pi_i^d h_i}{\sum_j \pi_j^d h_j} \tag{7.3}$$

CTMCs and SMPs are rarely used directly to specify a system's model in a typical modeling process because of the associated difficulties. First, the state space can grow much faster than the number of components in the system being modeled, making it difficult to specify a model correctly. Secondly, a Markov model is sometimes far removed in shape and general feel of the system being modeled. Thus, it becomes hard to translate real-world problems into Markov or non-Markov models. These difficulties can be overcome by using a higher-level model formalism that is more concise and closer to a designer's intuition about what a model should look like. Stochastic Petri net is one such high-level formalism. In the next subsection, we discuss stochastic Petri nets.

7.2.3 Higher-Level Model Formalisms

Many high-level modeling formalisms have been created to fill the gap between CTMC specifications and system design specifications. Examples of these formalisms include variants of stochastic Petri nets and interacting Markov chains. We describe stochastic Petri nets (SPNs) and their extension in detail.

SPNs and their extensions have been developed as extensions to untimed Petri nets (PNs) (originally introduced by C. A. Petri in 1962) with timed transitions for which the firing time distributions are assumed to be exponential. SPNs have been extensively used in the area of dependability analysis due to the small size of their descriptions and their visual/conceptual clarity. They allow a designer to focus more on the system being modeled rather than on error-prone and tedious manual construction of Markov chains.

A PN is a bipartite directed graph with two types of nodes: *places* and *transitions*. Each place may contain zero or more *tokens*. Graphically, places are depicted as circles, transitions are represented by bars, and tokens are represented by dots or integers in the places. All places from which arcs go to a particular transition are called *input places* of that transition. All places to which arcs go from a particular transition are called the *output places* of that transition. Each transition may have zero or more *input arcs*, coming from its input places, and zero or more *output arcs*, going to its output places. A transition is *enabled* if all its input places have at least as many tokens as the multiplicity of the corresponding input arc. A transition can *fire* when it is enabled and, upon firing a number of tokens equal to the multiplicity of the input arc, are removed from each of its input places, and a number of tokens equal to the multiplicity of the output arc are deposited in each of its output places. A *marking* depicts the *state* of a PN, which is characterized by a number of tokens in each place. The initial number of tokens assigned to the places in a PN determine the initial state (marking) of the PN. With respect to a given initial marking, the *reachability set* is defined as the set of all markings reachable through any possible firing sequences of transitions, starting from the initial marking.

Generalized stochastic Petri nets (GSPNs) extend the PNs by assigning a *firing time* to each transition. Transitions with exponentially distributed firing times are called *timed* transitions, while the transitions with zero firing times are called *immediate* transitions. A marking in a GSPN is called *vanishing* if at least one immediate transition is enabled; otherwise it is called a *tangible* marking. A *reachability graph* is generated with the markings of the reachability set as the nodes and some stochastic information attached to the arcs, thus connecting the markings to each other. Arcs are labeled with the name of the transitions whose firing caused the associated changes in the marking. Under the condition that only a finite number of transitions can fire in finite time with nonzero probability and firing times are exponentially distributed, it can be shown that for a given GSPN model, the reachability graph can be reduced to a homogeneous CTMC [12]. GSPN also introduces *inhibitor arcs*. An inhibitor arc from a place to a transition *disables* the transition if the place contains at least as many tokens as the cardinality of the inhibitor arc. Graphically, an inhibitor arc is represented by a line terminated with a small circle.

In order to make more compact models of complex systems, several extensions are made to GSPNs, leading to a stochastic reward net (SRN). One of the most important features of an SRN is its ability to allow extensive marking dependency. Each tangible marking can be assigned one or more *reward rates(s)*. Parameters, such as the firing rate of the timed transitions, multiplicities of input/output arcs, and reward rate in a marking, can be specified as functions of the number of tokens in any place in the SRN. All output measures are expressed in terms of the expected values of the reward rate functions. To get the performance and reliability/availability measures of a system, appropriate reward rates are assigned to its SRN.

The Symbolic Hierarchical Automated Reliability and Performance Evaluator (SHARPE) is a well-known modeling tool that combines the flexibility of Markov models and has been used for analysis of SPNs and their extensions. It contains support for multiple model types and provides flexible mechanisms for combining results so that models can be used in hierarchical combinations. It gives users direct and complete access to various models, such as Markov models, semi-Markov models, Markov reward models, and SPNs and their extensions, without making assumptions about an application domain. SPNs and their extensions can be specified using SHARPE and can be analyzed for system survivability and security attributes [13].

7.3   SECURITY MODELING

Information systems and networks are prone to security intrusions, where the range may vary from minor mischief for pleasure, DoS, and criminal interest for stealing or destroying critical information. This has made the security an important attribute for information systems and networks. Most of the reported research in the literature on security characterization has dealt with the qualitative aspects of security. A system is assigned a given security level with respect to the presence or absence of certain functional characteristics and the use of certain development techniques. Swiler et al. [14] and Jha et al. [15] use an attack graph to model the security vulnerabilities of a system and their exploitation by an attacker. Note that attack graphs are also discussed in Chapter 9. Ortalo et al. [16] proposed modeling of known system security vulnerabilities using privilege graphs and described a technique for transforming these privilege graphs into a Markov chain. The states of this Markov chain denote the privileges gained by an attacker and the deterioration of a system toward the security failed state due to the series of atomic attacks on the system. The effort spent by an attacker to bring about the transitions in a Markov chain is modeled as a random variable with an exponential distribution. This Markov chain is then solved to obtain the security attributes. Jonsson and Olovsson [17] attempted to build a quantitative Markov model of attacker behavior based on the empirical data collected from several intrusion experiments conducted over a period of two years. They postulated that the process representing an attack may be broken into several phases, each of which has an exponential distribution. The overall attacker behavior, therefore, required nonexponential characterization. Software is an important component in an inherently complex system. Despite the best efforts of software architects and coders, there are always some unintended faults or security vulnerabilities present in a software system. The OASIS program [18, 19] for information assurance has proposed a classification of secure software systems into three generations:

1. *First Generation:* Emphasis is on the protection or prevention of security intrusions.

2. *Second Generation:* Secure software systems put emphasis on detecting intrusions and alerting the system administrators for initiating remedial measures.

3. *Third Generation:* Secure software systems emphasize tolerating security intrusions and reconfiguring, regenerating, or rejuvenating a system after a security intrusion has occurred.

Our interest is in studying the third-generation intrusion-tolerant systems for quantifying their security attributes. The model should consider intrusions with different impacts (e.g., compromise of confidentiality, compromise of data integrity, and DoS attack), and should be able to capture the dynamic behavior of the system in response to these intrusions.

A security intrusion and the response of an intrusion-tolerant system to an attack is modeled as a random process. This facilitates the use of stochastic modeling techniques to capture an attacker's behavior as well as a system's response to a security intrusion. Since it is a challenging problem to properly characterize a security intrusion and a system's response in terms of probability distributions and their parameterizations, we concentrate on developing the security quantification model and use typical values for various model parameters.

7.3.1 Intrusion-Tolerant Systems

An intrusion-tolerant software system [3] should be capable of reorganizing itself, preferably automatically, in order to initiate the response to a security intrusion. The action of an attacker who is trying to cause security failures and the corrective actions taken by the intrusion-tolerant system under an attack are to be considered simultaneously. Therefore, we require a composite security model that incorporates the behavior of both these elements. An intrusion-tolerant architecture, for example, SITAR (Scalable Intrusion-Tolerant Architecture) provides intrusion tolerance by means of diversity and redundancy in a system [4].

SMP Model for Intrusion-Tolerant Systems

Figure 7.1 depicts the state transition model for representing system behavior for a specific attack and given system configuration that depends on the actual security requirements.

A system is in the vulnerable state V if it enables a user to read/modify information without authorization, or grant an entity access to a resource without authorization. Here, "without authorization" means a violation of a system's security policy. A vulnerability is the property of a system, its software and/or hardware, or its administrative procedures that causes it to enter a vulnerable state. If a vulnerability is exploited successfully, a system enters the active attack state A

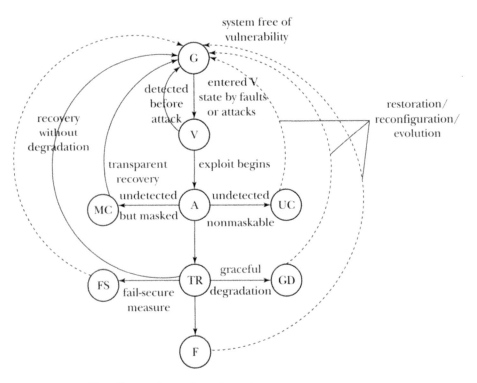

FIGURE   State transition diagram for an intrusion-tolerant system.

7.1

and then the damage may follow. Traditionally, first-generation software security systems rely on resistance to attacks. A system typically oscillates between the good state G and vulnerable state V. Some of the strategies that prevent a system from being vulnerable or reduce the time it remains in a vulnerable state includes the use of authentication, access control encryptions, firewalls, proxy servers, strong configuration management, dispersion of data, and application of system upgrades for known vulnerabilities. The four phases that form the basis for the design and implementation of an intrusion-tolerant system are error detection, damage assessment, error recovery, and fault treatment.

Strategies for detecting attacks and assessment of damage include intrusion detection (i.e., anomaly-based and signature-based detection), logging, and auditing. If the probing that precedes an attack is detected, the system will stay in the good state G. The other possibility is to detect the penetration and exploration phases of an attack and bring the system from the vulnerable state back to G. Otherwise, the system might enter the active attack state. Traditionally, the resistance and detection of attacks received most of the attention, and once an active attack state is entered, damage may start. Thus, it is critical to assess the damage and try the recovery during the exploitation phase of an intrusion. The recovery strategies include the use of redundancy for critical information and services, incorporation of backup systems in isolation from the network, isolation of damage, ability to operate with reduced services, or reduced user population.

In the presence of enough redundancy in a system, the delivery of error-free service is ensured and the system is back to good state G by measuring the attack's impact MC. On the other hand, if the intrusion-tolerance strategies fail to recognize an active attack state and limit the damage, it can lead to an undetected compromised state UC, without any service assurance. When an active attack in the exploitation phase is detected, a system will enter the triage state TR. In the triage stage, the system has to figure out different possible ways it can respond to an attack so as to recover and limit the damage that can be caused by an attack.

An ideal system should be capable of eliminating the impacts produced by an attack, providing successful restoration to the good state G. However, if it is not feasible, a system can attempt to limit the extent of damage while maintaining the essential services. Essential services are the functions of a system that must be maintained to meet system requirements even when the environment is hostile and may threaten the system. In an intrusion-tolerant system, the impact is more important than the causes. If the aim is to protect the system from a DoS attack, the system enters the graceful degradation state GD maintaining only essential services. However, if the aim is to protect the confidentiality and data integrity, the system must be made to stop functioning. This is called fail-secure state FS. If all the strategies fail, then the system enters the failed state F and signals an alarm to the system administrator. Here, dashed lines denote that full service is recovered by manual intervention and the system returns to the good state.

After describing the transition diagram, we now develop a stochastic model for the intrusion-tolerant system that could explain an attacker's response as well as a system's behavior to the attack. An attacker does not have complete knowledge of a system, and hence, the effect of attacks are uncertain. Similarly, a system designer/owner/operator is uncertain to the type, frequency, intensity, and duration of an attack. In order to solve this stochastic process, we first describe the events that trigger transitions among states in terms of probability and cumulative distribution functions (CDF).

Attacker's Behavior and System Responses

For analyzing the security attributes of an intrusion-tolerant system, we need to consider the actions undertaken by an attacker as well as the system's response to an attack. An attacker tries to send the system into a security-failed state. To plan his or her actions, he or she requires time and effort. The time/effort are modeled as a random variable that may follow one of the several distribution functions such as deterministic, exponential, hypoexponential, hyperexponential, Weibull, gamma, and log-logistic [9]. The hypoexponential distribution may be used to model transitions that may involve multistage activities. For example, the Code-Red worm first causes the parameter stack buffer to overflow by sending a long URL to the web server that is to be attacked. In the next stage, the normal return address (already stored on this stack) is overwritten with a bad return address placed in this URL. In the final stage, this bad return address points to a rogue piece of Code-Red code (also supplied as part of the long URL) that gets invoked the next time the return from a call is executed. The above discussion suggests that we need to consider a nonexponential type of distribution. The hypoexponential distribution may be used to model threat situations that can cause a monotonically increasing failure rate (IFR) of security. Similarly, a hyperexponential distribution may be used to model threats that can cause a monotonically decreasing failure rate (DFR). The Weibull distribution function may be used to model a constant failure rate (CFR), DFR, or IFR type of threat by suitably choosing its parameters. For more complex attack scenarios, which are characterized by having a decreasing rate of success initially, followed by an increasing rate of success (or vice versa), we can use the log-logistic type of distribution function. It should also be noted that an attacker may not always be successful in causing a security failure (i.e., probability of success ≤ 1).

In Figure 7.1, an attacker's actions are modeled by the states $\{G, V, A\}$. An intrusion-tolerant system needs to constantly evaluate the presence of security penetration, and on detection of attack, has to perform the remedial actions. The system will try to move back to a secure state from a security-compromised state. The time and effort of the system for performing these actions is also a random variable and are described by the suitable chosen probability distribution functions. Note that the system may not be able to detect an intrusion successfully. The system response may be described by the states $\{MC, UC, TR, FS, GD, F\}$. Let $\{X(t), t \geq 0\}$ be the underlying stochastic process with discrete state space $S = \{G, V, A, TR, MC, UC, FS, GD, F\}$. Since the time spent in at least one of the states is not exponential, $\{X(t), t \geq 0\}$ is an SMP. To analyze the SMP, we need to deal with two sets of parameters [9]: (1) mean sojourn time h_i in state i, $i \in S$, and (2) transition probability p_{ij} between different states $i, j \in S$.

The security attributes are described by the attributes of:

1. *Availability:* Readiness of usage.

2. *Integrity:* Data and programs are modified or destroyed only in a specified and authorized manner.

3 *Confidentiality:* Sensitive information is not disclosed to unauthorized recipients.

Thus, associating integrity and availability with respect to authorized actions, together with confidentiality, leads to security. The degree of each of these properties varies from application to application. For instance, confidentiality is the most important in defense applications while data integrity is of prime concern in banks and wireless networks that value the availability of their services. These attributes are computed by solving the SMP, whose state transition diagram is shown in Figure 7.1. First, we solve this SMP and obtain its steady-sate probabilities for obtaining the security attributes.

Computations of Steady-State Probabilities

The embedded DTMC for the above discussed SMP is shown in Figure 7.2. As mentioned earlier in subsection 7.2.2, we need the information of sojourn times in each state and the transition probabilities. The corresponding parameters are listed as follows:

h_G: Mean time for a system to resist becoming vulnerable to attacks.

h_V: Mean time for a system to resist attacks when vulnerable.

h_A: Mean time taken by a system to detect an attack and initiate triage actions.

h_{MC}: Mean time a system can keep the effects of an attack masked.

h_{UC}: Mean time that an attack remains undetected while doing damage.

h_{TR}: Mean time a system takes to evaluate how best to handle an attack.

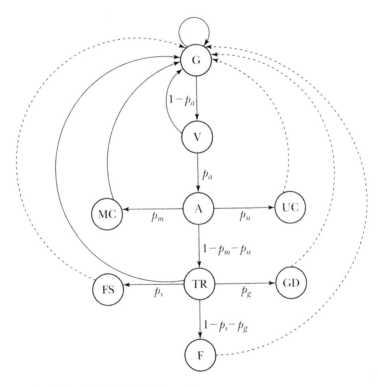

FIGURE 7.2 Embedded DTMC for the SMP model.

h_{FS}: Mean time a system operates in a fail-secure mode in the presence of an attack.

h_{GD}: Mean time a system is in the degraded state in the presence of an attack.

h_F: Mean time a system is in the failed state despite detecting an attack.

p_a: Probability of injecting a successful attack, given that a system is vulnerable.

p_u: Probability that a successful attack has remain undetected.

p_m: Probability that a system successfully masks an attack.

p_g: Probability that a system resists an attack by graceful degradation.

p_s: Probability that a system responds to an attack in a fail-secure manner.

For computing the security attributes in terms of availability, confidentiality, and integrity, we need to determine the steady-state probabilities $\{\pi_i, i \in S\}$ of the SMP states. These probabilities are to be determined in terms of the steady-state probabilities π_i^d and the mean sojourn time h_i of the states of the DTMC.

The matrix P that describes the state transition probabilities for this DTMC is written as:

$$P = \begin{bmatrix} 0 & 1 & 0 & 0 & 0 & 0 & 0 & 0 & 0 \\ \tilde{p}_a & 0 & p_a & 0 & 0 & 0 & 0 & 0 & 0 \\ 0 & 0 & 0 & p_m & p_u & \tilde{p}_{mu} & 0 & 0 & 0 \\ 1 & 0 & 0 & 0 & 0 & 0 & 0 & 0 & 0 \\ 1 & 0 & 0 & 0 & 0 & 0 & 0 & 0 & 0 \\ 0 & 0 & 0 & 0 & 0 & 0 & p_s & p_g & \tilde{p}_{sg} \\ 1 & 0 & 0 & 0 & 0 & 0 & 0 & 0 & 0 \\ 1 & 0 & 0 & 0 & 0 & 0 & 0 & 0 & 0 \\ 1 & 0 & 0 & 0 & 0 & 0 & 0 & 0 & 0 \end{bmatrix}$$

where $\tilde{p}_a = 1 - p_a, \tilde{p}_{mu} = 1 - p_m - p_u$, and $\tilde{p}_{sg} = 1 - p_s - p_g$. On solving the equation

$$\pi^d = \pi^d \times P, \ \sum_i \pi_i^d = 1, \ i \in S \tag{7.4}$$

where $\pi^d = [\pi_G^d, \pi_V^d, \pi_A^d, \pi_{MC}^d, \pi_{UC}^d, \pi_{TR}^d, \pi_{FS}^d, \pi_{GD}^d, \pi_F^d]$, the steady-state probabilities π_i^d are obtained.

Next, we compute the mean sojourn time h_i in each state i. The quantity h_i is determined by a random time the process spends in state i. The attacker behavior is described by the transitions $G \rightarrow V$ and $V \rightarrow A$. To model the wide range of attacks (from amateur mischief to cyber attacks), it is necessary to consider a variety of probability distributions. On the other hand, system response to an attack is algorithmic and automated. Based on the sojourn time distribution of state i, the mean sojourn time h_i for this state is calculated. For example, if sojourn time distribution for state G is hypoexponential with parameters λ_{g1} and λ_{g2}, then its mean sojourn time h_G is given as $h_G = \left(\dfrac{1}{\lambda_{g1}} + \dfrac{1}{\lambda_{g2}} \right)$. Similarly, the mean sojourn times for the other states $h_A, h_V, h_{MC}, h_{GD}, h_{TR}, h_{FS}, h_{GD}, h_F$ are also computed.

Steady-state probability for SMP states is expressed in terms of the steady-state probabilities π_i^d of the DTMC and their sojourn times h_i using Eq. 7.3. Substituting for π_i^d and h_i in Eq. 7.3, we get the steady-state probabilities for the SMP as:

$$\pi_G = \frac{h_G}{h_G + h_V + p_a[h_A + p_m h_{MC} + p_u h_{GD} + (1 - p_m - p_u)]},$$

$$\pi_V = h_V \frac{\pi_G}{h_G}, \ \pi_A = h_A p_a \frac{\pi_G}{h_G}, \ \pi_{MC} = h_{MC} p_m p_u \frac{\pi_G}{h_G},$$

$$\pi_{FS} = h_{FS} p_a p_s (1 - p_m - p_u) \frac{\pi_G}{h_G}, \ \pi_{TR} = h_{TR} p_a (1 - p_m - p_u) \frac{\pi_G}{h_G},$$

$$\pi_{GD} = h_{GD} p_a p_g (1 - p_m - p_u) \frac{\pi_G}{h_G},$$

$$\pi_F = h_F p_a (1 - p_a - p_g)(1 - p_m - p_u) \frac{\pi_G}{h_G}. \tag{7.5}$$

Once the steady-state probabilities are known, we now compute the security attributes such as availability, confidentiality, and integrity.

For calculating availability, we observe that a system is not available in states FS, F, and UC and is available in all the other states. Then, the availability is given as:

$$\mathcal{A} = 1 - (\pi_{FS} + \pi_F + \pi_{UC}) \tag{7.6}$$

In case of a DoS attack, a system is made to stop functioning, that is, bringing it to the FS state will accomplish the goal of a DoS attack. Therefore, the states FS and MC will not be part of the state transition diagram. For this attack, system availability is given as:

$$\mathcal{A}_{DoS} = 1 - (\pi_F + \pi_{UC}) \tag{7.7}$$

Similarly, confidentiality and integrity measures can be computed in the context of specific security attacks. For example, Microsoft IIS 4.0 suffered from the ASP vulnerability as documented in the Bugtraq ID 1002 [20]. Exploitation of this vulnerability allows an attacker to traverse the entire web server file system, thus compromising confidentiality. Therefore, in the context of this attack, states UC and F are identified with the loss of confidentiality. Similarly, if Code-Red worm is modified to inject a piece of code into a vulnerable IIS server to browse unauthorized files, states UC and F will imply loss of confidentiality. Therefore, the steady-state confidentiality measure is computed as:

$$C_{ASP} = 1 - (\pi_F + \pi_{UC}) \tag{7.8}$$

Consider another example, where a Common Gateway Interface (CGI) vulnerability present in the Samber server as reported in Bugtraq ID 1002 was reported [20]. Exploitation of this vulnerability permits an attacker to execute any MS-DOS command including deletion and modification of files in an unauthorized manner, thus compromising the integrity of a system. Here also, states UC and F indicate the loss of integrity, and thus the steady-state measure of integrity is given as:

$$I_{CGI} = 1 - (\pi_F + \pi_{UC}) \tag{7.9}$$

7.3.2   Security Modeling of SITAR Security System

In the last section, we saw how to model an intrusion-tolerant system and obtain the security attributes. Here we develop the stochastic model specific to the SITAR system [4] that describes the dynamic behavior of multiple intrusion tolerance strategies built into SITAR.

Basic SITAR Architecture

SITAR is an intrusion-tolerant system for making web and such other applications intrusion tolerant using spatial redundancy, diversity, automated intrusion detection, and reconfiguration. The main components of the SITAR architecture include proxy servers, acceptance monitors, ballot monitoring, audit control module, adaptive reconfiguration module (ARM), and Commercial-off-the-shelf (COTS) servers.

Proxy servers accept requests from clients. Acceptance monitors apply the acceptance testing algorithms on the requests. If passed, the request is sent to the designated COTS server and processed. Responses generated by the COTS servers are sent again to the acceptance monitors for applying validity checking on each response. This, in turn, is forwarded to the ballot monitors. If a sign of compromise is detected on the COTS server while checking the responses, the ballot monitor generates an intrusion trigger for the reconfiguration module. It also receives the responses sent from the acceptance monitors and votes to select the final response. This result is sent to the proxy servers to deliver the responses to the remote clients. Based on the received intrusion triggers from the other modules, ARM adaptively reconfigures the system. The audit control module monitors various resources used by all the internal components in SITAR.

Systems based on the SITAR security architecture can recover from security attacks that may otherwise result in loss of availability, integrity, and confidentiality. These goals are achieved by taking intrusion-tolerance measures at various stages during the processing of an operation, transaction, or request. To provide intrusion-tolerance, SITAR (or in general, any intrusion-tolerant system) performs two basic actions: detection of an intrusion and mitigating the adverse effects of a successful intrusion. In SITAR, detection of an attack is carried out by its multiple subsystems, whereas, the adverse effects are mitigated by using redundant and diverse internal components (e.g., acceptance monitors, ballot monitors, proxy modules) as well as redundant COTS servers.

Model of the SITAR Security System

Figure 7.3 shows the state transition diagram for the SITAR system with three redundant COTS servers. Initially, the system is in good state G with no

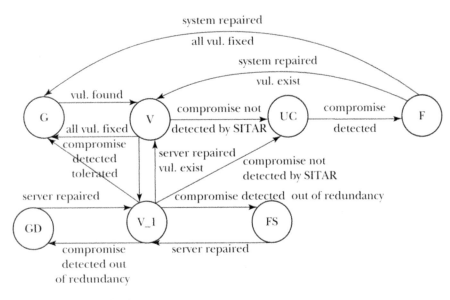

FIGURE   State transition model for SITAR.

7.3

vulnerabilities. Assume that an initial phase of an attack will move the system
to the vulnerable state V from state G. During the interval the system is in state
V; attackers try various ways to exploit these vulnerabilities in order to cause a
compromise to the system security. The other possibility is that the system administrators may locate some of the vulnerabilities and fix them. If these vulnerabilities
are fixed, the system returns to state G, otherwise the vulnerabilities are exploited
and an attack is injected into the system. In case SITAR security components detect
an attack before the damage, the system continues to stay in state V, otherwise
the attack may result in damage to the system. If the compromise is detected
by the security mechanisms in SITAR and the resulting damage is tolerated due
to the redundancies, the system returns to state V. If one of the COTS servers is
compromised by the malicious attack and the system detects the compromise, it
can tolerate the compromise by changing to state V_1 and continue providing services with two COTS servers up. If the system detects the compromise but cannot
mask the damage the attack caused, for example, when running out of the redundant COTS servers, based on the nature of the attack, the system will enter either
graceful degradation state GD (if the aim is to prevent the system from the DoS
attacks) or the fail-secure state FS (if the aim is to protect confidentiality or data
integrity).

In state GD, some of the services provided by the system are shutdown in
order to maintain the essential services. In the FS state, even though the parts

of the system are assumed to have failed, the confidentiality and integrity are still preserved, and further damage is prevented. If the compromise is not detected by all the security mechanisms in SITAR before the bad response is sent, the system is then in an undetected compromised state UC. In the state F, the system is undergoing a major diagnosis and recovery. A reconfiguration is also going on in state GD and FS so that the system can be returned to the normal operational state. In the meantime, the vulnerability may be fixed by upgrading the software, replacing the hardware, or modifying the system configuration to eliminate the vulnerability. When all the vulnerabilities have been fixed, the system returns to state G.

By incorporating sojourn time distributions and probabilities into the state transition model, we can obtain an SMP. On solving this SMP, the steady-state probabilities are obtained and hence the security attributes are computed, as in the example in Section 3.1.

7.4   SURVIVABILITY MODELING

Information survivability encompasses many aspects of security and reliability for computers and networks. Information survivability is more than preventing security breaches. Systems must be robust; they must be able to continue to operate despite accidental breakdowns, failures in their components and subsystems, and successful security attacks. Survivability is concerned with a system's transient behavior just after the occurrence of a failure until the system stabilizes, that is, gets repaired or recovered. By failure here, we mean a physical failure, an attack, or a natural disaster.

In recent years, a variety of survivable network techniques and architectures have been proposed and developed for better protection and restoration capability. For synchronous digital hierarchy networks, the architecture has evolved from the $1 + 1$ and $1:N$ automatic protection-switching point-to-point protection to a more robust two- or four-fiber ring architecture. The attention to the problem of survivability of wireless access networks (WANs) has focused primarily on survivability for the cellular network database (i.e., HLR, VLR). This work developed checkpoint algorithms and authentication techniques for the fault recovery of database content. In Tipper et al. [2, 21], a survivability framework for WANs consisting of four layers, with survivability strategies such as fault tolerance and redundancies, is possible in each layer proposed. The four layers are termed as radio access, access link level, transport, and intelligent. Each of the four layers consists of network functions, network components, and communication links. This framework includes metrics for quantifying network survivability, possible survivability strategies, and restoration techniques for each layer. Discrete event simulation is then used to analyze the survivability attributes for WANs.

Many survivability definitions have been given in different standard organizations, industrial institutes, and academic communities under different contexts. The National Communication Systems Technology and Standards Division created a definition of survivability for telecommunication systems as "the property of a system, subsystem, equipment, process or procedure that provides a defined degree of assurance that the named entity will continue to function during and after a natural and man-made disturbance." Deutsch and Willis [22] proposed a survivability definition for software systems as "the degree to which essential functions are still available even though some part of the system is down." Neumann [23] used the term survivability for computer systems and networks as the "the ability of a system to satisfy and to continue to satisfy critical requirements in the face of adverse conditions." Mead et al. [24] of the Software Engineering Institute defined survivability of critical information systems as "the capability of a system to fulfill its mission, in a timely manner, in the presence of attacks, failures or accidents." Although these definitions give a good conceptual description of survivability, none of them is clear and precise enough for carrying out a quantitative evaluation. The most precise definition was proposed by the T1A1.2 Working Group on Network Survivability Performance as follows [25]:

Suppose a measure of interest M has the value M_0 just before a failure occurs. Survivability behavior can be depicted by the following attributes: M_a is the value of M just after the failure occurs; M_u is the maximum difference between the value of M and M_a after the failure; M_r is the restored value of M after some time t_r; and t_R is the time for the system to restore the value M_0.

This definition depicts the transient or time-dependent system behavior after the failures occur. Many techniques for quantifying network survivability based on combinatorial methods, such as fault scenario graphs and attack tree methodologies, were proposed in Jha and Wing [26], Zhao et al. [27], and Cloth and Haverkort [28], but these did not provide the time-dependent behavior of the system. In Liu and Trivedi [29], a composite Markov model approach to evaluate the network survivability performance was proposed. It was based on a five-step procedure that is described as follows:

✦ **Step 1:** Develop the pure availability model in which the resources, such as hardware, software, and/or other components, fail and get repaired. An up state of the availability model may be labeled as i, which may in general be a vector.

✦ **Step 2:** Develop a pure performance model with resource availability as defined by the up-state vector i. Obtain the steady-state results of the pure performance model, which describe the resource usage before any failures occur. The performance model includes the arrival and service completions of the jobs arriving to the system.

✦ **Step 3:** Combine the availability and performance models obtained in the first two steps into a composite model. This composite model can be solved directly or by using a two-level hierarchical solution as in Ma et al. [30].

✦ **Step 4:** Truncate the composite model obtained in step 3 based on the survivability measure of interests. Different models may be constructed in different circumstances. In order to reflect a system's resource usage before a failure occurs, initial probability must be assigned for the truncated model. The steady-state results of the pure performance model are needed in this initialization.

✦ **Step 5:** Perform the transient analysis of the truncated composite model developed in step 4.

Following this procedure, survivability of a system or a network can be easily quantified. As an illustration to this procedure, we present a survivability model of a mobile cellular network, adapted from Jindal et al. [31].

7.4.1   System Description

In cellular networks, a given geographic region is divided into a number of cells, each covered by a base station (BS). A BS consists of antennas, transmitters, receivers, channel computing units, radio resources, and links to other network elements. The various types of failures that occur at BSs are categorized into channel failures and infrastructure failures. Channel failures include a failure in the radio channels due to the reduction in signal quality, noise, multipath fading, and interference. These failures can occur either in busy or idle channels. A single repair facility at the BS is provided for the repair of wireless channels. On the other hand, failures in BS infrastructure, such as hardware, software, electromechanical equipment, natural disasters (e.g., earthquakes, tornadoes, and floods), and malicious attacks, are collectively termed infrastructure failures. Arriving calls are not granted access and channel recovery is not accomplished until any infrastructure failures are recovered. Also, the prematurely terminated mobile users of the damaged BS attempt to reestablish their calls, which results in an increase in network congestion. The calls in the emerging cellular networks are categorized as real-time service (RTS) calls (e.g., voice and live video) and non-real-time service (NRTS) calls (e.g., SMS, video-on-demand). For this system, the measure of interest to quantify survivability is the call-blocking probabilities for RTS and NRTS calls.

In accordance with the five-step survivability framework discussed above, we present the availability, performance, and composite performance and availability model, in sequence. Finally, the survivability model is developed from the composite performance and availability model by truncating it accordingly. This survivability model is analyzed to obtain the survivability attributes for cellular networks.

Step 1: Pure Availability Model

Let the time for channel failures and repairs be exponentially distributed with rates γ and τ, respectively. Let the time for infrastructure failures and repairs be exponentially distributed with parameters α and β, respectively. Infrastructure failure may recover completely with coverage probability p or are not recovered with probability $(1 - p)$. In this case, the system is operating in a degraded mode. The assumptions of exponential failures and repairs are made to keep the mathematical analysis tractable. Nonexponential failure and repairs can also be accommodated in this analysis using phase-type expansions [13]. With the assumption of exponential distributions for failures and repairs, the availability model of a BS is a CTMC with the state transition diagram shown in Figure 7.4.

State index i represents the number of nonfailed (either busy or idle) channels, and state S_i corresponds to the state of infrastructure failure at the BS, with i nonfailed channels. A new call (RTS or NRTS) arriving at a BS gets connected if an idle channel is available, otherwise it is blocked. Therefore, states $i \in \{1, 2, \ldots, N\}$ are *up states*. On the other hand, arriving RTS or NRTS calls cannot be connected if idle channels are not available or the BS is in an infrastructure failure state. Therefore, states 0 and $S_i, i \in \{1, 2, \ldots, N\}$ are *down states*. Steady-state probabilities

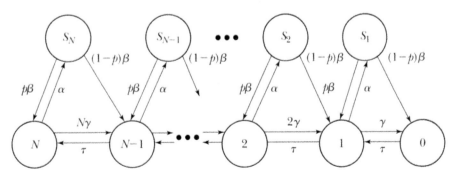

FIGURE 7.4   Pure availability model.

of states 0, i, and S_i; $i \in \{1,2,\ldots,N\}$ can be obtained by solving a system of linear equations corresponding to this CTMC. Also, the software tool SHARPE may be used to graphically represent this Markov chain and to obtain the numerical solutions.

The steady-state availability of the BS, denoted by P_A, is obtained as the sum of the steady-state probabilities of BS being in up states $\{1, 2,\ldots,N\}$. Therefore, we get

$$P_A = \sum_{k=1}^{N} \pi_k$$

where π_k is the steady-state probability of the CTMC being in state k.

Step 2: Performance Model

We consider the performance model of a single cell in a cellular network. Let RTS calls arrive in a Poisson stream at the rate λ_R and NRTS calls arrive in a Poisson stream at the rate λ_N. Let the channel holding times (CHTs) for both types of traffic be exponentially distributed with parameter μ. There is a limited number of channels, N, in the channel pool. Since RTS traffic is delay sensitive and requires guaranteed quality-of-service bounds, a fixed number of channels, $g(< N)$, are reserved exclusively for RTS traffic. When an idle channel is available and an RTS call arrives, it is accepted, otherwise it is blocked. Similarly, if an arriving NRTS call finds at least $g + 1$ channels idle, it is accepted, otherwise it is blocked. Let $N(t)$ denote the number of busy channels at time t. With the assumption of exponential distributions for interarrival times and CHTs of the calls, the stochastic process $\{N(t), t \geq 0\}$ is a CTMC since the Markov property is satisfied at all time points. The state transition diagram of this CTMC is shown in Figure 7.5, and state index i gives the number of busy channels.

We define $\lambda = \lambda_R + \lambda_N$. The arrival and departure rates in the CTMC depend on the state of a system. When the state of the system is i, $0 \leq i < N - g$, both RTS and NRTS calls are accepted. Therefore, in state i, $0 \leq i < N - g$, the arrival rate is λ. On the other hand, when the system state is i, $N - g \leq i < N$, only the RTS calls are accepted. In this case, the arrival rate to the CTMC is λ_R. The

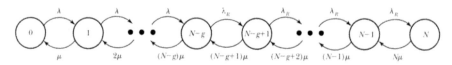

FIGURE   Pure performance model.

7.5

state-dependent departure rate is $i\mu$, $1 \leq i \leq N$. Let x_j denote the steady-state probability of being in state j. On solving this Markov chain using Eq. 7.2, the steady-state probabilities are obtained.

Let the steady-state blocking probabilities for RTS and NRTS calls be denoted as P_{BR} and P_{BN}, respectively, in the pure performance model. The RTS calls are blocked if all the channels are busy. Therefore, the blocking probability of RTS calls is given by:

$$P_{BR} = x_N$$

where x_N is the steady-state probability that N channels are busy.

NRTS calls are blocked if $N - g$ or more channels are busy. Hence, the blocking probability of NRTS calls is given as:

$$P_{BN} = \sum_{k=N-g}^{N} x_k$$

Step 3: Composite Availability and Performance Model

The composite performance and availability model discusses the performance of a network in the presence of failure. Figure 7.6 shows the state transition diagram where the parameters have usual meanings.

State (n, j) denotes n nonfailed channels with $j \leq n$ ongoing (RTS or NRTS) calls in a system and the state $S_{n,j}$ corresponds to the state of infrastructure failure with n nonfailed channels and j calls ongoing in the system. The transition rate from state (n, j) to $(n - 1, j)$ is $(n - j)\gamma$. It corresponds to the failure of any one of the $(n - j)$ idle channels. The transition rate from state (n, j) to state $(n - 1, j - 1)$ is $j\gamma$ due to the failure of one of the j channels carrying the calls. To obtain the steady-state probabilities $\pi_{k,j}$, this CTMC is input to the software tool SHARPE, and the numerical values of the probabilities are obtained. Once the state probabilities have been obtained, the performance measures of interest are obtained as follows.

The steady-state blocking probability for RTS calls is given by:

$$P_{BR} = \sum_{k=1}^{N} \sum_{i=0}^{k} \pi_{S_{k,i}} + \sum_{k=0}^{N} \pi_{k,k} \tag{7.10}$$

Similarly, the steady-state blocking probability for NRTS calls is given by:

$$P_{BN} = \sum_{k=g+1}^{N} \sum_{i=k-g}^{k} \pi_{k,i} + \sum_{k=0}^{g} \sum_{i=0}^{k} \pi_{k,i} + \sum_{k=1}^{N} \sum_{i=0}^{k} \pi_{S_{k,i}} \tag{7.11}$$

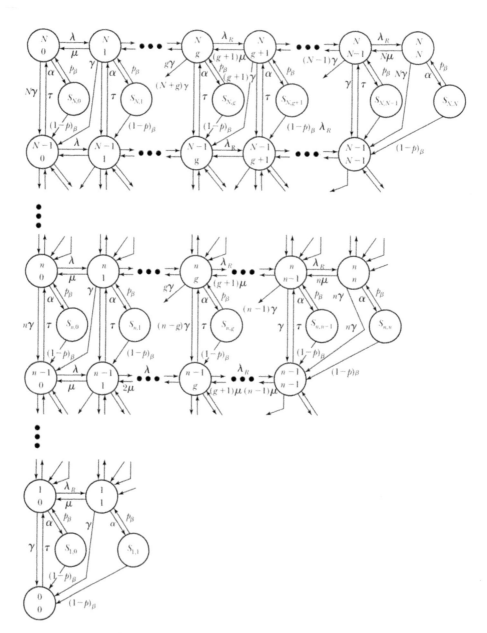

FIGURE   Composite performance and availability model.

7.6

The steady-state probability $\pi_{k,j}$ will provide the initial probability vector in the survivability model presented in the next step. Similarly, P_{BR} and P_{BN} provide the values of M_0^{BR} and M_0^{BN}, the call-blocking probabilities of RTS and NRTS traffic before a failure or natural disaster occurs.

Step 4: Survivability Model

The aftermath of malicious attacks and natural disasters induces frequent infrastructure failures and an increase in network congestion. Whenever a BS encounters an infrastructure failure, it can not provide connections to incoming RTS or NRTS calls. However, ongoing calls may not be lost due to fault tolerance employed in various components of the BS. We assume that infrastructure faults are recovered with probability p or are not recovered with probability $1 - p$. In this case, these failures are recovered after a graceful degradation of BS radio resources.

We next construct a survivability model from the composite model discussed in step 3. The definition of network survivability proposed by the T1A1.2 network survivability performance group emphasizes the time-dependent analysis of the behavior of a system after failures. Therefore, we determine transient blocking probabilities for RTS and NRTS calls immediately after the natural disaster has occurred.

Let the BS be in state (n, j), $\{1 \leq n \leq N,\ 0 \leq j \leq n\}$ at the time of occurrence of a failure or natural disaster. The composite performance and availability model shown in Figure 7.6 is truncated such that the rows corresponding to states with less than or n nonfailed channels are included, and the rows that correspond to states with more than n channels are truncated. The CTMC of composite performance and availability model is so truncated because the fault-tolerance techniques can maintain the continuity of service but the system is not repaired as good as new. The truncated model is also a CTMC and it represents the behavior of the system immediately after a natural disaster has occurred. Also, in the truncated model, the transitions from states (n, j), $0 \leq j \leq n$, to state $S_{n,j}$ are disabled since a disaster has already occurred and transition to $S_{n,j}$ would not occur again. Figure 7.7 shows the state transition diagram for the survivability model. In this model, arrival rates of RTS and NRTS traffic, λ_R and λ_N, are expected to increase due to an increase in network congestion. Further, the rate of infrastructure failures also increases as these failures become more frequent after a natural disaster has occurred in a geographic area. The initial probabilities $p_{i,j}(0)$ and $p_{S_{i,j}}(0)$ for the states (i, j) and $S_{i,j}, 0 \leq i \leq n, 0 \leq j \leq i$ in the truncated composite model give the probability with which the system will be in these states immediately after the

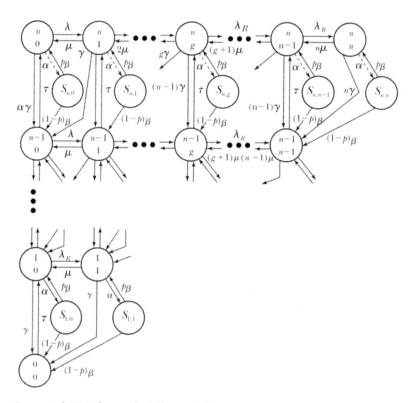

FIGURE

7.7
Truncated CTMC for survivability model.

occurrence of an infrastructure failure. We set $p_{i,j}(0) = 0$, $1 \le i \le n$, $0 \le j \le n$ since an infrastructure failure has already occurred due to a natural disaster. The initial probability for the system to be in state $S_{n,j}$, denoted by $p_{S_{n,j}}(0)$ depends on the probability that the system is in state (n, j) before the infrastructure failure has occurred. Therefore, for a fixed number of nonfailed channels n,

$$p_{S_{n,j}}(0) = \frac{\pi_{n,j}}{\sum\limits_{j=0}^{n} \pi_{n,j}}, \ 0 \le j \le n$$

$$p_{S_{i,j}}(0) = 0, \ 1 \le i \le n-1, \ 0 \le j \le i$$

Here, $\pi_{n,j}$ is the steady-state probability for state (n, j) in the composite model discussed earlier. If the number of nonfailed channels, n, is less than the number of guard channels (i.e., $n \leq g$), an NRTS call is not accepted because all the available channels will remain reserved for high-priority RTS calls. However, if $n > g$, then g channels out of n remain reserved for the RTS calls exclusively and the rest of the available $n - g$ channels are shared by both RTS and NRTS calls.

Step 5: Computation of Performance-Oriented Survivability Metrics

After the construction of the Markov chain for the survivability model of a cellular BS, the final step is to compute the survivability metrics in terms of time-dependent call-blocking probabilities of RTS and NRTS calls, denoted by $M_a^{BR}(t)$ and $M_a^{BN}(t)$, respectively.

We first compute the transient blocking probability $M_a^{BR}(t)$ for RTS calls in the wake of a natural disaster in a cellular network service area. An incoming RTS call is lost in the following two cases:

+ BS is in an infrastructure failure state.

+ All channels are busy at a BS.

Therefore, summing up the transient probabilities of the corresponding states, the transient blocking probability $M_a^{BR}(t)$ for RTS calls is given by:

$$M_a^{BR}(t) = \sum_{k=1}^{n} \sum_{i=0}^{k} p_{S_{k,i}}(t) + \sum_{k=0}^{n} p_{k,k}(t) \qquad (7.12)$$

where $p_{k,k}(t)$ and $p_{S_{k,i}}(t)$ are the transient probabilities of state (k, k) and $(S_{k,i})$ in the survivability model shown in Figure 7.7. Before the occurrence of a natural disaster, the blocking probability of RTS calls, denoted by M_0^{BR}, is given as $M_0^{BR} = P_{BR}$, where P_{BR} is obtained from Eq. 7.10.

Similarly, we obtain the expression for $M_a^{BN}(t)$. An NRTS call is blocked if on arriving, it finds the BS in any of the following cases:

+ BS is in an infrastructure failure state.

+ The number of available channels n is at most g (i.e., $n \leq g$). In this case, all channels are reserved for RTS calls and an incoming NRTS call is always blocked.

+ The number of available channels n is greater than g (i.e., $n > g$). In this case, out of n available channels, g channels are reserved for RTS calls and the remaining $n - g$ channels are shared by both RTS and NRTS calls. If an incoming NRTS call finds $n - g$ or more channels busy, it is blocked. Otherwise, it gets connected.

Therefore, $M_a^{BN}(t)$ is obtained by summing the transient probabilities of corresponding states and is given as follows:

$$M_a^{BN}(t) = \begin{cases} \displaystyle\sum_{k=g+1}^{n}\sum_{i=k-g}^{k} p_{k,i}(t) + \sum_{k=0}^{g}\sum_{i=0}^{k} p_{k,i}(t) + \sum_{k=1}^{n}\sum_{i=0}^{k} p_{S_{k,i}}(t), & n > g \\[4mm] \displaystyle\sum_{k=0}^{n}\sum_{i=0}^{k} p_{k,i}(t) + \sum_{k=1}^{n}\sum_{i=0}^{k} p_{S_{k,i}}(t), & n \leq g \end{cases} \qquad (7.13)$$

where $p_{k,i}(t)$ and $p_{S_{k,i}}(t)$ are the transient probabilities of states (k,i) and $(S_{k,i})$ in the truncated model of survivability shown in Figure 7.7. Before the occurrence of a natural disaster, the blocking probability of NRTS calls, denoted by M_0^{BN}, is given as $M_0^{BN} = P_{BN}$, where P_{BN} is obtained using Eq. 7.11. To obtain the above measures—M_0^{BR}, M_0^{BN}, $M_a^{BR}(t)$, and $M_a^{BN}(t)$—we have used the software package SHARPE.

Two distinct problems arise for this composite approach of Markov modeling of survivability: largeness and stiffness [5]. The largeness problem can be tolerated to some extent by using high-level specification techniques such as stochastic reward net (SRN) and automated methods for generating the Markov chain. We next develop an SRN model to compute the survivability metrics and study the transient effects of the failures on the performance of cellular networks.

Figure 7.8 shows the SRN model to obtain the survivability attributes of a cellular network. Initially, a token is put in place P_{no_inf} indicating that there are no infrastructure failures. The firing of the transition T_{inf} represents the occurrence of infrastructure failures. On its firing, a token moves from place P_{no_inf} to place P_{inf}. A token in place P_{inf} indicates that infrastructure failures have occurred. In this case, the BS does not accept the arriving RTS and NRTS calls. Also, repair of the failed channels is discontinued until the recovery of infrastructure failures. With probability p, infrastructure failures are recovered completely, and with probability $(1 - p)$, these failures are recovered partially, but with graceful degradation of the wireless channels. Transition T_{rep} represents the complete recovery of the infrastructure failures. On its firing, the token moves from place P_{inf} to place P_{no_inf}. Transitions $T_{degrep1}$ and $T_{degrep2}$ represent recovery of the infrastructure failures at the cost of a wireless channel. On firing of transitions $T_{degrep1}$ or $T_{degrep2}$, a token is removed from place P_{inf} and is deposited in place P_{no_inf}. Further, transition $T_{degrep1}$ is enabled if place P_{chpool} is nonempty. On its firing, a token is transferred from place P_{chpool} to place P_{fail}, where the number of tokens in places P_{chpool} and P_{fail} represent the number of nonfailed idle channels and failed channels, respectively. On the other hand, transition $T_{degrep2}$ is enabled if there are no idle channels, that is, place P_{chpool} is empty. In this case, recovery of the

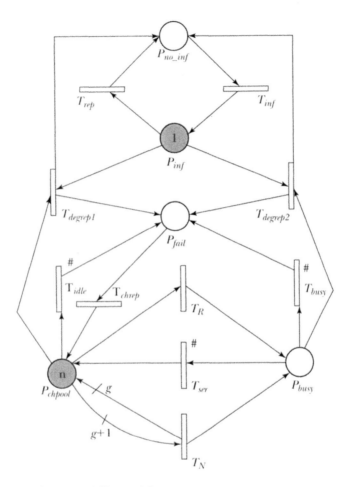

FIGURE   SRN for survivability model.

7.8

infrastructure failures is accompanied by a loss of one of the ongoing calls, and a token moves from place P_{busy} to place P_{fail}.

Tokens in place P_{busy} represent the number of busy channels. Transitions T_{idle} and T_{busy} represent the failure of an idle and a busy channel, respectively. The firing rates of transitions T_{idle} and T_{busy} are marking dependent and depend on the number of tokens in their respective input places P_{chpool} and P_{busy}. The # sign next to transitions T_{idle} and T_{busy} indicate the marking dependency. These transitions are enabled if their guard function $\#(P_{inf}) < 1$ is satisfied, in addition to the constraints imposed by the input arcs. Note that $\#(P_j)$ denotes the number of tokens in place P_j. On the firing of T_{idle} (T_{busy}), a token is removed from its input place P_{chpool} (P_{busy}) and is deposited in place P_{fail}. A single repair facility at the BS repairs the failed channels, which are represented by transition T_{chrep}. Whenever there is at least one token in place P_{fail} and its guard function $\#(P_{inf}) < 1$ holds true, transition T_{chrep} is enabled. On its firing, a token is moved to place P_{chpool}, thus representing the repair of the failed channel.

The idle nonfailed channels in place P_{chpool} are accessible by both RTS and NRTS calls. Transitions T_R and T_N represent the arrival of RTS and NRTS calls, respectively. Transition T_R is enabled if there is least one idle channel in place P_{chpool} and the guard function $\#(P_{inf}) < 1$ holds true; otherwise it is disabled. The transition T_N is disabled if there are less than $g + 1$ tokens in place P_{chpool}. This is represented by the input arc with multiplicity $g + 1$ from place P_{chpool} to transitions T_N and the output arc with multiplicity g from transition T_N to place P_{chpool}. Also, if the guard function $\#(P_{inf}) < 1$ is not satisfied, transition T_N remains disabled. Hence, T_N or T_R fires after enabling and a token is moved from place P_{chpool} to place P_{busy}. The number of tokens in place P_{busy} represents the number of channels being utilized in the cell. Transition T_{ser} represents the departure of a call from the cell. It is also enabled if its guard function $\#(P_{inf}) < 1$ holds true in addition to the input arc constraint. The firing rate of T_{ser} depends on the number of tokens in place P_{busy}. It is represented by the # sign next to transition T_{ser}. The rates and the guard functions for the transitions are listed in Table 7.1.

Based on the definition proposed by the T1A1.2 Working Group on Network Survivability Performance [25], the immediate effect of the failures on the cellular networks are to be quantified. We want to quantify the performance after the infrastructure failures have occurred. Thus, place P_{no_inf} is empty and a token is

Transition	Rate	Guard Function
T_R	λ_R	$\#(P_{inf}) < 1$
T_N	λ_N	$\#(P_{inf}) < 1$
T_{ser}	$\mu(\#P_{busy})$	$\#(P_{inf}) < 1$
T_{idle}	$\gamma(\#P_{chpool})$	$\#(P_{inf}) < 1$
T_{busy}	$\gamma(\#P_{busy})$	$\#(P_{inf}) < 1$
T_{chrep}	τ	$\#(P_{inf}) < 1$
T_{inf}	α	
T_{rep}	$p\beta$	
$T_{degrep1}$	$(1-p)\beta$	
$T_{degrep2}$	$(1-p)\beta$	$\#(P_{chpool}) < 1$

TABLE   Rates for timed transitions.

7.1

placed in place P_{inf}, which indicates that the system is in the infrastructure failure state. Due to the occurrence of natural disasters, some of the N channels are not available and BS is now operating with n channels. It is represented by placing n tokens in place P_{chpool}. The SRN model is solved to obtain the time-dependent behavior of network performance after a failure has occurred.

Survivability Metrics

The measures of interest are call-blocking probabilities for RTS and NRTS calls, denoted by M^{BR} and M^{BN}, respectively. The steady-state probability for RTS and NRTS calls before the natural disasters and malicious attacks, referred as M_0^{BR} and M_0^{BN}, respectively, are obtained using the expected steady-state reward rate.

To obtain M_0^{BR}, the reward rate assignment is:

$$r_{BR}^j = \begin{cases} 1, \text{ if } \#(P_{chpool_j}) = 0 \text{ or } \#(P_{inf_j}) = 1 \\ 0, \text{ otherwise} \end{cases} \tag{7.14}$$

Here, r_{BR}^j is the reward rate for marking j of the reachability graph of the SRN shown in Figure 7.8. For marking j, $\#(P_{chpool_j})$ denotes the number of tokens in place P_{chpool}, and $\#(P_{inf_j}) = 1$ indicates that the system is in the state of an infrastructure failure. Thus, a reward rate of 1 is assigned to the state where the channel pool is empty or place P_{inf} is nonempty (with one token) and reward rate 0 is assigned to other markings. Then, the steady-state call-blocking probability for RTS calls, M_0^{BR}, is calculated by:

$$M_0^{BR} = \sum_{j \in \Omega} r_{BR}^j \pi_j \tag{7.15}$$

where Ω is the set of all markings in the reachability graph and π_j is the steady-state probability of marking j.

Similarly, to obtain steady-state call-blocking probability, M_0^{BN}, the reward rate assignment is:

$$r_{BN}^j = \begin{cases} 1, \text{ if } \#(P_{chpool_j}) < g + 1 \text{ or } \#(P_{inf_j}) = 1 \\ 0, \text{ otherwise} \end{cases} \tag{7.16}$$

Here, r_{BN}^j is the reward rate for marking j of the reachability graph for the SRN shown in Figure 7.8. A reward rate 1 is assigned to marking j in which place P_{chpool} has less than or equal to g tokens or place P_{inf} is nonempty (with one token) and reward rate 0 is assigned to other markings. Then, the steady-state call-blocking probability for NRTS calls, M_0^{BN}, is calculated by:

$$M_0^{BN} = \sum_{j \in \Omega} r_{BN}^j \pi_j \tag{7.17}$$

where Ω is the set of all markings of the reachability graph, and π_j is the steady-state probability of marking j.

Next, the time-dependent call-blocking probabilities $M_a^{BR}(t)$ and $M_a^{BN}(t)$ for RTS and NRTS calls, respectively, are calculated immediately after the natural disasters are computed from the SRN model shown in the Figure 7.8. These measures are obtained using the expected reward rate at time t. Assigning the reward rate r_{BR}^j given by Eq. 7.14, the time-dependent call-blocking probability $M_a^{BR}(t)$ for RTS calls is calculated by:

$$M_a^{BR}(t) = \sum_{j \in \Omega} r_{BR}^j p_j(t) \tag{7.18}$$

where $p_j(t)$ is the transient probability of marking j.

Similarly, for computing the transient call-blocking probabilities for the NRTS calls, assign the reward rate r_{BN}^j given by Eq. 7.16 to state j. Then the call-blocking probabilities for NRTS calls are obtained as:

$$M_a^{BN}(t) = \sum_{j \in \Omega} r_{BN}^j p_j(t) \tag{7.19}$$

where $p_j(t)$ is the transient probability of marking j.

Note that the SRN description of the model is concise and allows us to vary the values of N without changing the model structure. However, the underlying CTMC model is very large. Therefore, the appropriate data structures for sparse matrix and sparsity preventing solution methods must be used. The stiffness problem arises when there is a large difference between failure and repair rates or failure and call arrival rates in the model. Stiffness is also caused by combining the performance and availability models in a single composite model. Solving an overall model can potentially yield more accurate results in comparison to solving two smaller, less stiff problems leading to approximate solutions. However, it was noted in Haverkort et al. [11] and Ma et al. [30] that numerical difficulties arising from largeness and stiffness in composite models may negate this gain.

Some of the other works related to survivability quantification based on the definition of survivability proposed by the TIA1.2 Working Group on Network Survivability Performance are reported in Liu et al. [29, 32]. In Chen et al. [33], a set of Markov models are presented to develop a survivability model for ad hoc networks. Here, the excess packet loss due to failures is taken as the survivability measure.

7.5 CONCLUSION

Analytical modeling is a cost-effective method for examining the behavior of various systems. To be useful, these models should be realistic and reflect important system characteristics such as failure, reconfiguration, recovery, fault tolerance, graceful degradation, and repair. The advances in the development of different model types and solution techniques from a high-level description enable large and realistic models to be developed and studied effectively. High-level model formalisms, such as stochastic Petri nets, are used to accurately model a system and to tolerate the problem of largeness in these analytic models. In this chapter, we discussed analytical models for security and survivability analysis of networked systems and also illustrated the stochastic Petri net model for these.

ACKNOWLEDGMENT

This work was supported by the Department of Science and Technology, India, under grant number RP 1907. Vaneeta Jindal would like to thank the CSIR, India, for the financial support provided to her.

References

[1] J.-P. Vasseur, M. Pickavet, and P. Demeester, *Network Recovery: Protection and Restoration of Optical, SONET-SDH, IP, and MPLS*. (San Francisco: Morgan Kaufmann, 2004).

[2] D. Tipper, S. Ramaswamy, and T. Dahlberg, "PCS Network Survivability," *Proceedings of the IEEE Wireless Communication and Networking Conference*, New Orleans, LA, 1999, pp. 1028–1032.

[3] B. B. Madan, K. Goseva-Popstojanova, K. Vaidyanathan, and K. S. Trivedi, "A Method for Modeling and Quantifying the Security Attributes of Intrusion Tolerant Systems," *Performance Evaluation* 56 (2004): 167–186.

[4] D. Wang, B. Madan, and K. S. Trivedi, "Security Analysis of SITAR Intrusion-Tolerant System," *Proceedings of the ACM workshop Survivable and Self-Regenerative Systems*, Fairfax, VA, 2003, pp. 23–32.

[5] D. M. Nicol, W. H. Sanders, and K. S. Trivedi, "Model-Based Evaluation: From Dependability to Security," *IEEE Transactions on Dependable and Secure Computing* 1 (2004): 48–65.

[6] K. Goseva-Popstojanova, F. Wang, R. Wang, F. Gong, K. Vaidyanathan, K. S. Trivedi, and B. Muthuswamy, "Characterizing Intrusion Tolerant Systems Using a State Transition Model," *Proceedings of the DARPA Information Survivability Conference and Exposition (DISCEX II)*, Anaheim, CA, 2001, pp. 211–221.

[7] Y. Liu and K. S. Trivedi, "A General Framework for Network Survivability Quantification," *Proceedings of the Measuring, Modeling and Evaluation of Computer and Communication Systems Conference*, Dresden, Germany Sept. 2004.

[8] G. Balbo, G. Conte, S. Donatelli, G. Franceschinis, M. Ajmone Marson, *Modeling with Generalized Stochastic Petri Nets*, 1st ed. (New York: John Wiley, 1995).

[9] K. S. Trivedi, *Probability and Statistics with Reliability, Queueing, and Computer Science Applications*, 2nd ed. (New York: John Wiley, 2001).

[10] R. M. Smith, K. S. Trivedi, and A. V. Ramesh, "Performability Analysis: Measures, an Algorithm, and a Case Study," *IEEE Transaction Computers* 37, No. 4 (1988): 406–417.

[11] B. R. Haverkort, R. Marie, G. Rubino, and K. S. Trivedi (Eds.), *Performability Modeling: Techniques and Tools* (New York: John Wiley, 2001).

[12] M. Ajmone-Marson, D. Kartson, G. Conte, and S. Donatelli, *Modeling with Generalized Stochastic Petri Nets* (New York: John Wiley, 1995).

[13] R. A. Sahner, K. S. Trivedi, and A. Puliafito, *Performance and Reliability Analysis of Computer Systems: An Example Based Approach Using the SHARPE Software Package* (Boston: Kluwer Academic Publishers, 1996).

[14] L. Swiler, C. Philips, and T. Gaylor, "A Graph-Based Network Vulnerability Analysis System," *Technical Report, SANDIA Report No. SANS97-3010/1*, Jan. 1998.

[15] S. Jha, O. Sheyner, and J. Wing, "Minimization and Reliability Analsis of Attack Graphs," *Technical Report, CMU Technical Report No. CMU-CS-2-109*, May 2002.

[16] R. Ortalo, Y. Deswarte, and M. Kaaniche, "Experimenting with Quantitative Evaluation Tools for Monitoring Operational Security," *IEEE Transaction Software Eng.* 25, No. 2 (1999): 207–217.

[17] E. Jonsson and T. Olovsson, "A Quantitative Model of the Security Intrusion Based on Attacker Behavior," *IEEE Transaction Software Eng.* 23, No. 4 (1997): 235–245.

[18] "Organically Assured and Survivable Information Systems," at http://www.tolerantsystems.org/oasis.html.

[19] R. Schantz, F. Webber, P. Pal, J. Loyall, and D. C. Schmidt, "Protecting Applications Against Malice with Adaptive Middleware," *Proceedings of the 17th IFIP World Computer Congress*, Montreal, Canada, August 2002.

[20] Bugtraq archive, at http://www.securityfocus.com.

[21] D. Tipper, T. Dahlberg, H. Shin, and C. Charnsripiryo, "Providing Fault Tolerance in Wireless Access Networks," *IEEE Communication Magazine* 40, No. 1 (2002): 58–64.

[22] M. S. Deutsch and R. R. Willis, *Software Quality Engineering: A Total Technical and Management Approach* (Englewood Cliffs, NJ: Prentice-Hall, 1988).

[23] P. G. Neumann, "Practical Architectures for Survivable Systems and Networks," Computer Science Laboratory, SRI International, Menlo Park, CA, 2000.

[24] N. R. Mead, R. J. Ellison, R. C. Linger, T. Longstaff, and J. McHugh, "Survivable Network Analysis Method," *Software Engineering Institute Technical Report CMU/SEI-2000-TR-013*, Sept. 2000.

[25] T1A1.2 Working Group on Network Survivability Performance, *Technical Report on Enhanced Network Survivability Performance*, Feb. 2001.

[26] S. Jha and J. M. Wing, "Survivability Analysis of Networked Systems," *Proceedings of the International Conference on Software Engineering, ICSE'01*, Toronto, Canada 2001, pp. 307–317.

[27] G. Zhao, H. Wang, and J. Wang, "A Novel Quantitative Analysis Method for Network Survivability," *Proceedings of the First International Multi-Symposiums on Computer and Computational Sciences, IMSCCS'06*, Hangzhou, China 2006, pp. 30–33.

[28] L. Cloth and B. R. Haverkort, "Model Checking for Survivability!," *Proceedings of the IEEE Second International Conference on the Quantitative Evaluation of Systems, QEST'05*, Torano, Italy 2005, pp. 145–154.

[29] Y. Liu and K. S. Trivedi, "Survivability Quantification: The Analytical Modeling Approach," *Int. Journal of Performability Engineering* 2 No. 1 (2006): 29–44.

[30] Y. Ma, J. Han, and K. S. Trivedi, "Composite Performance and Availability Analysis of Wireless Communication Networks," *IEEE Trans. Vehicular Technology* 50, No. 5 (2001): 1216–1223.

[31] V. Jindal, S. Dharmaraja, and K. S. Trivedi, "Analytical Model for Fault Tolerant Cellular Networks Supporing Multiple Services," *Proceedings of the International Conferenece SPECTS 2006*, Calgary, Canada, 2006, pp. 505–512.

[32] Y. Liu, B. Veena Mendiratta, and K. S. Trivedi, "Survivability Analysis of Telephone Access Network," *Proceedings of the IEEE International Symposium on Software and Reliability Engineering, ISSRE'04*, Saint-Malo, France 2004, pp. 366–377.

[33] D. Chen, S. Garg, and K. S. Trivedi, "Network Survivability Performance Evaluation: A Quantitative Approach with Applications in Wireless Ad Hoc Networks," *Proceedings of the ACM Int Workshop on Modeling, Analysis and Simulation of Wireless and Mobile Systems, MSWIM'02*, Atlanta, GA 2002, pp. 61–68.

8

CHAPTER

Integrated Dependability and Security Evaluation Using Game Theory and Markov Models

Bjarne E. Helvik   University of Science and Technology, Norway
Karin Sallhammar   University of Science and Technology, Norway
Svein J. Knapskog   University of Science and Technology, Norway

8.1   INTRODUCTION

Information and communication technologies (ICT) are tightly interwoven in every aspect of our modern society. The paradigm of ubiquitous computing and communication touches upon every activity in our everyday lives. High-capacity networks and web services have turned the Internet into today's main area for information interchange and electronic commerce. The Internet plays an increasingly important role in supporting critical applications. In summary, we have to trust ICT-based systems for the economical, social, and physical well-being of individuals and organizations. Hence, being able to analyze and quantify the trustworthiness of ICT systems is of utmost importance.

As indicated in Figure 8.1, trustworthiness is determined by the combined dependability and security of systems. Although the interrelation between these properties is recognized and has been known for a long time [1, 2], dependability and security have been analyzed separately and by different means in the past. There are several reasons why we should change this situation by pursuing a combined approach:

♦ It is desirable to have some overall quantification of the trustworthiness of a system. Some attributes are also common to the dependability and security

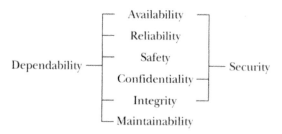

FIGURE

8.1

Dependability and security attributes. From Avizienis et al. [1].

domains (Figure 8.1). We are interested in the overall quality (here, lack of vulnerability) of a system.

✦ Many of the threats are common. It is too simplistic to regard random faults as threats toward the dependability, and intentional faults as threats toward security. This is illustrated in Figure 8.2.

✦ In order to have a model that sufficiently reflects the reality, it is necessary to include the coincident effect of combinations of various types of intentional and random faults, system management actions, automatic restoration actions, and the current state of a system.

The objective pursued in this chapter is to establish a modeling methodology that enables us to take into account both intentional and unintentional threats to a system, and to deal with the interrelated effect of these combined threats with actions related to system operation. Proceeding toward this objective, we recognize that in spite of all efforts to make a system secure, it is widely accepted that, due to the unavoidable presence of (undetected) vulnerabilities, design faults and administrative errors, an ICT system will never be totally secure. The threats making a system less than totally secure have a probabilistic nature. As pointed out in Greenwald et al. [3], the present security evaluation tools and methodologies are only adequate for securing systems on a small scale. For example, cryptography is one of the most well-studied and rigorously modeled aspects in the security field. Still, cryptography alone is not sufficient to secure a system. Most security breaches are caused by faulty software that can be exploited by, for example, buffer overflows, which unfortunately cannot be avoided by cryptographic techniques. As already mentioned, as a consequence 100% security is very difficult, if not impossible, to achieve. To be able to rely on the service that an ICT system provides, the users need to know to what extent it can be trusted. There is an urgent need for quantitative modeling

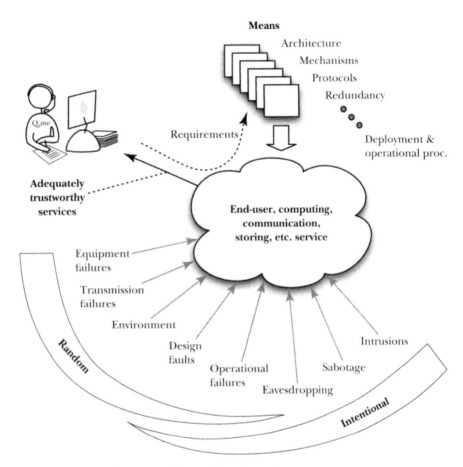

Means

Architecture

Mechanisms

Protocols

Redundancy

Deployment &
operational proc.

Requirements

Adequately
trustworthy
services

End-user, computing,
communication,
storing, etc. service

Equipment
failures

Transmission
failures

Environment

Random

Design
faults

Operational
failures

Eavesdropping

Sabotage

Intrusions

Intentional

FIGURE   Trustworthiness subject to random and intentional threats.

8.2

methods that can be used to analyze and evaluate the trustworthiness of systems. Today, there exists several methods for assessing the qualitative security level of a system, one of the most well-known being the Common Criteria [4]. However, even though such methods give an indication of the quality of the security achieved during design and implementation, they do not say anything about how a system will actually behave when operating in a particular threat environment. To be able to measure security, a new approach for quantitative evaluation is needed.

For these reasons, we seek to interpret and assess the security of a system in a probabilistic manner, where the goal is to provide a supplement to the established methods for security and dependability assessment. Probabilistic modeling and analysis to determine the dependability attributes of a system, or more precisely, the modeling and analysis under the assumption of randomly occurring faults, is well established and known. In this chapter, we will show how dependability modeling and analysis by means of a continuous-time Markov chain (CTMC) may be extended to include intentional faults (called attacks in the rest of the chapter) and also be used for obtaining quantitative probabilistic measures of system security as well as measures for system trustworthiness.

8.1.1   Previous Work

Challenges in obtaining quantitative measures of system security and trustworthiness have been recognized by other researchers. In the paper by Littlewood et al. [5], a first step toward operational measures of computer security is discussed. The authors point out the lack of quantitative measures for determining operational security and relate security assessment to the reliability domain. Quantitative measures, such as the *mean effort to security breach*, are defined and discussed. Ortalo et al. [6] present a quantitative model to measure known Unix security vulnerabilities using a privilege graph, which is transformed into a Markov chain. The model allows for the characterization of operational security expressed as the mean effort to security failure as proposed by Littlewood et al. [5]. Furthermore, Madan et al. and Wang et al. [7–9] use traditional stochastic modeling techniques to capture attacker behavior and a system's response to attacks and intrusions. A quantitative security analysis is carried out for the steady-state behavior of the system. In Singh et al. [10], an approach for probabilistic validation of an intrusion-tolerant replication system is described. They provide a hierarchical model using stochastic activity nets (SANs), which can be used to validate intrusion-tolerant systems and evaluate merits of various design choices. Finally, the paper by Nicol et al. [11] provides a survey over the existing model-based system dependability evaluation techniques, and summarizes how they are being extended to evaluate security.

The major challenge in establishing probabilistic models that properly reflect reality is to include attacks. The novelty in the approach introduced in this chapter is the recognition that a networked system is under continuous threat from an infinite number of attackers. Hence, the potential process of attacks may be assumed to be Poissonian. In each state of a system, the actions that attackers actually take should ideally be represented as a probability distribution over the possible attack actions. Therefore, we define and make use of attacker strategies as a part of the transition probabilities between states. To compute the expected attacker strategies, we use *stochastic game theory*. Game theory in a security-related context has been utilized in previous papers. A decision and control framework for a distributed intrusion detection system (IDS), where game theory is used to model and analyze attacker and IDS behavior, is proposed in Alpcan and Basar [12]. In Liu and Zang [13], a preliminary framework for modeling attacker intent, objectives, and strategies (AIOS) is presented. In Lye and Wing [14], a game-theoretic method for analyzing the security of computer networks is described. The interactions between an attacker and an administrator are modeled as a two-player stochastic game for which best-response strategies (Nash equilibrium) are computed. The approach presented in this chapter has been presented in a series of papers [15–18]. Stochastic game theory is used to compute the expected attacker behavior, where the use of the optimal strategies as a part of the transition probabilities in state transition models are introduced. The applied game theoretic method is heavily inspired by the work in Lye and Wing [14]. However, our main focus is on predicting attacker behavior rather than to find optimal defense strategies for system administrators. Hence, we use a zero-sum game rather than a general-sum model. Moreover, we model the outcome of the game elements as the possible consequences of an attacker's actions being detected or not.

8.1.2 Outline

Modeling and analysis of systems subject to random failures and handling of these is a well-established discipline, and it is assumed that the reader is familiar with dependability modeling by continuous time Markov chains (CTMCs). In this chapter, the focus is on including intrusions (intentional faults) and the detection and handling of these. Modeling attacks as a stochastic process and the construction of CTMCs for combined dependability and security evaluation are discussed in Section 8.2. Attacker behavior is predicted by game theory. The procedure for how this is done is detailed in Sections 8.3 and 8.4. In Section 8.5, it is discussed how attackers are expected to behave, depending on their risk awareness. A small case study of how our model can be used to evaluate the trustworthiness of a DNS system is presented in Section 8.6.

8.2 STOCHASTIC MODELING

At the highest level of a system's description is the specification of the system's functionality. The security policy is normally a part of this specification. This high-level description can be used to perform a qualitative assessment of system properties, such as the security levels obtained by Common Criteria evaluation [4]. Even though a qualitative evaluation can be used to rank a particular security design, its main focus is on the safeguards introduced during the development and design of a system. Moreover, such methods only evaluate static behavior of a system and do not consider dependencies of events or time aspects of failures. As a consequence, the achieved security level cannot be used to predict a system's actual robustness, that is, its ability to withstand attacks when running in a certain threat environment. To create a model suitable for quantitative analysis and assessment of operational security and dependability, one needs to use a fine-granular system description, which is capable of incorporating the dynamic behavior of a system. This is the main strength of state transition models where, at a low level, a system is modeled as a finite state machine.

A *state* in this context means an operational mode of a system characterized by which units of the system are operational or have failed, whether there are ongoing attacks, active countermeasures or, operational and maintenance activities, whether parts of the system have been compromised or not, and so on. It is assumed that a finite number N of such states $S_i, i = 1, \ldots, N$ may be defined. States are mutually exclusive, that is, a system is at any time in one and only one state. Most systems consist of a set of interacting components and the system state is therefore the set of its component states. Making such subdivisions may simplify the modeling. It would, however, complicate the presentation of the modeling approach and is omitted here.

Normally, a system will be subject to multiple failure causes, so that the model will have multiple failure modes. During its operational lifetime, a system will alternate between its different states. This may be due to normal usage as well as misuse, administrative measures and maintenance, and software and hardware failures and repairs. The behavior of a system is, therefore, characterized by the *transitions* between the states, each transition triggered by an event. The event that will occur next, as well as the time until the next event, is random. Hence, the behavior of a system is a stochastic process.

In a state transition model, one usually discriminates between good states and failed states, depending on whether the required service is delivered or not. Note that in required service, we also include whether the security requirements of a system are met or not. We may, of course, define more than one "good and failed state" classification in order to analyze the system with respect to several criteria. In other words, the system delivers service irrespective of whether the security requirements are met or not, versus a secure service is delivered. This simple binary working failed classification and corresponding measures are used for illustration. However, once CTMCs models are established, there is a potential to include rewards and the improved details from performability modeling [19, 20].

8.2.1   Failure Process

It has been shown in Avizienis et al. [1], Jonsson [2], and Powell and Stroud [21] that the "fault-error-failure" pathology, which is commonly used for modeling the failure process in a dependability context, can be applied in the security domain as well. Based on the results from this research, we demonstrate how a stochastic process can be used to model security failures in a similar way as the dependability community usually treats accidental and unintentional failures.

By definition, the fault-error-failure process is a sequence of events. A *fault* is an atomic phenomenon that can be either internal or external, which causes an error in a system. An *error* is a deviation from the correct operation of a system. An error is always internal and will not be visible from outside a system. Even though a system is erroneous it still manages to deliver its intended services. An error may lead to a *failure* of a system.

+ In a dependability context, a failure is an event that causes the delivered service to deviate from the correct service, as described in a system's functional specification.

+ Similarly, a security failure causes a system service to deviate from its security requirements, as specified in the security policy.

For each failure state, which conflicts with a system's intended functionality, we can assign a corresponding property that is violated (e.g., confidentiality-failed or availability-failed). Both security and dependability failures can be caused by a number of accidental fault sources, such as erroneous user input, administrative misconfiguration, software bugs, hardware deterioration, and so on. The failures originating from most of these faults can be modeled as randomly distributed in time, as is common practice in dependability modeling and analysis. However, the ones hardest to predict are the external malicious human-made faults, which are introduced with the objective of altering the functioning of a system during use [1].

In a security context, the result of such a fault is generally referred to as an *intrusion*. Because they are intentional in nature, intrusions cannot be modeled as truly random processes. Even though the time, or effort, to perform an intrusion may be randomly distributed, the *decision* to perform the action is not. As pointed out in Nicol et al. [11], security analysis must assume that an attacker's choice of action will depend on the system state, may change over time, and will result in security failures that are highly correlated.

8.2.2   Modeling Intrusion as Transitions

To be able to model the effect of an intrusion as a transition between a good system state and a failed system state, one needs to take a closer look at the intrusion process itself. According to Powell and Stroud [21], there are two underlying causes of any intrusion:

- At least one *vulnerability* (i.e., weakness) in a system. The vulnerability is possible to exploit, however, it will require a certain amount of time from an attacker.

- A *malicious action* that tries to exploit the vulnerability. Since the action is intentional, a decision is implicitly made by the attacker. All attackers will not choose the same course of action. Hence, there will be a probability that an attacker decides to perform a particular action.

An intrusion will, therefore, result from an action that has been successful in exploiting a vulnerability. Assume that i is a good (but vulnerable) system state and that j is a failed system state. To formalize the idea of an attacker's decision, we define $\pi_i(a)$ as the probability that an attacker will choose action a when the system is in state i. In a low-level system abstraction model, the successful intrusion will cause a transition of the system state, from the good state i to the failed state j. We assume that the system regarded is networked and may be attacked by a large number of intruders, n, as soon as it enters a vulnerable state (i.e., when a vulnerability is exposed and there is no vulnerability detection time). We model the accumulated failure intensity if all n potential attackers always take action a as $\lambda_{ij}(a)$. This corresponds to having a survival time distribution until a specific attack succeeds $\overline{F}(t)$, which for small t may be approximated by:

$$\overline{F}(t) = 1 - (\lambda_{ij}(a)t + o(t))/n \tag{8.1}$$

The survival time distribution under all attacks are $\overline{F}(t)^n$. If we let the rate of an immediately successful intrusion $\lambda_{ij}(a)/n$ decrease at the same speed as the number of intruders increase, the survival time distribution until a successful attack becomes

$$\lim_{n \to \infty} \overline{F}(t)^n = e^{\lambda_{ij}(a)t} \tag{8.2}$$

That is, a negatively exponentially distributed time until failure/intrusion. Taking the attack probability into account, the *failure rate* between state i and j becomes

$$q_{ij} = \pi_i(a)\,\lambda_{ij}(a) \tag{8.3}$$

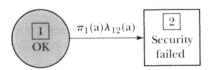

FIGURE

8.3

A two-state Markov model with assigned failure rate.

This is illustrated in Figure 8.3 where the good state $i = 1$ is depicted as a circle, and the failed state $j = 2$ as a square. A gray state symbol indicates that the system is vulnerable in this state.

By introducing the attack probability $\pi_i(a)$, the result from a successful intrusion can be modeled as one or more *intentional state changes* of the underlying stochastic process, which represents the dynamic behavior of the system. The adopted method for determining the attack probabilities will be explained in Sections 8.3 and 8.4.

In contrast to attack graphs, as used in e.g. Jha et al. [22] (see also Chapter 9), where each state transition corresponds to a single atomic step of a penetration, the modeling approach in this chapter aims to be more high level and focus on the *impact* of intrusions on a system rather than on the specific attack procedures themselves. This facilitates the modeling of unknown attacks in terms of generic state transitions. For example, in the stochastic model depicted in Figure 8.3, the attack a can simply be explained as "the action that seeks to transfer the system from the good state 1 to the failed state 2".

During the modeling process, the granularity of the state space needs to be carefully considered. Too simple models (as the one shown in Figure 8.3) will not provide any valuable insight into a system's behavior, whereas too complex models may quickly lead to state space explosion. The choice of what to include in the states definition will therefore be a trade-off between model representativeness and complexity. An example, primarily for illustration purposes, will be provided in Section 8.6.

8.2.3 Modeling the System

So far, the presentation has primarily been concentrated on how we may model attacks. In Section 8.4, we will discuss how actual attack intensities appear as the solution of a strategic game between attackers and a system, with its detection and defense mechanisms. The model of the entire system, including other events like failures, repairs, restorations, operations and maintenance (O&M) actions, and so on, defines the "battleground" (e.g., which are the vulnerable states) and influences the outcome (e.g., a restoration action may remove a vulnerability before it is exploited). The system model is also used to find the system properties of interest, like its availability or mean time to failure, as a result of the game and the parameters associated with the random events. Below we define the formalisms of the system model, and in Section 8.2.4, we explain how the measures of interest may be obtained from this model.

In the previous subsection it was established that successful attacks may be modeled as occurring with a constant intensity in a given state. With no further discussion, we also adopt the common assumption in dependability modeling and analysis that in a specific state of a system, all failure intensities, repair and restoration rates, intensities of operation and maintenance actions, and so on are either constant or may be approximated with a constant. Furthermore, these rates and intensities depend only on the current state of the system. Under these assumptions, we may formalize the ideas discussed above as a CTMC system model with a finite state space $S = \{S_1, \ldots, S_N\}$. The CTMC is defined by its $N \times N$ state transition rate matrix Q, whose elements $q_{ij} \in Q$ for $i \neq j$ are the transition rates between states i and j in the model and $q_{ii} = -\sum_{j \neq i} q_{ij}$. The q_{ij} for $i \neq j$ represent the attack success rates in Eq. 8.3, the failure intensities, intensities of operation and maintenance actions, restoration rates, etc. discussed above. An example is presented in Section 8.6.

8.2.4   Obtaining System Measures

Denote the state of a system at time t by $s(t) \in S$. Denote the probability of being in state i at t by $X_i(t)$, that is, $X_i(t) = P(s(t) = S_i)$. Let

$$X(t) = \{X_1(t), \ldots, X_N(t)\} \tag{8.4}$$

be the state probability vector. It is then well known [23, 24] that this vector may be obtained as the solution to the set of linear differential equations:

$$\frac{dX(t)}{dt} = X(0)Q \tag{8.5}$$

with the general (but not very useful) solution $X(t) = X(0)\exp(Qt)$, where $X(0)$ is the initial condition. However, a numerical solution to Eq. 8.5 is typically quite demanding due to the size of N and the stiffness of Q caused by the orders of magnitude in the ratios between the various rates in the system. Therefore, we concentrate on measures that may be obtained from the asymptotic (i.e., steady-state) behavior of the system. Let

$$\mathbf{X} = \lim_{t \to \infty} \mathbf{X}(t) \tag{8.6}$$

The asymptotic state probabilities of the system may now be obtained [23] as the solution to the set of linear equations:

$$\mathbf{XQ} = \mathbf{0}_N \tag{8.7}$$

with one of the equations in Eq. 8.7 replaced by:

$$\mathbf{X1}_N = 1 \tag{8.8}$$

In the above equations, $\mathbf{0}_N$ and $\mathbf{1}_N$ represent vectors of length N constituted of elements all being 0 and 1, respectively, the latter being a column vector.

Having obtained the asymptotic state probabilities $\mathbf{X}$ in Eq. 8.6, we may obtain operational measures of the system like the availability (A), the mean time between failures (MTBF), the mean time spent in the good states (MUT), and so on. The system measures of special interest in our context are:

✦ The mean time to first failure (MTFF) for the system (i.e., the expected time from the system is *as new* and until the first failure).

✦ The mean time to failure (MTTF) (i.e., the expected duration until a failure occurs when we start to observe the system when it is asymptotically in a good state).

See Figure 8.4 for an illustration of these two system measures.

To efficiently compute these measures, we adopt the approach of Buzacott [25]. The state space is partitioned into two disjoint sets $\mathbf{S} = \{\mathbf{S}_G, \mathbf{S}_F\}$, where

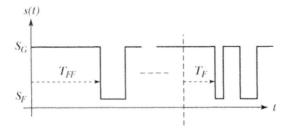

FIGURE 8.4 Sample behavior of a system alternating between good and failed states, where $MTFF = E(T_{FF})$ and $MTTF = E(T_F)$.

$\mathbf{S}_G = \{S_1,\ldots,S_K\}$ and $\mathbf{S}_F = \{S_{K+1},\ldots,S_N\}$, so that the states $1,\ldots,K$ are good states and the states $K+1,\ldots,N$ are failed states. Since the state set $\mathbf{S}$ is ordered, the $\mathbf{Q}$ matrix can be written in partitioned form as:

$$\mathbf{Q} = \begin{bmatrix} \mathbf{Q}_1 & \mathbf{Q}_2 \\ \mathbf{Q}_3 & \mathbf{Q}_4 \end{bmatrix} \tag{8.9}$$

where the size of $\mathbf{Q}_1$ is $K \times K$, the size of $\mathbf{Q}_2$ is $K \times (N - K)$, and so forth. To compute $MTFF$ one assumes that the system is as new at $t = 0$. Let this be state $S_1 \in \mathbf{S}_G$. Define $\mathbf{T} = \{T_1,\ldots,T_K\}$. By solving

$$-\mathbf{T}\mathbf{Q}_1 = \{1,0,\ldots,0\} \tag{8.10}$$

the $MTFF$ for the system can be computed as:

$$MTFF = \mathbf{T}\mathbf{1}_K \tag{8.11}$$

To obtain $MTTF$, the asymptotic state probabilities (Eq. 8.6) must be known. Since $\mathbf{S}$ is partitioned, $\mathbf{X}$ also can be partitioned as $\mathbf{X} = \{\mathbf{X}_G,\mathbf{X}_F\}$, where $\mathbf{X}_G = \{X_1,\ldots,X_K\}$ and $\mathbf{X}_F = \{X_{K+1},\ldots,X_N\}$. The asymptotic probability of being in one of the good states is from the Markov property:

$$\mathbf{X}_G^* = \lim_{t \to \infty} P(\{s(t) \in S_i\}_{i=1,\ldots,K} | s(t) \in \mathbf{S}_G) = \frac{\mathbf{X}_G}{\mathbf{X}_G \mathbf{1}_K} \tag{8.12}$$

Hence,

$$MTTF = \mathbf{X}_G^*(-\mathbf{Q}_1)^{-1}\mathbf{1}_K = \frac{\mathbf{X}_G(-\mathbf{Q}_1)^{-1}\mathbf{1}_K}{\mathbf{X}_G \mathbf{1}_K} \tag{8.13}$$

Having obtained the asymptotic state probabilities, the availability of the system is straightforwardly obtained as:

$$A = \lim_{t \to \infty} P(s(t) \in \mathbf{S}_G) = \mathbf{X}_G \mathbf{1}_K \tag{8.14}$$

8.2.5   Model Parametrization

In order to obtain measures (MTFF, MTTF), the stochastic model has to be parametrized (i.e., the elements $q_{ij} \in \mathbf{Q}$ need to be evaluated). The procedure of obtaining accidental failure and repair rates has been practiced for many years in traditional dependability analysis, and will therefore not be discussed in this chapter. However, choosing the accumulated attack intensities $\lambda_{ij}(a)$ remains a challenge. One solution is to let security experts assess the intensities based on subjective expert opinion, empirical data, or a combination of both. An example of empirical data is historical attack data collected from honeypots. The data can also be based on intrusion experiments performed by students in a controlled environment. Empirical data from such an experiment conducted at Chalmers University of Technology in Sweden [26] indicates that the time between successful intrusions during the standard attack phase is exponentially distributed. Another ongoing project at the Carnegie Mellon CyLab in Pittsburgh, PA [27] aims to collect information from a number of different sources in order to predict attacks. Even though the process of assessing the attack intensities is crucial, and an important research topic in itself, it is not the primary focus of this chapter.

Obtaining realistic $\pi_i(a)$ (i.e., the probabilities that an attacker chooses particular attack actions in certain system states) may be more difficult. In this chapter, we use *game theory* as a means for computing the expected attacker behavior. The procedure is summarized in Section 8.3.

8.3   PREDICTING ATTACKER BEHAVIOR

To compute the expected attacker behavior, in terms of attack probabilities as part of the transition rates between states in a CTMC (see Section 8.2.2), one needs to consider the underlying reasons of why attacks occur in the first place. One of the most crucial factors in the analysis of attacker behavior is motivation. In Project [28], six major factors that motivate an attacker's choices of action are identified:

1. Financial gain is the main source of motivation for actions such as credit card theft, blackmailing, or extraction of confidential information.

2. Entertainment can be the cause of hacking web sites or rerouting Internet browser requests.

3. The motive of ego is the satisfaction and rise in self-esteem that comes from overcoming technical difficulties or finding innovative solutions.

4. Cause, or ideology, can be based on culture, religion, or social issues, and in Project [28], it is pointed out that it is likely to increase as a motivation factor in the future.

5. For some attackers, entrance to a social group of hackers can be the driving force behind writing a particular exploit, or breaking into a particularly strong computer security defense.

6. Status is probably the most powerful motivation factor, and is currently motivating many of today's computer or network system intrusions.

On the other hand, a number of factors may reduce the attacker's motivation and make them refrain from certain attack actions. In our modeling framework, we include the aspect that attackers may be risk averse. For example, students with a user account at a university will put their enrollment status at risk if they use their insider privileges to abuse their local computer network. The gain from a successful break-in into the university file server may be smaller than the possible consequences if the intrusion is detected by the system administrators. As another example, the illegal aspect of actions (criminal offense) may prevent even remote attackers to use available tools to exploit vulnerabilities in corporate networks. To predict attacker behavior, in terms of attack probabilities for a stochastic model, both the underlying motivation factors as well as the possible deterrent aspects need to be carefully considered.

8.3.1   Reward and Cost Concept

To model the attacker's motivation in a situation with a realistic risk awareness, we make use of a reward and cost concept. In our model, an attacker accumulates *reward* during the events of an attack. Whenever an attacker performs an attack action, he or she receives an immediate reward. Furthermore, if the action succeeds, an additional reward may be gained. This is modeled in terms of expected future rewards, which is due to the ability to continue the attack. An attack action can be considered successful if the action causes an undesirable transformation of the current system state. The transition probabilities between states will, therefore, be an important aspect of the expected reward when an attacker decides what action to take. To model the possible consequences experienced by risk-averse attackers, a negative reward, or *cost*, is used to quantify the impact on an attacker as an attack action is detected and reacted to.

Both reward and cost are generic concepts that can be used to quantify the consequences of the actions both in terms of abstract values, such as social status and satisfaction versus disrespect and disappointment, as well as real values, such as financial gain and loss. For instance, in Lye and Wing [14], the reward of a successful attack action is the expected amount of recovery effort required from a system administrator, and in Liu and Zang [13], the reward is the degree of bandwidth occupied by a Distributed Denial of Service (DDoS) attack. In contrast to Lye and Wing [14] and Liu and Zang [13], we use the cost values in the game model to represent the fact that risk-averse attackers may sometimes refrain from certain attack actions due to the possible consequences of detection. In this chapter, the term "outcome" will be used to represent a consequence value, which can be either a reward or cost. Note that the outcome values themselves are not important, it is their size relative to each other that will affect the expected attacker behavior. This topic will be discussed further in Section 8.5.

8.3.2   Modeling Interactions as a Game

In order to create a generic and sound framework for computing the expected attacker behavior in terms of attack probabilities, this chapter applies game theory as the mathematical tool. Each atomic attack action, which may cause a transition of the current system state, is regarded as an action in a game where an attacker's choice of action is based on a consideration of the possible consequences. The interactions between the attackers and the systems can then be modeled as a game, as illustrated in Figure 8.5.

As can be seen, aspects that are included in the game are the detection probabilities of attack actions, operational activities that may affect the current system state, random software and hardware failures that may occur, and of course the outcome (reward and cost values) associated with the available attack

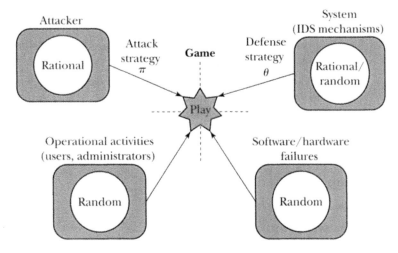

FIGURE

8.5

The interactions between an attacker and a system modeled as a game.

actions (not depicted in Figure 8.5). In this chapter, attackers are assumed to be rational, which, in a game theoretic context, means that they seek to maximize their own reward from attacks and, consequently, to minimize the cost associated with attacks.

8.3.3   Stochastic Game Model

In the context of attack prediction for evaluating security and dependability, the game is played by an attacker versus a system. In fact, the attacker's real counterplayer in the game is the system's IDS mechanisms, for simplicity referred to as "the system" hereafter. In this chapter, we use a two-player, zero-sum stochastic game to compute the expected attacker behavior, in terms of a set of attack probability vectors $\pi = \{\pi_i\}$. Even though in real life there may be numerous attackers attacking the system, simultaneously and independent of each other, a two-player game model is sufficient to predict their individual behavior, provided that they possess similar motives and skills. In contrast to previous research in the field of network security and game theory (see Section 8.1.1), we view the game entirely from an attacker's perspective. The purpose of our game model is to predict the behavior of attackers and not to perform any cost-benefit optimization of system defense strategies. Therefore, we assume that the set of system IDS mechanisms are fixed and do not change over time. Since the game is zero-sum, one player's gain will be the other player's loss. Hence, we do not need to specify separate outcome values for the system itself, as was done in Lye and Wing [14] and Alpcan and Basar [12]; it is sufficient to assign the attackers outcome values. The main benefit of our approach is that it does not assume that the attackers know the system outcome values. It also reduces the number of parameters that have to be assessed in the system evaluation model.

Formally, the game we use is a tuple $(\Gamma, A, D, \gamma, p)$, where $\Gamma = \{\Gamma_i\}$ is a state set, $A = \{a\}$ and $D = \{d\}$ are action sets, $\gamma : \Gamma \times A \times D \to \mathcal{R}$ is an outcome function, and $p : \Gamma \times A \times D \times \Gamma \to [0, 1]$ is a state transition probability function. To obtain the attack probabilities, a five-step procedure can be used:

1. Identify the game elements.

2. Construct the action sets.

3. Assign the outcome values.

4. Compute the transition probabilities.

5. Solve the game.

These steps will be explained in detail in Section 8.4.

8.4   DEFINING AND SOLVING THE GAME

To compute the expected attacker behavior by means of a stochastic game, the procedure is as follows.

Step 1: Identify the Game Elements

The first step is to identify the game elements. From the stochastic model, pick all states in **S** where the system is vulnerable to intrusions. Each of these states can be viewed as a game element Γ_i in a two-player, zero-sum stochastic game with state set Γ. For example, in Figure 8.6, the gray states V, L, and IS represent states where the system is vulnerable to one or more attack actions. Hence, the set of game elements for this model is $\Gamma = \{\Gamma_V, \Gamma_L, \Gamma_{IS}\}$. Note that even though the system state space **S** may be very large, the corresponding set with game elements Γ will often contain only a subset of all the states in **S**, as the example indicates.

Step 2: Construct the Action Sets

The next step is to construct the action sets A and D. Set A consists of all possible attack actions. For all transitions out of the game element states, which represent intrusions, identify the corresponding attack actions. Note that A must also contain an "inaction," which we will denote by ϕ, to represent that an attacker may not take any action at all. We use $A_i = \{a_1, \ldots, a_m\}$ to refer to the set of

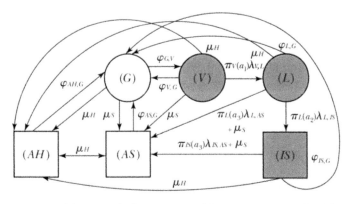

FIGURE   State transition model of DNS server with game elements identified.

8.6

actions available in game state i. All actions will not necessarily be available in all states (i.e., $A_i \subseteq A$, however, $A_i \cap \phi = \phi$). For instance, in Figure 8.6, the complete action set is $A = \{a_1, a_2, a_3, \phi\}$, where $A_V = \{a_1, \phi\}$, $A_I = \{a_2, a_3, \phi\}$, and $A_{IS} = \{a_3, \phi\}$.

Let π_i be a probability distribution over the action set A_i. In a game theoretic context, $\pi_i = (\pi_i(a_1), \ldots, \pi_i(a_m))$ is called the *attack strategy* of Γ_i. Hence, $\pi_i(a_k) \in \pi_i$ will be the probability that an attacker chooses action a_k when the system is in state i, as previously discussed. One must have $0 \leq \pi_i(a_k) \leq 1$, $\forall \pi_i(a_k) \in \pi_i$ and $\sum_{a_k} \pi_i(a_k) = 1$, $\forall \Gamma_i \in \Gamma$. The attack probability vectors π_i will now represent the degree of hostility in the network environment, or equivalently, the aggressiveness of the attackers targeting the system. The smaller the $\pi_i(a_k)$, the less probability of the particular attack a_k in system state i and, hence, the smaller the corresponding failure rate will be.

Set D consists of all possible defense actions, where $D_i = \{d_1, \ldots, d_m\}$ is the set of actions available in state i. The system *defense strategy* of Γ_i is $\theta_i = (\theta_i(d_1), \ldots, \theta_i(d_m))$. Hence, $\theta_i(d_k) \in \theta_i$ is the probability that an IDS alarm indicating action a_k will be triggered in system state i. As for A_i, also D_i must contain an ϕ element, since there may not be any reaction at all from the system. Also $0 \leq \theta_i(d_k) \leq 1$, $\forall \theta_i(d_k) \in \theta_i$ and $\sum_{d_k} \theta_i(d_k) = 1$, $\forall \Gamma_i \in \Gamma$.

A strategy is *stationary* if, for all states i, the corresponding strategy vector is independent of time. To avoid the mathematical obstacles of dynamic strategies, only stationary attack and defense strategies will be considered in this chapter.

Step 3: Assign the Outcome Values

To model the attacker's motivation, we make use of the reward and cost concept introduced in Section 8.3. As previously discussed, an outcome of a game element is a possible consequence of a play of the game, as experienced by an attacker. For each game element Γ_i, we assign an outcome value to each attack action and defense action pair (a_k, d_l). These values will be denoted r_{kl} or c_{kl}, depending on whether the outcome represents a reward or cost respectively. Since the game is zero-sum, we do not need to assign outcome values for the system; consequently, in our game model an attacker's gain will be the system's loss and vice versa.

As an example, the possible outcomes from game element Γ_V in Figure 8.6 are depicted in Figure 8.7. Since an attacker has two actions to choose between, $A_V = \{a_1, \phi\}$, and there are two possible response actions, $D_V = \{d_1, \phi\}$, there are four possible outcomes from that particular play. It could be argued that since nothing happens if the attacker does not take any action, the outcomes from the action pairs (ϕ, d_1) and (ϕ, ϕ) do not make any sense from an attacker's point of

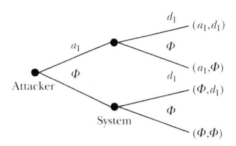

FIGURE

8.7
The possible outcomes from game element Γ_V.

view. We counter this by pointing out that what we aim to compute from Γ_V is the expected attacker behavior in terms of strategy $\pi_V = (\pi_V(a_1), \pi_V(\phi))$, which an attacker decides to adopt before the attack. So, if we assign a reward to the action pair (ϕ, d_1), it implies that if the attacker decides not to attack the system, no matter what, and that all the attacks will always be detected, then the attacker will experience this outcome as a gain: "It's good that I didn't try to attack the system, since I would have been detected if I did." This will be the case even though the system never gets a chance to actually detect any attack. The same line of reasoning is valid for the (ϕ, ϕ) outcome.

Step 4: Compute the Transition Probabilities

Given that an attack action is chosen in state i, and that the intrusion is successful and remains undetected, the system may transfer to another state j where the game can continue. The transition probability between game element Γ_i and Γ_j, denoted $p_{ij}(a_k, d_l)$, can be computed by conditioning on the chosen action a_k and the system response d_l. For example, if the system in Figure 8.6 is in state V and an attacker decides to attack the system, and the action remains undetected, then $\pi_V(a_1|(a_1, \phi)) = 1$. It is obtained from the Markov properties of the system that the probability of going from state V to L when an attack takes place becomes:

$$p_{VL}(a_1, \phi) = \frac{\lambda_{VL}}{\lambda_{VL} + \varphi_{VG} + \mu_S + \mu_H} \tag{8.15}$$

Here, φ_{VG}, μ_S, and μ_H are the rates of the competing events, which may disturb the attack. Hence, Eq. 8.15 is the probability that the game will continue in state L. Note that one must have $p_{ij}(a_k, d_l) \geq 0$ and $\sum_j p_{ij}(a_k, d_l) < 1, \forall \Gamma_i \in \Gamma$.

Recall that A_i and D_i are the action sets associated with state i. The possible outcomes of each game element Γ_i can now be represented by a $|A_i| \times |D_i|$ matrix, which has the form

$$\Gamma_i = \begin{array}{c||c|c|c} & d_1 & \cdots & d_m \\ \hline\hline a_1 & \gamma_{11} & \cdots & \gamma_{1m} \\ \hline \vdots & \vdots & & \vdots \\ \hline a_m & \gamma_{m1} & \cdots & \gamma_{mm} \end{array} \qquad (8.16)$$

where γ_{kl} is the total outcome associated with the action pair (a_k, d_l). The entries in Eq. 8.16, representing state i, are of the form

$$\gamma_{kl} = \begin{cases} r_{kl} + \sum_j p_{ij}(a_k, d_l)\Gamma_j & \text{for successful attacks,} \\ c_{kl} & \text{otherwise,} \end{cases} \qquad (8.17)$$

for which $r_{kl} \geq 0$ and $c_{kl} \leq 0$. When solving the game, the Γ_j element in Eq. 8.17 must be replaced by a value, as will be explained in the next subsection. The first case in Eq. 8.17 applies if the outcome represents a successful and undetected attack action. The attacker receives an immediate reward r_{kl} and there is also a possibility of future rewards, since the system may move to another game state. The second case normally applies if an attack action is detected, but can also apply if an attacker resigns even though any of the possible attacks would have been undetected. The attacker receives a cost c_{kl}. Implicitly, the formulation in Eq. 8.17 means that the game will end if an attack is detected and reacted to, if the attacker resigns, or if the system does not transfer to another game state, which will happen with probability $1 - \sum_j p_{ij}(a_k, d_l)$.

Step 5: Solve the Game

The last step is to solve the game. Here, solving means to compute the best strategies for the players who participate in the game. Our model relies on the basic assumption of game theory, which states that a rational player will always try to maximize his or her own reward. For each system state i, which is modeled as a game element Γ_i, we can therefore expect an attacker to behave in accordance with the probability distribution $\pi_i = (\pi_i(a_1), \ldots, \pi_i(a_m))$ that maximizes $E(\pi_i, \theta_i)$, where:

$$E(\pi_i, \theta_i) = \sum_{\forall a_k \in A_i} \sum_{\forall d_l \in D_i} \pi_i(a_k)\theta_i(d_l)\gamma_{kl} \qquad (8.18)$$

Recall that we use zero-sum game elements to model the interactions between an attacker and the system. This implies that an attacker who does not know the defense strategy θ_i will think of the system as a counterplayer in the game who tries to minimize the attacker's reward. Hence, the optimal attack strategy of Γ_i, and its corresponding defense strategy, are obtained by solving

$$\max_{\pi_i} \min_{\theta_i} E(\pi_i, \theta_i) \qquad (8.19)$$

These strategies will be denoted π_i^* and θ_i^*, respectively. The *value* of game element Γ_i, denoted $V(i)$, is defined as the expected outcome when π_i^* and θ_i^* are used, that is,

$$V(i) = E(\pi_i^*, \theta_i^*) \qquad (8.20)$$

The purpose of the stochastic game model is to predict the complete set of attack probability vectors $\pi^* = \{\pi_i^*\}$ to be used in the system rate matrix $\mathbf{Q}$. To find the π_i^* strategies for all game elements in the stochastic game, one can use Algorithm 8.1, which is based on the Shapley algorithm [29]. The functions Value[Γ_i] and Solve[Γ_i] refer to standard algorithms for solving zero-sum matrix games by linear programming. The former returns the expected value in Eq. 8.20 when an attacker and the system use their optimal strategies, whereas the latter returns the attacker's optimal strategy itself as resulting from Eq. 8.19. Note that Algorithm 8.1 replaces the game element Γ_j in Eq. 8.17 with its value component $V(j)$ iteratively when solving the stochastic game. For further details on the underlying assumptions and solution of the stochastic game model, the reader is referred to Owen [30, pp. 96–101].

We believe that the optimal attack strategy set $\pi^* = \{\pi_i^*\}$ will be a good indication of the expected attack probabilities for the vulnerable system states. This is because π^* gives a lower bound on the attacker outcome, regardless of the system defense strategy. When following π^*, the attacker has no reason to change strategy—the *no-regrets property* of game theory. This property means that the attacker has maximized his or her expected outcome from the attack, regardless if his or her actions are successful or not. Several experienced researchers indicate that this search for guarantees is a very strong motivation of human behavior. Assuming that the attacker population targeting the system will make rational choices relative to their objectives, their collected behavior will, in the long run, gravitate toward the optimal attack strategy [31].

Algorithm 8.1   Compute Expected Attacker Strategy

Require: $(\Gamma, A, D, \gamma, p)$ {a stochastic game}
Ensure: π^* {the optimal attack strategy}
  Initialize the value vector $V = \{V(i)\}$ arbitrarily
  repeat
    for each game element $\Gamma_i \in \Gamma$ **do**
      for all γ_{kl} **do**
        replace all Γ_j in Eq. 8.16 with $V(j)$
      end for
      compute the matrix $\Gamma_i(V) = [\gamma_{kl}]$,
    end for
    for each game element $\Gamma_i \in \Gamma$ **do**
      update the value vector $V(i) \leftarrow \text{Value}[\Gamma_i(V)]$
    end for
  until $V(i) = \text{Value}[\Gamma_i(V)], \forall \Gamma_i \in \Gamma$
  for each game element $\Gamma_i \in \Gamma$ **do**
    $\pi_i^* \leftarrow \text{Solve}[\Gamma_i(V)]$
  end for
  return the set of equilibrium vectors $\pi^* = \{\pi_i^*\}$

8.5   TUNING THE GAME PARAMETERS

The stochastic game model presented in the previous section is based on a reward and cost concept. As discussed in Section 8.3, these values will represent the attacker's motivation when deciding on attack actions. Whenever an attacker performs an attack action, he or she immediately receives a reward. Furthermore, if the action succeeds, additional rewards may be gained. We use negative rewards (i.e., costs) to make room for the possibility that attackers may be risk averse. The cost of a detected action will be an important demotivating factor when modeling, for example, insiders; legitimate users who override their current privileges. Similarly, commercial adversaries would lose reputation and market share if it is exposed that illegal means are used.

Since we have chosen to model the interactions between an attacker and the system as a zero-sum game rather than a general-sum one, an increasing cost value will play a deterrent role for an attacker. However, due to the inherent properties of the minimax solution in Eq. 8.19, an increasing reward value will indirectly play a deterrent role for an attacker. One must, therefore, vary the cost parameters rather than the reward parameters in order to get an intuitive corresponding attack strategy. This process will be further illustrated in the upcoming examples in this section. The purpose of the, relatively simple, analysis is to give the reader a better understanding of the case study in Section 8.6.

In Eq. 8.17, we set $r_{kl} = 1$ and $p_{ij}(a_k, d_l) = 0$, $\forall j,k,l$, and then let the cost value vary between $-10 \leq c_{kl} \leq 1$. This provides us with the possibility of analyzing, for example, how the cost of a detected attack versus the reward of an undetected one will affect the expected attacker behavior for a particular system state i.

8.5.1   One Possible Attack Action

As a first example, assume that a system is vulnerable to a single attack action in state i. An attacker can choose either to perform the attack (action a) or to resign (action ϕ). The system's response actions are then to either set an alarm (action d) or no reaction (action ϕ). Hence, $A_i = \{a,\phi\}$ and $D_i = \{\phi,d\}$. To model this scenario we use the 2×2 game element:

$$
\Gamma_i = \begin{array}{c|c|c} & \phi & d \\ \hline a & \gamma_{a\phi} & \gamma_{ad} \\ \hline \phi & \gamma_{\phi\phi} & \gamma_{\phi d} \end{array} = \begin{array}{c|c|c} & \phi & d \\ \hline a & 1 & c_{ad} \\ \hline \phi & c_{\phi\phi} & 0 \end{array}
\tag{8.21}
$$

where the cost value c_{ad} represents an attacker's cost of a detected action and $c_{\phi\phi}$ is the cost of resigning even though an attempted attack would have been undetected. By varying c_{ad} and $c_{\phi\phi}$, we can now demonstrate how the relation $\gamma_{ad}/\gamma_{a\phi}$ (i.e., the cost of a detected attack versus the reward of an undetected attack) and $\gamma_{\phi\phi}/\gamma_{a\phi}$ (i.e., the cost associated with resigning versus the reward of an undetected attack) will affect the expected attacker behavior, in terms of the attack probability $\pi_i^*(a)$. To compute $\pi_i^* = (\pi_i^*(a), \pi_i^*(\phi))$, we solve Eq. 8.19, as previously discussed.

Reducing c_{ad}. If $c_{ad} = -2$ and $c_{\phi\phi} = -3$ in Eq. 8.21, then the expected probability of attacking will be $\pi_i^*(a) = 0.50$. However, if the cost of a detected action is increased to $c_{ad} = -10$, then $\pi_i^*(a) = 0.21$. Hence, an increasing cost of a detected action will decrease the attacker's motivation.

Reducing $c_{\phi\phi}$. Again, if $c_{ad} = -2$ and $c_{\phi\phi} = -3$ in Eq. 8.21, then $\pi_i^*(a) = 0.50$. However, if $c_{\phi\phi} = -10$, then $\pi_i^*(a) = 0.77$. As the cost of resigning increases, the attacker's motivation will increase.

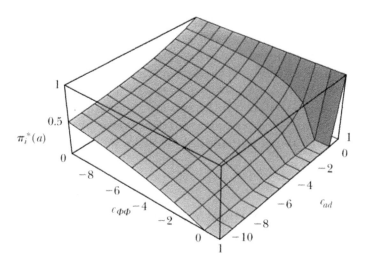

The expected attacker behavior $\pi_i^*(a)$ with respect to c_{ad} and $c_{\phi\phi}$.

Figure 8.8 depicts a more complete graph of a risk-averse attacker's expected behavior, according to Eq. 8.21. In the graph, we let $-10 \leq c_{ad}, c_{\phi\phi} \leq 1$. One can see that the expected probability of attacking is highest, $\pi_i^*(a) = 1.0$, when $c_{ad} = 1$. This is intuitive since an attacker who receives the same reward whether he or she is detected or not will always choose to attack. On the other hand, the expected probability of attacking is lowest, $\pi_i^*(a) = 0.0$, when $c_{\phi\phi} > 0$ and $c_{ad} < 0$. This can be interpreted as if the reward of an attack is small enough, so that it is not significantly greater than the cost of resigning, an attacker may not even bother to try (of course this is an ideal situation unlikely to occur in real life). In general, as the examples indicate and the graph illustrates, as the cost values increase, we can expect the attacker to act more carefully.

It is interesting to note that even though measures are taken to increase the cost of detected actions, legal proceedings for instance, a rapidly decreasing c_{ad} will only have marginal effect on the behavior of an attacker who has a strong reluctance of resigning. This is shown in Figure 8.8 as a slowly decreasing $\pi_i^*(a)$ along the "$c_{\phi\phi} = -10$" axis. In fact, the parameter that has the strongest influence on the expected attacker behavior with respect to Eq. 8.21 is $c_{\phi\phi}$. Unfortunately, since $c_{\phi\phi}$ represents a mental factor in this game (the attacker's reluctance to resign), it will be difficult for a system administrator to take preventive measures influencing $c_{\phi\phi}$ in a way that will reduce $\pi_i^*(a)$.

8.5.2 Two Possible Attack Actions

Assume that there are two possible attack actions available in system state i. This scenario can be represented by the 3×3 game element:

$$
\Gamma_i = \begin{array}{c|c|c|c}
 & \phi & d_1 & d_2 \\
\hline
a_1 & 1 & c_{a_1 d_1} & 1 \\
\hline
a_2 & 1 & 1 & c_{a_2 d_2} \\
\hline
\phi & c_{\phi\phi} & 0 & 0
\end{array} \tag{8.22}
$$

where $A_i = \{a_1, a_2, \phi\}$ and $D_i = \{\phi, d_1, d_2\}$. Now the expected attack probability π_i^* will depend on $c_{a_1 d_1}$, $c_{a_2 d_2}$, and $c_{\phi\phi}$. Figures 8.9–8.11 depict how $\pi_i^*(a_1)$ will vary for $-10 \leq c_{a_1 d_1}, c_{\phi\phi} \leq 1$, $-10 \leq c_{a_2 d_2}, c_{\phi\phi} \leq 1$, and $-10 \leq c_{a_1 d_1}, c_{a_2 d_2} \leq 1$ when $c_{a_2 d_2} = -3$, $c_{a_1 d_1} = -3$, and $c_{\phi\phi} = -2$, respectively.

Some interesting observations are:

- The general trend of the expected attacker behavior in Figures 8.9 and 8.10 is that $\pi_i^*(a_1) \to 0$ when $c_{\phi\phi} \to 0$ (i.e., the attack probability decreases as the cost of resigning decreases). However, $\pi_i^*(a_1)$ does not decrease as $c_{\phi\phi}$ decreases when $c_{a_1 d_1} > 0$ (Figure 8.9). Since there is no negative cost value associated with action a_1, regardless of the system's response, the cost associated with resigning will not affect the probability of attack a_1.

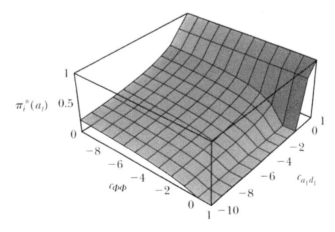

FIGURE 8.9 The attack probability $\pi_i^*(a_1)$ with respect to $c_{\phi\phi}$ and $c_{a_1 d_1}$ when $c_{a_2 d_2} = -3$.

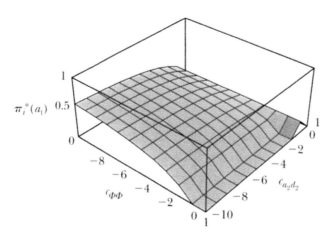

FIGURE

8.10

The attack probability $\pi_i^*(a_1)$ with respect to $c_{\phi\phi}$ and $c_{a_2 d_2}$ when $c_{a_1 d_1} = -3$.

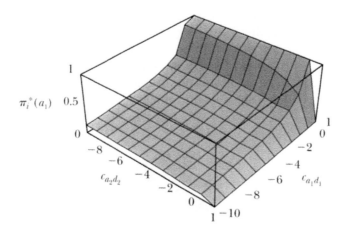

FIGURE

8.11

The attack probability $\pi_i^*(a_1)$ with respect to $c_{a_2 d_2}$ and $c_{a_1 d_1}$ when $c_{\phi\phi} = -2$.

♦ Naturally, $\pi_i^*(a_1)$ decreases as $c_{a_1 d_1}$ increases (Figure 8.9). On the contrary, $\pi_i^*(a_1)$ increases as $c_{a_2 d_2}$ increases (Figure 8.10). A higher cost of a detected action a_2 will increase the probability of action a_1, rather than a_2.

♦ In Figure 8.11, one can see that $\pi_i^*(a_1)$ will be close to 1 only when $c_{a_1 d_1} > 0$ and $c_{a_2 d_2} < 0$. As soon as there is a cost of a detected action a_1 (i.e., $c_{a_1 d_1} < 0$), the attack probability vector π_i^* will become more evenly distributed.

There are corresponding results for $\pi_i^*(a_2)$. These graphs are therefore not included in this chapter.

The same methodology can also be used to compute the expected attacker behavior for states where a system is vulnerable to a large number of attack actions. This has been demonstrated in Sallhammar et al. [18], which shows that, also for larger games, an increasing cost of a detected action will lead to a smaller probability of an attacker choosing that particular action.

8.5.3 Attacker Profiling

To distinguish between different types of attackers, it is common practice to make use of attacker profiles. A number of fine-granular classifications of attackers exist in the literature. In [32], Rogers summarizes earlier research on attacker categorization and provides a new taxonomy based on a two-dimensional circumflex classification model. *Skill* and *motivation* are identified as the primary classification criteria, which fit well into our mathematical framework where attacker skill is represented by attack intensities, as discussed in Section 8.2.2, and the motivation by the reward and cost concept. The advantage of Rogers circumflex approach is that it does not rely on any hard categorization model, but can rather serve as a basis when defining attacker profiles that share similar characteristics. Hence, to comply with the model in CERIAS [32], we suggest tuning, of the cost values of the game elements as well as the attack intensities in the stochastic model, to characterize the motivation and skill of the particular kind of attackers that are considered in the system's threat environment. The influence of the outcome values in the game model on the attack probabilities was demonstrated in this section.

In this chapter, we have implicitly assumed that all attackers are of the same type (i.e., share the same skills and motivation). It may, however, be more realistic to regard several types, for instance, skilled, risk-averse internal attackers and less skilled and risk-averse external attackers. This may be introduced in the model by replacing the intruder transition rates introduced in Section 8.2.2 (see Eq. 8.3) by:

$$q_{ij} = \sum_{\forall k} \pi_i^{(k)}(a)\lambda_{ij}^{(k)}(a) \tag{8.23}$$

where k denotes the type of attacker. The strategies for each attacker, $\pi_i^{(k)}(a)$, may be obtained by the procedure presented in this section, with the exception that we must take into account the coupling between attacks. For instance, the transition probability in Eq. 8.15 must be replaced by

$$p_{VL}^{(l)}(a_1, \phi) = -\frac{\lambda_{VL}^{(l)}}{\lambda_{VL}^{(l)} + \sum_{\forall k \neq l} \pi_V^{(k)}(a) \lambda_{VL}^{(k)}(a) + \varphi_{VG} + \mu_S + \mu_H} \qquad (8.24)$$

when modeling more than one type of attackers. It is seen that this also requires an iteration over the types of attackers, in addition to the iterations to find the strategies, which poses an increased computational effort.

8.6   CASE STUDY: DNS SERVICE

To further illustrate the approach, we model and analyze the trustworthiness (i.e., the security and dependability behavior) of a DNS service. The Domain Name System (DNS) provides a critical service to the Internet—the mapping between names and addresses. The original DNS specifications require that each domain name is served by (at least) two servers, usually referred to as the "primary" and "secondary" server. The primary DNS server holds the "master copy" of the data for a zone. When changes are made to zone data on the primary server, they must be distributed to the secondary server. The secondary server also periodically checks for changes. Contaminated data from the primary can, therefore, be transferred to the secondary server. For the purpose of redundancy, the recommended practice is to configure the primary and secondary DNS servers on separate machines, on separate Internet connections, and in separate geographic locations. Therefore, one can assume that both servers are attacked, will fail, and be repaired independently of each other.

The most important attributes of this service are availability and integrity; the service should be there when the clients need it, and it must provide correct replies to DNS requests. We distinguish between two different types of accidental failures: hardware availability failures, which require a manual repair, and software availability failures, which only require a system reconfiguration and/or reboot. Unfortunately, buffer overflow vulnerabilities are common in multiple implementations of DNS resolver libraries. During its operational lifetime, both servers will be subject to manual maintenance, upgrades, and reconfigurations. Humans frequently make mistakes. Therefore, it is realistic to assume that a server will alternate between a good state (G) where it is secure against these types of attacks and a vulnerable state (V) where buffer overflow attacks are possible. When a server is in the V state, an attacker who can send malicious DNS requests might exploit such a vulnerability to gain access to the server. This will transfer the server into a third state (L), from where it is possible to insert false entries in the server cache—software integrity failure (IS)—or to shut the server down—software availability failure (AS). Both servers are also subject to hardware availability failures (AH). State G, V, and L are considered to be good states. Even though a server is erroneous in state V and L, it still manages to deliver the intended service, that is, to provide clients with correct replies to DNS requests when requested.

8.6.1   Stochastic Model

The service provided by the duplicated DNS service can be described by 36 states: $\mathbf{S} = \{S_1,\ldots,S_{36}\} = \{(s_i,s_j)|s_i,s_j = G,V,L,IS,AS,AH\}$, where (s_i,s_j) means that the primary server is in state i and the secondary server in state j. As long as the primary server is in state G, V, or L, it will deliver the intended service regardless of the internal state of the secondary. There are four states where the DNS service is unavailable due to accidental software and hardware failures: (AS,AS), (AS,AH), (AH,AS), and (AH,AH). However, in states (IS,G), (IS,V), (IS,L), (IS,IS), (IS,AS), (IS,AH), (AS,IS), and (AH,IS), the service is available, but it provides erroneous results. All these states will, therefore, be included in the set of failed states $\mathbf{S}_F$ in the upcoming system analysis. Due to space limitations, we display the state transition model for the primary server only (Figure 8.12). The complete state set for the DNS service will be the cross product of this model and a similar model for the secondary server. The transitions labeled with μ_S and μ_H rates represent accidental software and hardware failures, the φ rates represent the system administrator's possible actions, and the λ rates represent the intensities of the possible attack actions. We use the rate values in Sallhammar et al. [17] when determining measures for the DNS service: $\lambda_{V,L} = 1/3$, $\lambda_{L,IS} = \lambda_{L,AS} = \lambda_{IS,AS} = 3$, $\varphi_{G,V} = 1/480$, $\varphi_{V,G} = 1/120$, $\varphi_{L,G} = \varphi_{IS,G} = 1$, $\varphi_{AS,G} = 3$, $\varphi_{AH,G} = 1/24$, $\mu_H = 1/3{,}600$, and $\mu_S = 1/120$ per hour. The rates are assumed to be the same for both the primary and the secondary servers. We also use $\varphi_{SYN} = 2$ as the synchronization rate of (possibly contaminated) zone data between the primary and secondary servers.

8.6.2   Stochastic Game

Since we assumed that an attacker will target only one of the servers at a time, there will be a single stochastic game representing the attack scenario for each of the servers. The game elements are the shaded states in Figure 8.12 (i.e., $\Gamma = \{\Gamma_V,\Gamma_L,\Gamma_{IS}\}$). The attack action set in the stochastic game is $A = \{a_1,a_2,a_3,\phi\} = \{$ "illegal log-in," "cache poisoning," "server shutdown," "do nothing"$\}$ and the defense action set is the corresponding $D = \{d_1,d_2,d_3,\phi\}$. Using the rate values in

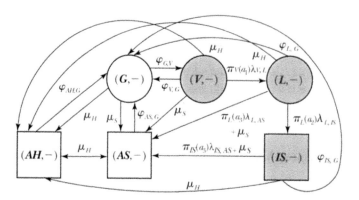

FIGURE

8.12

Internal state transitions for the primary DNS server. The vulnerable system states (i.e., the game elements) are gray. Note that the full expansion to 36 states including the behavior of the secondary server has been suppressed.

Section 8.6.1 to determine the transition probabilities between the game states (see Section 8.4), the game elements become:

$$
\Gamma_V = \begin{array}{c||c|c}
 & \phi & d_1 \\\hline
a_1 & r_{a_1\phi} + 0.952\Gamma_L & c_{a_1 d_1} \\
\phi & c_{\phi\phi} & 0
\end{array} ,
$$

$$
\Gamma_L = \begin{array}{c||c|c|c}
 & \phi & d_2 & d_3 \\\hline
a_2 & r_{a_2\phi} + 0.748\Gamma_{IS} & c_{a_2 d_2} & r_{a_2 d_3} + 0.748\Gamma_{IS} \\
a_3 & r_{a_3\phi} & r_{a_3 d_2} & c_{a_3 d_3} \\
\phi & c_{\phi\phi} & 0 & 0
\end{array}
\qquad (8.25)
$$

$$
\Gamma_{IS} = \begin{array}{c||c|c}
 & \phi & d_3 \\\hline
a_3 & r_{a_3\phi} & c_{a_3 d_3} \\
\phi & c_{\phi\phi} & 0
\end{array}
$$

similarly for both servers.

8.6.3   Four Scenarios

To determine security and dependability measures for the DNS service, the values for the outcome of the attacks in the various vulnerable states need to be set to obtain the attack probabilities. To illustrate the effect of the reward and cost values on the predicted system measures, we obtain the system measures for four different scenarios.

+ **The worst-case scenario.** First we look at the "worst-case scenario" when all attackers always try all possible attacks (i.e., $\pi_i(a_k) = 1, \forall i, k$ in $\mathbf{Q}$). In this case, we do not use the game model to determine the expected attacker behavior.

+ **Risk-averse attackers.** Now assume that the attackers will take into account the possible consequences of their actions. The following reward and cost values are used: $r_{a_1\phi} = r_{a_2\phi} = r_{a_3\phi} = 1$, $c_{a_1d_1} = -4$, $c_{a_2d_2} = -3$, $c_{a_3d_3} = -2$, $c_{\phi\phi} = -5$. Solving the stochastic game in accordance to Algorithm 8.1 provides the optimal attack strategy vectors $\pi_V^* = (0.568, 0.432)$, $\pi_L^* = (0, 0.625, 0.375)$, and $\pi_{IS}^* = (0.625, 0.375)$.

+ **Implementing countermeasures.** Assume that we want to evaluate the benefit of setting up a new logging and tracing mechanism for the DNS service, with the purpose of reducing the probability of illegal log-in attempts (action a_1). As in the previous scenario, we consider risk-averse attackers. All detected illegal log-in attempts will be recorded and prosecuted, which are modeled as an increasing cost value $c_{a_1d_1} = -7$ in game element Γ_V. Solving the game once again provides a new expected attack strategy for state V: $\pi_V^* = (0.394, 0.606)$.

+ **Accidental failures only.** Finally, assume that we do not consider attacks at all, but rather model accidental failure only (i.e., $\pi_i(a_k) = 0, \forall i, k$ in $\mathbf{Q}$).

8.6.4 Comparing the Scenarios

The measures for the system dependability and security presented in Section 8.2.4 for the four scenarios are presented in Table 8.1. From the worst case, we see that when potential attacks always are performed, the quantitative trustworthiness is significantly worse than in the other cases (i.e., incurring a risk averseness to the attacker community improves the system performance). The additional countermeasures introduced in the next case yield only a marginal improvement, even though $\pi_V^*(a_1)$ is decreased with 23%. As a conclusion, the DNS service will not benefit much from the new logging and tracing mechanism.

	Unavailability	MTTF [h]	MTFF [h]
Worst-case scenario	$3.4 \, 10^{-4}$	991	996
Risk-averse attackers	$9.56 \, 10^{-5}$	5,986	6,001
With countermeasures	$9.53 \, 10^{-5}$	6,018	6,034
Accidental failures only	$8.79 \, 10^{-5}$	7,088	7,104

TABLE Main system trustworthiness measures for the scenarios.

8.1

As can be seen from the case of accidental failures only, the system's expected availability time to failures will not increase noticeably when attacks are not included as possible fault sources. Hence, for the actual parametrization of this case study, the random failures dominate the trustworthiness of the DNS service.

It is also of interest to have a closer look at the detailed state probabilities. These are presented in Table 8.2, where probabilities less than 10^{-8} are shown as ≈ 0. An interesting observation from the table is that the first worst case dominates the asymptotic state probability distribution for system states where at least one of the servers has experienced a software integrity failure (i.e., the $(IS, -)$ and $(-, IS)$ states). This is to be expected, since the worst case considers the most aggressive type of attackers. On the contrary, case four with accidental failures only tends to dominate the states where either the primary or the secondary server is vulnerable to buffer overflow attacks (i.e., the $(V, -)$ and $(-, V)$ states). In fact, a substantial fraction of the time is spent in these states yielding a rather low probability for the "everything is OK" state, (G, G). Since this case models accidental failures only, there are no attacks that will bring the system out of this state. This is also the explanation of the counterintuitive result that the worst case has the largest probability of being in the "everything is OK" state, (G, G).

Regarding the probabilities of being in the failed states, $\mathbf{S}_F$, shown in the lower part of Table 8.2, it is seen, as pointed out above, that except for the worst case these are dominated by the random failures. Hence, although introducing countermeasures in the risk-averse scenario increases the probabilities of staying in the vulnerable states (G, V) and (V, G) notably, this has a small effect on the overall performance of the system as seen from Table 8.1. Studying the figures, it should be kept in mind that numerical values of reward and costs as well as failure rates are chosen for illustration purposes only and the findings may not conform with failure times for a real-life DNS server system.

8.7   CONCLUSION

More than ten years after the need for quantitative measures of security initially was brought up (see Littlewood et al. [5]), there still does not exist any common methodology which has been widely adopted for security quantification on a system-level basis. The efforts put in developing methods for quantitative security evaluation during the last decade can be viewed as either static or dynamic analysis methods. The static approach focuses on aspects such as how a system was built and what types of vulnerabilities it may contain, whereas the dynamic methods focus more on how a system is operated and how it behaves in a certain environment. The research presented in this chapter strives to follow the latter

Primary, Backup State	Worst Case	Risk Averse	With Countermeasures	Accident Only
G,G	0.967809	0.959767	0.952382	0.778212
G,V	$5.75\,10^{-3}$	$9.69\,10^{-3}$	$1.34\,10^{-2}$	$9.57\,10^{-2}$
G,L	$2.74\,10^{-4}$	$6.36\,10^{-4}$	$6.09\,10^{-4}$	0
G,IS	$2.26\,10^{-4}$	≈ 0	≈ 0	0
G,AS	$3.23\,10^{-3}$	$3.09\,10^{-3}$	$3.06\,10^{-3}$	$2.43\,10^{-3}$
G,AH	$6.52\,10^{-3}$	$6.49\,10^{-3}$	$6.46\,10^{-3}$	$5.84\,10^{-3}$
V,G	$5.76\,10^{-3}$	$9.69\,10^{-3}$	$1.34\,10^{-2}$	$9.57\,10^{-2}$
V,V	$3.42\,10^{-5}$	$9.79\,10^{-5}$	$1.88\,10^{-4}$	$1.18\,10^{-2}$
V,L	$1.63\,10^{-6}$	$6.43\,10^{-6}$	$8.56\,10^{-6}$	0
V,IS	$1.23\,10^{-6}$	≈ 0	≈ 0	0
V,AS	$1.9\,10^{-5}$	$3.12\,10^{-5}$	$4.31\,10^{-5}$	$2.98\,10^{-4}$
V,AH	$3.88\,10^{-5}$	$6.55\,10^{-5}$	$9.08\,10^{-5}$	$7.18\,10^{-4}$
L,G	$2.74\,10^{-4}$	$6.36\,10^{-4}$	$6.09\,10^{-4}$	0
L,V	$1.63\,10^{-6}$	$6.43\,10^{-6}$	$8.56\,10^{-6}$	0
L,L	$7.74\,10^{-8}$	$4.22\,10^{-7}$	$3.9\ 10^{-7}$	0
L,IS	$5.82\,10^{-8}$	≈ 0	≈ 0	0
L,AS	$9.02\,10^{-7}$	$2.05\,10^{-6}$	$1.96\,10^{-6}$	0
L,AH	$1.84\,10^{-6}$	$4.3\ 10^{-6}$	$4.14\,10^{-6}$	0
AS,G	$3.15\,10^{-3}$	$3.09\,10^{-3}$	$3.06\,10^{-3}$	$2.43\,10^{-3}$
AS,V	$1.85\,10^{-5}$	$3.12\,10^{-5}$	$4.31\,10^{-5}$	$2.98\,10^{-4}$
AS,L	$8.82\,10^{-7}$	$2.05\,10^{-6}$	$1.96\,10^{-6}$	0
AH,G	$6.52\,10^{-3}$	$6.49\,10^{-3}$	$6.46\,10^{-3}$	$5.84\,10^{-3}$
AH,V	$3.87\,10^{-5}$	$6.55\,10^{-5}$	$9.08\,10^{-5}$	$7.18\,10^{-4}$
AH,L	$1.84\,10^{-6}$	$4.3\ 10^{-6}$	$4.14\,10^{-6}$	0
IS,G	$1.51\,10^{-4}$	≈ 0	≈ 0	0
IS,V	$8.17\,10^{-7}$	≈ 0	≈ 0	0
IS,L	$3.88\,10^{-8}$	≈ 0	≈ 0	0
IS,IS	$3.8\,10^{-5}$	≈ 0	≈ 0	0
IS,AS	$1.69\,10^{-5}$	≈ 0	≈ 0	0
IS,AH	$1.38\,10^{-6}$	≈ 0	≈ 0	0
AS,IS	$1.7\,10^{-5}$	≈ 0	≈ 0	0
AS,AS	$2.68\,10^{-5}$	$9.96\,10^{-6}$	$9.86\,10^{-6}$	$7.57\,10^{-6}$
AS,AH	$2.14\,10^{-5}$	$2.09\,10^{-5}$	$2.08\,10^{-5}$	$1.82\,10^{-5}$
AH,IS	$1.38\,10^{-6}$	≈ 0	≈ 0	0
AH,AS	$2.14\,10^{-5}$	$2.09\,10^{-5}$	$2.08\,10^{-5}$	$1.82\,10^{-5}$
AH,AH	$4.39\,10^{-5}$	$4.39\,10^{-5}$	$4.39\,10^{-5}$	$4.39\,10^{-5}$

TABLE
8.2

Asymptotic state probabilities $\mathbf{X} = \{X_i\}$ for the four secnarios, subdivided with respect to the good $\mathbf{S}_G$ and failed $\mathbf{S}_F$ states.

approach. As was pointed out in Nicol et al. [11], to describe a system that is yet to be built or to describe an existing system whose vulnerabilities remain unknown, stochastic assumptions are needed. By using a stochastic modeling approach, a system's inherent random behavior due to the introduction and removal of vulnerabilities, attacker behavior, normal user behavior administrative activities, as well as accidental hardware and software failures, can be modeled and analyzed. This chapter presents a method for quantitative security and dependability evaluation, which is based on stochastic modeling techniques. The purpose of the method developed and used is to facilitate the process of obtaining measures of a system's trustworthiness, regardless if the failure cause is intentional or not. By using stochastic game theory, we can compute the expected attacker behavior for different types of attackers. The reward and cost concept makes it possible to use the stochastic model to predict security and dependability measures for a particular threat environment. Having solved the game, the expected attacker behavior is reflected in the transitions between states in the system model, by weighing the transition rates according to probability distributions. In the final step, the corresponding stochastic process is used to compute operational measures of a system.

Optimized strategies have frequently been used to derive predictions of what players in a game will do [33]. As discussed in Section 8.4, π^* will be an indication of the most likely strategy for attackers who do not know the probabilities that their actions will be detected. The game theoretic approach is based on the underlying assumption that the attackers have a complete overview of the system states, the possible transitions between states, and the existing vulnerabilities. This may not always be the case in real life. Other types of models, such as games with incomplete information, may be more appropriate in some cases. We would also like to point out that modeling attacker's interactions with a system as a zero-sum stochastic game will always provide us with a single unique solution to the game. Estimation of the parameters of a system model is a pertaining challenge.

As indicated in the case study, there are additional features of our model than just probabilistic predictions of a system. For instance, system administrators can use the approach presented in this chapter to answer questions such as "What is the effect of hardening security?" and "Should we perform additional monitoring?" The effect of these two countermeasures can be evaluated in our modeling and analysis framework before implementation, by changing the corresponding transition rates in the model and then comparing the results.

Currently, this model is being integrated into a framework for dynamic security and dependability evaluation. The framework is based on a method for real-time risk assessment using a distributed networked agent-sensor architecture, which has been published in Årnes et al. [34]. By using live data from network sensors, the current state and the future behavior of a system can be predicted, which makes it possible to compute system security and dependability measures in real time.

References

[1] A. Avizienis, J.-C. Laprie, B. Randell, and C. Landwehr, "Basic Concepts and Taxonomy of Dependable and Secure Computing," *IEEE Transactions on Dependable and Secure Computing* 1 (Jan.–Mar. 2004): 11–33.

[2] E. Jonsson, "Towards an Integrated Conceptual Model of Security and Dependability," *Proceedings of the First International Conference on Availability, Reliability and Security (AReS)*, Vienna, Austria, 2006.

[3] M. Greenwald, C. A. Gunter, B. Knutsson, A. Scedrov, J. M. Smith, and S. Zdancewic, "Computer Security Is Not a Science (But It Should Be)," *Proceedings of the Large-Scale Network Security Workshop*, Reston, VA, 2003.

[4] "ISO 15408: Common Criteria for Information Technology Security Evaluation," 1999, at http://www.commoncriteria.org.

[5] B. Littlewood, S. Brocklehurst, N. Fenton, P. Mellor, S. Page, D. Wright, J. Dobson, J. McDermid, and D. Gollmann, "Towards Operational Measures of Computer Security," *Journal of Computer Security* 2 (Oct. 1993): 211–229.

[6] R. Ortalo, Y. Deswarte, and M. Kaaniche, "Experimenting with Quantitative Evaluation Tools for Monitoring Operational Security," *IEEE Transactions on Software Engineering* 25 Sept./Oct. 1999: 633–650.

[7] B. Madan, K. Vaidyanathan, and K. Trivedi, "Modeling and Quantification of Security Attributes of Software Systems," *Proceedings of the International Conference on Dependable Systems and Networks (DSN'02)*, Washington, DC, 2002.

[8] D. Wang, B. Madan, and K. Trivedi, "Security Analysis of Sitar Intrusion Tolerance System," *Proceedings of ACM SSRS'03*, Fairfax, VA, 2003.

[9] B. B. Madan, K. Goseva-Popstojanova, K. Vaidyanathan, and K. S. Trivedi, "A Method for Modeling and Quantifying the Security Attributes of Intrusion Tolerant Systems," *Performance Evaluation* 56 (2004) pp. 167–186.

[10] S. Singh, M. Cukier, and W. Sanders, "Probabilistic Validation of an Intrusion-Tolerant Replication System," *International Conference on Dependable Systems and Networks (DSN'03)*, edited by J. W. de Bakker, W.-P. de Roever, and G. Rozenberg, San Francisco, CA, June 2003.

[11] D. M. Nicol, W. H. Sanders, and K. S. Trivedi, "Model-Based Evaluation: From Dependability to Security," *IEEE Transactions on Dependable and Secure Computing* 1 (Jan.–Mar. 2004): 48–65.

[12] T. Alpcan and T. Basar, "A Game Theoretic Approach to Decision and Analysis in Network Intrusion Detection," *Proceedings of the 42nd IEEE Conference on Decision and Control*, Lahaina, HI, Dec. 2003.

[13] P. Liu and W. Zang, "Incentive-Based Modeling and Inference of Attacker Intent, Objectives, and Strategies," *Proceedings of the 10th ACM Conference on Computer and Communication Security*, Washington, DC, 2003, pp. 179–189.

[14] K. Lye and J. M. Wing, "Game Strategies in Network Security," *International Journal of Information Security*, 4, No. 1–2, (2005): 71–86.

[15] K. Sallhammar, S. J. Knapskog, and B. E. Helvik, "Using Stochastic Game Theory to Compute the Expected Behavior of Attackers," *Proceedings of the 2005 International Symposium on Applications and the Internet (Saint2005) Workshops*, Trento, Italy, 2005.

[16] K. Sallhammar, B. E. Helvik, and S. J. Knapskog, "Incorporating Attacker Behavior in Stochastic Models of Security," *Proceedings of the 2005 International Conference on Security and Management (SAM'05)*, Las Vegas, NV, 2005.

[17] K. Sallhammar, B. E. Helvik, and S. J. Knapskog, "Towards a Stochastic Model for Integrated Security and Dependability Evaluation," *Proceedings of the First International Conference on Availability, Reliability and Security (AReS)*, Vienna, Austria, 2006.

[18] K. Sallhammar, B. E. Helvik, and S. J. Knapskog, "A Game-Theoretic Approach to Stochastic Security and Dependability Evaluation," *Proceedings of the 2nd IEEE International Symposium on Dependable, Autonomic and Secure Computing (DASC'06)*, Indianapolis, IN, 2006.

[19] E. de Souza e Silva and H. R. Gail, "Performability Analysis of Computer Systems: From Model Specification to Solution," *Performance Evaluation* 14 (Feb. 1992): 135–275.

[20] B. R. Haverkort, R. Marie, G. Rubino, and K. Trivedi (Eds.), *Performability Modelling: Techniques and Tools* (New York: Wiley, 2001).

[21] D. Powell and R. Stroud (Eds.), "Malicious- and Accidental-Fault Tolerance for Internet Applications—Conceptual Model and Architecture," Technical Report CS-TR-749 Newcastle University, Newcastle,UK, 2001.

[22] S. Jha, O. Sheyner, and J. Wing, "Two Formal Analyses of Attack Graphs," *Proceedings of the 2002 Computer Security Foundations Workshop*, Nova Scotia, Canada, 2002.

[23] D. R. Cox and H. D. Miller, *The Theory of Stochastic Processes* (Boston: Chapman and Hall, 1965).

[24] S. M. Ross, *Introduction to Probability Models*, 8 ed. (Boston: Academic Press, 2003).

[25] J. A. Buzacott, "Markov Approach to Finding Failure Times of Repairable Systems," *IEEE Transactions on Reliability* R-19(Nov. 1970): 128–134.

[26] E. Jonsson and T. Olovsson, "A Quantitative Model of the Security Intrusion Process Based on Attacker Behavior," *IEEE Transactions of Software Engineering* 23 (April 1997): 235–245.

[27] A. Arora, "A Statistical Analysis of Computer Attacks Using Data From the Honeynet Project," Carnegie Mellon CyLab, at http://www.cylab.cmu.edu/.

[28] T. H. Project, *Know Your Enemy*, 2nd ed. (Boston: Addison-Wesley, 2004).

[29] L. S. Shapley, "Stochastic Games," *Proceedings of the National Academy of Science USA* 39 (1953): 1095–1100.

[30] G. Owen, *Game Theory*, 3rd ed. (Boston: Academic Press, 2001).

[31] S. Stahl, *A Gentle Introduction to Game Theory* (Providence, RI American Mathematical Society, 1991).

[32] CERIAS, "The Development of a Meaningful Hacker Taxonomy: A Two-Dimensional Approach," CERIAS Technical Report 2005–43, 2005.

[33] C. A. Holt and A. E. Roth, "The Nash Equilibrium: A Perspective," *Proceedings of the National Academy of Sciences*, 101, March 23, 2004.

[34] A. Årnes, K. Sallhammar, K. Haslum, T. Brekne, M. E. G. Moe, and S. J. Knapskog, "Real-Time Risk Assessment with Network Sensors and Intrusion Detection Systems," *International Conference on Computational Intelligence and Security (CIS)*, Xian, China, Dec. 2005.

9 Scenario Graphs Applied to Network Security

Jeannette M. Wing   Carnegie Mellon University, USA

9.1   INTRODUCTION

Model checking is a technique for determining whether a formal model of a system satisfies a given property. If the property is false in the model, model checkers typically produce a single counterexample. The developer uses this counterexample to revise the model (or the property), which often means fixing a bug in the design of the system. The developer then iterates through the process, rechecking the revised model against the (possibly revised) property.

Sometimes, however, we would like *all* counterexamples, not just one. Rather than just producing one example of how the model does not satisfy a given property, why not produce all of them at once? We call the set of all counterexamples a *scenario graph*. For a traditional use of model checking (e.g., to find bugs), each path in the graph represents a counterexample (i.e., a failure scenario). In our application to security, each path represents an attack, that is, a way in which an intruder can attack a system. *Attack graphs* are a special case of scenario graphs.

This chapter first gives two algorithms for producing scenario graphs: The first algorithm was published in Jha and Wing [1], and the second in Hughes and Sheyner [2]. Then, we interpret scenario graphs as attack graphs. We walk through a simple example to show how to model the relevant aspects of a computer network and we present some example attack graphs. We highlight two automated analyses that system administrators might perform once they have attack graphs at their disposal. We summarize our practical experience with generating attack graphs using our algorithms and discuss related work. We close with some suggestions for future work on scenario graphs in general and attack graphs more specifically.

9.2 ALGORITHMS FOR GENERATING SCENARIO GRAPHS

We present two algorithms for generating scenario graphs. The first is based on symbolic model checking and produces counterexamples for only safety properties, as expressed in terms of a computational tree logic. The second is based on explicit-state model checking and produces counterexamples for both safety and liveness properties, as expressed in terms of a linear temporal logic.

Both algorithms produce scenario graphs that guarantee the following informally stated properties:

+ *Soundness:* Each path in the graph is a violation of the given property.

+ *Exhaustive:* The graph contains all executions of the model that violate the given property.

+ *Succinctness of states:* Each node in the graph represents a state that participates in some counterexample.

+ *Succinctness of transitions:* Each edge in the graph represents a state transition that participates in some counterexample.

These properties of our scenario graphs are not obvious, in particular for the second algorithm. See Sheyner [3] for formal definitions and proofs.

9.2.1 Symbolic Algorithm

Our first algorithm for producing scenario graphs is inspired by the symbolic model checking algorithm as implemented in model checkers such as NuSMV [4]. Our presentation and discussion of the algorithm in this section is taken almost verbatim from Sheyner et al. [5].

In the model checker NuSMV, the model M is a finite labeled transition system and p is a property written in *Computation Tree Logic* (CTL). In this section, we consider only safety properties, which in CTL have the form $\mathbf{AG}f$ (i.e., $p = \mathbf{AG}f$, where f is a formula in propositional logic). If the model M satisfies the property p, NuSMV reports "true." If M does not satisfy p, NuSMV produces a counterexample. A single counterexample shows a scenario that leads to a violation of the safety property.

Scenario graphs depict ways in which the execution of the model of a system can lead into an unsafe state. We can express the property that an unsafe state cannot be reached as:

$$\mathbf{AG}(\neg unsafe)$$

When this property is false, there are unsafe states that are reachable from the initial state. The precise meaning of *unsafe* depends on the system being modeled. For security, *unsafe* might mean that an intruder has gained root access to a host on a network.

We briefly describe the algorithm (Figure 9.1) for constructing scenario graphs for the property **AG**($\neg$*unsafe*). We start with a set of states S, a state transition relation R, a set of initial states S_0, a labeling function L, and a safety property p. The labeling function defines what atomic propositions are true in a given state. The first step in the algorithm is to determine the set of states S_{reach} that are reachable from the initial states. (This is a standard step in symbolic model checkers, where S_{reach} is represented symbolically, not explicitly.) Next, the algorithm computes the set of reachable states S_{unsafe} that have a path to an unsafe state. The set of states S_{unsafe} is computed using an iterative algorithm derived from a fixed-point characterization of the **AG** operator [6]. Let R be the transition relation of the model, that is, $(s, s') \in R$ if and only if there is a transition from state s to s'. By restricting the domain and range of R to S_{unsafe}, we obtain a transition relation R^p that encapsulates the edges of the scenario graph. Therefore,

Input:
    S—set of states
    $R \subseteq S \times S$—transition relation
    $S_0 \subseteq S$—set of initial states
    $L: S \rightarrow 2^{AP}$—labeling of states with propositional formulas
    $p = $ **AG**($\neg$*unsafe*)—a safety property

Output:
    Scenario graph $G_p = \langle S_{unsafe}, R^p, S_0^p, S_s^p \rangle$

Algorithm: *GenerateScenarioGraph*(S, R, S_0, L, p)

1. $S_{reach} = reachable(S, R, S_0, L)$
(* Use model checking to find the set of states S_{unsafe} that violate the safety property **AG**($\neg$*unsafe*). *)

2. $S_{unsafe} = modelCheck(S_{reach}, R, S_0, L, p)$.
(* Restrict the transition relation R to states in the set S_{unsafe} *)

3. $R^p = R \cap (S_{unsafe} \times S_{unsafe})$.
$S_0^p = S_0 \cap S_{unsafe}$.
$S_s^p = \{s | s \in S_{unsafe} \wedge unsafe \in L(s)\}$.

4. Return $G_p = \langle S_{unsafe}, R^p, S_0^p, S_s^p \rangle$.

FIGURE   Symbolic algorithm for generating scenario graphs.

9.1

the scenario graph is $\langle S_{unsafe}, R^p, S_0^p, S_s^p \rangle$, where S_{unsafe} and R^p represent the set of nodes and set of edges of the graph, respectively, $S_0^p = S_0 \cap S_{unsafe}$ is the set of initial states, and $S_s^p = \{s | s \in S_{unsafe} \wedge unsafe \in L(s)\}$ is the set of success states.

In symbolic model checkers, such as NuSMV, the transition relation and sets of states are represented using ordered binary decision diagrams (BDDs) [7], a compact representation for Boolean functions. There are efficient BDD algorithms for all operations used in our algorithm.

9.2.2   Explicit-State Algorithm

Our second algorithm for producing scenario graphs uses an explicit-state model checking algorithm based on ω-automata theory. Model checkers such as SPIN [8] use explicit-state model checking. Our presentation and discussion of the algorithm in this section is taken almost verbatim from Hughes and Sheyner [2].

Figure 9.2 contains a high-level outline of our second algorithm for generating scenario graphs. We model our system as a Bücchi automaton M. Bücchi automata are finite-state machines that accept infinite executions. A Bücchi automaton specifies a subset of *acceptance* states. The automaton accepts any infinite execution that visits an acceptance state infinitely often. The property p is specified in *Linear Temporal Logic* (LTL). The property p induces a language $L(p)$ of

Input:
> M—the model Bücchi automaton
> p—an LTL property

Output:
> Scenario graph $M_p = M \cap \neg p$

Algorithm: *GenerateScenarioGraph(M, p)*
1. Convert LTL formula $\neg p$ to equivalent Bücchi automaton N_p.
2. Construct the intersection automaton $I = M \cap \neg N_p$.
   I accepts the language $L(M) \setminus L(p)$, which is precisely the set of of executions of M forbidden by p.
3. Compute SCC, the set of strongly connected components of I that include at least one *acceptance* state.
4. Return M_p, which consists of SCC plus all the paths to any component in *SCC* from any initial state of I.

FIGURE   Explicit-state algorithm for generating scenario graphs.

9.2

executions that are permitted under the property. The executions of the model M that are *not* permitted by p thus constitute the language $L(M) \setminus L(p)$. The scenario graph is the automaton, $M_p = M \cap \neg p$, accepting this language. The construction procedure for M_p uses Gerth et al.'s algorithm [9] for converting LTL formulas to Bücchi automata (step 1). The Bücchi acceptance condition implies that any scenario accepted by M_p must eventually reach a strongly connected component of the graph that contains at least one acceptance state. Such components are found in step 3 using Tarjan's classic strongly connected component algorithm [10]. This step isolates the relevant parts of the graph and prunes states that do not participate in any scenarios.

9.3 ATTACK GRAPHS ARE SCENARIO GRAPHS

In the security community, Red Teams construct *attack graphs* to show how a system is vulnerable to attack. Each path in an attack graph shows a way in which an intruder can compromise the security of a system. These graphs are drawn by hand. A typical result of such intensive manual effort is a floor-to-ceiling, wall-to-wall "white board" attack graph, such as the one produced by a Red Team at Sandia National Labs for DARPA's CC20008 information battlespace preparation experiment (Figure 9.3). Each box in the graph designates a single intruder action. A path from one of the leftmost boxes in the graph to one of the rightmost boxes is a sequence of actions corresponding to an attack scenario. At the end of any such scenario, the intruder has broken the network security in some way. The graph is included here for illustrative purposes only, so we omit the description of specific details.

Since these attack graphs are drawn by hand, they are prone to error: They might be incomplete (missing attacks), they might have redundant paths or redundant subgraphs, or they might have irrelevant nodes, transitions, or paths.

The correspondence between scenario graphs and attack graphs is simple. For a given desired security property, we generate the scenario graph for a model of the system to be protected. An example security property is that an intruder should never gain root access to a specific host. Since each scenario graph is property specific, in practice, we might need to generate many scenario graphs to represent the entire attack graph that a Red Team might construct manually.

Our main contribution is that we automate the process of producing attack graphs: (1) our technique scales beyond what humans can do by hand, and

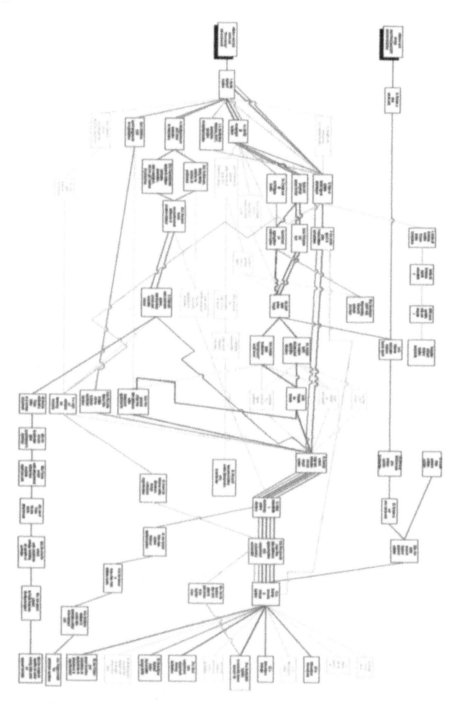

(2) since our algorithms guarantee to produce scenario graphs that are sound, exhaustive, and succinct, our attack graphs are not subject to the errors that humans are prone to make.

9.4 NETWORK ATTACK GRAPHS

Network attack graphs represent a collection of possible penetration scenarios in a computer network. Each penetration scenario is a sequence of actions taken by the intruder, typically culminating in a particular goal—administrative access on a particular host, access to a database, service disruption, and so on. For appropriately constructed network models, attack graphs give a bird's-eye view of every scenario that can lead to a serious security breach.

9.4.1 Network Attack Model

We model a network using either the tuple of inputs, $\langle S, R, S_0, L \rangle$, in the first algorithm (Figure 9.1) or the Bücchi automaton, M, of the second algorithm (Figure 9.2).

To be concrete, for the remainder of this chapter we will work in the context of the second algorithm. Also, rather than use the full Bücchi automaton to model attacks on a network, for our application to network security, we use a simpler attack model $M = \langle S, \tau, s_0 \rangle$, where S is a finite set of states, $\tau \subseteq S \times S$ is a transition relation, and $s_0 \in S$ is an initial state. The state space S represents a set of three agents $I = \{E, D, N\}$. Agent E is the attacker, agent D is the defender, and agent N is the system under attack. Each agent $i \in I$ has its own set of possible states S_i, so that $S = \times_{i \in I} S_i$.

With each agent $i \in I$ we associate a set of actions A_i, so that the total set of actions in the model is $A = \bigcup_{i \in I} A_i$. A state transition in a network attack model corresponds to a single action by the intruder, a defensive action by the system administrator (or security software installed on the network), or a routine network action. The single root state s_0 represents the initial state of each agent before any action has taken place. In general, the attacker's actions move the system toward some undesirable (from the system's point of view) state, and the defender's actions attempt to counteract that effect. For instance, in a computer network, the attacker's actions would be the steps taken by the intruder to compromise the network, and the defender's actions would be the steps taken by the system administrator to disrupt the attack.

Agent $i \in I$	S_i	A_i
E	I	A
D	Ids	$\{alarm\}$
N	$H \times C \times T$	$\varnothing$

TABLE

9.1

Network attack model.

Real networks consist of a large variety of hardware and software pieces, most of which are not involved in cyber attacks. We have chosen six network components relevant to constructing network attack models. The components were chosen to include enough information to represent a wide variety of networks and attack scenarios, yet keep the model reasonably simple and small. The following is a list of the components:

1. H, a set of hosts connected to the network.

2. C, a connectivity relation expressing the network topology and interhost reachability.

3. T, a relation expressing trust between hosts.

4. I, a model of the intruder.

5. A, a set of individual actions (exploits) that the intruder can use to construct attack scenarios.

6. Ids, a model of the intrusion detection system (IDS).

We construct an attack model M based on these components. Table 9.1 defines each agent i's state S_i and action set A_i in terms of the network components. This construction gives the system administrator an entirely passive "detection" role, embodied in the *alarm* action of the intrusion detection system. For simplicity, regular network activity is omitted entirely.

It remains to make explicit the transition relation of the attack model M. Each transition $(s_1, s_2) \in \tau$ is either an action by the intruder or an *alarm* action by the system administrator. An *alarm* action happens whenever the IDS is able to flag an intruder action. An action $a \in A$ requires that the preconditions of a hold in state s_1 and the effects of a hold in s_2. Action preconditions and effects are explained in Section 9.4.2.

9.4.2   Network Components

We now give details about each network component.

Hosts

Hosts are the main hubs of activity on a network. They run services, process network requests, and maintain data. With rare exceptions, every action in an attack scenario will target a host in some way. Typically, an action takes advantage of vulnerable or misconfigured software to gain information or access privileges for the attacker. The main goal in modeling hosts is to capture as much information as possible about components that may contribute to creating an exploitable vulnerability.

A host $h \in H$ is a tuple $\langle id, svcs, sw, vuls \rangle$, where

+ *id* is a unique host identifier (typically, name and network address).

+ *svcs* is a list of service name/port number pairs describing each service that is active on the host and the port on which the service is listening.

+ *sw* is a list of other software operating on the host, including the operating system type and version.

+ *vuls* is a list of host-specific vulnerable components. This list may include installed software with exploitable security flaws (e.g., a *setuid* program with a buffer overflow problem), or misconfigured environment settings (e.g., existing user shell for system-only users, such as *ftp*).

Network Connectivity

Following Ritchey and Ammann [11], connectivity is expressed as a ternary relation $C \subseteq H \times H \times P$, where P is a set of integer port numbers. $C(h_1, h_2, p)$ means that host h_2 is reachable from host h_1 on port p. Note that the connectivity relation incorporates firewalls and other elements that restrict the ability of one host to connect to another. Slightly abusing notation, we say $R(h_1, h_2)$ when there is a network route from h_1 to h_2.

Trust

We model trust as a binary relation $T \subseteq H \times H$, where $T(h_1, h_2)$ indicates that a user may log in from host h_2 to host h_1 without authentication (i.e., host h_1 "trusts" host h_2).

Services

The set of services S is a list of unique service names, one for each service that is present on any host on the network. We distinguish services from other software because network services so often serve as a conduit for exploits. Furthermore, services are tied to the connectivity relation via port numbers, and this information must be included in the model of each host. Every service name in each host's list of services comes from the set S.

Intrusion Detection System

We associate a Boolean variable with each action, abstractly representing whether or not the IDS can detect that particular action. Actions are classified as being either *detectable* or *stealthy* with respect to the IDS. If an action is detectable, it will trigger an alarm when executed on a host or network segment monitored by the IDS; if an action is *stealthy*, the IDS does not see it.

We specify the IDS as a function *ids*: $H \times H \times A \rightarrow \{d, s, b\}$, where $ids(h_1, h_2, a) = d$ if action a is *detectable* when executed with source host h_1 and target host h_2; $ids(h_1, h_2, a) = s$ if action a is stealthy when executed with source host h_1 and target host h_2; and $ids(h_1, h_2, a) = b$ if action a has *both* detectable and stealthy strains, and success in detecting the action depends on which strain is used. When h_1 and h_2 refer to the same host, $ids(h_1, h_2, a)$ specifies the IDS component (if any) located on that host. When h_1 and h_2 refer to different hosts, $ids(h_1, h_2, a)$ specifies the IDS component (if any) monitoring the network path between h_1 and h_2.

Actions

Each action is a triple $\langle r, h_s, h_t \rangle$, where $h_s \in H$ is the host from which the action is launched, $h_t \in H$ is the host targeted by the action, and r is the rule that describes how the intruder can change the network or add to his or her knowledge about it. A specification of an action rule has four components: *intruder preconditions*, *network preconditions*, *intruder effects*, and *network effects*. The *intruder preconditions* component places conditions on the intruder's store of knowledge and the privilege level required to launch the action. The *network preconditions* specifies conditions on the target host state, network connectivity, trust, services, and vulnerabilities that must hold before launching the action. Finally, the *intruder* and *network effects* components list the action's effects on the intruder and network, respectively.

Intruder

The intruder has a *store of knowledge* about the target network and its users. The intruder's store of knowledge includes host addresses, known vulnerabilities, user passwords, information gathered with port scans, and so on. Also associated with the intruder is the function *plvl: Hosts* $\rightarrow$ $\{none, user, root\}$, which gives the level of privilege that the intruder has on each host. For simplicity, we model only three privilege levels. There is a strict total order on the privilege levels: *none* ≤ *user* ≤ *root*.

Omitted Complications

Although we do not model actions taken by user services for the sake of simplicity, doing so in the future would let us ask questions about effects of intrusions on service quality. A more complex model could include services provided by the network to its regular users and other routine network traffic. These details would reflect more realistically the interaction between intruder actions and regular network activity at the expense of additional complexity.

Another activity worth modeling explicitly is administrative steps taken either to hinder an attack in progress or to repair the damage after an attack has occurred. The former corresponds to transitioning to states of the model that offer less opportunity for further penetration; the latter means "undoing" some of the damage caused by successful attacks.

9.5   EXAMPLE NETWORK

Figure 9.4 shows an example network. There are two target hosts, Windows and Linux, on an internal company network, and a web server on an isolated "demilitarized zone" (DMZ) network. One firewall separates the internal network from the DMZ and another firewall separates the DMZ from the rest of the Internet. An IDS watches the network traffic between the internal network and the outside world.

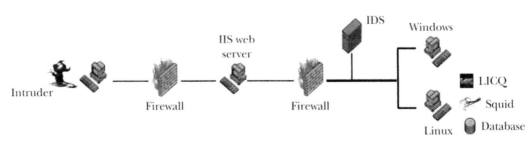

FIGURE   Example network.

9.4

The Linux host on the internal network is running several services—Linux "I Seek You" (*LICQ*) chat software, *Squid* web proxy, and a *Database*. The *LICQ* client lets Linux users exchange text messages over the Internet. The *Squid* web proxy is a caching server. It stores requested Internet objects on a system closer to the requesting site than to the source. Web browsers can then use the local Squid cache as a proxy, reducing access time as well as bandwidth consumption. The host inside the DMZ is running Microsoft's Internet Information Services (IIS) on a Windows platform.

The intruder launches his or her attack starting from a single computer, which lies on the outside network. To be concrete, let us assume that his or her eventual goal is to disrupt the functioning of the database. To achieve this goal, the intruder needs root access on the database host Linux. The five actions at his or her disposal are summarized in Table 9.2.

Each of the five actions corresponds to a real-world vulnerability and has an entry in the Common Vulnerabilities and Exposures (CVE) database. CVE [12] is a standard list of names for vulnerabilities and other information security exposures. A CVE identifier is an eight-digit string prefixed with the letters "CVE" (for accepted vulnerabilities) or "CAN" (for candidate vulnerabilities).

The IIS buffer overflow action exploits a buffer overflow vulnerability in the Microsoft IIS Web Server to gain administrative privileges remotely.

The Squid action lets the attacker scan network ports on machines that would otherwise be inaccessible to him or her, taking advantage of a misconfigured access control list in the Squid web proxy.

The LICQ action exploits a problem in the URL parsing function of the LICQ software for Unix-flavor systems. An attacker can send a specially crafted URL to the LICQ client to execute arbitrary commands on the client's computer with the same access privileges as the user of the LICQ client.

The scripting action lets the intruder gain user privileges on Windows machines. Microsoft Internet Explorer 5.01 and 6.0 allow remote attackers to execute arbitrary code via malformed Content-Disposition and Content-Type header

Action	Effect	Example CVE ID
IIS buffer overflow	Remotely get root	CAN-2002-0364
Squid port scan	Port scan	CVE-2001-1030
LICQ gain user	Gain user privileges remotely	CVE-2001-0439
Scripting exploit	Gain user privileges remotely	CAN-2002-0193
Local buffer overflow	Locally get root	CVE-2002-0004

TABLE   Intruder actions.

9.2

fields that cause the application for the spoofed file type to pass the file back to the operating system for handling rather than raising an error message. This vulnerability may also be exploited through HTML-formatted email. The action requires some social engineering to entice a user to visit a specially formatted web page. However, the action can work against firewalled networks, since it requires only that internal users be able to browse the Web through the firewall.

Finally, the local buffer overflow action can exploit a multitude of existing vulnerabilities to let a user without administrative privileges gain them illegitimately. For the CVE number referenced in Table 9.2, the action exploits a buffer overflow flaw in the *at* program. The *at* program is a Linux utility for queueing shell commands for later execution.

Some of the actions that we model have multiple instantiations in the CVE database. For example, the local buffer overflow action exploits a common coding error that occurs in many Linux programs. Each program vulnerable to local buffer overflow has a separate CVE entry, and all such entries correspond to the same action rule. Table 9.2 lists only one example CVE identifier for each rule.

9.5.1   Example Network Components

Services, Vulnerabilities, and Connectivity

We specify the state of a network to include services running on each host, existing vulnerabilities, and connectivity between hosts. There are five Boolean variables for each host, specifying whether any of the three services are running and whether either of two other vulnerabilities are present on that host (Table 9.3).

The model of the target network includes connectivity information among the four hosts. The initial value of the connectivity relation R is shown in Table 9.4. An entry Table 9.4 corresponds to a pair of hosts (h_1, h_2). IIS and Squid listen on port 80 and the LICQ client listens on port 5190, and the connectivity relation specifies which of these services can be reached remotely from other hosts.

Variable	Meaning
w3svc$_h$	IIS web service running on host h
squid$_h$	*Squid* proxy running on host h
licq$_h$	*LICQ* running on host h
scripting$_h$	HTML scripting is enabled on host h
vul-at$_h$	*at* executable vulnerable to overflow on host h

TABLE   Variables specifying a host.

9.3

Host	Intruder	IIS Web Server	Windows	Linux
Intruder	y,y,y	y,y,n	n,n,n	n,n,n
IIS Web Server	y,n,n	y,y,y	y,y,y	y,y,y
Windows	n,n,n	y,y,n	y,y,y	y,y,y
Linux	n,n,n	y,y,n	y,y,y	y,y,y

TABLE   Connectivity relation.

9.4

Each entry consists of three Boolean values. The first value is "y" if h_1 and h_2 are connected by a physical link, the second value is "y" if h_1 can connect to h_2 on port 80, and the third value is "y" if h_1 can connect to h_2 on port 5190.

We use the connectivity relation to reflect the settings of the firewall as well as the existence of physical links. In the example, the intruder machine initially can reach only the web server on port 80 due to a strict security policy on the external firewall. The internal firewall is initially used to restrict internal user activity by disallowing most outgoing connections. An important exception is that internal users are permitted to contact the web server on port 80.

In this example, the connectivity relation stays unchanged throughout an attack. In general, the connectivity relation can change as a result of intruder actions. For example, an action may enable the intruder to compromise a firewall host and relax the firewall rules.

Intrusion Detection System

A single network-based IDS protects the internal network. The paths between hosts Intruder and IIS Web Server and between Windows and Linux are not monitored; the IDS can see the traffic between any other pair of hosts. There are no host-based intrusion detection components. The IDS always detects the LICQ action but cannot see any of the other actions. The IDS is represented with a two-dimensional array of bits, shown in Table 9.5. An entry in Table 9.5 corresponds to a pair of hosts (h_1, h_2). The value is "y" if the path between h_1 and h_2 is monitored by the IDS, and "n" otherwise.

Intruder

The intruder's store of knowledge consists of a single Boolean variable "scan." The variable indicates whether the intruder has successfully performed a port scan on

Host	Intruder	IIS Web Server	Windows	Linux
Intruder	n	n	y	y
IIS Web Server	n	n	y	y
Windows	y	y	n	n
Linux	y	y	n	n

TABLE

9.5

IDS locations.

the target network. For simplicity, we do not keep track of specific information gathered by the scan. It would not be difficult to do so, at the cost of increasing the size of the state space.

Initially, the intruder has root access on his or her own machine Intruder, but no access to the other hosts. The "scan" variable is set to *false*.

Actions

There are five action rules corresponding to the five actions in the intruder's arsenal. Throughout the description, S is used to designate the source host and T the target host. $R(S,T,p)$ says that host T is reachable from host S on port p. The abbreviation $plvl(X)$ refers to the intruder's current privilege level on host X.

Recall that a specification of an action rule has four components: *intruder preconditions*, *network preconditions*, *intruder effects*, and *network effects*. The *intruder preconditions* component places conditions on the intruder's store of knowledge and the privilege level required to launch the action. The *network preconditions* component specifies conditions on target host state, network connectivity, trust, services, and vulnerabilities that must hold before launching the action. Finally, the *intruder* and *network effects* components list the action's effects on the intruder and network, respectively.

Sometimes the intruder has no logical reason to execute a specific action, even if all technical preconditions for the action have been met. For instance, if the intruder's current privileges include root access on the web server, the intruder would not need to execute the IIS buffer overflow action against the web server host. We have chosen to augment each action's preconditions with a clause that disables the action in instances when the primary purpose of the action has been achieved by other means. This change is not strictly conservative, as it prevents the intruder from using an action for its secondary side effects. However, we feel that this is a reasonable price to pay for removing unnecessary transitions from the attack graphs. The five action rules are discussed in turn below.

IIS buffer overflow. This remote-to-root action immediately gives a remote user a root shell on the target machine.

action IIS-buffer-overflow **is**

> **intruder preconditions**
>
> > $plvl(S) \geq$ user   *User-level privileges on host S*
> >
> > $plvl(T) <$ root   *No root-level privileges on host T*
>
> **network preconditions**
>
> > w3svc$_T$ *Host T is running vulnerable IIS server*
> >
> > $R(S,T,80)$ *Host T is reachable from S on port 80*
>
> **intruder effects**
>
> > $plvl(T) :=$ root   *Root-level privileges on host T*
>
> **network effects**
>
> > $\neg$w3svc$_T$ *Host T is not running IIS*

end

Squid port scan. The Squid port scan action uses a misconfigured Squid web proxy to conduct a port scan of neighboring machines and report the results to the intruder.

action squid-port-scan **is**

> **intruder preconditions**
>
> > $plvl(S) =$ user   *User-level privileges on host S*
> >
> > $\neg$scan   *A port scan has not occurred*
>
> **network preconditions**
>
> > squid$_T$ *Host T is running vulnerable Squid proxy*
> >
> > $R(S,T,80)$ *Host T is reachable from S on port 80*
>
> **intruder effects**
>
> > scan   *A port scan was performed on the network*
>
> **network effects**
>
> > $\oslash$ *No changes to the network component*

end

LICQ remote to user. This remote-to-user action immediately gives a remote user a user shell on the target machine. The action rule assumes that a port scan has been performed previously, modeling the fact that such actions typically become apparent to the intruder only after a scan reveals the possibility of exploiting software listening on lesser-known ports.

action LICQ-remote-to-user **is**

    intruder preconditions

        $plvl(S) \geq$ user   *User-level privileges on host S*

        $plvl(T) =$ none   *No user-level privileges on host T*

        scan   *A port scan was performed on the network*

    network preconditions

        $licq_T$ *Host T is running vulnerable LICQ software*

        $R(S,T,5190)$ *Host T is reachable from S on port 5190*

    intruder effects

        $plvl(T) :=$ user   *User-level privileges on host T*

    network effects

        ⊘   *No changes to the network component*

end

Scripting action.   This remote-to-user action immediately gives a remote user a user shell on the target machine. The action rule does not model the social engineering required to get a user to download a specially created web page.

action client-scripting **is**

    intruder preconditions

        $plvl(S) \geq$ user   *User-level privileges on host S*

        $plvl(T) =$ none   *No user-level privileges on host T*

    network preconditions

        $scripting_T$ *HTML scripting is enabled on host T*

        $R(T,S,80)$ *Host S is reachable from T on port 80*

    intruder effects

        $plvl(T) :=$ user   *User-level privileges on host T*

    network effects

        ⊘   *No changes to the network component*

end

Local buffer overflow. If the intruder has acquired a user shell on the target machine, this action exploits a buffer overflow vulnerability on a *setuid root* file (in this case, the *at* executable) to gain root access.

action local-setuid-buffer-overflow **is**

> **intruder preconditions**
>
> > $plvl(T) = \text{user}$ *User-level privileges on host T*
>
> **network preconditions**
>
> > vul-at$_T$ *There is a vulnerable* at *executable*
>
> **intruder effects**
>
> > $plvl(T) := \text{root}$ *Root-level privileges on host T*
>
> **network effects**
>
> > $\oslash$ *No changes to the network component*

end

9.5.2   Sample Attack Graphs

Figure 9.5 shows a screenshot of the attack graph generated with our attack graph toolkit (see Section 9.7.2) for the security property

$$\mathbf{G}\ (intruder.privilege[lin] < root)$$

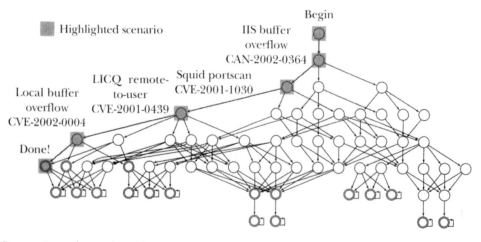

FIGURE   Example attack graph.

9.5

which states that the intruder will never attain root privileges on the Linux host. In Figure 9.5, a sample attack scenario is highlighted with solid square nodes, with each attack step identified by name and CVE number. Since the external firewall restricts most network connections from the outside, the intruder has no choice with respect to the initial step—it must be a buffer overflow action on the IIS Web Server. Once the intruder has access to the web server machine, his or her options expand. The highlighted scenario is the shortest route to success. The intruder uses the web server machine to launch a port scan via the vulnerable Squid proxy running on the Linux host. The scan discovers that it is possible to obtain user privileges on the Linux host with the LICQ exploit. After that, a simple local buffer overflow gives the intruder administrative control over the Linux machine. The last transition in the action path is a bookkeeping step, signifying the intruder's success.

Any information explicitly represented in the model is available for inspection and analysis in the attack graph. For instance, with a few clicks using our graphical user-interface tool, we are able to highlight portions of the graph "covered" by the IDS. Figure 9.6 shades the nodes where the IDS alarm has been sounded. These nodes lie on paths that use the LICQ action along a network path monitored by the IDS. It is clear that while a substantial portion of the graph is covered by the IDS, the intruder can escape detection and still succeed by taking one of the paths on the right side of the graph. One such attack scenario is

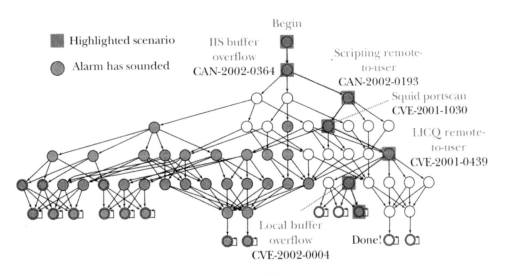

FIGURE

9.6

Alternative attack scenario avoiding the IDS.

highlighted with square nodes in Figure 9.6. It is very similar to the attack scenario just discussed, except that the LICQ action is launched from the internal Windows machine, where the intrusion detection system does not see it. To prepare for launching the LICQ action from the Windows machine, an additional step is needed to obtain user privileges in the machine. For that, the intruder uses the client scripting exploit on the Windows host immediately after taking over the web machine.

9.6   ATTACK GRAPH ANALYSIS

Attack graphs serve as the basis of further analysis in several areas of network security, including intrusion detection, defense, and forensic analysis. System administrators use attack graphs for the following reasons:

◆ *To gather information:* Attack graphs can answer questions like "What attacks is my system vulnerable to?" and "From an initial configuration, how many different ways can an intruder reach a final state to achieve his or her goal?"

◆ *To make decisions:* Attack graphs can answer questions like "Which set of actions should I prevent to ensure the intruder cannot achieve his or her goal?" or "Which set of security measures should I deploy to ensure the intruder cannot achieve his or her goal?"

Since we can produce attack graphs automatically, we make it convenient for system administrators to do "What if?" analysis. Administrators can look at a graph we produce and determine what would happen if they were to change firewall rules, add an IDS, install a software patch, or remove a host from the network. Does making a change to the system make the graph smaller, and in what way?

In this section, we look at two kinds of analyses that we can perform on an attack graph: single action removal and critical action set minimization. The first lets administrators see the effect of removing a single action from the intruder's arsenal. The second identifies a set of actions that if removed would then prevent an intruder from achieving his or her goal.

To demonstrate the analyses, we expand the example from Section 9.5.1 with an extra host User on the external network and several new actions. An authorized user W of the internal network owns the new host and uses it as a terminal to work remotely on the internal Windows host. The new actions permit an intruder to take over the host User, sniff user W's log-in credentials, and log in to the internal Windows host using the stolen credentials. We omit the details of the new actions, as they are not essential to understanding the examples. Figure 9.7(a) shows the full graph for the modified example. The graph is significantly larger, reflecting the expanded number of choices available to the intruder.

9.6.1 Single Action Removal

A simple kind of analysis determines the impact of removing one action from the intruder's arsenal. Recall from Section 9.4 that each action is a triple $\langle r, h_s, h_t \rangle$, where $h_s \in H$ is the host from which the attack is launched, $h_t \in H$ is the host targeted by the attack, and r is an action rule. The user specifies a set A_{rem} of action triples to be removed from the attack graph. Our toolkit deletes the transitions corresponding to each triple in the set A_{rem} from the graph and then removes the nodes that have become unreachable from the initial state.

As demonstrated in Figure 9.7, this procedure can be repeated several times, reducing the size of the attack graph at each step. The full graph in Figure 9.7(a) has 362 states. Removing one of two ways the intruder can sniff user W's log-in credentials produces the graph in Figure 9.7(b), with 213 states. Removing one of the local buffer overflow actions produces the graph in Figure 9.7(c), with 66 states. At each step, the user is able to visually judge the impact of removing a single action from the intruder's arsenal.

9.6.2 Critical Action Set Minimization

Let us turn to a more sophisticated analysis, which is a kind of *minimization analysis* [13]. Suppose the system administrator must decide among several different firewall configurations, several vulnerabilities to patch, or several IDSs to set up. Each choice prevents a different subset of actions. What should the system administrator do?

We cast this question in terms of the *Minimum Critical Set of Actions* (MCSA) problem: What are the minimum set of actions that must be prevented to guarantee the intruder cannot achieve his or her goal? The sketch of our solution is:

1. Reduce MCSA to the Minimum Hitting Set (MHS) problem [13].

2. Reduce MHS to the Minimum Set Covering (MSC) problem [14].

3. Use a textbook Greedy Approximation Algorithm to approximate a solution [15].

The first reduction can be briefly understood as follows. Each path in the graph is an attack. Label each edge in the path with the action that causes the

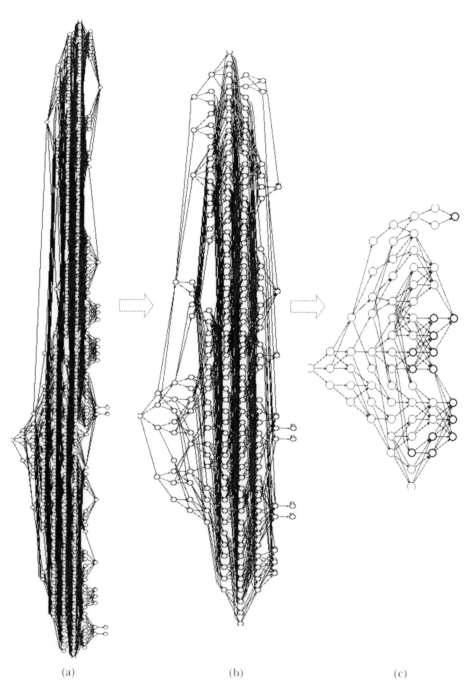

(a)　　　　　　　　　(b)　　　　　　　　　(c)

FIGURE　　　Reducing action arsenal.

9.7

state transition (note that an action might label more than one edge in the path). Thus, the path defines a set of actions used to "realize" an attack. Thus, an attack graph is a set, R, of "realizable" sets of actions. We need to hit each set in R. If we hit each set in R, then we cut the graph. If we cut the graph, then there is no path from the initial state to any final (success) state in the graph. Finding a minimum critical set of actions then reduces to finding a minimum hitting set for R. That is, a minimum hitting set for R will identify a set of actions that the intruder *must have* in his or her arsenal in order for him or her to succeed (achieve his or her goal). This set is a *critical set of actions*.

In short, once an attack graph is generated, we can use an approximation algorithm to find an approximately optimal critical set of actions that will completely disconnect the initial state from states where the intruder has achieved his or her goals [3]. A related algorithm can find an approximately optimal set of security measures that accomplish the same goal. With a single click using our graphical user-interface tool, the user can invoke both of these exposure minimization algorithms.

The effect of the critical action set algorithm on the modified example attack graph is shown in Figure 9.8(a). The algorithm finds a critical action set of size 1, containing the port scan action exploiting the Squid web proxy. The graph nodes and edges corresponding to actions in the critical set computed by the algorithm are highlighted in the toolkit by shading the relevant nodes. The shaded nodes are seen clearly when we zoom in to inspect a part of the graph on a larger scale (Figure 9.8b).

Since the computed action set is always critical, removing every action triple in the set from the intruder's arsenal is guaranteed to result in an empty attack graph. In the example, we might patch the Linux machine with a new version of the Squid proxy, thereby removing every action triple that uses the Squid port scan rule on the Linux machine from the intruder's arsenal.

9.7   PRACTICAL EXPERIENCE

9.7.1   Performance

In practice we found that the explicit-state algorithm has good performance: the speed to generate the attack graph is linear in the number of reachable state transitions [3]. We also found that for our limited number of examples, our explicit-state algorithm is better than our symbolic algorithm in terms of time to generate graphs. In all of our examples, our models are large due to their large

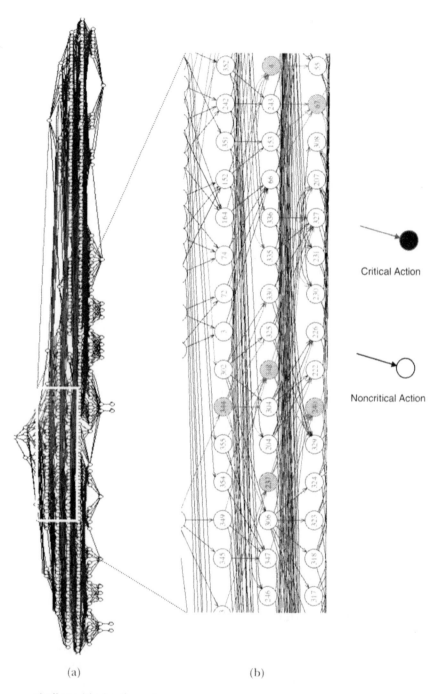

(a)   (b)

FIGURE   Finding critical action sets.

9.8

number of state variables, but at the same time they have a very small reachable state space. Thus, we have a double whammy against the symbolic algorithm: smaller reachable state spaces are better for explicit-state model checking, and larger numbers of state variables are worse for symbolic model checking.

These performance results, however, are not definitive. For one, we did not try to fine-tune the implementation of our symbolic model-checking algorithm. But most importantly, our application to security biases our experimental results in favor of our explicit-state algorithm. For other applications, the symbolic algorithm might be the better choice, in particular for general scenario graphs.

9.7.2 Toolkit

We built a toolkit that allows us to model networked systems [16]. We write XML input specifications that model the following kinds of information of a system: connectivity between hosts on the network, services running on each host, firewall rules, host-based and network-based IDSs, and most importantly, the actions an intruder might take in attempting to attack a system. We chose XML as our input specification language for modularity. We can plug in any model checker as our attack graph generator and translate our XML input specifications into the input language of the model checker. In our toolkit, we use our modifications of the NuSMV and SPIN model checkers, reflecting our two algorithms, to produce attack graphs.

One of the challenges to using our tools is providing a model of the network. We rely on external data sources to supply information necessary to build a network attack model. Specifically, it is necessary to know the topology of the target network, configuration of the network hosts, and vulnerabilities present on the network. In addition, we require access to a database of action rules to build the transition relation of the attack model.

We could expect the user to specify all of the necessary information manually, but such a task is tedious, error-prone, and unrealistic for networks of more than a few nodes. Thus, we recommend deploying the attack graph toolkit in conjunction with information gathering systems that automatically supply some of the data and with existing vulnerability databases. In our work, to give us network topology and host configuration data, we integrated the attack graph generator with two such systems: MITRE Corp.'s Outpost and Lockheed Martin's ANGI [16]. For our action rules, we specified a library of actions based on a vulnerability database provided to us by SEI/CERT. This database has over 150 actions representing many published CVEs. We wrote precondition/effects specifications as in Section 9.5.

9.8   RELATED WORK

Generating a set of all counterexamples is a novel addition to the repertoire of model checking techniques. Sheyner's dissertation [3] gives the most comprehensive description of scenario graphs and algorithms for generating them. We restrict the remainder of our discussion of related work to attack graphs.

Phillips and Swiler [17] propose the concept of attack graphs that is similar to the one described here. However, they take an "attack-centric" view of the system. Since we work with a general modeling language, we can express in our model both seemingly benign system events (such as failure of a link) and malicious events (such as attacks). Therefore, our attack graphs are more general than the one proposed by Phillips and Swiler. Swiler et al. [18] describe a tool for generating attack graphs based on their previous work. Their tool constructs the attack graph by forward exploration starting from the initial state.

The advantage of using model checking instead of forward search is that the technique can be expanded to include liveness properties, which can model service guarantees in the face of malicious activity. For example, a model of a banking network could have a liveness security property such as

$$\mathbf{G}\left(CheckDeposited \ \rightarrow \ (\mathbf{F} \ CheckCleared)\right)$$

which specifies that every check deposited at a bank branch must eventually clear.

Templeton and Levitt [19] propose a requires/provides model for attacks. The model links atomic attacks into scenarios, with earlier atomic attacks supplying the prerequisites for the later ones. Templeton and Levitt point out that relating seemingly innocuous system behavior to known attack scenarios can help discover new atomic attacks. However, they do not consider combining their attack scenarios into attack graphs.

Cuppens and Ortalo [20] propose a declarative language (LAMBDA) for specifying attacks in terms of pre- and postconditions. LAMBDA is a superset of the simple language we used to model attacks in our work. The language is modular and hierarchical; higher-level attacks can be described using lower-level attacks as components. LAMBDA also includes intrusion detection elements. Attack specifications include information about the steps needed to detect the attack and the steps needed to verify that the attack has already been carried out. Using a database of attacks specified in LAMBDA, Cuppens and Miege [21] propose a method for alert correlation based on matching postconditions of some attacks with preconditions of other attacks that may follow. In effect, they exploit the fact that alerts about attacks are more likely to be related if the corresponding attacks can be a part of the same attack scenario.

Dacier [22] proposes the concept of privilege graphs. Each node in the privilege graph represents a set of privileges owned by the user; edges represent vulnerabilities. Privilege graphs are then explored to construct attack state graphs, which represents different ways in which an intruder can reach a certain goal, such as root access on a host. He also defines a metric, called the *mean effort to failure* or METF, based on the attack state graphs. Orlato et al. [23] describe an experimental evaluation of a framework based on these ideas. At the surface, our notion of attack graphs seems similar to the one proposed by Dacier. However, as is the case with Phillips and Swiler, Dacier takes an "attack-centric" view of the world. As pointed out above, our attack graphs are more general. From the experiments conducted by Orlato et al., it appears that even for small examples the space required to construct attack state graphs becomes prohibitive. By basing our algorithm on model checking we take advantage of advances in representing large state spaces and can thus hope to represent large attack graphs.

Ritchey and Ammann [11] also use model checking for vulnerability analysis of networks. They use the (unmodified) model checker SMV [24]. They can obtain only one counterexample (i.e., only one attack corresponding to an unsafe state). In contrast, we modified the model checker NuSMV to produce attack graphs, representing all possible attacks. We also described postfacto analyses that can be performed on these attack graphs. These analysis techniques cannot be meaningfully performed on single attacks.

Graph-based data structures have also been used in network IDSs, such as *NetSTAT* [25]. There are two major components in NetSTAT: a set of probes placed at different points in the network and an analyzer. The analyzer processes events generated by the probes and generates alarms by consulting a network fact base and a scenario database. The network fact base contains information (such as connectivity) about the network being monitored. The scenario database has a directed graph representation of various atomic attacks. For example, the graph corresponding to an IP spoofing attack shows various steps that an intruder takes to mount that specific attack. The authors state that "in the analysis process the most critical operation is the generation of all possible instances of an attack scenario with respect to a given target network."

Ammann et al. [26] present a scalable attack graph representation. They encode attack graphs as dependencies among exploits and security conditions, under the assumption of monotonicity. Informally, monotonicity means that no action an intruder can take interferes with the intruder's ability to take any other actions. The authors treat vulnerabilities, intruder access privileges, and network connectivity as atomic Boolean attributes. Actions are treated as atomic transformations that, given a set of preconditions on the attributes, establish a set of postconditions. In this model, monotonicity means that (1) once a postcondition is satisfied, it can never become unsatisfied, and (2) the negation operator cannot be used in expressing action preconditions.

The authors show that under the monotonicity assumption it is possible to construct an efficient (low-order polynomial) attack graph representation that scales well. They present an efficient algorithm for extracting minimal attack scenarios from the representation, and suggest that a standard graph algorithm can produce a critical set of actions that disconnect the goal state of the intruder from the initial state.

This approach is less general than our treatment of attack graphs. In addition to the monotonicity requirement, it can handle only simple safety properties. Further, the compact attack graph representation is less explicit, and therefore harder for a human to read. The advantage of the approach is that it has a worst-case bound on the size of the graph that is polynomial in the number of atomic attributes in the model, and, therefore, can scale better than full-fledged model checking to large networks.

9.9   FUTURE WORK AND CONCLUSION

We are now producing scenario graphs so large that humans have a hard time interpreting them. We plan to address the problem of size in several ways:

+ Apply optimization techniques from the model checking literature to reduce the size of scenario graphs. For example, we can use symmetry and partial-order reduction techniques. One open problem is what a set of "all counterexamples" means when using the counterexample-guided abstraction and refinement model checking technique.

+ Find ways to compress either or both the internal representation of the scenario graph and the external one displayed to the user.

  • One novel approach we took was to apply the Google PageRank algorithm to the graphs we produce [27]. We use the in-degree and out-degree of a node in the graph as an estimate of how likely an attacker is to visit a state in a given attack (i.e., path in the graph).

  • Rather than generate the entire scenario graph, we could do "query-directed" scenario graph generation. An example query might be "What are all paths in the scenario graph that involve a particular action?" For attack graphs, the system administrator might want to see subgraphs involving a particular host, service, or IDS. We could use such queries to reduce the graph that is then displayed to the user.

- Design and implement new graph-based analyses on scenario graphs. The minimization analysis discussed in Section 9.6.2 is only the tip of the iceberg. We would like to explore more such analyses for scenario graphs in general.

We are also interested in pursuing further uses of attack graphs, for example, in using them in conjunction with online IDSs and in using them to help with alert correlation. One potential approach is to use the edit-distance algorithm (e.g., used on DNA sequences) to match an abstraction of a sequence of alerts with a subpath of some attack in an attack graph [28]. The closer the match, the higher the likelihood that the alerts signal a real attack.

Finally, we are interested in exploring applications of scenario graphs to other domains. The model checking algorithms we present for producing all counterexamples are both extremely general. Model checkers, which produce a single counterexample, are already used for a broad range of applications, including hardware design, software debugging, embedded systems verification, program analysis, e-commerce, authentication protocols, and computational biology. We leave for future work what the analog of "all counterexamples" means in these and other applications.

ACKNOWLEDGMENTS

Oleg Sheyner deserves all the credit for the technical contributions summarized in this chapter. The initial idea of using model checking to produce attack graphs is due to my collaboration with Somesh Jha.

All the ideas in this chapter can be found in greater detail in Oleg Sheyner's doctoral dissertation [3]. Portions of his dissertation have appeared in conference and journal papers [1, 2, 5, 13, 16, 29]. This chapter draws largely from Wing's summary paper [29] and Sheyner and Wing's conference paper [16]; specific sections are reprinted in part from Wing [29], pp. 229–234, with permission from IOS Press, and Sheyner and Wing [16], pp. 344–371, Figures 2–7, with kind permission of Springer Science and Business Media.

This research is sponsored in part by the Army Research Office under contract no. DAAD19-01-1-0485 and DAAD19-02-1-0389, the National Science Foundation under grant no. CCR-0121547 and CNS-0433540, and the Software Engineering Institute through a U.S. government funding appropriation.

The views and conclusions contained herein are those of the authors and should not be interpreted as necessarily representing the official policies or endorsements, either expressed or implied, of the sponsoring institutions, the U.S. Government, or any other entity.

References

[1] S. Jha and J. M. Wing, "Survivability Analysis of Networked Systems," *Proceedings of the International Conference on Software Engineering*, Toronto, Canada, May 2001.

[2] T. Hughes and O. Sheyner, "Attack Scenario Graphs for Computer Network Threat Analysis and Prediction," *Complexity* 9, No. 2 (Nov./Dec. 2003): 15–18.

[3] O. Sheyner, "Scenario Graphs and Attack Graphs," CMU Computer Science Department Technical Report CMU-CS-04-122, Ph.D. Dissertation, April 2004.

[4] NuSMV: A New Symbolic Model Checker, at *http://afrodite.itc.it:1024/nusmv/*.

[5] O. Sheyner, J. Haines, S. Jha, R. Lippman, and J. M. Wing, "Automated Generation and Analysis of Attack Graphs," *Proceedings of the IEEE Symposium on Security and Privacy*, Oakland, CA, May 2002.

[6] E. M. Clarke, Orna Grumberg, and Doron Peled, *Model Checking* (Boston: MIT Press, 2000).

[7] R. E. Bryant, "Graph-Based Algorithms for Boolean Function Manipulation," *IEEE Transactions on Computers* C-35, No. 8 (Aug. 1986): 677–691.

[8] G. J. Holzmann, *The SPIN Model Checker: Primer and Reference Manual* (Boston: Addison-Wesley, 2004). Also at *http://www.spinroot.com/spin/whatispin.html*.

[9] R. Gerth, D. Peled, M. Y. Vardi, and P. Wolper, "Simple On-the-Fly Automatic Verification of Linear Temporal Logic," *Proceedings of the 6th Symposium on Logic in Computer Science*, Amsterdam, The Netherlands, July 1991, pp. 406–415.

[10] R. E. Tarjan, "Depth First Search and Linear Graph Algorithms," *SIAM Journal of Computing* 1, No. 2 (June 1972): 146–160.

[11] R. W. Ritchey and P. Ammann, "Using Model Checking to Analyze Network Vulnerabilities," *Proceedings of the IEEE Symposium on Security and Privacy*, Oakland, CA, May 2001, pp. 156–165.

[12] Common Vulnerabilities and Exposures, at *http://www.cve.mitre.org*.

[13] S. Jha, O. Sheyner, and J. M. Wing, "Minimization and Reliability Analysis of Attack Graphs," *Proceedings of the Computer Security Foundations Workshop*, Nova Scotia, Canada, June 2002, pp. 49–63.

[14] G. Ausiello, A. Datri, and M. Protasi. "Structure Preserving Reductions among Convex Optimization Problems," *Journal of Computational System Sciences (JCSS)* 21 (1980): 136–153.

[15] T. H. Cormen, Charles E. Leiserson, Ronald L. Rivest, and Clifford Stein, *Introduction to Algorithms*, 2nd ed. (Boston: MIT Press and McGraw-Hill, 2001).

[16] O. Sheyner and J. M. Wing, "Tools for Generating and Analyzing Attack Graphs," *Proceedings of Formal Methods for Components and Objects*, Second

International Symposium, FMCO 2003, Leiden, The Netherlands, Nov. 2003, edited by F. S. de Boer, M. M. Bonsangue, S. Graf, and W.-P. de Roever, *Lecture Notes in Computer Science 3188* (Berlin, Germany Springer-Verlag, 2004), pp. 344–371.

[17] C. A. Phillips and L. P. Swiler, "A Graph-Based System for Network Vulnerability Analysis," New Security Paradigms Workshop, 1998, pp. 71–79.

[18] L. P. Swiler, C. Phillips, D. Ellis, and S. Chakerian, "Computer-Attack Graph Generation Tool," *Proceedings of the DARPA Information Survivability Conference and Exposition*, Hilton Head Island, SC, June 2000.

[19] S. Templeton and K. Levitt, "A Requires/Provides Model for Computer Attacks," *Proceedings of the New Security Paradigms Workshop*, Cork, Ireland, 2000.

[20] F. Cuppens and R. Ortalo, "LAMBDA: A Language to Model a Database for Detection of Attacks," *Proceedings of the Third International Workshop on the Recent Advances in Intrusion Detection (RAID)*, LNCS 1907 (Toulouse, France Springer-Verlag, 2000), pp. 197–216.

[21] F. Cuppens and A. Miege, "Alert Correlation in a Cooperative Intrusion Detection Framework," *Proceedings of the 23rd IEEE Symposium on Security and Privacy*, Oakland, CA, May 2002.

[22] M. Dacier, "Towards Quantitative Evaluation of Computer Security," Ph.D. Thesis, Institut National Polytechnique de Toulouse, Dec. 1994.

[23] R. Ortalo, Y. Deswarte, and M. Kaaniche, "Experimenting with Quantitative Evaluation Tools for Monitoring Operational Security," *IEEE Transactions on Software Engineering* 25, No. 5 (Sept./Oct. 1999): 633–650.

[24] SMV: A Symbolic Model Checker, at *http://www.cs.cmu.edu/modelcheck/*.

[25] G. Vigna and R. A. Kemmerer, "NetSTAT: A Network-Based Intrusion Detection System," *Journal of Computer Security* 7, No. 1 (1999): pp. 37–71.

[26] P. Ammann, D. Wijesekera, and S. Kaushik, "Scalable, Graph-Based Network Vulnerability Analysis," *Proceedings of the 9th ACM Conference on Computer and Communications Security*, Washington, DC 2002, pp. 217–224.

[27] V. Mehta, C. Bartzis, H. Zhu, E. M. Clarke, and J. M. Wing, "Ranking Attack Graphs," *Proceedings of Recent Advances in Intrusion Detection*, Hamburg, Germany, Sept. 20–22, 2006.

[28] O. Dobzinski, "Alert Abstraction Using Attack Graphs," Master's Project, Department of Electrical and Computer Engineering, Carnegie Mellon University, Pittsburgh, PA, May 2006.

[29] J. M. Wing, "Scenario Graphs Applied to Security (Extended Abstract)," *Verification of Infinite-State Systems with Applications to Security*, edited by E. Clarke, M. Minea, and F. L. Tiplea (Washington DC IOS Press, 2006), pp. 229–234.

10 | Vulnerability-Centric Alert Correlation

Lingyu Wang   Concordia University, Canada
Sushil Jajodia   George Mason University, USA

10.1   INTRODUCTION

With 20 years of research on vulnerability analysis and intrusion detection, most critical computer networks are now under the protection of various security measures, such as access control, firewalls, intrusion detection systems (IDSs), and vulnerability scanners. With proper implementations, such measures can effectively thwart intrusion attempts made by amateur attackers and so-called script kiddies. However, real nightmares to a security administrator are usually caused by more experienced attackers who can easily circumvent basic security controls and detections through *multistep* intrusions. In such an intrusion, an attacker launches multiple attack steps that prepare for each other such that privileges can be gradually obtained and escalated on a series of intermediate hosts before he or she reaches the final goal.

Security administrators usually find it challenging to defend against multistep intrusions because most existing security tools have been designed to cope with individual incidents of attacks rather than correlated attacks. IDSs, such as Snort [1], can report intrusion alerts on isolated attack steps, but these systems are typically unaware of the relationships among attacks. It is generally difficult to identify correlated attacks corresponding to a multistep intrusion by manually inspecting the large amount of intrusion alerts reported by IDSs. Attackers can hide their intentions by deliberately triggering false attack attempts and by spreading an intrusion over a longer time period, both of which will make it more difficult for administrators to identify the intrusion. Similarly, vulnerability scanners can identify individual weaknesses in a host or network, but each identified vulnerability by itself usually does not seem to be a serious threat until it is combined with others in a cleverly-crafted multistep intrusion.

Penetration testing can sometimes reveal a potential multistep intrusion thanks to the heavy human intervention used in such a testing. However, due to the same reason, the effectiveness of such testing critically depends on the capabilities of the red team (representing attackers) and is prone to human errors. *Topological vulnerability analysis* can be regarded as an automated version of penetration testing [2, 3]. The result of such an analysis, the attack graph, can be used to harden a network such that critical resources can be protected at a minimal cost [2, 4, 5]. This approach provides an ideal solution to defending against multistep intrusions. However, the solution is not always feasible due to its incurred administrative costs and its potential impact on the availability of network services. In practice, we may have to live with some vulnerability, and to take actions only when an actual intrusion has been detected. This, though at a different level, is analogous to the fact that we need IDSs even though we already have vulnerability scanners. Finally, to ignore the correlation between attack steps and respond to each individual attack will cause large volumes of false-positive intrusions and effectively render a network useless.

In this chapter, we discuss real-time detection and prediction methods for less-than-ideal situations where vulnerabilities have to be tolerated. The methods will help administrators to monitor and predict the progress of actual multistep intrusions, and hence to take appropriate countermeasures in a timely manner. We first review the literature on *alert correlation*. Adding the missing relationships among attack steps, alert correlation techniques reassemble isolated IDS alerts into more meaningful attack scenarios. Previous alert correlation techniques typically either rely on domain knowledge about alert types or rely on statistical methods to identify the relationships among alerts. A more recent approach uses the knowledge obtained through topological vulnerability analysis to correlate alerts [6, 7]. Inspired by an ancient Chinese saying, "Know your enemy, know yourself, fight a hundred battles, win a hundred battles," this *vulnerability-centric* approach starts from the knowledge about one's own weaknesses (vulnerabilities) and incorporates information about one's enemies (intrusion alerts). The approach shows a promising direction toward defeating multistep intrusions, because it inherits advantages from both alert correlation and topological vulnerability analysis. In particular, the knowledge about a network helps to filter out irrelevant alerts that do not correspond to vulnerabilities in the network.

In addition to filtering out irrelevant alerts, the vulnerability-centric approach also makes alert correlation immune to the so-called *slow attack*. Most previous alert correlation methods have been designed for offline applications, such as computer forensics. Thus, those methods typically have a computational complexity and memory requirement that are both proportional to (or worse than) the number of received alerts. This fact implies that only a limited number of alerts can be processed for correlation with a fixed amount of resources, such as memory. Such a limitation does not cause apparent problems in an offline application, because the number of alerts is already known and resources can be accordingly allocated. However, alert correlation in the real-time defense against ongoing intrusions brings a new challenge that renders many existing methods ineffective. A *live* attacker may be aware of the above-mentioned limitation. Thus, the attacker can exploit the limitation by following slow attacks. To prevent any two attack steps from being correlated, the attacker may either passively delay the second step or actively trigger false alerts between the two attack steps. In either case, correlation methods would be defeated.

To remove the above limitation, the vulnerability-centric alert correlation method first makes the key observation that not all alerts need to be explicitly correlated due to the transitive property of correlation relation. That is, if two attacks exploit the same vulnerability on the same host, and they both occur before a third attack that exploits a different vulnerability, then either both of the first two attacks prepare for the third attack (if the two vulnerabilities are related) or neither of them do (if the vulnerabilities are not related). To take advantage of this observation, the method materializes attack graphs as a special *queue graph* data structure. The queue graph only keeps in memory the last alert of each type, and only records explicit correlation relationship between two alerts if they are both in memory. As a result, both the time complexity and the memory requirement of alert correlation are now independent of the number of received alerts. Correlation can thus be established between any two alerts that may be separated by arbitrarily many others. Therefore, the correlation method is immune to the slow attack.

The method is also extended for the hypothesis of attacks missed by IDSs, for the prediction of possible future attacks and for the aggregation of repetitive alerts. Roughly speaking, we compare the *knowledge* encoded in the attack graph with the *fact* reflected in correlated alerts. An inconsistency between the knowledge and the facts implies potential attacks missed by IDSs, whereas extending the facts in a way that is consistent with the knowledge can indicate future attacks. To represent the analysis result in a compact way, an alert aggregation mechanism is also incorporated in the method, which ensures that no transitive edges will be introduced in the result graph and *indistinguishable* alerts will be aggregated. This capability is important because repetitive brute-force attempts may trigger a large number of similar alerts in a short time, and these alerts will render the result graph incomprehensible if not aggregated. Previously, alerts need to be aggregated prior to correlation, which adds extra overhead. Instead, the method described here interleaves alert aggregation with alert correlation, and the aggregation may actually make alert correlation faster. The described method can thus correlate, hypothesize, predict, and aggregate alerts all at the same time. Empirical results show that these tasks can be fulfilled faster than IDSs can report alerts. The method thus provides security administrators a practical tool in monitoring and predicting ongoing multistep intrusions.

The rest of this chapter is organized as follows. The next section reviews previous alert correlation and topological vulnerability analysis techniques. Section 10.3 introduces relevant concepts on attack graphs that will be needed in later sections. Section 10.4 then focuses on the vulnerability-centric method for alert correlation, hypothesis, prediction, and aggregation. Section 10.5 concludes the chapter.

10.2   REVIEW OF ALERT CORRELATION AND RELATED TECHNIQUES

Although most alert correlation techniques share the same objective of discovering relationships among isolated alerts, these techniques have evolved with respect to the different relationships they discover. Early work on alert correlation usually focused on the syntax similarity between alerts. That is, they group alerts with similar attributes into natural clusters to simplify the further examination of alerts [8–11]. These techniques are especially useful as preprocessing steps prior to other analyses. Some of the techniques correlate similar alerts based on their statistical or temporal similarity [12, 13]. Such methods can provide supplementary results about unknown attacks or unknown relationships among attacks.

Rather than relying on the syntax similarity, such as between similar attributes, other techniques aim to discover semantic similarity between attacks, such as the case that one attack is used by attackers to prepare for another. Some techniques use knowledge about known attack strategies or scenarios to find correlated attacks that match these strategies or scenarios [14–18]. These methods are analogous to misuse detection in that the strategies or scenarios play the role of signatures. Treating a complete strategy or scenario as a signature also leads to the limitation that variations from the signature will usually be ignored. This limitation was soon addressed by splitting the strategy or scenario into pairs of alert types that can be correlated with common pre- and postconditions [18–20].

The correlation between alerts discovered in Templeton and Levitt [18], Cuppens and Miege [19], and Ning et al. [20] is sometimes called a *causal* relationship. This reflects a key difference from the afore-mentioned work that defines a complete strategy or scenario as a signature in matching alerts. With respect to the causal relationship, two alerts are correlated if the former satisfies at least one security-related condition required by the latter. The role of the former attack can be regarded as contributory since it makes the second attack easier but not necessarily possible. On the other hand, previous approaches correlate a set of alerts to another alert, only if the former collectively satisfies *all* the conditions required by the latter.

Using the causal relationship between alerts reduces the complexity of alert correlation, because the relationship exists between a pair of alerts instead of between two sets of alerts. The causal relationship also makes it possible to tolerate attacks missed by IDSs because an alert will be correlated with others even if some of its required preconditions are not satisfied. On the other hand, correlation based on the causal relationship may introduce false positives, and the results also lack high-level attack strategies used by the attacker. A later work aims to extract such strategies from correlated alerts based on knowledge about different types of attacks that may play the same role in a multistep intrusion [21]. This work also attempts to reduce noises in the correlation result through verification against raw audit logs.

Combining domain knowledge with other information, such as the statistical or temporal similarity between alerts and common resources shared by alerts, leads to hybrid approaches that can discover unknown relationships among alerts [22, 23]. A recent work attempts to increase the validity of correlation by borrowing a technique for tracking operating system (OS) level events [24]. The assumption there is that each network attack will also trigger a series of interdependent OS events, such as the reads or writes of the same file. Thus, the correlation between two alerts is more convincing if the OS events they trigger are correlated. The interdependency between OS events is considered as hard evidence since it is inherent to the operating system and not prune to potential human errors in domain knowledge. Alert correlation is also shown to be helpful in dealing with insider threats [25, 26].

Closely related to the vulnerability-centric alert correlation method we describe below, topological vulnerability analysis techniques address the lack of relationships among vulnerabilities reported by security scanners. The interdependency between vulnerabilities and security conditions has long been investigated [27–31]. By regarding each exploitation of vulnerability as a state transition between the set of preconditions and that of postconditions, model checking was first used to analyze whether the given goal condition is reachable from the initially satisfied conditions [32, 33]. Later, a modified version of the model checker was used to enumerate all possible sequences of exploits between the two [2, 34]. The result of such an analysis was called an *attack graph*.

The above notion of attack graph explicitly includes all sequences of attacks that lead to compromises of given critical resources. However, attack graphs also face a scalability issue due to an exponential explosion in the number of potential attack sequences. A more compact representation of attack graphs was thus proposed to address this issue [3]. Underlying the new representation of attack graphs is the monotonicity assumption that says an attacker never needs to relinquish any obtained capability. Under the assumption, each exploit appears at most once in any sequence of attacks. In another word, each exploit (or condition) corresponds to no more than one vertex in the attack graph. This fact guarantees that an attack graph always has a polynomial size in the total number of vulnerabilities and security conditions. In this chapter, we shall assume such a compact representation of the attack graph.

10.3   ATTACK GRAPH

Attack graph is the basis of the vulnerability-centric approach we are going to discuss in the rest of this chapter. This section briefly reviews relevant concepts and states our assumptions. Attack graphs represent prior knowledge about network connectivity and the dependency between vulnerabilities. There have been two different representations for an attack graph. First, an attack graph can explicitly enumerate possible sequences of vulnerabilities (i.e., attack paths) that an attacker can follow [2,34]. Second, an attack graph can be represented by the dependency relationships among vulnerabilities, whence attack paths are encoded implicitly [3]. This representation does not lose any information under the monotonicity assumption, which states that an attacker never needs to relinquish any obtained capability. The resulting attack graph has no duplicate vertices, and hence has a polynomial size in the number of vulnerabilities multiplied by the number of connected pairs of hosts. We shall assume this latter notion of attack graphs.

An attack graph of the second notion is usually represented as a directed graph with two types of vertices: exploits and pre- or postconditions. An exploit is a tuple $(v, h_s, h_{m1}, h_{m2}, \ldots, h_d)$. This indicates an exploitation of the vulnerability v on the destination host h_d, initiated from the source host h_s and through a series of intermediate hosts h_{m1}, h_{m2}, and so on. In particular, for exploits involving two hosts (with no intermediate host) or one host (in local exploits), we use (v, h_s, h_d) and (v, h), respectively. Similarly, a security condition is a triple (c, h_s, h_d) that indicates a security-related condition c involving the source host h_s and the destination host h_d. When a condition involves a single host, we simply write (c, h). Here, conditions typically refer to the existence of vulnerability or the connectivity between two hosts (while there might be abundant security-related conditions in each host, we only include those that are either precondition or postcondition of at least one exploit in the attack graph). Two types of directed edges interconnect exploits and conditions, with no edge going directly between exploits or between conditions. First, an edge pointing from a condition to an exploit denotes the *require* relation, which means the exploit cannot be executed unless the condition is satisfied. Second, an edge pointing from an exploit to a condition denotes the *imply* relation, which means executing the exploit will satisfy the condition. For example, an exploit usually requires existence of the vulnerability on the destination host and connectivity between the two hosts. We call the composition of the *require* and *imply* relations the *prepare-for* relation, and denote it as an arrow. Later, when we map alerts to exploits, the prepare-for relation will be abused to relate the alerts, too.

Example 10.1

Figure 10.1 shows an attack graph where exploits are represented as triples (*source host, target host, vulnerability*) in ovals and security conditions as pairs (*host, condition*) in plaintext. The attack graph depicts a scenario where an attacker may exploit the *sadmind buffer overflow* vulnerability (Nessus ID 11841) on any of the two hosts h_1 and h_2 from his or her own machine h_3 since he or she already has the required user privilege on h_3. Once the attacker gains user privilege on h_1 or h_2, he or she can then use it as a stepping stone to further attack other hosts.

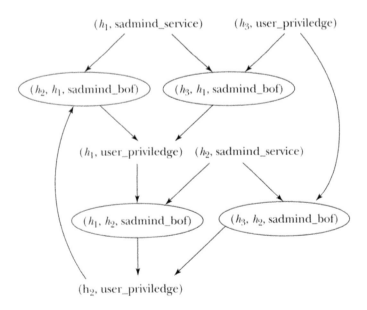

FIGURE   An example of an attack graph.

10.1

In interpreting an attack graph, an important aspect is that the *require* relation is always *conjunctive*, whereas the *imply* relation is always *disjunctive*. More specifically, an exploit cannot be realized until *all* of its required conditions have been satisfied, whereas a condition is satisfied if *any* of the realized exploits implies the condition. During further discussions, we assume attack graphs can be obtained with existing tools, such as the Topological Vulnerability Analysis (TVA) system [35]. We assume the attack graph is updated in a timely fashion upon changes in network topology and configurations. We assume the attack graph can be placed in memory for the given network. It is worth noting that this assumption depends on the size of a network and the complexity of its configurations and, therefore, may not always hold. We do not assume external host addresses to be trustful and hence use wildcards to match them. This may cause false correlations when multiple attackers concurrently launch similar attacks while they do not intend to cooperate with each other. The vulnerability-centric correlation approach needs to match alerts with exploits such that the alerts can be correlated using the knowledge encoded in an attack graph. To match alerts with exploits, the event-type attributes of alerts need to be mapped to the vulnerability attributes of exploits using domain knowledge, such as the correspondence between Snort identifiers and Nessus identifiers [36]. For simplicity, we denote the matching between alerts and exploits as a function *Exp*() from the set of alerts to the set of exploits. In some cases, an event type matches multiple vulnerabilities, which will be handled by creating a copy of alert for each matched exploit, indicating a simultaneous exploitation of multiple vulnerabilities.

Starting from the knowledge about one's own network, the vulnerability-centric correlation approach can mitigate the negative impact of disruptive alerts. For example, if an attacker blindly launches some Windows-specific attacks on UNIX machines, then the reported alerts will be ignored by the approach. On the other hand, the limitation lies in that relevant alerts do not always match exploits. For example, an ICMP PING matches no vulnerability, but it may signal the probing preparation for the attacks that follow. Such relevant alerts can be identified based on attack graphs and the knowledge about alert types. The concept of exploits needs to be extended to include alert types in the place of vulnerability attributes. Such special exploits are added to attack graphs and the function *Exp* will be extended accordingly. Because the vulnerability-centric approach processes incoming alerts in exactly one pass, the correlation method critically depends on temporal characteristics of alerts, such as the order of arrivals and the timestamps. In practice, those characteristics will exhibit much more uncertainty due to various delays in hosts and networks, especially when alerts are collected from multiple sensors placed in different places in a network. We shall address such temporal impreciseness in more details in later sections. However, we assume the clocks of IDS sensors are loosely synchronized with the correlation engine. This can be achieved in many ways depending on specific IDS systems. For example, Snort has built-in support of automatic time synchronization through the network time protocol (NTP) [1].

10.4 ALERT CORRELATION, HYPOTHESIS, PREDICTION, AND AGGREGATION

This section discusses the vulnerability-centric approach to the correlation, hypothesis, prediction, and aggregation of intrusion alerts. First, Section 10.4.1 discusses alert correlation in offline applications and its limitations. Then, Section 10.4.2 describes the vulnerability-centric alert correlation method, Section 10.4.3 discusses alert hypothesis and prediction, Section 10.4.4 discusses alert aggregation, and finally, Section 10.4.5 presents experimental results.

10.4.1 Alert Correlation in Offline Applications

In a typical offline alert correlation method, when a new alert arrives, it searches the previously received alerts to find those that prepare for it. This process is repeated for each new alert. This procedure involves two nested loops, and is thus called the *nested loop* approach. Figure 10.2 illustrates this approach. The left side of the figure shows a sequence of alerts with ascending timestamps (we shall discuss later the case when two alerts have exactly the same timestamps), $a_0, a_1, \ldots, a_n$. For $i = 1, 2, \ldots, n$, the nested loop approach searches $a_0, a_1, \ldots, a_{i-1}$ for those a_j's that satisfy $Exp(a_j) \rightarrow Exp(a_i)$. The search for the alerts that prepare for a_i can be optimized with an index on $a_0, a_1, \ldots, a_{i-1}$. After a_i is processed, an entry corresponding to a_i is inserted into the index.

As the number of received alerts keeps increasing, any finite amount of memory will eventually be insufficient for storing the index. A *sliding window* approach comes to the rescue. That is, only the alerts close enough to the new alert

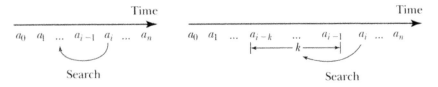

FIGURE

10.2 The nested loop approach, with or without a sliding window.

are considered for correlation. As in the right side of Figure 10.2, for the alert a_i the search is only performed on $a_{i-k}, a_{i-k+1}, \ldots, a_{i-1}$, where k is a given window size determined by available memory. However, this sliding window approach leads to another problem. The need for performance requires k to be small enough so the index can fit in memory, whereas a smaller k means less alerts will be considered for correlation with the new alert and hence an incomplete result. This situation can be worsened by experienced attackers who are aware of the correlation efforts. They can employ a *slow attack* to defeat such efforts. Specifically, given an arbitrarily large window size k, for any two attacks that trigger two correlated alerts, the attacker can delay the second attack until at least k other alerts have been raised since the first alert is triggered (based on an estimation of k), so the sliding window will be filled and the two alerts will not be correlated. Instead of passively awaiting, a smarter attacker can actively launch bogus attacks between the two real attack steps to fill in the sliding window in a shorter time. The attacker can even script bogus attack sequences between the real attack steps, such that a deceived correlation engine will be kept busy in producing falsely correlated alerts, while the real intrusion will be advanced in peace of mind.

To remove this limitation of the nested loop approach, we observe that the correlation between alerts does not always need to be explicitly recorded. Note that the correlation between two alerts actually mean two things. First, the prepare-for relationship exists between the exploits to which the two alerts are mapped. Second, the alert preparing for the other must occur before it. Knowing these facts, a new alert only needs to be explicitly correlated with the last alert matching each exploit. Its correlation with other earlier alerts matching the same exploit can be kept implicit through the temporal order and with the matching between alerts and exploits. This is illustrated in Example 10.2.

Example 10.2

In Figure 10.3, suppose the first three alerts a_i, a_j, and a_k, all match the same exploit $Exp(a_k)$ (i.e., their event types match the same vulnerability and they involve the same source and destination hosts). The alert a_h matches another exploit $Exp(a_h)$, and $Exp(a_k)$ prepares for $Exp(a_h)$. Hence, a_i, a_j, and a_k should all be correlated with a_h. However, if the correlation between a_k and a_h has been explicitly recorded (shown as a solid line in Figure 10.3), then the correlation between a_j and a_h can be kept implicit (shown as a dotted line). This observation is important because it can significantly reduce the complexity and memory requirement. Intuitively, for each exploit the correlation algorithm only needs to search backward for the first (a_k in the above case) alert matching that exploit. In the nested loop approach, however, the correlation is always explicit, and hence each new alert must unnecessarily search all the received alerts, as discussed before.

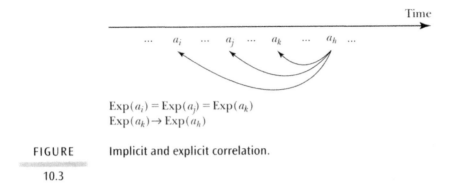

$$\text{Exp}(a_i) = \text{Exp}(a_j) = \text{Exp}(a_k)$$
$$\text{Exp}(a_k) \rightarrow \text{Exp}(a_h)$$

FIGURE   Implicit and explicit correlation.

10.3

10.4.2   Vulnerability-Centric Alert Correlation

We design an in-memory data structure called a *queue graph* (the name queue graph comes from the fact that the data structure is a graph and works like a queue). A queue graph is basically an in-memory materialization of the given attack graph with enhanced features (the purpose of the features will be made clear in the following sections). In a queue graph, each exploit is realized as a queue of length one (i.e., a bucket) and each condition as a variable. The realization of edges is based on a bidirectional, layered structure as follows. Starting from each exploit e_i, a breadth-first search (BFS) is performed in the attack graph by following the directed edges. For each edge encountered during the search, a forward pointer is created to connect the corresponding queue and variable. Similarly, another search is performed by following the directed edges in their reversed direction, and a backward pointer is created for each encountered edge. Later, we shall use the backward edges for correlation purposes and use the forward edges for prediction purposes. The pointers are then placed at a separate layer tailored to the queue corresponding to the exploit e_i. The reason for separating pointers into layers is as follows. A BFS always creates a tree (namely, the BFS tree), and hence later, another BFS starting from the same queue can follow only the pointers at that layer. This later BFS will then be performed within a tree instead of a graph, reducing the complexity from quadratic to linear. We illustrate the concepts in Example 10.3.

Example 10.3

In Figure 10.4, from left to right, are a given attack graph: the corresponding queues (shown as buckets), variables (shown as texts), and the (both forward and backward) pointers at different layers. Notice that the layer-one pointers do not include those connecting v_2 and Q_3, because a BFS in the attack graph

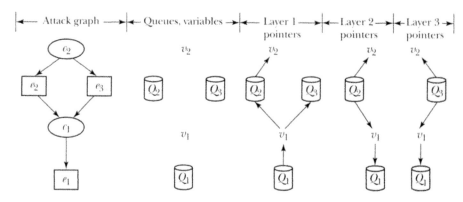

FIGURE   An example queue graph.

10.4

starting from e_1 will reach e_2 only once (either via e_2 or e_3, but we assume e_2 in this example). The layer-one pointers thus form a tree rooted at Q_1.

We have discussed how a nested loop approach correlates alerts. As a comparison, we now perform the same correlation using a queue graph (we discuss other correlation requirements later). Intuitively, we let the stream of alerts flow through the queue graph, and at the same time, we collect correlation results by searching the queue graph. Specifically, each incoming alert is first matched with an exploit and placed in the corresponding queue. Then, because the length of each queue is one, a nonempty queue must dequeue the current alert before it can enqueue a new alert. The results of correlation are collected during this process as a directed graph, namely, the *result graph*. First, each new alert is recorded as a vertex in the result graph. Second, when a new alert forces an old alert to be dequeued, a directed edge between the two alerts is added into the result graph, which records the temporal order between the two alerts and the fact that they both match the same exploit. Third, after each new alert is enqueued, a search starts from the queue and follows two consecutive backward pointers; for each nonempty queue encountered during the search, a directed edge from the alert in that queue to the new alert is added into the result graph. This is illustrated in Example 10.4.

Example 10.4

Consider correlating the four alerts a_i, a_j, a_k, and a_h in Figure 10.3 with the queue graph given in Figure 10.4, and suppose $Exp(a_h) = e_1, Exp(a_k) = e_2$, and no other alerts match e_1 or e_2 besides a_i, a_j, a_k, and a_h. First, when a_i arrives, it is placed in the empty queue Q_2. Then, a_j forces a_i to be dequeued from Q_2, and a directed edge (a_i, a_j) in the result graph records the facts that a_i is before a_j and they both match e_2. Similarly, a_k replaces a_j in Q_2, and a directed edge (a_j, a_k) is recorded. Finally, a_h arrives and occupies Q_1, a search starting from Q_1 and following two layer-one backward pointers will find the alert a_k in Q_2. Hence, a directed edge (a_k, a_h) records the only explicit correlation.

The above correlation process is sufficient for demonstrating the advantages of the queue graph approach, although some of the features of the queue graph, such as the variables and forward pointers, are not yet used and will be needed in the next section. First, the time for processing each new alert with the queue graph approach is linear in $(m + n)$, that is, the number of vertices in the attack graph. In the above process, the correlation step visits at most $(m + n)$ edges because it searches in a tree (that is, the BFS tree rooted at Q_i) by following the layered pointers in P_i; the other steps of the procedure take almost constant time. Hence, the performance of the queue graph approach is independent of the number of received alerts, as n and m are relatively stable for a given network. Second, the memory usage of the queue graph approach is roughly $O(n(n + m))$ due to n layers of maximally $(n + m)$ pointers (the correlation only appends to the result graph but does not read from it, hence, the result graph does not need to reside in memory), which does not depend on the number of received alerts, either. Third, the queue graph approach is not vulnerable to slowed attacks. During the correlation, an alert is no longer considered for correlation only if a new alert matching the same exploit arrives. Hence, if one alert prepares for another, then no matter how many unrelated alerts are injected between them, the first alert will always sit in the queue graph waiting for the second alert.

When an alert is dequeued from the queue graph, it will no longer be needed for correlation. This critically depends on the assumption that alerts arrive in the correct order. However, both the order suggested by timestamps and the actual order of arrivals can be wrong, since the temporal characteristics of alerts are typically imprecise. Instead, we adopt the following conservative approach. First, any two alerts whose timestamps have a difference no greater than a given threshold t_{con} are treated as concurrent; the correct order of concurrent alerts is always the one that allows the alerts to be correlated. Second, for nonconcurrent alerts, the correct order is the one suggested by their timestamps, but alerts are allowed to arrive in a different (and incorrect) order. This conservative approach enables us to tolerate varying delays in a network and small differences between the clocks of sensors (as discussed earlier, we assume the clocks of sensors are loosely synchronized). However, the basic queue graph approach does not work properly on alerts arriving in incorrect order. Consider an alert a_1 that prepares for another alert a_2 but arrives later then a_2. As described before, the procedure queue graph alert correlation will only look for those alerts that prepare for a_1, but not those that a_1 prepares for (a_2 in this case). Moreover, if another concurrent alert a_3 matches the same exploit as a_2 does and arrives after a_2 but before a_1, then a_2 is already dequeued by the time a_1 arrives, and the correlation between a_1 and a_2 will not be discovered.

To address the above issue, we cache alerts inside a time window before the queue graph and reorder them in a conservative way as follows. Assume the varying delay is bound by a threshold t_{max}. We postpone the processing of an alert a_1 with a timestamp t_1 until t_{max} (the larger one between t_{max} and t_{con}, when concurrent alerts are also considered) time has passed since the time we receive a_1. We reorder the postponed alerts, so they arrive at the correlation engine in the correct order. Then after t_{max} time, any alert a_2 will have a timestamp t_2 satisfying $t_2 > t_1$. The worst case is when a_1 is not delayed but a_2 is delayed t_{max} time, and the fact that a_2 is received t_{max} later than a_1 indicates $t_2 + t_{max} - t_{max} > t_1$, and hence $t_2 > t_1$. Notice here a time window is used only for reordering alerts and no alert will be excluded from correlation due to the use of a time window. This is different from the sliding window used by the nested loop approach, and this time window does not make the correlation vulnerable to slow attacks. However, the capability of dealing with concurrent alerts and varying delays comes at a cost. The additional delay introduced for reordering alerts causes an undesired decrease in the timeliness of alert correlation. Nevertheless, if we choose to report results immediately as each alert arrives, then the imprecise temporal characteristics of alerts may cause incorrect and confusing results that diminish the value of the correlation effort.

10.4.3   Alert Hypothesis and Prediction

Attack graphs provide unique opportunities for hypothesizing alerts missed by IDSs and for predicting possible consequences of current attacks. Intuitively, missing alerts will cause *inconsistency* between the knowledge encoded in attack graphs and the facts represented by received alerts. By reasoning about such inconsistency, missing alerts can be plausibly hypothesized. On the other hand, by extending the facts in a consistent way with respect to the knowledge, possible consequences of an intrusion can be predicted. To elaborate on those ideas, we first illustrate the concepts Example 10.5.

Example 10.5

The sequence of alerts shown on the left-hand side of Figure 10.5 (that is, a_0, a_3) is inconsistent with respect to the attack graph, because the condition c_3 is not

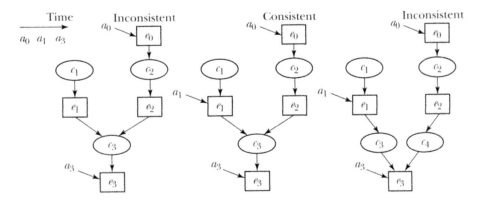

FIGURE   Consistent and inconsistent alert sequences.

10.5

satisfied before the exploit e_3 is executed (as indicated by the alert a_3). On the other hand, the sequence a_0, a_1, a_3 is consistent, because executing the exploit e_1 (as indicated by the alert a_1) satisfies the only condition c_3 that is required by the execution of e_3 (as indicated by a_3). The sequence shown on the right-hand side of Figure 10.5 is inconsistent, because the condition c_4 is not satisfied before the execution of e_3.

We have been correlating alerts only to adjacent ones. Such an approach only works for consistent alert sequences. For inconsistent sequences, such as those in Example 10.5, the search will stop at empty queues that correspond to missing alerts and the correlation result will be incomplete. A natural question is, "Can we continue to search and hypothesize missing alerts if necessary?" The question motivates us to extend the correlation method to hypothesize missing alerts. Intuitively, we want to explain the occurrence of a new alert by including it in a consistent sequence of alerts (by alert correlation) and missing alerts (by alert hypothesis). More specifically, a search starts from the queue containing the new alert and hypothesizes about missing alerts for encountered empty queues. It stops at each nonempty queue because it knows that the alert in that queue must have already been processed previously. The search expands its frontier in a breadth-first manner after each hypothesis is made, since the hypothesis itself may also need an explanation. Such attempts continue until satisfactory explanations for the new alert and all the hypothesized ones have been obtained. The explanations of all received alerts collectively form the result graph, which is now composed of alerts, hypothesized alerts, and conditions that are either satisfied or hypothetically satisfied. This is illustrated in Example 10.6.

Example 10.6

Consider again the three cases, from left to right, in Figure 10.5 when the alert a_3 is received. For the first case, two missing alerts matching e_1 and e_2 need to be hypothesized and then a_3 can be correlated to a_0 (through one of the hypothesized alerts). For the second case, no alert needs to be hypothesized because the sequence is already consistent, and a_3 needs to be correlated to a_1. For the third case, a_0 needs to be correlated to a_1, and it also needs to be correlated to a_0 through a hypothesized alert matching e_2.

The correlation process described in the previous section can be modified by replacing the correlation step with a new subprocedure that correlates and hypothesizes alerts as follows. Take a queue graph Q_g with n queues Q and m variables V. Each variable in V can now have one of the three values *TRUE*, *FALSE*, and *HYP*, together with a timestamp, which respectively denote a satisfied condition, an unsatisfied one, a hypothetically satisfied one, and the time of the last update. Each queue in Q can contain alerts or hypothesized alerts. The result graph $Gr(V, E_l \bigcup E_r)$ is similar to that described in the last section. However, the vertex set V now includes not only alerts but also hypothesized alerts and conditions. Now suppose a new alert a_{new} with timestamp t_{new} is received and placed in the queue $Q_i (1 \leq i \leq n)$. First, we start from Q_i and follow the pointers in PR_i to set each variable $v_j (1 \leq j \leq m)$ adjacent to Q_i with the value *TRUE* and the timestamp t_{new}. This step records the conditions satisfied by a_{new}. Second, we start from Q_i and make a partial BFS by following the pointers in P_i. The BFS is partial, because it stops upon leaving (given that a BFS is implemented by manipulating a separate queue as usual, we shall refer to the enqueues as reaching and the dequeues as leaving to avoid confusion) a variable with the value TRUE or the value HYP or a queue that contains a hypothesized alert. This step correlates a_{new} to previously received or hypothesized alerts.

The result graph G_r is updated during the above process as follows. First, after we enqueue a_{new} into Q_i and make changes to each v_j adjacent to Q_i, we add a_{new} and v_j (that is, the value and timestamp of v_j) as vertices, and an edge from a_{new} pointing to v_j into the result graph G_r. This step records the fact that the new alert a_{new} satisfies its implied conditions at time t_{new}. Second, during the partial BFS, we record each hypothesis. Whenever we change the value of a variable v_j from *FALSE* to *HYP*, we record this update in G_r; similarly, whenever we enqueue a hypothesized alert into an empty queue, we record this hypothesized alert in G_r. Third, whenever we leave a variable v and reach a queue Q, we insert into G_r a directed edge from each queue Q to v; similarly, we insert edges from a queue to its connected variables when we leave the queue. Example 10.7 illustrates the above procedure.

Example 10.7

Consider the left-hand side of Figure 10.5. The first alert a_0 will only cause the condition c_2 to be changed from *FALSE* to *TRUE*. The result graph will be updated with the alert a_0, the satisfied condition c_2, and the directed edge connecting them. When a_3 is received, a search starts from (the queue corresponding to) e_3; it changes c_3 from *FALSE* to *HYP*, it inserts a hypothesized alert a_1 into e_1 and a_2 into e_2, respectively; and it stops at c_1 (which is initially set as *TRUE*) and c_2 (which has been set as *TRUE* when a_0 arrived). The result graph will be updated with the alert a_3, the hypothesized alerts a_1 and a_2, the hypothetically satisfied condition c_3, and the directed edges between them.

Although a BFS takes quadratic time in the number of vertices of a graph, the above process has a linear time complexity. This is because a queue graph organizes its pointers in separate layers, and each layer is a BFS tree rooted at a queue. Hence, a BFS in each layer will be equivalent to a tree traversal, which takes linear time $(n + m)$. This performance gain seems to be obtained at the price of more memory requirement as there are duplicate pointers among layers. However, the memory requirement is quadratic, that is, $O(n(n + m))$, which is indeed asymptotically the same as that of the original attack graph.

For alert hypothesis, we *explain* the occurrence of a new alert by searching backwards in the reversed direction of the edges in attack graphs for correlated (or hypothesized) alerts. Conversely, we can also predict possible consequences of each new alert by searching forwards. A BFS is also preferred in this case, because the predicted conditions will be discovered in the order of their (shortest) distances to the new alert. This distance roughly indicates how imminent a predicted attack is, based on the alerts received so far (although not pursued in this chapter, probability-based prediction techniques [22] can be easily incorporated based on the queue graph data structure to more precisely measure how imminent each attack is).

The process for alert prediction is similar to that of correlation and hypothesis except as follows. After the correlation and hypothesis completes for a new alert, the prediction process starts. It begins at the conditions satisfied by the new alert and makes a partial BFS in the queue graph by following the pointers in PR_i (suppose the new alert is enqueued by Q_i). The search stops at previously received (or hypothesized) alerts and their (hypothetically) satisfied conditions to avoid repeating the previous prediction. The result of the prediction process is a sequence of nonempty sets $Con_1, Con_2, \ldots, Con_m$ containing the conditions that can possibly be satisfied in i steps from now. Unlike in correlation and hypothesis, the prediction process does not reason about the disjunctive and conjunctive relationship between exploits. Instead, a condition c will appear in the set Con_i as long as there exists a path of length $2i$ (the path consists of both security conditions and exploits) from c to some previously satisfied condition. Hence, the number i provides a lower bound to the number of exploits that must be executed before c can be satisfied.

10.4.4   Alert Aggregation

This section studies how to aggregate alerts in the result graph such that no redundant information will be introduced by transitive edges. In previous sections, avoiding unnecessary searches has allowed the time for correlation to be independent of the number of received alerts. As a side effect, this also reduces the size of result graphs by having less transitive edges. However, the queue graph approach does not completely remove transitive edges from result graphs, as illustrated in Example 10.8. In practice, brute-force attempts of the same attack with different parameters can lead to a large number of alerts in a short time (the treasure-hunt data set provided by the University of California-Santa Barbara (UCSB) is a good example for such brute-force attempts). In Example 10.8, if the b_i's happen to be such an attack, then a large number of transitive edges will make the result graph less perceptible. Therefore, it is desirable to remove such transitive edges. The transitive edges also cause redundant information in alerts. Following the above example, b_1, b_2, and b_3 are indistinguishable in terms of alert correlation. That is, any other alert prepares for (or is prepared for by) either all or none of them. The three alerts can thus be aggregated as a single vertex in the result graph, with the edge connecting these alerts deleted. Similarly, a_2 and a_3 are also indistinguishable. On the other hand, a_1, a_2, and a_3 are not indistinguishable, because c prepares for a_2 and a_3 but not a_1. The right side of Figure 10.6 shows a more compact version of the result graph, with transitive edges deleted and indistinguishable alerts aggregated.

Example 10.8

The left side of Figure 10.6 shows the result graph of correlating a series of alerts using the queue graph approach. Transitive edges such as (a_1, b_1) and (a_2, b_1) are not present, since the queue graph approach immediately stops after it reaches a_3. However, the edges (a_3, b_2) and (a_3, b_3) are both transitive edges. When b_2 and b_3 arrive, the queue graph approach repeats the same search as it does for b_1 and thus the two transitive edges are inserted into the result graph. Similarly, the edge (c, a_3) is also transitive.

Existing alert correlation approaches usually take extra efforts in making the result graph more compact, such as aggregating alerts before correlating

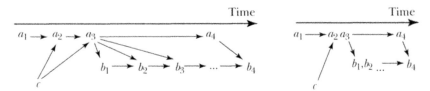

$\mathrm{Exp}(a_i) = \mathrm{Exp}(a_j), = \mathrm{Exp}(b_i) = \mathrm{Exp}(b_j)$, and $= \mathrm{Exp}(c_i) = \mathrm{Exp}(c_j)$ for $1 \le i, j \le 4$
$\mathrm{Exp}(a_i) \to \mathrm{Exp}(b_i)$ and $\mathrm{Exp}(c_i) \to \mathrm{Exp}(b_i)$

FIGURE   An example of compressing result graphs.

10.6

them [20]. The additional step increases the performance overhead of alert correlation. We show that our queue graph approach can be modified to directly produce a compact result graph. We also show that the modified queue graph approach may actually be more efficient. We first modify the queue graph approach to avoid inserting transitive edges into the result graph. For this purpose, we let each backward pointer in a queue graph have one of the two states: *on* and *off*. Initially, all the backward pointers are on. The backward pointers are then switched between the two states as follows. Whenever a directed edge (a_i, a_j) is inserted into the result graph, we turn off the backward edges between the corresponding queues Q_i and Q_j. Whenever an alert is enqueued in a queue Q_i, all the backward pointers arriving at Q_i will be turned on. Finally, when we search for older alerts that prepare for a new alert, we follow a backward edge only if it is currently turned on. This process is illustrated in Example 10.9.

Example 10.9

In the left side of Figure 10.6, suppose the alerts a_i, b_i, c correspond to the queues Q_a, Q_b, and Q_c, respectively. When the alert b_1 arrives, it searches through the backward pointers from Q_b to Q_a and inserts an edge (a_3, b_1) into E_r. Then, according to the above discussion, the backward pointers from Q_b to Q_a will be turned off. Consequently, the alerts b_2 and b_3 will not follow those pointers, and the transitive edges (a_3, b_2) and (a_3, b_3) are avoided. This remains true until the alert a_4 arrives, which turns on all the backward pointers arriving at the queue Q_a. Then later when b_4 arrives, it follows the backward pointers from Q_b to Q_a and inserts the edge (a_4, b_4).

Alerts are aggregated during the above process as follows. Suppose an alert a_i arrives and the corresponding queue Q_i already contains another alert a_{ii}. Then a_i is aggregated with a_{ii} if the following two conditions are true. First, all the backward pointers arriving at Q_i are on. Second, all the backward pointers leaving Q_i

are off. The first condition ensures that a_{ii} does not prepare for any other alerts that arrive between a_{ii} and a_i, because otherwise a_i and a_{ii} would not be indistinguishable. The second condition ensures that a_{ii} and a_i are prepared for by the same collection of alerts, so they are indistinguishable with respect to those alerts. This process is illustrated in Example 10.10. This new procedure not only produces a more compact result graph, but is also more efficient than the original one in most of the cases. This is because unnecessary searches corresponding to transitive edges are avoided. In Figure 10.6, the alerts a_3, b_2, and b_3 will not lead to a search in the modified approach because the backward pointers have been turned off by earlier alerts. The performance gain can be significant in the case of brute-force attempts where a large number of searches can be avoided.

Example 10.10

Following the above example, a_3 is aggregated with a_2 because the backward pointers from Q_b to Q_a are on and those from Q_a to Q_c have been turned off by the alert a_2. Similarly, b_2 and b_3 are aggregated with b_1, because the backward pointers from Q_b to Q_a have been turned off by b_1. On the other hand, the alert b_4 will not be aggregated, because the backward pointers from Q_b to Q_a must have been turned on by a_4 by the time b_4 arrives.

10.4.5   Empirical Results

The correlation engine is implemented in C++ and tested on a Pentium III 860 MHz server with 1 G RAM running RedHat Linux. We use Snort-2.3.0 [1] to generate isolated alerts, which are directly pipelined into the correlation engine for analyses. We use Tcpreplay 2.3.2 [37] to replay network traffic from a separate machine to the server running the correlation engine. Two data sets are used for experiments: the DARPA 2000 intrusion detection LLDOS 1.0 by MIT Lincoln Labs [38], and the treasure-hunt data set by the UCSB [39]. The attack scenario in the DARPA 2000 data set has been extensively explored before, such as in Ning and Xu [40]. Our experiments with the data set show similar results, validating the correctness of our correlation algorithm. The treasure-hunt data set generates a large amount of alerts (about two million alerts taking about 1.4 G of disc space, with most of them being brute-force attempts of the same attacks), which may render a nested loop–based correlation method infeasible (we found that even running a simple database query over the data will paralyze the system). In contrast, our correlation engine processes alerts with negligible delays (Snort turns out to be the bottleneck).

To evaluate the performance of the correlation engine, we use the performance metric of resource usage (computer processing unit (CPU) and memory) and the processing time of each alert. The correlation engine measures its own processing time and compares the processing time to the delay between receiving two consecutive alerts from Snort. All the results have 95% confidence intervals within about 5% of the reported values. Figure 10.7 shows the CPU usage (on the left-hand side) and memory usage (on the right-hand side) over time for the DARPA data set. The correlation engine clearly demands less resources than Snort (on average, the correlation engine's CPU usage and memory usage are both under 10% of Snort's).

The left chart in Figure 10.8 shows the processing time per alert (averaged per 22 alerts). Clearly, the correlation engine works faster than Snort in processing the entire data set. The result also proves that the performance does not decrease over time. Indeed, the processing time per alert remains fairly steady. We examine

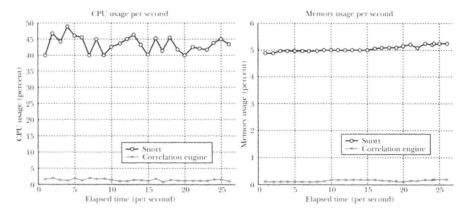

FIGURE 10.7 The CPU and memory usage.

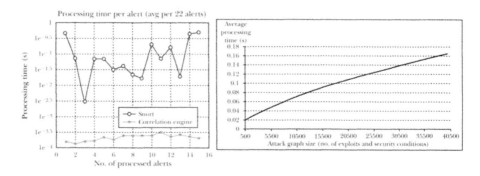

FIGURE 10.8 The processing time and its relationship with the size of the attack graph.

the scalability of the correlation engine in terms of the number of exploits and conditions. The treasure-hunt data set is used for this purpose. The original attack graph only has about 100 exploits. We increase the size of attack graphs by randomly inserting dummy exploits and conditions. The inserted exploits increase the complexity of correlation because the correlation engine must search through them. The right chart in Figure 10.8 shows that the average processing time scales with the size of attack graphs as expected.

We replay network traffic at relatively high speed (e.g., the DARPA data set is replayed in about 26 seconds while the actual duration of the data set is several hours). Real-world attacks are usually less intensive, and consequently our correlation engine will exhibit a better performance. However, we are aware that real-world traffic may bring up new challenges that are absent in synthesized data sets. For example, we currently set the time window used to reorder alerts (i.e., t_{max}) as discussed before as one second to deal with identical timestamps of alerts. In a real network, the windows size must be decided based on the actual placement of IDS sensors and the typical network delays.

10.5   CONCLUSION

This chapter has described a vulnerability-centric alert correlation method for defending against multistep intrusions in networks. We have described methods that can be used in less-than-ideal situations where not all vulnerabilities can be easily removed through network hardening, and multistep intrusions must be defended in real time. We identified a key limitation in applying the nested loop–based correlation methods and described a novel queue graph approach to remove this limitation. The method has a linear time complexity and a quadratic memory requirement and can correlate alerts arbitrarily far away in time. The correlation method was then extended to a unified approach to the hypothesis, prediction, and aggregation of intrusion alerts. Empirical results showed that the correlation engine can process alerts faster than IDS can report them, making the method a promising solution for administrators to monitor the progress of intrusions.

10.6   ACKNOWLEDGMENTS

This material is based upon work supported by National Institute of Standards and Technology Computer Security Division; by Homeland Security Advanced

Research Projects Agency under the contract FA8750-05-C-0212 administered by the Air Force Research Laboratory/Rome; by Air Force Research Laboratory/Rome under the contract FA8750-06-C-0246; by Army Research Office under grant W911NF-05-1-0374; by Federal Aviation Administration under the contract DTFAWA-04-P-00278/0001; by National Science Foundation under grants CT-0627493, IIS-0242237, and IIS-0430402; and by Natural Sciences and Engineering Research Council of Canada under Discovery Grant N01035. Any opinions, findings, and conclusions or recommendations expressed in this material are those of the authors and do not necessarily reflect the views of the sponsoring organizations. The authors are grateful to the anonymous reviewers for their valuable comments.

References

[1] M. Roesch, "Snort: Lightweight Intrusion Detection for Networks," *Proceedings of the 1999 USENIX LISA Conference*, Seattle, WA, November 7–12, 1999, pp. 229–238.

[2] O. Sheyner, J. Haines, S. Jha, R. Lippmann, and J. Wing, "Automated Generation and Analysis of Attack Graphs," *Proceedings of the 2002 IEEE Symposium on Security and Privacy (S&P'02)*, 2002, pp. 273–284.

[3] P. Ammann, D. Wijesekera, and S. Kaushik, "Scalable, Graph-Based Network Vulnerability Analysis," *Proceedings of the 9th ACM Conference on Computer and Communications Security (CCS'02)*, Washington, DC, 2002, pp. 217–224.

[4] S. Noel, S. Jajodia, B. O'Berry, and M. Jacobs, "Efficient Minimum-Cost Network Hardening via Exploit Dependency Graphs," *Proceedings of the 19th Annual Computer Security Applications Conference (ACSAC'03)*, Las Vegas, NV, 2003, pp. 86–95.

[5] L. Wang, S. Noel, and S. Jajodia, "Minimum-Cost Network Hardening Using Attack Graphs," *Computer Communications* 29, No. 18, November 2006, pp. 3812–3824.

[6] L. Wang, A. Liu, and S. Jajodia, "An Efficient and Unified Approach to Correlating, Hypothesizing, and Predicting Intrusion Alerts," *Proceedings of the 10th European Symposium on Research in Computer Security (ESORICS 2005)*, 2005, pp. 247–266.

[7] L. Wang, A. Liu, and S. Jajodia, "Using Attack Graphs for Correlating, Hypothesizing, and Predicting Intrusion Alerts," *Computer Communications* 29, No. 15 (2006): 2917–2933.

[8] F. Cuppens, "Managing Alerts in a Multi-Intrusion Detection Environment," *Proceedings of the 17th Annual Computer Security Applications Conference (ACSAC'01)*, New Orleans, Louisiana, 2001, p. 22.

[9] O. Dain and R. Cunningham, "Building Scenarios from a Heterogeneous Alert Stream," *Proceedings of the 2001 IEEE Workshop on Information Assurance and Security*, 2001, pp. 231–235.

[10] S. Staniford, J. Hoagland, and J. McAlerney, "Practical Automated Detection of Stealthy Portscans," *Journal of Computer Security* 10, No. 1/2 (2002): 105–136.

[11] A. Valdes and K. Skinner, "Probabilistic Alert Correlation," *Proceedings of the 4th International Symposium on Recent Advances in Intrusion Detection*, 2001, pp. 54–68.

[12] K. Julisch and M. Dacier, "Mining Intrusion Detection Alarms for Actionable Knowledge," *Proceedings of the Eighth ACM SIGKDD International Conference on Knowledge Discovery and Data Mining*, Edmonton, Canada, 2002, pp. 366–375.

[13] X. Qin and W. Lee, "Statistical Causality Analysis of INFOSEC Alert Data," *Proceedings of the 6th International Symposium on Recent Advances in Intrusion Detection (RAID 2003)*, 2003, pp. 591–627.

[14] O. Dain and R. Cunningham, "Fusing a Heterogeneous Alert Stream into Scenarios," In *Proceedings of the ACM Workshop on Data Mining for Security Applications*, 2001, pp. 1–13.

[15] H. Debar and A. Wespi, "Aggregation and Correlation of Intrusion-Detection Alerts," *Proceedings of the 3rd International Symposium on Recent Advances in Intrusion Detection (RAID'01)*, 2001, pp. 85–103.

[16] F. Cuppens and R. Ortalo, "LAMBDA: A Language to Model a Database for Detection of Attacks," *Proceedings of the 3rd International Symposium on Recent Advances in Intrusion Detection (RAID'01)*, 2001, pp. 197–216.

[17] S. Eckmann, G. Vigna, and R. Kemmerer, "STATL: An Attack Language for State-Based Intrusion Detection," *Journal of Computer Security* 10, No. 1/2 (2002): 71–104.

[18] S. Templeton and K. Levitt, "A Requires/Provides Model for Computer Attacks," *Proceedings of the 2000 New Security Paradigms Workshop (NSPW'00)*, 2000, pp. 31–38.

[19] F. Cuppens and A. Miege, "Alert Correlation in a Cooperative Intrusion Detection Framework," *Proceedings of the 2002 IEEE Symposium on Security and Privacy (S&P'02)*, 2002, pp. 187–200.

[20] P. Ning, Y. Cui, and D. Reeves, "Constructing Attack Scenarios through Correlation of Intrusion Alerts," *Proceedings of the 9th ACM Conference on Computer and Communications Security (CCS'02)*, Washington, DC, 2002, pp. 245–254.

[21] P. Ning and D. Xu, "Learning Attack Strategies from Intrusion Alerts," *Proceedings of the 10th ACM Conference on Computer and Communications Security (CCS'03)*, Washington, DC, 2003, pp. 200–209.

[22] X. Qin and W. Lee, "Discovering Novel Attack Strategies from INFOSEC Alerts," *Proceedings of the 9th European Symposium on Research in Computer Security (ESORICS 2004)*, 2004, pp. 439–456.

[23] D. Xu and P. Ning, "Alert Correlation through Triggering Events and Common Resources," *Proceedings of the 20th Annual Computer Security Applications Conference (ACSAC'04)*, Tucson, Arizona, 2004, pp. 360–369.

[24] Y. Zhai, P. Ning, and J. Xu, "Integrating IDS Alert Correlation and OS-Level Dependency Tracking," *IEEE International Conference on Intelligence and Security Informatics (ISI 2006)*, San Diego, CA, 2006, pp. 272–284.

[25] I. Ray and N. Poolsappasit, "Using Attack Trees to Identify Malicious Attacks from Authorized Insiders," *Proceedings of the 10th European Symposium on Research in Computer Security (ESORICS'05)*, 2005, pp. 231–246.

[26] R. Chinchani, A. Iyer, H. Ngo, and S. Upadhyay, "Towards a Theory of Insider Threat Assessment," *Proceedings of the IEEE International Conference on Dependable Systems and Networks (DSN'05)*, Yokohama, Japan, 2005, pp. 108–117.

[27] D. Farmer, and E. Spafford, "The COPS Security Checker System," *USENIX Summer*, 1990, pp. 165–170.

[28] D. Zerkle and K. Levitt, "Netkuang: A Multi-Host Configuration Vulnerability Checker," *Proceedings of the 6th USENIX Security Symposium (USENIX'96)*, 1996.

[29] C. Phillips L. and Swiler, "A Graph-Based System for Network-Vulnerability Analysis," *Proceedings of the New Security Paradigms Workshop (NSPW'98)*, 1998, pp. 71–79.

[30] M. Dacier, "Towards Quantitative Evaluation of Computer Security," Ph.D. Thesis, Institut National Polytechnique de Toulouse, Toulouse, France, 1994.

[31] R. Ortalo, Y. Deswarte, and M. Kaaniche, "Experimenting with Quantitative Evaluation Tools for Monitoring Operational Security," *IEEE Trans. Software Eng.* 25, No. 5 (1999): 633–650.

[32] R. Ritchey and P. Ammann, "Using Model Checking to Analyze Network Vulnerabilities," *Proceedings of the 2000 IEEE Symposium on Research on Security and Privacy (S&P'00)*, 2000, pp. 156–165.

[33] C. Ramakrishnan and R. Sekar, "Model-Based Analysis of Configuration Vulnerabilities," *Journal of Computer Security* 10, No. 1/2 (2002): 189–209.

[34] S. Jha, O. Sheyner, and J. Wing, "Two Formal Analysis of Attack Graph," *Proceedings of the 15th Computer Security Foundation Workshop (CSFW'02)*, 2002, pp. 49–63.

[35] S. Jajodia, S. Noel, and B. O'Berry, "Topological Analysis of Network Attack Vulnerability," in *Managing Cyber Threats: Issues, Approaches and Challenges*, edited by V. Kumar, J. Srivastava, and A. Lazarevic (Boston: Kluwer Academic Publisher, 2003).

[36] OSSIM, "Open Source Security Information Management," at http://www.ossim.net.

[37] A. Turner, "Tcpreplay: Pcap Editing and Replay Tools for *nix," at http://tcpreplay.sourceforge.net/.

[38] Darpa, "2000 Darpa Intrusion Detection Evaluation Data Sets," at http://www.ll.mit.edu/IST/ideval/data/2000/2000 data index.html.

[39] Treasurehunt, "Treasure Hunt Data Sets," at http://www.cs.ucsb.edu/vigna/treasurehunt/index.html.

[40] P. Ning and D. Xu, "Adapting Query Optimization Techniques for Efficient Intrusion Alert Correlation," Technical report, North Carolina State University, Department of Computer Science, 2002.

PART III

DESIGN AND ARCHITECTURAL ISSUES FOR SECURE AND DEPENDABLE SYSTEMS

CHAPTER 11 Monitoring and Detecting Attacks in All-Optical Networks
(Arun K. Somani and Tao Wu, Iowa State University, USA)

CHAPTER 12 Robustness Profiling of Operating Systems
(Andréas Johansson and Neeraj Suri, Technische Universität
of Darmstadt, Germany)

CHAPTER 13 Intrusion Response Systems: A Survey
(Bingrui Foo, Matthew W. Glause, Gaspar M. Howard, Yu-Sung Wu,
Saurabh Bagchi, and Eugene H. Spafford, Purdue University, USA)

CHAPTER 14 Secure and Resilient Routing: A Framework for Resilient
Network Architectures
(Deep Medhi, University of Missouri–Kansas City, USA, and Dijang Huang,
Arizona State University, USA)

CHAPTER 15 Security and Survivability of Wireless Systems
(Yi Qian, University of Puerto Rico at Mayaguez, Puerto Rico, and Prashant Krishnamurthy
and David Tipper, University of Pittsburgh, USA)

CHAPTER 16 Integrated Fault and Security Management
(Ehab Al-Shaer, DePaul University, USA, and Yan Chen, Northwestern University, USA)

11 Monitoring and Detecting Attacks in All-Optical Networks

Arun K. Somani Iowa State University, USA
Tao Wu Iowa State University, USA

11.1 INTRODUCTION

Optical fiber-based networks have emerged as the predominant transport layer technology for telecom service providers [1–6]. These networks provide very high bit rates to support a broad class of applications. The ability to route large amounts of data and access different channels make them a very appealing option for providing very high-rate access in wide-area networks (WANs), metropolitan area networks (MANs), and even local-area networks (LANs). In particular, if they can be used in an all-optical network (AON) mode where a signal does not have to go through optical-to-electrical-to-optical (O-E-O) conversion, the benefits are larger.

The high capacity of a fiber channel can be efficiently utilized by deploying either time division multiplexed (TDM) or wavelength division multiplexed (WDM) modes [2]. In this chapter, we focus on the AON employing the WDM mode. Fiber bandwidth is divided into multiple optical wavelength channels and each wavelength can support 10 Gbps or higher data rates. A fiber in the future is likely to carry 100 Gbps and hundreds of such channels. However, such networks have four important security ramifications:

1. Any attack, even that of a short duration and perhaps infrequent, can result in large amounts of data being corrupted or compromised.

2. End users may be using security protocols designed for slower networks, which may not be efficient or sufficient to detect attacks at very high

speeds, resulting in effective service denial attacks using high-bandwidth methods.

3. The large physical spans in WANs with very high data rates produce high latencies. Such latencies imply that large amounts of data on the wire may be beyond the reach of anti-attack measures.

4. The transparency feature in AONs has large implications in ensuring security (see Section 11.1.1).

11.1.1   Security Problems in All-Optical Networks

Security in AONs is different from communication and computer security in general. This is because AONs introduce physical-layer mechanisms that cause potential models of attack to be different from those that are well known for traditional electronic networks [7]. The transparency characteristic of AONs means that data do not undergo optical-to-electrical or electrical-to-optical conversion. Thus, connections in such networks are only amplified but not regenerated at intermediate components [8]. This creates many security vulnerabilities that do not exist in traditional networks. Transparency and nonregeneration features make attack detection and localization much more difficult.

11.1.2   Possible Attacks

Attacks on a network can be broadly categorized into six areas:

1. *Traffic analysis attack.* The ciphertext length usually reveals the plaintext length from which an attacker can get valuable information. An attacker can tap into fibers and obtain this information.

2. *Eavesdropping.* This occurs when an attacker covertly listens in on traffic to get sensitive information.

3. *Data delay.* An attacker intercepts the data sent by the user for later use.

4. *Spoofing.* This attack is defined as the acquisition of privileges, capabilities, trust, and anonymity by pretending to be a more privileged or trusted process/user. This attack includes masquerading and Trojan horse attacks.

5. *Service denial.* This attack deprives a user or an organization of the services of a resource that they would normally expect to have. A denial of service (DoS) attack can also destroy programs and files in a computer system.

6. *Quality of service (QoS) degradation.* An attacker overpowers legitimate signals to degrade or deny services.

11.1.3   All-Optical Network Attack Types

AON attacks can be roughly divided into two different types: service disruption attacks and tapping attacks.

Service Disruption Attacks

This type of attack include service denial attacks and QoS degradation attacks. Physically, this type of attack can be carried out using the following three methods.

Fiber attacks.   Fibers ideally propagate information on different wavelengths with only frequency-dependent delay and attenuation. They typically have very low radiation loss, that is, under normal operating conditions, there is a negligible radiation of power from the fiber. However, unprotected fiber is very vulnerable against any attacker with physical access (e.g., service is easily disrupted by cutting or bending a fiber).

Optical amplifier attacks.   Optical amplifiers are critical and necessary components for AONs. The erbium doped fiber amplifier (EDFA) is commonly used in current optical networks. EDFA consists of an optical fiber having a core doped with the rare-earth element erbium. Light from one or more external semiconductor lasers is coupled into the fiber, exciting the erbium atoms. Optical signals entering the fiber stimulate the excited erbium atoms to emit photons at the same wavelength as the incoming signal. This amplifies a weak optical signal to higher power. EDFAs can simultaneously amplify signals over a range of wavelengths, making them compatible with WDM systems. However, the nature of EDFA operation in WDM communication links and nodes can lead to a phenomenon known as gain competition, whereby multiple independent WDM wavelengths share a limited pool of available upper-state photons within the fiber. The result is that a stronger signal (possibly from an attack) can deprive a weaker signal of signal amplification gain. This gain competition, combined with the fact that a fiber has extremely low loss, means that EDFA is susceptible to power jamming from remote locations. In some cases, an attacker from a legitimate network access point can cause service denial to many other users in this manner.

Switching node attacks.   Wavelength selective switches (WSSs) have significant crosstalk levels. Crosstalk causes signals to leak onto unintended outputs and permits inputs to cause interference on other optical signals that are passing through these devices. The level of crosstalk greatly depends on the particular components and architecture of a switch. However, crosstalk is additive and thus the aggregate effect of crosstalk over a whole AON may be much worse than the effect of a single point of crosstalk. An attacker could inject a very strong signal into a switch.

Although only a small fraction of it may leak onto another channel, a sufficiently powerful signal modulated in a malicious way can be highly disruptive.

Tapping Attacks

This type of attack includes both eavesdropping attacks and traffic analysis attacks. Physically, this can be achieved in two different ways: fiber or EDFA attacks and switching node attacks. Some of the possible attacks, like fiber cuts, can be treated as a component failure. Other attacks, like correlated jamming, have limited spreading capability as they affect only those connections that share a link or a node with the attack connections.

11.1.4   Issues in Crosstalk Attack Diagnostic Algorithms

Attack monitoring and localization is important for the security of AON. There has been some work [3,9–11] in the area of attack localization in AONs, and some detection methods have been proposed. However, it is not clear if these methods guarantee the localization of every attack. Other studies [12,13] describe the capability of an optical monitoring module. Generally, an optical monitor can measure a single connection's optical power as well as its optical SNR (signal-to-noise ratio). But placing monitors at each node in a network is not an attractive and efficient option. Supervisory connection concepts have also been proposed. A network management system using supervisory connections [14,15] can detect and monitor the performance of devices in the network. The advantage of this scheme is that a monitoring device can be put in a remote place. The major drawback of such a scheme is that extra supervisory connections are needed to send control signal and detection data. However, this method provides the means required for sparse monitoring.

The goal of this chapter is to provide quantitative answers to questions about the level of resources needed to support a modern attack management system. Our research in attack-diagnostic problems broadly lies in three areas: *modeling* (i.e., how to model crosstalk attacks); *characterization and algorithms* (i.e., how to devise methods for detection and localization of crosstalk attacks); and *policies* (i.e., how to implement the various steps involved in the diagnosis of crosstalk attacks).

Crosstalk Attack Modeling

To establish clear models for crosstalk attacks and monitoring nodes, we study the special properties of crosstalk attacks and analyze the power levels for attack signals, affected signals, and unaffected signals according to the origination and propagation mechanism for crosstalk attacks. We assume that using different power levels implies that different signals have different attack capabilities. With these assumptions, a reasonable crosstalk attack model is established. The monitoring model is based on power-level detection.

Characterization and Algorithms

The next important question then is how to locate the attack source. We develop necessary and sufficient conditions for a one-crosstalk attack diagnosable network and a k-crosstalk attack diagnosable network. We also develop a diagnosis algorithm.

Sparse Monitoring Policies

An interesting problem in the attack diagnosis system is whether a sparse monitoring network can provide sufficient information for detection and localization purpose. Based on the necessary and sufficient conditions, we develop solutions that only require sparse monitoring in the network. It is shown that these solutions are sufficient to detect a single crosstalk attack. We also develop methods for a k-crosstalk attack diagnosable system.

11.2   CROSSTALK ATTACK FEATURES AND MONITORING TECHNIQUES

Among the attack methods listed previously, the crosstalk attack has the highest damage capabilities. In this case, an attacker injects a malicious signal with a very high power, far beyond the expected value. When this connection passes through a wavelength selective switch, the leakage energy (crosstalk) of this malicious connection significantly affects the normal connections passing through the same switch. Unlike other attacks, a crosstalk attack not only affects those connections that are sharing the same link or node with it, but also may induce attack capabilities to those connections that are attacked [3, 16–19] as explained below. We first describe the characteristics of crosstalk attacks and possible anti-attack mechanisms.

11.2.1   Crosstalk Attack Features

As depicted in Figure 11.1, the crosstalk attack happens at a wavelength switch and only affects the normal connections on the same wavelength. The attacker injects a strong signal into a switch, and the power leakage (crosstalk) from the malicious channel is superimposed on a normal channel that shares the same wavelength

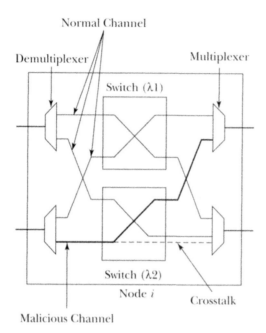

FIGURE

11.1

Example of crosstalk attack using wavelength selective switches.

switch. The power of the malicious channel is high enough that just simply the power leakage can still greatly disturb a normal channel. It is also possible that the high energy on one wavelength may affect the signals on other wavelengths. However, for now we assume that the probability of such occurrences is low, and therefore, do not pursue this aspect further here.

A crosstalk attack may also propagate as depicted in Figure 11.2. The original crosstalk attack occurs on node i, which carries connections 1 and 2. Connection 1 is originally a malicious attack connection. Because of the crosstalk attack from connection 1, the power of connection 2 is also beyond a certain threshold, so connection 2 itself has crosstalk attack capability. Thus, at node j, which carries connections 2 and 3, power leakage from connection 2 also superimposes on connection 3, therefore, connection 3 is also disturbed. This characteristic makes localization of the attack connection much more difficult.

11.2.2   Security Consideration

Security vulnerabilities that are specific to AONs stem from the characteristics of the physical devices, such as fiber and amplifiers. Thus, attack avoidance can only

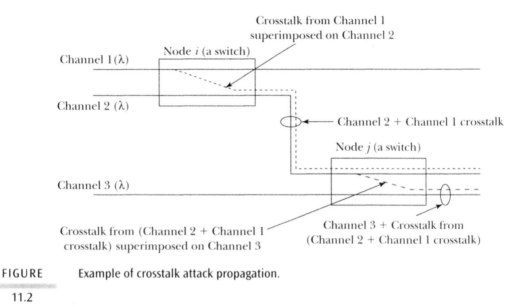

FIGURE   Example of crosstalk attack propagation.

11.2

be achieved by a judicious design of components after understanding the security vulnerabilities and the techniques for detection, localization, and response to attacks. Network management in AONs must be able to differentiate an attack from normal network traffic problems caused, for example, by a physical failure. The strategy for protection and restoration of service due to hardware failure is simply to reroute the disturbed traffic connections [20–23]. However, these methods cannot be used to solve the problems caused by an attack. For example, consider an attack caused by connection 1 on node i, which has two connections, 1 and 2. If the network management system treats such an attack as a component failure, then it assumes that node i has failed and reroutes connections 1 and 2 to some other node, say j. After this rerouting, node j will appear as having failed because connection 1 will attack other normal connections on node j. The network management system may reroute all these channels to some other node k, and so on. Therefore, it is important for node i, which is under attack, to be able to identify an attack within its traffic stream and to differentiate it from a physical component failure.

11.2.3   Overview of Current Monitoring Methods

To detect attack signals, a sophisticated optical monitoring technique is required. With current techniques, we can monitor and detect some important features of optical signals. Typically, a monitoring device should be capable of measuring the following: the signal wavelength, signal power, and optical SNR. The following testing methods are available. We also describe their limitations.

Power Detection

Power detection over a wide band may be used to record an increase or decrease in power with respect to the expected value. The power detection technique is well suited to some problems such as amplifier failures. However, this alone is insufficient to detect a combination of in-band jamming attacks that increase average power and out-of-band jamming attacks that decrease power, as they might yield no difference in average received power. The power detection technique is also not satisfactory in the detection of gain competition attacks.

Optical Spectral Analyzers

Optical spectral analyzers (OSAs) display the spectrum of an optical signal. A significant programming effort is required to analyze the output of the OSA and map it to the generation of different types of alarms. Therefore, it is an expensive diagnostic tool for the automatic generation of network alarms. However, OSAs can detect those jamming attacks that seriously affect the optical spectrum.

Bit Error Rate Testers

Bit error rate testers (BERTs) operate by comparing a received pattern with the pattern that was known to have been sent. Given the number of discrepancies that are found, the bit error rate (BER) of the transmission is estimated. BERTs only examine a given test data sequence when this special sequence is transmitted. They do not test the actual data. The time it takes for a BERT to establish the BER will depend on the BER and the data rate. For instance, at 1 Gbps, it takes several seconds for a BERT to establish with good statistical accuracy that the BER has been degraded from 10^{-8} to 10^{-3}. Moreover, some of the attacks may not seriously affect BER.

Pilot Tones

Pilot tones are signals that travel along the same links and nodes as the communication payload, but are distinguishable from the communication payload. Pilot tones are often at different carrier frequencies than the transmitted signal, and may also be distinguished from the communication payload by certain time slots or codes. The pilot tone technique may generate an alarm only if an attack is at the pilot wavelength. Thus, jamming attacks, for example, cannot be detected. Moreover, pilot tones themselves can be masked by malicious signals, such as gain competition attacks.

Optical Time Domain Refractometry

Optical time domain refractometries (OTDRs) are a special application of pilot tones. Rather than analyzing a pilot tone at the point where the communication signal is received, the pilot tone's echo is analyzed. OTDRs are generally used to diagnose faults, bends, and losses in fibers. Thus, they are usually better adapted to detecting attacks that involve tampering. Since they operate by reflecting a signal back through the fiber, they may also provide information about other attacks that might be taking place. OTDRs with modulated signals can be used to detect jamming attacks as jamming attack signals can be returned in the reflections and observed. The detection efficiency for gain competition is dependent on the type of device. For example, a unidirectional amplifier, if attacked, cannot be detected.

11.3   NODE, ATTACK, AND MONITOR MODELS

11.3.1   Node Model

A node in the network performs routing and switching. With the switching capability, a node can propagate a crosstalk attack from one attack channel to other normal connections. Some nodes can also support monitoring capabilities. Such a node is referred to as a *monitor node*. Otherwise, it is a *nonmonitor node*.

11.3.2   Crosstalk Attack Model

As shown in Figure 11.1, a crosstalk attack connection usually only affects another connection on the same wavelength. We define the following terms to describe a crosstalk attack model:

♦ *Upstream* and *downstream neighbor nodes.* For a node on a certain path, its *upstream neighbor node* (UNN) is the previous node on that path. Similarly, its *downstream neighbor node* (DNN) is the next node on that path. $UNN(node\ A, connection\ C)$ denotes the UNN of node A on connection C.

Similarly, $DNN(node\ A,\ connection\ C)$ denotes the DNN of node A on connection C.

◆ A connection causing crosstalk attack results in different types of nodes and flows as follows:

  ◆ The *original attack flow* (OAF) has a much higher energy level than permitted on a normal connection. The leakage of energy at a switch from the attack connection influences all other normal connections using the same wavelength on other fibers. The ability of an OAF to influence normal connections is the same at every node on its path. A node is called a *primary attacked node* (PAN) if there is an OAF originating at, terminating at, or passing through this node.

  ◆ A normal connection sharing a node with an OAF is called a *secondary attacked flow* (SAF). The SAF has limited attack capability. If a normal connection C gets affected by an OAF at node u, then the connection C has attack capability only at node $DNN(u, C)$, and we call $DNN(u, C)$ a *secondary attacked node* (SAN).

  ◆ A normal connection influenced by an SAF is called a *final attacked flow* (FAF). The FAF does not have the attack propagation capability.

  ◆ A connection not affected by either OAF or SAF is called an *attack-free flow* (AFF). Similarly, a node that is neither a PAN nor a SAN is called an *attack-free node* (AFN). The union of AFF, SAF, and FAF is called an *innocent flow* (IF) set.

    We illustrate the conncetion types by an example. As shown in Figure 11.3, connection C_1 is the OAF, connection C_2 is an SAF, connection C_3 is an FAF, and connection C_4 is an AFF. Nodes 1, 2, 3, and 6 are PANs. Node 5 is a SAN. The rest—nodes 4, 7, 8, and 9—are AFNs. Connection C_1 can propagate its attack to connection C_3 by affecting connection C_2. According to this, it is expected that the OAF pollutes any connections passing through the PAN, and the SAF pollutes any normal connections passing through a SAN. Connections C_2, C_3, and C_4 comprise the IF set.

◆ Since the OAF, SAF, and FAF have different attack capabilities, the power level of these connection channels are as follows:

$$P(OAF) \gg P(SAF) > P(FAF) > P(AFF)$$

where $P(OAF)$ denotes the power level of OAF, and so on. For example, as shown in Figure 11.3, $P(C_1) > P(C_2) > P(C_3) > P(C_4)$.

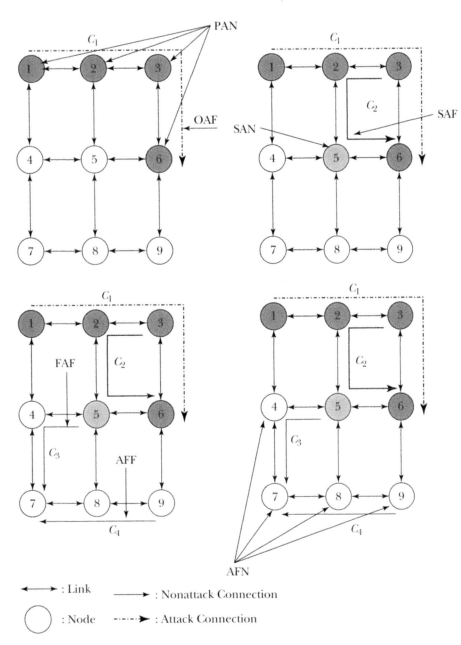

FIGURE Example of attack flow and affected flow.

11.3

11.3.3   Monitor Node Model

A monitor needs to be as simple and cheap as possible. Because crosstalk attacks only change the optical power of normal signals, we only need the crosstalk detection method to detect the change in signal power, however, more than that seems unnecessary. Detection of the power level method is used as the core technique for monitoring. The following describes the monitor model in detail.

+ A monitor node can monitor all traffic passing through it, including the traffic that originates/terminates at the node.

+ The monitor node can detect the input/output connection power in all parts, including its demultiplexer, multiplexer, and switch plane, and distinguish them as needed to identify OAF, SAF, and FAF. We also use power detection methods to monitor the input and output connection signal power levels on all wavelengths in the input and the output fibers, as shown in Figure 11.4.

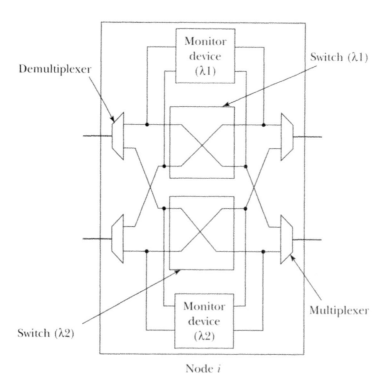

FIGURE   Attack monitoring mechanism for selective wavelength switches.

11.4

◆ A connection can be in an attack/nonattack status at a monitor. We use $A/\bar{A}$ to indicate the attack/nonattack status of the connection.

◆ It is possible that a monitor node may have multiple attacked connections passing through it. We consider three possibilities and the corresponding three responses from a monitor respectively:

1. One connection is an OAF while all the others are SAFs. Because $P(OAF) > P(SAF)$, the monitor considers only the OAF connection to have attack capability. Thus, we assume that only the state of the OAF is set as A, while the other SAFs states are set as $\bar{A}$.

2. More than one connection is an SAF, but none is an OAF. In this situation, the monitor can detect several connections that have similar unexpected high power. We assume that the monitor sets all SAFs to A state.

3. Two or more connections are OAFs. In this situation, similar to step 1 above, the monitor can detect several connections that have high power, and set states of these connections to A and sets states of other connections to $\bar{A}$.

Figure 11.5 shows a 3×3 mesh network. Connections C_1 and C_6 are two OAFs. Nodes 2, 4, 6, and 8 are monitors. On node 2, because connection

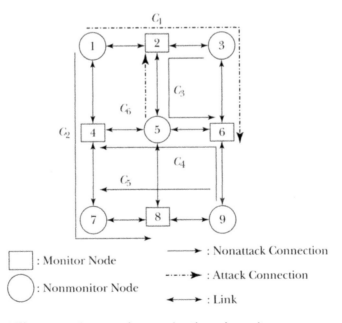

FIGURE

11.5

Different attack connections passing through monitors.

C_1 and C_6 are two OAFs passing through this monitor, connections C_1 and C_6's statuses are set as A, while connection C_3 is set as $\bar{A}$ because it is an SAF. On node 4, both connections C_2 and C_4 are SAFs, and no OAF passes through node 4. Thus, node 4 sets both C_2 and C_4 as A. On node 6, OAF connection C_1 is set as A while C_3 and C_4 are set as $\bar{A}$. On node 8, because C_2 does not have attack capability on this node, both C_2 and C_5 are set as $\bar{A}$.

11.4   NECESSARY AND SUFFICIENT CONDITIONS FOR CROSSTALK ATTACK DETECTION

In this section, we first prove that we can localize all crosstalk attacks in an AON with sparse monitors. Initially, we focus on a special situation where only one crosstalk attack exists on each wavelength in the whole network. Later, we extend this result to a general case where more than one crosstalk attack exists on a wavelength. This work is based on the general principle theory of system level diagnosis [24, 25].

11.4.1   Single Crosstalk Attack in a Network

A network is called one-OAF diagnosable if a single OAF can always be detected and localized. For a given graph $G(V, E)$, let M denote the set of monitor nodes, and let N denote the set of nonmonitor nodes, $M \subseteq V$, $N \subset V$, and $M \bigcup N = V$. Let $C = R \bigcup T$ denote the set of connections that exist in the network, where R is the regular set of connections and T is the set of test connections.

Let c_i be a connection consisting of nodes $\{u_0, u_1, u_2, \ldots, u_k, \ldots\}$. Let $U(c_i)$ denote the set of nodes on connection c_i's path. Then, c_{ij} denotes a one-hop segment $(u_j \rightarrow u_{j+1})$ on connection c_i.

11.4.2   Monitoring Relationship

There are three kinds of relations between a monitor and a connection:

1. *Direct-Monitor.* A monitor m is a direct-monitor of a connection c if $m \in U(c)$. As shown in Figure 11.6, monitor m_2 is a direct-monitor of connection c_1 because m_2 is on connection c_1's path: $m_2 \in U(c_1)$.

2. *One-Hop Monitor.* A monitor m is a one-hop monitor of a connection c if $m \notin U(c)$ and $\exists (u \rightarrow m)$, where $u \in U(c)$. As shown in Figure 11.6, monitor

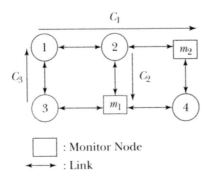

FIGURE

11.6

Relation between a monitor and a connection.

m_1 is a one-hop monitor of connection c_1 because m_1 is not on connection c_1's path: $m_1 \notin U(c_1)$ and $\exists\, (2 \to m_1) \subseteq$ connection c_2, where node $2 \in U(c_1)$.

3. *Nonmonitor.* A monitor m is a nonmonitor of a connection c if $m \notin U(c)$ and $\not\exists\, (u \to m)$, where $u \in U(c)$. In Figure 11.6, both monitors m_1 and m_2 are nonmonitors of connection c_3, because $m_1, m_2 \notin U(c_3)$, and $\not\exists\, (u \to m_1 \ or \ m_2)$ in any existing connection, where $u \in U(c_3)$.

Monitor-Segment

A monitor-segment msc_{ij} is a one-hop segment c_{ij}, where node u_{j+1} is a monitor. Let MSC denote the set of the monitor-segments. Let msc_{ij} denote this particular monitor-segment. Mostly, we use msc to denote a common monitor segment. Two monitor-segments are shown in Figure 11.7: one is made by connection c_2 and monitor node m_1, denoted by $m_1 c_2$, while the other is made by a one-hop segment on connection c_1, from node 2 to node m_2, and monitor node m_2, denoted by $m_2 c_1$.

A monitor-segment $msc = (u \to m)$ is monitoring a connection c if the monitor m is a *direct-monitor* of this connection, where the segment $(u \to m) \in c$, or if the monitor m is a *one-hop monitor* of a connection c, where $u \in U(c)$, and $m \notin U(c)$.

For example, in Figure 11.7, monitor m_2 is a direct-monitor for connection c_1, and monitor m_1 is a one-hop monitor for connection c_1. According to our definition, both monitor-segments $m_1 c_2$ and $m_2 c_1$ are monitoring connection c_1, and neither of them is monitoring connection c_3. Let (msc, c) denote this relation between monitor-segment msc and connection c. Consequently, the status of the segment $(u \to m)$ indicated by monitor m is the *status of the monitor-segment*, denoted by $S(msc)$. $S(msc)$ can be either A or $\bar{A}$. For example, in Figure 11.7, if the status of c_2 in monitor m_1 is indicated as A, then the status of the monitor segment $S(m_1 c_2)$ is A.

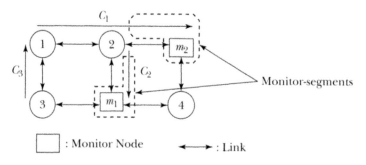

: Monitor Node   : Link

FIGURE

11.7

Attack monitoring mechanism and monitor-segment

Relation	$S(msc)$	$S(c)$
msc monitoring c	A	uncertain
(msc, c)	$\bar{A}$	IF
msc nonmonitoring c	A	IF
	$\bar{A}$	uncertain

TABLE

11.1

Monitor-segment and its monitoring/nonmonitoring connections.

The *status of a connection* can be either *innocent flow* (IF) or *uncertain*. *IF* means that the connection is determined as IF, and *uncertain* means that the connection cannot be determined either as IF or as OAF. Let $S(c)$ denote the status of connection c. Table 11.1 shows the relations between a monitor-segment status and its monitoring connection's status. For a connection c, which is not being monitored by msc, we say that msc has *nonmonitoring* relation with c. Table 11.1 shows the relations between a monitor-segment and its nonmonitoring connection.

Figure 11.8 depicts two special cases of monitor-segments. Figure 11.8(a) shows the monitor m as the originating node of the connection c. For this case, monitor m and connection c make up a special monitor-segment msc, and only connection c is monitored by this monitor-segment, while all other connections are not monitored. If $S(msc) = A$, all other connections can be identified as *IF*. Figure 11.8(b) shows the relation between a monitor segment msc_1 and a connection c_2, where $c_1 \notin c_2$, and $n, m \in U(c_2)$. In this case, both c_1 and c_2 share the same nodes n and m. While it seems that c_2 is monitored by msc_1, in fact the relation between connection c_2 and the monitor-segment msc_1 is *nonmonitoring*. This can be explained as follows. According to our definition of *monitoring*, the only

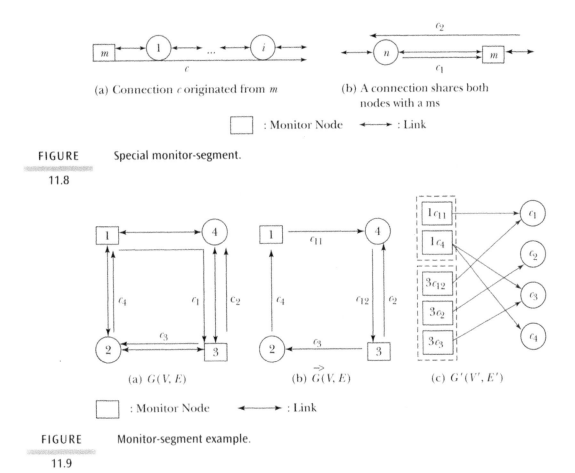

(a) Connection c originated from m (b) A connection shares both
nodes with a ms

☐ : Monitor Node   ⟷ : Link

FIGURE   Special monitor-segment.

11.8

(a) $G(V, E)$ (b) $\overrightarrow{G}(V, E)$ (c) $G'(V', E')$

☐ : Monitor Node   ⟷ : Link

FIGURE   Monitor-segment example.

11.9

two cases of monitoring are either the segment is a part of the monitored connection (that is clearly not the case here), or the monitored connection does not pass through the monitor (which is also not true here). The example provided by Figure 11.8(b) does not fit either of these definitions and the statement is true. Hence this is a *nonmonitor* relation.

We represent the connections and monitors using a bipartite graph. Figure 11.9(a) shows the network graph $G(V, E)$. Figure 11.9(b) shows a graph with all connections separated into one-hop segments, for example, c_{1-1} is the first segment of connection c_1. Figure 11.9(c) depicts the bipartite graph $G'(V', E')$ for the shown connections. In graph $G'(V', E')$, the vertices set $V' = \{mc_{ij}\} \bigcup \{C_k\}$ consists of the monitor-segments and the connection (i.e., $mc_{ij} \in MC$), and $c_k \in C$. For example, $3c_{12}$ is a monitor-segment made up by monitor node 3 and one-hop segment c_{12}, shown in Figure 11.9(b). An edge in G' depicts a relation between a monitor segment and a connection. In the figure, a directed edge from a monitor-segment *msc* to a connection *c* describes the monitoring relation between this pair of monitor-segment and connection, and (*msc*, *c*) denotes the edge.

Let $\Gamma(msc_i) = \{c_j|(msc_i, c_j) \in E'\}$ denote the set of connections monitored by a monitor-segment msc_i. Let $\Gamma^{-1}(c_i) = \{msc_j|(msc_j, c_i) \in E'\}$ denote the set of monitor-segments monitoring a connection c_i.

A connection is called *unidentified* if we cannot obtain the status of the connection directly from the status of the set of all monitor-segments in the network. Figure 11.10 shows an example to help understand this concept. A network and its connections are shown in Figure 11.10. If connection c_1 is the *OAF*, according to the truth table, we can identify the status for both the monitor-segments and connections, as shown in Table 11.2. The monitor-segments can only identify the

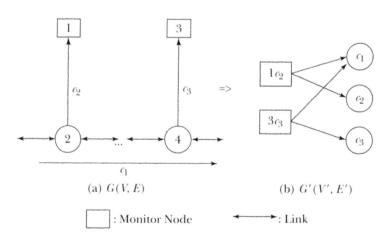

(a) $G(V, E)$ (b) $G'(V', E')$

□ : Monitor Node   ⟷ : Link

FIGURE 11.10   Unidentified connection.

Monitor-Segments	$S(msc)$	$S(c_1)$	$S(c_2)$	$S(c_3)$
$S(1c_2)$	A	uncertain	uncertain	IF
$S(3c_3)$	A	uncertain	IF	uncertain

TABLE 11.2   Status of the connections and the monitor-segments shown in Figure 11.10.

status of c_2 and c_3 as IF and the status of connection c_1 as *uncertain* according to both monitor-segments' results.

11.5   ONE-CROSSTALK ATTACK DIAGNOSABLE CONDITIONS

In this section, we establish the exact diagnosis conditions by using a set of lemmas and theorems.

Lemma 1. In any network, if this system is one-OAF diagnosable, then, $|unidentified\ connection| \leq 1$.

Proof: Obvious.

Lemma 2. For an arbitrary connection c_i, if c_i is unidentified, then $S(msc_i) = A$ for $\forall\ msc_i \in \Gamma^{-1}(c_i)$.

Proof: Suppose one $msc_k \in \Gamma^{-1}(c_i)$ has $S(msc_k) = \bar{A}$. Then, according to Table 11.1, $S(c_i) = IF$, and this contradicts the condition of the statement of Lemma 2.

Theorem 1 (Necessary and Sufficient Condition for One-Crosstalk Attack). In a network with at most one OAF existing at a time, $\forall c_i, c_j \in C, c_i \neq c_j$, if $\Gamma^{-1}(c_i) \neq \Gamma^{-1}(c_j)$, then for this network with the connection set C, $|unidentified\ connection| \leq 1$ holds.

What this theorem states is that for any arbitrary pair of connections c_i and c_j in a given monitor-segment graph G', if the set of monitor-segment of connection c_i is not the same as the set of monitor-segment of connection c_j, then there is no more than one unidentified connection for this network with the connection set C.

Proof: Necessity. Suppose $\Gamma^{-1}(c_i) = \Gamma^{-1}(c_j)$, then there are two possibilities:

1. $\Gamma^{-1}(c_i) = \Gamma^{-1}(c_j) = \emptyset$ Then, for all $msc_x \in MSC$, there always exists a *nonmonitoring* relation to both c_i and c_j. If for all $msc_x \in MSC$, $S(msc_x) = \bar{A}$, then according to Table 11.1, the status for both c_i and c_j will be uncertain. All other connections will have a status of IF. Thus, these two connections will be unidentified, and $|unidentified\ connection| > 1$.

2. $\Gamma^{-1}(c_i) = \Gamma^{-1}(c_j) \neq \emptyset$ Figure 11.11(a) shows a network that has three nodes and two connections, c_i and c_j. The only way to make $\Gamma^{-1}(c_i) = \Gamma^{-1}(c_j) \neq \emptyset$ is to let nodes 1 and 3 be monitor nodes and node 2 be a nonmonitor node, as shown in Figure 11.11(b). Figure 11.11(c) shows the monitor-segment graph G'. Suppose c_i is the OAF. Then both monitor-segments would have state A, which makes both c_i and c_j in uncertain status. Again, $|unidentified\ connection| > 1$.

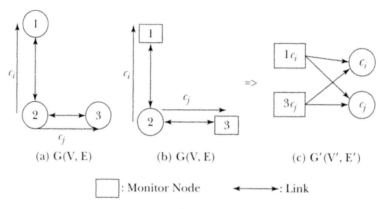

(a) G(V, E)   (b) G(V, E)   (c) G'(V', E')

☐ : Monitor Node   ——————▶ : Link

FIGURE   Two connections with the same $\Gamma^{-1}(c)$ sets.

11.11

Sufficiency: Suppose $|unidentified\ connection| > 1$. Then, there are only three possibilities:

1. At least two unidentified connections have $\Gamma^{-1}(c) = \emptyset$. Arbitrarily pick a pair of connections c_i and c_j from this unidentified connection set, and we get $\Gamma^{-1}(c_i) = \Gamma^{-1}(c_j) = \emptyset$. Obviously, this contradicts our original statement of the theorem.

2. One unidentified connection c_i has $\Gamma^{-1}(c_i) = \emptyset$, and at least another unidentified connection c_j has $\Gamma^{-1}(c_j) \neq \emptyset$. Then, according to Lemma 2, in graph G', there exists at least one edge (msc_j, c_j), while $S(msc_j) = A$. Because of $\Gamma^{-1}(c_i) = \emptyset$, the monitor-segment msc_j has nonmonitoring on c_i. According to Table 11.1, if $S(msc_j) = A$, then $S(c_i) = IF$. Thus, c_i is not unidentified. This contradicts the assumption.

3. At least two unidentified connections have $\Gamma^{-1}(c) \neq \emptyset$. Arbitrarily select two connections c_i and c_j from this set. There are two possible cases:

   ✦ Case I: $\Gamma^{-1}(c_i) \neq \Gamma^{-1}(c_j)$. Suppose one monitor-segment $msc_i \in \Gamma^{-1}(c_i)$ but $msc_i \notin \Gamma^{-1}(c_j)$. Then, edge (msc_i, c_j) does not exist in graph G'. Thus, monitor-segment msc_i must have nonmonitoring on c_j. Because c_i is unidentified, according to Lemma 2, $S(msc_i) = A$, which implies that $S(c_j) = IF$, referring to Table 11.1. Thus, c_j is not unidentified, which contradicts our assumption.

   ✦ Case II: $\Gamma^{-1}(c_i) = \Gamma^{-1}(c_j)$. This contradicts the condition.

Thus, if $\Gamma^{-1}(c_i) \neq \Gamma^{-1}(c_j)$, then $|unidentified\ connection| \leq 1$ always holds.

11.5.1 Detecting the Status of a Connection under One–Original Attack Flow Conditions

For a given monitor-segment msc_i, there are only two relations between msc_i and an arbitrary connection c_j: monitoring or nonmonitoring. Let monitoring and nonmonitoring relations be denoted by values 1 and 0, respectively. Then, a vector $\vec{r_i}$ can be used to denote such a relation between each msc_i and all connections in the network: $\vec{r_i} = \{r_i(c_j)|c_j \in C\}$, and a *relation matrix* $\mathbb{R}$ can be created as follows:

$$\mathbb{R} = \begin{pmatrix} \vec{r_1} \\ \vec{r_2} \\ \cdots \\ \vec{r_m} \end{pmatrix} = \begin{pmatrix} r_1(c_1) & r_1(c_2) & \cdots & r_1(c_n) \\ r_2(c_1) & r_2(c_2) & \cdots & r_2(c_n) \\ \cdots & \cdots & \cdots & \cdots \\ r_m(c_1) & r_m(c_2) & \cdots & r_m(c_n) \end{pmatrix}$$

where $r_i(c_j)$ denotes the relation between msc_i and c_j, i.e.,

$$r_i(c_j) = \begin{cases} 1, & \textit{if } msc_i \textit{ monitors } c_j \\ 0, & \textit{if } msc_i \textit{ not monitoring } c_j \end{cases}$$

With a given status of the monitor-segment, we can get the corresponding status of all connections. For example, in Table 11.2, according to the status of monitor-segment $S(1c_2)$, the status of all three connections—$S(c_1)$, $S(c_2)$, and $S(c_3)$—can be derived. Monitor-segment $1c_2$ monitors c_1 and c_2, but does not monitor c_3. Because $S(1c_2)$ is A, according to Table 11.1, the status of c_1 should be $S(c_1) = uncertain$, the status of c_2 should be $S(c_2) = uncertain$, and the status of c_3 should be $S(c_3) = IF$. Let us assume that there are a total of n connections and m monitor-segments in the network. Let vector $\vec{S_i(c)} = \{S_i(c_1), S_i(c_2), \ldots, S_i(c_n)\}$ denote all connections' status given by msc_i, where $S_i(c_j)$ denotes the status of c_j derived from the status of msc_i.

Now, set two possible connection statuses, IF and $uncertain$, as 1 and 0, respectively. Similarly, set two possible monitor-segment status, A and $\bar{A}$, as 1 and 0, respectively. Then, according to the truth table, Table 11.1, we can derive $S_i(c_j)$ from $S(msc_i)$ and $r_i(c_j)$:

$$S_i(c_j) = S(msc_i) \oplus r_i(c_j)$$

and while $\vec{S_i(c)}$ from $S(msc_i)$ and $\vec{r_i}$:

$$\vec{S_i(c)} = [S(msc_i) \times \vec{1}] \oplus \vec{r_i}$$

where $\vec{1}$ is a $1 \times n$ vector, and $\oplus$ is *XOR*.

Then, a *status matrix* can be obtained as follows:

$$
\begin{pmatrix} \overrightarrow{S_1(c)} \\ \overrightarrow{S_2(c)} \\ \cdots \\ \overrightarrow{S_m(c)} \end{pmatrix} = \begin{pmatrix} S_1(c_1) & S_1(c_2) & \cdots & S_1(c_n) \\ S_2(c_1) & S_2(c_2) & \cdots & S_2(c_n) \\ \cdots & \cdots & \cdots & \cdots \\ S_m(c_1) & S_m(c_2) & \cdots & S_m(c_n) \end{pmatrix}
$$

$$
= \left\{ \begin{pmatrix} S(msc_1) \\ S(msc_2) \\ \cdots \\ S(msc_m) \end{pmatrix} \times \overrightarrow{1} \right\} \oplus \begin{pmatrix} \overrightarrow{r_1} \\ \overrightarrow{r_2} \\ \cdots \\ \overrightarrow{r_m} \end{pmatrix}
$$

Let $S(c_j)$ denote the logical *OR* of jth column in the above matrix, and let $\bigvee$ denote the logical *OR* operation:

$$
S(c_j) = \bigvee_{i=1}^{m} S_i(c_j) = \bigvee_{i=1}^{m} [S(msc_i) \oplus r_i(c_j)]
$$

Now, if we define a new operation $*$ as:

$$
\overrightarrow{X} * \overrightarrow{Y}^T = \bigvee_{i=1}^{n} [x_i \oplus y_i]
$$

where $\overrightarrow{X}$ and $\overrightarrow{Y}$ are $1 \times n$ vectors and x_i and y_i are their elements, then vector $\overrightarrow{S(c)}$ can be denoted by $S(msc_i)$ and its relation matrix as following:

$$
\overrightarrow{S(c)} = (S(c_1) \dots S(c_n))
$$

$$
= (S(msc_1) \dots S(msc_m)) * \begin{pmatrix} r_1(c_1) & \cdots & r_1(c_n) \\ \cdots & \cdots & \cdots \\ r_m(c_1) & \cdots & r_m(c_n) \end{pmatrix}
$$

The global status of connection c_j can be obtained as:

$$
\text{Status of } c_j = \begin{cases} IF, & if\ S(c_j) = 1 \\ unidentified, & if\ S(c_j) = 0 \end{cases}
$$

As shown in Figure 11.10, if connection c_1 is the OAF, then $S(1c_2) = A = 1$ and $S(3c_3) = A = 1$. According to Figure 11.10(b), we can get the relation between $1c_2$ and other connections as:

$$\overrightarrow{r_{1c_2}} = \{r_{1c_2}(c_1), r_{1c_2}(c_2), r_{1c_2}(c_3)\} = \{1,1,0\}$$

and the relation between $3c_3$ and other connections as:

$$\overrightarrow{r_{3c_3}} = \{r_{3c_3}(c_1), r_{3c_3}(c_2), r_{3c_3}(c_3)\} = \{1,0,1\}.$$

Then,

$$\begin{aligned}
\overrightarrow{S(c)} &= (\ S(c_1)\ \ S(c_2)\ \ S(c_3)\ ) \\
&= (\ S(1c_2)\ \ S(3c_3)\ ) * \begin{pmatrix} r_{1c_2}(c_1) & r_{1c_2}(c_2) & r_{1c_2}(c_3) \\ r_{3c_3}(c_1) & r_{3c_3}(c_2) & r_{3c_3}(c_3) \end{pmatrix} \\
&= (\ 1\ \ 1\ ) * \begin{pmatrix} 1 & 1 & 0 \\ 1 & 0 & 1 \end{pmatrix} \\
&= (\ 0\ \ 1\ \ 1\ )
\end{aligned}$$

Because $S(c_1) = 0$, connection c_1 must be the OAF in the network.

11.5.2   Computational Complexity

This method can be easily applied to any large- or small-size network. Let $D(u)$ denote the degree of node u. Suppose we have $|M|$ monitors in a network, and $Max\{D(m)\} = d_M, m \in M$, then the total number of monitor-segment will be no more than $|M| \times d_M$. Also, if we assume that there are no more than $|C|$ connections in the whole network, then the relation matrix size will be no more than $(|M| \times d_M) \times |C|$. Thus, for determining one OAF, the computation complexity will be $O((|M| \times d_M)^2 \times |C|)$, and the only operations needed in the computation are $+$ and $\oplus$.

11.6   *k*-CROSSTALK ATTACKS IN THE NETWORK

In some cases, it is possible that attackers introduce more than one attack signal into a network simultaneously. Thus, we need to extend the one-OAF diagnosable condition into a *k*-OAF diagnosable network [18]. In this case, the status identification in Table 11.1 changes. In a one-OAF diagnosable network, if the status of

Relation	$S(msc)$	$S(c)$
msc monitoring c	A	uncertain
(msc, c)	$\bar{A}$	IF
msc nonmonitoring c	A	uncertain
	$\bar{A}$	uncertain

TABLE 11.3   Truth table for monitor-segment and connections with more than one OAF in a network.

Monitor-Segments	$S(msc)$	$S(c_1)$	$S(c_2)$	$S(c_3)$
$S(1c_2)$	A	uncertain	uncertain	uncertain
$S(3c_3)$	$\bar{A}$	uncertain	uncertain	IF

TABLE 11.4   Status of the connections and the monitor-segments shown in Figure 11.10.

one msc is A, then all connections not monitored by this msc can be automatically set to $\bar{A}$. However, if there is more than one OAF in the network simultaneously, this conclusion is not true. Those connections not monitored by this msc can still be either OAF or IF. Table 11.3 shows the relations between a monitor-segment status and its monitoring connection's status.

The major difference between Table 11.1 and Table 11.3 is that in Table 11.1, an A status monitor-segment implies that all its nonmonitoring connections' statuses are IF, while in Table 11.3, an A status monitor-segment cannot conclude that the status of any of its nonmonitored connections' is IF.

Similarly, a connection is called *unidentified* if we cannot obtain the status of the connection directly from the set of all monitor-segments' statuses in the network. A network and its connections are shown in Figure 11.10. If connection c_2 is the OAF, then according to the truth table, Table 11.3, we can identify the status for both the monitor-segments and connections, as shown in Table 11.4. The monitor-segments can only identify the status of c_3 as IF and the status of connections c_1 and c_2 as *uncertain* according to both monitor-segments' results.

11.6.1   *k*-Crosstalk Attack Diagnosable Condition

We establish the diagnosis conditions for k-crosstalk attacks using a set of lemmas, theorems, and corollaries.

Lemma 3. If $msc \notin \Gamma^{-1}(c)$, c cannot affect the msc status even if c is an OAF.

Proof: According to Table 11.3, no matter whether a connection c is in *uncertain* status or in *IF* status, if a $msc \notin \Gamma^{-1}(c)$, then the status of this monitor-segment msc is always unknown.

Lemma 4. For a connection $c_i \notin \{c_{j_1}, \ldots, c_{j_k}\}$, $c_i \in C$, and $\{c_{j_1}, \ldots, c_{j_k}\} \subseteq C$, if $\Gamma^{-1}(c_i) \not\subseteq \bigcup_{j=j_1}^{j_k} \Gamma^{-1}(c_j)$, then $\Gamma^{-1}(c_i) \not\subseteq \bigcup_{j=j_m}^{j_n} \Gamma^{-1}(c_j)$, where $\{c_{j_m}, \ldots, c_{j_n}\} \subseteq \{c_{j_1}, \ldots, c_{j_k}\}$.

Proof: Since $\{c_{j_m}, \ldots, c_{j_n}\} \subseteq \{c_{j_1}, \ldots, c_{j_k}\}$, $\bigcup_{j=j_m}^{j_n} \Gamma^{-1}(c_j) \subseteq \bigcup_{j=j_1}^{j_k} \Gamma^{-1}(c_j)$ is always true. Moreover, since $\Gamma^{-1}(c_i) \not\subseteq \bigcup_{j=j_1}^{j_k} \Gamma^{-1}(c_j)$, $\Gamma^{-1}(c_i) \not\subseteq \bigcup_{j=j_m}^{j_n} \Gamma^{-1}(c_j)$ is also always true.

Lemma 5. If a connection c is an OAF, then c must be in *unidentified* status.

Proof: If c is an OAF, all $msc \in \Gamma^{-1}(c)$ are in A status, thus, all $msc \in \Gamma^{-1}(c)$ indicate that c's status is uncertain. According to the definition, c is in *unidentified* status.

Corollary 1. If there is a total of m *unidentified* connections in a network, then there are no more than m OAFs in the network simultaneously.

Proof: If there are more than m OAFs in the network simultaneously, then according to Lemma 5, all these OAFs must be in *unidentified* status, which contradicts our assumption. Thus, if there are total m *unidentified* connections in the network, then there are no more than m OAFs in the network simultaneously.

Theorem 2. For any connection $c_i \notin \{c_{j_1}, \ldots, c_{j_k}\}$, where $c_i \in C$, and $\{c_{j_1}, \ldots, c_{j_k}\} \subseteq C$ is an arbitrary subset of existing connections in a network, if $\Gamma^{-1}(c_i) \not\subseteq \bigcup_{j=j_1}^{j_k} \Gamma^{-1}(c_j)$, and there are $k+1$ *unidentified* connections in the network, then there must be at least $k+1$ OAFs in the network.

Proof: We prove this theorem by induction.

Initial step. Suppose $k = 1$. Then, $\Gamma^{-1}(c_i) \not\subseteq \Gamma^{-1}(c_j)$, for $\forall c_i, c_j \in C$. Assume an arbitrary pair of connections c_a and c_b are *unidentified* connections, but there is no more than one OAF in a network. There can be three possibilities:

1. There is no OAF in the network. Then, every msc in the network should be in $\bar{A}$ status, thus, all connections should be in *IF* status. This contradicts our assumption.

2. One of c_a or c_b is an OAF. Without loss of generality, assume c_b is an OAF. Since $\Gamma^{-1}(c_a) \not\subseteq \Gamma^{-1}(c_b)$, there exists at least one msc m such that $m \in \Gamma^{-1}(c_a)$ and $m \notin \Gamma^{-1}(c_b)$. According to Lemma 3, c_b cannot affect the status of m. Then, m must be in $\bar{A}$ status, which implies c_a is not an *unidentified* connection. This again contradicts our assumption.

3. Another OAF c_m exists. According to the given condition, $\Gamma^{-1}(c_a) \not\subseteq \Gamma^{-1}(c_m)$. Thus, there exists at least one msc m such that $m \in \Gamma^{-1}(c_a)$ and $m \notin \Gamma^{-1}(c_m)$

must exist. According to Lemma 3, c_m cannot affect the status of m. Then, m must be in $\bar{A}$ status, which implies c_a is not an *unidentified* connection. This again contradicts our assumption.

Thus, the number of OAFs, $|OAF|$, is at least two, which implies that this theorem is true when $k = 1$.

Induction step. Suppose this theorem is true for $k - 1$ (i.e., $\Gamma^{-1}(c_i) \not\subseteq \bigcup_{j=j_1}^{j_{k-1}} \Gamma^{-1}(c_j)$, where $c_i \notin \{c_{j_1}, \ldots, c_{j_{k-1}}\}$, $c_i \in C$, and $\{c_{j_1}, \ldots, c_{j_{k-1}}\} \subseteq C$ are an arbitrary subset of existing connections in the network), then there must be at least k OAFs in the network simultaneously if there exist k *unidentified* connections in the network.

Suppose $\Gamma^{-1}(c_i) \not\subseteq \bigcup_{j=j_1}^{j_k} \Gamma^{-1}(c_j)$ is true for all $c_i \notin \{c_{j_1}, \ldots, c_{j_k}\}$, and suppose $k + 1$ *unidentified* connections in the network are $c_{n_1}, \ldots, c_{n_{k+1}}$. Since $\Gamma^{-1}(c_i) \not\subseteq \bigcup_{j=j_1}^{j_k} \Gamma^{-1}(c_j)$, from Lemma 4, $\Gamma^{-1}(c_i) \not\subseteq \bigcup_{j=j_1}^{j_{k-1}} \Gamma^{-1}(c_j)$ is also satisfied. Since there are at least k *unidentified* connections in the network, at least k OAFs, $c_{m_1}, \ldots, c_{m_k}$, exist. According to our assumption, $\Gamma^{-1}(c_{n_i}) \not\subseteq \bigcup_{m=m_1}^{m_k} \Gamma^{-1}(c_m)$, there exists a monitor-segment msc_{n_i} such that $msc_{n_i} \in \Gamma^{-1}(c_{n_i})$ and $msc_{n_i} \notin \bigcup_{m=m_1}^{m_k} \Gamma^{-1}(c_m)$.

According to Lemma 3, all $c_m \in \{c_{m_1}, \ldots, c_{m_k}\}$ cannot affect msc_{n_i}. Thus, there must exist at least one extra OAF that affects the status of msc_{n_i}. Therefore, at least $k + 1$ OAFs must exist in the network. Thus, the theorem holds for all values of k.

Theorem 3.   (Necessary and Sufficient Conditions for k-Crosstalk Attacks). In a network containing up to k OAFs simultaneously, $\forall c_i, c_{j_1}, \ldots, c_{j_k} \in C$, $c_i \notin \{c_{j_1}, \ldots, c_{j_k}\}$, if

$$\Gamma^{-1}(c_i) \not\subseteq \bigcup_{j=j_1}^{j_k} \Gamma^{-1}(c_j)$$

then for this network with the connection set C, $|unidentified\ connection| \leq k$ holds.

What this theorem states is that for one connection c_i and an arbitrary set of k connections $\{c_{j_1}, \ldots, c_{j_k}\}$, where c_i is not in $\{c_{j_1}, \ldots, c_{j_k}\}$, if the set of monitor-segments of connection c_i is not a subset of the union of monitor-segment sets for connections $\{c_{j_1}, \ldots, c_{j_k}\}$, then there is no more than k *unidentified* connections for this network if there are at most k OAFs existing simultaneously in the network.

Proof: Necessity. Without loss of generality, suppose in a subset of k connections (i.e., $\{c_{j_1}, \ldots, c_{j_k}\}$) all are OAFs. According to Lemma 5, all OAFs are unidentified. Then, for some connection $c_i \notin \{c_{j_1}, \ldots, c_{j_k}\}$, there are two possibilities:

1. $\Gamma^{-1}(c_i) = \varnothing$. Obviously, $\Gamma^{-1}(c_i) \subseteq \bigcup_{j=j_1}^{j_k} \Gamma^{-1}(c_j)$. Since there is no $msc \in \Gamma^{-1}(c_i)$, c_i is unidentified. According to Lemma 5, all OAFs are unidentified along

with $\{c_{j_1}, \ldots, c_{j_k}\}$, and thus, $|unidentified\ connection| > k$, this contradicts our assumption.

2. $\Gamma^{-1}(c_i) \neq \emptyset$ and suppose $\Gamma^{-1}(c_i) \subseteq \bigcup_{j=j_1}^{j_k} \Gamma^{-1}(c_j)$. Then, for all $msc \in \Gamma^{-1}(c_i)$, $msc \in \bigcup_{j=j_1}^{j_k} \Gamma^{-1}(c_j)$. Obviously, all $msc \in \bigcup_{j=j_1}^{j_k} \Gamma^{-1}(c_j)$ must be in A status. Therefore, $msc \in \Gamma^{-1}(c_i)$ are also in A state, thus, c_i is also *unidentified* and $|unidentified\ connection| > k$. This contradicts our assumption again.

Sufficiency: Suppose $|unidentified\ connection| \geq k+1$, and for every unidentified connection c, $\Gamma^{-1}(c) \neq \emptyset$. Assume that for any connection c_i and any arbitrary subset of k connections $\{c_{j_1}, \ldots, c_{j_k}\}$, $c_i \notin \{c_{j_1}, \ldots, c_{j_k}\}$, $\Gamma^{-1}(c_i) \not\subseteq \bigcup_{j=j_1}^{j_k} \Gamma^{-1}(c_j)$ is always satisfied. According to Theorem 2, at this time, the number of OAFs is at least $k+1$, which contradicts our assumption that there are no more than k OAFs in the network simultaneously. Thus, the theorem holds.

Corollary 2. For any connection $c_i \notin \{c_{j_1}, \ldots, c_{j_k}\}$, where $c_i \in C$ and any arbitrary subset $\{c_{j_1}, \ldots, c_{j_k}\} \subseteq C$ in a network, if $\Gamma^{-1}(c_i) \not\subseteq \bigcup_{j=j_1}^{j_k} \Gamma^{-1}(c_j)$ is always true, then for $m \leq k$:

1. There are no more than m *unidentified* connections in the network if there are only m OAFs in the network.

2. There are exactly m OAFs if there exist m *unidentified* connections.

3. If there exist m *unidentified* connections, these m connections must be m OAFs.

Proof:

1. According to the condition, if c_i is not an OAF, then $\Gamma^{-1}(c_i) \not\subseteq \bigcup_{j=j_1}^{j_m} \Gamma^{-1}(c_j)$, where c_j is one of m OAF connections, is always true. Thus, there exists an $msc_i \in \Gamma^{-1}(c_i)$ but $msc_i \notin \bigcup_{j=j_1}^{j_m} \Gamma^{-1}(c_j)$. According to Lemma 3, none of these OAFs can affect the state of msc_i. Thus, no connections except OAFs will have *unidentified* status.

2. According to Corollary 1, $|OAF| \leq m$, while according to Theorem 2, $|OAF| \geq m$, thus $|OAF| = m$.

3. According to result 2, if there are $m \leq k$ *unidentified* connections, there must be exactly m OAFs; while according to result 1, if there are $m \leq k$ OAFs, then no more than m connections will be *unidentified* connections. According to Lemma 5, all OAFs must be *unidentified* connections. Therefore, all these m OAFs should have *unidentified* status. Thus, if there are $m \leq k$ *unidentified* connections in the network, these m connections must be the OAFs.

11.6.2   Detecting Global Status of Connections

As we did in the case of one-OAF diagnosable networks, we define the relation between the status of *msc* and connections in vector $\vec{r_i}$ and a *relation matrix* $\mathbb{R}$ as above. With a given status of the monitor-segment, we can get the corresponding status of all connections. We can derive $S_i(c_j)$ from $S(msc_i)$ and $r_i(c_j)$:

$$S_i(c_j) = \{S(msc_i) \times r_i(c_j)\} \oplus r_i(c_j)$$

while $\overrightarrow{S_i(c)}$ from $S(msc_i)$ and $\vec{r_i}$ is:

$$\overrightarrow{S_i(c)} = \{[S(msc_i) \times \vec{1}] \times \vec{r_i}\} \oplus \vec{r_i}$$

where $\vec{1}$ is a $1 \times n$ vector, $\times$ is *AND*, and $\oplus$ is *XOR*.

Let $S(c_j)$ denote the logical *OR* of *j*th column in the above matrix, and let $\bigvee$ denote the logical *OR* operation:

$$S(c_j) = \bigvee_{i=1}^{m} S_i(c_j) = \bigvee_{i=1}^{m} \{[S(msc_i) \times r_i(c_j)] \oplus r_i(c_j)\}$$

Now, we define a new operation $*$ as:

$$\vec{X} * \vec{Y}^T = \bigvee_{i=1}^{n} \{[x_i \times y_i] \oplus y_i\}$$

where $\vec{X}$ and $\vec{Y}$ are $1 \times n$ vectors and x_i and y_i are their elements; then, vector $\overrightarrow{S(c)}$ can be denoted by $S(msc_i)$ and its relation matrix.

The global status of connection c_j is obtained as:

$$Status\ of\ c_j = \begin{cases} IF, & if\ S(c_j) = 1 \\ unidentified, & if\ S(c_j) = 0 \end{cases}$$

According to Corollary 2, if the status of connection c_j is *unidentified*, then c_j must be an OAF. This provides the algorithm for locating the attack connections of each wavelength.

For example, as shown in Figure 11.12, there are two crosstalk attack connections, c_1 and c_2, and c_3 is a nonattack connection. There are three monitor-segments: $1c_1$, $1c_2$, and $1c_3$. According to the monitor-segment definition, $\Gamma^{-1}(c_1) = \{1c_1\}$, $\Gamma^{-1}(c_2) = \{1c_2\}$, and $\Gamma^{-1}(c_3) = \{1c_3\}$. This satisfies the *k*-crosstalk diagnosable condition. Thus, we can determine which connections are attack

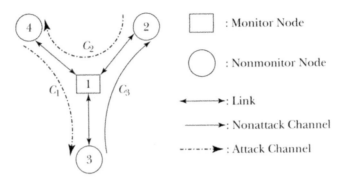

FIGURE

11.12
Two attacks in AON.

connections according to these monitor-segments' statuses. In this example, the relation matrix $\mathbb{R}$ is:

$$\mathbb{R} = \begin{pmatrix} 1 & 0 & 0 \\ 0 & 1 & 0 \\ 0 & 0 & 1 \end{pmatrix}$$

and the status of all monitor-segments is:

$$\overrightarrow{S(msc)} = \begin{pmatrix} S(1c_1) & S(1c_2) & S(1c_3) \end{pmatrix}$$
$$= \begin{pmatrix} 1 & 1 & 0 \end{pmatrix}$$

Thus,

$$\overrightarrow{S(c)} = \begin{pmatrix} 0 & 0 & 1 \end{pmatrix}$$

Because $S(c_1) = 0$, $S(c_2) = 0$, and $S(c_3) = 1$, connections c_1 and c_2 must be the OAFs in this network.

11.6.3   Computational Complexity

Suppose we have $|M|$ monitors in a network and $Max\{D(m)\} = d_M, m \in M$, then the total number of monitor-segments will be no more than $|M| \times d_M$. Also, if we assume that there are no more than $|C|$ connections in the whole network, then the relation matrix size will be no more than $(|M| \times d_M) \times |C|$. The computational complexity of the first part, $[S(msc_i)] \times \mathbb{R}$, is $O((|M| \times d_M)^2 \times |C|)$, while the computational complexity of the second part, two $(|M| \times d_M) \times |C|$ size matrices $\oplus$, is $O(|M| \times d_M \times |C|)$. Thus, for determining k OAFs, the computation complexity will be $O((|M| \times d_M + 1) \times |M| \times d_M \times |C|) = O((|M| \times d_M)^2 \times |C|)$, and the only operations needed in the computation are $+$ and $\oplus$. Thus, this method is scalable and can be easily applied to a large network.

11.7   SPARSE MONITORING AND ROUTING ALGORITHMS

Thus far we established conditions for monitoring and diagnosing attacks. To find out the exact location of an OAF in a network, we have to determine monitor placement and a routing policy that work together in such a way that we can meet the necessary and sufficient conditions. We cannot satisfy the conditions if several connections neither traverse a monitor nor pass through nodes next to a monitor.

We develop several sparse monitoring and the corresponding routing policies. The conditions require that there must be at least one monitor-segment on every connection. Thus, with a given monitor placement policy, the routing policy needs to route connections through at least one monitor or its neighbor. Obviously, a smaller number of monitors places more restrictions on the routing policies. This has an adverse impact on the blocking probability. Since sparse monitor placement is a difficult problem, only heuristic solutions are given here.

11.7.1   Sparse Monitoring, Test Connection, and Routing for a Single Original Attack Flow Policy I

To detect a single OAF, we need the following definitions. If a monitor is connected directly to a nonmonitor node u, then the monitor is said to be a one-hop-distance monitor (OHM). $OHM(u)$ denotes the set of OHMs for node u. The degree of node u is denoted by $D(u)$. A node with a degree of one is called a *pendant node.*

To guarantee the exact location of the OAF in a network, we suggest the following sparse monitor placement policy: (1) every nonmonitor node u should have $D(u) \geq 2$, (2) a nonmonitor node u must have $D(u)$ OHMs, and (3) a node u with a pendant node as its neighbor must be a monitor node.

We assume that each link in the network is bidirectional so that there is one fiber in each of two directions on each link. In the network, there are two kinds of connections set up: one is the *normal connection,* which is set up by users and the other is the *test connection*, which is requested by the network management system. A test connection is used to determine if a node is a PAN or not. For a nonmonitor node, if there is a normal connection on wavelength λ terminating at this node and no normal connection provides a monitor-segment on the corresponding link, then one test connection from this node to each OHM is needed.

We normally use shortest-path routing except in one case to guarantee the exact location of the OAF in a network. For any two normal connections (excluding test connections) originating from the same nonmonitor node, at least one must pass through three different (including source and destination) nodes (i.e., $\forall c_i, c_j \in R$, and $c_i = \{u_0, \dots\}$, $c_j = \{u_0, \dots\}$, then either $\exists \{u_a, u_b, u_c\} \subset c_i$ but $\not\subset c_j$ or $\exists \{u_a, u_b, u_c\} \subset c_j$ but $\not\subset c_i$).

According to our crosstalk attack model, the crosstalk attack only affects the same wavelength connections at the wavelength selective switch. To simplify our analysis, we assume that (1) there is no wavelength converter (in case there is one, then the monitor is required to detect attack conditions across conversions) in the whole network, and (2) for each link only one fiber exists in each direction. Then we claim the following.

Claim 1. With the above monitor placement, test connection setup, and routing policy, a network with one fiber on each link and without a wavelength converter is one-OAF diagnosable on each wavelength.

Proof: We only provide an outline of a proof. Since each fiber (wavelength) link has a monitor node on at least one of the ends, each monitor segment is monitored. Thus, $\Gamma^{-1}(c) \neq \emptyset$ holds $\forall c \in C$. Moreover with the routing policy, no two connections have the same segments, and therefore, $\Gamma^{-1}(c_i) \neq \Gamma^{-1}(c_j)$. Thus, under this condition, the network is one-OAF diagnosable.

Since attacks do not propagate from one wavelength to another, therefore, we can always detect OAFs on all wavelengths in the whole network, if there is only one OAF on each wavelength.

11.7.2 Examples

Figure 11.13(a) depicts a four-node bidirectional mesh network with two monitor nodes, 2 and 4, and only one wavelength.

Suppose the following connections exist and one of them is an OAF. The connection set consists of $\{c_1(1 \rightarrow 4), c_2(1 \rightarrow 2 \rightarrow 3), c_3(3 \rightarrow 4 \rightarrow 1), c_4(3 \rightarrow 2 \rightarrow 1)\}$. For each nonmonitor node, one normal connection exists from this node to everyone of its OHMs, thus according to our test connection setup policy, no test connection is necessarily needed.

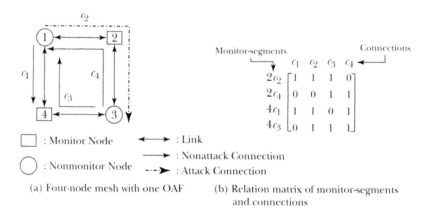

: Monitor Node   ◄──► : Link

: Nonmonitor Node   ──► : Nonattack Connection

                   ┈► : Attack Connection

(a) Four-node mesh with one OAF   (b) Relation matrix of monitor-segments and connections

FIGURE   Diagnose the OAF in a network without a test connection.

11.13

Thus, the current monitor-segment set is $msc = \{2c_2, 2c_4, 4c_1, 4c_3\}$, and the relation matrix between these monitor-segments and the connections is shown in Figure 11.13(b).

Let us assume that connection $\{c_2(1 \rightarrow 2 \rightarrow 3)\}$ is the OAF. Then, we can get the status of all monitor-segments as folllows: $S(2c_2) = A = 1$, $S(2c_4) = \bar{A} = 0$, $S(4c_1) = A = 1$, and $S(4c_3) = A = 1$. Thus, $S(msc) = (S(2c_2)\ S(2c_4)\ S(4c_1)\ S(4c_3)) = (1\ 0\ 1\ 1)$ and vector $S(c) = (1\ 0\ 1\ 1)$.

Since $S(c_1)$, $S(c_3)$, and $S(c_4)$ are all greater than 0, this means that connections c_1, c_3, and c_4 are all IFs. Also $S(c_2) = 0$, which means that c_2 is in *unidentified* status. Thus, the only *unidentified* connection c_2 must be an OAF.

Now, let us assume that connection c_3 does not exist. Then, according to our test connection setup policy, a test connection t_3 is established from node 3 to node 4 because of a lacking monitor-segment on link (3, 4), as shown in Figure 11.14(a). Then, as shown in Figure 11.14(b), we can get the relation matrix of monitor-segments and connections. By using the same method as shown in the previous example, we obtain the vector $S(c) = (1\ 0\ 1\ 1)$, from which we can determine the only unidentified connection c_2 as the OAF.

11.7.3   Sparse Monitoring, Test Connection, and Routing Policy II

The previous method requires a lot of monitor nodes in a network (more than half). To reduce the total number of monitor nodes in a network, we propose another heuristic method. With this new method, fewer monitors are required

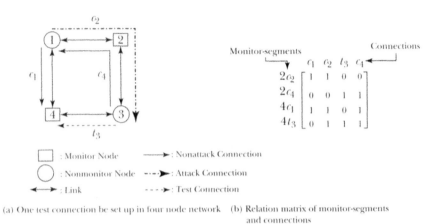

(a) One test connection be set up in four node network   (b) Relation matrix of monitor-segments
and connections

FIGURE   Diagnose the OAF in a network with a test connection.

11.14

in the whole AON. In this case, we need to change the test connection and routing scheme.

We require that any nonmonitor node u must have at least one OHM. Moreover, for any monitor or nonmonitor node, if there is a normal connection passing through or terminating at this node, then there must be one test connection from this node to each OHM (if an OHM exists) that must exist if there is no normal connection that exists on the corresponding link. In other words, there must be either a regular or a test connection from a node to each of its OHMs.

For routing, we use shortest-path routing except in the following cases:

1. For any arbitrary pair of connections c_i and c_j, if neither source node is a monitor node, then $U(c_i) \neq U(c_j)$ should always be satisfied (i.e., ($\forall c_i, c_j \in R$, $U(c_i) = \{u_i, \dots\}$, $U(c_j) = \{u_j, \dots\}$, and $u_i, u_j \notin M$, then $U(c_i) \neq U(c_j)$).

2. For any arbitrary pair of connections c_i and c_j that share at least one node u, if neither source node is a monitor node, then at least one of the following conditions should be satisfied: ($\forall c_i, c_j \in R$, $U(c_i) = \{u_i, \dots\}$, $U(c_j) = \{u_j, \dots\}$, $u_i, u_j \notin M$, and $u \in \{U(c_i) \cap U(c_j)\}$. Then, either u is a monitor node, or either $UNN(u, c_i)$ or $UNN(u, c_j)$ should be a monitor node, or at least one node v, $v \in U(c_i)$ but $v \notin U(c_j)$, exists, such that $DNN(v, c_i) \in M$ exists or one of its OHM $m \notin U(c_i)$ exists.

Comparing this policy with the previous sparse monitor policy (Policy I) where any nonmonitor node u requires $D(u)$ OHMs, we see that this new method only requires one OHM for each nonmonitor node. Considering the expense of a monitor, this is a big advantage. Now we make the following claim.

Claim 2. With the above new sparse monitoring policies, a network is one-OAF diagnosable.

Proof: Again we provide an informal proof. It is easy to see that we cannot find two connections in the network such that $\Gamma^{-1}(c_i) = \Gamma^{-1}(c_j)$. Thus, under this condition, the network is one-OAF diagnosable. More details can be found in Wu and Somani [16, 19].

11.7.4   Connection Routing Algorithm in One–Original Attack Flow Networks

In this section we develop a practical routing algorithm. Without loss of generality, we develop a variant of the shortest-path algorithm that satisfies the above routing constraints. The pseudo code for the algorithm is given below.

BEGIN:

    Given a node request.

    Run Shortest-Path-Algorithm to find the source-destination path. /*Test connections are ignored to compute the path and removed if the path uses links with test connections*/.

    IF Fail to find any available path, reject this request,

    ELSE find one path P1,

        IF source node s is a monitor node,

        THEN accept this request and set up this connection with path P1.

        ELSE source node s is a nonmonitor node,

            Check number of nodes n on P1,

            IF $n \geq 3$,

            THEN accept this request and set up this connection with path P1.

            ELSE check all existing connections originated from s,

                IF all existing connections' paths include at least three nodes,

                THEN accept this request and set up this connection with path P1.

                ELSE remove one link on path P1 from original graph and reiterate the algorithm.

                ENDIF

            ENDIF

        ENDIF

    ENDIF

END

Suppose the maximum output degree of network nodes is $Max\{D(u)\} = d_N$, then, with this routing algorithm, at most d_N connections need to be checked before we can make a decision for the connection request.

11.7.5 Example

Figure 11.15(a) depicts a nine-node bidirectional mesh network. According to the sparse monitor placement policy, only three monitor nodes are necessary in this network. Here, we choose nodes 4, 5, and 6 as the monitor nodes and the remaining nodes as nonmonitor nodes. By considering attack connections that are on the same wavelength to simplify our example, we assume that only one wavelength is supported in this network.

Suppose a normal connection set consists of $\{c_1(1 \to 2 \to 3 \to 6), c_2(2 \to 1 \to 4 \to 5), c_3(3 \to 2 \to 5 \to 6), c_4(9 \to 6 \to 5 \to 4)\}$, and only one of them is an OAF.

According to our test connection setup policy, no test connection is necessarily needed. Thus, the current monitor-segment set is $msc = \{4c_2, 4c_4, 5c_3, 5c_4, 6c_1, 6c_3, 6c_4\}$, and the relation matrix between these monitor-segments and the connections is shown in Figure 11.15(b).

Let us assume that connection $\{c_1(1 \to 2 \to 3 \to 6)\}$ is the OAF. Then, we can get the status of all monitor-segments immediately: $S(4c_2) = A = 1$, $S(4c_4) = \bar{A} = 0$, $S(5c_3) = A = 1$, $S(5c_4) = A = 1$, $S(6c_1) = A = 1$, $S(6c_3) = \bar{A} = 0$, and $S(6c_4) = \bar{A} = 0$. Thus, $\overrightarrow{S(msc)} = (S(4c_2)\,S(4c_4)\,S(5c_3)\,S(5c_4)\,S(6c_1)\,S(6c_3)\,S(6c_4)) = (1\ 0\ 1\ 1\ 1\ 0\ 0)$ and vector $S(c) = (0\ 1\ 1\ 1)$ are obtained.

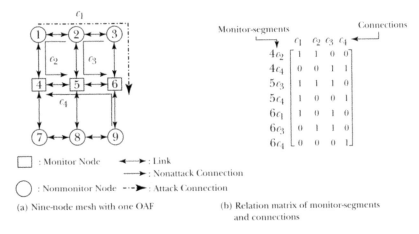

(a) Nine-node mesh with one OAF

(b) Relation matrix of monitor-segments and connections

FIGURE 11.15 Single-wavelength crosstalk attack diagnosable network.

The values of $S(c_2)$, $S(c_3)$, and $S(c_4)$ are greater than 0, implying that connections c_2, c_3, and c_4 are all IFs, while $S(c_1) = 0$ implies that connection c_1 is in the unidentified status. Thus, the only unidentified connection c_1 must be an OAF.

11.8   SPARSE MONITORING, TEST CONNECTION, AND ROUTING FOR MORE THAN ONE ORIGINAL ATTACK FLOW

To place the monitors and set up test connections for more than one OAF is still an open question. In this section, we extend the results of the previous section and propose a sparse monitoring scheme, which includes monitor placement as well as regular and test connection setting policies for a two-OAF diagnosable network. We call it policy III.

For a two-diagnosable system, we propose that a nonmonitor node u must have $D(u)$ OHMs, and a node u with a pendant node as its neighbor must be a monitor node. Again in a network with bidirectional fiber links and no wavelength conversion, we use test connections in addition to regular connections to make them two-diagnosable.

For test connections, for every nonmonitor node u, if there is a normal connection c on wavelength λ passing through or terminating at u, then one test connection from node u to each OHM is needed if no normal connection provides a monitor-segment on the corresponding link, except when u's upstream neighbor node is $UNN(u, c)$.

For routing, we use shortest-path routing except in certain specific situations where the routing policy is needed to guarantee the exact location of the OAFs. If the source of a connection c_i is a nonmonitor node that is also on the path of another connection c_j, then c_i must pass through three continuous nodes $(n_1, n_2, n_3) \not\subseteq U(c_j) \cup U(c_k)$, where $c_k \neq c_i$, c_j is an arbitrary connection in the network.

In the following, we prove that a network is always two-OAF diagnosable if it is designed using the models and policies described above.

Lemma 6. If a connection c_i passes through three continuous nodes that are not in $U(c_j)$, then there is at least one monitor segment msc_i such that $msc_i \in \Gamma^{-1}(c_i)$, but $msc_i \notin \Gamma^{-1}(c_j)$.

Proof: Suppose that the three continuous nodes are $\{n_1, n_2, n_3\}$ on c_i. If n_2 is not a monitor node, then both n_1 and n_3 must be monitor nodes. Then, $msc_i = (n_2 \rightarrow n_3) \in \Gamma^{-1}(c_i)$, but is not in $\Gamma^{-1}(c_j)$, and the Lemma holds. If n_2 is a monitor node, then since both n_1 and n_2 are not in $U(c_j)$, monitor segment $msc_i = (n_1 \rightarrow n_2) \in \Gamma^{-1}(c_i)$, but is not in $\Gamma^{-1}(c_j)$. Again the result holds.

Thus, we can make the following claim.

Claim 3. A network using Policy III for monitor placement, test connection setup, and routing in a network with bidirectional fiber links and no wavelength converters is two-OAF diagnosable on each wavelength.

Proof: First, it is obvious that for each connection c, at least one monitor node $m \in U(c)$. Thus, at least one monitor-segment monitors this connection (i.e., $\Gamma^{-1}(c) \neq \emptyset$ holds $\forall c \in C$).

According to Theorem 3, for any three arbitrary connections, c_i, c_j, and c_k, the necessary and sufficient condition for a two-OAF diagnosable network is $\Gamma^{-1}(c_i) \nsubseteq \Gamma^{-1}(c_j) \cup \Gamma^{-1}(c_k)$. Because at least one monitor exists on each link, it is easy to argue that, assuming $\Gamma^{-1}(c_i) \subseteq \Gamma^{-1}(c_j) \cup \Gamma^{-1}(c_k)$, this leads to a contradiction whether the source of connection c_i is a monitor node or not. Thus, under Policy III, the network is two-OAF diagnosable.

11.8.1 Examples

Figure 11.16(a) depicts a nine-node bidirectional mesh network. In this example, this network is a two-OAF diagnosable network. According to our sparse monitor placement policy, four monitor nodes are necessary. Let us say we choose nodes 2, 4, 6, and 8 as the monitor nodes and consider connections on only one wavelength.

The current set of connections consists of $\{c_1(1 \to 2 \to 3)$, $c_2(1 \to 4 \to 7 \to 8)$, $c_3(3 \to 2 \to 5 \to 6)$, $c_4(9 \to 6 \to 5 \to 4)\}$. Two of which are OAFs.

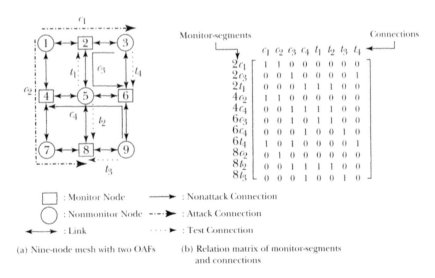

(a) Nine-node mesh with two OAFs

(b) Relation matrix of monitor-segments and connections

FIGURE 11.16   Diagnose two OAFs in a network.

According to our test connection setup policy, for each nonmonitor node, at least one normal connection or one test connection must exist from this node to each of its OHMs, therefore, the test connection set consists of $\{t_1(5 \to 2),$ $t_2(5 \to 8), t_3(9 \to 8) \ t_4(3 \to 6)\}$.

Thus, the current monitor-segment set is:

$$msc = \{2c_1, 2c_3, 2t_1, 4c_2, 4c_4, 6c_3, 6c_4, 6t_4, 8c_2, 8t_2, 8t_3\}$$

and the relation matrix between these monitor-segments and the connections is shown in Figure 11.16(b).

Let us assume that connections $\{c_1(1 \to 2 \to 3)\}$ and $\{c_2(1 \to 4 \to 7 \to 8)\}$ are OAFs. Then, we obtain the status of all monitor-segments immediately: $S(2c_1) = A = 1, S(2c_3) = \bar{A} = 0, S(2t_1) = \bar{A} = 0, S(4c_2) = A = 1, S(4c_4) = \bar{A} = 0,$ $S(6c_3) = \bar{A} = 0, S(6c_4) = \bar{A} = 0, S(6t_4) = A = 1, S(8c_2) = A = 1, S(8t_2) = \bar{A} = 0,$ and $S(8t_3) = \bar{A} = 0.$ Thus, $\overrightarrow{S(msc)} = (1\ 0\ 0\ 1\ 0\ 0\ 0\ 1\ 1\ 0\ 0)$ is obtained. This results in vector $\overrightarrow{S(c)} = (0\ 0\ 1\ 1\ 1\ 1\ 1\ 1).$ Since $S(c_3), S(c_4), S(t_1), S(t_2), S(t_3),$ and $S(t_4)$ are greater than 0, which means connections $c_3, c_4, t_1, t_2, t_3,$ and t_4 are all IFs. Since $S(c_1) = 0$ and $S(c_2) = 0$, it implies that both c_1 and c_2 have unidentified status. Thus, according to Corollary 2, the unidentified connections c_1 and c_2 must be OAFs.

Now, let us assume that only connection c_1 is an OAF in the same network, as shown in Figure 11.17. Because the sets of connections are the same in both cases, the monitor-segment set and the relation matrix will be the same as the

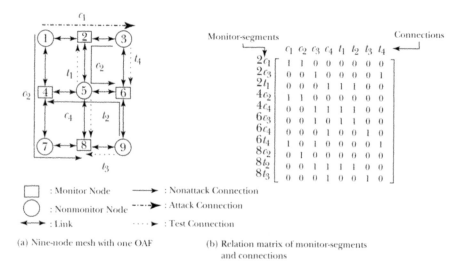

: Monitor Node   ⟶ : Nonattack Connection

: Nonmonitor Node   ┄⟶ : Attack Connection

⟷ : Link   ⋯⟶ : Test Connection

(a) Nine-node mesh with one OAF   (b) Relation matrix of monitor-segments and connections

FIGURE
11.17   Diagnosing only one OAF in a one- *OAF* diagnosable network.

previous example. Since we assume that connection $\{c_1(1 \to 2 \to 3)\}$ is an OAF, then we can get the status of all monitor-segments immediately: $S(2c_1) = A = 1$, $S(2c_3) = \bar{A} = 0$, $S(2t_1) = \bar{A} = 0$, $S(4c_2) = A = 1$, $S(4c_4) = \bar{A} = 0$, $S(6c_3) = \bar{A} = 0$, $S(6c_4) = \bar{A} = 0$, $S(6t_4) = A = 1$, $S(8c_2) = \bar{A} = 0$, $S(8t_2) = \bar{A} = 0$, and $S(8t_3) = \bar{A} = 0$. Thus, $\overrightarrow{S(msc)} = (1\ 0\ 0\ 1\ 0\ 0\ 0\ 1\ 0\ 0\ 0)$ is obtained. This results in vector $\overrightarrow{S(c)} = (0\ 1\ 1\ 1\ 1\ 1\ 1\ 1)$. Since $S(c_2)$, $S(c_3)$, $S(c_4)$, $S(t_1)$, $S(t_2)$, $S(t_3)$, and $S(t_4)$ are greater than 0, which means connections c_2, c_3, c_4, t_1, t_2, t_3, and t_4 are all IFs. Since $S(c_1) = 0$, it implies that only c_1 has unidentified status. Thus, according to Corollary 2, the unidentified connection c_1 must be the OAF.

11.9   CONCLUSION

In this chapter, we have discussed the physical security problems in an AON and mainly focused on crosstalk attacks because of their propagation capability. We have developed a crosstalk attack as well as a monitor model. Based on these models, we proposed the concept of a monitor-segment and developed necessary and sufficient conditions for a one-crosstalk attack diagnosable and k-crosstalk attack diagnosable network. We have also developed several sparse monitor placement algorithms and an attack diagnosis (location) algorithm based on the observations made during monitor operation.

We have shown that it is possible to design diagnosable networks with sparse monitoring as long as appropriate routing and test connection strategies are followed. We have also shown that less than half the nodes need to monitor nodes to satisfy one-OAF diagnostic requirements, and about half of the nodes need to monitor nodes to satisfy two-OAF diagnostic requirements. Considering the fact that the monitor devices are expensive, this really provides a big advantage.

The algorithms require the setting up of test connections in case all regular connections do not exist. This, however, will not have any resource overhead as the resources are not in use anyway.

The results of this research will enable designing better and more efficient fault-and attack-tolerant optical fiber–based networks. Since society is very dependent on fully functional computing and networking systems, this research will have significant economic impact as well.

References

[1] R. C. Alferness, "The All-Optical Networks," *WCC—ICCT 2000* 1 Beijing, China (Aug. 2000): 14–15.
[2] J. Fee, "All-Optical Network Technology Enablers," *OFC 97*, Dallas, TX Feb. 1997.

[3] Advanced Networks Group, "All-Optical Network Security," *MIT Lincoln Laboratory*, Dec. 1998.

[4] M. L. Jones, "A Carrier Perspective on All-Optical Networks," *IEEE/LEOS All-Optical Networking: Existing and Emerging Architecture and Applications*, 2002, pp. 31–32.

[5] S.-K. Liu, "Challenges of All-Optical Network Evolution," *IEEE LEOS '98* 1 Orlando, FL (Dec. 1998): 182–183.

[6] M. Marciniak, "Optical Transparency in Next Generation IP over All-Optical Networks," *Proceedings of 2001 3rd International Conference on Transparent Optical Networks*, Cracow, Poland June 2001, pp. 329–332.

[7] A. Amrani, J. Roldan, and G. Junyent, "Optical Monitoring System for Scalable All-Optical Networks," *Proceeding of IEEE LEOS '97 10th Annual Meeting* 2 San Franscisco, CA (Nov. 1997): 270–271.

[8] M. W. Maeda, "Management and Control of Transparent Optical Networks," *IEEE Journal on Selected Areas in Communications* 16, No. 7 (Sept. 1998): 1008–1023.

[9] R. Bergman, M. Medard, and S. Chan, "Distributed Algorithms for Attack Localization in All-Optical Networks," *Network and Distributed System Security Symposium*, San Diego, CA 1998.

[10] M. Medard, D. Marquis, R. A. Barry, and S. G. Finn, "Security Issues in All-Optical Networks," *IEEE Network* 11, No. 3 (May/June 1997): 42–48.

[11] M. Medard, D. Marquis, and S. R. Chinn, "Attack Detection Methods for All-Optical Networks," *Network and Distributed System Security Symposium*, San Diego, CA 1998.

[12] W. T. Anderson, J. Jackel, G.-K. Chang, and H. Dai et al., "The Monet Project—A Final Report," *IEEE Journal of Lightwave Technology* 18, No. 2 (Dec. 2000): 1988–2009.

[13] N. Golmie, T. D. Ndousse, and D. H. Su, "A Differentiated Optical Services Model for WDM Networks," *IEEE Communication Magazine* (Feb. 2000): 68–73.

[14] C.-S. Li and R. Ramaswami, "Fault Detection, Isolation, and Open Fiber Control in Transparent All-Optical Networks," *GlobeCom '96* 1 London, UK (1996): 157–162.

[15] C.-S. Li and R. Ramaswami, "Automatic Fault Detection, Isolation, and Recovery in Transparent All-Optical Networks," *IEEE Journal of Lightwave Technology* 15 (Oct. 1997): 1784–1793.

[16] T. Wu, "Attack Monitoring and Localization in All-Optical Network," Ph.D. Dissertation, Department of Electrical and Computer Engineering, Iowa State University, 2003.

[17] T. Wu and A. K. Somani, "Attack Monitoring and Localization in All-Optical Networks," *OptiComm '02 Proceedings*, Boston, MA July 2002.

[18] T. Wu and A. K. Somani, "Necessary and Sufficient Condition for k-Crosstalk Attacks Localization in All-Optical Networks," *GlobeCom '03*, San Francisco, CA 2003.

[19] T. Wu and A. K. Somani, "Cross-Talk Attack Monitoring and Localization in All-Optical Networks," *IEEE/ACM Transactions on Networking* 13, No. 6 (Dec. 2005): 1390–1401.

[20] R. Antosik, "Protection and Restoration in Optical Networks, *Proceedings of 2nd International Conference on Transparent Optical Networks*, Gdańsk, Poland 2000.

[21] G. Conte, M. Listanti, M. Settembre, and R. Sabella, "Strategy for Protection and Restoration of Optical Paths in WDM Backbone Networks for Next-Generation Internet Infrastructures," *Journal of Lightwave Technology* 20, No. 8 (Aug. 2002): 1264–1276.

[22] I. Rubin and L. Jing, "Failure Protection Methods for Optical Meshed-Ring Communications Networks," *IEEE Journal on Selected Areas in Communications* 18, No. 10 (Oct. 2000): 1950–1960.

[23] D. Zhou and S. Subramaniam, "Survivability in Optical Networks," *IEEE Network* 14, No. 6 (Nov. 2000): 16–23.

[24] A. K. Somani, "Sequential Fault Occurrence and Reconfiguration in System-Level Diagnosis," *IEEE Trans. Comput.* 39, No. 12 (Dec. 1990): 1472–1475.

[25] A. K. Somani, "System Level Diagnosis: A Review," Technique Report, Dependable Computer Laboratory, Iowa State University, 1997.

12 — Robustness Evaluation of Operating Systems[1]

CHAPTER

Andréas Johansson   Technische Universität Darmstadt, Germany
Neeraj Suri   Technische Universität Darmstadt, Germany

12.1   INTRODUCTION

The operating system (OS) constitutes a key building block in virtually all computer-based systems. Consequently, the ability of a computing system to provide the desired services to its users depends on the ability of the OS to correctly support the applications running on the computing system, even in the presence of operational perturbations. The degree to which an OS can handle the perturbations and provide sustained correct operations is termed as the "OS robustness" [1,2]. Such perturbations include malfunctioning hardware, software bugs, invalid inputs from external components, and application-level stress/loading. OSs are typically highly complex functional entities with countless environment interaction scenarios. This limits the use of static analytical approaches, hence, typically experimental evaluations of OS robustness form the preferred approach.

This chapter specifically deals with experimental methods for the evaluation of OS robustness. It covers the aspects of target system definition, choice of evaluation strategy, metrics to use, and interpretation of the results. Throughout the chapter, examples are provided on how different aspects of OS robustness evaluation have been treated in the literature. Emphasis is also given to a representative OS case study, which outlines some important aspects of robustness evaluation.

The robustness of a system relates to its behavior when subjected to invalid inputs and/or exposure to stressful situations, such as low-resource situations, high-volume invocations, and so on. The thrust of this chapter is primarily on robustness to invalid inputs. Hence, the focus is on the interactions among system

[1]   This research has been supported, in part, by Microsoft Research, EU FP6 NoE ReSIST, EU FP6 IP DECOS and DFG TUD GK MM.

components to establish how they behave when other components fail. Consequently, a key aspect is the interface between components, where errors manifest and propagate [3]. Generally faults can be either related to data or to control flow. With focus on interfaces, the focus of this chapter is primarily on data value faults.

Typically, methods for evaluating robustness do not consider functional correctness as the key objective and such issues will consequently not be covered in this chapter in any depth. This is instead the area of software testing. There are good introductory textbooks on the topic of software testing [4–7]. Similarly, formal correctness techniques, such as static analysis [8] and model checking [9], are also beyond the scope of this chapter. Operational profiling of OS behavior based on field data, such as in [10–14], is taken as the general basis behind OS operations and the reader is encouraged to use that as supplemental background.

This chapter covers robustness evaluation via the use of experimental and quantifiable techniques, focusing on invalid inputs and unexpected behavior in the environment. As in any experimental process, the robustness evaluation typically follows a series of progressive steps which will also constitute the organization of this chapter. The chapter sections will detail the evaluation steps as follows:

✦ Section 12.2, Evaluation Goals. Prior to initiating robustness evaluation, the goals of the study must be articulated clearly. There can be many reasons for the study to be carried out, such as part of acceptance tests in complementing functional testing or benchmarking. The goal of the study can contain guidelines for how the evaluation is to be performed by specifying the system under study, interfaces targeted, error model considered, or metrics used. The goals are specified without considering the details of the target system to the extent possible.

✦ Section 12.3, Target System. The target of the evaluation needs to be precisely defined, as supported by the goals set up previously. This step establishes the boundaries of the targeted system by specifying the individual components of the system with their respective input/output interfaces. This step is important as it tells an evaluator where and how the system under study interacts with its environment. Consequently, it guides the process of selecting the invalid inputs and/or stressful conditions the system is to be subjected to (i.e., the chosen error model). Furthermore, the level of access to the system is defined, such as access to source code, compilers, debuggers, and other tools.

As OSs are large software components, one cannot typically consider all its interfaces at one time. A selection of the targeted interfaces is an integral part of defining the system boundary. Usually, the system boundary is tied to the goals set out for the evaluation. If the goals specify that a certain target (OS component and/or interface) is to be used, this step specifies how the system boundary is defined and precisely which interfaces are targeted. This step uses details of the target system for which the evaluation is to be performed.

✦ Section 12.4, Error Model and Workload Selection. The intent of this step is to select the representative error model to be used. Again, the goals set up can guide the selection of error model, for instance, by specifying the type of model (e.g., single event upsets in network packets or memory, misuse of pointers in APIs (application programming interfaces), resource exhaustion). This step specifies the error model at a level of detail, sufficient to allow for an implementation. When the goals do not specify any error model, this step also entails the selection of an appropriate error model.

The workload specifies what the system is doing at the time of the evaluation. It is typically defined as a set of applications and associated inputs. However, for networked systems, it could also include the network traffic experienced by the system. The workload can be purely synthetic one or based on real applications.

✦ Section 12.5, Robustness Metrics. The metrics used to evaluate robustness are guided by the goals set up in the first step. One also needs to define their implementation together with their specifications. This step is important as it entails exploring the implementation space. Some metrics may be hard, or even impossible to measure as planned due to lack of access, tools, skills, or time.

✦ Section 12.6, Presentation and Interpretation of Results. Depending on the goals, metrics, and audience, the level of detail and the type of presentation will differ. The case study presented in this section details the implementation of the approach and presents the results of the study. It shows how useful information pertaining to the robustness of a system can be deduced. Depending on the goals and the audience, different types of presentations of the results may be warranted. Most commonly, tables and charts are used.

Based on this organization, the chapter details each of these issues in a progressive manner.

12.1.1   Case Study

To tangibly exemplify the overall OS evaluation process, a case study of a real OS (Windows CE .Net) is presented. Windows CE .Net is an OS by Microsoft for the embedded market. It is used, for instance, in mobile phones, PDAs, ATMs, embedded controllers, set-top boxes, and so on. It supports multiple hardware architectures, like MIPS, ARM, SHx, and x86, and features many of the protocols and APIs of the Windows family. This includes networking, USB, PCMCIA, and many Microsoft-specific technologies, such as .Net, COM, and ActiveSync. The experiments reported in the case study are implemented for Windows CE .Net 4.2 running on a reference board using the Intel XScale processor architecture.

The concluding part of each section is dedicated to showing how the process is applied to the targeted OS in the case study. The last section of this chapter presents the results of the study and interprets them in the context of error propagation. The case study is based on the work reported in Johansson and Suri [15].

12.2   EVALUATION GOALS

Clearly articulating the goals for an evaluation greatly simplifies the overall evaluation steps. The goals of a study are typically set by the person or company ordering the study. When a study is conducted as a part of a larger project, its goals may be guided by the goals of the project as well. One can distinguish two main classes of goals: *comparative* and *quantitative*.

Comparative goals aim to set up a basis for comparing systems (or components). Important aspects include specifying system boundaries such that the comparison can be made across several systems. In Gu et al. [16], the robustness of the Linux kernel was investigated on two different hardware platforms. Another level for comparison is to specify a certain interface as the target interface, such as POSIX, C-libraries, or Windows device drivers [17–21]. This type of specification limits the number of target systems possible to only those supporting the specified interface.

One special case of comparative approaches is benchmarking. For benchmarks, fairness and repeatability are key drivers. Several robustness benchmarks have been proposed in the literature. Early benchmarks include the crashme and CMU crashme benchmarks for UNIX systems, where random data are used to try to crash a system [22,23]. Later efforts include the Ballista project for benchmarking OSs implementing the POSIX interface [20, 24] and the DBench project, a European Union project on dependability benchmarking [25]. Other examples of OS benchmarks are presented in Siewiorek et al. [21], Durães and Madeira [26], Kalakech et al. [27], and Kanoun et al. [28].

The second class of goals are quantitative in nature, that is, the aim is to quantify a specific attribute of robustness for the system at hand, for instance, failure modes and error propagation [29–34] or error detection capabilities [35]. Other studies focus on robustness in terms of security vulnerabilities [36–38]. Another goal could be to enhance the robustness of an existing system using robustness wrappers. This is especially useful in the case of Commercial-Off-The-Self (COTS) components, where source code may not be available or changes may be prohibited due to lack of resources, legal constraints, and so on [3, 19, 30, 39].

12.2.1   Case Study

The goals of a study can also be both comparative and quantitative, as is the case for our case study of Windows CE .Net. In OSs, device drivers have been identified as a prominent source of failures [10, 11, 40]. Thus, the goal is to quantitatively estimate error propagation in an OS for errors in device drivers, that is, estimate the degree to which errors that arise in device drivers can spread (propagate) to other parts of the system and cause a failure there. This goal drives all of the subsequent steps of the process by specifying the interface of the system (device drivers), error model (errors in device drivers), and metrics (error propagation). At the same time, we are interested in a comparison across device drivers to be able to rank them in terms of their participation in error propagation. A related goal is to allow a system designer to be able to choose between competing device drivers or to guide driver robustness enhancement by error propagation analysis. As source code access may not always be accessible to third-party device drivers, the evaluation process should not depend on code availability, neither for the drivers nor for the OS itself.

12.3   TARGET SYSTEM

The target system is the entity under test. As robustness relates to input and environmental stresses, the target system definition is a key issue. Typically, a layered model of a system is used to indicate the different entities in the system. The OS is split into a suitably large number of components, as in Figure 12.1, depending on the goals of the study. A model similar to the one in Figure 12.1 allows for defining the input/output interfaces in the system and to isolate the target system under test.

The model chosen should be general enough to make the approach applicable to more than a specific target. This becomes even more important when the goal is to benchmark a system, as the benchmark is used to compare multiple systems. In Koopman and DeVale [20], the POSIX interface (an API to OS services) is used as a benchmark target (i.e., the components "below" this level in the system are considered to be the target system). Any system supporting this API can then potentially be benchmarked.

Often the OS is split into components, allowing characterization of intercomponent interaction. Arlat et al. [30] considers microkernel-based systems, where

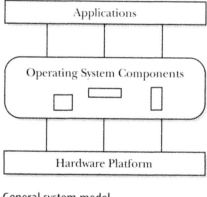

FIGURE   General system model.

12.1

interactions between the different functional components comprising the kernel are studied. Gu et al. [16, 41] study the Linux OS, dividing it into functional subsystems, allowing characterization of error propagation across subsystems.

12.3.1   Case Study

The system used in this case study consists of the OS software and hardware components depicted in Figure 12.2. The goal is comparing device drivers and system services on their effect on OS robustness. The *target system* is the OS. The interfaces to the system under test thus become the software interfaces between the OS and the drivers and the interface between applications and the OS, as depicted in Figure 12.2. The first step (evaluation goals), has already pointed out device drivers as being separate from the rest of the OS, and thus Figure 12.2 highlights this key interface.

Drivers handle the interaction between the OS and the hardware. They are responsible for implementing the interface that the OS expects and are typically implemented by the hardware vendors. We do not consider direct interaction by the OS (or applications for that matter) with the hardware. This type of interaction is indeed possible in some OSs, but we focus on the more common model using device drivers.

The drivers in the system are labeled D_1, D_2,..., D_N in Figure 12.2. A driver exports services (service $ds_{x,y}$ is the yth service of driver D_x) that the OS uses to interact with the driver. For implementing its functionality, a driver may use other services provided by the OS ($os_{x,y}$), for instance, system calls. The two types of service interactions are considered individually in the case study.

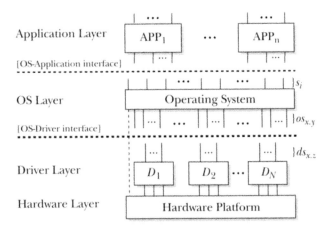

FIGURE

12.2

The target system model in our case study. From Johansson and Suri [15].

The OS layer includes shared libraries present in the system. This corresponds to a programmer's view of the system, that is, the libraries are present in the system to provide services for applications (and drivers). The OS layer is part of two important interfaces: the OS-Application and OS-Driver interfaces. The OS-Application interface (also known as API) provides services s_1, s_2,..., s_s to be used by applications. The OS-Driver interface contains the services the OS provides for drivers to use. For a specific driver D_x, the OS services it uses are labeled $os_{x.1}$, $os_{x.2}$,..., $os_{x.K}$. Note that it is possible for the OS to provide the same service for applications as well as for drivers.

The applications executing in the system provide services to users by the use of application code and services provided by the OS. Since different OS services may have different failure characteristics, the set of used services influences the behavior of the application when faults are present in the system. For the robustness evaluation presented in this chapter, the workload is defined as a set of applications and Section 12.4 discusses the choice of workload in more detail.

12.4   ERROR MODEL AND WORKLOAD SELECTION

A robust system functions correctly in the presence of external perturbations and stresses. As such perturbations and stressful situations are typically infrequent during normal operations of a system, special techniques have been developed to speed up the process of testing. Fault injection is the process of inserting errors from a specified error model into a system while observing the behavior of the system. By carefully selecting which errors to insert, where and when, the outcome of the evaluation reveals how the system behaves in the presence of real perturbations. In this chapter, we focus solely on error models for OS robustness evaluations. Good introductory texts on fault injection in general can be found in Arlat et al. [42], Carreira et al. [43], and Hsueh et al. [44].

The types of perturbations considered are specified in the error model.[2] There are many models proposed and used in the literature, and the choice of model to use for a specific study is influenced by multiple factors, such as the goals of the study, the system's operational environment, and cost in terms of implementation time and execution time.

Each error model can be classified along three dimensions: type, location, and timing. The following sections discuss each of these dimensions in turn and give examples of how they have been applied in reported robustness studies.

12.4.1   Error Type

The error type relates to the implementation of the error model, such as flipping bits in CPU registers, corrupting system call parameters, or providing random input to system utilities. It is important to distinguish the implementation from the origin of the hypothesized error model, which could be different. Jarboui et al. [45] defines dr as the distance between the injected error and the reference fault. For instance, if the hypothesized fault is a bit-flip in a CPU register due to radiation and the injected error changes register contents directly, dr is 0. When errors are injected as corrupted parameters to kernel functions, we get $dr > 0$ instead. Jarboui et al. note that it is important to ensure that the error propagation paths from the two levels converge before the level where errors/failures are observed. The relation between faults and errors at different levels is still an open issue for many fault/error models. Most robustness studies do not aim at finding reliability estimates, and can, therefore, do without an explicit relationship between faults and errors.

One of the first systematic and comparative studies of OS robustness was carried out by Miller et al. [22], where a series of utility programs where tested on several commercial UNIX implementations. The target system was not the OS kernel, but rather a set of utility programs present in most UNIX systems, allowing

---

[2] Even though we use the term *error model*, a perturbation may not always be considered strictly "erroneous."

for OS level comparisons. The error model supplied random strings as input to the utility programs, which should not crash or hang the system, but provide error messages in a robust manner. Miller et al. found a surprising number of robustness deficiencies and significant differences between different systems. The experiments were later repeated with similar results [32, 46, 47]. This error model is called *Fuzz* and has since been applied by others [48–50].

Errors in hardware components commonly manifest themselves as erroneous bit values when reading memory/registers. This has given rise to a plethora of fault injection techniques for such errors [51–53]. To increase control and flexibility, new software-implemented fault injection techniques have been proposed. More recently, the bit-flip model has been proposed to be also used for more general robustness evaluations [16, 30, 41, 54]. Its main advantage is at the same time its biggest disadvantage, namely, its simplicity. A bit is selected as a target, and its value is changed (flipped) and a system is allowed to continue executing. This typically leads to a large number of injection cases needed, which can negatively influence the execution time required for injection. Bit-flips have been applied at several levels in a system, such as memory, CPU registers, and function call parameters.

For software faults (bugs), techniques have been developed to inject typical programmer errors by using code mutations, without access to the actual source code [18, 26].

The most commonly used error model for robustness testing of OSs is corruption of parameters to a system or library calls. A good reason for the popularity of this error model is that it closely relates to the definition of robustness (invalid inputs) and the fact that it facilitates comparative studies using standard interfaces. As an example, the Ballista project [17, 20, 24] corrupts the parameters of function calls made to standard APIs to compare the robustness of OSs. The type of corruption employed is based on the data type of the selected parameter. For each parameter type, a set of error cases are defined that could represent both erroneous values, correct values, and values whose correctness is not known. The approach is attractive as it scales well. The number of data types used, even in very large APIs, is relatively low, thus, adding new functions becomes a simple and fast process. Similar techniques have also been applied in, for instance, [15, 19, 27, 29, 45, 55, 56]. Ghosh et al. [57, 58] use a similar approach, but with the intent to simulate erroneous behavior by the OS by replacing return values with error codes and exceptions.

Some studies combine several error types, for instance, in Kalakech et al. [27], the authors benchmark three versions of Windows (NT, 2000, and XP) by corrupting functions in the API, using both data type corruption and bit-flips.

The goals and objectives of the study typically guide the decision on which error model to use. When considering effects of software bugs in application programs, injecting errors in APIs becomes relevant, as shown by several researchers including Fetzer and Xiao [19] and Koopman and DeVale [20]. When evaluating a system for use in space, bit-flips in hardware become relevant [54].

12.4.2   Error Location

The location of an error is related to the type of error, but refers to the location where the error is injected and not where the fault appears. Injecting errors at the same location where the faults appears ($dr = 0$) may not be possible in some circumstances due to lack of access (to source code, for instance) or for scalability reasons (each bit in RAM). Therefore, a common technique is to inject higher-level errors that represent several kinds of lower-level faults. Following the general system model in Figure 12.1, the location of the injection must be outside the targeted component, and as discussed in the previous section, it should be close to the hypothesized fault.

12.4.3   Error Timing

The timing dimension can be further split into two subdimensions: *time of injection* and *duration*. The time of injection is often defined relative to some event in the system or when the system is in a certain state. Examples include injecting errors in the system scheduler after a new process has been created or in the file handling utilities when certain file properties have changed. It can also be defined as a specified time from system startup or when some code location is reached [44]. The duration of the error may be defined in terms of physical time (e.g., 2 ms) or in terms of events (e.g., three times). Errors may also be permanent in nature (i.e., never disappearing after appearing).

12.4.4   Workload Selection

Another key attribute of the selected target system is the system workload, that is, what the system is executing during the test. The workload is external to the system under test and is used to stimulate the system. It is important to differentiate between the workload and the error model (sometimes referred to as fault load). The workload represents the "normal" load on the system, whereas the abnormal load is part of the error model. Sometimes the difference between workload and fault load is fuzzy, for instance, when testing a client server–based system where the work/fault load may be defined as the requests sent to the server.

The workload can be implicitly defined together with the error model, as is the case in Ballista [20], where the functions of system APIs are tested individually.

Ideally, the starting point for the workload for robustness testing is the anticipated workload of the system in its operational environment. If such knowledge is not available, the best option is to use a synthetic workload mimicking typical system load, or exercising system resources in a proscribed manner. When the goal is comparative evaluation, it is common to use benchmark applications which are either part of standard benchmarking suites or exercise common OS features.

12.4.5   Case Study

This section discusses the choice of error model and workload for the Windows CE case study.

Error Model

The goals of the case study do not completely specify the type of errors, only that they occur in device drivers. We have chosen a specific error model, namely transient data level errors, which allow us to inject errors directly at the OS-Driver interface without requiring source code access. Errors at the interface level represent multiple potential fault locations within the driver. Transient data level errors are the result of implementation defects in the driver or value faults related to malfunctioning hardware. The following subsections discuss the choice of error model along the three dimensions: error type, location, and timing.

Error type.   For this study, data-level errors were chosen, based on the data type of each parameter. C-types are used as the OS-Driver interface for this target, which is defined using the C language. Data errors are of high interest as they are hard to detect with general error detection techniques (like tracking of memory accesses) and may still lead to severe failures [40]. They also allow for flexible insertion using a black-box view of the system.

Table 12.1 presents an overview of the 27 C-types for which the error model was implemented. The table shows the basic and user defined data types required to perform the case study. For each type, multiple data values are chosen for injection. Values are chosen to cover both boundary values and values for different generic equivalence classes as well as offset values. Table 12.2 illustrates this for the type int. Note that underflow and overflow can occur for cases 1 and 2.

Data Type	C-Type	Number of Cases
	int	7
	unsigned int	5
	Long	7
Integers	unsigned long	5
	Short	7
	unsigned short	5
	LARGE_INTEGER	7
Void	* void	3
	Char	7
Characters	unsigned char	5
	wchar_t	5
Boolean	bool	1
Enums	multiple cases	# identifiers
Structs	multiple cases	1

TABLE

12.1

Error types used in the case study.

Error location. As already mentioned, the focus is on data errors at the OS-Driver interface. By introducing errors at the parameters used in this interface, errors occurring within the driver in question are simulated. An example of an OS service in this interface is:

```
LONG RegQueryValueEx(
HKEY                hKey,
LPCWSTR             lpValueName,
LPDWORD             lpReserved,
LPDWORD             lpType,
LPBYTE              lpData,
LPDWORD             lpcbData
);
```

Using the available documentation the parameters for each service are identified. Each output parameter of a driver service $ds_{x.y}$ and each input parameter for the OS-Driver services $os_{x.q}$ are targeted for injection. Errors are injected after calls to/from a driver by modifying the value of a parameter and then continuing the execution with the corrupted value.

Error timing. By injecting each error only once a transient error behavior is simulated. As permanent errors are expected to have been found in nominal

Case Number	New Value
1	(Original value) − 1
2	(Original value) + 1
3	1
4	0
5	−1
6	INT_MIN
7	INT_MAX

TABLE
12.2

Error cases for type int.

testing of the system these are not considered here. Transient errors represent rare cases which are not easily detectable with normal testing techniques.

Errors are injected the first time a service is called, i.e., using a "first occurrence" approach. Previous studies for OS's have indicated that first occurrence injection gives similar results as other injection strategies [62].

Workload

In the case study, no specific application context is specified. Therefore, a general synthetic benchmark is used, implemented as a set of test applications. The purpose of the test applications is to exercise the OS services. The use of custom test applications simplifies the task of exercising specific parts of the OS and detection of propagating errors.

A set of test applications are used, each stimulating the OS in different ways. Three applications are dedicated to test (1) the memory management subsystem, (2) thread management and synchronization primitives, and (3) file system operations. The fourth application type is dedicated to the specific driver being tested. Driver-specific applications are echo applications, exchanging data with a host server. All applications are manually equipped with assertions, checking calls to the OS for any irregularities. Assertions are based on the imported OS services by an application. These are matched to calls made in the application using the service specifications.

12.5   ROBUSTNESS METRICS

In order to quantify the robustness of a target system, metrics of robustness are needed. The most commonly used metrics are failure modes and error propagation. A robust system is one where fewer perturbations result in severe failures and where error propagation is minimized.

In failure mode analysis, the possible outcomes of injections are postulated beforehand (they may be iteratively refined, of course) as a set of failure modes or classes [17, 30, 41, 53]. The modes are defined to be disjoint, such that the outcome of an experiment can be unambiguously determined to be a member of a specific class. The failure classes can typically be listed in order of severity, but severity is also a subjective viewpoint and there is no universal severity scale.

As a representative example, the CRASH severity scale presented in Koopman et al. [59] is shown in Table 12.3. The API of the OS is tested by creating a specific task that calls the targeted function and the outcome is classified according to the CRASH scale.

The concept of error propagation studies how errors percolate through a system and affect components other than the source component of the fault [14, 60]. In order to measure error propagation, the target system must be equipped with enough observation points such that the propagation across modules can be observed.

Tsai et al. [61] present a benchmark for fault-tolerant systems using the number of catastrophic incidents and performance degradation as the key metrics. Performance degradation is an important aspect for fault-tolerant systems as it allows us to compare the effectiveness of the tolerance techniques. Kalakech et al. [27], the time to perform system calls and the time required for a restart are used as measures of performance degradation. Similar measures are used together with the file system benchmark PostMark™ in Kanoun et al. [28].

Failure Mode	Description
Catastrophic	System crash
Restart	The task is hung and requires restart
Abort	The task terminates abnormally
Silent	No error report is generated by the OS, even though the operation tested cannot be performed and should generate an error
Hindering	Incorrect error returned

TABLE 12.3   The CRASH scale.
Source: Koopman et al. [59].

12.5.1 Case Study

The goal of the case study is to assess error propagation paths in the system and to compare device drivers in terms of error propagation potential. For this purpose, three metrics are defined as follows [15]:

* Measure for degree of error porosity of an OS service: **service error permeability**.
* Measure for error exposure of an OS service: **OS service error exposure**.
* Measure of driver error corelation with service set: **driver error diffusion**.

It is important to note that the presented metrics implicitly use a uniform distribution of errors. This is a consequence of the fact that no operational profile exists describing how the system is used in a real scenario.

Service Error Permeability

Two metrics for error permeability are defined: one for a driver's export of services (PDS) and one for its import of OS services (POS), where a driver D_x has a set of export services $(ds_{x.1}, \ldots, ds_{x.N})$ and import services $(os_{x.1}, \ldots, os_{x.M})$. The service error permeabilities for exports $(PDS^i_{x.y})$ and imports $(POS^i_{x.z})$ define the error propagation relation between one driver service and one OS service. The service error permeability is the conditional probability that an error in a specific driver service $(ds_{x.y})$ or in the use of OS-Driver service $(os_{x.z})$ will propagate to a specific OS service (s_i). For an OS service s_i and a driver D_x:

$$PDS^i_{x.y} = Pr\left(error\ in\ s_i\ |error\ in\ ds_{x.y}\right)$$

$$POS^i_{x.z} = Pr(error\ in\ s_i\ |error\ in\ use\ of\ os_{x.z})$$

The service error permeability gives an estimate of the permeability for a particular OS service, that is, how *easily* does the service let errors in the driver propagate to applications. A higher permeability naturally means that either (1) an add-on software component that "wraps" the driver is needed to protect the OS from driver errors, or (2) application developers making use of the affected services need to ensure proper use, including error handling. Note that $POS^i_{x.z}$ allows comparing the same OS service used by different drivers. Thus, the impact of the context induced by different drivers can be studied.

OS Service Error Exposure

To get information on which OS services are more likely exposed to propagating errors, the full set of drivers needs to be considered. Service error permeability (E^i) is used to compose the OS service error exposure for an OS service s_i:

$$E^i = \sum_{D_x} \sum_{os_{x,j}} POS^i_{x,j} + \sum_{D_x} \sum_{ds_{x,j}} PDS^i_{x,j}$$

The OS service error exposure E^i accounts for all drivers and provides a relative ordering across OS services based on their susceptibility to propagating errors. Thus, its use is mainly to identify weaknesses in services on the OS-Application level. Note that the OS service error exposure implies aggregating all imported and exported service error permeabilities.

Driver Error Diffusion

Driver error diffusion locates drivers that are more likely to spread errors when faulty, by estimating one particular driver's influence on multiple services. Driver error diffusion is a measure of a driver's impact on OS services (at the OS-Application interface). The more services and the higher the diffusion impact (permeability) a driver has, the higher the diffusion value. For a driver D_x and a given set of OS services, the driver error diffusion D^x is:

$$D^x = \sum_{s_i} \sum_{os_{x,j}} POS^i_{x,j} + \sum_{s_i} \sum_{ds_{x,j}} PDS^i_{x,j}$$

By aggregating service error permeabilitiy values on a driver basis, driver error diffusion ranks drivers based on their potential for spreading errors in the system. This guides the system designer on where addition of protection wrappers will be most effective. Note that drivers are not tested per se, driver error diffusion only identifies drivers that *may* corrupt the system by spreading errors. Also, the emphasis of the measure is *not* for absolute values, but to obtain a relative rankings.

Once a ranking across drivers exists, the driver(s) with the highest driver error diffusion value should be the first target(s) for robustness-enhancing activities, such as the addition of protection wrappers. Details on specific propagation paths can then be used to guide composition and placement of wrappers.

Error Exposure versus Error Impact

Error propagation profiling is used to expose prominent error propagation paths as well as to identify paths having a severe impact on system services. The measures previously described aid in identifying the common error propagation paths. However, the impact can range from no effect at all to the whole system being rendered unusable. Thus, it is important to not only identify *if a failure occurred*, but also to identify what *type of failure it was and how severe its consequences were*. Failure mode analysis is an approach that accomplishes this. A set of failure modes are defined and the outcome of each experiment is classified as belonging to one of them. The classes used in this study are similar to the classes established in DeVale and Koopman [17], Arlat et al. [30], and Gu et al. [41]:

+ *Class NF.* When no visible effect can be seen as an outcome of an experiment, the *no failure* class is used. This indicates that the error was either not activated or was masked by the OS.

+ *Class 1.* Class 1 is when the error propagated but still satisfied the OS service specification as defined in the documentation. Examples of Class 1 outcomes are when an error code or exception is returned that is a member of the set of allowed codes for this call, or if a data value was corrupted and propagated to the service but did not violate the specification.

+ *Class 2.* Class 2 is when the error propagated and violated a service specification. For example, returning an unspecified error code or if a call directly causes an application to hang or crash but other applications in the system remain unharmed result in this category.

+ *Class 3.* Class 3 is when the OS hung or crashed due to the error. If the OS hangs or crashes, no progress is possible. For a crashed OS, this state must be detected by an outside monitor unless it is automatically detected internally and the machine is rebooted.

Using the severity scale, further analysis of the results can be performed. Starting with the most severe class of failures (Class 3), one can study the exposure to these errors separately and then progressively consider the remaining classes.

To detect Class 1 and Class 2 failures, each of the workload applications have been equipped with assertions. The system is first executed without performing any injections to establish a baseline for expected behavior, a so called *golden run*. The application assertions detect if the OS returns from a system call in an unexpected way.

12.6   PRESENTATION AND INTERPRETATION OF RESULTS

This section presents the results of the case study and discusses some of the conclusions that can be drawn from the data. The metrics defined in Section 12.5 are used.

Table 12.4 shows an overview of the drivers used for this case study. The number of services provided by the two drivers is similar (60 and 54), translating into a similar number of injections performed. The number of injections depends on the number of services, the number of parameters targeted, and the injection cases defined for each type. The drivers differ in the number of activated injections (i.e., injected errors actually executed), where the network driver has a higher activation rate (55% compared to 43%). The activation rate is a measure of how many experiments actually execute the error. The time required for executing the experiment depends on the number of experiments performed.

Table 12.5 details the results of the experiments for the serial port driver cerfio_serial.dll with respect to the OS services used by the driver. Only services resulting in failures are shown together with the number of error propagation observations, not their location. Table 12.6 shows the results for the Ethernet driver 91C111.dll, which shows more services leading to failure than cerfio_serial.dll. The rows in the tables are ordered according to the severity of the failures. For cerfio_serial.dll, it can be seen that no service leads to a crash of the system. However, for 91C111.dll FreeLibrary and LoadLibrary are both vulnerable services. 91C111.dll does not have as many cumulative Class 2 failures as cerfio_serial.dll, indicating that addition of a few robustness enhancing wrappers would remove all severe error propagation paths (Class 2 and Class 3 failures).

From the OS service point of view, Tables 12.7 and 12.8 show the used OS services, together with the OS service error exposure values. Alongside the number of failures for Class 1, the number of No Failure (NF) observations is also

| Driver | Number of Services | | Test Cases | Activated Cases |
	Imported	Exported		
Serial	50	10	411	43%
Ethernet	42	12	414	55%

TABLE   Overview of the targeted drivers.

12.4

OS Service	Tests	Failure Class			
		NF	1	2	3
CreateThread	13	6	4	3	0
CreateEventW	6	4	0	2	0
InterruptInitialize	14	3	10	1	0
memcpy	11	7	3	1	0
Sleep	5	4	0	1	0
LeaveCriticalSection	1	0	0	1	0
LocalAlloc	9	4	5	0	0
EnterCriticalSection	1	0	1	0	0
InitializeCriticalSection	1	0	1	0	0
memset	15	14	1	0	0
Cumulative	76	42	25	9	0

TABLE 12.5   Serial driver service errors for cerfio_serial.dll.

OS Service	Tests	Failure Class			
		NF	1	2	3
FreeLibrary	3	1	0	0	2
LoadLibraryW	3	2	0	0	1
NdisAllocateMemory	20	19	0	1	0
VirtualCopy	16	2	14	0	0
KernelIoControl	18	5	13	0	0
VirtualAlloc	18	7	11	0	0
memset	15	6	9	0	0
NdisMSetAttributesEx	16	10	6	0	0
NdisMSetAttributesEx	16	10	6	0	0
NdisMRegisterInterrupt	17	11	6	0	0
RegOpenKeyExW	17	12	5	0	0
NdisOpenConfiguration	3	0	3	0	0
memcpy	11	8	3	0	0
CreateMutexW	5	3	2	0	0
NKDbgPrintfW	3	2	1	0	0
GetProcAddressoftware	6	5	1	0	0
Cumulative	187	103	80	1	3

TABLE 12.6   Ethernet driver service errors for 91C111.dll.

shown. The Class 2 and Class 3 failures affect all used OS service listed collectively. This effect is specific to the experiments conducted and does not translate into a general statement of OS behavior. For Class 2 failures, only the driver-specific test application was affected. Consequently, the OS service error exposures are calculated using only Class 1 failures. From these tables, one can find the services that are more exposed to propagating errors. For some services, the number of propagated errors is zero, indicating that the function was not affected by any of the injected errors (Class 1). On top of the tested OS services (Table 12.7), the correctness assertions are also included, which detect whether the correct information was received from the host computer. In this case, Correctness 1 failed 27 times, indicating that the first round of testing done in the application failed, where as the second round (Correctness 2) did not. This is not surprising given that each error is injected only once.

Tables 12.7 and 12.8 show that the results of the experiments "cluster" (i.e., an error in one service implies an error in another). This indicates dependencies across services, as well as nondependencies (or at least indication of weaker dependency). Some of these dependencies are expected, for instance that CreateFile affects ReadFile and WriteFile (Table 12.7). Some nondependencies are more unexpected, for instance that SetCommState is not affected by CreateFile. For both drivers, only one cluster appears, with 27 cases for seven services for the serial driver cerfio_serial.dll and 85 cases for three services for the Ethernet driver 91C111.dll.

OS Service	Failure Class				
	NF	1	2	3	$\hat{E}^j$
Correctness 1	384	27	9	0	0.666
CreateFile	384	27	9	0	0.666
GetCommState	384	27	9	0	0.666
GetCommTimeouts	384	27	9	0	0.666
SetCommTimeouts	384	27	9	0	0.666
ReadFile	384	27	9	0	0.666
WriteFile	384	27	9	0	0.666
CloseHandle	411	0	9	0	0.0
Correctness 2	411	0	9	0	0.0
SetCommState	411	0	9	0	0.0
strlen	411	0	9	0	0.0

TABLE   OS service error exposure for cerfio_serial.dll.

12.7

OS Service	Failure Class				$\hat{E^j}$
	NF	1	2	3	
connect	274	85	1	3	0.205
closesocket	274	85	1	3	0.205
shutdown	274	85	1	3	0.0
getaddrinfo	414	0	1	3	0.0
getnameinfo	414	0	1	3	0.0
getpeername	414	0	1	3	0.0
memset	414	0	1	3	0.0
select	414	0	1	3	0.0
sendto	414	0	1	3	0.0
socket	414	0	1	3	0.0
strcpy	414	0	1	3	0.0
WSACleanup	414	0	1	3	0.0
WSAStartup	414	0	1	3	0.0

TABLE 12.8   OS service error exposure for 91C111.dll.

Driver	Failure Class Distribution			Total
	D_{C1}^k	D_{C2}^k	D_{C3}^k	
cerfio_serial.dll	0.460	0.022	0.0	0.482
91C111.dll	0.616	0.002	0.007	0.625

TABLE 12.9   Results of injection experiments.

For this case study, no OS service experienced failure as a result of propagating errors from more than one. This suggests that there is little correlation between failures in the OS services tested for both drivers, indicating the OS being able to limit error propagation in many cases.

Finally, Table 12.9 shows the resulting driver error diffusion values. The failure classes are presented separately as they have different failure impacts, with a Class 3 failure having higher impact than a Class 2, and so on. Table 12.9 shows that when considering error impact the network driver has more severe errors, whereas the serial driver has more Class 2 failures. Thus, these two classes of failures should be the first focus of the robustness enhancing activities. The network driver has overall more failures, but mainly of lesser impact.

12.7   CONCLUSION

This chapter has presented a systematic process for robustness evaluation of operating systems. Robustness is the ability of a system to withstand external perturbations arising in its environment. The key steps involved in evaluating the robustness of an OS are:

- ✦ Definition objectives and goals.
- ✦ Definition system model and the target of a study.
- ✦ Definition of fault models and workload.
- ✦ Definition of the robustness metrics.

A case study shows how each of the steps can be implemented for a real OS, and the last section shows that the results from such a study are very useful for comparing system components, in this case, device drivers.

References

[1] IEEE, "IEEE Standard Glossary of Software Engineering Terminology," IEEE Standard 610.12-1990, 1990.

[2] P. A. Laplante, *Dictionary of Computer Science Engineering and Technology* (Boca Raton, FL: CRC Press, 2001).

[3] J. Voas, "Building Software Recovery Assertions from a Fault Injection-Based Propagation Analysis," *Proceedings of the International Computer Software & Applications Conference*, Washington D.C., 1997, pp. 505–570.

[4] B. Beizer, *Black-Box Testing* (New York: John Wiley & Sons, 1995).

[5] C. Kaner, J. Falk, and H. Q. Nguyen, *Testing Computer Software* (New York: John Wiley & Sons, 1999).

[6] G. J. Myers, *The Art of Software Testing*, 2nd ed. (New York: John Wiley & Sons, 2004).

[7] J. A. Whittaker, *How to Break Software* (Boston: Addison-Wesley, 2003).

[8] T. Ball and S. Rajamani, "The SLAM Project: Debugging System Software via Static Analysis," *Proceedings of Principles of Programming Languages*, Portland, OR, 2002, pp. 1–3.

[9] S. Kumar and K. Li, "Using Model Checking to Debug Device Firmware," *Proceedings of Symposium On Operating Systems Design and Implementation*, Boston, 2002, pp. 61–74.

[10] A. Chou, J. Yang, B. Chelf, S. Hallem, and D. Engler, "An Empirical Study of Operating System Errors," *Proceedings of Symposium on Operating System Principles*, Banff, 2001, pp. 73–88.

[11] A. Ganapathi, V. Ganapathi, and D. Patterson, "Windows XP Kernel Crash Analysis," *Proceedings of Large Installation System Administration Conference*, Washington D.C., 2006.

[12] J. Gray, "Why Do Computers Stop and What Can We Do About It," Tandem Technical Report 85.7, 1985.

[13] R. Iyer and P. Velardi, "Hardware-Related Software Errors: Measurement and Analysis," *IEEE Transactions on Software Engineering* SE-11, No. 2 (Feb. 1985): 223–231.

[14] I. Lee and R. K. Iyer, "Faults, Symptoms, and Software Fault Tolerance in the Tandem GUARDIAN90 Operating System," *Proceedings of the International Symposium on Fault-Tolerant Computing*, Toulouse, France, 1993, pp. 20–29.

[15] A. Johansson and N. Suri, "Error Propagation in Operating Systems," *Proceedings of the International Conference on Dependable Systems and Networks*, Yokohama, Japan, 2005, pp. 86–95.

[16] W. Gu, Z. Kalbarczyk, and R. K. Iyer, "Error Sensitivity of the Linux Kernel Executing on PowerPC G4 and Pentium 4 Processors," *Proceedings of the International Conference on Dependable Systems and Networks*, Florence, Italy, 2004, pp. 887–896.

[17] J. DeVale and P. Koopman, "Performance Evaluation of Exception Handling in I/O Libraries," *Proceedings of the International Conference on Dependable Systems and Networks*, Göteborg, Sweden, 2001, pp. 519–524.

[18] J. Durães and H. Madeira, "Multidimensional Characterization of the Impact of Faulty Drivers on the OS Behavior," *IEICE Transactions*, E86-D(12) (Dec. 2003): 2563–2570.

[19] C. Fetzer and Z. Xiao, "An Automated Approach to Increasing the Robustness of C Libraries," *Proceedings of the International Conference on Dependable Systems and Networks*, 2002, Bethesda, MD, pp. 155–164.

[20] P. Koopman and J. DeVale, "Comparing the Robustness of POSIX OSs," *Proceedings of the International Symposium on Fault-Tolerant Computing*, Madison, 1999, pp. 30–37.

[21] D. P. Siewiorek, J. J. Hudak, B.-H. Suh, and Z. Segal, "Development of a Benchmark to Measure System Robustness," *Proceedings of the International Symposium on Fault-Tolerant Computing*, Toulouse, France, 1993, pp. 88–97.

[22] B. P. Miller, L. Fredriksen, and B. So, "An Empirical Study of the Reliability of UNIX Utilities," *Communications of the ACM* 33, No. 12 (Nov. 1990): 32–43.

[23] A. Mukherjee and D. P. Siewiorek, "Measuring Software Dependability by Robustness Benchmarking," *IEEE Transaction on Software Engineering* 23, No. 6 (June 1997): 366–378.

[24] Ballista project, Carnegie Mellon University, at http://www.ballista.org.

[25] DBench, EC-IST Dependability Benchmarking Project, at http://www.dbench.org.

[26] J. Durães and H. Madeira, "Generic Faultloads Based on Software Faults for Dependability Benchmarking," *Proceedings of the International Conference on Dependable Systems and Networks*, Florence, Italy, 2004, pp. 261–270.

[27] A. Kalakech, K. Kanoun, Y. Crouzet, and J. Arlat, "Benchmarking the Dependability of Windows NT4, 2000 and XP," *Proceedings of the International Conference on Dependable Systems and Networks*, Florence, Italy, 2004, pp. 681–686.

[28] K. Kanoun, Y. Crouzet, A. Kalakech, A. E. Rugina, and P. Rumeau, "Benchmarking the Dependability of Windows and Linux using PostMark^{TM} Workloads," *Proceedings of the International Symposium on Software Reliability Engineering*, Chicago, IL, 2005, pp. 11–20.

[29] A. Albinet, J. Arlat, and J.-C. Fabre, "Characterization of the Impact of Faulty Drivers on the Robustness of the Linux Kernel," *Proceedings of the International Conference on Dependable Systems and Networks*, Florence, Italy, 2004, pp. 807–816.

[30] J. Arlat, J.-C. Fabre, M. Rodríguez, and F. Salles, "Dependability of COTS Microkernel-Based Systems," *IEEE Transactions on Computers* 51, No. 2 (Feb. 2002): 138–163.

[31] J.-C. Fabre, M. Rodriguez, J. Arlat, F. Salles and J.-M. Sizun, "Building Dependable COTS Microkernel-Based Systems Using Mafalda," *Proceedings of the* Pacific Rim International Symposium on Dependable Computing, Los Angeles, CA, 2000, pp. 85–92.

[32] B. P. Miller, D. Koski, C. P. Lee, V. Maganty, R. Murthy, A. Natarajan, and J. Steidl, "Fuzz Revisited: A Reexamination of the Reliability of UNIX Utilities and Services," Computer Sciences Technical Report #1268, University of Wisconsin-Madison, 1995.

[33] T. Mitchem, R. Lu, R. OäBrien and K. Larson, "Linux Kernel Loadable Wrappers," Proceedings of DARPA Information Survivability Conference, Vol. 2, Hilton Head, SC, 2000, pp. 296–307.

[34] B. Murphy and B. Levidow, "Windows 2000 Dependability," *Proceedings of the Workshop on Dependable Networks and OS*, New York, 2000, pp. D20–28.

[35] K. Whisnant, R. K. Iyer, P. Jones, R. Some, and D. Rennels, "An Experimental Evaluation of the REE SIFT Environment for Spaceborne Applications," *Proceedings of the International Conference on Dependable Systems and Networks*, Bethesda, MD, 2002, pp. 585–594.

[36] S. Chen, J. Xu, R. K. Iyer, and K. Whisnant, "Evaluating the Security Threat of Firewall Data Corruption Caused by Instruction Transient Errors," *Proceedings of the International Conference on Dependable Systems and Networks*, Bethesda, MD, 2002, pp. 495–504.

[37] W. Du and A. P. Mathur, "Testing for Software Vulnerability Using Environment Perturbation," *Proceedings of the International Conference on Dependable Systems and Networks*, New York, NY, pp. 603–612.

[38] J. Xu, S. Chen, Z. Kalbarczyk, and R. K. Iyer, "An Experimental Study of Security Vulnerabilities Caused by Errors," *Proceedings of the International Conference on Dependable Systems and Networks*, Göteborg, Sweden, 2001, pp. 421–432.

[39] J. Voas, "Certifying Off-the-Shelf Software Components," *IEEE Computer* 31, No. 6 (1998): 53–59.

[40] M. M. Swift, B. Bershad and H. Levy, "Improving the Reliability of Commodity OSs," *Proceedings of Symposium on Operating System Principles*, Bolton Landing, NY, 2003, pp. 207–222.

[41] W. Gu, Z. Kalbarczyk, R. Iyer and Z. Yang, "Characterization of Linux Kernel Behavior Under Errors," *Proceedings of the International Conference on Dependable Systems and Network*, San Francisco, CA, 2003, pp. 459–468.

[42] J. Arlat, A. Costes, Y. Crouzet, J.-C. Laprie, and D. Powell, "Fault Injection and Dependability Evaluation of Fault-Tolerant Systems," *IEEE Transactions on Computers* 42, No. 8 (Aug. 1993): 913–923.

[43] J. V. Carreira, D. Costa, and J. G. Silva, "Fault Injection Spot-Checks Computer System Dependability," *IEEE Spectrum* 36, No. 8 (Aug. 1999): 50–55.

[44] M.-C. Hsueh, T. K. Tsai, and R. K. Iyer, "Fault Injection Techniques and Tools," *IEEE Computer* 30, No. 4 (April 1997): 75–82.

[45] T. Jarboui, J. Arlat, Y. Crouzet, K. Kanoun, and T. Marteau, "Impact of Internal and External Software Faults on the Linux Kernel," *IEICE Transactions on Information and Systems* E86-D, No. 12 (Dec. 2003): 2571–2578.

[46] J. E. Forrester and B. P. Miller, "An Empirical Study of the Robustness of Windows NT Applications Using Random Testing," *USENIX Windows Systems Symposium*, Seattle, WA, 2000.

[47] B. P. Miller, G. Cooksey, and F. Moore, "An Empirical Study of the Robustness of MacOS Applications Using Random Testing," *International Workshop on Random Testing*, Portland, ME, 2006, pp. 46–54.

[48] A. K. Ghosh, M. Schmid, V. Shah, "Testing the Robustness of Windows NT Software," *Proceedings of the International Symposium on Software Reliability Engineering*, Paderborn, Germany, 1998, pp. 231–235.

[49] M. Howard and S. Lipner, *The Security Development Lifecycle* Redmond: Microsoft Press, 2006).

[50] P. Oehlert, "Violating Assumptions with Fuzzing," *IEEE Security & Privacy Magazine* 3, No. 2 (2005): 58–62.

[51] J. V. Carreira, H. Madeira, and J. G. Silva, "Xception: A Technique for the Experimental Evaluation of Dependability in Modern Computers," *IEEE Transactions on Software Engineering* 24, No. 2 (Feb. 1998): 125–136.

[52] G. Kanawati, N. A. Kanawati, and J. A. Abraham, "FERRARI: A Flexible Software-Based Fault and Error Injection System," *IEEE Transactions on Computers* 44, No. 2 (Feb. 1995): 248–260.

[53] M. Rodríguez, A. Albinet, and J. Arlet, "MAFALDA-RT: A Tool for Dependability Assessment of Real-Time Systems," *Proceedings of the International Conference on Dependable Systems and Network*, Bethesda, MD, 2002, pp. 267–272.

[54] H. Madeira, R. R. Some, F. Moreira, D. Costa, and D. Rennels, "Experimental Evaluation of a COTS System for Space Applications," *Proceedings of the International Conference on Dependable Systems and Network*, Bethesda, MD, 2002, pp. 325–330.

[55] C. P. Dingman, J. Marshall, and D. P. Siewiorek, "Measuring Robustness of a Fault-Tolerant Aerospace System," *Proceedings of the International Symposium on Fault-Tolerant Computing*, Pasadena, CA, 1995, pp. 522–527.

[56] T. Jarboui, J. Arlat, Y. Crouzet, K. Kanoun, and T. Marteau, "Analysis of the Effects of Real and Injected Software Faults," *Proceedings of the Pacific Rim International Symposium on Dependable Computing*, 2002, pp. 51–58.

[57] A. K. Ghosh, M. Schmid, and F. Hill, "Wrapping Windows NT Software for Robustness," *Proceedings of the International Symposium on Fault-Tolerant Computing*, Madison, WI, 1999, pp. 344–347.

[58] A. K. Ghosh, V. Shah, and M. Schmid, "An Approach to Testing COTS Software for Robustness to Operating System Exceptions and Errors," *Proceedings of the International Symposium on Software Reliability Engineering*, Boca Raton, FL, 1999, pp. 166–174.

[59] P. Koopman, J. Sung, C. Dingman, D. Siewiorek, and T. Marz, "Comparing Operating Systems Using Robustness Benchmarks," *Proceedings of the International Symposium on Reliable Distributed Systems*, Durham, NC, 1997, pp. 72–79.

[60] J. Voas, G. McGraw, and A. Gosh, "Gluing Together Software Components: How Good Is Your Glue?," *Proceedings of Pacific Northwest Software Quality Conference*, 1996.

[61] T. Tsai, R. K. Iyer, and D. Jewitt, "An Approach Towards Benchmarking of Fault-Tolerant Commercial Systems," *Proceedings of the International Symposium on Fault-Tolerant Computing*, Sendai, 1996, pp. 314–323.

[62] T. Tsai and N. Singh, "Reliability Testing of Applications on Windows NT," *Proceedings of DSN*, 2000, pp. 427–436.

Further Reading

M. Hiller, et al., "EPIC: Profiling the Propagation and Effect of Data Errors in Software," *IEEE Transactions on Computers* 53, No. 5 (May 2004): 512–530.

A. Johansson, N. Suri, and B. Murphy, "On the Selection of Error Model(s) for OS Robustness Evaluation", *Proceedings of DSN*, Edinburgh, Scotland, 2007, pp. 502–511.

13 | Intrusion Response Systems: A Survey

Bingrui Foo Purdue University, USA
Matthew W. Glause Purdue University, USA
Gaspar M. Howard Purdue University, USA
Yu-Sung Wu Purdue University, USA
Saurabh Bagchi Purdue University, USA
Eugene H. Spafford Purdue University, USA

13.1   INTRODUCTION

The occurrence of outages due to failures in today's information technology infrastructure is a real problem that still begs a satisfactory solution. The backbone of the ubiquitous information technology infrastructure is formed by distributed systems—distributed middleware, such as CORBA and DCOM; distributed file systems, such as NFS and XFS; distributed coordination-based systems, such as publish-subscribe systems and network protocols; and above all, the distributed infrastructure of the World Wide Web. Distributed systems support many critical applications in the civilian and military domains. Critical civilian applications abound in private enterprise, such as banking, electronic commerce, and industrial control systems, as well as in the public enterprise, such as air traffic control, nuclear power plants, and protection of public infrastructures through Supervisory Control and Data Acquisition (SCADA) systems. The dependency dramatically magnifies the consequence of failures, even if transient. There is little wonder that distributed systems, therefore, are called upon to provide always-available and trustworthy services. The terminology that we will use in this chapter is to consider the distributed systems as composed of multiple services and the services interact with one another through standardized network protocols. Consider, for example, a distributed e-commerce system with the traditional three-tier architecture of a web server, application server, and database server. The services are typically located on multiple hosts.

The importance of distributed systems has led to a long interest in securing such systems through prevention and runtime detection of intrusions. The prevention is traditionally achieved by a system for user authentication and identification (e.g., users log in by providing some identifying information such as log-in signature and password, biometric information, or smart card); access control mechanisms (rules to indicate which user has what privileges over what resources in the system); and building a "protective shield" around the computer system (typically a firewall that inspects incoming and optionally outgoing network traffic and allows it if the traffic is determined to be benign). The prevention mechanism by itself is considered inadequate, because without being too restrictive, it is impossible to block out all malicious traffic from the outside. Also, if a legitimate user's password is compromised or an insider launches an attack, then prevention may not be adequate.

Intrusion detection systems (IDSs) seek to detect the behavior of an adversary by observing its manifestations on a system. The detection is done at runtime when the attack has been launched. There are many IDSs that have been developed in research and as commercial products. They fundamentally operate by analyzing the signatures of incoming packets and either matching them against known attack patterns (misuse-based signatures) or against patterns of expected system behavior (anomaly-based signatures). There are two metrics for evaluating IDSs: rate of false alarms (legitimate traffic being flagged as malicious) and rate of missed alarms (malicious traffic not flagged by the IDS).

However, in order to meet the challenges of continuously available trustworthy services from today's distributed systems, intrusion detection needs to be followed by response actions. This has typically been considered the domain of system administrators who manually "patch" a system in response to detected attacks. The traditional mode of performing response was that first, the system administrator would get an alert from the IDS. Then, he or she would consult logs and run various system commands on the different machines comprising the entire system in an effort to determine if the attack was currently active and what damage had been caused by it. There were several sophisticated but ad hoc tools that system administrators would execute to aid in the determination process, such as a script to log into all the machines in a system to determine if .rhosts files had been tampered with and if so, set them to some overly restrictive privileges. Clearly, this process, still the dominant method today, is ad hoc and very human intensive. By the nature of the actions, this process cannot reasonably hope to respond in real time and is therefore considered offline. However, as distributed systems become larger, more complex, and ubiquitous, the number of users increases and sophisticated automated script-based attacks gain ground, automated tools for intrusion response become vitally important.[1]

The autonomous intrusion response systems (IRSs) are designed to respond at runtime to an attack in progress. The goals of an IRS may be a combination of the following: to contain the effect of a current attack if the underlying model is that it is a multistage attack, to recover the affected services, and to take longer-term actions of reconfiguration of a system to make future attacks of a similar kind less likely to succeed. There are several challenges in the design of an IRS. First, attacks through automated scripts are fast moving through the different services in a system. Second, the nature of the distributed applications enables the spread of an attack, since under normal behavior the services have interactions among them and a compromised service can infect another. Third, the owner of a distributed system does not have knowledge of or access to the internals of the different services. For example, the source code may not be available, or even if available, the expertise to understand the internals may not be available. Hence, an IRS should ideally work at the interfaces rather than in the internals. Fourth, it may not be possible to deploy detectors at each service for performance reasons (e.g., the performance overhead imposed by the packet matching at a network-based detector is excessive for a host) or deployment conditions (e.g., no host-based detector is available for the particular platform). Additionally, the detectors, if installed, may be faulty and produce false alarms or missed alarms. The IRS, therefore, has to suppress inaccurate detections and extrapolate from the available detectors to determine the appropriate services at which to take the response action. Finally, the distributed systems are often complex enough that the universe of attacks possible against such systems is not enumerable and, therefore, the IRS has to work with possibly unanticipated attacks.

The current IRSs meet only a subset of the above challenges and none that we are aware of addresses all of them. The general principles followed in the development of the IRS naturally classify them into four categories.

1. *Static decision making.* This class of IRS provides a static mapping of the alert from the detector to the response that is to be deployed. The IRS includes a basic look-up table where an administrator has anticipated all alerts possible in a system and an expert indicated responses to take for each. In some cases, the response site is the same as the site from which the alarm was flagged, as with the responses often bundled with anti-virus products

---

[1]   We will discuss response systems in the context of distributed systems since their application to standalone systems is simpler and does not have many of the challenges that makes this topic intellectually challenging. To distinguish between the system that the IRS protects from the IRS itself, we will call the former the *payload system.*

(disallow access to the file that was detected to be infected) or network-based IDSs (terminate a network connection that matched a signature for anomalous behavior). The systems presented in [1–4] fall in this category.

2. *Dynamic decision making.* This class of IRS reasons about an ongoing attack based on the observed alerts and determines an appropriate response to take. The first step in the reasoning process is to determine which services in a system are likely affected, taking into account the characteristics of the detector, network topology, and so on. The actual choice of the response is then taken dependent on a host of factors, such as the amount of evidence about the attack, the severity of the response, and so on. The third step is to determine the effectiveness of the deployed response to decide if further responses are required for the current attack or to modify the measure of effectiveness of the deployed response to guide future choices. Not all IRSs in this class include all the three steps. A wide variety is discernible in this class based on the sophistication of the algorithms. The systems presented in [5–13] fall in this category.

3. *Intrusion tolerance through diverse replicas.* This class of IRS implicitly provides the response to an attack by masking the effect of the response and allowing the affected computer system to continue uninterrupted operation. The basic approach is to employ a diverse set of replicas to implement any given service. The fault model is the replicas are unlikely to share the same vulnerabilities and, therefore, not all will be compromised by any given attack. A voting process on the outputs or the state of the replicas can mask the compromised replicas, provided less than half are compromised. An advantage of this approach is the system can continue operation without a disruption. This approach is reminiscent of active replication in the fault-tolerance field. The systems presented in [14–18] fall in this category.

4. *Responses to specific kinds of attacks.* This class of IRS is customized to respond to specific kinds of attacks, most commonly, distributed denial of service (DDoS) attacks. The approach is to trace back as close to the source of an attack as possible and then limit the amount of resources available to the potentially adversarial network flows. A characteristic of this approach is cooperation is required from entities outside the computer system being protected for an accurate trace back. The systems reported in [19–21] fall in this category.

In this chapter, we will describe the primary IRSs that have been reported in the literature and label each in one of these four categories.

Next, we consider the metrics that are relevant for evaluating an IRS. Both low-level metrics and high-level metrics need to be considered for this purpose.

Low-level metrics are those that look at specific activities within an IRS, such as the latency in deploying a response, and the fraction of times a given response is successful in terminating an attack. However, these metrics need to be combined in application and domain-specific ways to evaluate the impact of the IRS on the distributed system being protected. An example of the high-level metric is the net value of transactions that could not be completed in an e-commerce system due to an attack, when an IRS is deployed. We provide a scientific basis for the high-level metrics in this chapter.

The rest of the chapter is organized as follows. Sections 13.2–13.5 present the IRSs that belong to each class introduced above. Section 13.6 presents a discussion of metrics used to evaluate an IRS and gives an example with the ADEPTS IRS applied to protect a distributed e-commerce system. Section 13.7 describes our thoughts for future evolution of the work on IRSs.

13.2   STATIC DECISION-MAKING SYSTEMS

The characteristic that defines this class of IRSs is that they respond to attacks defined exactly, prior to deployment, and using responses that are enumerated and completely configured. They are in generally simple to understand and deploy and work well for a large class of systems that have determinism in the kinds of workload and where the attack modes are enumerable a priori. However, they are not very effective for dynamic systems with changing workloads, new kinds of services installed, and new vulnerabilities introduced due to hardware or software changes.

13.2.1   Generic Authorization and Access Control—Application Programming Interface

Introduction

The Generic Authorization and Access Control—Application Programming Interface (GAA-API), developed by the Information Sciences Institute [3], is a signature-based intrusion detection and response system that provides a dynamic authorization mechanism at the application layer of a computer system. The basic idea is to integrate access control policy with intrusion detection and some countermeasure according to policy, such as generating audit records. GAA-API supports access control policies and conditions defined by a BNF-syntax language. It is a generic tool that has been integrated with many applications, including Apache, SSH, SOCKS5, and FreeS/WAN (IPSec VPN), running on Linux and Sun Solaris platforms. It is designed as a generic interface based on standard C language APIs, so it can be easily ported to other platforms and applications.

Details

GAA-API extends the access control capabilities from an application, while providing the opportunity to identify application-level attacks and specify different types of real-time responses to intrusions (Figure 13.1). A key component of the API is its Extended Access Control List (EACL) language, which allows the formulation of policies for the API to evaluate, decide, and respond to possible attack scenarios. Each object in the application is associated with an EACL, where the access rights are defined along with a set of conditions necessary for the rights

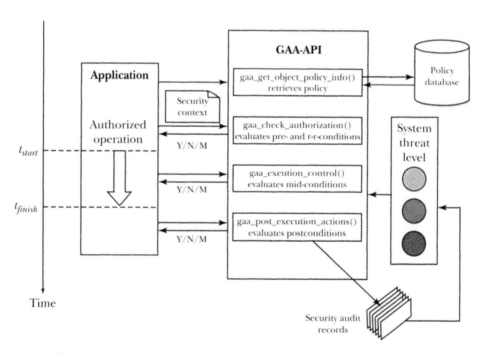

FIGURE

13.1

Application interacting through the GAA-API to enforce policies at different stages of interaction (preconditions, request-result, mid-conditions, and postconditions). The policy in effect is dependent on the threat level as communicated by the IDS. From USC, Information Sciences Institute [22].

to be matched. The conditions can state the requirements necessary to grant or deny access (preconditions), determine what to do when an access request arrives (request-result), what must hold while the access is granted (mid-conditions), and what to do after the access ends (postconditions).

The conditions allow for the API to interact with IDSs, modify existing policy rules, and trigger a response. As an example of the interaction with an IDS, the API can report attack information such as a violation of threshold conditions and access requests with parameters that do not comply with a site's policy. The API can also request an IDS for network-based attack information, such as spoofed addresses. The API can deploy responses according to the conditions previously defined. The API might, for example, limit the consumption of resources, increase the auditing level, or request user authentication to access a certain application. Nevertheless, it is unclear as to which type of language or protocol is used for the framework to exchange messages with an IDS.

GAA-API defines two types of policies: system-wide policies, which can be applied to all the objects in an application, and local policies, which are selectively applied to individual objects. The final policy application to an object, for which both system-wide and local policies exist, depends on the composition mode selected. There are three alternatives: expand, which provides access to an object if either system or local policy allows it; narrow, where mandatory access control rules defined by system-wide policies overrule any discretionary rule defined at the local policy level; and stop, where local policies are ignored if a corresponding system-wide policy exists.

The policies defined and implemented allow for the GAA-API framework to also interact with system administrators. An administrator can receive messages and validate the impact and effectiveness of the response actions taken by the framework. An example would be a rule defined for an Apache web server that states updating the list of malicious Internet provider (IP) addresses after a potential attack is detected and sending an email with the IP address of the potential attacker, the URL attempted, and the reported time of the attack. The administrator would later validate the effectiveness of the response.

The authors at USC [22] report that GAA-API functions introduce a 30% overhead for an Apache web server function call when email notification to administrators is disabled. If the email notification is enabled, the overhead rises to 80%.

Significance

The authors at USC [22] present an extended approach to the regular access control model found in popular Unix-based applications. The access control policies interact with other important security mechanisms such as IDS and firewalls, allowing for a richer set of potential responses in the presence of attacks. More recently, the authors further developed the concepts presented in GAA-API with the introduction of dynamic detection and response mechanisms during the trust negotiation phase between two parties, usually client and server, and the support they can provide for stronger access control. A potential drawback to this model could be the complexity introduced by such policies, with many variables and the interaction among them, making it hard to administer in a large environment.

13.2.2   Snort Inline

Introduction

Snort Inline is a mode of operation for Snort, the popular open-source IDS. Originally developed as an independent, modified version of Snort, it was integrated in version 2.3.0 RC1 of the Snort project to provide intrusion prevention capabilities. It requires the Netfilters/IPtables software developed by the same project. Snort Inline provides detection at the application layer to the IPtables firewall so it can dynamically respond to real-time attacks that take advantage of vulnerabilities at the application level.

Details

Snort Inline is the intrusion prevention component of Snort, a popular network intrusion detection and prevention system capable of real-time IP network traffic analysis. Snort was originally developed by Martin Roesch and is currently owned and developed by Sourcefire, a company founded by Roesch. Snort Inline started as a separate project that used Snort for its packet logging and traffic analysis capabilities, but has since been included in the Snort distribution, providing the intrusion response capabilities that the popular IDS had hitherto lacked.

The Netfilter/IPtables software allows for the implementation of the response mechanism while Snort Inline provides the policies based on which IPtables make the decision to allow or deny packets. After an incoming packet to a network is provided by IPtables, Snort performs the rule matching against the packet. There are three new rule types included in Snort for Snort Inline to define the actions that IPtables might take after receiving an incoming packet. All three rule types drop the packet if it matches a predefined rule. The second type of rule also logs the packet and the third type sends a control message back. The rules are applied before any alert or log rule is applied. The current version of Snort also allows a system to replace sections of a packet payload when using Snort Inline. The only limitation is that the payload selected must be replaced by a string of the same length. For example, an adversary that is looking to propagate malicious code through the PUT command could have it replaced by the TRACE command, thus halting further propagation of the code.

In order for Snort Inline to interface with IPtables, two C libraries are needed: libipq and libnet. Libipq [23] is a library for IPtables packet queuing that allows Snort Inline to exchange messages with IPtables. Libnet is the popular networking interface to construct, handle, and inject packets into a network.

Significance

The inclusion of Snort Inline to the popular Snort project is a good example of the evolution of IDSs as more proactive—dynamic capabilities are necessary to assist systems against today's attacks. However, the rule matching is against a statically created rule base and thus needs a prior estimate of the kinds of attacks that will be seen and the action is taken at the site of detection.

13.2.3   McAfee Internet Security Suite

Introduction

The McAfee Internet Security Suite (ISS) is a commercial product developed for the Windows operating system platform that integrates many security technologies to protect desktop computers from malicious code, spam, and unwanted or unauthorized access. The suite also includes monitoring and logging capabilities as well as backup, file and print sharing, privacy, spam filtering, and file wiping utilities. The interaction between several of these technologies allows for prevention, detection, and response of various types of attacks, chief among them being attacks related to malicious code. However, for this system, it is impossible to find detailed technical material while there is an overabundance of documents listing the features of the solution.

Details

The two main components of ISS are an anti-virus subsystem and a firewall subsystem. The anti-virus subsystem allows for the detection of viruses, worms, and other types of malicious code by using a signature-based approach along with a heuristic engine for unknown attacks. The firewall subsystem can be configured to scan multiple points of data entry, such as email, storage devices, instant messaging, and web browser. An intrusion detection module allows the firewall to interact with the anti-virus, providing a limited set of automatic responses to ongoing attacks. Another component of the ISS that is relevant to intrusion response is a system monitor. The system monitor detects and blocks changes on important components of the operating system, such as configuration files, browser settings, startup configuration, and active protocols and applications.

Significance

The evolution from an anti-virus product to an all-in-one security solution is a natural transformation that vendors such as McAfee and Symantec have experimented with in the last few years. The increase in complexity, speed, and variety for malicious code, along with the requirement to respond to attacks in real time, have led these vendors to integrate multiple security mechanisms. The response mechanisms implemented are still static and limited but one could expect more dynamic responses in future versions of these suites.

13.2.4   Other Systems

McAfee IntruShield Intrusion Prevention System

This forms part of the Network Intrusion Prevention product offering from McAfee. There is no technically rigorous publication describing the product. Our discussion is based on the documents put on the specific McAfee web page [24]. This system can be described as a network intrusion prevention system (IPS). It provides real-time prevention of encrypted attacks, while its ASIC-based architecture provides deep packet inspection and shell-code detection leading to zero-day protection. It employs purpose-built appliances (i.e., specialized hardware). The hardware is of different types depending on deployment—at the core of the network or the perimeter of the corporate network. It claims to prevent a wide variety of attacks, such as botnets, voiceover IP (VoIP) vulnerability-based attacks, and encrypted attacks.

In terms of response, it provides hints for creating some offline response in the manner of forensics. It delivers unique forensic features to analyze key characteristics of known and zero-day threats and intrusions. IntruShield's forensic capabilities provide highly actionable and accurate information and reporting related to intrusion identification, relevancy, direction, impact, and analysis. There is a host-based intrusion prevention system also from McAfee [25].

13.3   DYNAMIC DECISION-MAKING SYSTEMS

13.3.1   Broad Research Issues

Dynamic decision-making-based IRS involves the process of reasoning about an ongoing attack based on observed alerts and determining an appropriate response to take. There have been various designs and architectures proposed for this kind of dynamic decision-making-based IRS system. However, the core issue underlying all these systems is how the decision making should be achieved. Many factors can contribute to and complicate the decision-making process. For instance, a response can come with a certain cost such as the computation resource required for executing the response and the negative impact on the system after the execution of this response. Also, a response can fail with some probability. So, at the highest level of abstraction for each applicable response option, an IRS has to consider both the outcome from deploying the specific response and not deploying it, and makes a decision between these two choices based on some metric. From this point, we can see three potential research issues regarding dynamic decision-making-based IRSs. One is modeling the effect of an attack on a system, and this is directly related to the outcome from a decision on not using any response. The second issue is modeling the effect of the responses, and this is related to the outcome from a decision on using responses. Finally, there's the issue of how to decide the *set of responses* for deployment for a given attack, considering that responses are deployed on different hosts or services in a distributed environment and that they are not all independent.

There has been some work done on modeling the effect from responses and incidents. For example, Balepin et al. [5] propose the "gain matrix," which formulates the effect of using response A_k in a system with M potential states $S_1, S_2, \ldots, S_M$ as:

$$(q_1 a_{k1} + q_2 a_{k2} + \ldots + q_m a_{km})$$

where q_i is the probability of the system being in state S_i and a_{ki} is the benefit from using response A_k in state S_i. The benefit is derived from the response cost (say, in terms of negative impact on functional services), the likelihood of success of the response, and the potential damage from the system remaining in that system state. Following this formulation, the "optimal" response A_i from a set of response alternatives $\{A_1, A_2, \ldots, A_N\}$ is determined by:

$$i = \arg \max_{1 \leq k \leq N} (q_1 a_{k1} + q_2 a_{k2} + \ldots + q_m a_{km})$$

The gain matrix brings out two challenging facts in the design and implementation of a dynamic decision-making-based IRS. One is the number of system states to be considered. There are likely to be a vast number of states for a real production system and this would preclude any approach that relies on statically enumerating the states and creating the responses in each state. This underpins the desirability of dynamic intrusion response approaches. An example is the work by Toth and Kruegel [10], in which they use a dependency tree structure to dynamically calculate the impact on a system from a response.

The second challenge is about selecting the optimal set of responses in real time. A *response plan* is composed of multiple response operations that will be carried out in a certain sequence and at specific times. For example, {tightening the firewall rules for the entry point to the network at time x, rebooting the web server at time y, and resetting the firewall rules at time z} is a response plan composed of three response operations. Now, consider that the IRS has a choice of N response operations, say one each at a service site. There can be at least $2^N - 1$ possible response plans even without considering the timings in the sequence of response operations. This imposes a challenge on the response decision process, which is to pick the best choice from all potential plans. A naive dynamic approach of scanning through the gain matrix and evaluating the expected gain for the large number of response plans will not work well, in general, since an IRS usually has to respond to incidents in a timely manner. Existing work, such as ADEPTS [26, 27], relies on heuristics for limiting the size of the set of response plans by considering only the response operations that are applicable near the sites where an incident was detected. ADEPTS also evaluates the responses with respect to a local optimality criterion (e.g., effect on the specific service, rather than on the system as a whole). While this is certainly an improvement over static decision-making-based IRS systems, much work needs to be done to determine how good a given heuristic is for a specific payload system. Now we provide the details of some representative dynamic IRSs.

13.3.2   ADEPTS

Design Approach

ADEPTS [26, 27] makes use of the characteristics of a distributed application in guiding its response choices. It considers the interaction effects among the multiple services both to accurately identify patterns of the intrusions relevant to the response process (e.g., cascading failures due to service interactions) and to identify the effectiveness of the deployed response mechanism. In designing an IRS, a possible approach is to consider different attacks and provide a customized sequence of response actions for each step in an attack. A second approach, subtly yet significantly different, is to consider the constituent services in the system and the different levels of degradation of each individual service due to a successful attack. For easier understanding, one may visualize a malicious adversary who is trying to impact the constituent services (the subgoals) with the overall goal of either degrading some system functionality (e.g., no new orders may be placed to the e-store) or violating some system guarantee (e.g., credit card records of the e-store customers will be made public). In ADEPTS, the authors take the latter approach. This is motivated by the fact that the set of services and their service levels are finite and reasonably well understood, while the possible universe of attack sequences is potentially unbounded. They focus on the manifestations of the different attacks as they pertain to the services rather than the attack sequence itself. This leads them to use a representation called an intrusion graph (I-Graph), where the nodes represent subgoals for the intrusion and the edges represent preconditions/postconditions between the goals. Thus, an edge may be OR/AND/Quorum indicating any, all, or a subset, respectively, of the goals of the nodes at the head of the edge that need to be achieved before the goal at the tail can be achieved.

In ADEPTS, the response choice is determined by a combination of three factors: static information about the response, such as how disruptive the response is to normal users; dynamic information, which is essentially the history of how effective the response has been for a specific class of intrusion; and out-of-band parameters of the response, such as expert system knowledge of an effective response for a specific intrusion or policy-determined response when a specific manifestation occurs. Importantly and distinct from other work, ADEPTS points out the need for the IRS to provide its service in the face of unanticipated attacks. Thus, it does not assume that the I-Graph is complete nor that there is a detector to flag whenever an I-Graph node is achieved. However, it assumes that the intrusion will ultimately have a manifested goal that is detectable. ADEPTS also considers the imperfections of the detection system that inputs alerts to it. The detectors would have both type I and type II errors, that is, false alarms and missed alarms. If false alarms are not handled, this can cause the IRS to take unnecessary responses, potentially degrading the system functionality below that of an unsecured system. If missed alarms (or delayed alarms) are not compensated for, the system functionality may be severely degraded despite the IRS. ADEPTS can coexist with off-the-shelf detectors and estimates the likelihood that an alarm from the detection system is false or there is a missing alarm. The algorithm is based on following the pattern of nodes being achieved in the I-Graph with the intuition that a lower-level subgoal is achieved with the intention of achieving a higher-level subgoal.

The design of ADEPTS is realized in an implementation that provides intrusion response service to a distributed e-commerce system. The e-commerce system mimics an online bookstore system and two auxiliary systems for the warehouse and the bank. Real attack scenarios are injected into the system with each scenario being realized through a sequence of steps. The sequence may be nonlinear and have control flow, such as trying out a different step if one fails. ADEPTS' responses are deployed for different runs of the attack scenarios with different speeds of propagation, which bring out the latency of the response action and the adaptive nature of ADEPTS. The survivability of the system is shown to improve over a baseline system, with a larger number of runs leading to greater improvement.

Contributions and Further Work

ADEPTS presents a worthy framework for reasoning about and responding to multistage attacks in systems that have the nondeterminism and imperfections of real-world distributed systems. It provides fundamental algorithms for diagnosis of the affected service, taking proactive response and evaluating the effect of a response by observing further alerts in the system.

However, the responses in ADEPTS only achieve a local optima and are deployed in sites close to where the detector flagged the alarm. It is unclear how close ADEPTS can get to the theoretically best achievable response. Also, ADEPTS needs to consider variants of previously observed attack scenarios and completely unanticipated attack scenarios.

13.3.3   ALPHATECH Light Autonomic Defense System

Design Approach

This is a host-based autonomic defense system (ADS) using a partially observable Markov decision process (PO-MDP) that is developed by a company called ALPHATECH, which has since been acquired by BAE systems [28–30]. The system ALPHATECH Light Autonomic Defense System (α LADS) is a prototype ADS constructed around a PO-MDP stochastic controller. The main thrust of the work has been the development, analysis, and experimental evaluation of the controller. At the high level, Armstrong et al. [28, 29] and Kriedl and Frazier [30] have two goals for their ADS: it must select the correct response in the face of an attack and it must not take actions to attacks that are not there, notwithstanding noisy signals from the IDS.

The overall framework is that the system has a stochastic feedback controller based on PO-MDP that takes its input from a commercially available anomaly sensor (CylantSecure, from Software Systems International, Cyland

Division, http://www.cylant.com/), calculates the probability that the system may be in an attack state, and invokes actuators to respond to a perceived attack. The system is partially observable because the sensors (the intrusion detectors) can give imperfect alerts; the system is also partially controllable since the effect of an action by the ADS will not deterministically bring the system back to a functional state.

The authors set up PO-MDP formulas to determine for each $x \in X, b_k(x) = Pr(x_k = x/I_k)$, where I_k denotes the set of the first k observations received and all controls selected through the $(k-1)$st decision stage. Let $B_k = \{b_k(x) : x \in X\}$ be the set of all individual state estimates after the kth observation. The objective is to choose a response policy μ that outputs the selected control $u_k = \mu(B_k)$ (as a function of B_k). The choice of the optimal response is given by:

$$\mu^*(B_k) = \arg \min_{u \in U} \left[\sum_{x \in X} \alpha^*(u,x) b_k(x) \right]$$

where $\alpha^*(u,x)$, for each $u \in U$ and $x \in X$, is proportional to the optimal cost-to-go, given current state $x_k = x$ and current decision $u_k = u$. That is, $\alpha^*(u,x)$ is the expected cost obtained through an optimal selection of controls at future decision stages, given current state $x_k = x$ and current decision $u_k = u$. However, determining the optimal response policy that minimizes the infinite horizon cost function is intractable and heuristics must be applied to find near-optimal policies. The heuristics Armstrong et al. [28, 29] and Kriedl and Frazier [30] apply is to consider the single-step combination of current state and control.

For the evaluation, the authors build a Markov state model for the worm attack on a host. The prototype ADS receives observations from two intrusion detector sensors. One intrusion detector sensor monitors activities on the IP port and the other sensor monitors processes operating on the host computer. These two sensors are calibrated against activity that is determined to be representative of how the computer system will typically be used. For the experiments, the training data were a combination of stochastic http and ftp accesses plus random issuances of commands that are commonly used by operators of Linux. The first experiment demonstrates that an ADS built on a feedback controller is less likely to respond inappropriately to authorized system activity than a static controller (i.e., is less susceptible to noises from the detection system) and is thus able to effectively use a more sensitive anomaly detector than a static controller. The second experiment demonstrates the ability to respond to attacks not seen before—α LADS was trained with a worm attack on the ftp server and able to thwart similar worm attacks to the named and rpcd servers. The surprising result is αLADS is able to thwart every single instance of the not-seen-before attacks. To interpret the results, a crucial piece of information is the degree of similarity between the different worms, which is not available in the published papers.

Contributions and Further Work

The work is significant in its use of a formal modeling technology (i.e., PO-MDP) in intrusion response. The design is rigorous and while the modeling technique has the challenge of determining the correct transition matrix from suitable training data, this challenge is not unique to the αLADS system. It is expected that the work will mature and use more sophisticated techniques for creation of the matrices that are available in related literature.

What has gotten short shrift in this work is the development of the actual responses that would be effective in a distributed environment. In fact, their experiments only use the ability to kill a process or shutdown a computer (apart from just observation or human notification). The system has to be made hierarchical and distributed so that it can respond to attacks in different parts of a distributed infrastructure.

13.3.4   Cooperating Security Managers and Adaptive, Agent-Based Intrusion Response Systems

Design Approach

Both systems come from the same research group with cooperating security managers (CSMs) preceding adaptive, agent-based intrusion response system (AAIRSs) in chronology. CSM is designed to be used as an intrusion detection tool in a large network environment. CSM follows an approach in which individual intrusion detection monitors can operate in a cooperative manner, without relying on a centralized director to perform the network intrusion detection. To stress the role of the individual components in managing intrusions, not just monitoring them, the term used is *security managers*. CSM employs no centralized director; instead, each of the individual managers assumes this role for its own users when that manager suspects suspicious activity. Each CSM reports all significant activity to the CSM for the host from which the connection originated. This enables CSM to track a user as he or she travels from one host to another in a distributed environment.

If an intruder is suspected or detected, it is up to the intruder-handling (IH) component to determine which action to take. This is where the intrusion response capability is embedded in CSM. The responsibility of the IH module is to take appropriate actions when intrusive activity is detected. Performing a specific action in response to an abuse will depend on the perceived severity of the detected abuse. Simple notification of the system manager on the detecting system is still the first step. The second step is to also notify all other CSMs in the trail for this user. This information is obtained from the user-tracking module. Beyond this, several other activities may be deemed appropriate. Two actions would be to kill the current session of the suspected intruder and to lock the account that was used to gain access so the intruder cannot simply return. However, they have to be done with care only when the evidence is strong and the disruption due to lack of response is severe.

A later work coming from the same group is the AAIRS [20, 21]. In AAIRS, multiple IDSs monitor a computer system and generate intrusion alarms. The interface agents receive the alerts and use an iteratively built model of false alerts and missed alerts from the detectors to generate an attack-confidence metric. The agents pass this metric along with the intrusion report to the master analysis agent. The master analysis agent classifies whether the incident is a continuation of an existing incident or is a new attack using several different parameters, such as the target application and target port. The decision algorithm for determining if an alarm corresponds to a new attack or an existing attack is adopted by other systems, such as ADEPTS.

If the master analysis agent determines this is a new attack, it creates a new analysis agent for handling this attack. The analysis agent analyzes an incident and generates an abstract course of action to resolve the incident, using the response taxonomy agent from Hiltunen et al. [18] to classify the attack and determine a response goal. The analysis agent passes the selected course of action to the tactics agent, which decomposes the abstract course of action into very specific actions and then invokes the appropriate components of the response toolkit.

The proposed methodology provides response adaptation through three components: the interface, analysis, and tactics agents. The interface agent adapts by modifying the confidence metric associated with each IDS. As the analysis components receive additional incident reports, these reports may lead to reclassification of the type of attacker and/or type of attack. This reclassification may lead to the formulation of a new plan or a change in how the response goal is accomplished. The analysis component may change the plan steps being used to accomplish the goal if alternative steps are available and can be substituted into the plan. Alternatively, the tactics components may have multiple techniques for implementing the plan step and adapt by choosing alternate steps. These components maintain success metrics on their plans and actions, respectively, and weight the successful ones so that they are more likely to be taken in subsequent instances of an attack.

The work provides a good framework on which the IRS can be built. However, it does not provide any of the system-level techniques and algorithms that will be required for the AAIRS to work in practice. It leaves many unanswered questions, most important of which are: How is the algorithm to determine a sequence of response actions to an incident, how does the system measure the success of previous responses, or how are multiple concurrent attacks handled?

Contributions and Further Work

CSM highlights the trade-offs to be made in any autonomous response system. Its module for tracking a user and the architecture for distributed detection are valuable in an IRS for a distributed system. However, the work is lacking in system-level details and actual design decisions made for a specific application context. The evaluation does not shed any light on the IH component of the system.

AAIRS presents a compelling architecture with different modules that make up an IRS. The modules are at two basic levels of abstraction: application system neutral and application system specific. These levels are important to the extensibility of an IRS to new applications. AAIRS also raises important concerns for any IRS: the imperfections of any IDS both for false alarms and missed alarms have to be accounted for in the IRS and there should be feedback about the success or failure of a deployed response. However, the work is lacking in specific algorithms for any of the steps of an IRS. There are no system-level details provided and this is especially critical for IRS since many trade-offs in algorithms are brought out by actual implementations and deployments. The system description indicates competent system administrators may still need to be involved in the loop (e.g., in manually determining if an alert from an IDS was a false one).

13.3.5   EMERALD

Design Approach

Event Monitoring Enabling Responses to Anomalous Live Disturbances (EMERALD) developed an architecture that inherits well-developed analytical techniques for detecting intrusions and cast them in a framework that is highly reusable, interoperable, and scalable in large network infrastructures [8, 31]. Its primary goal is not to perform automated intrusion response. However, its modular structure and tools can enable effective response mechanisms.

The primary entity within EMERALD is the monitor, with multiple monitors deployed within each administrative domain. The monitors may interact with the environment passively (reading activity logs or network packets) or actively (via probing that supplements normal event gathering). The monitors may interact with one another. An EMERALD monitor has a well-defined interface for sending and receiving event data and analytical results from third-party security services. An EMERALD monitor is capable of performing both signature analysis and statistical profile-based anomaly detection on a target event stream. The work on these components represent state-of-the-art development in the intrusion detection literature within each domain. In addition, each monitor includes an instance of the EMERALD resolver, a countermeasure decision engine capable of fusing the alerts from its associated analysis engines and invoking response handlers to counter malicious activity.

A feature that makes EMERALD well suited to intrusion response in a distributed environment is its capability for alert aggregation. This is achieved through a tiered arrangement of monitors and exchange of CIDF-based [32] alert information. Thus, resolvers are able to request and receive intrusion reports from other resolvers at lower layers of the analysis hierarchy, enabling the monitoring and response to global malicious activity. Each resolver is capable of invoking real-time countermeasures in response to malicious or anomalous activity reports produced by the analysis engines. The countermeasures are defined in a field specific to the resource object corresponding to the resource in which the monitor is deployed. Included with each valid response method are evaluation metrics for determining the circumstances under which the method should be dispatched. These criteria are the confidence of the analysis engine that the attack is real and the severity of the attack. The resolver combines the metrics to formulate its monitor's response policy.

Contributions and Further Work

An important lesson from the design of EMERALD is the separation of generic and target-specific parts of the system. Target-specific refers to the service (FTP, SSH) and the hardware resource (router) that EMERALD is deployed on. This design approach simplifies reusability of components and extensibility and enhances integration with other data sources, analysis engines, and response capabilities. While we see the great potential in EMERALD to build automatic responses in the resolver, we did not find any detailed description of its capabilities or its application. The infrastructure provides the common EMERALD API, event-queue management, error-reporting services, secondary storage management (primarily for the statistical component), and internal configuration control. The statistical and P-BEST (Production-Based Expert System Tool) components are integrated as libraries and provide powerful intrusion detection capabilities. The EMERALD API can likely be used to build a powerful intrusion response engine. However, this has not been reported in the project.

13.3.6   Other Dynamic Intrusion Response Systems

There are some other systems that employ dynamic decision making for intrusion response. In the interest of space, we will limit the discussion of these systems to their key contributions.

1. In Toth and Kruegel [10], the authors propose a network model that allows an IRS to evaluate the effect of a response on the network services. There exist dependencies between entities in the system either as a direct dependency (user A depends on DNS service) or an indirect dependency that needs to be satisfied for the direct dependencies (if DNS service on a different subnet, then firewall rules must allow access to that subnet). A dependent entity may become unavailable either because no path exists in the network topology or firewall rules disallow access. Indirect dependencies are determined automatically by analyzing the network topology (which is encoded in routing tables) as well as firewall rules. Dependencies are represented using an AND-OR tree and the degree of dependency is represented by a number between 0 and 1. Capability of an entity is the portion of the entity's functionality that is available under the current response strategy (number between 0 and 1). The capability is computed from the dependency tree. A penalty is assigned for the unavailability of each entity. The net penalty cost of an entity is capability × penalty. At each step, the system takes the response that minimizes the penalty. This is a greedy algorithm and does not necessarily lead to a global optima.

2. Security agility [33] is a software flexibility technique that extends the functionality of software components to accommodate the dynamic security properties of their environment. Thus, when access control is tightened in the environment, the software does not fail. The security agility toolkit provides the means to integrate more sophisticated response capabilities (than simply killing an offending process) into processes to realize more flexible intrusion-tolerant systems. At its heart, the response actions are changes to access control rules with activation criteria specified. The chief contribution of this work is policy reconfiguration techniques at runtime. A secondary contribution is that the reconfiguration capability enables reconfiguration as part of a response.

In general, dynamic decision-making-based IRS is a promising technology that is still in its nascent phase. There is scarce deployment of them in real-world production systems, at least what is reported in open literature. Part of the reason is the many open issues that need to be solved before generalizable design principles can be presented. For example, the heterogeneity among real-world systems has been an obstacle for modeling the effect on a system from incidents and responses. In a sense, an IRS has to figure out what are the services in the system, what are their functionalities, what are the interactions among them, and what are the effects of a response on the system. Each of these is a topic of active research in distinct fields, such as system management. Besides, there are many properties in the response decision-making process that need to be quantitatively modeled and analyzed, such as the optimality of a response. There is surprisingly little in the way of comparative evaluation of the different techniques with respect to each other and with respect to an idealized scenario. We believe this is an exciting field of development in IRS technology and we hope to see many worthwhile research efforts in it in the years to come.

13.4   INTRUSION TOLERANCE THROUGH DIVERSE REPLICAS

The use of diverse replicas in IRS borrows ideas from the field of natural fault tolerance and from observations of biological systems. By introducing artificial diversity, a common phenomenon in biological systems, an attack specific to a vulnerability in a system cannot affect another system that lacks that vulnerability. Coupled with redundancy, the effect of an attack can be masked, allowing the system to provide continued service in the presence of disruptions. The basic approach is to employ a diverse set of replicas for a given service, such that they provide the same high-level functionality with respect to other services, but their internal designs and implementations differ. The fault-masking techniques used are similar to methods in natural fault tolerance, such as voting and agreement protocols. The use of diverse replicas is attractive because provable theoretical improvements to the survivability or security of the system can be obtained, compared to other techniques that are more suitably classified as heuristics. Evaluation techniques from the mature field of natural fault tolerance are more readily adapted to this class of IRSs.

A common assumption is to assume, at most, a fraction of the servers in a network may fail. This assumption is strengthened through the use of active and periodic recovery. Another common assumption is that failures in the system are independent, which motivates the use of diversity. Extending this argument to vulnerabilities, the assumption states that vulnerabilities do not occur across different operating systems and applications.

13.4.1   Broad Research Issues

Two main issues that arise are (1) how to introduce diversity into a system and (2) how to achieve redundancy that improves survivability and security of a system. To handle the first issue, most system architects have chosen to manually introduce diversity, such as installing different operating systems and applications. Taking it a step further, different versions of an application are also used. Introducing diversity automatically is a topic of much ongoing research, such as through the OASIS and SRS programs within DARPA [14, 16, 34, 35]. We survey two of these papers here. The second issue is system specific and, in general, advances in the fields of cryptography and dependability have given us a better idea of how redundancy impacts the survivability of the system. The following are sample systems in this domain.

13.4.2   Building Survivable Services Using Redundancy and Adaptation

Hiltunen et al.'s paper [18] advocates the use of redundancy and adaptation to build survivable services and presents a general approach to do so. The authors introduce various forms of redundancy: redundancy in space and time and the use of redundant methods. Redundant methods enforce a security attribute and the attribute remains valid if at least one of the methods remains uncompromised. An example is to perform multiple encryption operations using different cipher systems. They motivate the use of redundancy to avoid single points of vulnerability and to introduce artificial diversity and unpredictability into a system. They provide a useful characterization of the effectiveness of redundancy as the independence of the redundant elements, and the main goal of the design is to maximize this independence.

As an example, they apply redundancy to a secure communication service called *SecComm*. SecComm provides customizable secure communication by allowing user-specified security attributes and algorithms for implementing these attributes. The traditional approach of selecting a better encryption algorithm or increasing the key size to increase security is not survivable, since they in essence still contain single points of vulnerability. Therefore, they propose using two or more techniques to guarantee an attribute rather than a single method. For maximal independence, a different key established using different key distribution methods is used for each method. Fragmentation is also proposed when there are multiple connections. At a basic level, they implement redundancy by sequentially applying multiple methods to the same data. They suggest numerous general ideas to vary the application of the methods, with the main goal being to maximize the independence as mentioned above. The increase in survivability is relatively hard to quantify, therefore, their experimental results only measure the cost of redundancy against performance.

Hiltunen et al. have done a good job motivating the use of redundancy and diversity with respect to the security of computer systems. They provided many examples on how to use diverse replicas for various purposes, and the next two sections illustrate specific architectures that use diverse replicas.

13.4.3   Scalable Intrusion-Tolerant Architecture

Design Approach

Scalable Intrusion-Tolerant Architecture (SITAR) is an intrusion-tolerant system that relies heavily on redundancy [14]. The main components of the SITAR architecture are proxy servers that validate incoming and outgoing traffic and detect failures within the application servers and among themselves. The mitigation of adverse effects due to intrusions is through the use of redundant and diverse internal components. The diversity is achieved manually by choosing different server codes (e.g. Apache, Internet Information Server for web servers) and different operating systems (e.g. Linux, Solaris, MS). Through this, the authors of [14] assume that only one server can be compromised by a single attack, allowing them to build a simple model for their system.

A specific subsystem that employs redundancy is their ballot monitor subsystem. The monitors receive responses from acceptance monitors, perform validation of responses, and apply a voting algorithm to detect the presence of an attack and respond to the attack by choosing the majority response as the final response.

Contributions and Further Work

SITAR is a good example of using diverse replicas to improve the survivability of a system. The architecture used clearly illustrates the practical benefits of diversity and replication, and how they can be used to detect and respond to attacks. However, the work does not lay down generalizable design principles for diverse replicas.

13.4.4   Survival by Defense Enabling

Design Approach

Pal et al. [16] propose an approach to survivability and intrusion tolerance called *survival by defense*. The main idea is to introduce defense mechanisms that enhance the common protection mechanisms with a dynamic strategy for reacting to a partially successful attack. Due to their assumption that they lack control over the environment (e.g., OS, network), they focus on ensuring correct functioning of the critical applications. Therefore, defense enabling is performed around the application, with the assumption that it can be modified.

The type of attack considered is the corruption that results from a malicious attack exploiting flaws in an application's environment (they conclude it is most likely). Since the knowledge and actions within the environment are limited, an assumption they make is that administrator privileges will eventually be obtained by an attacker. In this context, defense enabling is divided into two complementary goals: (1) attacker's privilege escalation is slowed down and (2) defense responds and adapts to the privileged attacker's abuse of resources. Therefore, an application is defense enabled if mechanisms are in place to cause most attackers to take significantly longer to corrupt it (these mechanisms tend to be in the middleware).

To prevent the quick spread of privilege, the main idea is to divide a system into distinct security domains consisting of user-defined elements (e.g., host, LAN, router), such that each domain has its own set of privileges. Pal et al. suggest the use of a heterogeneous environment (various types of hardware, OS) to prevent domain administrator privileges from one domain to be converted into domain administrator privileges in another domain. Also, applications are distributed across the security domains (i.e., application redundancy) to reduce the effect of privilege escalation within a domain. Not limited to replicating applications, Pal et al. suggest other forms of replication such as communication redundancy.

A strong assumption made is that attacks proceed sequentially (staged attacks) instead of concurrently, that is, an attack on an application in multiple domains is slower than an attack on one single domain. Their design approach is to design applications intelligently distributed across security domains, so that privilege in a set of domains is needed to compromise the application. However, there is no discussion on how the staging is to be enforced.

Contributions and Further Work

With respect to the use of diverse replicas, the significance of this work is their higher-level approach to the use of redundancy. This is illustrated by partitioning a network into various domains, such that an attack on a domain only has a limited affect on another domain.

13.4.5 Implementing Trustworthy Services Using Replicated State Machines

Schneider and Zhou's article [17] is a comprehensive survey on techniques to implement distributed trust. In essence, the problem of distributing trust is solved by using replicas, and the issues faced are the same as the general theme of this section. By distributing trust, it is possible for the fault tolerance of the distributed system to exceed the fault tolerance of any single server. The first emphasis of the authors is the use of proactive recovery to transform a system that tolerates t failures in its lifetime to a system that tolerates t failures within a time window. This is useful because it strengthens the assumption that not more than t failures will exist at any one time, though additional complexity to the system design is introduced. Next, they discuss service key refresh and scalability, which is achieved through the use of secret sharing protocols. This allows periodic changes to the shared secret keys to be transparent to the clients. With regards to server key refresh, Schneider and Zhou discuss three solutions, namely the use of trusted hardware, offline keys, or read-only service public key.

The independence assumption of failures is discussed and methods to reduce correlated failures are mentioned. They are:

1. Developing multiple server implementations, which is generally an expensive endeavor.

2. Employing preexisting diverse components, such as using different operating systems.

3. Introducing artificial diversity during compile or runtime, which will not eliminate flaws inherent in the algorithms implemented.

The next important requirement in distributed trust is replica coordination. This is mainly required for consensus, which is impossible to implement deterministically in the asynchronous model. The solutions provided are:

1. Abandon consensus and use quorum systems or embrace all the sharings of a secret (rather than having to agree on one sharing).

2. Employ randomization to solve Byzantine agreement.

3. Sacrifice liveness (temporarily) for weaker assumptions of the asynchronous model.

Finally, Schneider and Zhou discuss the problems and solutions that arise when confidential data is involved. The main problems of confidential data are that they cannot be changed by proactive recovery, and at any time they are unencrypted, their confidentiality may be lost. By using either reencryption or blinding, it is possible for clients to retrieve encrypted data in the case where services implement access control.

Schneider and Zhou's article is a well-written introduction to the issues and solutions of distributing trust, which are the same issues one would face when using diverse replicas in a system. The next section presents a specific approach to this problem.

13.4.6   Distributing Trust on the Internet

Design Approach

Cachin [15] presents an architecture for secure state machine replication in an asynchronous and adversarial network. This is achieved through recent advances in threshold cryptography and protocols for atomic broadcast. Depending on the level of diversity in the replicated servers, guarantees of liveness and safety can be made under certain assumptions (e.g., there are n static servers and at most t may fail). The designer of the distributed system can easily define meaningful attributes, such as the location and type of operating system, which represent the different measures of diversity within the system. From these attributes, one can produce a description of how the servers may be compromised simultaneously (which is formalized as a general adversary structure in [15]) and design a secret sharing scheme that ensures that the guarantees of the distributed system are kept.

The use of diversity enables the authors of [15] to avoid making the standard independence assumption of faults, allowing the system to tolerate malicious acts and better approximate reality. The consensus protocol described within Cachin [15] is part of the Secure Intrusion-Tolerant Replication Architecture (Sintra) toolkit.

Contributions and Further Work

Cachin [15] presents specific techniques for distributing trust in an untrusted environment. This work is significant in that a clear approach is presented that allows a system designer or administrator to easily incorporate this architecture into a network with no existing use of diverse replicas and obtain an improvement in the survivability of the system.

Extensions to the scheme are discussed, such as using proactive recovery, dynamic grouping of servers, hybrid failure structures that distinguish between natural and malicious failures, and optimistic protocols that adapt their speeds depending on the presence of adversaries (due to the significant overhead of the atomic broadcast protocols).

13.5   RESPONSES TO SPECIFIC KINDS OF ATTACKS

This class of IRS is customized to respond to specific kinds of attacks, most commonly, DDoS attacks. There are scarce efforts at responses to other kinds of specialized attacks. One example is responding to internal attacks, where approaches proposed include changing the access control rules or dropping some connections when a high threat level is perceived [36]. However, such techniques so far have been human intensive and little exists in the literature in terms of rigorous validation of an automated system against different internal attacks. Hence, we focus on the DDoS attack response technology here.

DDoS attacks present a growing problem for network administrators around the world. On the Internet, a DDoS attack is one in which a multitude of compromised systems attack a single target, thereby causing denial of service (DoS) for users of the targeted system. The flood of incoming messages to the target system essentially forces it to shutdown, thereby denying service to the system to legitimate users. An adversary begins a DDoS attack by exploiting a vulnerability in one computer system and making it the DDoS "master." It is from the master system that the intruder identifies and communicates with other systems that can be compromised. The intruder loads cracking tools available on the Internet onto multiple—sometimes thousands of—compromised systems. With a single command, the intruder instructs the controlled machines to launch one of many flood attacks against a specified target. The inundation of packets to the target causes a denial of service.

Increasingly powerful DDoS toolkits are readily available to potential attackers and essential systems are ill prepared to defend themselves. Both their ease of use and effectiveness make them the perfect tool for malicious individuals attempting to disrupt networks and web services. Accordingly, corporations and academia are working overtime to solve this complex problem and several systems exist that work to address DDoS. Unfortunately, none of the solutions fully handles the ever-evolving DDoS toolkits being used today and fail to present an all encompassing solution to the problem. Despite this failing of existing DDoS handling systems, systems such as Cooperative Intrusion Traceback and Response

Architecture (CITRA) and the cooperative architecture hold much promise for the future.

13.5.1   Primitives for Responding to DDoS

DDoS attacks typically require four components: an attacker, master hosts, zombie hosts, and a victim host. Using exploits in a remote system, an attacker installs the attack program that can be remote controlled by the master host. When the attack begins, it usually falls in to one of two classes: *bandwidth depletion* and *resource depletion*. Attackers can perform these attacks directly or through reflection. Reflection makes it more difficult to track down the source of the problem and offers a greater challenge to DDoS handling systems by bouncing packets off other hosts. The first line of defense against DDoS attacks is intrusion prevention. Rate-limiting filters are commonly used for preventing DDoS attacks [37, 38]. The reason why intrusion prevention and intrusion detection are unlikely to solve all kinds of DDoS attacks is that it is often difficult to tell the two kinds of traffic apart. Although some DDoS traffic can be easily distinguished from legitimate traffic, this is not true in the general case. More sophisticated DDoS toolkits generate traffic that "blends in" with legitimate traffic and, therefore, cannot be blocked. Hence, autonomous intrusion response is called for. Responses when a DDoS attack is detected usually involve some type of trace back or packet marking procedure to locate the source of the attack and block it.

Fundamentally, response mechanisms for DDoS attacks have to be distributed in nature as pointed out in Koutepas et al. [21]. This is due to several factors: (1) attackers most of the time spoof the packet source IP's address, (2) the possibility of the attack initiating from a wide range of networks worldwide, and (3) the inability of a domain to enforce incoming traffic shaping. Detected malicious flows can be blocked locally but the assistance of the upstream network is still needed in order to free the resources occupied on the incoming link.

13.5.2   CITRA

Design Approach

CITRA is one of these systems currently in development working to handle bandwidth depletion attacks [19, 39]. Originally, CITRA (and the Intruder Detection and Isolation Protocol (IDIP) on which CITRA is based) did not have DDoS response as their goal. They were developed to provide an infrastructure enabling

IDSs, firewalls, routers, and other components to cooperatively trace and block network intrusions as close to their sources as possible. Later CITRA was adapted for responding to DDoS attacks. CITRA is used by creating a cooperative network of nodes, each installed with the CITRA software. A node registers itself and coordinates efforts with the rest of the nodes through the discovery coordinator (DC). When an attack is detected, the CITRA nodes trace back toward the source through the use of network audit data. Along the path of the trace back, temporary action lasting only two minutes is taken to decrease the network flooding. During this two-minute window, the DC formulates a more reasoned plan of how to handle the attack.

At each CITRA component along the path of attack, responses are taken in accordance with the CITRA policy mechanisms. Traffic rate limiting is used rather than packet filtering, because of the difficulty of telling a legitimate packet from one that is part of the adversarial stream of packets. This response strategy is approximate since some DoS traffic may get through while some legitimate traffic may get blocked out. But with well-chosen parameters, enough bandwidth should be available for legitimate traffic even though it may be at a reduced speed. So the authors of CITRA [19, 39] integrated a rate limiter function using a token bucket rate limiting service available with netfilter. Experiments using RealPlayer were carried out on a test bed composed of several subnets, each with their own CITRA-enabled router. Results showed that when the system was active it allowed uninterrupted viewing but at reduced quality. It took ten seconds to slow the attack even on their small-scale test bed, bringing up a possible issue of scalability. On more powerful hardware, however, the delay was reduced to two seconds and the quality was not reduced.

Contributions and Further Work

The architecture presented is appealing and points in the direction of further development for DDoS mitigation. It does not require universal deployment to be meaningful, which is a big positive factor for any DDoS response mechanism.

Possible problems with the system involve slower-than-optimal trace back and scalability limitations. The system currently needs more effective means of dealing with attacks than simply limiting the bandwidth due to more sophisticated, multi-pronged attacks. Also, monitoring all packets coming in from all other networks is not scalable without smart algorithms. There is considerable ongoing work in the area of making routers fast by developing high-speed algorithms for packet lookups and classification (see work by George Varghese et al. from University of California at Davis and Nick McKeown et al. at Stanford University).

13.5.3   Cooperative Counter-DDoS Entity

Design Approach

Similar to CITRA, the cooperative architecture [21] attempts to locate the source of an attack but through the use of cooperative domains that internally check if they are sending a DDoS attack, and if so, alert the other networks that may be affected. To deal with the scalability of this system and increased network congestion from the message, the system uses multicast transmission of alerts. Multicast allows a source host to send a message to multiple hosts through an optimal spanning tree by only sending the message once and replicating it only when the path along the spanning tree splits. Within each domain, there are entities that determine the probability of an attack internally by looking at the alerts coming in from other entities and domains and the results of local IDSs. If one entity fails, another entity has the ability to take over. Once the number of alerts exceeds a threshold, the entities take action through use of a reaction table. This reaction table provides the action that should be taken given the current state. This system lacks any experimental evidence to support its claims and offers a different approach than CITRA. By not using a traditional trace-back mechanism, the system can react faster and more efficiently. However, it heavily relies on the multicast backbone, and should an attacker target the backbone, the system may be rendered ineffective.

Contributions and Further Work

The work lays out an impressive architecture for quickly reacting to DDoS attacks. It moves away from the reliance on trace back that underlies the vast majority of approaches in this domain. However, problems facing the systems in existence today are how to detect legitimate packets sent to a network and packets intended to perform a DDoS attack without disrupting the legitimate users. This is no easy task when one considers that a network may simply be undergoing an increase in legitimate traffic or a DDoS attack may even use legitimate requests. Another problem deals with determining the source of an attack. How does one find the source of the attack if it is constantly switching sources or it passes through a network with a less-than-helpful network administrator? Lastly, what is the universe of responses that should be included with any DDoS mitigation system—are the current ones of bandwidth throttling or packet filtering sufficient?

DDoS handling systems today have several weaknesses that can be exploited. They still need a better way of determining the source of an attack and better ways of responding to a detected attack. Blocking the remote host at the source would be optimal but trace-back procedures are too slow and resource intensive. Also, they rely on the cooperation of other networks and a limited set of responses. The aforementioned actions either fail to stop the attack and only slow it down or stop the attack but in the process block legitimate users. Better response, detection, and trace-back technology will have to be developed if these systems are to be deployable in real-world systems.

13.6 BENCHMARKING INTRUSION RESPONSE SYSTEMS

It is important to benchmark any IRS using quantifiable metrics. This is a nascent field within IRS design and development and one which needs significant work to get to maturity. Hence, this section is based around a suggested course of action for future development and an example from an existing IRS, ADEPTS. The metrics should capture the two essential goals of IRSs: to provide gracefully degraded functionality in the presence of attacks and to make a system more robust to future attacks. These two notions are addressed respectively by the metrics *survivability* and *vulnerability*.

One commonly accepted definition of *survivability* is the capacity of a system to provide essential services in the face of intrusions [40, 41]. The challenge with this definition is how to define essential services: Is this by the different categories of users for the different services, or by business criticality, or by some other measure? Also, the question arises if there exists a minimum essential service level that can be guaranteed. In Jha et al. [42], the authors inject errors into a network specification and visualize effects in the form of scenario graphs. Model checking is used to verify if states that violate certain temporal properties can be reached. Hiltunen et al. [18] present Cactus, which is a framework for constructing highly customizable and dynamically adaptable middleware services for networked systems. The fine-grained customization allows customized trade-offs between QoS attributes, including performance, reliability, and survivability, while the dynamic adaptation allows services to change behavior at runtime as a reaction to incoming intrusions.

To start, consider a simple combinatorial model for survivability. Let us define G as the overall goal of the system (e.g., sell products or services on the Internet), which is accomplished through several subgoals G_i (e.g., the different transactions that are possible on the system), $i = 1, \ldots, N$. Each subgoal G_i is given a weight W_i indicating its importance in the achievement of the system goal G, ($\sum_i W_i = 1$). This can be estimated by the number of users who reach the subgoal as a fraction of the total number of users, a fraction of the usage of the subgoal, or a quantity defined by the system owner. Each subgoal G_i is decomposed into a conjunction of sets of services $\vec{S}_{ij}$, $j = 1,\ldots,N_i$, such that each set of services must be functional for goal G_i to be reached. Each such set can be further decomposed to be a disjunction of basic services $\vec{S}_{ijk}$, $k = 1,\ldots,N_{ij}$, such that any service of this set being functional causes the set to be functional. Let p_x denote the probability that a service X is affected by a disruption and cannot be used, and P_Y denote the probability that a goal y cannot be reached. Then, $P_{G_i} = \text{Max}\,(\text{Min}\,(p_{S_{ijk}})$, over all $k = 1,\ldots,N_{ij})$, over all $j = 1,\ldots,N_i$, $P_G = \sum_i W_i P_{G_i}$. The survivability is given by $1 - P_G$.

To apply this formulation, we will have to decompose a goal into the services and estimate the probability of a service being nonfunctional. The former can be deduced from a Service Net (network indicating interactions between services during normal operation) through a training phase when the transaction corresponding to a particular subgoal G_i is executed and the service interactions observed. We may use techniques from software reliability engineering of path testing [43] to determine the conjunction and disjunction of services.

To illustrate the concept, let us consider an example of its application as shown by Foo et al. in ADEPTS[26]. Figure 13.2 depicts the test bed that is used for experiments on ADEPTS. The payload system mimics an e-commerce web store, which has two Apache web servers running web store applications based on Cube-Cart [44] and are written in the PHP scripting language. In the backend, there is a MySQL database that stores all the store's information, which includes products inventory, products description, customer accounts, and order history. There are two other organizations with which the web store interacts: a bank and a warehouse. The bank is a home-grown application that verifies credit card requests from the web store. The warehouse is also a home-grown application that takes shipping requests from the web store, checks inventory, applies charges on the customers' credit card accounts, and ships the products. The clients submit transactions to the web store through a browser. Some important transactions are given in Table 13.1.

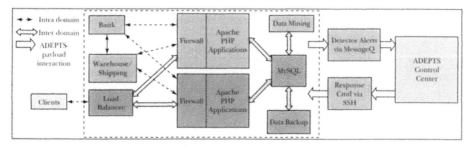

FIGURE

13.2

Layout of e-commerce test bed for the experiments on ADEPTS.

Name	Description	Services Involved	Weight
Browse web store	Customer uses web browser to access web store and browse the products available	Apache, MySQL	10
Add merchandise to shopping cart	Customer adds products to shopping cart	Apache, MySQL	10
Place order	Customer can input credit card inform-ation, submit orders, and web store will authenticate credit card with bank	Apache, MySQL, bank	10
Charge credit card	Warehouse charges credit card through bank when order is shipped	Warehouse, bank	5
Administrative work	Admins/webmasters can modify various source codes	Variable	10

TABLE 13.1 List of important transactions in e-commerce system. The weight is unitless and gives the relative importance of each transaction to the system owner.

Illegal read of file (20)	Corruption of MySQL database (70)	Unauthorized credit card charges (80)
Illegal write to file (30)	Confidentiality leak of customer information stored in MySQL database (100)	Cracked administrator password (90)
Illegal process being run (50)	Unauthorized orders created or shipped (80)	

TABLE 13.2 List of security goals for e-commerce test bed.

There are certain security goals for the system, the complement of which are specified in Table 13.2, along with the weights. Thus, adding the word "prevent" before each gives the goal. The attached weights to the transactions and security goals are used for survivability computation as discussed below.

The authors define survivability based on the high-level transactions and security goals. Thus, the metric shows the effect of ADEPTS on the high-level functioning of the e-commerce system:

$$\text{Survivability} = 1000 - \sum \text{unavailable transactions} - \sum \text{failed security goals}$$

When a transaction became unavailable or the security goal is violated, the survivability drops by its corresponding weight, which was given in Tables 13.1 and

Table 13.2. Transactions become unavailable due to ADEPTS responses, such as rebooting a host or due to attacks. Security goals may be violated due to the successful execution of an attack step or an erroneous response action. If a security goal is violated multiple times during an attack, then each violation causes a decrease in the survivability.

The survivability metric considers the state of the system at the present time and does not consider the resilience of the system to future disruptions. This is an important measure and is captured by the *vulnerability* metric. The basic idea of this metric is to fit a temporal distribution for the probability that a given goal in a multistage attack is reached. This curve is analogous to unreliability curves seen in traditional fault-tolerant systems. To get the vulnerability at a point in time T, we aggregate the individual unreliability curves using some structure as an attack graph and map the nodes to the services that are affected. Then an analysis similar to the survivability analysis above is performed. Note that the different curves are not independent. Given the Service Net with times for interaction between services, the edges in the attack graph will also have time for the delay between a lower-level goal and a higher-level goal being achieved. We believe the dependence introduces substantial complexity in the analysis and requires further investigation.

13.7   THOUGHTS ON EVOLUTION OF IRS TECHNOLOGY

We anticipate that for IRSs to be widely deployed, they will have to evolve in several directions over the coming years, including:

+ *Ability to withstand unpredictable attack scenarios.* It is inconceivable that all attack scenarios would be "programmed" in the IRS. The IRS should, therefore, be able to extrapolate strategies available in its knowledge base and take responses to hitherto unseen attacks. This will be an important requirement since polymorphic worms, viruses, and other forms of attacks are rampant in today's security landscape. In this matter, there is a delicate balancing game between learning from the past and being agile to respond to future attacks. It is possible to build up large knowledge bases and do exact matches with them to choose appropriate responses from the history. However, this may affect the ability of the system to respond quickly. Also, in taking lessons from the past, the IRS should take into account the fact that the impact of the attack may be different even though the attack steps may be the same. Thus, a more drastic or quicker response may be called for.

✦ *Dynamic responses with changing network configurations.* The IRS will have to deal with topology and configuration changes in the distributed system. It may take inputs from change notification software systems, such as Tripwire, and modify its response strategies accordingly. In any medium- to large-size distributed system, there are multiple administrators responsible for maintaining the system. The tools are often not standardized or uniform across different administrators. Thus, modifying the tools to send notification to the IRS seems daunting. A more feasible approach appears to be software to observe the resultant changes and notify the IRS. A change in the configuration may render some responses unnecessary (such as a critical service being made accessible from only inside the corporate network) or some responses more critical (such as a service being made Web accessible).

✦ *Interaction with other components of the security framework.* The response strategy decided on by the IRS is predicated on confidence placed on other components of the security framework, such as IDS, change notification software, firewalls, and so on. The confidence placed on these components should not be predefined constant values. The confidence should change as new software is installed, rules updated, or configurations change. This also indicates why a probabilistic framework for the IRS seems the promising avenue, rather than deterministic response decisions. On another point, the IRS may depend on various basic functionalities in the system, such as firewalls or an access control system, to deploy the computed responses.

✦ *Separation of policy and mechanism.* It is important for the IRS to provide mechanisms for determining the appropriate response based on security policy settings. As far as practicable, the two aspects should be clearly delineated. This will enable a system administrator to set the policy, which can be at various levels of abstraction, such as a paranoid versus *laissez faire* policy at the system-wide level, to policy levels for individual services. In the absence of this, an IRS will not have buy-in for production systems.

✦ *User interface design.* Visualizing the different effects of an attack and its responses in a distributed environment is inherently challenging. The speed of the processes (attacks as well as responses) makes this a particularly daunting task. However, for critical functions, all the stake holders (system administrators to chief information officers of an organization) will likely have a human-digestible form of the information available to them. This should include online tools that let them visualize the network while an attack or its responses are being deployed, as well as offline tools that will aid in forensics action.

13.8   CONCLUSION

In this chapter, we present the motivation for designing IRSs for distributed systems. We lay out the design challenges in designing and implementing IRSs. Then, we present existing work in the field, classified into four classes. The first category of IRSs, called *static decision making*, provides a static mapping of the alert from the detector to the response that is to be deployed. The second class, called *dynamic decision making*, reasons about an ongoing attack based on the observed alerts and determines an appropriate response to take. The third class, called *intrusion tolerance through diverse replicas*, provides masking of security failures through the use of diverse replicas concurrently for performing security critical functions. The fourth class includes IRSs meant to target specific kinds of attacks, with our focus being on DDoS attacks. Then, we present a discussion on the nascent field of benchmarking of IRSs. Finally, we present five key areas in which IRSs need to evolve for a widespread adoption. In summary, we find that the design and development of IRSs have been gaining in research attention and we expect that they will become mainstream in the computer security landscape in the near future.

References

[1] W. Metcalf, V. Julien, D. Remien and N. Rogness, "Snort Inline," http:// sourceforge.net/projects/snort-inline/.

[2] Symantec Corp., "Norton Antivirus," at http://www.symantec.com/home_ homeoffice/products/overview.jsp?pcid=is&pvid=nav2007.

[3] T. Ryutov, C. Neuman, K. Dongho, and Z. Li, "Integrated Access Control and Intrusion Detection for Web Servers," *Proceedings of the 23rd International Conference on Distributed Computing Systems (ICDCS)*, Providence, RI, 2003, pp. 394 – 401.

[4] McAfee Inc., "Internet Security Suite," at http://us.mcafee.com/root/ package.asp?pkgid=272.

[5] I. Balepin, S. Maltsev, J. Rowe, and K. Levitt, "Using Specification-Based Intrusion Detection for Automated Response," *Proceedings of the 6th International Symposium on Recent Advances in Intrusion Detection (RAID)*, Pittsburgh, PA, 2003, pp. 136–154.

[6] S. M. Lewandowski, D. J. Van Hook, G. C. O'Leary, J. W. Haines, and L. M. Rossey, "SARA: Survivable Autonomic Response Architecture," *Proceedings of the DARPA Information Survivability Conference & Exposition II (DISCEX)*, Anaheim, CA, 2001, vol. 1, pp. 77–88.

[7] G. B. White, E. A. Fisch, and U. W. Pooch, "Cooperating Security Managers: A Peer-Based Intrusion Detection System," *Network, IEEE* 10 (1996): 20–23.

[8] P. G. Neumann and P. A. Porras, "Experience with EMERALD to Date," *Proceedings of the Workshop on Intrusion Detection and Network Monitoring*, Santa Clara, CA, 1999, pp. 73–80.

[9] D. Ragsdale, C. Carver, J. Humphries, and U. Pooch, "Adaptation Techniques for Intrusion Detection and Intrusion Response Systems," *Proceedings of the IEEE International Conference on Systems, Man, and Cybernetics*, Nashville, TN, 2000, pp. 2344–2349.

[10] T. Toth and C. Kruegel, "Evaluating the Impact of Automated Intrusion Response Mechanisms," *Proceedings of the 18th Annual Computer Security Applications Conference (ACSAC)*, Las Vegas, Nevada, 2002, pp. 301–310.

[11] M. Atighetchi, P. Pal, F. Webber, R. Schantz, C. Jones, and J. Loyall, "Adaptive Cyber Defense for Survival and Intrusion Tolerance," *Internet Computing, IEEE* 8 (2004): 25–33.

[12] M. Tylutki, "Optimal Intrusion Recovery and Response Through Resource and Attack Modeling," Ph.D. Thesis, University of California at Davis, 2003.

[13] W. Lee, W. Fan, M. Miller, S. J. Stolfo, and E. Zadok, "Toward Cost-Sensitive Modeling for Intrusion Detection and Response," *Journal of Computer Security* 10 (2002): 5–22.

[14] D. Wang, B. B. Madan, and K. S. Trivedi, "Security Analysis of SITAR Intrusion Tolerance System," *Proceedings of the ACM Workshop on Survivable and Self-Regenerative Systems*, Fairfax, VA, 2003, pp. 23–32.

[15] C. Cachin, "Distributing Trust on the Internet," *Proceedings of the International Conference on Dependable Systems and Networks (DSN)*, Göteborg, Sweden, 2001, pp. 183–192.

[16] P. Pal, F. Webber, and R. Schantz, "Survival by Defense-Enabling," *Foundations of Intrusion Tolerant Systems (Organically Assured and Survivable Information Systems)*, Jaynarayan H. Lala, ed., IEEE Computer Society, Los Alamitos, CA, 2003, pp. 261–269.

[17] F. B. Schneider and L. Zhou, "Implementing Trustworthy Services Using Replicated State Machines," *Security & Privacy Magazine, IEEE* 3 (2005): 34–43.

[18] M. A. Hiltunen, R. D. Schlichting, and C. A. Ugarte, "Building Survivable Services Using Redundancy and Adaptation," *IEEE Transactions on Computers* 52 (2003): 181–194.

[19] D. Sterne, K. Djahandari, B. Wilson, B. Babson, D. Schnackenberg, H. Holliday, and T. Reid, "Autonomic Response to Distributed Denial of Service Attacks," *Proceedings of the 4th International Symposium on Rapid Advances in Intrusion Detection (RAID)*, Davis, CA, 2001, pp. 134–149.

[20] C. Douligeris and A. Mitrokotsa, "DDoS Attacks and Defense Mechanisms: Classification and State-of-the-Art," *Computer Networks* 44 (2004): 643–666.

[21] G. Koutepas, F. Stamatelopoulos, and B. Maglaris, "Distributed Management Architecture for Cooperative Detection and Reaction to DDoS Attacks," *Journal of Network and Systems Management* 12 (2004): 73–94.

[22] University of Southern California, Information Sciences Institute, "Generic Authorization and Access-control API (GAA-API)," at http://gost.isi.edu/info/gaaapi/.

[23] Netfilter Core Team, "Libipq—Iptables Userspace Packet Queuing Library," at http://www.cs.princeton.edu/~nakao/libipq.htm.

[24] McAfee Inc., "Network Intrusion Prevention," at http://www.mcafee.com/us/smb/products/network_intrusion_prevention/index.html.

[25] McAfee Inc., "McAfee Host Intrusion Prevention," at http://www.mcafee.com/us/local_content/datasheets/partners/ds_hips.pdf.

[26] B. Foo, Y. S. Wu, Y. C. Mao, S. Bagchi, and E. Spafford, "ADEPTS: Adaptive Intrusion Response Using Attack Graphs in an E-commerce Environment," *Proceedings of the International Conference on Dependable Systems and Networks (DSN)*, Yokohama, Japan, 2005, pp. 508–517.

[27] Yu-Sung Wu, Bingrui Foo, Yu-Chun Mao, Saurabh Bagchi, and Eugene H. Spafford, "Automated Adaptive Intrusion Containment in Systems of Interacting Services," *Elsevier Computer Networks Journal*, Special Issue on "From intrusion detection to self-protection", vol. 51, Issue 5, pp. 1334–1360, April 2007.

[28] D. Armstrong, S. Carter, G. Frazier, and T. Frazier, "Autonomic Defense: Thwarting Automated Attacks via Real-Time Feedback control," *Wiley Complexity* 9 (2003): 41–48.

[29] D. Armstrong, G. Frazier, S. Carter, T. Frazier, and I. Alphatech, "A Controller-Based Autonomic Defense System," *Proceedings of the DARPA Information Survivability Conference and Exposition*, Washington, DC, 2003, vol. 2, pp. 21–23.

[30] O. P. Kreidl and T. M. Frazier, "Feedback Control Applied to Survivability: A Host-Based Autonomic Defense System," *IEEE Transactions on Reliability* 53 (2004): 148–166.

[31] P. A. Porras and P. G. Neumann, "EMERALD: Event Monitoring Enabling Responses to Anomalous Live Disturbances," *Proceedings of the National Information Systems Security Conference*, Baltimore, MD, 1997, pp. 353–365.

[32] P. Porras, D. Schnackenberg, S. Staniford-Chen, M. Stillman, and F. Wu, "The Common Intrusion Detection Framework," CIDF working group document, at http://www.gidos.org.

[33] M. Petkac and L. Badger, "Security Agility in Response to Intrusion Detection," *Proceedings of the 16th Annual Computer Security Applications Conference (ACSAC)*, New Orleans, LA, 2000, pp. 11–20.

[34] P. P. Pal, F. Webber, R. E. Schantz, and J. P. Loyall, "Intrusion Tolerant Systems," *Proceedings of the IEEE Information Survivability Workshop (ISW-2000)*, Boston, MA, 2000, pp. 24–26.

[35] V. Stavridou, B. Dutertre, R. A. Riemenschneider, and H. Saidi, "Intrusion Tolerant Software Architectures," *Proceedings of the 2001 DARPA Information Survivability Conference & Exposition*, 2001. pp. 230–241

[36] S. M. Khattab, C. Sangpachatanaruk, D. Mosse, R. Melhem, and T. Znati, "Roaming Honeypots for Mitigating Service-Level Denial-of-Service Attacks," *Proceedings of the the 24th International Conference on Distributed Computing Systems (ICDCS)*, 2004, pp. 328–337.

[37] W. J. Blackert, D. M. Gregg, A. K. Castner, E. M. Kyle, R. L. Hom, and R. M. Jokerst, "Analyzing Interaction between Distributed Denial of Service Attacks and Mitigation Technologies," *Proceedings of the DARPA Information Survivability Conference and Exposition (DISCEX)*, 2003, vol. 1, pp. 26–36.

[38] D. K. Y. Yau, J. C. S. Lui, L. Feng, and Y. Yeung, "Defending against Distributed Denial-of-Service Attacks with Max-Min Fair Server-Centric Router Throttles," *IEEE/ACM Transactions on Networking* 13 (2005): 29–42.

[39] D. Schnackenberg, K. Djahandari, and D. Sterne, "Infrastructure for Intrusion Detection and Response," *Proceedings of DARPA Information Survivability Conference and Exposition (DISCEX)*, 2000, vol. 2, pp. 3–11.

[40] Carnegie Mellon University, Software Engineering Institute, "Survivable Network Technology," at http://www.sei.cmu.edu/organization/programs/nss/surv-net-tech.html.

[41] R. J. Ellison, R. C. Linger, T. Longstaff, and N. R. Mead, "Survivable Network System Analysis: A Case Study," *IEEE Software*, vol. 16. no. 4, pp. 70–77, Jul/Aug. 1999.

[42] S. Jha, J. Wing, R. Linger, and T. Longstaff, "Survivability Analysis of Network Specifications," *Proceedings of International Conference on Dependable Systems and Networks (DSN)*, New York, NY, 2000, pp. 613–622.

[43] J. R. Horgan, S. London, and M. R. Lyu, "Achieving Software Quality with Testing Coverage Measures," *Computer* 27 (1994): 60–69.

[44] Devellion Limited, "CubeCart: PHP and MySQL Shopping Cart," at http://www.cubecart.com/.

[45] V. Srinivasan, G. Varghese, and S. Suri, "Packet Classification Using Tuple Space Search," in *Proc. ACM SIGCOMM*, Sept. 1999, pp. 135–146.

[46] M. Waldvogel, G. Varghese, J. Turner, and B. Plattner, "Scalable High Speed IP Routing Lookups," in *Proc. ACM SIGCOMM*, Sept. 1997, pp. 25–36.

[47] P. Gupta and N. McKeown, "Algorithms for Packet Classification," *IEEE Network*, vol. 15, no. 2, pp. 24–32, 2001.

[48] P. Gupta and N. McKeown, "Packet Classification Using Hierarchical Intelligent Cuttings," *Hot Interconnects VII*, Aug. 1999.

[49] P. Gupta, S. Lin, and N. McKeown, "Routing Lookups in Hardware at Memory Access Speeds," *Proc. IEEE INFOCOM*, pp. 1240–1247, Mar. 1999.

Secure and Resilient Routing: Building Blocks for Resilient Network Architectures

Deep Medhi   University of Missouri–Kansas City, USA
Dijiang Huang   Arizona State University, USA

14.1   INTRODUCTION

A common paradigm for a network service architecture is to provide a number of different services or applications in which all of them share resources; the routing framework provides the best path to all services. A simple twist to this basic notion is if we were to architect in a way to virtualize the network so that different services are clustered into different virtual, adaptive partitions to provide different levels of services. In considering this notion, it is important to note that a service offering can span the entire spectrum from complete sharing to physically dedicated partitioning. Furthermore, even without a shared environment, prioritization is also possible, for example, in packet scheduling for different service classes at a router. Typically, to provide a certain quality of service, which might be agreed upon through a service-level agreement, a shared environment requires less network bandwidth due to statistical gain as opposed to a completely dedicated, partitioned environment to each different service—this is from the angle of a network service provider. However, in many instances, a middle-of-the-road approach can be a viable alternative in which through virtualization, services can be offered as guaranteed prioritized services, and more importantly, such virtualization can be adaptively configured, without requiring complete physical partitioning.

Our middle-of-the-road approach is motivated by a different service paradigm. Consider the simple scenario of two service classes—survivable critical (SC) services and normal services—in which the objective is to provide a certain level of service quality or protection to SC services even under an attack or a network stress situation. This attack or stress can be either of the following forms: (1) injection of excessive dummy traffic to overload the network or network elements or (2) overtaking of a part of the network (e.g., some routers) so that some network elements become untrusted for use by SC services. An important driver then is that the network has the framework to consider trustworthiness and the routing protocol has the appropriate functionality that can support trustworthiness as well as resilience.

In this work, we present a routing perspective for a resilient network architecture in which different services with different priority can coexist in a virtualized environment. For resiliency, it is necessary to provide robustness in the routing architecture to protect against attacks as well as network overload. More importantly, we present a general framework for secure and resilient routing that can be conducive to providing secure traffic engineering as well. We, however, take a sort of backward-direction approach; specifically, instead of starting with what we require or assume in the network architecture, we start with the need for the service requirement for resiliency in a prioritized environment and work backward to identify what are the different components desirable in the network architecture to support this service paradigm. Implicit in our presentation is then the basic understanding that we do not necessarily consider the components identified to be efficient nor do we claim that all components or solutions have been identified; at times, we leave some problems identified as open, research problems.

We conclude this introduction with a general note about terminology. We use the term *router* as a generic routing node; in other words, it is not to be confused with an IP router and its capabilities as is understood in the context of the current Internet. This also means that the router is not necessarily limited to doing a shortest-path-based computation for route selection. Similarly, we use the term *link-state routing protocol* to indicate that information would need to be exchanged for the purpose of route computation that uses a link-state framework. Thus, within this framework we also mean that node-state information may need to be communicated as well. Hence, we will use link-state update (LSU) and extended node/link update (ENLU) interchangeably. For comparison purpose, however, we consider Open Shortest Path First (OSPF) to identify and contrast what it provides and what we envision a link-state routing framework needs, or how OSPF can be extended for the benefit of the resilient network architecture.

Network resiliency has been addressed over the years by many researchers. We note here two works: (1) Resilient overlay networks [1] present an approach for robustness over the current Internet for path diversity; our work addresses the infrastructure itself for the future Internet both from the perspective of robustness and security of routing information. (2) BGP/MPLS [2] architecture provides the ability to separate between routing update, path determination, and resource reservation; our architecture can potentially be deployed in a similar environment while we also address security of routing information exchange as well as how the nodes might be differentiated in the presence of an attack.

The rest of the chapter is organized as follows. In Section 14.2, we present the overall traffic engineering perspective as a motivating discussion toward resilient architecture, while in Section 14.3 we briefly identify the components of a resilient architecture. In Section 14.4, we discuss threats and countermeasures for link-state routing. We then present the resilient architecture in Section 14.5 in which we discuss routing protocol extension, virtualization of routing domain, and preliminary analysis. We then conclude with our summary.

14.2   TRAFFIC ENGINEERING PERSPECTIVE AND ITS RELATION TO NETWORK ROBUSTNESS

In order to provide prioritization to different services under an attack or an overload condition, a key requirement is allocation of resources. For our discussion here, we will use bandwidth as the resource. While theoretically any network can be overprovisioned to the point where such resources are unlimited, from a practical perspective, this is not so. There are two important issues to consider: (1) the cost of overprovisioning can be prohibitive and (2) a sudden surge in traffic due to a number of events (legitimate or otherwise) can overwhelm a network to the point where it becomes nonfunctional or poorly functional. The first issue can be addressed somewhat by providing some level of overprovisioning, allowable within the capital and operational expenditure budget. However, the second issue brings out the importance of the point that *not* all events can be predicated, and thus, a network requires some form of protection. Combining both of them, we can say that protection or prioritization might not be necessary all the time, but the network must have the capability to have that, if and when necessary.

An important question then is how do we protect resources such as bandwidth in a shared environment. While there are a number of approaches in a shared virtualized environment, we take the approach of hiding resources, for example, by *not* announcing all available information in routing updates in a link-state routing environment. Before we delve into this aspect on how to do it, we first take a traffic engineering perspective with regard to hiding information in a dynamic routing environment.

To illustrate the hidden information idea in the context of a link-state advertisement, we consider a generic link $i - j$ in a network. If $C_{i,j}$ is the total bandwidth of this link, and the currently used bandwidth is $u_{i,j}$, then the free bandwidth is $a_{i,j} = C_{i,j} - u_{i,j}$. Thus, the obvious thing to do is to advertise $a_{i,j}$ in the link-state advertisement. This information is flooded through the network and is used by (source) routers when doing routing computation in determining, say, the least-loaded route (e.g., the route with the most available bandwidth, also known as the widest path) to a destination router; this is then used for setting up a new request or a service class.

Suppose that we want to provide a built-in protection mechanism. That is, we want to reserve some bandwidth, say $s_{i,j}$, on link $i - j$ for SC services. The link-state advertisement is SC capable when the available bandwidth advertised is $w_{i,j} = C_{i,j} - u_{i,j} - s_{i,j}$. In effect, we would like normal services to use the quantity $w_{i,j}$ in determining route computation. At the same time, we want to let SC services know that there is really $s_{i,j}$ amount of bandwidth *also* available on link i-j for their use in route computation *and* for traffic flow; this bandwidth is, however, not available to normal services. Note that the SC traffic has access to both the available bandwidth for normal traffic and the bandwidth set aside for SC traffic. To accomplish this, in the link-state advertisement, we actually want to advertise $w_{i,j}$ *as well as* $s_{i,j}$; while the normal service sees $w_{i,j}$, the $s_{i,j}$ amount is "hidden" to them. On the other hand, the SC service sees $s_{i,j}$, but based only on a properly specified authorization. Furthermore, if some routers are untrusted, we do not want them to "see" this hidden bandwidth. This mechanism provides a way to accomplish service priority to critical services in computing and selecting routes that uses the hidden bandwidth. This can be critical during an attack or an overload. Given the assumption that some routers (or users) may be untrusted, we propose to transmit the hidden bandwidth information in an encrypted mode. In this way, only the trusted routers can decipher this information. Note that while we focus here on available bandwidth information to be hidden, other resources that are critical to SC services could also be encrypted and disseminated through a link-state update.

The basic paradigm works on a semi-reservation-based mode. We use *semi* in two different ways. If in the above mechanism, $s_{i,j}$ is set to zero, then there is no special reservation for SC services. Secondly, updating $w_{i,j}$ with a new value does not mean that a hard reservation is needed; a soft reservation mechanism suffices. The network state maintenance at the routers can be threshold based with regard to access control. For example, access control may be activated if the link utilization is above a certain value and/or if notified by an intrusion detection system (IDS).

Finally, despite the hidden bandwidth protection mechanism, it is possible that an attacker may still want to consume resources by generating excessive dummy traffic. In the earlier scenario, we assume that an attacker may not use the hidden bandwidth in route computation since it cannot decipher this information. This, however, does not stop the attacker from still trying to inject traffic into the "hidden" parts of the network. To avoid this attack traffic from spreading, we need an access control mechanism at the entry point to check if this traffic should be allowed and a reservation mechanism that protects resources dedicated to SC services. Thus, a dynamic access control mechanism to check such requests is needed. The second possible scenario is that the attacker somehow manages to access the SC traffic class (at some source router) and starts injecting excessive traffic to a certain destination (resulting in, for example, a distributed denial-of-service (DoS) attack). In this case, through active monitoring, it is desirable to substantially limit the injection of this traffic at different entry points rather than letting it reach its destination. This allows us to contain the attack (closer to the source) rather than let it spread throughout the network for an extended period of time. Either of these scenarios would require some adaptive feedback mechanisms between different entry-point routers and possible destinations (choke points) in a network and a new level of trust generation among routers.

It may be noted that a feature similar to SC service bandwidth protection, called *trunk reservation* (TR), is currently used in dynamic call routing telephone networks [3]. The TR concept [4–6] is essentially equivalent to the protection we have described here. Note that TR in such settings is typically used to avoid bistability in a network [5] rather than the type of protection we are considering. Also, note that TR has been discussed in the context of quality-of-service (QoS) routing in the Internet [7].

14.2.1 An Illustrative Example

We consider an example to address some of the issues related to adaptiveness, routing, and the SC service protection. Consider a three-node network. We will assume a flow-based reservation for the purpose of this illustration; note that this is *not* a requirement in general in semi-reservation-based mode. A new flow request requires a fixed bandwidth rate for the time duration of the flow. Note that in general, a flow does not mean a call or a microflow in our framework; it may be a request that is the result of a virtual tunnel that needs to be set up with certain guarantees for a certain time duration, which in turn serves as a bearer of microflows. However, for the purpose of this simple illustration, a flow may be thought of as a microflow or a call.

We assume dynamic flow-based routing (a flow request for a traffic node pair can either use the direct path or use the alternate two-link path). The traffic between two traffic pairs (i.e., between nodes 1 and 2 denoted by pair {1:2}, and between nodes 1 and 3 denoted by pair {1:3}) is assumed to be stationary (and has the traffic volume). On the other hand, the third pair (i.e., between nodes

2 and 3 denoted by {2:3}) has overloaded traffic caused by an attack, which is represented by a dynamic traffic stream using a time-dependent arrival rate that follows a sinusoidal behavior. Now assume that all of the traffic for both pairs {1:2} and {1:3} are for SC services, while the dynamic traffic behavior for pair {2:3} is for the normal service that contains traffic due to the attack. It may be noted that this is a special case of the framework discussed in Section 14.2. Specifically, in this case, we have reservations for normal and SC services with the following condition: $s_{2,3} = 0$, while $s_{1,2} > 0, s_{1,3} > 0$.

We have performed a simulation of this scenario using the MuSDyR simulator [8]. In Figure 14.1, we plot the flow-blocking probability for the normal service and SC service over time. As can be seen from Figure 14.1(a) (where the SC service protection amount is low), it is clear that as the dynamic traffic for the normal service peaks, it *also* drastically affects the SC services by increasing the denial rate even though the traffic for the SC service did *not* have increase in traffic during this period (since a stationary traffic pattern was used). On the other hand, in Figure 14.1(b) (by adjusting the SC service protection parameter values appropriately), we can show that the SC service is receiving essentially the same service guarantee during the entire time while the attack traffic is dynamically increasing during this period, and in fact, the attack traffic is facing heavy blocking as is desirable during this time. On the other hand, when the attack traffic dies away (the right part on each plot), having a low level of protection for SC services can be acceptable.

It is important to note that the protection amount for the SC service needs to be adjusted although the traffic itself may remain at the same level in a dynamic traffic environment. The second observation is that the reservation parameter

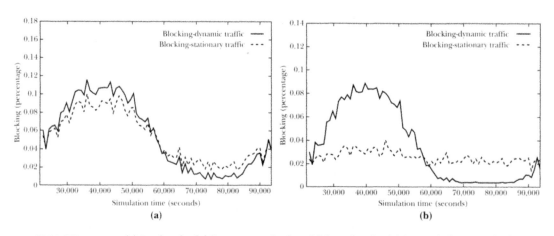

FIGURE   (a) Service denial (low reservation) and (b) service denial (extended reservation).

14.1

values need to be adaptive based on the traffic changes in a network. In other words, a semi-reservation-based mode can be the operational mode.

14.3   COMPONENTS OF A RESILIENT NETWORK ARCHITECTURE

Based on the discussion presented so far, we ask ourselves the basic question of what needs to be addressed in a resilient network architecture for such a service paradigm. Our thesis is that (1) the network needs to operate in a semi-reservation-oriented mode, (2) security and authentication need to be built-in factors, (3) routing can operate and hide information from untrusted elements, and (4) entry points to the network have the ability to do authorization checks and/or control traffic when necessary so that SC services can have priority (under stress).

Consider first one of the basic premises of our approach: the semi-reservation-oriented operation of the network. This means that the network has the ability to reserve resources to be made available to some services (e.g., SC services) *when* they need them. Note that the reservation need not be on a per-flow basis [9] such as in int-serv; a per class-based-type reservation, such as in diff-serv [10], suffices when needed. For brevity, we will refer to this network as the *semi-reservation-oriented network* (SRON). In this network, any reservation that is set does not necessarily remain static over a long duration; in fact, the SRON, in our view, operates in an adaptive reservation mode and can run without reservation until needed.

Secondly, security is a dynamic built-in factor in the SRON. This allows us to do at least the following: (1) determine if a router cannot be trusted, (2) check if a request has the authority to use reserved parts of the network, and (3) hide certain information in the network through encryption that can only be "seen" by authorized users. This aspect affects the operation of the routers and information exchanged among themselves. Since our interest is to provide priority to SC services, especially under a stress/attack, it is imperative that we periodically check the routers to see if they are trustworthy. Furthermore, we want the capability to hide resources (e.g., bandwidth) in the network that can be used by critical services at the right time using the trusted routers.

Since the network operates in the SRON mode and for the routers to determine good/acceptable routes, the routers need to exchange information about resource availability. For simplicity of illustration, we will use available bandwidth to be the resource of interest. For the purpose of this illustration, we assume that a link-state protocol is used to disseminate this information. The question then is, what should be included in this link-state advertisement, and more importantly, how do we ensure that the information advertised cannot be deciphered by an entity in the middle of the network? Given this premise, we next consider in depth both insider and outsider threats and countermeasures in a link-state routing framework.

14.4   THREATS AND COUNTERMEASURES IN LINK-STATE ROUTING

14.4.1   Link-State Routing Model and Threat Model

In this section, our discussion focuses on the origination, verification, and transmission of routing data. We start with a brief description of link-state routing and security threats specific to it. We discuss the security mechanisms that are known, as of now, to prevent some of these threat actions from taking place. Furthermore, we discuss the vulnerabilities of existing network routing security mechanisms and the improvements that can be done by using stronger authentication and a new method to manage routing data through encryption.

Link-State Routing Model

The link-state routing model is composed of physical entities (routers and communication links) and logical entities (the link-state routing protocol running in the routers). Within a link-state routing domain, each router generates the link-state information for the link that has the direct connection with the router (the link-state information is directional) and floods[1] this information to its neighbors. A receiving router will forward the routing information (unmodified) via flooding again. Therefore, each router will have the same view of a network. When a router joins the network, it needs to synchronize the link-state database with its neighbors. The routing information carried by a link-state routing protocol is typically the link-state of a router's interface. This information is called the *link-state advertisement* (LSA). During flooding, multiple LSAs can be encapsulated in a single *link-state update* (LSU) routing packet.

The security issues related to the link-state routing model can be broadly classified as security for the network device, operational security, and communication security. Security for the network devices concerns the physical access to the

---

[1] Flooding provides robust data transmission, in which a router forwards the link-state routing information packet to every interface except the one that receives the link-state routing information packet.

routers and communication links. Operational security includes the access control of the operating system of a router, privilege mode of a router, and so on. Communication security is related to the transmission, reception, and processing of routing data (LSAs and LSUs). Note that all data security-related issues discussed here are based on routing data but not on user data, and we focus on the communication security aspect of the link-state routing protocol.

Threats to Link-State Routing

In order to categorize the security threats to the routing protocol, we first need to identify the possible threat sources and their actions. We will follow definitions (such as threats, insider/outsider, etc.) provided in *RFC 2828* [11] for this purpose and use them in the context of network routing and routing protocols.

Threat sources.   The threat sources for link-state routing can be through communication links and routers. In the context of a deliberate attack, a threat source is defined as a motivated, capable adversary. Attacks can come from outside as well as from inside. As such, it is equally important to provide adequate safeguards for both internal and external threat sources. Here, internal threat sources are called insiders and external threat sources are called outsiders. In other words, the legitimate participants in network routing are called insiders. On the contrary, the illegitimate participants in the network routing are called outsiders. The outsiders can reside anywhere in a network and have the ability to observe routed traffic on a link or send attack packets to routers. Note that an outsider can masquerade to generate routing information as an insider. However, an outsider has no valid identifier and is not authorized to perform routing functions. An insider can also masquerade as another authorized router and generate forged routing information. It has a valid identifier, but it is not authorized to impersonate other routers or forge other routers' routing information (by "authorized" we mean the permission for overall routing operational functionalities). In this sense, we can say an outsider is unauthorized and an insider is authorized.

Threat actions.   Threat actions are also called attacks. Here, all our discussions focus on the origination, verification, and transmission of routing data. The attacks can be active or passive. Defined in *RFC 2828*: "An *active attack* attempts to alter system resources or affects their operation; a *passive attack* attempts to learn or makes use of information from the system but does not affect system resources." Attacks can also be classified based on threat sources—insiders and outsiders. This classification helps to categorize corresponding preventive cryptographic countermeasures, which will be discussed in Section 14.4.2. Note that we focus on the attack model that an attacker uses to compromise other routers' resources. Thus, we exclude the discussion of insider attackers that over-claim/underclaim/misclaim network resources that are under its control. For example, a subverted router claims that the bandwidth attached to one of its interfaces is w, but in fact, the actual bandwidth is r, where $w \neq r$.

Outsider attacks.　There are several types of outsider attacks:

  a. *Sniffing (passive)*: Monitoring and recording routing data transmitted on the communication links among routers (Figure 14.2a).

  b. *Falsification and masquerading (active)*: This attack can be of three kinds:

   1. *Substitution*: Altering or replacing valid routing information with false routing information (i in Figure 14.2b).

   2. *Insertion*: Introducing false routing data that serve to deceive an authorized router (ii in Figure 14.2b),

   3. *Masquerading*: Impersonating an authorized link/router (iii in Figure 14.2b). Masquerading is usually executed concurrently with substitution and/or insertion.

  c. *Obstruction (active)*: This attack can be of two types:

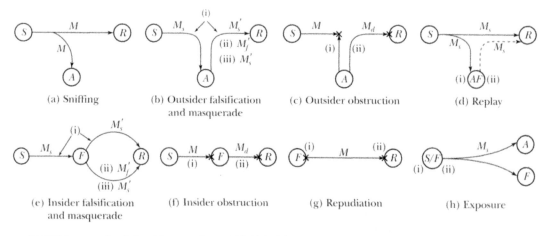

(a) Sniffing   (b) Outsider falsification and masquerade   (c) Outsider obstruction   (d) Replay

(e) Insider falsification and masquerade   (f) Insider obstruction   (g) Repudiation   (h) Exposure

FIGURE
14.2

(a–d) Outsider attacks and (d–h) insider attacks. Key: S: sender, R: receiver (or victim), A: outsider (attacker), F: insider (attacker), M: any routing message, M_s: routing message from sender, M'_s: forged routing message of sender, M'_f: malicious routing message generated by subverted routers, M_d: dummy routing traffic that cause overload, and $\rightarrow$: delayed transmission.

1. *Interference*: An attacker can block the transmission link, by cutting off the transmission link or by introducing noise into the transmission link to prevent the victims from receiving the routing information correctly (i in Figure 14.2c).

2. *Overload*: An attacker can place excess dummy routing traffic that can saturate the victim's input buffer or exhaust victim's computer processing unit (CPU) capacity (ii in Figure 14.2c).

d.1. *Replay (active)*: A valid routing data transmission is maliciously or fraudulently repeated by an outsider (i in Figure 14.2d).

Insider attacks.   There are several types of insider attacks:

d.2. *Replay (active)*: A valid routing data transmission is maliciously or fraudulently repeated by insiders (ii in Figure 14.2d).

e. *Falsification and masquerading (active)*: This is the same as specified in outsiders' threat actions (see Figure 14.2e). Thus, there are three sub-cases: (e.1) substitution, (e.2) insertion, and (e.3) masquerading. Compared to an outsider's falsification and masquerading, the insider attack can be more effective. Since the insider is a legitimate participant, he or she might know the shared key or serve as an intermediate forwarder, which makes the attack easier but more difficult to detect.

f. *Obstruction (active)*:

1. *Stop forwarding*: The subverted router does not forward received routing packets (i in Figure 14.2f).

2. *Overload*: Excessive routing information processing burden is placed on the router in order to saturate the victim's input buffer or exhaust the victim's CPU capacity (ii in Figure 14.2f). This is the same as the outsider's overload attack.

g. *Repudiation (active)*:

1. *False denial of origin*: A subverted router denies the operations that it has made on the transmitted routing information (i in Figure 14.2g).

2. *False denial of receipt*: A subverted router denies receiving the routing data (ii in Figure 14.2g). Although an outsider can repudiate what he or she has done, it is more critical for insider attacks. A subverted router can cause a more serious problem when it is authorized to perform routing functions. Quickly identifying the subverted routers/links will help to reduce the recovery time imposed by the attacks.

h. *Exposure (active)*:

1. *Nondeliberate exposure*: A router unintentionally releases sensitive routing data to attackers, both insiders and outsiders (i in Figure 14.2h).

2. *Deliberate exposure*: A subverted router intentionally releases sensitive routing data to attackers, both insiders and outsiders (ii in Figure 14.2h).

We note that in our classification all attacks originating from outsiders occur on the routing transmission links (e.g., Figures 14.2a–d). Among these, attacks interference (c.1) and replay (active) (d.2) need to get access to the transmission link first and then attackers can launch attacks. Attacks originating from insiders are generated by the subverted routers (e.g., Figures 14.2d–h). When an outsider successfully takes over an authorized router, it becomes an insider (or subverted router). In other words, the outsider usurps the rights of a legitimate router.

14.4.2   Preventive Cryptographic Countermeasures against Attacks

The challenges posed due to the enormity and diversity of threats has led to various research activities in recent years that address techniques to safeguard a network. On the other hand, the current standards for network routing protocols have not incorporated all of the techniques required to make them as foolproof as possible. A set of unplugged security holes remain that an adversary can use to paralyze a network. In this section, we first analyze the possible preventive cryptographic countermeasures, and then describe how they can completely or partially prevent attacks from taking place.

Preventive Cryptographic Countermeasures

Computer security rests on confidentiality, integrity, and availability. Table 14.1 enlists two preventive cryptographic countermeasures that are described in the literature, including those that have found a place in protocol standards. The two main preventive cryptographic countermeasures that have been suggested for routing protocols are confidentiality and integrity. Confidentiality ensures that no unauthorized entities can decipher the routing information on its way to its destination. Integrity refers to the trustworthiness of data or resources, and it is usually phrased in terms of preventing improper or unauthorized change.

Integrity includes data integrity (the content of the information) and origin integrity (the source of the data, often called authentication). The interpretations of integrity and authentication vary, as do the contexts in which they arise. In a link-state routing context/setting, authentication is generally considered as both

Methods		Label	Description	Protection
Authentication	Packet level	$PLA_{P2P}{}^{\dagger}$	Packet level, point-to-point authentication	Data and
(A)		$PLA_{E2E}{}^{\P}$	Packet level, end-to-end authentication	origin
	Information	$ILA_{P2P}{}^{\S}$	Information level, point-to-point authentication	integrity
	level	$ILA_{E2E}{}^{\ddagger}$	Information level, end-to-end authentication	
Confidentiality		$PLC^{\dagger}$	Confidentiality for the whole packet	Information
(C)		$ILC^{\P}$	Confidentiality for the information within the packet	availability

$\dagger$: OSPFv2 RFC 2328 and OSPFv3.
$\P$: Not in current literature.
$\S$: Proposed in Huang et al. [12].
$\ddagger$: OSPF extension RFC 2154.

TABLE   Security mechanisms.

14.1

data integrity and origin integrity [12]. For example, a keyed-hashing message authentication (HMAC) code can be used as the cryptographic authentication for OSPF (see *RFC 2328* [13]). It provides data integrity and only an authorized user (possesses a shared key) can generate and verify the HMAC. Similarly, digital signatures for OSPF (see *RFC 2154* [14]) also provide both data integrity and origin integrity. In the following, we consider authentication as providing both data integrity and origin integrity.

Availability refers to the ability to use the information or resource desired. The aspect of availability that is relevant to security is that someone may deliberately arrange to deny access to data or to a service by making them unavailable, such as a DoS attack. Preventive cryptographic countermeasures, by themselves, can do little to prevent DoS attacks. Most of the current solutions to DoS attacks are reactive solutions (i.e., solutions that depend on IDSs), which are beyond the scope of this research. We will show later on how to create multiple trusted routing domains to mitigate the consequence of a DoS attack.

Here, we focus on the following two preventive cryptographic countermeasures: confidentiality and authentication. These two countermeasures can provide protection at either the packet level (PL) or at the information level (IL). If we assume a routing packet to be a bus filled with a group of passengers, PL and IL represent the cryptographic countermeasures being provided for the bus and each individual passenger, respectively. Besides authentication and confidentiality, there are two other important concepts we need to introduce: point-to-point (P2P) and end-to-end (E2E) authentication. In terms of authentication, P2P means that the generation and verification of an authentication code are performed by every forwarding router. E2E means that the generation of an authentication code is performed only at the source; all the forwarding routers and termination routers are part of the end system, and they only perform verification. In Table 14.1, we provide a summary of the two main preventive cryptographic countermeasures for link-state routing protocols.

In the link-state routing protocol, pieces of routing information, *link-state advertisements* (LSAs), are encapsulated in a *link-state update* (LSU) packet. Most of the current implementations fall into the category of PLA_{P2P}. If PLA_{P2P} is provided for the entire LSU packet, then PLA_{P2P} can guard against the "man-in-the-middle" attack [11]. But, in link-state routing, flooding is used for distributing LSAs within a link-state routing domain. PLA_{P2P} cannot prevent any intermediate subverted router from modifying forwarded LSAs or a router from originating forged LSAs. E2E is more desirable to provide stronger protection for LSAs. But another difficulty of link-state routing is that multiple LSAs are encapsulated within a single LSU packet and the content of each LSU that originated from different routers may be *different*. This prevents PLA_{E2E} from being implemented efficiently. Hence, ILA_{E2E} and ILA_{P2P} are required to provide information-level protection. OSPF with digital signatures [14] is an example of ILA_{E2E}, while the double authentication scheme [12] is an example of ILA_{P2P}.

For confidentiality, too, we differentiate between packet level and information level, which are shown in Table 14.1. OSPF running over IPSec [15] is an example of providing PLC, which provides confidentiality for the internet provider (IP) payload. Providing confidentiality for each LSA individually is represented by ILC.

Using Preventive Cryptographic Countermeasures to Guard against Attacks

Next, we analyze how to use cryptographic countermeasures presented in Table 14.1 to guard against threat actions illustrated in Figure 14.2. Table 14.2 presents the mapping of threats and corresponding countermeasures. Threat actions that are marked with $\surd$ are solvable via well-known solutions and are outsider attacks. Attacks presented in (b) can be easily guarded against by using PLA_{P2P}. The dummy routing traffic due to attack (c.2) can be filtered out using PLA_{P2P}. Although, a cryptographic-based operation can aggravate the computer processing unit (CPU) computation burden, the overload attack is usually limited within a small range of where it happens. This is because the excess routing traffic cannot get through a router. This may be useful in preventing *distributed denial of service* (DDoS).

It may be noted that preventive countermeasures, such as authentication and confidentiality, cannot prevent attacks that are marked with ✤ (see (e.2) and (f.1)). These attacks need other security mechanisms such as admission/access control, intrusion detection, and so on.

| Threats | | Attack Types | | | Preventive | |
Threat Actions (Attacks)	Label	I/O	P/A	Countermeasures	Remarks
Wiretapping	Sniffing	(a)	O	Passive	*PLC* or *ILC*	★★
Outsider	Substitution	(b.1)	O	Active	*PLA$_{P2P}$*	√
falsification and	Insertion	(b.2)	O	Active	*PLA$_{P2P}$*	√
masquerade	Masquerading	(b.3)	O	Active	*PLA$_{P2P}$*	√
Outsider obstruction	Interference	(c.1)	O	Active	*PLC* or *ILC*	★★★
	Overload	(c.2)	O	Active	*PLA$_{P2P}$*	√
Replay	Outsider replay	(d.1)	O	Active	New keys	★★
	Insider replay	(d.2)	I	Active	New keys and *ILC* or *ILA$_{E2E}$*	★★★
Insider	Substitution	(e.1)	I	Active	*ILA$_{E2E}$*	★
falsification and	Insertion	(e.2)	I	Active	n/a	✣
masquerade	Masquerading	(e.3)	I	Active	*ILA$_{E2E}$*	★
Insider obstruction	Stop forwarding	(f.1)	I	Active	n/a	✣
	Overload	(f.2)	I	Active	*ILC*	★★★
Repudiation	False denial of origin	(g.1)	I	Active	*ILA$_{E2E}$* or *ILA$_{P2P}$*	★
	False denial of receipt	(g.2)	I	Active	*PLA$_{P2P}$*	★★★
Exposure	Nondeliberate exposure	(h.1)	I	Active	*PLC*† or *ILC*‡	★★
	Deliberate exposure	(h.2)	I	Active	*ILC*	★★★

I/O: Insider/Outsider (attacks).
P/A: Passive/Active (attacks).
†: Guard against outsider attacks.
‡: Guard against insider attacks.
★: Solvable via well known solutions but less deployed.
√: Solvable via well known solutions and widely deployed.
★★★: Partially solvable via our proposed solution.
★★: Solvable via solutions proposed here.
✣: Unsolvable via authentication and confidentiality.

TABLE   Threats and corresponding cryptographic preventive countermeasures.

14.2

Our discussion here will focus only on the countermeasures marked by ★, ★★, or ★★★. The countermeasures marked by ★ are specified in the current literature, such as OSPF with digital signatures [14]. We note that end-to-end authentication is considered as a strong preventive cryptographic countermeasure. A widely accepted proposal uses the public key scheme to sign each LSA. The reason we separate it from *PLA*, marked by √, is because of the deployment difficulty of digital signatures, which comes with a high computation overhead compared with the traditional authentication schemes (e.g., the keyed hash function (HMAC) [16]). Countermeasures marked by ★★ are barely addressed in the current literature, while countermeasures marked by ∗∗∗ have not been addressed so far.

Guarding against Attacks on Communication Links

As shown in Table 14.2, attacks from (a) to (d.1) are injected on the communication link. Here, we investigate the possible use of preventive cryptographic countermeasures when attacks (a), (c.1), and (d.1) occur (marked with ∗∗ and ∗∗∗).

Outsider wiretapping attack (a). *PLC* or *ILC* can be used to prevent outsiders from sniffing packets containing routing information. This is a straightforward method to prevent passive attacks. When *PLC* is provided for the entire IP payload, the outsider would not know general information, such as link-state type, advertising router, and sequence number, that is contained within the routing packet header. This information can help an attacker to derive network topology and traffic patterns. *ILC* cannot prevent an attacker from knowing the information within the routing packet header, but it can prevent subverted routers from decrypting the routing information when they use different encryption/decryption keys. The combination of *PLC* and *ILC* provides strong security features to guard against ineligible entities.

Outsider interference attack (c.1). We assume that there is an admission control mechanism to prevent outsiders from using network tools to derive the network topology. This can also be done by simply disabling those network services. Then an attacker might arbitrarily wiretap any possible communication links to intercept the routing information. Plaintext routing information can help attackers to derive network topology and traffic patterns. Due to flooding of the routing information used by the link-state routing protocol, tapping one link can help attackers to intercept all flooded LSAs within its routing domain. The intercepted routing information can be valuable for attackers to decide the location of an attack target, such as the weakest communication links or the partition routers. We note that providing confidentiality cannot prevent an attacker from doing active attacks. However, without the network topology and traffic pattern information, it is hard for attackers to deploy attacks successfully. Note that most of the active attacks presented here require the network topology or traffic pattern information.

Outsider replay attack (d.1). Although link-state routing protocols typically use a nondecreasing sequence number to prevent replay attack, the replay attack can still take place when the sequence number is rolled over or a router reboots.

Guarding against Attacks on Routers

We next discuss possible use of preventive cryptographic countermeasures when attacks take place on a router. Insider attacks (d.2), (e.1), (f.2), (g), and (h) are some examples of attacks on routers (marked by *, **, and ***).

Insider replay attack (d.2). The analysis of attack (d.2) is similar to the outsider replay attack (d.1). The difference is that information-level confidentiality is required. We illustrate the reason through a simple example; the LSA contains the bandwidth information of a particular link l, which is c_l. When all routers share a common key to sign/encrypt LSAs, any subverted insider can replay an LSA. Preventing this form of attack in the current framework is difficult. Therefore, a new framework should be such that one can allocate a different set of keys to routers and sign/encrypt only a subportion of bandwidth of link l, say c_l'. The insider attacker can only replay the old routing information c_l', which only affects parts of a network's resources. This would mean that not all routers within the link-state routing domain share the same network resource information. If we consider a link-state routing domain as a trust domain (TD), through ILC we can differentiate it as multiple subtrust domains. Hence, if one of the subrouting systems is compromised, it does not affect others or can only cause minimal damage to other subtrust domains. Since routers within a TD share the crypto key, the replay attack can still occur, and updating the crypto key will not be helpful to prevent the subverted routers from replaying the old routing packets. Thus, building multiple trust domains through ILC can only limit the effect of attack (d.2).

Insider substitution attack (e.1) and insider masquerading attack (e.3). In the case of attacks (e.1) and (e.3), ILA_{E2E} can prevent subverted routers from substituting the routing information and masquerading as other routers when data origin authentication is provided for each LSA and is guaranteed E2E.

Insider overload attack (f.2). This scenario occurs when there is an excessive routing information burden on routers, overloading the routers' input buffer or CPU. It is different from outsider overload attack (c.2), which only aims to overload the neighboring routers' input buffers or CPU. Insider overload can cause more damage, because the attacked routers will forward the excessive routing information to the next hop due to flooding. Although some link-state routing protocols set a minimal arrival interval to limit LSA updating, a subverted router can circumvent this protection via constantly inventing new LSA instances. Thus, the attacking traffic can be spread throughout a network due to flooding.

In order to limit the routing data traffic overload attack, we again need to divide the link-state routing domain into multiple smaller link-state routing (sub)domains. We assume here that the network has the link bandwidth management capability. An illustrative example is shown in Figure 14.3, which represents a network segment composed of three routers and two links. The capacity of a communication link 1–2 is c_{1-2}. TD_1 and TD_2 are configured to run through link 1–2. The bandwidth allocated for these two TDs are μ^1_{1-2} and μ^2_{1-2} (the superscript is the identifier of a TD and the subscript is the identifier of a link). The available bandwidth of link 1–2 is given by α_{1-2}. Then, we have $c_{1-2} = \mu^1_{1-2} + \mu^2_{1-2} + \alpha_{1-2}$. Similarly, the capacity allocation of link 2–3 is $c_{2-3} = \mu^2_{2-3} + \alpha_{2-3}$. Note that the reserved bandwidth is guaranteed through both bandwidth management and confidentiality provided for each TD. A particular encryption/decryption session key is used to provide confidentiality for a TD. In our example, both routers R1 and R2 can decrypt LSAs for TD_1 and TD_2, and R3 can only see the available bandwidth allocated for TD_2. R3 does not possess the session key used by TD_2, and it cannot forge routing information to announce allocated bandwidth on link 2–3 for TD_1. If the subverted router R3 overloads R2, then R2 would not forward the excessive routing traffic that exceeds μ^2_{1-2}. The traffic control is done through bandwidth management and the TD identification is done through providing confidentiality (ILC) to hide the network resources.

Insider false denial of origin attack (g.1). In the case of attack (g.1), ILA_{E2E} can prevent insiders from denying the original sources that sent the false routing information. The authentication code should provide evidence that the sender cannot deny (e.g., a digital signature).

Insider false denial of receipt attack (g.2). The acknowledgment mechanism of a link-state routing protocol is neighbor-to-neighbor based. Multiple LSAs can be acknowledged by a single link-state acknowledgment packet. The acknowledgment packet can use a shared key between the communication

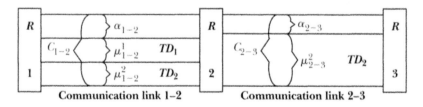

FIGURE
14.3

Communication link under attack.

peers to authenticate the received packet. However, by using a shared-key based neighbor-to-neighbor authentication mechanism, there is no way to explicitly determine who generates the packets. Use of ILA_{E2E} and ILA_{P2P} for acknowledgment of every LSA is impractical and unnecessary. Moreover, the receiver can stop sending back acknowledgments. Thus, using PLA_{P2P} for acknowledgment is optional and can only benefit in preventing the "man-in-the-middle" attack.

Insider nondeliberate exposure attack (h.1).   An insider may unintentionally expose routing information to outsiders or other insiders that are not necessarily receiving the routing information (e.g., if the communication is via a wireless link). The analysis of this scenario is the same as scenario (a). PLC ensures no outsider can reveal the content. Within the multiple TD's framework, ILC ensures only eligible TD members can reveal the content within their TD.

Insider deliberate exposure attack (h.2).   An insider can deliberately expose the routing information to anyone. But, with the routing information protected by ILC, a subverted/compromised router cannot expose the routing information of other TDs to which it does not belong.

14.5 RESILIENT ARCHITECTURE: VIRTUALIZATION AND ROUTING

Having discussed so far our original premise along with the routing protocol framework and the attack models in detail, we are now ready to discuss the resilient network architecture and the role of routing that has the benefit of enabling a virtualized environment.

14.5.1 An Enabling Framework for Adaptive and Secure Virtualized Networking

Network virtualization to provide prioritized critical/emergency services is a critical need for cybertrust in next-generation networks. In this section, we present a new secure, extended node/link update (ENLU) framework by extending a link-state routing framework through a secure group communication approach for enabling network virtualization. This scheme allows dissemination of ENLU messages to be encoded in such a way that only nodes with the proper key can take advantage of the encoded information for prioritized services. We invoke a many-to-many group communication keying scheme to virtualize network resources to support multiple service domains; the scheme has been described in detail Huang et al. [17] and is summarized in Appendix 14.A at the end of the chapter.

Cryptographic Approaches for Network Resource Prioritization

In general, confidentiality ensures that no unauthorized entities can decipher the routing information on its way to a destination; integrity refers to the trustworthiness of data or resources and it is usually phrased in terms of preventing improper or unauthorized change. Integrity includes data integrity (the content of the information) and origin integrity (the source of the data, often called authentication).

As discussed earlier, our approach considers two preventive cryptographic countermeasures: confidentiality and authentication. These two countermeasures can provide protection at either the PL or the IL, shown in Figure 14.4(a). Recall that if we assume a routing packet to be a bus filled with a group of passengers, PL and IL represent the cryptographic countermeasures being provided for the bus and each individual passenger, respectively.

To date, there has been no information-level confidentiality (ILC) schemes proposed for routing protocols that can be used for network virtualization. Our approach is to use ILC and information-level authentication (ILA) as the foundation to build a new secure routing framework. To deploy ILC, routing information (i.e., metric) is categorized by multiple groups. By carefully assigning group keys to nodes, we can partition network resources into multiple routing domains.

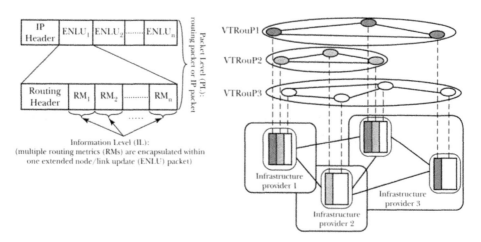

FIGURE 14.4 (a) Granularity of attributes at the packet level and information level and (b) VTRouP: conceptual framework.

For example, consider a node with several outgoing links; it can encrypt routing metrics (RMs) for some links using one key and encrypt RMs for other links using another key. Thus, only nodes that have the correct key can decrypt the routing information. This strategy can also be applied to a single link, that is, a node can partition the bandwidth of a link into multiple portions and create/encrypt an RM for each portion. This approach has several benefits:

+ It prevents outsiders' sniffing attacks. We assume that the crypto key length is long enough to prevent brute-force attack: within a maintenance cycle (i.e., periodically updating the window of the crypto keys).

+ It mitigates outsiders' traffic-analysis attacks. Since extended node/link attributes are encrypted and a node may or may not possess the decrypting key, nodes can maintain different network topology information and shortest-path tree or other provisioned paths. Thus, the data flow may not follow the same shortest path, which can prevent attackers from deriving the correct network topology or traffic allocation pattern.

+ An insider has limited information of a network, which can mitigate routing analysis and deliberate exposure attacks.

To implement ILC and ILA, an efficient secure group key management scheme, which supports many-to-many secure group communication, is needed. Many-to-many secure group communication requires that each group member (node in our case) with a group population of size n can communicate with any subgroup of members securely and on a real-time basis without requiring a new set of keys for each subgroup communication. In general, this means a group member would need to possess $2^{n-1} - 1$ keys; however, our secure many-to-many group communication keying scheme [18], summarized in Appendix 14.A, has been designed for the purpose of virtualization and has much less complexity. Briefly, our many-to-many secure group communication keying scheme has the following advantages:

1. During the communication phase, group members can self-derive desired subgroup keys.

2. No group/subgroup setup delay, although there is some processing overhead incurred due to the key agreement protocol.

3. Less communication overhead incurred compared to other methods.

4. It is suitable where subgroup formation is frequent.

5. A node cannot partner with another node to move to a different (unauthorized) subgroup.

The above advantages are ideal for the encrypted ENLU framework since it allows us to disseminate ENLU messages in a way that is meant only for a subgroup of nodes. Recall that we initially considered two services, normal services and SC services, with the important requirement that SC services encompass normal services as well. This can be accomplished by defining two subgroups for extended node/link-state dissemination using the many-to-many secure group communication scheme we have developed. Note that although there are only two subgroups in this case, which are mapped to two categories of services, the formations of subgroups can be changed frequently with respect to the use of different subgroup keys.

Note that our keying scheme addresses the problem of undesirable node partnering with other nodes to read all attributes of an advertised LSA, thus preventing a node from moving from a normal service state to a prioritized service state without having the credentials (i.e., the set of secrets to derive desired group/subgroup keys).

Our keying scheme has an additional advantage since it allows dynamic subgroup formation. This means that if a network wants to dynamically define multiple prioritized service levels, our approach allows it with the added advantage that a node can be in different prioritized groups and yet it cannot become an undesirable node (i.e., to move to a higher prioritized service class).

It may be noted that if a number of nodes in a network is likely to grow, then our scheme can be deployed with overprovisioned keys. For example, if the overall group size is currently around 50, and it is expected to grow to about 100, then the initial deployment can be done assuming the total group members to be, say, 101, since our scheme requires the overall population size to be odd numbered. This would mean that there would be some fictitious group members to start with. This approach then avoids redistribution of keys frequently (at the expense of overprovisioning) to nodes in the entire network. Our current approach has the following limitations: (1) the storage complexity of the keying scheme is $O(n^2)$, and the overall group size is restricted to a few hundred nodes, and (2) a centralized key server is required to do initial key predistribution. An important research goal is to overcome these limitations.

Virtual Trust Routing and Provisioning Domain

Using our many-to-many secure group keying scheme and information-level encryption and authentication approach, the entire routing domain can be divided into multiple routing/provisioning subdomains. We refer to such a subdomain as a virtual trust routing and provisioning domain (VTRouP) (Figure 14.4b). The framework may not need/imply the division of the administrative domain into VTRouPs.

Every node that belongs to a particular VTRouP will have complete routing information of its own VTRouP, but not others. We use the cryptographic techniques ILA and ILC to build the VTRouP framework. Each node can be provided by a different infrastructure provider; however, each node would need to support our framework that includes secure many-to-many communication as well as the capability of link bandwidth control and virtualization. For example, the bandwidth of a communication link of each node would be divided by using different encryption/decryption/authentication keys. While bandwidth partitioning is not directly available in most of today's routers, this can be accomplished through the concept of multiple virtual links due to availability of the virtual link concept in the current generation of routers. Thus, a subset of network resources, which is composed of multiple network links using the same encryption/decryption/authentication key, will build a VTRouP.

We now briefly discuss how the overall system framework is affected (see Figure 14.5). Typically, from a systems perspective, traffic management and network resource management components are necessary for monitoring and managing a network. For a resilient environment, there are three additional components involved IDS, key management, and VTRouP. Note that intrusion detection is outside the scope of the present work, however, its role is important in the overall system framework.

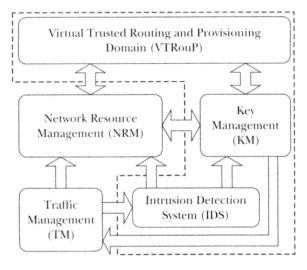

FIGURE   System framework.

14.5

14.5.2   Routing Protocol Extension: OSPF-E

In this section we present an extension to OSPF, to be referred to as OSPF-E, for use in a VTRouP environment. A basic notion is that our approach benefits from a traffic engineering extension of OSPF, known as OSPF-TE. Here, we go beyond that to address the encryption of information. To achieve this, we also use the opaque LSA option (*RFC 2370* [19]). The opaque LSA consists of a standard LSA header followed by application-specific information and it provides a generalized mechanism to allow for the future extensibility of OSPF. We include the details of our proposed LSA packet format. We then introduce a key numbering scheme in order to identify the trust level of the routers and the key that has been used to encrypt the routing information. We also discuss processing overhead of the LSU packet which is critical in an operational environment.

OSPF Opaque Link-State Advertisement: Extension

Opaque LSA [19] provide three LSA types: type 9, 10, and 11. These three LSA types provide the advertisement within a network, area, and autonomous system, respectively. We define the opaque LSA format to provide confidentiality for these three types of advertisements. In addition to these three types of opaque LSAs, we can define other types of opaque LSAs for particular use, such as a key distribution LSA or a routing control LSA.

In our scheme, authentication is based on the packet level of LSA, since the LSA header is not encrypted. We do not intend to provide a way to prevent insider attacks, rather, we show how OSPF-E works by introducing confidentiality. Murphy et al. [14] use digital signatures for each LSA to prevent impersonation attacks, which can be added to our scheme when needed. Here, we assume the network has the capability to detect insider attacks.

We now summarize the changes we propose in opaque LSA. The modified opaque LSA header is shown in Table 14.3.

1. *Options.* In *RFC 2370*, O bit of option field is set in the database description packet to indicate that the router is opaque capable. In the LSA's header, we use S bit in the same position to indicate the confidentiality provided.

2. *LSA type (8 bits).* Three types of opaque LSAs exist (type 9, 10, and 11), each of which has a different flooding scope. We provide confidentiality for these three types.

3. *OType (8 bits).* This field specifies the LSA type encrypted. The various Otypes are defined as follows: 1—Router-LSAs, 2—Network-LSAs, 3—Summary-LSAs

```
1                                      31
┌──────────────┬──────────┬──────────┐
│   LS age     │ Options  │ LSA type │
├───────┬──────┼──────────┼──────────┤
│ OType │ Pri  │  EType   │  Key ID  │
├───────┴──────┴──────────┴──────────┤
│        Advertising router           │
├─────────────────────────────────────┤
│        LS sequence number           │
├──────────────┬──────────────────────┤
│ LS checksum  │       Length         │
├──────────────┴──────────────────────┤
│          LSA subheader               │
│              . . .                   │
└─────────────────────────────────────┘
```

TABLE   Opaque LSA header.

14.3

(destination to network), 4—Summary-LSAs (destination to AS boundary routers), and 5—AS-external-LSAs.

4. *EType (8 bits).* The encryption type specifies the encryption/decryption method used, such as DES, 3DES, AES, and so on.

5. *Key ID (8 bits).* This field specifies the type of cryptographic scheme used to encrypt a propagated LSA. Some of the schemes are shared key, public key, and so on.

6. *LSA subheader.* The LSA subheader just follows the opaque LSA's header and identifies what encryption/decryption key is used.

We also propose changes to the LSA subheader (Table 14.4):

1. *Format (16 bits).* This field specifies what type of key is used. It can be Globe/level/subgroup key, individual key, and so on.

2. *Levels (n).* This field represents the number of levels between the key used and the top-level key.

3. *Num of bits (16 bits).* Based on our proposed master key scheme, this field specifies the number of concatenated hash values.

4. *Var 1~16*(n−1).* This field identifies the location of the key in the hierarchical key structure. It contains each level's information from the top down to the level in which the key is located; here, *n* is specified in the "Levels" field.

5. *SKey len (8 bits).* This field specifies the length of a session key when it is used.

6. *Var/Encrypted session key.* The session key is encrypted by the individual or globe/level/subgroup key. The length is variable and depends on the field of "SKey len."

1		31
Format	Levels (n)	Num of Bits
	...	
	Var $1 \sim 16*(n-1)$...	
	...	
SKey len	...	
	Var/Encrypted Session Key ...	
	...	
	Encrypted Data	
	...	

**TABLE
14.4**   Opaque LSA subheader.

Key Numbering Scheme

We use dot notation to present our key numbering scheme. The dot separates the levels of the hierarchical key structure.

An OSPF-E key numbering example is shown in Figure 14.6 in which both the trusted group (TG) and the keys are labeled with a dot notation. The leading number stands for the top level of the group. The succeeding numbers following the "." represent subgroup, sub-subgroup members, and so on. So, it can be conveniently represented as: *root.group.subgroup.sub-subgroup....*

When a router receives an encrypted routing information packet with a key label as *a.b.c.d*, it compares its key label with the one received to find out the common parts. In the example, in group TG(0.1), there are four routers with key labels 0.1.1, 0.1.2, 0.1.3, and 0.1.4. The router labeled with $K_{0.1}$ is the trusted group leader (TGL) of TG(0.1). Using its predistributed key set, the TGL can derive all the keys that are distributed to its group members (using the group key management scheme discussed in Appendix 14.A). We use suffix 0 in a key label to represent a group key. Thus, the group key for this TG is given by 0.1.0. If 0.1.2 and 0.1.3 want to set up subgroup communication, then they can use subgroup key with the label 0.1.2–3, where "–" denotes communication within a subgroup.

OSPF-E and Link-State Advertisement Packet Processing

In order to incorporate the encryption/decryption process into the LSU packet processing, the flow chart presented Shaikh and Greenberg [20] for OSPF needs to be modified. Figure 14.7 represents the new flow chart for the OSPF-E processes initiated, once the LSU packet is received by the router. It can be observed that on receiving an LSU packet, the router processes the LSAs contained in that packet

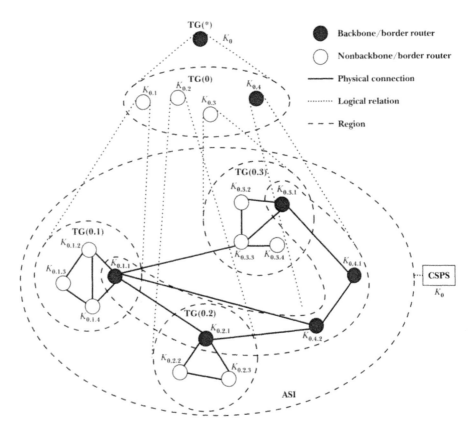

FIGURE

14.6

Key allocations of OSPF-E hierarchical trust structure.

one by one. It looks up the LSA packet header to find which level the key resides in. If the key (the one used to encrypt the LSA) resides at a higher level than the router, then it simply bundles the LSA into the LSU packet. If the key belongs to the same level or lower, the router will either use its own key or generate the key using the group keying scheme presented in Appendix 14.A and decrypt the LSA. Once the LSA is decrypted, it is checked for duplicates. OSPF-E updates its link-state database for every new LSA it receives. The flooding of LSA is similar to OSPF. It also needs to schedule the best route calculation module.

Before the router creates the LSU packet to be sent on its interfaces, it encrypts the information using various keys. The choice of the encryption key for a particular LSA depends on the level of the router and also the scope of the information as defined by the network policy. Once all the LSAs are encrypted, they are bundled into the LSU packet and flooded through the interface.

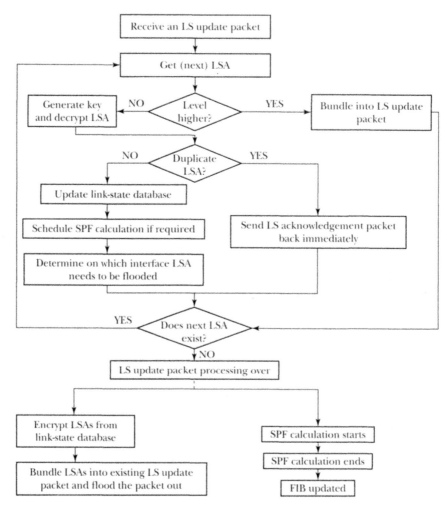

FIGURE

14.7

Flow chart depicting the OSPF-E processes initiated on receipt of LSU packets.

14.5.3   Network Analysis: Preliminary Results

An important question is: Can we quantify the benefit in a network that protected services do get allocated prioritized provisioning in a network virtualization framework based on secure encryption? To be able to quantify such a benefit, we have recently started the development of a *virtual network analysis simulator* (VNAS), which is extended from MuSDyR [8].

In VNAS, we have incorporated protected and dynamic network virtualization by allowing for different service classes, such as in SC service class over the normal service class. In our preliminary prototype, we have implemented a rudimentary version of the ENLU message passing framework for different service classes. In our current implementation, virtualization is performed on a per-link basis, that is, to simulate the affect, a user can decide which links to be considered for virtualization. If it is not considered for virtualization, then all services share the link equally. For activating network virtualization, attribute values of a link are encoded differently for the prioritized service on a link basis compared to the normal services. This is done so that ENLU messages are recorded by nodes as appropriate for different services in computing routes and service provisioning.

For our preliminary study, we have considered an eight-node network (Figure 14.8a). Traffic load was considered in such a way that the network is in a stressed situation where the prioritized service requires better performance than the normal service while both have the same amount of offered load. In Figure 14.8(b), we plot service blocking performance for prioritized and normal services. At the left end is the case when all links in the network are considered as fully shared by both service classes; thus, naturally, both service classes have the same performance. Then, we increase the number of links virtualized (one at time), and plot service blocking for both classes. Thus, using VNAS, we can observe that service blocking performance is significantly lower for the prioritized class over the normal service class as more and more links are virtualized. More important, our tool allows us to quantify *how much* is the benefit. Currently, additional feature development on VNAS is planned in order to study a series of scenarios.

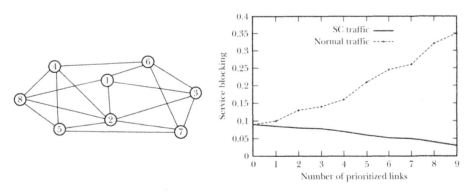

FIGURE 14.8   Network topology and service performance: (a) eight-node network topology, and (b) performance: service blocking.

14.6   CONCLUSION

In this chapter, we present a traffic engineering perspective for resilient services, including an illustration. We discuss the key components needed in the resilient network architecture so that such an adaptive environment is possible, especially to guard against both insider and outsider attacks on a routing infrastructure.

To summarize, the basic problem domain leads us to consider a virtualized trusted routing and provisioning domain, which is complemented with an adaptive traffic engineering mechanism in a semi-reservation-oriented mode to provide prioritized services, especially for resiliency under attacks or overload conditions. We present mechanisms to extend the link-state routing protocol to facilitate such an environment.

There are many issues that remain to be addressed. For instance, when many virtualized domains are created, is there any routing stability problem? In a multiprovider environment, how can the trustedness of different information be extended, and how can the secure group communication framework be applied? How does the routing framework interact with distributed controls? Furthermore, scalability of secure group communication in a large network environment is another direction to explore. We are currently investigating these issues.

ACKNOWLEDGMENTS

We thank Amit Sinha, Lein Harn, Cory Beard, and Tian Li for many discussions. The preliminary analysis result presented in Section 14.5.3 is discussed in [21]. We thank David Tipper and James Joshi for carefully reading a draft of this paper. This work was partially supported by a grant from the University of Missouri Research Board.

References

[1] D. G. Andersen, H. Balakrishnan, M. F. Kaashoek, R. Morris, "Resilient Overlay Networks," *Proceedings of the 18th ACM SOSP*, Banff, Canada, Oct. 2001.

[2] E. Rosen and Y. Rekhter, "BGP/MPLS IP Virtual Private Networks (VPNs)," *IETF RFC 4364*, Feb. 2006.

[3] G. R. Ash, *Dynamic Routing in Telecommunication Networks* (New York: McGraw-Hill, 1997).

[4] J. M. Akinpelu, "The Overload Performance of Engineered Networks with Nonhierarchical and Hierarchical Routing," *AT&T Bell Labs Technical Journal* 63(1984): 1261–1281.

[5] R. S. Krupp, "Stabilization of Alternate Routing Networks," *Proceedings of IEEE ICC'82*, Philadelphia, PA, June 1982, pp. 31.2.1–31.2.5.

[6] J. H. Weber, "A Simulation Study of Routing and Control in Communication Networks," *Bell Systems Technical Journal* 43(1964): 2639–2676.

[7] D. Medhi and K. Ramasamy, *Network Routing: Algorithms, Protocols, and Architectures* (San Francisco: Morgan Kaufmann, 2007).

[8] D. Medhi, et al., "MuSDyR: Multi-Service Dynamic Routing simulator, v 1.1.," Computer Networking Research Lab, University of Missouri–Kansas City, at http://conrel.sice.umkc.edu/simulator/Musdyr1.1.pdf.

[9] R. Braden, D. Clark, and S. Shenker, "Integrated Services in the Internet Architecture: An Overview," *IETF RFC 1633*, July 1994.

[10] S. Blake, D. Black, M. Carlson, E. Davies, Z. Wang, W. Weiss "An Architecture for Differentiated Services," *IETF RFC 2475*, Dec. 1998.

[11] R. W. Shirey, "Internet Security Glossary," *RFC 2828*, May 2000.

[12] D. Huang, A. Sinha, and D. Medhi, "A Double Authentication Scheme to Detect Impersonation Attack in Link State Routing Protocols," *Proceedings of IEEE International Conference on Communications (ICC)*, Anchorage, AK, 2003, pp. 1723–1727.

[13] J. Moy, "OSPF Version 2," *RFC 2328*, Apr. 1998.

[14] S. Murphy, M. Badger, and B. Wellington, "OSPF with Digital Signatures," *RFC 2154*, June 1997.

[15] M. Gupta and N. S. Melam, "Authentication/Confidentiality for OSPFv3," at http://www.ietf.org/internet-drafts/draft-ietf-ospf-ospfv3-auth-05.txt, Oct. 2004.

[16] H. Krawczyk, M. Bellare, and R. Canetti, "HMAC: Keyed-Hashing for Message Authentication," *RFC 2104*, Feb. 1997.

[17] D. Huang, Q. Cao, A. Sinha, M. Schniederjans, C. Beard, L. Harn, and D. Medhi, "New Architecture for Intra-Domain Network Security Issues," *Communications of the ACM* 49, No. 11 (2006): 64–72.

[18] D. Huang and D. Medhi, "A Key-Chain Based Keying Scheme for Many-to-Many Secure Group Communication," *ACM Transactions on Information and System Security* 7, No. 4 (2004): 523–552.

[19] R. Coltun, "The OSPF Opaque LSA Option," *RFC 2370*, July 1998.

[20] A. Shaikh and A. Greenberg, "Experience in Black-Box OSPF Measurement," *Proceedings of ACM SIGCOMM Internet Measurement Workshop (IMW)*, San Francisco, CA, Nov. 2001.

[21] T. Li, "Virtual Route: An Analysis to Ensure Resource Availability for Critical Services in a Dynamic Routing Environment," M.S. thesis, University of Missouri–Kansas City, May 2005.

[22] D. Huang, A. Sinha, and D. Medhi, "On Providing Confidentiality in Link State Routing Protocol," *Proceedings of IEEE Consumer Communications and Networking Conference*, Las Vegas, NV, 2006, pp. 671–675.

[23] F. Harary, *Graph Theory* (Boston: Addison-Wesley, 1969).

[24] D. Naor, M. Naor, and J. Lotspiech, "Revocation and Tracing Schemes for Stateless Receivers," *Lecture Notes in Computer Science* 2139 (2001): 41–62.

[25] A. T. Sherman and D. A. McGrew, "Key Establishment in Large Dynamic Groups Using One-Way Function Trees," *IEEE Transactions on Software Engineering* 29, No. 5, (2003): 444–458.

14.A Secure Group Communication

For the secure link-state routing protocol problem, we have recently proposed a novel key chain–based secure group key management scheme [18]. Our approach captures the merits of both centralized and distributed approaches and targets minimizing the communication and delay overhead due to key management that is critical in link-state flooding. Briefly, a set of secrets are first distributed to each user (node) from a centrally controlled key server before the secure group communication phase. During the actual communication, every group member can self-derive desired group/subgroup keys and then communicate with any possible subgroups *without* any help from the key server. Our work in many-to-many secure group communication [18] helps to develop secure link-state routing protocols [22] to construct future reliable and trusted routing frameworks [17].

14.A.1 USING ONE-WAY FUNCTION CHAIN TO BUILD KEY CHAIN

In order to reduce the storage overhead, we build a key forest structure via multiple key chains. Each "tree" (a linear key chain) in the key forest structure represents a particular key derivative relation among all group members. Here, we first show how we can use a one-way function to construct a one-way function chain, and subsequently, to form a key chain. Finally, we present how to systematically distribute key elements from multiple key chains to each group member.

We start with function $h(\cdot)$, which is a one-way function that maps an arbitrary-length message M to a fixed-length message MD. It satisfies the following properties:

1. Function $h(\cdot)$ is publicly known.
2. Given M, it is relatively easy to compute $h(M)$.

3. Given MD, it is computationally infeasible to find a message M such that $h(M) = MD$.

4. Given M and $h(M)$, it is computationally infeasible to find a message M' ($\neq M$) such that $h(M') = h(M)$.

A one-way function chain (OFC) is a sequence of values with the linear derivative relations among these values. Thus, we use $h^j(\cdot)$ to denote the result of one-way function $h(\cdot)$ on a message j times. The outputs of the multiple one-way operations construct an OFC. An OFC maintains a linear derivative relation among multiple values (i.e., $h^j(\cdot)$ can derive $h^r(\cdot)$ when $j < r$).

Consider message M_i to be the ith initial key element that is used by a user to generate the cryptographic key denoted by k_{i_0}, where $k_{i_0} = f(M_i)$, and where $f(\cdot)$ is a key-generating function. This key-generating function is publicly known and generates the exact length of the cryptographic key. Thus, we have the following relation:

$$k_{i_j} = f(h^j(M_i)) \quad (j > 0)$$

Since $h(\cdot)$ is publicly known, we know that the derivative relations of an OFC are:

$$M_i \Rightarrow h^1(M_i) \Rightarrow \cdots \Rightarrow h^j(M_i) \Rightarrow \cdots \Rightarrow h^r(M_i)$$

$$(1 < j < r)$$

Then, using function $f(\cdot)$, the key chain derivative relations corresponding to the above are (see also Figure 14.9):

$$k_{i_0} \Rightarrow k_{i_1} \cdots \Rightarrow k_{i_j} \Rightarrow \cdots \Rightarrow k_{i_r}, \quad \text{where } 1 < j < r \qquad (14.1)$$

The derivative relations among multiple keys form a linear hierarchical structure from the top level (k_{i_0}) to the bottom level (k_{i_r}). In Figure 14.9, a straightforward key allocation example is shown that is composed of six keys ($r = 5$). If we allocate a key to each group member from u_c to u_{c+5}, each group member can derive its lower-level keys. Then, a key chain can be formed by six subgroups, denoted by S_{i_0} to S_{i_5} (Figure 14.9). Note that these subgroups are *noncolluding* subgroups, that is, a subset of members cannot *collude* or *partner* to derive the keys used by a specific subgroup unless at least one of the members belongs to that subgroup.

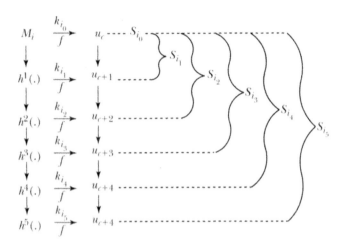

FIGURE

An example of keys allocation ($n = 6, r = 5$).

14.9

14.A.2   KEY DISTRIBUTION

We extend the linear structure of a key chain to a nonlinear structure by combining multiple key chains (a key forest). These properties provide critical ingredients to our keying science due to efficiency and flexibility. We describe how to utilize graph theory to model our key distribution scheme.

Assigning more than one key from multiple key chains to a user is very similar to arranging the group members' positions in different key chains. To give a more visualized view of our scheme, we consider every group member to be a vertex of a graph $\mathcal{K}(\mathcal{E}, \mathcal{V})$, that is, each group member in $\mathcal{U}$ is mapped to a vertex in $\mathcal{V}$: $v_c \in \mathcal{V}$, $u_c = v_c$ and $c = \{1, 2, \ldots, n\}$. Assume that a group has n members thus, we can associate them to n vertices in a graph, and when n is odd, we can write $n = 2s + 1$ for some s. These n vertices can form a fully connected graph that we refer to as $\mathcal{K}_{2s+1}$. We now state the following important graph theory result [23] that is applicable in our work.

Theorem 14.A.1   The fully-connected graph $\mathcal{K}_{2s+1}$ is the sum of s spanning cycles, where $s \in \mathcal{N}$. (For Proof, refer to Harary [23], p. 89.)

Theorem 14.A.1 states that any fully connected graph $\mathcal{K}_{2s+1}$ can be constructed by s independent *spanning* cycles. These s spanning cycles have no overlapping edges, and each cycle has exactly n edges. Since our keying scheme is based on a sequence of one-way function values, we use the term *Hamiltonian* cycles instead of *spanning* cycles. A Hamiltonian cycle visits each vertex exactly once in sequence. There are many ways to create s independent Hamiltonian cycles. We present an algorithm that creates s *Hamiltonian* cycles for graph $\mathcal{K}_{2s+1}$, where $2s + 1$ is a prime.

For any group of users $\mathcal{U}$ ($|\mathcal{U}| = n$ and $n = 2s + 1$, $s \in \mathcal{N}$), we can always find s Hamiltonian cycles (or spanning cycles or permutation cycles) that have no overlapping edges. For illustration, we use an overall group with seven members. This illustration is important due to its connection to the key agreement protocol described later.

14.A.2.1   An Example of Keying Protocol

Consider seven group members as seven vertices in a graph as shown in Figure 14.10. Using Algorithm 14.A.1, we can build three separate Hamiltonian cycles. Node 1 is the starting point of each of these Hamiltonian cycles. The group key distribution requires two levels of cycle tours: the node-level tour and the chain-level tour. Figure 14.11 shows the two-level tour of key distribution based on the first Hamiltonian cycle shown in Figure 14.10. For example, the key distribution tour starts from the node-level tour and the beginning node is u_1. Then the tour goes to the chain-level tour: The first key element in chain 1 (the head of the key chain $c1$) is distributed to u_1; the second key element in chain 2 ($c2$) is distributed to u_1; this process continues until the seventh key element in chain 7 ($c7$) is distributed to u_1. After the chain-level tour is complete, the key

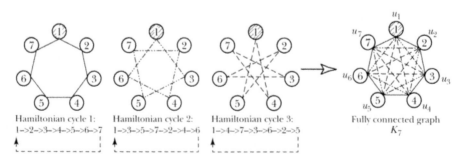

Hamiltonian cycle 1:   Hamiltonian cycle 2:   Hamiltonian cycle 3:   Fully connected graph
1->2->3->4->5->6->7   1->3->5->7->2->4->6   1->4->7->3->6->2->5 K_7

FIGURE   An example of Hamiltonian cycles for seven nodes ($n = 7$, $s = 3$).

14.10

Algorithm 14.A.1   (Hamiltonian cycles creation algorithm)

Initial: Given n entities: $v_1, v_2, \ldots, v_n$, where $n = 2s + 1$, $s \in \mathcal{N}$

Procedures: Construct a set of s paths denoted by $\mathcal{P}_l$, on the points
$v_1, v_2, \ldots, v_{2s+1}$ as follows:

1. Create s paths: $\mathcal{P}_l = v_1 v_{l+1} v_{2l+1} v_{3l+1} \ldots v_{2sl+1}$, where
   $l = \{1, \ldots, s\}$. All the subscripts are taken as integers
   ($mod\ 2s + 1$).

2. The Hamiltonian cycle Z_l is then constructed by joining
   v_1 to the endpoints of $\mathcal{P}_l$.

End

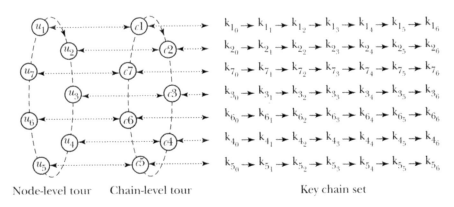

Node-level tour   Chain-level tour   Key chain set

FIGURE   An example of a key distribution tour for seven group members ($n = 7$, $s = 3$).

14.11

distribution tour goes back to the node-level tour and visits node u_2. Next, the
tour goes to the chain-level tour: The first key element in chain 2 is distributed
to u_2, the second key element in chain 3 is distributed to u_2, and so on, until the
seventh key element in chain 1 is distributed to u_2. The key distribution tour then
goes back to the node-level tour and visits node u_3. This process is continued until
the tour is complete at node 7. Thus, each Hamiltonian cycle corresponds to a set
of key chains. For $n = 7$ and $s = 3$, we need $3 \times 7 = 21$ key chains in total and each
group member possesses 21 keys.

In Table 14.5, each group member has 21 keys (in a column) that belong to
three different cycles (for ease of readability, we only list subscripts ($_{i_j}$) of the k_{i_j}
in each row). Here, $K_{\hat{i}}^{(l)}$ is a key chain that is constructed by following the lth

$\mathcal{K}_7$ nodes	1	2	3	4
Member	u_1	u_2	u_3	u_4
Cycle 1	$1_0 2_6 3_5 4_4 5_3 6_2 7_1$	$1_1 2_0 3_6 4_5 5_4 6_3 7_2$	$1_2 2_1 3_0 4_6 5_5 6_4 7_3$	$1_3 2_2 3_1 4_0 5_6 6_5 7_4$
Cycle 2	$1_0 2_6 3_5 4_4 5_3 6_2 7_1$	$1_4 2_3 3_2 4_1 5_0 6_6 7_5$	$1_1 2_0 3_6 4_5 5_4 6_3 7_2$	$1_5 2_4 3_3 4_2 5_1 6_0 7_6$
Cycle 3	$1_0 2_6 3_5 4_4 5_3 6_2 7_1$	$1_4 2_4 3_3 4_2 5_1 6_0 7_6$	$1_3 2_2 3_1 4_0 5_6 6_5 7_4$	$1_1 2_0 3_6 4_5 5_4 6_3 7_2$

$\mathcal{K}_7$ nodes	5	6	7
Member	u_5	u_6	u_7
Cycle 1	$1_4 2_3 3_2 4_1 5_0 6_6 7_5$	$1_5 2_4 3_3 4_2 5_1 6_0 7_6$	$1_6 2_5 3_4 4_3 5_2 6_1 7_0$
Cycle 2	$1_2 2_1 3_0 4_6 5_5 6_4 7_3$	$1_6 2_5 3_4 4_3 5_2 6_1 7_0$	$1_3 2_2 3_1 4_0 5_6 6_5 7_4$
Cycle 3	$1_6 2_5 3_4 4_3 5_2 6_1 7_0$	$1_4 2_3 3_2 4_1 5_0 6_6 7_5$	$1_2 2_1 3_0 4_6 5_5 6_4 7_3$

TABLE 14.5 $n = 7$ group (only subscript $_{i_j}$ of k_{i_j} is shown in this table).

Hamiltonian cycle ($t = \{1, 2, \ldots, s\}$) to allocate keys to group members. Similarly, we can add notation $^{(t)}$ to key $k_{i_j}^{(t)}$.

Figure 14.10 shows that any two group members are connected by a direct link and they both can derive a two-member subgroup key to form a secure communication channel. For example, if we randomly select u_1 and u_4, then, for Hamiltonian cycle 3, u_1 and u_4 are adjacent, and in the third key chain, u_4 has the key $k_{1_1}^{(3)}$ and u_1 can derive it from its $k_{1_0}^{(3)}$. These relations can be applied to any combination of two group members. Note that these Hamiltonian cycles cannot cover every combination of selected group members. In a Hamiltonian cycle with n entities, the number of t different group members in a continuous path is n, where $t < n$. Thus, in a group with n members, using Algorithm 14.A.1 there will be s cycles formed. The number of adjacent members in s cycles is $s \times n$. In the example, when $s = 3$, the number of three-member subgroups is $\binom{7}{3} = 35$ and $s \times n = 21$. Thus, we can infer that three Hamiltonian cycles cannot completely cover every possible combination of subgroup members. We have developed a novel way to build relations among the cycles to solve this problem—this is accomplished through the key agreement protocol described next.

14.A.3   KEY AGREEMENT PROTOCOL

We can use a session key k' to encrypt data and use subgroup keys as *key-encrypting keys* (KEKs) to encrypt the session key that is attached to the encrypted data.

Multiple subgroup keys can be used as KEKs to fulfill desired subgroup composition. Using the encrypting function $E(\cdot)$ and decrypting function $D(\cdot)$, we can encrypt the data to be transmitted as follows:

$$\langle [i_{1j_1}, \ldots, i_{rj_r}, E_{k_{i_{1j_1}}^{(t_1)}}(k'), \ldots, E_{k_{i_{rj_r}}^{(t_r)}}(k')], E_{k'}(Data)\rangle \tag{14.2}$$

$$(i_1 \ldots i_r \in \{1, 2, \ldots, n-1\}; j_1 \ldots j_r \in \{1, 2, \ldots, n-1\}; t_1 \ldots t_r \in \{1, 2, \ldots, s\})$$

The receivers check the key chain list $\{i_1, \ldots, i_r\}$ to see if they belong to the group. The checking method is straightforward: A receiver compares each element in the list with j_k in the key chains that he or she possesses; he or she belongs to the group if and only if $j_r \geq j_k$; and then he or she can use one-way function $j_r - j_k$ times on the key $k_{i_r j_k}^{t_r}$ to derive key $k_{i_r j_r}^{t_r}$. To decrypt the data received, the receiver first decrypts the session key:

$$k' = D_{k_{i_r j_r}^{(t_r)}}(E_{k_{i_r j_r}^{(t_r)}}(k')) \tag{14.3}$$

and then uses k' to decrypt the received cypher data:

$$Data = D_{k'}(E_{k'}(Data)) \tag{14.4}$$

We have proved the following key result (see [18] for a proof).

Theorem 14.A.2 Using the proposed key agreement protocol, s sets of key chains can be built where group size is n and $s = (n-1)/2$. For those arbitrarily selected subgroup members, we can always find b $(0 \leq b \leq s)$ encryption relations that provide secure subgroup communication.

In the seven-member example, if we consider subgroup members u_2, u_6, and u_7, we cannot find any continuous path in the three Hamiltonian cycles for these three group members. We prune graph $\mathcal{K}_7$ to $\mathcal{K}_3$, which is shown in Figure 14.12. When u_2 wants to send messages to subgroup $\{u_2, u_6, u_7\}$, u_2 sends out the cyphertext as follows:

$$\langle [5_1, 4_1, E_{k_{5_1}^{(3)}}(k'), E_{k_{4_1}^{(2)}}(k')], E_{k'}(Data)\rangle$$

The encrypted session key is attached to the cyphertext. Only u_6 and u_7 can decrypt the encrypted session key and thus can decrypt the message. In the worst case, the number of encryption/decryption operations is equal to the number

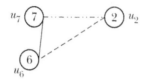

FIGURE

14.12   Subgraph $\mathcal{K}_3$.

of Hamiltonian cycles. We have proved that based on the predistributed keys, a group member can derive all possible subgroup keys (for proof, see Huang and Medhi [18]). It is important to note that this subgroup keying scheme can completely avoid KDC being involved in the subgroup's communication, and the secure subgroup's communication can be freely accomplished.

It may be noted that the work described here is for a group with n members where n is odd. We can easily take care of a group with an even number of members by adding a fictitious member to increase the group size to an odd number of members.

14.A.4   ASSESSMENT

For assessment of our key agreement protocol, we use S to represent the desired subgroup that user $u_i \in S$ wants to set up, where $S \subset \mathcal{U}$ and $|S| = L$. User u_i (the sender) is required to find r ($1 \leq r \leq L$) keys to encrypt session key k', then, the session key is used to encrypt the message. To find the minimal number of subgroup keys to cover all possible desired group members is an NP-complete problem (can be reduced from the minimal set covering the problem). We have developed two heuristic search algorithms to find subgroup keys:

1. *Addition algorithm.* When $|S| \leq (|\mathcal{U}| + 1)/2$, we have $L = |S|$.

2. *Eviction algorithm.* When $|S| > (|\mathcal{U}| + 1)/2$, we have $L = |\mathcal{U}| - |S|$. This is equivalent to evicting L group members from the system.

For details, refer to Huang and Medhi [18].

Using either the addition or the eviction algorithm, each group member can derive the desired subgroup keys. We have tested the addition and eviction subgroup key-searching algorithms. Through regression fitting, we have found that the function $f(L) = a + bL + cL \ln(L)$ matches our results from this test. The

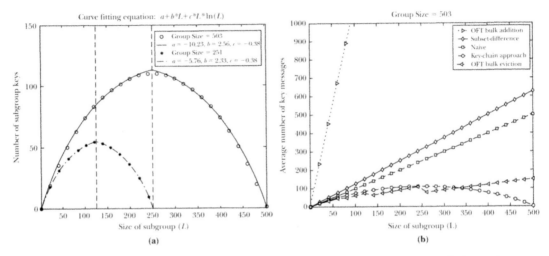

FIGURE

14.13

Performance of keying protocol: (a) addition/eviction algorithm complexity, and (b) comparison of the number of key messages for many-to-many communication schemes.

test results and curve-fitting function are shown in Figure 14.13(a) (results are shown for an overall group size of 251 and 503 members). In Figure 14.13(b), we compare our scheme with three typical shared key–based group keying scheme: a nave scheme, subset difference scheme [24], and one-way function tree–based scheme [25]. In terms of communication overhead in a networking environment requiring frequent subgroup formations, our key chain–based scheme performs better than these schemes.

15 Security and Survivability of Wireless Systems

Yi Qian   University of Puerto Rico at Mayaguez, Puerto Rico
Prashant Krishnamurthy   University of Pittsburgh, USA
David Tipper   University of Pittsburgh, USA

15.1   INTRODUCTION

Recent trends indicate that the next-generation wireless networks will consist of hybrid wireless access networks and wireless sensor networks [1–3]. The wireless access networks will be hybrid, that is, they will consist of wide-area mobile data services providing extensive coverage but lower data rates and wireless local-area networks (WLANs) for covering local area hot spots with much higher data rates [2]. Wireless ad hoc connections can assist with missing connections between a wireless device and the rest of a network [1, 3]. Wireless sensor networks (WSNs) are becoming increasing relevant for sensing physical phenomenon for a variety of applications (e.g., structural health monitoring, sampling soil quality). All of these wireless networks are expected to be interconnected in the future.

Already, the public's demand for and dependence on mobile services makes existing wireless networks a part of the nation's critical network infrastructure (CNI), and ongoing development of next-generation wireless networks only increases their importance. The continually increasing reliance on wireless networks by businesses, the general public, and government services, and their role in the CNI of the country, make it imperative to have information assurance (IA) built into them. IA for wireless networks is an emerging research area with relatively little literature in comparison to wired networks. While individual wireless technologies currently incorporate some in-built security features, these have been implemented in a largely uncoordinated manner. Availability features for wireless systems are either nonexistent or not well understood [4]. Moreover,

IA techniques employed in wired networks have limited direct applicability in wireless networks because of the unique aspects of wireless networks (e.g., user mobility, wireless communication channel, power conservation, limited computational power in mobile nodes, security at the link layer). IA in wireless sensor networks is unique in that the faults and threats that need to be considered are quite different from those in other kinds of networks or distributed systems. Sensor networks consist of perhaps thousands of low-cost, battery-operated units with limited computational power and memory that need to communicate potentially with one another and some sink or base station using wireless links. Consequently, scalability (because of the sheer numbers of nodes), energy efficiency, necessity of lightweight cryptographic protocols, and methods to overcome wireless vulnerabilities are important. Also, it is not possible to assume that sensor units will not be compromised or tampered with for the same reasons. Hence, it is important to consider both outsider and insider threats in sensor networks. Low-cost sensor nodes are likely to fail randomly or stop working due to limited battery life.

Finally, to the best of our knowledge, there is very little literature on how the components of IA, namely availability and security, interact with each other in a wireless network environment. Components failures or coordinated physical/cyber attacks on network equipment will result in security breaches and impact network performance simultaneously. Thus, there is a need to study the coupling between network survivability and security and create design strategies consistent with both sets of requirements [5, 6].

In this chapter, we investigate the security and survivability issues for wireless systems and networks. We first provide a background of hybrid wireless access networks and sensor networks (Section 15.2). We discuss the current survivability and security approaches in hybrid wireless infrastructure networks in Sections 15.3 and 15.4. We then present a premliminary study on the design of security and survivability for wireless ad hoc and sensor networks in Section 15.5. We also discuss with two case studies the issues that relate to the interaction between security and survivability in hybrid wireless access networks and sensor networks in Section 15.6.

15.2   BACKGROUND

In this section, we give a brief discussion on hybrid wireless access networks, wireless ad hoc and sensor networks, and security and survivability for wireless networks in general.

Traditionally, wireless networks have been homogeneous with limited or no interoperability between various technologies. However, no single wireless technology is capable of supporting all the various application requirements such as coverage, data rates, error rates, mobility, and so on. The evolutionary trend is toward a mixture of various technologies and networks that must coexist and interoperate to provide required services [2]. Cellular service providers are currently deploying such hybrid architectures in the United States and Europe. As an example, a WLAN may be employed for local coverage, low mobility, and high data rates while an overlaid mobile data network (such as the General Packet Radio Service, GPRS, or Third-Generation Universal Mobile Telecommunications Service, 3G-UMTS) is used for wide-area coverage and high mobility, but lower data rates [7]. Figure 15.1 shows the architecture of a future hybrid wireless network with 3G-UMTS, IEEE 802.11 infrastructure WLANs, a backhaul mesh network (perhaps using 802.16 WiMAX), a single ad hoc network cluster, and a sensor network. MSs participating in such a hybrid network must have the capability to operate with multiple technologies and possess the intelligence to appropriately switch among technologies

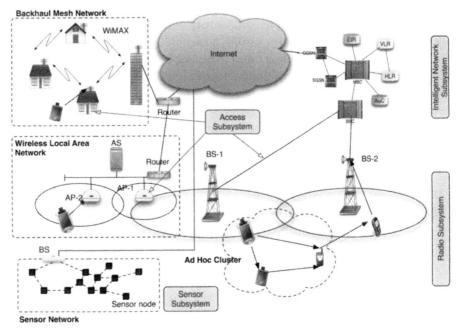

FIGURE

15.1

A hybrid wireless network architecture.

and networks. Entities in Figure 15.1 are grouped into different subsystems (such as the access subsystem), which are considered in more detail later in the chapter.

In Figure 15.1, the mobile switching center (MSC) in conjunction with several databases—the home and visitor location registers (HLR/VLR), the equipment identity register (EIR), and the authentication center (AuC)—manage access control (via authentication) and mobility for MSs. The base station/radio network controller (BSC/RNC) is involved in allocating and deallocating radio channels, handoff decisions, transmit powers, and so on. GPRS support nodes (GSNs) that support data traffic also play a role in mobility management. The serving GSN (SGSN) handles communications to and from MSs in its service area and is similar to the foreign agent (FA) in the mobile Internet Protocol (mobile IP). The gateway GSN (GGSN) is similar to the home agent (HA) in mobile IP. WLANs do not have the full range of mobility and radio resource management functions as the cellular network and rely on the AP (or mobile IP) to provide some of these services. Since LANs are broadcast in nature (there is no need to track MS locations) and based on carrier sensing, they do not require sophisticated management techniques. Authentication using 802.1X or RADIUS servers is also possible in WLANs and this is now a standard (802.11i). In backhaul mesh networks, *mesh routers* form a network through self-configuration and may also provide connectivity to isolated base stations or access points [8]. Mesh networking is possible using 802.11 WLAN technology or 802.16 WiMAX technology. Mobile stations in ad hoc clusters communicate in peer-to-peer fashion directly or in multihop fashion using mobile ad hoc networks (MANET) routing protocols.

Wide-area cellular systems are far more sophisticated than their local-area, metro-area, and ad hoc counterparts. There are little or no mechanisms or entities (like the HLR/VLR, BSC, or AuC) to handle mobility management, radio resources management, billing, or security in WLANs or ad hoc networks. For seamless operation between different technologies, some interworking functions are required [2, 7] that are not discussed here in great detail. Five different approaches for roaming between GPRS and WLANs were suggested in Pahlavan and Krishnamurthy [2]. The approaches can be broadly considered as using an emulator entity that makes the WLAN look like a location area or routing area of a UMTS network, using mobile IP or a proxy mobility gateway to reconcile the two networks. A network where the cellular operator owns the WLAN is considered in Salkintzis et al. [7]. A loose coupling approach where the WLAN is complementary to GPRS and only uses the GPRS databases (for authentication and subscriber information) but not the GPRS interfaces is proposed. The WLAN directly transports data to the Internet in this case. A tight coupling approach where data from a WLAN first goes through the GPRS core network is also proposed in Salkintzis et al. [7]. In this case, the WLAN looks like a GPRS radio access network with a different air interface. These two approaches are similar to the ones proposed in Pahlavan and Krishnamurthy [2] but include more operational details. Details of the messages and protocols used in these approaches can be found in Pahlavan and Krishnamurthy [2] and Salkintzis et al. [7]. Similarly, mesh routers with gateway bridges are used for interworking with base stations or MSs in mesh networks [8].

Recently, interconnecting MANETs and infrastructure wireless networks has been considered in Luo et al. [9] where the primary motivation is to allow MSs that have poor connectivity to a base station to get higher throughputs by using intermediate relays or proxies that have better connectivity. In this work, greedy and on-demand algorithms have been developed for discovering the proxies with the best connectivity and routing between the MSs. While the greedy algorithm generates lesser overhead on the cellular uplink, it results in larger energy consumption at the MSs compared to the on-demand algorithm. However, this work does not consider survivability or interworking aspects of the hybrid network.

Wireless sensor networks consist of hundreds of sensor nodes deployed over the environment to be sensed. Typically, a high-power, high-capability base station communicates with all the nodes through broadcast messages for network activities such as synchronization, querying, topology control, transmission schedules, and so on. [3]. Sensor nodes have low transmission powers, so they have to use multihop communications to report sensed data to sensor nodes closest to the base station. These closest nodes then relay the information (perhaps fused, aggregated, or processed cooperatively by all the sensor nodes) to the base station, which may be connected to the Internet. We consider a different kind of sensor network with heterogeneous sensor nodes and no base station in Section 15.6.3.

15.3   CURRENT SECURITY APPROACHES IN WIRELESS NETWORKS

Unlike wired networks that have some degree of physical security, physical security in wireless networks is impossible to achieve on wireless links (because of their broadcast nature) and, therefore, security attacks on information flow can be widespread (e.g., passive interception of data, active injection of traffic, and overloading the access point with garbage packets). Modification of information is possible because of the nature of the channel and the mobility of nodes.

The radio channel is harsh and subject to interference, fading, multipath, and high error rates. As a result, packet losses are common even without security threats. An opponent can make use of these natural impairments to modify information and also render the information unavailable.

Most wireless networks use mild variations of wired security mechanisms. The primary vulnerabilities in the past were fraud and exposure of information and, thus, only confidentiality (privacy of voice calls) and identification (entity authentication) are given importance in second-generation (2G) wireless networks. For this, they employ challenge-response schemes [10]. The key sizes range from 40–128 bits, in many cases being insufficient for good security. The security mechanisms are not designed from the perspective of *data integrity* or potential attacks like replay or overload. The drawbacks of existing security in wireless networks, ranging from the flaws in encryption algorithms in the Global System for Mobile Communications (GSM), Cellular Digital Packet Data (CDPD), Bluetooth, and IEEE 802.11 to the more obvious protocol flaws, are discussed in many papers (e.g., see Fluhrer et al. [11] for attacks on RC-4 used in CDPD and IEEE 802.11). Third-generation wireless systems and emerging standards address some of these drawbacks. The Kasumi algorithm (for confidentiality) and the Milenage algorithm (for authentication) employed by the third-generation partnership project (3GPP) use larger key sizes (128 bits long) and stronger algorithms [12]. There are also mechanisms for data integrity and message authentication. In CDPD and in 3GPP, two sets of identification information are maintained: the latest update and the previous one in case the latest update is lost due to bad radio conditions [12]. The IEEE 802.11i standard proposes the use of the advanced encryption standard (AES) in one of its many modes of operation (countermode) for WLANs with 802.1X entity authentication for IEEE 802.11 WLANs [13]. Key management makes use of preinstalled master keys (or passwords) that are used with nonces to generate fresh session keys. Research groups have also suggested the use of IPSec at the network layer for all IP traffic on the air. Very little work exists in the evaluation of security of backhaul wireless mesh networks.

Security for sensor networks is still in the research stage. Threats to sensor networks can be at the physical layer (e.g., jamming), eavesdropping of sensed data, attacks against routing of data through multiple hops, corruption of fused or aggregated data by compromised nodes, and so on. The IEEE 802.15.4 low-rate wireless personal area networking standard employs mechanisms similar to IEEE 802.11i (AES countermode and cipher-block chaining message authentication code) for security. However, key distribution and management in sensor networks is not simple (see the case study in Section 15.6.3). The interested reader is referred to Djenouri et al. [14] for a survey of security issues in the superset of ad hoc networks; to Zheng et al. [15] for security in low-rate wireless networks; and to Shi and Perrig [16] for a discussion of design issues for security in sensor networks.

15.4 CURRENT SURVIVABILITY APPROACHES IN WIRELESS NETWORKS

Survivability of wireless networks has recently begun to receive attention, mainly focusing on database survivability tailored to the cellular network databases (HLR and VLR) architecture [17–19]. This work focuses on the development of checkpoint algorithms and authentication techniques for the fault recovery of database contents. Literature on the design of a survivable landline topology for wireless networks [20–23] concentrates on formulating various optimization models for single-link failure survivable landline mesh-topology and capacity allocation design. However, the approach and assumptions used are identical to techniques used for wired backbone network design. None of the unique aspects of wireless networks are incorporated into the models. In Snow et al. [24], the importance of survivability for wireless networks is discussed and the difficulty in applying standard wired metrics for quantifying wireless survivability is shown.

We believe that survivability approaches for wired networks are not entirely applicable to the mobile and wireless domain. Consider that the failure of nodes and links is a primary survivability consideration. Wired networks are characterized by relatively high-speed, highly reliable, fixed-capacity links serving fixed users. The number of physical cables and their interconnection configuration influences system capacity. Diversity techniques often consist of adding spare capacity by the addition of physical cables, which are primarily subject to cost constraints. In contrast, the wireless domain is characterized by variable capacity and unreliable links serving mobile users. Wireless link capacity is influenced by the continually changing network conditions such as cell congestion, environmental factors, and interference. Diversity techniques are constrained by cost and a regulated frequency spectrum. Spectrum is a scarce resource in wireless networks and allocating spare capacity is much more difficult since, unlike wired networks, duplicating the medium is not easy. Furthermore, wireless network survivability approaches must account for user mobility and radio resource management. It has been shown that *user mobility worsens transient conditions* as disconnected users move among geographical areas to attempt to reconnect to the wireless access network [25–27]. In [25–27], the results of a sample survivability analysis of a typical GSM cellular network are presented using simulation. The steady-state and transient behavior of standard performance metrics, such as the call-blocking rate and location registration delay, were measured for a variety of failure cases. One significant result from these studies is that the *impact of failure is larger than the failed area*. For example, the failure of a BSC knocking out a group of four adjacent cells (in a network of 100) results in the mean time to process a location update for the entire group of 100 cells to exceed (by a factor of 10) the recommended International Telecommunications Union (ITU) benchmark value, resulting in protocol timeouts. Further, the magnitude and duration of a failure impact depend on a complex set of factors including the location of the failure (e.g., center or edge of location area), shape of the failed area (e.g., adjacent or disjoint cells), user mobility patterns, and user behavior in attempting reconnection. Thus, the network design should consider transient conditions in the capacity allocation and restoration techniques must consider *spatial* and *temporal* properties and address both the *transient* and steady-state periods. Current literature also does not consider the impact a failure in the wireless access networks has on the signaling network. In fact, our studies [26, 27] show that radio-level failure (e.g., loss of a base station, BS) causes a large increase in transient congestion in the signaling network. Similar results from network measurement on a GSM after an earthquake have been reported in the IST Caution project [28]. Incorporating such transient effects into the network topology design was recently proposed in [29].

A framework for cellular network survivability at the access layer, transport layer, and intelligent layer is presented in Tipper et al. [4, 25] along with potential survivability approaches at each layer. An extension of this framework to packet based 3G cellular networks was presented in [30]. Note that hybrid wireless networks offer alternatives to restoration schemes by enabling the use of overlays or underlays after failure of components of one particular technology. However, such schemes have also not been studied extensively for their benefits.

An overview of survivability issues and possible approaches for mobile ad hoc networks was presented in [31], including store-and-forward when end-to-end paths do not exist and store-and-haul in which nodes physically transport data. More recently, work on delay tolerant networking [32] has developed an architecture that has lead to work in disruption-tolerant networking. Disruption tolerant networking addresses the problem of how to communicate when wireless channel environments and mobility are so severe that stable end-to-end paths never exist and conventional communication that assumes routing convergence breaks down. In sensor networks, partitioning of the network due to failed sensor nodes (either hardware failure or battery exhaustion) can lead to the sensor network being unable to sense data or transmit the sensed data reliably to the base station. Work has been done to reduce the energy consumption in WSNs and load balancing among sensor nodes, but this is primarily at the academic research level.

15.5 FRAMEWORK FOR WIRELESS NETWORK SURVIVABILITY AND SECURITY

In light of the limitations indicated by the current literature, we have developed a framework for the comprehensive treatment of the problems of IA in hybrid wireless access networks. To facilitate the work, a hybrid wireless access network survivability/security framework [5] is developed similar to the approaches of Zolfaghari and Kaudel [33] for wired backbone networks. The wireless access network is viewed as having radio, sensor, access, and intelligent layers, as shown in Figure 15.1, with survivability/security strategies possible at each layer as detailed in Shin et al. [26], Krishnamurthy et al. [5], and Tipper et al. [4]. The components and functions supported at each layer are listed in Table 15.1. The radio network subsystem (RNS) includes the APs, BSs, BSC/RNC, and radio resource management schemes. The sensor subsystem (SenS) consists of a sensor network of sensor nodes with a base station connected to the Internet. The access network subsystem (ANS) supports packet switching, connection management, call management, and mobility management functions using the wired interconnection of APs, BSs, BSC, and MSC. The MSC, HLR, and VLR at the transport layer use the signaling network and services provided by service data management functions, implemented at the intelligent layer, to support connection and mobility management. The intelligent network subsystem (INS) supports security, location, service data and mobility management functions.

Subsystem	Components	Communication Links	Function
RNS	MS, BS, ad hoc clusters, WLAN AP, and BSC	Digital radio channels with TDMA, FDMA, or CDMA, wireline links, and/or terrestrial microwave	Define physical interface for radio communication, BS cluster management, radio channel management, and MAC signaling
ANS	BS, BSC, MSC, WAP, SGSN, GGSN, and signaling network	Wireline links and/or terrestrial microwave	Connection management and mobility management
INS	MSC, HLR, VLR, EIR, AuC, mobile IP signaling, and RADIUS	Wireline links and/or terrestrial microwave	Service management, security, location services and mobility management
SenS	Sensor nodes and BS	Wireless multihop links on the uplink and broadcast wireless downlink	Deliver sensed data to BS and broadcast control messages for network operation to sensor nodes

TABLE 15.1   Wireless network subsystems for survivability and security.

Given the framework above to conduct a survivability analysis, performance-oriented *survivability metrics* along with techniques for evaluating the metrics over various *modes of operation* are identified. The modes of operation include normal, single-failure, and multiple-failure/attack/disaster modes. Table 15.2 lists examples of possible *survivability metrics* and *failure conditions* at each layer in the framework, as well as some of the potential *impacts* of a failure in terms of the area affected and network service disruption. The survivability of a particular network is based on the ability of the network to meet performance goals stated in terms of *service thresholds* for each survivability metric, over each operational mode. For example, a performance goal with respect to packet delivery may be 1% packet loss for all cells during normal operation and 2% steady-state packet loss for cells adjacent to or near a failed cell with a maximum transient peak of 10% packet loss. While many of the survivability metrics listed in Table 15.2 have target mean and 0.95 percentile values recommended by ITU [34] for voice, no corresponding values exist for data.

For a network to be fault tolerant, alternate routes must exist between the network components or spare components must be provisioned (e.g., spare link between the BS-BSC with automatic protection switching at the end points). At the ANS and INS levels, traditional survivability strategies such as a mesh-type

Subsystem	Failure Scenario	Potential Impact	Possible Metrics
RNS	Loss of AP or BS/Node B	Partial/full-service loss in cell and increased traffic in cells adjacent to failure. Increased signaling	Packet loss rate, TCP session timeout, connection blocking probability, forced connection termination probability, throughput, and handover request rate
ANS	Loss of BSC-MSC or AP link	Partial/full-service loss in a cell or cluster of cells and increased traffic in cells adjacent to failure. Increased signaling	Packet loss rate, TCP session timeout, connection blocking probability, forced connection termination probability, connection setup/release delay, and paging/location update/registration delays
INS	Loss of VLR	Loss of roaming service in a coverage area or network/subnetwork	Lost user load (Erlangs or packets), database access delay, and information accuracy probability
SenS	Failure of sensor nodes or links	Partitioning of network leading to more energy consumption for data delivery, or congestion	Network lifetime, throughput, delay, packet delivery ratio, and energy efficiency

TABLE   Typical failure scenarios and survivability metrics at each layer.

15.2

architecture (at least two connected) are feasible. For example, all of the base stations in a cluster together with their associated BSC could be connected with a self-healing ring.

Table 15.3 lists examples of the types of survivable network design strategies that can be implemented. In addition, specific network controls (e.g., routing) are required to support the restoration of service to connections disrupted by a failure/attack, while maintaining network performance goals. This should enable a network to provide service continuity if possible, while minimizing network congestion. Table 15.3 also lists examples of the type of restoration technique for a given redundancy approach at a particular layer. As an example, a *self-healing ring* (SHR) at the ANS layer is shown in Figure 15.2. The SHR can provide full restoration capability against a single cable cut and equipment failure. Each node in the SHR uses one add/drop multiplexer (ADM) to access either the primary (outer) ring or the secondary (inner) ring. In normal operation, the system uses the primary ring for both transmitting and receiving data, and the secondary ring is served as a protection system. In the ANS, the SHR could be used to connect a BS and a BSC, BSC and an MSC, or multiple MSCs as a ring topology. Figure 15.2 illustrates an example of employing SHR between an MSC and multiple BSCs in a mobile cellular network. The SHR is simple, fast, and provides full-capacity restoration. However, it can protect a system from failures that occur only in its physical rings and ADMs. Also, it is expensive to implement.

Thus far we have considered failure conditions, in Table 15.4 we look at the layers of Table 15.1 from a security standpoint. At each layer, the messages and protocols are identified that have security implications and the types of security

Subsystem	Robustness and Redundancy	Traffic Restoration
RNS	Spare RF components, NICs, overlapping/scaleable cells, corner excited overlapping cells, ad hoc relays, spare BS-BSC links, dual-homing APs, multihoming BS to BSCs, and ring topology for BS-BSC interconnect	Load-sharing protocols, dynamic channel allocation, adaptive channel quality protocols, MANET routing protocols, automatic protection switching, dynamic rerouting protocols, and self-healing rings
ANS	Spare BSC-MSC link, ring topology for BSC-MSC interconnect, multihoming BSC to MSCs, and dual-homing APs	Automatic protection switching, self-healing rings, dynamic rerouting, call gapping/selective packet dropping
INS	Physical diversity in signal networking links and physical database diversity	Dynamic routing and checkpoint protocols
SenS	Spare sensor nodes with alternating sleep and waking schedules and multipath routing	Creating new routes upon failure and control messaging from BS for restoring routes and time synchronization

TABLE   Typical survivability strategies.

15.3

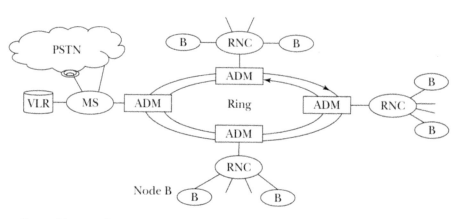

FIGURE   Ring architecture for ANS diversity.

15.2

attacks that are possible at each layer. Currently in WLANs, the only repository of the shared key is the AP (or Authentication Server) and the MS. In cellular networks, different entities have possession of different secrets. The subscriber identity is kept in the HLR, MS, and SGSN. For random nonces used in session key generation, the challenge messages are known to the HLR, SGSN, BSC, MS, and BS. Only the MS and AuC know the master key. The AuC maintains a different master key for each MS that belongs to its network. This master key is utilized for securely generating session keys for encrypting voice calls. Table 15.5 shows examples of security breaches at each level and the impact on a network. In a hybrid wireless access network, several security features will have to be in place to prevent or quickly detect security attacks such as those listed in Table 15.5. Table 15.6 provides some typical security features and mechanisms (and network entities that need to share secret information) that can prevent or detect the attacks in Table 15.5.

15.6   INTERACTION BETWEEN SURVIVABILITY AND SECURITY IN WIRELESS NETWORKS

A major area of research that has been neglected is the interaction between survivability and security. Survivability and security have been usually studied separately. A system may be survivable under component failures but may make itself vulnerable to security attacks because of the restoration mechanisms

Subsystem	Network Components	Secret Information	Messages	Information to be Secured
RNS	MS, BS, ad hoc clusters WLAN AP, and BSC	Subscriber identity, shared secret master key, session key(s), random nonces	Signaling messages (RRM, MM), challenge, response voice/data traffic	Beacon needs to be checked for integrity; challenge, response, nonces to be authenticated; and voice/data traffic confidentiality
ANS	BS, BSC, MSC, WAP, SGSN, GGSN, and signaling network	Shared keys between entities for each session, and random nonces	Signaling messages, voice/data traffic	All traffic needs authentication especially nonces and RRM and MM messages
INS	MSC, HLR, VLR, EIR, AuC, mobileIP signaling, and RADIUS	Certificates, shared secret master key, subscriber ID, session keys, and nonces	Challenge, response, session key, and nonces	Session key to be confidential, challenge, response, and nonces need to be tested for integrity and authentication
SenS	Sensor nodes and BS	Predistributed secret keys and public keys	Sensed/fused/ data, routing control data, and broadcast control messages	Authenticity and confidentiality of different types of information (control and data)

TABLE

15.4

Wireless network layers and security implications.

Subsystem	Attack Scenario	Potential Impact
RNS	Modify beacon or BCCH to falsify information	Loss of access, changed sleep times, and false signal strength measurements
ANS	Replay nonce	Creation of wrong session key, exposure of session key, and failure to detect replayed data
INS	Man-in-the-middle attack for session key generation	Interception of traffic on-air link and modification of traffic on-air link
SenS	Eavesdropping and jamming, fabricated messages	Loss of confidential information, partition of network, lifetime reduction, delivered data are unreliable, data delivery impacted, and network operations fail

TABLE

15.5

Typical security breaches and potential impacts.

Subsystem	Attack Scenario	Entities Involved	Security Feature/Mechanism	Required Shared Secret
RNS	Modify beacon or BCCH to falsify information	MS and BS	Message authentication code, encryption algorithm/hash, and digital signature	Shared secret key > 80 bits, known algorithm like AES and nonce, and authenticated public key of BS/network through certificate
ANS	Replay nonce	BSC and BS	Message authentication code and encryption algorithm/hash	Shared secret key > 80 bits
INS	Man-in-the-middle attack	AuC, BSC/BS, AuC, and AP	Authenticated and secure key establishment	Public key certificates at both ends (not secret)
SenS	Eavesdropping or jamming fabrication	Sensor nodes and BS	Encryption, obfuscation, broadcast and unicast authentication	Secret keys between sensor node pairs and sensor nodes-BS pairs

TABLE 15.6   Typical security features and mechanisms that need to be in place.

employed. Also, automatic recovery from a security breach in wireless networks is not very well understood. Very few works exist in the literature that consider the two aspects together even for wired networks. Furthermore, in wireless networks, the two aspects are closely related because of the need to secure the broadcast wireless link and also keep a network survivable. Recent activities in Network Reliability and Interoperability Council (NRIC) VI Wireless Network Reliability Focus Group indicate that network interoperability and security are considered to the extent that they can impact network survivability. In addition, access to remote wireless network elements (e.g., cell sites) for restoration of service can often be delayed due to security concerns. The security and survivability and their interoperability in the wireless networks need to be improved [35].

15.6.1   Extending the Framework to Include Interactions between Security and Survivability

The framework for security and survivability in last section can also be used to understand the interaction between security and survivability in wireless networks. A range of issues exists such as the impact of node and link failures and restoration schemes on the security architecture and the impact of attacks on components of the survivability strategies and methods of recovery. Table 15.7 shows some examples of each case at the RNS, ANS, INS, and SenS levels. At each of the levels, possible failure/attack scenarios, the impact of the failure/attack scenarios, survivability measures related to security, and security measures related to survivability are identified.

At the RNS level, an example of a failure/attack scenario is the loss of a BS/Node B or compromise of the BCCH message in a cell. When a BS or Node B fails, several MSs will try to reconnect to nearby Node Bs that may have overlapping coverage. The survivability measures related to security are now required to generate spare keys for the failure scenario, while the security measures related to survivability now need to perform authentication of failure and reconnect messages. When the attack scenario is the compromise of the BCCH, MSs will likely lose access to the cell, and it also has potential impact on signal strength measurements. Now the survivability measures related to security are required to generate a redundant BCCH first, perhaps sending the information through neighboring Node Bs. The security measures related to survivability need to quickly detect the compromise and authenticate the updated BCCH to the MSs.

At the ANS level, an example of a failure/attack scenario is the loss of a BSC-SGSN link or compromise of the SGSN. When a BSC-SGSN link fails, there will be partial- or full-service loss in a cell or cluster of cells, and there will be increased traffic in cells adjacent to the failed link. The survivability measures related to security are required to hold spare session keys in SGSNs targeted for handoff and in neighboring clusters, while the security measures related to survivability need authentication of messages to MSs asking them to defer new calls. When compromise of the SGSN happens, there will be loss of data integrity and exposure of session keys. Now the survivability measures related to security are required to reroute traffic to another SGSN from a BSC, while the security measures related to survivability need the set up of new session keys and authentication of a new session between the affected BSC and secondary SGSN.

At the INS level, an example of a failure/attack scenario is the loss of the VLR or compromise of the HLR-VLR link. When a VLR fails, there will be loss of roaming service in the coverage area of a network/subnetwork. The survivability measures related to security will be required to have a spare subset of nonces and keys for the VLR with physical diversity, while the security measures related to survivability need to authenticate the spare VLR and ensure that new nonces and keys rapidly replace the spare subset. When compromise of the HLR-VLR link happens, the session key could be exposed and man-in-the-middle attacks can be launched. Now the survivability measures related to security are required to physically separate the spare link, while the security measures related to survivability quickly need to detect the compromise and need to check the integrity of the spare link.

Subsystem	Failure/Attack Scenario	Impact	Survivability Measures Related to Security	Security Measures Related to Survivability
RNS	Loss of BS/Node B	Service loss requiring MSs to move to neighboring cell	Generate spare keys for failure scenario	Need authentication of failure and reconnect messages
	Compromise of BCCH	Loss of access to cell and potential impact on signal strength measurements	Generate redundant BCCH	Quick detection of compromise, and authenticate the updated BCCH to MS
ANS	Loss of BSC–SGSN link and compromise of SGSN	Partial/full-service loss in a cell or cluster of cells, increased traffic in cells adjacent to failure, and loss of data integrity and exposure of session keys	Hold spare session keys in SGSNs targeted for handoff and in neighboring clusters and reroute traffic to another SGSN from a BSC	Need authentication of messages to MSs asking them to defer new calls and set up of new session keys and authentication of new session between BSC and secondary SGSN
INS	Loss of VLR	Loss of roaming service in a coverage area or network/subnetwork	VLR with physical diversity must have a spare subset of nonces and keys	Need to authenticate the spare VLR and ensure that new nonces and keys replace the spare subset rapidly
	Compromise of HLR-VLR link	Man-in-the-middle attack exposes the session key	Physically separate spare link	Detection of compromise and check integrity of spare link
SenS	Failed sensor node(s) and compromise of sensor nodes	Network partition or impact on data delivery, and false data injected into the network	Wake up sleeping nodes to fill holes, wake up additional nodes to verify sensed data, and rekeying protocols	Woken nodes need to establish secure links (check for nodes that they share keys with), and detection of compromise and check integrity of received data

TABLE
15.7   Typical survivability and security features and mechanisms that need to be in place.

At the SenS level, one example of failure is a group of sensor nodes dying due to hardware failures or battery exhaustion. The network may be partitioned unless redundant nodes that are sleeping are woken up by broadcast messages from a BS. However, such nodes may not share keys with neighboring sensor nodes, or they may have to discover those nodes with which they share a key to secure the new links and routes created in the sensor network. Similarly, if some sensor nodes are compromised and they inject fabricated data into the network, upon detection of such compromise, other nodes in their vicinity may have to be queried to send sensed data that may be essential for the application. It may be necessary to have some restoration schemes for rekeying the sensor nodes that are not compromised if keys are revealed by the compromised nodes.

15.6.2   Case Study I: Idle Handoffs

Figure 15.3 shows another example of the interaction between survivability and security. In a UMTS-WCDMA system, an *idle handoff* occurs upon detecting a stronger pilot (when an MS moves to another cell while it is not making a call). The request from the MS is sent through the new Node B and RNC to a new MSC/VLR if necessary. The VLR contacts the HLR for an authentication request. In response, several authentication vectors (AVs) are sent to the VLR, one of which is used to authenticate the MS as a challenge and obtain the MS response. The others are kept in reserve if necessary. Suppose now a Node B fails and several MSs will try to simultaneously make idle handoffs to nearby Node Bs that may have overlapping coverage. All of these requests will congest the connection to the VLR. If AVs are instead stored in neighboring Node Bs and some time-limited authentication can be done while a traffic restoration protocol can schedule a more rigorous authentication, the performance could be improved significantly.

In a hybrid network scenario, the interaction between survivability and security becomes more complex. In the case of failure of a Node B in a cellular network, MSs may benefit from connecting to an underlay 802.11 WLAN that may be providing coverage in the same geographical area. When the MSs try to connect to the 802.11 AP, the process involved will be similar to a handoff. The only difference is that the handoff is performed to a different type of wireless access network. As part of this handoff, MSs need to be authenticated. Only then can a MS associate itself with an AP and resume communications. Even assuming loose coupling (described earlier), the time taken to authenticate an MS in a 802.11 WLAN can be fairly large, (1) because of the time taken to obtain information about the WLAN availability through the beacon messages [36, 37] and (2) because of the numerous message exchanges and cryptographic functions.

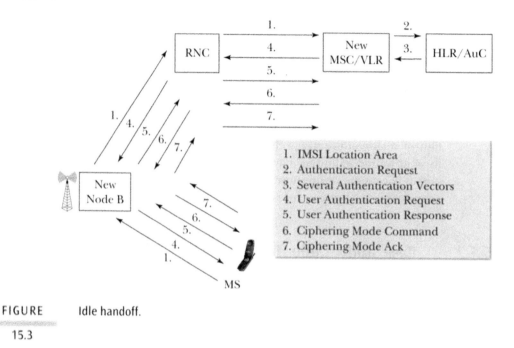

FIGURE   Idle handoff.

15.3

In the case of tight coupling, this delay could be worse because of the need to communicate with the GPRS core network. Survivability and security measures will have to carefully interact to ensure that the quality of communications is maintained according to the specified metrics, while adequate security levels are maintained. Moreover, the examples of failure/attack scenarios described above can be more complex in this case.

15.6.3   Case Study II: Key Management in Heterogeneous Sensor Networks

To understand the interaction between survivability and security of our WSN security architecture with heterogeneous sensor nodes, we conduct a case study for the key management scheme. Our study shows that the WSN can achieve higher key connectivity and higher resilience with our proposed key management scheme, with a small percentage of heterogeneous nodes that have reasonable storage, processing, and communication capabilities. We can also see the trade-off between the reliability and the security in some examples.

Key management is one of the most important prevention and protection schemes for security mechanisms of WSNs. To provide secure communications for WSNs, all messages should be encrypted and authenticated. Consequently, security solutions for such applications depend on the existence of strong and efficient key distribution mechanisms for uncontrolled environments of WSNs. We illustrate how to design an effective key management framework under the general heterogeneous WSN security architecture. Up to now, almost all the existing key management schemes for distributed WSNs assume that the sensor nodes are homogeneous with the same capabilities for each sensor network. Therefore, it is of significance to investigate how to design a suitable key management scheme for heterogeneous WSNs. Consequently, it is also important to address the reliability issue in the design of a key management scheme. Energy conservation is a critical issue in WSNs since batteries are the only limited-life energy source to power the sensor nodes. The key management schemes designed for WSNs should be energy aware and efficient.

Obviously, using a single shared key in a whole WSN is not a good idea because an adversary can easily obtain the key. Therefore, as a fundamental security service, pair-wise key establishment shall be used, which can enable the sensor nodes to communicate securely with each other using cryptographic techniques. However, due to resource constraints on sensor nodes, it is not feasible for sensors to use traditional pair-wise key establishment techniques such as public key cryptography and key distribution center [38]. Instead, sensor nodes can use pre-distributed keys directly or use keying materials to dynamically generate pair-wise keys. In such a case, the main challenge is to find an efficient way of distributing keys and keying materials to sensor nodes prior to deployment.

In this case study, we assume that there are I classes of sensor nodes in the network, with Class 1 consisting of the least powerful nodes and Class I the most powerful nodes, in terms of communication range, node processing capability, and energy level. Particularly, in terms of communication range, we assume the existence of bidirectional links between any two nodes. Let r_i denote the communication range of Class i nodes; we always have $r_m < r_n$ if $m < n$. Therefore, if a Class m node is within the range of a direct communication link of a Class n node, the Class m node might need multiple links to reach the Class n node if $m < n$. The heterogeneity of the sensor nodes are distributed in the WSN, with p_i the percentage of the Class i nodes, and $p_1 + p_2 + \ldots \ldots + p_I = 1$. Here, it is important to notice the fundamental difference between the heterogeneous WSNs assumed in this section and the hierarchical WSNs in Law et al. [39] and Zhu et al. [40]. In the hierarchical WSNs, the base stations (or cluster supervisors) are centralized nodes, and more importantly, they are acting like key distribution centers. In contrast, in the heterogeneous WSNs, except that the higher class nodes are more powerful in terms of communication range, node capability, and energy level, the communications between all different classes of nodes are still peer-to-peer and distributed.

The security requirements and services can be described by the following metrics: scalability, efficiency, resilience, and reliability. Scalability is the ability to support a large number of wireless sensor nodes in a network. The security mechanisms must support a large network and be flexible against a substantial increase in the size of the network even after deployment. Efficiency is the consideration of storage, processing, and communication limitations on sensor nodes. Resilience is about the resistance to node capture. A compromise of security credentials, which are stored on a sensor node or exchanged over radio links, should not reveal information about security of any other links in the WSN. A higher resilience means a lower number of compromised links. Reliability is the capability to keep the functionality of the WSN even if some sensor nodes are failed. The survivability concerns can be provided with the design goals of scalability, efficiency, key connectivity, resilience, and reliability. Key connectivity is the probability that two or more sensor nodes store the same key or keying material. Enough key connectivity must be provided for a WSN to perform its intended functionality.

The key generation in heterogeneous-distributed WSNs here is based on the random key distribution [41] and the polynomial based key predistribution protocol [42], and is inspired by the approaches of Liu and Ning [43]. In a manner similar to the studies in Eschenauer and Gligor [41], we consider that there are three steps in the framework to establish pair-wise keys between the sensor nodes:

1. Initialization.

2. Direct key setup.

3. Path key setup.

The initialization step is performed to initialize the sensors by distributing polynomial shares to them, with the consideration of the heterogeneity of the sensor nodes. The direct key setup step is for any two nodes trying to establish a pair-wise key, in which they always first attempt to do so through direct key establishment. If the second step is successful, there is no need to start the third step. Otherwise, these sensor nodes may start the path key setup step, trying to establish a pair-wise key with the help of other sensors.

Our scheme uses a pool of randomly generated bivariate polynomials to establish pair-wise keys between sensor nodes, with the consideration of I classes of heterogeneity among the wireless sensor nodes. In this manner, existing distributed key management schemes can all be included in the framework. For example, if $I = 1$, which means that the sensor network is homogeneous, we have the following special cases: when all the polynomials are 0-degree ones and the sensor network is homogeneous, the polynomial pool degenerates into a key pool [41]; and when the polynomial pool has only one polynomial and the sensor network is homogeneous, the key distribution scheme degenerates into the polynomial-based key predistribution [42].

The main challenge in this scheme is how to assign polynomial shares to different classes of nodes. We can clearly observe that the major issue in our scheme is the subset assignment problem, which specifies how to determine the set of polynomials and how to assign the polynomial shared for each sensor node in group j with class i. During the key distribution procedure, a number of factors must be considered, including the probability that adjacent nodes can share a common key, the resilience of the network when it is under attack, and importantly, the nature of the heterogeneity.

The proposed new key generation scheme is essentially different from most existing schemes in that the heterogeneity features can now be taken into account. To illustrate the advantages of the new scheme, we consider a typical heterogeneous WSN that is established to collect data in a distributed scenario. In this scenario, a sensor node shall submit its observation to a sink node (or sink nodes, depending on the configuration of the network) through the sensor network in a hop-by-hop manner, as shown in Figure 15.4, in which there are two classes of sensor nodes in addition to the sink node.

Since the high-class nodes have a larger transmission range, it is nature that a low-class node will tend to utilize the link between itself and a high-class node to submit the observations. For example, in Figure 15.4, class-one node A will tend to use the path "A-X-Sink" (the solid lines) to submit its report, instead of passing the message by all class-one nodes "A-B-C-Sink" (the dash lines). Clearly, a high-class node will more likely be chosen as the next hop neighbor of nearby low-class nodes to forward data. Consequently, in this heterogeneous sensor network, the connectivity between a low-class node and a high-class node will be more important than the connectivity between two low-class nodes.

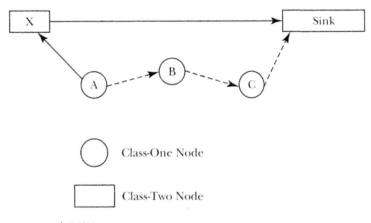

We now design a special key management scheme within the new framework for the above scenario. Specifically, we consider that there are two classes of the heterogeneous sensor nodes (i.e., $I = 2$). To simplify the discussion, we also assume that there is only one group, denoted as group 0, in the network.

The special key management scheme is a key-pool-based key distribution scheme. In this scheme, we denote C_1 as the class of the less powerful sensor nodes and C_2 the class of the more powerful sensor nodes. We consider that a C_2 node X is *in the neighborhood of* a C_1 node A, if A can directly receive the message from X. Since the transmission range of A is less than the transmission range of X, A may need to send messages to X through a multihop path. We define that a C_1 node is *connected to the network if it shares at least one key with C_2 nodes in its neighborhood.* We then define the key connectivity as the probability that a C_1 node is connected to the network. For simplicity, we only consider the direct key setup between a C_1 node and adjacent C_2 node.

An example of this scheme is illustrated in Figure 15.5, where node A is a C_1 node and nodes X, Y, and Z are C_2 nodes. In this example, nodes X, Y, and Z are the only C_2 neighbor nodes of node A. In addition, node A shares key K_1 with node X, K_2 with node Y, and K_1 and K_3 with node Z, respectively. In this example, node A is connected to the network through three different keys: K_1, K_2, and K_3. In such a case, if node A wants to submit new information to the sink node, it can first randomly select a key from K_1 to K_3; then, it can randomly select a neighbor node that shares the same key with it. For example, in Figure 15.5, if K_1 is chosen as the key, then node X and Z can be randomly selected. In this manner, we can see that the communication is more resilient, while the connectivity can also be maintained.

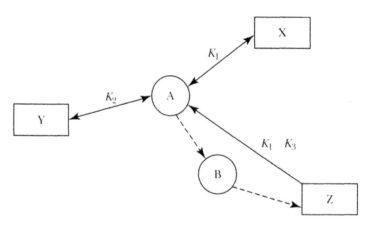

FIGURE   The proposed key management scheme for the example WSN.

15.5

To understand the behavior of the key management scheme above, we have conducted extensive quantitative studies to evaluate the performance, in terms of key connectivity, reliability, and resilience. In our experiments, we consider a small area of WSN that consists of 200 C_1 nodes and a number of C_2 nodes, denoted as N_2. We also assume that the size of key pool is 50,000 and the number of keys in any C_2 node is fixed to 2,000.

Reliability of the New Schemes: Key Connectivity of the New Schemes in Normal Conditions

According to the definition, *key connectivity* is the probability that two or more sensor nodes store the same key. Clearly, enough key connectivity must be provided for a WSN to perform its intended functionality. Figure 15.6 shows the connectivity of the proposed scheme versus the number of keys in a C_1 node with a different number of C_2 nodes. We can first observe that the connectivity can increase with the increase of the number of keys. For a fixed number of keys in each C_1 node, we can see that a small increase of the number of C_2 nodes can significantly increase the connectivity, especially when the number of keys in C_1 node is small and medium. From another perspective, we can see that, to achieve

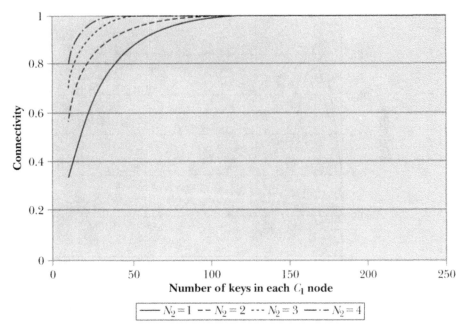

FIGURE

15.6

Connectivity of proposed key management scheme in normal conditions.

a specific connectivity, the number of keys that must be stored in each C_1 node can be decreased with the increase of N_2. For instance, if the connectivity is 0.99, then about 113 keys are required for $N_2 = 1$, about 57 keys are required for $N_2 = 2$, about 38 keys are required for $N_2 = 3$, and about 29 keys are needed for $N_2 = 4$.

To highlight the impact of the number of C_2 nodes, we demonstrate in Figure 15.7 the probability distribution of the number of shared keys with different N_2. In this example, we assume the number of keys in each C_1 node is 60. We can observe that, with the increase of N_2, the shape of the distribution tends to shift to the right-hand side, which implies that a C_1 node can share more keys with neighboring C_2 nodes. With the increase of shared keys, the network becomes more reliable.

Resilience of the New Schemes: Key Connectivity of the New Schemes in Attack Conditions

To evaluate the resilience of the new schemes, we study the performance of the sensor network when some C_1 nodes are compromised. Here we assume that C_2 nodes are more tamper resistant. In Figure 15.8, we consider the scenario in which the keys per C_1 node will be selected in a manner such that the

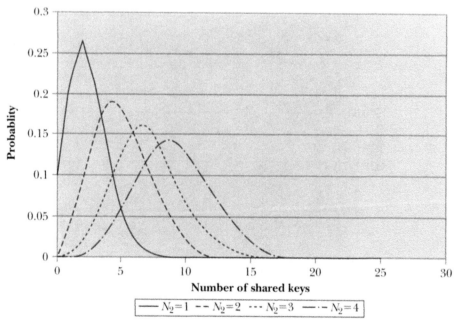

FIGURE 15.7   Probability of the number of shared keys.

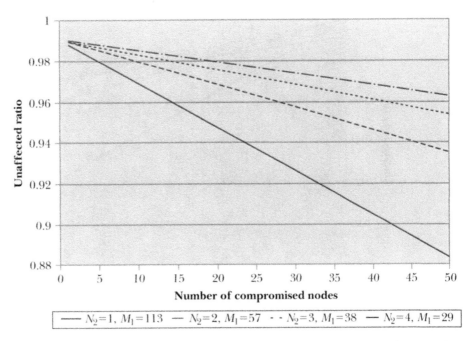

FIGURE

15.8

Resilience of the key management scheme in attack conditions (connectivity = 99% in normal conditions).

network connectivity is 99% under normal conditions. We also assume that the compromised C_1 nodes cannot be detected. In such a scenario, the data transmission from an unaffected C_1 node may be eavesdropped by a nearby compromised node. Therefore, it is important to study the percentage of communications that are not affected. From Figure 15.5, we can see that with our schemes, a C_1 node can still securely transmit data to C_2 nodes even if some of the keys are compromised. For example, if K_1 is the only key that is compromised, then we can see that node A still has a 66% chance to forward the data to any one of the C_2 nodes (with K_2 or K_3). This phenomenon can be clearly observed from Figure 15.8, where we find that a high percentage of secured communications can still be maintained even if a large number of C_1 nodes have been compromised. Moreover, we can see that more C_2 nodes can help to increase the fraction of unaffected communications, given the same number of compromised C_1 nodes.

In Figure 15.9, we consider scenarios in which we fix $N_2 = 4$ and let M_1 be 29, 38, 57, and 113, where M_1 is the number of keys that can be stored in a C_1 node. In this case, $M_1 = 29$ can represent the lowest reliability because the connectivity of the network will be less than 99% if one C_2 node is failed. On the other extreme, we notice that $M_1 = 113$ can represent the situation with the highest reliability

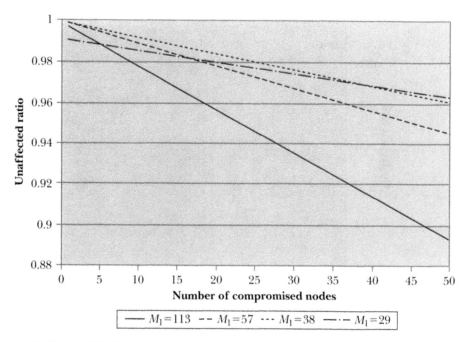

FIGURE   Resilience of the key management scheme in attack conditions ($N_2 = 4$).

15.9

because the connectivity of the network will be greater than 99% even if three C_2 nodes are failed. Clearly, we can first observe the trade-off between the reliability and resilience from this example. For example, if the number of compromised nodes is larger than 5, $M_1 = 29$ can have better resilience than that of $M_1 = 113$. Moreover, we also notice that, given a certain number of compromised nodes, an optimum configuration may exist that can lead to the highest resilience. For instance, if the number of compromised nodes is 20, than $M_1 = 38$ has the best performance in terms of unaffected ratio.

15.7   CONCLUSION

Information assurance techniques employed in wired networks have limited direct applicability in wireless networks because of the unique aspects of wireless networks (user mobility, wireless channel, power conservation, limited computational power in mobile nodes, and security at the link layer). In this chapter, we study the survivability and security in wireless networks, both for hybrid wireless infrastructure networks and wireless ad hoc and sensor networks. The issues that are related to the interaction between survivability and security in hybrid wireless infrastructure networks are discussed. We provide a framework that can be used to understand the implications of failures or security breaches on the performance and design of hybrid wireless infrastructure networks. We also address the design issues for secure and survivable wireless sensor networks, which are vulnerable to physical and network-based security attacks, accidents, and failures. Based on the study about the security requirements and survivability requirements, we develop architecture for security and survivability in WSNs with heterogeneous sensor nodes. To better understand the interactions between survivability and security, we also design and analyze a key management scheme within the architecture. The experiment results show that a good design can improve both security and survivability of WSNs. It also illustrates that there is a trade-off between security and survivability in some scenarios.

References

[1] J. J.-N. Liu and I. Chlamtac, "Mobile Ad-Hoc Networking with a View of 4G Wireless: Imperatives and Challenges," in *Mobile Ad Hoc Networking*, edited by S. Basagni, M. Conti, S. Giordano, and I. Stojmenovic (New York: IEEE Press, Wiley-Interscience, 2004).

[2] K. Pahlavan, P. Krishnamurthy, et al., "Handoff in Hybrid Mobile Data Networks," *IEEE Personal Communications* (April 2000).

[3] I. Akyildiz, W. Su, Y. Sankarasubramanian, and E. Cayirci, "A Survey on Sensor Networks," *IEEE Communications Magazines* (Aug. 2002).

[4] D. Tipper, T. Dahlberg, H. Shin, and C. Charnsripinyo, "Providing Fault Tolerance in Wireless Access Networks," *IEEE Communications Magazine* (Jan. 2002): 58–64.

[5] P. Krishnamurthy, D. Tipper, and Y. Qian, "The Interaction of Security and Survivability in Hybrid Wireless Networks," *WIA 2004, Proceedings of IEEE IPCCC 2004*, Phoenix, AZ, April 14–17, 2004.

[6] Y. Qian, K. Lu, and D. Tipper, "Towards Survivable and Secure Wireless Sensor Networks," *WIA 2007, Proceedings of IEEE IPCCC 2007*, New Orleans, LA, April 11–13, 2007.

[7] A. K. Salkintzis, C. Fors, and R. Pazhyannur, "WLAN-GPRS Integration for Next Generation Mobile Data Networks," *IEEE Wireless Communications* (Oct. 2002).

[8] I. Akyildiz and X. Wang, "A Survey on Wireless Mesh Networks," *IEEE Communications Magazine*, (Sept. 2005): 23–30.

[9] H. Luo, R. Ramjee, P. Sinha, L. Li, and S. Lu, "UCAN: A Unified Cellular and Ad Hoc Network Architecture," *ACM Mobicom* (Sept. 2003): 353–367.

[10] K. Pahlavan and P. Krishnamurthy, *Principles of Wireless Networks: A Unified Approach* (Englewood Cliffs, NJ: Prentice Hall PTR, 2002).

[11] S. Fluhrer, I. Martin, and A. Shamir, "Weaknesses in Key Scheduling Algorithm of RC4," *Eighth Annual Workshop on Selected Areas in Cryptography,* Aug. 2001.

[12] TR 33.102, "3GPP Security Architecture," 3GPP release, 1999.

[13] D. Simon, B. Aboba, and T. Moore, "IEEE 802.11 Security and 802.1X," *IEEE 802.11 WG Document doc: IEEE 802.11–00/034r1,* Mar. 2000.

[14] D. Djenouri, L. Khelladi, and N. Badache, "A Survey of Security Issues in Mobile Ad Hoc and Sensor Networks," *IEEE Communications Surveys* 7, No. 4 (2005).

[15] J. Zheng, M. J. Lee, and M. Anshel, "Toward Secure Low Rate Wireless Personal Area Networks," *IEEE Transactions on Mobile Computing* 5, No. 10 (Oct. 2006): 1361–1373.

[16] E. Shi and A. Perrig, "Designing Secure Sensor Networks," *IEEE Wireless Communications* (Dec. 2004): 38–43.

[17] P. E. Wirth, "Teletraffic Implications of Database Architectures in Mobile and Personal Communications," *IEEE Communications Magazine* (June 1995): 54–59.

[18] Y. Lin, "Failure Restoration of Mobility Databases for Personal Communication Networks," *Wireless Networks,* Vol. 1, No. 3, pp. 365–372, 1995.

[19] Y. Lin, "Per-User Checkpointing for Mobility Database Failure Restoration," *IEEE Transactions on Mobile Computing,* Vol. 4, No. 1, Jan.–March, 2005.

[20] A. Hilt and P. Berzethy, "Recent Trends in Reliable Access Networking for GSM Systems," *Proceedings of Third International Workshop on the Design of Reliable Communication Networks,* Budapest, Hungary, Oct. 2001.

[21] A. Dutta, and P. Kubat, "Design of partially survivable networks for cellular telecommunication systems," *European Journal of Operational Research,* Vol. 118, (1999), pp. 52–64.

[22] Louis A. Cox, Jr., and Jennifer R. Sanchez, "Designing least-cost survivable wireless backhaul networks," Journal of Heuristics, Vol. 6, (2000), pp. 525–540.

[23] P. Kubat, J. M. Smith and C. Yum, "Design of Cellular Networks with Diversity and Capacity Constraints," *IEEE Transactions on Reliability,* Vol., 49, No. 2, (June 2000), pp. 165–175.

[24] A. P. Snow, U. Varshney, and A. D. Malloy, "Reliability and Survivability of Wireless and Mobile Networks," *IEEE Computer* 33 (July 2000): 49–55.

[25] D. Tipper, S. Ramaswamy, and T. Dahlberg, "PCS Network Survivability," *Proceedings of IEEE Wireless Communications and Networking Conference (WCNC'99),* New Orleans, LA, Sept. 1999.

[26] H. Shin, C. Charnsripinyo, D. Tipper, and T. Dahlberg, "The Effects of Failures in PCS Networks," *Proceedings of DRCN*, Budapest, Hungary, Oct. 2001.

[27] D. Tipper, C. Charnsripinyo, H. Shin, and T. Dahlberg, "Survivability Analysis for Mobile Cellular Networks," Proceedings CNDS 2002, San Antonio, TX, Jan. 27–31, 2002.

[28] The IST Caution Project at: http://www.telecom.ntua.gr/caution/start.html

[29] C. Charnsripinyo and D. Tipper, "Topological Design of 3G Wireless Backhaul Networks for Service Assurance," *Proceedings Fifth IEEE International Workshop on the Design of Reliable Communication Networks, (DRCN 2005)*, Oct. 17–19, 2005, Ischia, Italy.

[30] T. Dahlberg, D. Tipper, B. Cao, and C. Charnsripinyo, "Survivability in Wireless Mobile Networks," pp. 81–114 in Reliability, Survivability, and Quality of Large Scale Telecommunication Systems, *Ed. P. Stavroulakis*, John Wiley & Sons, London, UK, 2003.

[31] J. Sterbenz, R. Krishnan, R. Hain, A. Jackson, D. Levin, R. Ramanathan, and J. Zhao, "Survivable Mobile Wireless Networks: Issues, Challenges, and Research Directions," *Proceedings of ACM Wireless Security Workshop (WiSe'02)*, Sept. 28, 2002, Atlanta, GA.

[32] K. Fall, "A Delay-Tolerant Network Architecture for Challenged Internets", *Proceedings of the ACM SIGCOMM 2003*, Karlsruhe Germany, Aug. 2003, pp. 27–34.

[33] A. Zolfaghari and F. J. Kaudel, "Framework for Network Survivability Performance," *IEEE Journal on Sel. Areas in Comm.* 12, No. 1 (Jan. 1994): 46–51.

[34] D. Grillo, "Personal Communications and Traffic Engineering in ITU-T: Developing E.750 Series of Recommendations," *IEEE Personal Communications* (Dec. 1996): 16–28.

[35] NRIC, at http://www.nric.org/.

[36] M. Shin, A. Mishra, and W. Arbaugh, "Improving the Latency of 802.11 Hand-offs Using Neighbor Graphs," *Proceedings of MobiSys'04*, Boston, MA, June 6–9, 2004.

[37] H. Velayos and G. Karlsson, "Techniques to Reduce the IEEE 802.11b Handoff Time," *Proceedings of IEEE ICC 2004*, Paris, France, June 2004.

[38] S. Avancha, J. Undercoffer, A. Joshi, and J. Pinkston, "Security for Wireless Sensor Networks," in *Wireless Sensor Networks*, edited by C. S. Raghavendra, K. M. Sivalingam, and T. Znati (New York: Kluwer Academic Publishers, 2004).

[39] Y. Law, R. Corin, S. Etalle, and P. Hartel, "A Formally Verified Decentralized Key Management for Wireless Sensor Networks," *Personal/Wireless Communications, LNCS* 2775 (2003): 27–39.

[40] S. Zhu, S. Setia, and S. Jajodia, "LEAP: Efficient Security Mechanisms for Large-Scale Distributed Sensor Networks," *Proceedings of IEEE Symposium on Research in Security and Privacy*, May 2003.

[41] L. Eschenauer and V. D. Gligor, "A Key-Management Scheme for Distributed Sensor Networks," *Proceedings of 9th ACM Conference on Computer and Communication Security*, Nov. 2002.

[42] C. Blundo, A. De Santis, A. Herzberg, S. Kutten, U. Vaccaro, and M. Yung, "Perfectly- Secure Key Distribution for Dynamic Conferences," *Proceedings of Advances in Cryptology, CRYPTO'92, LNCS* 740 (1993): 471–486.

[43] D. Liu, and P. Ning, "Establishing Pairwise Keys in Distributed Sensor Networks," *Proceedings of the 10th ACM Conference on Computer and Communications Security*, Oct. 2003.

16 — Integrated Fault and Security Management

CHAPTER

Ehab Al-Shaer   DePaul University, USA
Yan Chen   Northwestern University, USA

16.1   INTRODUCTION

Network problems such as faults and security attacks are expressed in a network as one or more symptoms (e.g., alarms, logs, troupe tickets). Network problem diagnosis is the process of correlating or analyzing the observed symptoms in order to identify the root cause. As network faults and security attacks might show similar symptoms, it is possible to incorrectly identify faults as security attacks or vice versa. For example, host/network reachablility problems could be due to either a denial of service (DoS) attack or link or protocol failure. These cause more false alarms and incorrect response actions. Therefore, integrating fault and security management is important for practical network management systems in order to diagnose and fix problems accurately.

Fault and security intrusion diagnosis exhibit a similar reasoning process that includes symptom collection, correlation, and evaluation. This makes the integration of fault and security management even more sensible. However, to achieve an optimal integration, a number of challenges need to be addressed. First, the root cause for a symptom should be accurately identified even with incomplete symptom information. Second, the problem identification should be fast to account for high-speed networks and wide distribution of sensors (e.g., intrusion detection system, or IDS).

In Section 16.2, we present an active problem diagnosis framework for integrating the reasoning of fault or security alarms within the same engine. The presented framework uses this active diagnosis approach to deal with incomplete symptom information and identify faults and intrusions. In Section 16.3, we show an architecture for network-based IDSs that analyzes traffic collected from different sensors on a high-speed network, identifies faults and intrusions, and initiates proper mitigation actions for various intrusions.

16.2   ACTIVE INTEGRATED FAULT IDENTIFICATION FRAMEWORK

16.2.1   Background

Fault localization is a basic component in fault management systems, because it identifies the reason for the fault that can best explain the observed network disorders (namely, symptoms). Examples of fault symptoms include unreachable hosts or networks, slow response, high utilization, and so on. Most fault reasoning algorithms use a bipartite directed acyclic graph to describe the symptom-fault correlation, which represents the causal relationship between each fault f_i and a set of its observed symptoms S_{f_i} [1]. Symptom-fault causality graphs provide a vector of correlation likelihood measures $p(s_i|f_i)$ to bind a fault f_i to a set of its symptoms S_{f_i}. Similarly, symptom-intrusion causality graphs can be constructed based on *attack graphs* [2] (see also Chapter 9) to describe the alarm-intrusion correlation. For simplicity, in the rest of this section, we will focus on fault reasoning and diagnosis. However, similar techniques are applicable to identification of security attacks/intrusions.

Two approaches are commonly used in fault reasoning and localization: passive diagnosis [1, 3–5] and active probing [6–9]. In the passive approach, all symptoms are passively collected and then processed to infer the root faults. In the active approach, faults are detected by conducting a set of probing actions. The passive approach causes less intrusiveness in management networks. However, it may take a long time to discover the root faults, particularly if the symptom loss ratio is high. On the other hand, although an active probing approach is more efficient to quickly identify faults, probing might cause significant overhead, particularly in large-scale networks. In this section, we will show a novel fault localization technique that integrates the advantage of both passive and active monitoring into one framework, called *active integrated fault reasoning* (AIR). In our approach, if the passive reasoning is not sufficient to explain the problem, AIR selects optimal probing actions to discover the most critical symptoms that are important to explain the problem. But such symptoms may have been lost or corrupted during passive fault reasoning. Our approach significantly improves the performance of fault localization while minimizing the intrusiveness of active fault reasoning.

AIR consists of three modules: fault reasoning (FR), fidelity evaluation (FE), and action selection(AS). The *fault reasoning* module passively analyzes observed symptoms and generates a fault hypothesis. The fault hypothesis is then sent to a *fidelity evaluation* module to verify whether the fidelity value of the reasoning result is satisfactory. If the correlated symptoms necessary to explain the fault hypothesis are observed (i.e., there is high fidelity), then the fault reasoning process terminates. Otherwise, a list of most likely unobserved symptoms that can contribute to the fault hypothesis fidelity is sent to the *action selection* module. The AS module then performs selected actions to determine which symptoms have occurred but are not observed (i.e., lost) and accordingly adjusts the hypothesis fidelity value. If the new fidelity value is satisfactory, then the reasoning process terminates; otherwise, the new symptom evidence is fed into the FR module to create a new hypothesis. This process is recursively invoked until a highly credible hypothesis is found.

The section is organized as follows. In Section 16.2.2, related work is discussed. In Section 16.2.3, we discuss our research motivation and the problem formalization. In Section 16.2.4, we describe the components and algorithms of AIR. In Section 16.2.5, we present a simulation study to evaluate AIR performance and accuracy.

16.2.2   Related Work

Many proposed solutions have been presented to address fault localization problems in communication networks. A number of these techniques use different causality models to infer the observation of network disorder to the root faults. In our survey, we classify the related work into two general categories: passive approach and active probing approach.

Passive Approach

Passive fault management techniques typically depended on monitoring agents to detect and report network abnormality using alarms or symptom events. These events are then analyzed and correlated in order to reach the root faults. Various event correlation models were proposed including the rule-based analyzing system [10], model-based system [11], case-based diagnosing system, and model traversing techniques. Different techniques are also introduced to improve the performance, accuracy, and resilience of fault localization. In Appleby and Goldszmidt [5], a model-based event correlation engine is designed for multilayer fault diagnosis. In Kliger et al. [3], a coding approach is applied to the deterministic model to reduce the reasoning time and improve system resilience. A novel incremental event-driven fault reasoning technique is presented in Steinder and Sethi [1, 4] to improve the robustness of the fault localization system by analyzing lost, positive, and spurious symptoms.

The above techniques were developed based on passively received symptoms. If the evidence (symptoms) is collected correctly, the fault reasoning results can be accurate. However, in real systems, symptom loss or spurious symptoms (observation noise) are unavoidable. Even with a good strategy [1] to deal with observation noise, such techniques have limited resilience to noise because of their underlying passive approach, which might also increase the fault detection time.

Active Probing Approach

Recently, some researchers incorporate active probing into fault localization. In Brodie et al. [6], an active probing fault localization system is introduced, in which preplanned active probes are associated with system status by a dependency matrix. An online action selection algorithm is studied in Rish and Brodie [7] to optimize action selection. In Guo and Kermani [9], a fault detection and resolution system is proposed for a large distributed transaction processing system.

The active probing approach is more efficient in locating faults in a timely fashion and is more resilient to observation noise. However, this approach has the following limitations:

- Lack of integrating passive and active techniques in one framework that can take advantage of both approaches.
- Lack of a scalable technique that can deal with multiple simultaneous faults.
- Limitation of some approaches to track or isolate intermittent network faults and performance-related faults because they solely depend on the active probing model.
- The number of required probes might be increased exponentially to the number of possible faults [7].

Both passive and active probing approaches have their own good features and limitations. Thus, integrating passive and active fault reasoning is the ideal approach. Our approach combines the good features of both passive and active approaches and overcomes their limitations by optimizing the fault reasoning result and action selection process.

16.2.3   Challenges and Problem Formalization

In general, active fault management does not scale well when the number of managed nodes or faults grows significantly in the network. In fact, some faults, such as an intermittent reachability problem, may not even be identified if only active fault management is used. However, this can be easily reported using passive fault management systems because agents are configured to report abnormal system conditions or symptoms such as high average packet drop ratios. On the other hand, symptoms can be lost due to noisy or unreliable communications channels, or they might be corrupted due to spurious symptoms generated as a result of malfunctioning agents or devices. This significantly reduces the accuracy and the performance of passive fault localization. Only the integration of active and passive reasoning can provide efficient fault localization solutions.

To incorporate actions into traditional symptom-fault models, we propose an extended symptom-fault-action model as shown in Figure 16.1. In our model, actions (e.g., a_1) are properly selected probes or test transactions that are used to detect or verify the existence of observable symptoms. Actions can simply include commonly used network utilities, like ping and trace route, or some proprietary fault management system, like Simple Network Management Protocol (SNMP)based multicast reachability monitoring (SMRM) [8]. We assume that symptoms are verifiable, which means that, if a symptom ever occurred, we could verify the symptom's existence by executing some probing actions or checking the system status such as system logs.

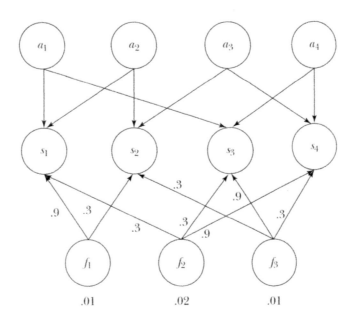

FIGURE   Action-symptom-fault model.

16.1

Notation	Definition
S_{f_i}	A set of all symptoms caused by the fault f_i
F_{s_i}	A set of all faults that might cause symptom s_i
S_O	A set of all observed symptoms so far
S_{O_i}	A set of observed symptoms caused by fault f_i
S_{U_i}	A set of not-yet-observed (lost) symptoms caused by the fault f_i
h_i	A set of faults that constitute a possible hypothesis that can explain S_O
Φ	A set of all different fault hypotheses, h_i, that can explain S_O
S_N	A set of correlated but not-yet-observed symptoms associated with any fault in a hypothesis
S_Y	A subset of S_N, which includes symptoms that their existence is confirmed
S_U	A subset of S_N, which includes symptoms that their nonexistence is confirmed

TABLE   Active integrated fault reasoning notation.

16.1

In this section, we use $F = \{f_1, f_2, \ldots, f_n\}$ to denote the *fault set*, and $S = \{s_1, s_2, \ldots, s_m\}$ to denote the *symptom set* that can be caused by one or multiple faults in F. A causality matrix $P_{F \times S} = \{p(s_i | f_j)\}$ is used to define causal certainty between fault $f_i (f_i \in F)$ and symptom $s_i (s_i \in S)$. If $p(s_i | f_j) = 0$ or 1 for all (i, j), we call such a causality model a deterministic model, otherwise, we call it a probabilistic model. We also use $A = \{a_1, \ldots, a_k\}$ to denote the list of actions that can be used to verify symptom existence. We describe the relation between actions and symptoms using an *action codebook* represented as a bipartite graph, as shown in Figure 16.1. For example, the symptom s_1 can be verified using action a_1 or a_2. The action codebook can be defined by network managers based on symptom type, the network topology, and the available fault diagnostic tools. The extended symptom-fault-action graph is viewed as a five-tuple (S, F, A, E_1, E_2), where the fault set F, symptom set S, and action set A are three independent vertex sets. Every edge in E_1 connects a vertex in S and another vertex in F to indicate causality relationship between symptoms and faults. Every edge in E_2 connects a vertex in A and another vertex in S to indicate the action codebook. For convenience, in Table 16.1, we introduce the notations used in our discussion throughout this section. The basic symptom-fault-action model can be described as the following:

+ For every action, associate an action vertex a_i, $a_i \in A$.

+ For every symptom, associate a symptom vertex s_i, $s_i \in S$.

+ For every fault, associate a fault vertex f_i, $f_i \in F$.

+ For every fault f_i, associate an edge to each s_i caused by this fault with a weight equal to $p(s_i | f_i)$.

+ For every action a_i, associate an edge of weight equal to the action cost to each symptom verifiable by this action.

Performance and accuracy are the two most important factors for evaluating fault localization techniques. Performance is measured by fault detection time T, which is the time between receiving the fault symptoms and identifying the root faults. The fault diagnostic accuracy depends on two factors: (1) the detection ratio (α), which is the ratio of the number of *true* detected root faults (F_d is the total detected fault set) to the number of *actual* occurred faults F_h, formally $\alpha = \frac{|F_d \cap F_h|}{|F_h|}$; and (2) false positive ratio (β), which is the ratio of the number of *false* reported faults to the total number of detected faults, formally $\beta = \frac{|F_d - F_d \cap F_h|}{|F_d|}$ [1]. Therefore, the goal of any fault management system is to increase α and reduce β in order to achieve high accurate fault reasoning results.

The task of the fault reasoning is to search for root faults in F based on the observed symptoms S_O. Our objective is to improve fault reasoning by minimizing the detection time T and false positive ratio β and maximizing the detection ratio α.

In order to develop this system, we have to address the following three problems:

1. Given the fault-symptom correlation matrix and the set of observed symptoms (S_O), construct a set of the most possible hypotheses, $\Phi = \{h_1, h_2, \ldots, h_p\}, h_i \subseteq F$, that can explain the current observed symptoms.

2. Given a set of possible hypotheses, find the most credible hypothesis h that can give the best explanation for the current observed symptoms.

3. If the selected hypothesis does not satisfy fidelity requirements, then given the unobserved symptoms S_N, select the minimum-cost actions to search for an acceptable hypothesis.

In the following, we will discuss the solution for each problem.

16.2.4   Integrated Fault Intrusion Reasoning

The active integrated fault reasoning (AIR) process (Figure 16.2) includes three functional modules: fault reasoning (FR), fidelity evaluation (FE), and action selection (AS), as mentioned previously. The module takes passively observed symptoms S_O as input and returns a fault hypothesis set Φ as output. The fault/intrusions hypothesis set Φ might include a set of hypotheses ($h_1, h_2, \ldots, h_n$) where each one contains a set of faults or intrusions that explains all observed symptoms so far. Then, Φ is sent to the FE module to check if any hypothesis h_i ($h_i \in \Phi$) is satisfactory. If the most correlated symptoms necessary to explain the fault hypothesis h_i are observed (i.e., high fidelity), then the FR process terminates. Otherwise, a list of unobserved symptoms/alarms S_N that contributes to explain the fault hypothesis h_i of the highest fidelity is sent to the AS module to determine which symptoms have occurred or to distinguish between faults and security breaches. As a result, the fidelity value of hypothesis h_i is adjusted accordingly. The conducted actions return the test result with a set of existing symptoms S_V and nonexisting symptoms S_U. The corresponding fidelity value might be increased or decreased based on the results of the action return. If the newly calculated fidelity is satisfactory, then the reasoning process terminates, otherwise, S_O and S_U are sent as new input to the FR module to create a new hypothesis. This process is repeated until a hypothesis with high fidelity is found.

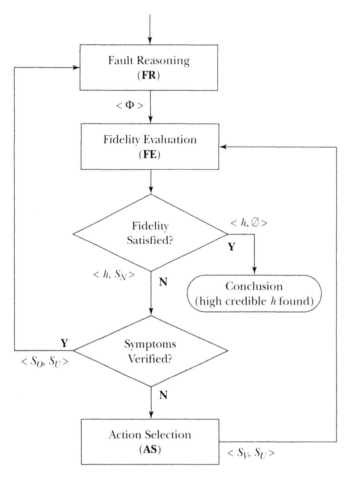

FIGURE

16.2

Active action integrated fault reasoning.

Fidelity calculation is explained later in this section. In the following, we describe the three modules in detail and then we discuss the complete AIR algorithm.

Heuristic Algorithm for Fault Reasoning

In the FR module, we use a *contribution function* $C(f_i)$ as the criteria to find faults or intrusions that have the maximal contribution to the observed symptoms. In the probabilistic model, symptom s_i can be caused by a set of faults $f_i, (f_i \in F_{s_i})$ with different probabilities $p(s_i|f_i) \in (0, 1]$. We assume that the symptom-fault correlation model is sufficient enough to neglect other undocumented faults (i.e., prior fault probability is very low). Thus, we can also assume that symptom s_i will not occur if none of the faults in F_{s_i} has occurred. In other words, if s_i occurred, at least one f_i ($f_i \in F_{s_i}$) must have occurred. However, the conditional probability $p(s_i|f_i)$ itself may not truly reflect the chance of fault f_i's occurrence through observing symptom s_i. For example, in Figure 16.1, by observing s_1, there are three possible scenarios: f_1 happened, f_2 happened, or both happened. Based on the heuristic assumption that the possibility of multiple faults occurring simultaneously is low, one of the faults (f_1 or f_2) should explain the occurrence of s_1. In order to measure the contribution of each fault f_i to the creation of s_i, we normalize the conditional probability $\hat{p}(s_i|f_i)$ to the normalized conditional probability $\hat{p}(s_i|f_i)$ to reflect the relative contribution of each fault f_i to the observation of s_i, where:

$$\hat{p}(s_i|f_i) = \frac{p(s_i|f_i)}{\sum_{f_i \in F_{s_i}} p(s_i|f_i)} \tag{16.1}$$

With $\hat{p}(s_i|f_i)$, we can compute the normalized posterior probability $\hat{p}(f_i|s_i)$ as follows:

$$\hat{p}(f_i|s_i) = \frac{\hat{p}(s_i|f_i)p(f_i)}{\sum_{f_i \in F_{s_i}} \hat{p}(s_i|f_i)p(f_i)} \tag{16.2}$$

where $\hat{p}(f_i|s_i)$ shows the relative probability of f_i happening by observing s_i. For example, in Figure 16.1, assuming all faults have the same prior probability, we have $\hat{p}(f_1|s_1) = 0.9/(0.9 + 0.3) = 0.75$ and $\hat{p}(f_2|s_1) = 0.3/(0.9 + 0.3) = 0.25$. The following contribution function $C(f_i)$ evaluates all contribution factors $\hat{p}(f_i|s_i)$, $s_i \in S_{O_i}$ with the observation S_{O_i}, and decides which f_i is the best candidate with maximum contribution value $C(f_i)$ to the currently not-yet-explained symptoms:

$$C(f_i) = \frac{\sum_{s_i \in S_{O_i}} \hat{p}(f_i|s_i)}{\sum_{s_i \in S_{f_i}} \hat{p}(f_i|s_i)} \tag{16.3}$$

Therefore, fault reasoning becomes a process of searching for the fault or security breach (f_i) with maximum $C(f_i)$. This process continues until all observed symptoms are explained. The contribution function $C(f_i)$ can be used in both deterministic and probabilistic models.

In the deterministic model, the more the number of symptoms observed, the stronger the indication that the corresponding fault has occurred. Meanwhile, we should not ignore the influence of prior fault probability $p(f_i)$, which represents long-term statistical observations. Since $p(s_i|f_j) = 0$ or 1 in the deterministic model, the normalized conditional probability reflects the influence of prior probability of fault f_i. Thus, the same contribution function can seamlessly combine the effect of $p(f_i)$ and the ratio of $\frac{|S_{O_i}|}{|S_{f_i}|}$ together.

The fault reasoning algorithm first finds the fault candidate set F_C, including all faults that can explain at least one symptom s_i $(s_i \in S_O)$. It then calls the function $HU()$ to generate and update the hypothesis set Φ until all observed symptoms S_O can be explained. According to the contribution $C(f_i)$ of each fault f_i $(f_i \in F_C)$, Algorithm 16.1 searches for the best explanation of S_K, which is currently an observed but not-yet-explained symptom by the hypothesis h_i (lines 2–12). Here, $S_K = S_O - \cup_{f_i \in h_i} S_{O_i}$ and initially $S_K = S_O$. If multiple faults have the same contribution, multiple hypotheses will be generated (lines 13–17). The searching process (HU) will recursively run until all observed symptoms are explained (lines 18–24). Notice that only those hypotheses with a minimum number of faults that cover all observed symptoms are included into Φ (lines 23–24).

The fault reasoning algorithm can be applied to both deterministic and probabilistic models with the same contribution function $C(f_i)$ but different conditional probability $p(s_i|f_i)$.

Fidelity Evaluation of Fault Hypotheses

As explained previously, the fault hypotheses created by the fault reasoning algorithm may not accurately determine the root faults because of lost or spurious symptoms. The task of FE is to measure the credibility of the hypothesis created in the reasoning phase given the corresponding observed symptoms. How the reasoning result is objectively evaluated is crucial in fault localization systems.

We use the fidelity function $FD(h)$ to measure the credibility of hypothesis h given the symptom observation S_O. We assume that the occurrence of each fault is independent.

- For the deterministic model:

$$FD(h) = \frac{\sum_{f_i \in h} |S_{O_i}| / |S_{f_i}|}{|h|} \tag{16.4}$$

Algorithm 16.1   Hypothesis Updating Algorithm $HU(h, S_K, F_P)$

Input: hypothesis h, observed but uncovered symptom set S_K, fault candidate set F_P Output: fault hypothesis set Φ

1: $c_{max} = 0$
2: **for all** $f_i \in F_P$ **do**
3:    **if** $C(f_i) > c_{max}$ **then**
4:       $c_{max} \leftarrow C(f_i)$
5:       $F_S \leftarrow \emptyset$
6:       $F_S \leftarrow F_S \cup \{f_i\}$
7:    **else**
8:       **if** $C(f_i) = c_{max}$ **then**
9:          $F_S \leftarrow F_S \cup \{f_i\}$
10:      **end if**
11:    **end if**
12: **end for**
13: **for all** $f_i \in F_S$ **do**
14:    $h_i \leftarrow h \cup \{f_i\}$
15:    $S_{K_i} \leftarrow S_K - S_{O_i}$
16:    $F_{P_i} \leftarrow F_P - \{f_i\}$
17: **end for**
18: **for all** $S_{K_i} = \emptyset$ **do**
19:    **if** $S_{K_i} = \emptyset$ **then**
20:       $\Phi \leftarrow \Phi \cup \{h_i\}$
21:    **end if**
22: **end for**
23: **if** $\Phi \neq \emptyset$ **then**
24:    return $< \Phi >$
25: **else**
26:    /* No h_i can explain all S_O*/
27:    **for all** h_i **do**
28:       $HU(h_i, S_{K_i}, F_{P_i})$
29:    **end for**
30: **end if**

◆ For the probabilistic model:

$$FD(h) = \frac{\prod_{s_i \in \bigcup_{f_i \in h} S_{f_i}} (1 - \prod_{f_i \in h}(1 - p(s_i|f_i)))}{\prod_{s_i \in S_O}(1 - \prod_{f_i \in h}(1 - p(s_i|f_i)))} \tag{16.5}$$

Obviously in the deterministic model, if the hypothesis h is correct, $FD(h)$ must be equal to 1, because the corresponding symptoms can be either observed or verified. In the probabilistic model, if related symptoms are observed or verified, $FD(h)$ of a credible hypothesis can still be less than 1, because some symptoms may not occur even when the hypotheses are correct. In either case, this fidelity algorithm takes into consideration a target fidelity threshold, $FD_{THRESHOLD}$, that the user can configure to accept the hypotheses. System administrators can define the threshold based on long-term observation and previous experience. If the threshold is set too high, even correct hypotheses will be ignored, but if the threshold is too low, then less credible hypotheses might be selected.

The fidelity evaluation function is used to evaluate each hypothesis, and a decision is made if the result is satisfactory by comparing the output to the pre-defined threshold value. If an acceptable hypothesis that matches the fidelity threshold exists, the fault localization process can terminate. Otherwise, the best available hypothesis and a nonempty set of symptoms (S_N) would be verified in order to reach a satisfactory hypothesis in the next iteration.

Action Selection Heuristic Algorithm

The main purpose of this component is to verify or investigate the existence of symptoms/alarms that have the most contribution to identify faults or intrusions. We verify symptoms rather than faults because they are the manifestation of faults in the network and easily trackable. The AS also performs actions to identify if the problem is fault related or security intrusion related. The AS finds the least-cost actions to verify S_N (unobserved symptoms) of the hypothesis that has the highest fidelity. As the size of S_N grows very large, the process of selecting the minimal-cost action that verifies S_N becomes nontrivial. The action-symptoms correlation graph can be represented as a three-tuple (A, S, E) graph, such that A and S are two independent vertex sets representing actions and symptoms, respectively, and every edge e in E connects a vertex $a_j \in A$ with a vertex $s_i \in S$ with a corresponding weight (w_{ij}) to denote that a_j can verify s_i with cost $w_{ij} = w(s_i, a_j) > 0$. If there is no association between s_i and a_j, then $w_{ij} = 0$. Because a set of actions might be required to verify one symptom, we use a virtual action vertex v_j to represent this case. The virtual action vertex v_j is used to associate a set of conjunctive actions to the corresponding symptom(s). However, if multiple actions are directly connected to a symptom, then this means any of these actions can be used disjunctively to verify this symptom (Figure 16.3). To convert this to a bipartite graph, (1) we set the weight of v_j, $w(s_i, v_j)$ to the total cost of the conjunctive action set, (2) we then eliminate the associated conjunctive set to the v_j, and (3) we associate v_j with all symptoms that can be verified by any action in the conjunctive action set.

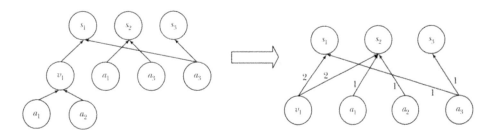

FIGURE   Symptom-action bipartite graph.

16.3

The symptom-action graph in Figure 16.3 presents the verification relationship between symptoms $\{s_1, s_2, s_3\}$ and actions $\{a_1, a_2, a_3\}$. Symptom s_1 can be verified by taking a combination of action a_1 and a_2, which causes a new virtual action vertex v_1 to be created with weight 2. Action v_1 can verify all symptoms (s_1, s_2) that are verifiable by either a_1 or a_2. After converting action combinations into a virtual action, the symptom-action correlation can be represented as a bipartite graph.

The goal of the AS algorithm is to select the actions that cover all symptoms S_N with a minimal-cost action. With the representation of the symptom-action bipartite graph, we can model this problem as a weighted set-covering problem. Thus, the AS algorithm searches for A_i, such that A_i includes the set of actions that cover all the symptoms in the symptoms-action correlation graph with total minimum cost. We can formally define A_i as the covering set that satisfies the following conditions: (1) $\forall s_i \in S, \exists a_j \in A_i$ such that $w_{ij} > 0$, and (2) $\sum_{a_i \in A_i, s_j \in S_N} w_{ij}$ is the *minimum*.

The weighted set covering is an NP-complete problem. Thus, we developed a heuristic greedy set-covering approximation algorithm to solve this problem. The main idea of the algorithm is as follows. First, it simply selects the action $(a_i$ or $v_i)$ that has the maximum *relative covering ratio*, $R_i = \frac{|S_{a_i}|}{\sum_{s_j \in S_{a_i}} w_{ij}}$, where this action is added to the final set A_f and removed from the candidate set A_c that includes all actions. Here, S_{a_i} is the set of symptoms that action a_i can verify, $S_{a_i} \subseteq S_N$. Then, we remove all symptoms that are covered by this selected action from the unobserved symptom set S_N. This search continues to find the next action a_i $(a_i \in A_c)$ that has the maximum ratio R_i until all symptoms are covered (i.e., S_N is empty). Thus, intuitively, this algorithm appreciates actions that have more symptom correlation or aggregation. If multiple actions have the same relative covering weight, the action with more covered symptoms (i.e., larger $|S_{a_i}|$ size) will be selected. If multiple actions have the same ratio R_i and same $|S_{a_i}|$, then each action is considered independently to compute the final selected sets for each action, and the set that has the minimum cost is selected. Finally, it is important to note that each single action in the A_f set is necessary for the fault determination process, because each one covers unique symptoms.

Algorithm for Active Integrated Fault Reasoning

Here, we incorporate active actions into fault reasoning. Passive fault reasoning could work well if enough symptoms can be observed correctly. However, in most cases, we need to deal with interference from symptom loss and spurious symptoms, which could mislead fault localization analysis. As a result of fault reasoning, the generated hypothesis suggests a set of selected symptoms S_N that are unobserved but expected to occur based on the highest fidelity hypothesis. If the result of fidelity evaluation of such hypothesis is not acceptable, optimal actions are selected to verify S_N. Action results will either increase fidelity evaluation results of the previous hypothesis or bring new evidence to generate a new hypothesis. By taking actions selectively, the system can evaluate fault hypotheses progressively and reach root faults.

Algorithm 16.2 illustrates the complete process of the AIR technique. Initially, the system takes an observed symptom S_O as input. Fault reasoning is used to search the best hypothesis ϕ (line 3). Fidelity is the key to associate passive reasoning to active probing. Fidelity evaluation is used to measure the correctness of the corresponding hypothesis h ($h \in \phi$) and produce expected missing symptoms S_N (line 3). If the result with h is satisfied, the process terminates with current hypothesis as output (lines 5–6). Otherwise, the AIR algorithm waits until an *initial passive period* (IPP) expires (line 8) to initiate actions to collect more evidence of verified symptoms S_V and symptoms S_U that have not occurred (line 10). New evidence will be added to reevaluate the previous hypothesis (line 13). If fidelity evaluation is still not satisfactory, the new evidence with previous observation is used to search another hypothesis (line 3) until the fidelity evaluation is satisfactory. At any point, the program terminates and returns the current selected hypothesis, if either the fidelity evaluation does not find symptoms to verify (S_N is ϕ), or none of the verified symptoms had occurred (S_V is ϕ).

16.2.5   Simulation Study

In this section, we describe our simulation study to evaluate the AIR technique. We conducted a series of experiments to measure how AIR improves the performance and accuracy of the fault localization compared with *passive fault reasoning* (PFR). The evaluation study considers fault detection time T as a performance parameter, and the detection rate α and false positive rate β as accuracy parameters.

Algorithm 16.2   Active Integrated Fault Reasoning S_O

Input: S_O
Output: fault hypothesis h

1: $S_N \leftarrow S_O$
2: **while** $S_N \neq \emptyset$ **do**
3:     $\Phi = FR(S_O)$
4:     $< h, S_N >= FE(\Phi)$
5:     **if** $S_N = \emptyset$ **then**
6:         return $< h >$
7:     **else**
8:         **if** IPP experied **then**
9:             /*used to schedule active fault localization periodically*/
10:             $< S_V, S_U >= AS(S_N)$
11:         **end if**
12:     **end if**
13:     $S_O \leftarrow S_O \cup S_V$
14:     $< h, S_N >= FE(\{h\})$
15:     **if** $S_N = \emptyset \parallel S_V = \emptyset$ **then**
16:         return $< h >$
17:     **end if**
18: **end while**

In our simulation study, the number of monitored network objects D ranged from 60–600. We assume every network object can generate different faults and each fault could be associated with 2–5 symptoms uniformly distributed. The number of simulated symptoms vary from 120–3,000 uniformly distributed. We use *fault cardinality* (FC), *symptom cardinality* (SC), and *action cardinality* (AC) to describe the symptom-fault-action matrix such that FC defines the maximal number of symptoms that can be associated with one specific fault, SC defines the maximal number of faults one symptom might correlate to, and AC defines the maximal number of symptoms that one action can verify. The independent prior fault probabilities $p(f_i)$ and conditional probabilities $p(s_i|f_j)$ are uniformly distributed in ranges [0.001, 0.01] and (0, 1], respectively. Our simulation model also considers the following parameters: initial passive period (IPP), symptom active collecting rate (SACR), symptom passive collecting rate (SPCR), symptom loss ratio (SLR), spurious symptom ratio (SSR), and fidelity threshold ($FD_{THRESHOLD}$).

The major contribution of this work is to offer an efficient fault reasoning technique that provides accurate results even in worst cases like when SPCR is low,

and/or SLR and SSR are high. We show how these factors affect the performance
(T) and accuracy (α and β) of our approach and passive fault reasoning approach.

The Impact of Symptom Loss Ratio

Symptom loss hides fault indications, which negatively affect both accuracy and
performance of the fault localization process. In order to study the improvement
in both the performance and the accuracy of the AIR approach, we fix the value
of the spurious symptom ratio (SSR = 0), initial passive period (IPP = 10 sec),
symptom active collecting rate (SACR = 100 symptoms/sec), and symptom passive collecting rate (SPCR = 20 symptoms/sec). In this simulation, we use SLR
values that vary from 10–30%. With the increase of symptom loss ratio, the passive
fault reasoning system becomes infeasible. Therefore, in this experiment, we had
to reduce the fidelity threshold to a relatively lower value based on the symptom
loss ratio so the passive reasoning process can converge in reasonable time. From
Figure 16.4(a), in contrast to the passive approach, the AIR system can always
reach a relatively high fidelity threshold with average performance improvement of 20–40%. Hence, when SLR increases, the advantage of active fault
reasoning in the performance aspect is more evident. In addition to performance improvement, the AIR approach shows high accuracy. With the same
settings, Figure 16.4(b, c) show that the active approach gains 20–50% improvement in the detection rate and 20–60% improvement in the false detection rate, even with much different fidelity criteria over the passive reasoning
approach.

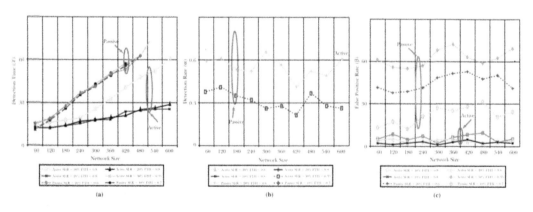

FIGURE   The impact of symptom loss ratio: (a) detection time T, (b) detection rate α, and
                (c) false positive rate β.

16.4

The Impact of Network Size

In this section, we examine the scalability of AIR when the network size and number of symptoms significantly increase. To show this, we measure AIR detection time under different scenarios: (1) without symptom loss and spurious symptom (Figure 16.5a), (2) with symptom loss only (Figure 16.5b), and (3) with spurious symptoms only (Figure 16.5c). In all three cases, when the network size increases 10 times (from 100% to 1,000%), the detection time has slowly increased by 1.7 times (170%), 3.7 times (370%), and 5.8 times (580%) in Figures 16.5(a, b, and c), respectively. This shows that even in the worst-case scenario (Figure 16.5c), the growth in network size causes a slow linear increases in AIR performance.

The Impact of Symptom Loss on AIR Intrusiveness

AIR intrusiveness is measured by the number of total actions performed to localize faults. As shown in Section 16.2.4, the intrusiveness of AIR was algorithmically minimized by (1) considering the fault hypothesis of high credibility and (2) selecting the minimum-cost actions based on the greedy algorithm described in the section on the heuristic algorithm. We also conducted experiments to assess the intrusiveness (i.e., action cost) when the loss ratio increases. Loss ratio and network size are the most significant factors that might affect the intrusiveness of AIR. Figure 16.6 shows that, with different scale of network sizes and prior fault probability as high as 10%, the number of actions required for fault localization slowly increases linearly (from 1–22) even when the loss ratio significantly increases (from 2–35%). For example, in a large-scale network of size 600 objects and a fault rate of 60 faults per iteration, the number of actions performed did not exceed 0.37 actions/fault ratio.

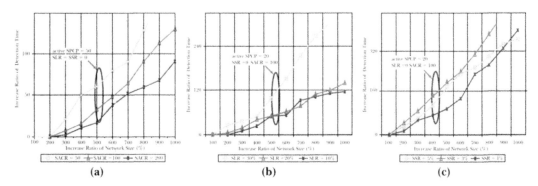

FIGURE

16.5

The impact of network size: (a) without symptom loss and spurious symptoms, (b) with symptom loss, and (c) with spurious symptoms.

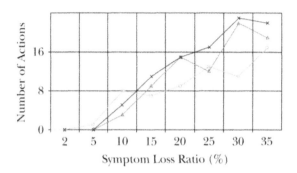

FIGURE   Intrusiveness evaluation.

16.6

In addition, AIR was deliberately designed to give the user the control to adjust the intrusiveness of active probing via configuring the following fault reasoning parameters: fidelity threshold, IPP, and action coverage.

16.3   FAULT AND SECURITY MANAGEMENT ON HIGH-SPEED NETWORKS

16.3.1   Background

In this section, we discuss network-level faults (i.e., anomalies) and intrusion detection, particularly for high-speed networks. It is very important to have integrated fault and intrusion detection because many network faults are often misidentified as intrusions. Such false alerts often make network administrators turn off the IDS systems. Thus, it is of crucial importance to rapidly and accurately identify both faults and intrusions for network-based IDS systems. With the rapid growth of network bandwidth and fast emergence of new attacks/viruses/worms, existing network IDSs are insufficient due to the lack of the following features.

First, separating anomalies from intrusions for false-positive reduction. To detect unknown attacks and polymorphic worms, statistics-based intrusion detection has been widely adopted instead of signature-based intrusion detection. However, many network element faults (e.g., router misconfigurations and polluted DNS entries) can lead to traffic anomalies that may be detected as attacks.

Second, scalability to high-speed networks. Today's fast propagating viruses/worms (e.g., SQL Slammer worm) can infect most vulnerable machines within ten minutes [12]. Thus, it is crucial to identify such outbreaks in their early phases, which is achievable only in high-speed routers. However, existing schemes are not scalable to the link speeds and number of flows for high-speed networks.

In general, it is difficult for software-based data recording approaches in IDSs to keep up with the link speed in a high-speed router. Thus, the data recording of high-speed IDSs has to be hardware implementable, and it is strongly desirable to achieve the following three capabilities:

1. Small memory usage.

2. Sparse memory accesses per packet [13].

3. Scalability to large key sizes.

Third, attack resiliency. To bypass an IDS, attackers can execute DoS attacks, or fool the IDS to raise many false positives to conceal the real attack. Thus, the attack resiliency of an IDS is very important. However, existing IDSs often keep per-flow states for detection, which is vulnerable.

Fourth, attack root cause analysis for mitigation. Accurate attack mitigation requires IDSs to pinpoint the attack type and flows. This advocates detecting intrusions at the *flow level* instead of the overall traffic level. Furthermore, we want to differentiate different types of attacks to choose different mitigation schemes accordingly.

Fifth, aggregated detection over multiple vantage points. Most existing network IDSs assume detection to be on a single router or gateway. However, as multihoming, load balancing–based routing, and policy routing become prevalent, even for a connection between a certain source and destination, the packets may traverse different paths [14]. Thus, observation from a single vantage point is often incomplete and affects detection accuracy. Meanwhile, it is very hard to copy all traffic from one router to other routers/IDSs due to the huge data volume.

To meet the above requirements, we propose a new paradigm called DoS resilient High-speed Flow-level INtrusion Detection (HiFIND), leveraging recent work on data streaming computation and, in particular, sketches [15]. Sketches are a kind of compact data streaming data structure that record traffic for given keys and are capable of reporting heavy traffic keys. Essentially, we want to detect as many attacks as possible. As the first step toward this ambitious goal, we aim to detect various port scans (which covers most large-scale worm propagation) and TCP SYN flooding.

While each of these attacks seems relatively easy to be detected, it is indeed very hard to detect a mixture of attacks online at the flow level. To the best of our knowledge, HiFIND is the *first* DoS resilient high-speed flow-level IDS for port scans and TCP SYN flooding for high-speed networks.

To this end, we leverage and improve sketches to record flow-level traffic as the basis for statistical intrusion detection. First proposed in Schweller et al. [15, 16], sketches have not been applied to building IDSs for the following challenges:

+ Sketches can only record certain aggregated metrics for some given keys. Since it is not feasible to try all possible combinations of the metrics, what would be the minimal set of metrics for monitoring?

+ Existing sketches are all one dimensional. However, various forms of attacks are often hard to identify with such single-dimensional information.

In this section, we address these two challenges and build the HiFIND prototype system to meet the aforementioned five requirements. We make the following contributions:

+ We analyze the attributes in TCP/IP headers and select an optimal small set of metrics for flow-level sketch-based traffic monitoring and intrusion detection. Based on that, we build the HiFIND online high-speed flow-level IDS prototype that is DoS resilient.

+ To analyze the attack root cause for mitigation, we design efficient two-dimensional (2D) sketches to distinguish different types of attacks.

+ We aggregate the compact sketches from multiple vantage points (e.g., routers) to detect intrusion in the face of asymmetric routing and multipath routing caused by per-packet load balancing of routers.

+ For false-positive reduction, we propose several heuristics to separate SYN floodings from network/server congestions and misconfigurations.

As shown in Figure 16.7, HiFIND detection systems can be implemented as black boxes attached to high-speed routers (edge or backbone routers) of ISPs without affecting the normal operation of the routers.

For evaluation, we tested the router traffic traces collected at Northwestern University (NU) and Lawrence Berkeley National Labs (LBL). We validated TCP SYN flooding and detected port scans and found the HiFIND system is highly accurate. The 2D sketches successfully separate the SYN flooding from port scans and the heuristics effectively reduce false positives related to SYN flooding. Our approach is also very fast in terms of data recording and detection.

16.3.2   Related Work

Intrusion Detection Systems

While some vendors claim to have multigigabit statistical IDSs [17], these claims usually refer to *average* traffic conditions and use packet sampling [18]. Recent

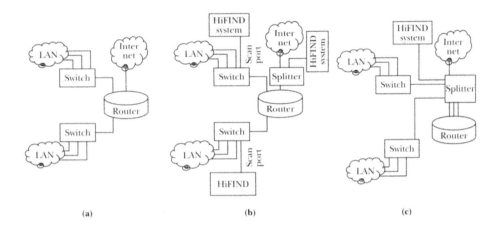

FIGURE

16.7

Attaching the HiFIND systems to high-speed routers: (a) original configuration, (b) distributed configuration for which each port is monitored separately, and (c) aggregate configuration for which a splitter is used to aggregate the traffic from all the ports.

work has proposed detecting large-scale attacks, like DoS attacks, port scans, and so on, based on the statistical traffic patterns. They can roughly be classified into two categories: detecting based on the overall traffic [19, 20] and flow-level detection [21].

With the first approach, even when we can detect the attack, we still do not have any flow or port knowledge for mitigation. Moreover, attacks can be easily buried in the background network traffic. Thus, such detection schemes tend to be inaccurate; for example, Change-Point Monitoring (CPM) [20] will detect port scans as SYN floodings as verified in Section 16.3.4. For the second approach, such schemes usually need to maintain a per-flow table (e.g., a per-source IP table for Threshold Random Walk (TRW) [21]) for detection, which is not scalable and thus provides a vulnerability to DoS attacks with randomly spoofed IP addresses, especially on high-speed networks. TRW was recently improved by limiting its memory consumption with approximate caches (TRW-AC) [22]. However, spoofed DoS attacks will still cause collisions in TRW-AC, and leave the real port scans undetected. As Weaver et al. [22] mentioned, when the connection cache size of 1 million entries reaches about 20% full, each new scan attempt has a 20% chance of not being recorded because it aliases with an already-established connection. Actually, during spoofed DoS attacks, such collisions can become even worse.

The existing schemes can detect specific types of attacks, but will perform poorly when facing a mixture of attacks as in the real world. People may attempt

Approaches	Spoofed DoS	Nonspoofed DoS	HScan	VScan
HiFIND	Yes	Yes	Yes	Yes
TRW(AC)	No	No	Yes	(Yes)
CPM	Yes, but with high FP with port scans		No	No
Backscatter	Yes	No	No	No
Superspreader	No	No	Yes	No

TABLE   Functionality comparison.

16.2

to combine TRW-AC and CPM to detect both scans and SYN flooding attacks. However, each of these two approaches can work properly only when the other one works well.

Table 16.2 shows the high-level functionality comparison of our approach to the other methods. Backscatter detects the spoofed SYN flooding attacks by testing the uniform distribution of destination Internet Providers (IPs) to which the same source (potential victim) sends SYN/ACK [19]. We use this for validating the SYN flooding detected by HiFIND. Venkataraman et al. [23] propose efficient algorithms to detect superspreaders, sources that connect to a large number of distinct destinations. But they may have high false positives with P2P traffic where a single host may connect to many peers for download. Partial Completion Filters (PCF) was recently proposed for scalable network detection [24]. They do not differentiate among various attacks.

Sketches for Network Monitoring

There is a significant amount of prior work on efficient and online heavy-hitter detection [13, 25]. However, these approaches are limited in their applicability to online intrusion detection in that (1) they lack the ability to differentiate different types of attacks, (2) they cannot work with time series analysis-based detection algorithms, and (3) they cannot be applied to asymmetric routing environments.

To this end, we designed the original k-ary sketchs [26], and further enhanced them to be reversible sketches [15, 16], which allow us to have separate stages for update, combine, and inference, so that we can easily solve the problems mentioned before. In Table 16.3, we summarize the functions supported by sketches.

Functions	Descriptions	k-ary Sketch	Reversible Sketch
UPDATE(S, y, v)	Update the corresponding values of the given key into the sketch in the monitoring module	√	√
v = ESTIMATE (S, y)	Reconstruct the signal series for statistical detection for a given key in the anomaly detection module	√	√
S = COMBINE $(c_1, S_1,..., c_k, S_k)$	Compute the linear combination of multiple sketches $S = \sum_{k=1}^{l} c_k \times S_k$ (c_i is coefficient) to aggregate signals in the anomaly detection module	√	√
Y = INFERENCE (S, t)	Return the keys whose values are larger than the threshold in the anomaly detection module		√

TABLE 16.3   Function of sketches (S–sketch, v–value, y–key, Y–set of keys, t–threshold).

16.3.3   Architecture of the HiFIND System

System Architecture

Figure 16.8 shows the architecture of the HiFIND system. First, we record the network traffic with sketches in each router. Based on linearity of the sketches, we summarize the sketches over multiple routers into an aggregate sketch and apply time series analysis methods for aggregate sketches to obtain the forecast sketches for change detection. The forecast time series analysis method (e.g., EWMA, or exponentially weighted moving average) can help remove noise. By subtracting the forecast sketch from the current one, we obtain the forecast error sketches. Intuitively, a large forecast error implies there is an anomaly, thus, the forecast

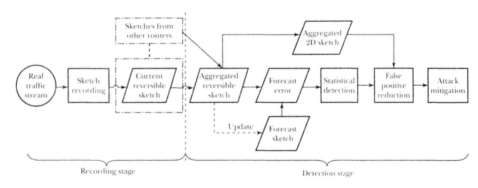

FIGURE 16.8   HiFIND system architecture.

error is the key metric for detection in our system. Moreover, we aggregate the 2D sketches in the same way and adopt them to further distinguish different types of attacks. We also apply other false-positive reduction techniques as discussed later. Finally, we use the key characteristics of the culprit flows revealed by the reversible sketches to mitigate the attacks. Note that the streaming data recording process needs to be done continuously in real time, while the detection process can be run in the background executing only once every interval (e.g., every second or minute) with more memory (DRAM).

To deal with asymmetric routing (Figure 16.9), for most existing IDS systems, all the packet traces or all connection states have to be transported from one router to the other. Obviously' this is very expensive. Moreover, if the link is congested when an attack happens, transmission of these data can be very slow. Furthermore, some routers may use per-packet load balancing so that packets of the same flow may traverse different paths.

In contrast, for HiFIND, we summarize the traffic information with compact sketches at each edge router, and deliver them quickly to some central site. Then, with the linearity of the sketches, we can aggregate them and the resulting sketch has all the information as if all the traffic went through the same router.

Threat Model

Ultimately, we want to detect as many different types of attacks as possible. As a first step, we focus on detecting the two most popular intrusions: TCP SYN flooding (DoS) attack and port Scans/worm propagation, which include *horizontal scan*

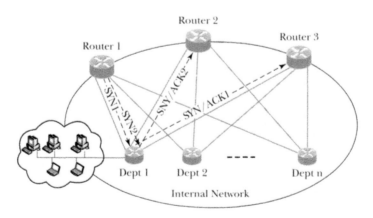

FIGURE

16.9

Sample network topology with asymmetric routing and multipath routing.

(Hscan), *vertical scan* (Vscan), and *block scan* [27]. It is also crucial to distinguish them because network administrators need to apply different mitigation schemes for different attacks.

Sketch-Based Detection Algorithm

We denote the key of a sketch as K, the feature value recorded as V, and the reversible sketch as RS(K,V). We also denote the number of SYN packets as #SYN, and the number of SYN/ACK packets as #SYN/ACK.

Here, we only consider the attacks in TCP protocol, that is, the TCP SYN flooding attacks and TCP port scans. Normally, attackers can choose source ports arbitrarily, so Sport is not a good metric for attack detection. For the other three fields, we can consider all the possible combinations of them, but the key (SIP, DIP, Dport) can only help detect nonspoofed SYN flooding, so we do not use it in the detection process. Table 16.4 shows the other combinations and their uniqueness. Here, we define the *uniqueness* of a key as the capability of differentiating among different types of attacks. For example, the count of unsuccessful connections aggregated by {SIP} can be used to detect nonspoofed SYN flooding attacks (we count it as 0.5), horizontal scans, and vertical scans, so its value of uniqueness is 2.5. The best key would ideally correspond to only one type of attack. Normally a key can be related to several types of attacks, so we need to use more than one dimension to differentiate these attacks as shown in Li and Chen [28]. In this section, we use the tree combinations of two fields as keys for the reversible sketches. Our detection has the following three steps.

Step 1. We use RS({DIP, Dport}, #SYN-#SYN/ACK) to detect SYN flooding attacks, because it usually targets a certain service as characterized by the Dport on a small set of machine(s). The value of #SYN-#SYN/ACK means that for each

Keys	SYN Flooding	Hscan	Vscan	Uniqueness
{SIP,Dport}	Nonspoofed	Yes	No	1.5
{DIP,Dport}	Yes	No	No	1
{SIP,DIP}	Nonspoofed	No	yes	1.5
{SIP}	Nonspoofed	Yes	Yes	2.5
{DIP}	Yes	No	Yes	2
{Dport}	Yes	Yes	No	2

TABLE 16.4   The uniqueness of different types of keys.

incoming SYN packet, we will update the sketch by incrementing one, while for each outgoing SYN/ACK packet, the sketch will be updated by decrementing one. In fact, similar structures can be applied to detect any partial completion attacks [24]. The reversible sketch can further provide the victim IP and port number for mitigation as in the threat model just described. We denote this set of DIPs as *FLOODING_DIP_SET*.

Step 2. We use RS({SIP, DIP}, #SYN-#SYN/ACK) to detect any intruder trying to attack a particular IP address. The detected attacks can be nonspoofed SYN flooding attacks or vertical scans. For each {SIP, DIP} entry, if DIP ∈ *FLOODING_DIP_SET*, we put the SIP into the *FLOODING_SIP_SET* for the next step; otherwise, the {SIP, DIP} is the attacker's IP and victim IP of a vertical scan.

Step 3. We use RS({SIP, Dport}, #SYN-#SYN/ACK) to detect any source IP which causes a large number of uncompleted connections to a particular destination port. For each {SIP, Dport} entry, if SIP ∈ *FLOODING_SIP_SET*, it is a nonspoofed SYN flooding, otherwise, it is a horizontal scan.

Here, we apply the EWMA algorithm as the forecast models to do change detection. If we denote $M_0(t)$ as the current #SYN-#SYN/ACK at the time interval t, and $M_f(t)$ as the forecasted #SYN-#SYN/ACK at the time interval t, we have:

$$\mathbf{M}_f(t) = \begin{cases} \alpha\mathbf{M}_0(t-1) + (1-\alpha)\mathbf{M}_f(t-1) & t > 2 \\ \mathbf{M}_0(1) & t = 2 \end{cases} \tag{16.6}$$

The difference between the forecasted value and the actual value, $\mathbf{e}_t = \mathbf{M}_0(t) - \mathbf{M}_f(t)$, is then used for detection.

Separating Faults/Anomalies from SYN Flooding

There can be a number of factors other than SYN flooding that may cause a particular destination IP and port with a large number of unacknowledged SYNs. For instance, flash crowds, network/server congestions/failures, and even polluted or outdated DNS entries may cause a large number of SYNs without SYN/ACK at the edge routers. These may cause high false positives in our detection scheme. For the flash crowds, it is difficult, if not impossible, to differentiate them from the SYN flooding attacks without payload information as discussed in Jung et al. [21]. Thus, we aim at reducing the false positives caused by the other two behaviors listed above.

First, we add filters to reduce false positives caused by bursty network/server congestions/failures based on the ratio of #SYN comparing with #SYN/ACK and the fact that attacks may last some time. Second, we add filters to reduce the false positives caused by misconfigurations or related problems based on the fact that DoS attacks attack some active IP addresses and services.

16.3.4   Evaluation

Evaluation Methodology

In this section, we evaluate HiFIND with two data sets. One is the router traffic traces collected at LBL, which consists of about 900 M netflow records. The other is the traffic traces of NU, which has several class B networks, edge routers. The router exports netflow data continuously, which is recorded with sketches of HiFIND on the fly. The one-day experiment in May 2005 consisted of 239 M netflow records, which comes to 1.8 T total traffic.

Unless denoted otherwise, the default time interval for constructing the time series is one minute. The data recording part of the HiFIND system consists of (1) three reversible sketches (RSs), one for {SIP, Dport}, one for {DIP, Dport}, and the other for {SIP, DIP}; (2) one original sketch (OS) for {DIP, Dport}; and (3) two 2D sketches for {SIP, Dport} × {DIP} and {SIP, DIP} × {Dport}. For all the RS and 2D sketches, we update #SYN - #SYN/ACK as the value, and only for the OS, we use #SYN as the value.

The following parameters are chosen based on systematic study as in Schweller et al. [15] and Krishnamurthy et al. [26]. We adopt six stages for each RS and OS and five stages for each 2D sketch in our system. We use 2^{12} buckets for each stage in 48-bit RS, 2^{16} buckets for each stage in the 64-bit RS, and 2^{14} buckets for all their verification sketches. 2^{14} buckets are applied for each stage in OS. We also use $2^{12} \times 64$ buckets for each stage of the 2D sketches. Therefore, the total memory is 13.2 MB.

Both NU and LBL have a large amount of traffic, so we set the detection threshold to be one unresponded SYN packet per second.

Accuracy of Sketches in Recording Traffic for Detection

Table 16.5 shows the three phases of our detection results. We first detect attacks using reversible sketches with algorithms described previously. The results are shown as "raw results" (phase 1) in Table 16.5. Two-dimensional sketches reduce the false positives for port scans introduced by SYN flooding attacks (phase 2

Traces	Attack Type	Phase 1: Raw Results	FP Reduction	
			Phase 2: Port Scan	Phase 3: Flooding
	SYN flooding	157	157	32
NU	Hscan	988	936	936
	Vscan	73	19	19
	SYN flooding	35	35	0
LBL	Hscan	736	699	699
	Vscan	40	1	1

TABLE   Detection results under three phases

16.5

of Table 16.5). The heuristics previously discussed reduce false positives of SYN flooding attacks (phase 3).

To evaluate the errors introduced by sketches, we compare the results obtained from the same detection algorithm but with two different types of traffic recording: sketches and accurate flow table to hold per-flow information (we call it the nonsketch method). We find that we detect exactly the same attacks for the two configurations with very different amounts of memory (see memory consumption discussion later. There is no false positive in our results. This shows sketches are highly accurate in recording the traffic for detection.

Comparison of HiFIND and Other Existing Network IDSs

Detection over a single router.   We compare the HiFIND with other state-of-the-art work as introduced in Section 16.3.2: The TRW [21] for port scan detection and the CPM [20] for SYN flooding detection.

For TRW experiments, we choose similar parameters as those in Jung et al. [21]. We apply the TRW on both data sets with the same threshold. Repeated alerts are removed from the results of both methods. Table 16.6 shows the comparison results of our methods with TRW for Hscan detection. We observe that the scans detected by these two methods have very good overlap, except for a few special

Data	TRW	HiFIND	Overlap Number
NU	497	512	488
LBL	695	699	692

TABLE   Horizontal scans detection comparison of HiFIND and TRW aggregated by source IP.

16.6

cases. There are a small number of Hscans detected by HiFIND but not TRW, because some attacks have both successful and unsuccessful connection attempts, but TRW cannot detect those suspicious ones in this category. There are also a very small number of Hscans detected by TRW but not HiFIND because they are the combination of multiple small scans, which are too stealthy to be captured by our threshold. It is our future work to further investigate this.

Next, we compare our method with CPM for SYN flooding attack detection. The results are shown in Table 16.7. In the LBL traces, there is no SYN flooding, but a very large number of scans. CPM cannot differentiate them. On the other hand, CPM and HiFIND have very similar results for the NU data because most time intervals contain SYN flooding. Meanwhile, there is a small number of intervals in which SYN flooding is buried in the rest of the normal traffic, so CPM cannot detect them.

Aggregated detection over multiple routers. In this section, we consider the network topology of Figure 16.9 and evaluate the performance of HiFIND and TRW under such scenarios. To simulate asymmetric routing and multipath routing caused by per-packet load balancing on routers, we split the packet level trace from an NU edge router into three routers randomly, for both inbound and outbound packets. For each packet, we randomly select an edge router to deliver (i.e., for any single connection) the incoming SYN packet and the outgoing SYN/ACK packet, which have two-thirds probability to go through different routers.

For HiFIND, we obtain the same results as those when the traffic goes through the same router. In comparison, we apply TRW to the data on each router for detection and then sum up the result. We found their approach had high false positives or negatives in this case.

Validation of Successfully Detected Intrusions

In this section, we manually examine a certain number of attacks for validation.

SYN flooding. We validate our SYN flooding detection results with backscatter [19]. Among the 32 SYN floodings detected, there are 21 matched with

Data	CPM	HiFIND	Overlap Number
NU	1,422	1,427	1,422
LBL	1,426	0	0

TABLE
16.7

TCP SYN flooding detection comparison of HiFIND and CPM.

Anonymized SIP	Dport	#DIP	Cause
204.10.110.38	1,433	56,275	SQLSnake scan
109.132.101.199	22	45,014	Scan SSH
95.30.62.202	3,306	25,964	MySQL Bot scans
162.39.147.51	6,101	24,741	Unknown scan
15.192.50.153	4,899	23,687	Rahack worm

TABLE   Five major senarios of the top five Hscans in NU experiment.

16.8

Anonymized SIP	Dport	#DIP	Cause
98.198.251.168	135	64	Nachi or MSBlast worm
3.66.52.227	445	64	Sasser and Korgo worm
2.0.28.90	139	64	NetBIOS scan
98.198.0.101	135	64	Nachi or MSBlast worm
165.5.42.10	5,554	62	Sasser worm

TABLE   Five major scenarios of the bottom ten Hscans in NU experiment.

16.9

backscatter results. For the other 11 attacks, three are due to threshold boundary effect.

Horizontal scans.   We manually validate horizontal scans, in particular, the top five and bottom five attacks in terms of their change difference. Due to limited space, Table 16.8 shows the top five Hscans and Table 16.9 shows the bottom five Hscans from the NU experiment. Detailed evaluation can be found in our technical report [29].

Vertical scans.   We also manually validate vertical scans. In the LBL trace, we found one vertical scan. It scanned some well-known service ports, such as HTTPS(81) and HTTP-Proxy(8000,8001,8081). In the NU experiment, we found in total 19 vertical scans. We manually checked all of them and found the vertical scans are mostly interested in the well-known service ports and Trojan/Backdoor ports.

Evaluation Results for Online Performance Constraints

Small memory consumption.   In our experiments, we only use a total memory of 13.2 MB for traffic recording. Note that such settings work well for a large range of link speeds.

Methods	2.5 Gbps		10 Gbps	
	1 min	5 min	1 min	5 min
HiFIND w/ sketch	13.2M		13.2M	
HiFIND w/ complete info	10.3G	51.6G	41.25G	206G
TRW	5.63G	28G	22.5G	112.5G

TABLE   Memory comparison (bytes).

16.10

On the other hand, if hash tables are used to record every flow, much larger memory is required, as shown in Table 16.10. We consider the worst-case traffic of all 40-byte packet streams with 100% utilization of the link capacity. There is a spoofed SYN flooding attack with a different source IP for each packet. For the method without sketch, it needs at least three hash tables corresponding to the three reversible sketches in our detection methods.

Small memory access per packet.   There are 15 memory accesses per packet for 48-bit reversible sketches and 16 per packet for 64-bit reversible sketches [21]. For each 2D sketch, we only need 5 memory accesses per packet, one for each 2D hash matrix. Thus, when recording these sketches in parallel or in pipeline, the HiFIND system has a very small number of memory accesses per packet and is capable of online monitoring.

High-speed traffic monitoring.   In the HiFIND system, the speed of 2D sketches is much faster than that of the reversible sketches. Thus, the speed is dominated by the latter. With our prototype single FPGA board implementation, we are able to sustain 16.2 Gbps throughput for recording all 40-byte packet streams (the worst case) with a reversible sketch.

We can also use multiprocessors to simultaneously record multiple sketches in software. We record 239 M items with one reversible sketch in 20.6 seconds (i.e., 11 M insertions/sec). For the worst-case scenario with all 40-byte packets, this translates to around 3.7 Gbps. These results are obtained from code that is not fully optimized and from a machine that is not dedicated to this process.

For the on-site NU experiments, the HiFIND system used 0.34 seconds on average to perform detection for each one-minute interval, and the standard deviation is 0.64 seconds. The maximum detection time (for which the interval contains the largest number of attacks) is 12.91 seconds, which is still far less than one minute. In order to show the scalability of HiFIND, we do some further stress experiments. We compress the NU data by the factor of 60 and detect the top 100 anomalies in each interval. The HiFIND system used 35.61 seconds on average in detection for each interval. The maximum detection time is 46.90 seconds.

16.4   CONCLUSION

Analyzing fault and security alarms is very crucial for identifying and localizing network problems such as failure or intrusions. In this chapter, we show how to integrate fault and security management to relieve the heavy burden of manual diagnostics by system administrators and improve the accuracy of fault and intrusion identification. In the first section, a novel technique called *active integrated fault reasoning*, or AIR, is presented. This technique is the first to seamlessly integrate passive and active fault reasoning in order to reduce fault detection times as well as improve the accuracy of fault diagnosis. AIR can be similarly used to correlate security alarms and identify potential intrusions or attacks. In case of incomplete symptoms to identify the root cause, AIR initiates an optimal active probing to investigate and identify the problem with reasonable certainly. The AIR approach is designed to minimize the intrusiveness of active probing via enhancing the fault hypothesis and optimizing the action selection process. Our simulation results show that AIR is robust and scalable even in extreme scenarios such as large network sizes and high spurious and symptom loss rates.

In the second section, we show how network-level intrusion detection systems can integrate fault and intrusion detection to avoid wrongly identifying faults as intrusions. This decreases false alerts that often make network administrators turn off IDS systems. Thus, it is of crucial importance to rapidly and accurately identify both faults and intrusions for network-based IDS systems. We propose the HiFIND system that leverages data streaming techniques such as the reversible sketch. In contrast to existing IDSs, HiFIND (1) separates anomalies to limit false positives in detection, (2) is scalable to flow-level detection on high-speed networks, (3) is DoS resilient, (4) can distinguish SYN flooding and various port scans (mostly for worm propagation) for effective mitigation, and (5) enables aggregate detection over multiple routers/gateways. Both theoretical analysis and evaluation with several router traces show that HiFIND achieves these properties.

References

[1] M. Steinder and A. S. Sethi, "Probabilistic Fault Diagnosis in Communication Systems through Incremental Hypothesis Updating," *Computer Networks* Vol. 45. (2004): pp. 537–562.

[2] X. Ou, W. F. Boyer, and M. A. McQueen, "A Scalable Approach to Attack Graph Generation," *13th ACM Conference on Computer and Communications Security (CCS 2006)*, Alexandria, VA, October 2006.

[3] S. Klihger, S. Yemini, Y. Yemini, D. Ohsie and S. Stolfo, "A Coding Approach to Event Correlation," *Proceedings of the Fourth International Symposium on Intelligent Network Management*, 1995.

[4] M. Steinder and A. S. Sethi, "Increasing Robustness of Fault Localization through Analysis of Lost, Spurious, and Positive Symptoms," *Proceedings of IEEE INFOCOM*, New York, NY, 2002.

[5] K. Appleby G. Goldszmidt and M. Steinder, "Yemanja: A Layered Fault Localization System for Multidomain Computing Utilities," *Journal of Network and Systems Management* Vol. 10 pp. 171–194 (2002).

[6] R. I. Brodie, M. Ma, and S. Ma, "Optimizing Probe Selection for Fault Localization," *IEEE/IFIP (DSOM)*, Nancy, France 2001.

[7] I. Rish, M. Brodie, N. Daintsova, S. Ma, G. Grabarnik, "Real-Time Problem Determination in Distributed Systems Using Active Probing," *IEEE/IFIP (NOMS)*, Seoul, S. Korea, 2004.

[8] Al-Shaer, Y. Tang, "QoS Path Monitoring for Multicast Networks," *Journal of Network and System Management (JNSM)*, 2002. Vol. 10, pp. 357–381.

[9] J. Gao, G. Ker and P. Kermani, "Approaches to Building Self-Healing System Using Dependency Analysis," *IEEE/IFIP (NOMS)*, Seoul, S. Korea, 2004.

[10] G. Liu, A. K. Mok, E. J. Yang, "Composite Events for Network Event Correlation" *Integrated Network Management VI*, Boston, MA, 1999, pp. 247–260.

[11] G. Jakobson and M. D. Weissman, "Alarm Correlation," *IEEE Network* Vol. 7, (1993) pp. 52–59.

[12] D. Moore, V. Paxson, S. Savage, C. Shainon, S. Staniford, and N. Weaver, "The Spread of the Sapphire/Slammer Worm," at http://www.caida.org, 2003.

[13] G. Cormode and S. Muthukrishnan, "What's New: Finding Significant Differences in Network Data Streams," *Proceedings of IEEE Infocom*, Hong Kong, China, 2004.

[14] Cisco Inc, "Per-Packet Load Balancing, 2003," at http://www.cisco.com/univercd/cc/td/doc/product/software/ios120/120newft/120limit/120s/120s21/pplb.pdf.

[15] R. Schweller, Z. Li, Y. Chen, Y. Gao, A. Gopra, Y. Zhang, P. Dinda, M-Y. Kao, and G. Memik et al., "Reverse Hashing for High-Speed Network Monitoring: Algorithms, Evaluation, and Applications," *Proceedings of IEEE Infocom*, Barcelona, Spain, 2006.

[16] R. Schweller, A. Gupta, E. Parsons, and Y. Chen, "Reversible Sketches for Efficient and Accurate Change Detection over Network Data Streams," *IMC, Proceedings of the 4th ACM SIGCOMM Conference on Interner Measurement* (2004). pp. 207–212.

[17] Arbor Networks, "Intelligent Network Management with Peakflow Traffic," at http://www.arbornetworks.com/download.php.

[18] N. Duffield, C. Lund, and M. Thorup, "Flow Sampling under Hard Resource Constraints," *Proceedings of ACM SIGMETRICS*, New York, NY, 2004.

[19] D. Moore, "Inferring Internet Denial of Service Activity," *Proceedings of the 2001 USENIX Security Symposium*, Washington, DC, Aug. 2001.

[20] H. Wang, D. Zhang, and K. G. Shin, "Detecting SYN Flooding Attacks," *Proceedings of IEEE INFOCOM*, New York, NY, 2002.

[21] J. Jung, V. Paxson, A.W. Berger, H. Balakrishnan, "Fast Portscan Detection Using Sequential Hypothesis Testing," *Proceedings of the IEEE Symposium on Security and Privacy*, Oakland, CA, 2004.

[22] N. Weaver S. Staniford, and V. Paxson, "Very Fast Containment of Scanning Worms," *USENIX Security Symposium*, San Diego, CA, 2004.

[23] S. Venkataraman, D. Song, P. Gibbons, and A. Blum, "New Streaming Algorithms for Superspreader Detection," *The Annual Network and Distributed System Security Symposium (NDSS)*, San Diego, CA, 2005.

[24] R. R. Kompella, S. Singh, and G. Varghese, "On Scalable Attack Detection in the Network," *Proceedings of ACM/USENIX IMC*, Sicily, Italy, 2004.

[25] Q. G. Zhao, A. Kumar, and J. J. Xu, "Joint Data Streaming and Sampling Techniques for Detection of Super Sources and Destinations," *Proceedings of ACM/USENIX Internet Measurement Conference*, Berkeley, CA, 2005.

[26] B. Krishnamurthy, S. Sen, Y. Zhang, and Y. Chen, "Sketch-Based Change Detection: Methods, Evaluation, and Applications," *Proceedings of ACM SIGCOMM Internet Measurement Conference (IMC)*, Miami FL, 2003.

[27] V. Yegneswaran, P. Barford, J. Ullrich, "Internet Intrusions: Global Characteristics and Prevalence," *Proceedings of ACM SIGMETRICS*, San Diego, CA, 2003.

[28] G. Y. Z. Li and Y. Chen, "A Dos Resilient Flow-Level Intrusion Detection Approach for High-Speed Networks," *Proceedings of the IEEE International Conference on Distributed Computing Systems (ICDCS)*, Lisboa, Portugal, 2006.

[29] Y. Gao, Z. Li, and Y. Chen, "Towards a High-Speed Router-Based Anomaly/Intrusion Detection System," at http://list.cs.northwestern.edu/hpnaidm.html.

Index

A

*-property
  see no-write-down rules
1 + 1 automatic protection switching, 92–3
α LADS
  see ALPHATECH light autonomic defense
    systems
AAIRS
  see adaptive, agent-based intrusion
    response systems
access control, 39–40, 46–8
  based on subject-object relationships, 48
  models, 47–8. *see also individual models, e.g.,*
    protection matrix model
access control in distributed systems, 8–9,
    60–1, 76
  advanced approaches, 65–72
  multidomain, 69–70
  spatially-aware, 65, 70–2
  standards, 9, 61–5
access control lists (ACL), 50
  multiple principals and, 51
  packet filtering, 28
access masks, 48, 49, 53
access networks, 84, 85, 107–8
accidents, 172, 173
accountability, 3
accuracy
  for evaluation of fault localization
    techniques, 495
ACL
  see access control lists
active attacks, 26, 181–2
  definition, 425

insider, 427–8
outsider, 426
active integrated fault reasoning (AIR), 490,
    520
  challenges and problem formalization,
    492–5
  modules, 490–1, 495–502
  related work, 491–2
  simulation study, 502–6
active probing fault management
    approaches, 490, 491, 492, 520
  limitations, 492–3
adaptive, agent-based intrusion response
    systems (AAIRS), 392, 393–4
address resolution protocols
    (ARP), 21
address spoofing, 24, 273
ADEPTS intrusion response systems, 381,
    388–90
  evaluation, 408–10
ad hoc wireless networks, 459, 462
  security, 460
  survivability, 466
AFF
  see attack-free flow
AFN
  see attack-free node
agent security
  scheduling, 138
AH
  see authentication header
AIR
  see active integrated fault reasoning
alert aggregation, 281
  in result graphs, 296–8

alert correlation, 280–2
    in offline applications, 287–9
    previous work, 282
    vulnerability-centric approach, 11, 280–1,
        289–92, 298–300
alert hypothesis
    attack graphs for, 292–5
alert prediction
    attack graphs for, 295–6
all-optical networks (AON), 307
    security attack types, 309–10
    security considerations, 11–12, 307–8,
        312–13, 345
    security modeling, 315–20
    security monitoring methods, 313–15
    security monitoring relationships, 320–5
ALPHATECH light autonomic defense
        systems (α LADS), 390–2
analytical modeling, 205
    security, 179–87
    survivability, 192–204
    techniques, 174–9
    types, 173–4
anomaly-based intrusion detection, 35, 167
anonymous credential systems, 75–6
AON
    see all-optical networks
APS
    see automatic protection switching
arbitrary faults, 117
arc-path approaches, 102–3
ARP
    see address resolution protocols
asymmetric faults, 117, 119, 120, 158
attack-free flow (AFF), 316
attack-free node (AFN), 316
attack graphs, 11, 179, 247, 251–3, 280,
        283–4, 284–7
    for alert hypothesis and prediction, 292–6
    analysis, 266–7
    future work, 275
    illustration, 264–6
    monotonicity assumption, 273–4, 284
    network attack model, 253–4
    related work, 272–4
attribute assertions, 62
audit trail processing, 35
authentication, 26, 84, 165, 428–9, 436
    assertions, 45–6, 62
    biometric, 165–6
    cryptographic-based, 165
    distributed systems, 43–6
    entity, 32–3

link-state routing, 429
    types, 41–3
authentication header (AH), 34
authentication servers, 44
authorization, 61
    negative, 51–3
authorization decision assertions, 62
authorization service, 46
    implementation, 49–51
automatic protection switching (APS), 92–3
autonomous intrusion response systems,
        379, 404
autonomous mobile agents, 139–41
availability, 3, 27, 84, 152, 429
    wireless systems, 13, 460
availability faults, 159, 160–1, 163

B

Ballista project, 356
bandwidth protection, 419–21
Bell-LaPadula models, 9, 55–6
benchmarking
    intrusion response systems, 380–1, 407–10
    robustness, 352
benign faults, 117, 119
BGP
    see border gateway protocols
bidirectional line-switched rings (BLSR), 95
biometric identification, 165–6
bit-flips, 356, 357, 358
block ciphers, 30, 31, 32
BLSR
    see bidirectional line-switched rings
border gateway protocols (BGP), 21
brute-force attacks, 41, 281, 296, 298
Bücchi automata, 250–1
Byzantine faults
    see asymmetric faults

C

capability lists, 50
CardSpace, 73, 74–5
causal relationship between alerts, 282–3
CBC-MAC
    see cipher block chaining message
        authentication codes
CDI
    see constrained data items
challenge-response systems, 42–3
change-point monitoring (CPM), 509, 510
    HiFIND, 517

cipher block chaining message
authentication codes (CBC-MAC), 32,
464
ciphertext, 30
CITRA
see cooperative intrusion traceback and
response architecture
Clark-Wilson model, 56–7
certification rules, 57–8
enforcement rules, 58–9
CMU crashme benchmarks, 352
CNI
see critical national infrastructure
Code Red worms, 24, 183
combinatorial models
see nonstate space models
commission faults, 158
common-mode faults, 124–5
common pool protection, 107
communication faults, 160
computation tree logic (CTL), 248
confidentiality, 3–4, 26, 39, 84, 152, 172, 428,
436
information flow policy for, 53–5
link-state routing, 429
confidentiality faults, 159, 161, 164
prevention, 164
constrained data items (CDI), 57
constrained GEO-RBAC, 71
continuous-time Markov chains (CTMC),
10, 174–5
limitations, 177
network survivability modeling, 193–204
state transition, 216–17, 218
cooperating security managers (CSM),
392–3, 394
cooperative counter-DDoS entity, 406–7
cooperative intrusion traceback and
response architecture (CITRA), 404–5
corrective maintenance, 166
corruption of parameters error model, 357
CPM
see change-point monitoring
crash faults, 116
crashme benchmarks, 352
credential management, 75–6
credibility-based approaches, 129
credibility threshold principle, 129
critical action set minimization, 266, 267,
269, 270
critical national infrastructure (CNI), 81,
459
crosstalk attacks, 12, 309–10, 311, 345

conditions for detection, 320–5
current monitoring methods, 313–15
diagnostic algorithms, 310–11
features, 311–12
models, 315–20
monitoring policies, 311
nodes and flows, 316
cryptographic faults, 159, 161, 162
minimizing, 164
cryptographic protocols, 27, 30–2, 33–4,
164–5
phases, 32–3
cryptographic techniques, 3, 428–30, 436
CSM
see cooperating security managers
CTL
see computation tree logic
CTMC
see continuous-time Markov chains

D

data delay, 308
data distribution schemes, 126–7
data-level errors, 359
data value faults, 350
DDoS attacks
see distributed denial of service attacks
decentralization
survivability and, 9, 125, 126–7, 128–33,
141
decimation $(1, n, n)$ schemes, 127
deliberate exposure, 428
cryptographic countermeasures, 435
demand-wise shared protection (DSP), 93
demilitarized zones (DMZ), 29
denial of service (DoS) attacks, 23–4, 84,
159, 308
dependability 1–2, 150
attributes, 3, 152, 156–7
definition, 150–1, 155
fault models, 116–17, 118
ontology, 151, 152
quantitative analysis, 10, 172–3
see also information assurance
design for survivability, 9, 120–1, 122–3
decentralization, 125, 126–7
design for testability, 119–20
DHCP
see dynamic host configuration protocols
digital credentials, 67
digital identity, 72

digital identity management, 72, 76
  frameworks, 73–5
  research approaches, 75–6
digital signatures, 31–2, 35, 165
direct-monitors, 320
disclosure policies, 67
discrete logarithms, 31
discretionary security property, 56
disruption-tolerant networking, 466
distributed denial of service (DDoS) attacks,
      24, 380, 403
  prevention in link-state routing, 430
  primitives for responding to, 404
distributed denial of service (DDoS)
      handling systems, 380, 403–6, 412
  limitations, 406–7
distributed systems, 377–8
  access control, 8–9, 60–1, 76
  access control advance approaches, 65–72
  access control standards, 9, 61–5
  authentication, 43–6
  intrusion detection, 35, 213, 378
  intrusion response systems, 378–81, 412
  survivability of large systems, 128–33
distributing trust, 401–2
  on Internet, 402–3
disturbances, 154
diversity, 86–7, 125
  intrusion tolerance through diverse
      replicas, 398
  research issues, 398
  techniques for wireless systems, 465
DMZ
  see demilitarized zones
DNN
  see downstream neighbor nodes
DNS
  see domain name servers; domain name
      service
domain name servers (DNS), 124
domain name service (DNS), 21
  cache poisoning, 24, 25–6
domain name service (DNS)
      trustworthiness, 236–7
  scenarios, 238–40, 241
  stochastic game, 237–8
  stochastic model, 237
DoS attacks
  see denial of service attacks
downstream neighbor nodes (DNN), 315–16
driver error diffusion, 363, 364, 369
DSP
  see demand-wise shared protection

dynamic decision making intrusion response
      systems, 380, 388–97, 412
  research issues, 387–8
dynamic host configuration protocols
      (DHCP), 20–1
dynamic packet filters
  see stateful firewalls

E

EACL
  see extended access control list language
eavesdropping, 26, 308, 310, 464, 471,
      472
EDFA attacks
  see erbium doped fiber amplifier attacks
EMERALD
  see event monitoring enabling responses
      to anomalous live disturbances
encapsulated security payload (ESP), 34
end-to-end Internet resiliency, 107–8
end-to-end principle, 90
ENLU frameworks
  see extended node/link update
      frameworks
entity authentication, 32–3
erbium doped fiber amplifier (EDFA)
      attacks, 309
error models
  for OS robustness, 356–8
error propagation, 362, 365
  metrics, 363–5
error tolerance boundary, 155
escalation strategy, 106
ESP
  see encapsulated security payload
event monitoring enabling responses to
      anomalous live disturbances
      (EMERALD), 394–5
evil twins, 25
explicit-state algorithms, 250–1
  performance, 269, 271
exploit events, 158
exposure, 428
  cryptographic countermeasures, 435
extended access control list (EACL)
      language, 382
extended node/link update (ENLU)
      frameworks, 418
  for virtualized networking, 435–45
extensible access control markup language
      (XACML), 9, 40, 52, 61, 63–5

F

FAF
  see final attacked flow
fail-secure state, 181, 182–3, 187, 189–90
failure(s), 172, 215
  network, 81–2
  service, 155
failure avoidance
  see fault tolerance
failure-dependent path protection (FDPP)
  see shared path restoration
failure-independent path protection (FIPP)
  see shared backup path protection
failure mode analysis, 361, 362, 365
false denial of origin, 427
  cryptographic countermeasures, 434
false denial of receipt, 427
  cryptographic countermeasures, 434–5
fault(s), 155, 489
  dependability considerations, 116–17, 118
  notion, 115–16, 215
  prevention, 164–6
  prevention techniques, 82, 83–4, 92–3
  proposed novel framework, 157–64
  survivability considerations, 118–19
fault and security management
  integrated, 14, 489–90, 520. *see also* active integrated fault reasoning
  on high-speed networks, 506–8, 520. *see also* high-speed flow-level intrusion detection
fault-error-failure processes, 215
fault forecasting, 166
fault injection, 356
  timing, 358, 360–1
fault localization, 490
  active probing approaches, 490, 492
  passive approaches, 490, 491–2, 493
  see also active integrated fault reasoning
fault management
  functions, 87–8
  see also fault and security management
fault-masking techniques, 397
fault models
  dependability considerations, 116–17, 118
  survivability considerations, 118–19, 141
fault prevention
  proposed novel framework, 164–6
fault propagation, 105–6
fault reasoning, 490–1, 495–6
  heuristic algorithm for, 497–8

fault removal
  proposed novel framework, 166–7
faults with unauthorized access (FUA), 158–60
fault tolerance, 9, 121, 123–4
  performance degradation, 362
  proposed novel framework, 166
feedback control systems, 154–5
fiber attacks, 309
fidelity evaluation
  fault hypotheses, 491, 495, 498–500
filters, 154
final attacked flow (FAF), 316
fingerprint-based authentication, 165
firewalls, 27–30, 257
five-fault hybrid fault models, 117
five-stage transformation models, 133–6
FUA
  see faults with unauthorized access
fuzz error models, 356–7

G

GAA-API
  see generic authorization and access control-application programming interface
gain competition attacks, 309, 315
GCP
  see global computing platforms
generalized stochastic Petri nets (GSPN), 178–9
generalized trunk diversity, 92–3
general packet radio service (GPRS), 461
  seamless operation between WLAN and, 462–3
generic authorization and access control-application programming interface (GAA-API), 381–3
  significance, 383–4
GEO-RBAC, 71–2
GID
  see group identifiers
global computing platforms (GCP), 130–1
  resources, 131
GPRS
  see general packet radio service
graceful degradation, 122
group identifiers (GID), 41, 42, 48, 50–1
GSPN
  see generalized stochastic Petri nets

H

Hamiltonian cycles, 452–4
hash functions, 31, 32, 127
hierarchical GEO-RBAC, 71
HiFIND
    see high-speed flow-level intrusion
        detection
Higgins Trust framework, 75
higher-level modeling formalisms, 10, 177–9
high-speed flow-level intrusion detection
        (HiFIND), 507, 508, 520
    algorithm, 513–14
    evaluation, 515–19
    related work, 508–11
    system architecture, 511–12
    threat model, 512–13
    existing network IDSs, 516–17
HMF
    see human-made faults
honeypots
    see Internet traps
horizontal scans (Hscan), 512–13
    detection, 513–17
    detection validation, 518
host(s), 255
host-based intrusion detection, 35
Hscan
    see horizontal scans
human-made faults (HMF), 158
    categories, 158–64
hybrid crypto-biometric protocols, 165–6
hybrid fault models, 118–19
hybrid wireless networks, 461
    architecture, 461–2
hypoexponential distribution
    threat modeling, 183

I

IA
    see information assurance
ICMP PING, 286
Idemix, 75–6
identifiers, 72
    group, 41, 42, 48, 50–1
    id, 255
    security, 41
    subject, 48
identity management federations, 72–3
identity provider(s), 72
identity provider-centric frameworks,
        73–4

idle handoffs, 475–6
IDS
    see intrusion detection systems
IF
    see innocent flow
I-Graphs
    see intrusion graphs
IKE
    see Internet key exchange
ILA schemes
    see information-level authentication
        schemes
ILC schemes
    see information-level confidentiality
        schemes
ILP
    see integer linear programming problems
information assurance (IA), 2, 3–6, 19,
        152–3
    proposed novel framework, 9–10, 154–5,
        168
    rationale, 209–10
    wireless networks, 459–60, 484–5
information flow policy, 53–5
information-level authentication (ILA)
        schemes
    routing frameworks, 436–7
information-level confidentiality (ILC)
        schemes
    routing frameworks, 436–7
innocent flow (IF), 316, 322
insertion attacks, 426, 427
insider deliberate exposure attacks, 428
    cryptographic countermeasures, 435
insider false denial of origin attack, 427
    cryptographic countermeasures, 434
insider false denial of receipt attack, 427
    cryptographic countermeasures, 434–5
insider masquerading attacks, 427
    cryptographic countermeasures, 433
insider nondeliberate exposure attacks, 428
    cryptographic countermeasures, 435
insider overload attacks, 427
    cryptographic countermeasures, 433–4
insider replay attack, 427
    cryptographic countermeasures, 433
insider substitution attacks, 427
    cryptographic countermeasures, 433
integer linear programming (ILP)
        problems, 103–4
integrity, 3–4, 26, 39, 84, 152, 172, 428, 436
integrity faults, 159, 161, 163
    prevention, 164–5

integrity verification procedures (IVP), 57
intentional faults, 119
interference attacks, 427, 428
  cryptographic countermeasures, 432
Internet
  distributing trust, 402–3
  typical network architecture, 84–5
Internet key exchange (IKE), 34
Internet protocol (IP), 20
Internet protocol (IP) addresses
  finding, 21
  spoofing, 24, 273
Internet traps, 36
intruders, 256–7
intrusion(s), 158, 215
  causes, 216
  intrusion response systems, 378–81, 412
  modeling, 216–17
intrusion detection, 34–6
intrusion detection systems (IDS), 11, 35–6, 167, 256, 378
  distributed systems, 35, 213, 378
  for high-speed networks, 506–7. *see also* high-speed flow-level intrusion detection
  limitations, 279
  network-based, 489–90, 520
  scheduling, 138–9
  traffic conditions and flow-level detection, 508–10
intrusion graphs (I-Graphs), 389
intrusion prevention systems (IPS), 12–13, 27, 36, 378
  see also McAfee Intrushield intrusion prevention systems; Snort
intrusion response systems (IRS), 12–13, 36, 378–9, 412
  autonomous, 379, 404
  benchmarking, 380–1, 407–10
  classification, 379–80
  DDoS attacks, 380, 403–7
  future work, 410–11
intrusion tolerance through diverse replicas, 380, 397, 398–403, 412
intrusion-tolerant systems, 180–1
  semi-Markov process modeling, 181–4
  stochastic modeling, 183–4
IP
  see Internet protocol
IPS
  see intrusion prevention systems
IPSec, 33–4

IRS
  see intrusion response systems
IVP
  see integrity verification procedures

J

JCA
  see joint-capacity allocation
joint-capacity allocation (JCA), 102

K

Kasumi algorithms, 464
KEK
  see key-encrypting keys
Kerberos, 33, 44, 45
key connectivity, 481–4
key-encrypting keys (KEK), 454–5
key management
  heterogeneous sensor networks, 476–84
  link-state routing and, 449
  third-generation wireless systems, 464
Keynote, 67, 68
knapsack problems, 122–3
k-original attack flow diagnosable networks, 329–30
  connection status detection, 334–5
  diagnostic conditions, 330–3
Krings five-stage transformation model, 133–6

L

LAMBDA, 272
linear temporal logic (LTL), 248, 250
link-based survivability schemes, 91
link restoration
  see span restoration
link-state advertisement (LSA), 419–20, 423–4, 430
  definition, 424
link-state routing model, 424–5
  cryptographic countermeasures against attacks, 428–35
  insider attacks, 426, 427–8
  outsider attacks, 426–7
  threats, 425–8, 429
link-state routing protocols, 418
  secure group key management, 449–57
local policies
  GAA-API frameworks, 383

LSA
  see link-state advertisement
LTL
  see linear temporal logic

——— M

MAC
  message authentication codes
MAC address
  see medium access control address
macro data-flow graph *G*, 131
maintainability, 151, 152, 153, 156, 157, 210
makespan, 137
malicious attempt faults, 159–60, 161, 162,
    168
malicious faults
  see asymmetric faults
malware, 159
MAN
  see metropolitan area networks
MANET
  see mobile ad hoc networks
man-in-the-middle attacks, 159, 473
  prevention, 42
Markov models, 6, 174–6
  network survivability, 191–2
  security modeling, 179–80
Markov reward models, 175–6
masquerading attacks, 26, 308, 425, 426, 427
  cryptographic countermeasures, 431, 433
massive attacks, 121, 128, 130, 132
McAfee Internet Security Suite (ISS), 385–6
McAfee Intrushield Intrusion Prevention
    Systems, 386
MCSA problems
  see minimum critical set of action
    problems
MCT
  see Monte Carlo tests
mean effort to failure (METF), 273
medium access control (MAC) address, 20–1
mesh survivability, 86, 96–102
message authentication, 26
message authentication codes (MAC), 31, 32
message integrity checks (MIC), 31, 32
METF
  see mean effort to failure
metropolitan area networks (MAN), 84, 85
MIC
  see message integrity checks
Microsoft Windows 2000

negative authorization, 52–3
Milenage algorithms, 464
minimum critical set of action (MCSA)
    problems, 267, 269
MIP problems
  see mixed integer linear programming
    problems
misuse-based intrusion detection, 167
mixed integer linear programming (MIP)
    problems, 103–4
mobile ad hoc networks (MANET), 463
  current survivability approaches, 466
mobile cellular networks, 81, 85
  composite availability and performance
    model, 195–7
  computation of performance-oriented
    survivability metrics, 199–204
  current survivability approaches, 465–6
  hybrid wireless architecture, 461–2,
    467–70
  performance model, 194–5
  pure availability model, 193–4
  survivability, 190
  survivability modeling, 197–9
  system description, 192–3
  wide-area systems, 462–3
model checking, 247, 407
  advantage, 272
  explicit-state, 250–1, 269, 271
  future work, 275
  related work, 272–4
  symbolic, 248–50, 269, 271
monitor models, 345
monitor nodes, 315
  models, 318–20
monitor-segments, 321–5, 345
Monte Carlo tests (MCT), 132
MPLS networks
  see multiprotocol label switched networks
multilayer survivability, 105–7
multiprotocol label switched (MPLS)
    networks, 83
  mesh survivability, 96
  survivability, 105–6
multistep network intrusions, 279
  countermeasures, 11, 279–80, 300. *see also*
    vulnerability-centric alert correlation

——— N

negative authorization, 51–3
negotiation trees, 69

nested-loop correlation approach, 287–8
  limitations, 288, 300
  using queue graph, 290
NetSTAT, 273
network(s)
  attack model, 253–4
  components, 255–7
  illustration, 257–64
  modeling toolkit, 271
network attack graphs, 253–7, 264–6
  analysis, 266–9
network-based intrusion detection, 35
network communications, 20–3
networked information systems, 1–2, 10,
    209, 210
network failures, 81–2
network service architecture, 417–18
network survivability, 9, 82, 190
  analytical modeling, 10, 192–204
  definition, 191
  modeling, 190–2. *see also* mobile cellular
    networks
  multilayer networks, 105–7
  research, 86, 107–8
  security, 172–3
  techniques, 82–3, 107
  wireless systems, 460, 465–6, 467–70
  wireless systems, interactions between
    security, 460, 470, 472–5
node models, 315
nondeliberate exposure, 428
nonhuman-made faults (NHMF), 158, 160
nonmalicious faults, 158
nonmonitors, 321, 322–3
nonrepudiation, 3, 10, 26–7, 84, 156–7, 165
nonstate space models, 173–4
nontechnical prevention techniques, 83
no-read-up rules, 54
no-write-down rules, 54–5, 56
NuSMV, 248, 250
N-version software, 125
nyms, 72

O

OAF
  see original attack flow
obstruction attacks
  insider, 427
  outsider, 426–7
OFC
  see one-way function chains

offline alert correlation, 287–9
OHM
  see one-hop monitors
omission faults, 116, 158
  strictly asymmetric, 117
  symmetric, 117
one-hop monitors (OHM), 320–1, 336, 339
one-original attack flow diagnosable
    networks, 320
  connection routing algorithms, 340–2
  connection status detection, 327–9
  diagnosable conditions, 325–6
  sparse monitoring, 336–40
one-way function chains (OFC), 449–51
open-loop control systems, 155
open shortest path first (OSPF), 21, 418, 430
  cryptographic authentication, 429
open shortest path first-extension (OSPF-E),
    440–2
  packet processing, 442–4
operating systems (OS)
  service error exposure, 364, 366, 368–9
operating systems (OS) robustness
    evaluation, 12, 349, 370
  case study, 351–2, 353, 354–5, 359–61,
    363–6
  error model and workload selection, 351,
    355–9
  goals, 350, 352–3
  target system, 350–1, 353–4
  techniques, 350
operational profiling
  operating system behavior, 350
OPPR
  see optical path protection rings
optical amplifier attacks, 309
optical fiber-based networks, 307
optical path protection rings (OPPR), 94
optical shared protection rings (OSPR), 95
optical time domain refractometries
    (OTDR), 315
optimality, 125-6, 133
original attack flow (OAF), 316
  sparse monitoring and routing
    algorithms, 336–42
OS
  see operating systems
OSPF
  see open shortest path first
OSPF-E
  see open shortest path first-extension
OSPR
  see optical shared protection rings

OTDR
   see optical time domain refractometries
outsider interference attacks, 427
   cryptographic countermeasures, 432
outsider replay attacks, 427
   cryptographic countermeasures, 432
outsider wiretapping attacks, 432
   cryptographic countermeasures, 432
overload attacks, 427
   cryptographic countermeasures, 430, 431,
     433–4

P

packet filters, 27–30
PAN
   see primary attacked nodes
partial execution on reliable resources, 129
PASIS project, 126
passive attacks, 26
   cryptographic countermeasures, 431, 432
   definition, 425
   outsider, 426
passive fault management techniques, 490,
    491–2, 493
   active integrated fault reasoning, 502–5
password-based authentication, 32–3, 41–2,
    43–4
path-based survivability schemes, 91
path restoration
   see shared path restoration
p-cycles, 99–102
PD
   see policy decision points
PDP
   see policy decision points
pendant nodes, 336
penetration tests, 36, 280
PEP
   see policy enforcement points
performability, 3
performance
   correlation engine, 298–9
   decentralized storage and, 126–7
   evaluation techniques, 108
   explicit-state vs. symbolic algorithms, 269,
    271
   fault localization techniques, 495
   large distributed systems, 128–33
   network survivability, 191–204
performance degradation
   fault-tolerant systems, 362

performance management, 87, 88
perimeter security, 27–30
permission masks
   see access masks
pharming attacks, 25–6
phishing attacks, 25–6
ping, 167
plaintext, 30
$p - m - n$ threshold schemes, 126
policy decision points (PD), 46–7, 63–4
policy enforcement points (PEP), 46,
    63, 64
port numbers, 20, 21–2
port scans
   detection, 507
   detection using HiFIND, 512–18
   existing detection schemes, 511–12
   HiFIND vs. other existing IDSs, 516–17
preventive maintenance, 166
primary attacked nodes (PAN), 316
primitives, 30–2
   classification, 31
   for responding to DDoS, 404
private key encryption, 31
privilege graphs, 273
probabilistic certification, 131–2
problem transformation, 133–6
protection
   mechanisms, 27–34
   vs. restoration, 88–90
protection matrix model, 48–9
protection state, 47, 55
provider-centric identity management
    frameworks, 73, 74–5
proxy firewalls, 28–9
public key cryptography, 45
public key encryption, 31–2

Q

QoS
   see quality of service
quality of service (QoS) degradation, 81, 82,
    88, 308, 309
quantitative security evaluation, 10, 210–12,
    240, 242
   based on stochastic modeling, 214–21
   lack of viable techniques, 5–6
   previous work, 212–13
queue graphs, 281, 289–92
   defined, 289–90

R

rate-based intrusion prevention systems, 36
RBAC models
  see role-based access control models
real-time detection, 280
reconnaissance, 26
redundancy, 86, 87, 101–2
  building survivable services, 398–9
  fault tolerance, 123–4
reexecution on reliable resources, 129–30,
    132
reference monitors
  see authentication service
regulators, 155
relative covering ratio, 501–2
reliability, 3, 152, 153, 156, 157
  key management schemes heterogeneous
    sensor networks, 481–2
  optimization of, 126
relying parties
  see service providers
replay attacks, 165
  cryptographic countermeasures, 432, 433
replicated state machines
  trustworthy services using, 401–2
repudiation attacks, 426, 427, 431
rerouting
  algorithms, 91
  location of, 90–1
resiliency, 418–19, 446
  end-to-end Internet, 107–8
  of key management schemes for
    heterogeneous sensor networks, 482–4
resilient network routing architectures
  components, 423–4
  routing perspectives, 418, 446
  virtualization and routing, 13, 435–45
resilient overlay networks, 418
restoration of service, 88, 89–90
  all-optical networks, 313
  DeNISSE(RN), 88, 89
  layer responsible for, 90
  rerouting location, 90–1
result graphs, 290
  alert aggregation, 296–8
ring-based survivability, 93–4
  types, 94–5
  vs. *p*-cycles, 99–101
RIP
  see routing information protocols
robustness evaluation of operating systems,
    12, 349, 370

  case study, 351–2, 353, 354–5, 359–61,
    363–6
  error model and workload selection, 351,
    355–9
  goals, 350, 352–3
  target system, 350–1, 353–4
  techniques, 350
Roger circumflex approach, 235
role-based access control (RBAC) models, 9,
    59–60, 70–1
  multidomain, 69–70
role hierarchy, 60
root name servers, 21
routers
  cryptographic countermeasures against
    attacks, 433–5
  defined, 418
  hidden information idea, 419–20
  ongoing research, 405
routing algorithms
  single original attack flow networks,
    336–42
  two original attack flow networks, 342–5
routing information protocols (RIP), 21
routing protocol(s), 21, 418
routing protocol extension, 440–4

S

SAF
  see secondary attacked flow
safety, 3, 4, 151, 152, 153, 156, 157, 210, 248,
    249
SAML
  see security assertion markup language
SAN
  see secondary attacked nodes
SBPP
  see shared backup path protection
SCA
  see spare-capacity allocation
scalable intrusion-tolerant architecture
    (SITAR), 399
  analytical modeling, 188–90
  basic architecture, 188
scenario graphs, 11, 247
  algorithms, 248–51
  future work, 274–5
scheduling problems, 135, 136–9
SC services
  see survivable critical services
SecComm, 398

secondary attacked flow (SAF), 316
secondary attacked nodes (SAN), 316
secret key encryption, 30
secret sharing (*m*, *m*, *n*) schemes, 127
secure sockets layer (SSL), 34
secure software systems
    classification, 180
secure state, 55, 56
secure state machine replication
    architecture, 402–3
security, 1–2, 8, 19, 150, 172
    analytical modeling, 179–80
    attributes, 3–4, 152, 156–7, 172
    problems, 22–3
    quantitative evaluation. *see* quantitative
        security evaluation
    survivability, 172–3
    wireless systems. *see* under wireless
        network(s)
    see also information assurance
security agility, 396
security assertion markup language (SAML),
    9, 45–6, 61–3
security assurances, 3
security attack(s), 20, 22–3, 172, 489
    categories, 308
    examples, 23–6
    link-state routing, 425–8, 429
    types, 26
    see also all-optical networks
security attacker behavior
    game theoretic method, 223–4
    motivations, 221–2
    reward and cost, 222–3, 230–1
    stochastic game model, 223–35, 242
security attacker profiling, 235–6
security groups, 50–1
security identifiers (SID), 41, 48
security modeling, 179–83
    attacker's behavior and system responses,
        183–4
    SITAR security system, 188–90
    steady state probabilities, 184–7
security services, 8, 26–7
self-healing rings (SHR), 469, 470
semi-Markov processes (SMP), 176–7
    model for intrusion-tolerant systems,
        181–3, 185
sequence number guessing attacks, 24
service disruption attacks, 309–10
service error permeability, 363, 366, 367
service failure, 155
service providers, 72

service restoration, 88, 89–90
    all-optical networks, 313
    DeNISSE(RN), 88, 89
    layer responsible for, 90
    rerouting location, 90–1
shared backup path protection (SBPP),
    96–8
shared keys, 44
shared path protection (SPP)
    see shared backup path protection
shared path restoration (SPR), 98–9
shared-risk link groups (SRLG), 106
SHARPE
    see symbolic hierarchical automated
        reliability and performance evaluator
Shibboleth, 73–4
SHR
    see self-healing rings
SID
    see security identifiers
simple security property
    see no-read-up rules
single sign-on, 45–6, 52, 62
SITAR
    see scalable intrusion-tolerant architecture
sliding window approach, 287–8
slow attacks, 11, 280, 288
SNA methods
    see survivability network analysis methods
sniffing, 84, 426, 431, 437
    cryptographic countermeasures, 432
Snort, 35–6, 279, 287, 298–9, 384
Snort inline, 384–5
spanning cycles, 451–2
span restoration, 96
spare-capacity allocation (SCA), 102, 104
sparse monitoring, 345
    one-original attack flow, 336–40
    two-original attack flow, 342–5
spatially-aware access control systems, 65,
    70–2
spatial role schema, 71
SPIN model checkers, 250, 271
splitting (*n*, *n*, *n*) scheme, 127
SPN
    see stochastic Petri nets
spoofing, 308
    address, 24, 273
spot-checking, 129–30
SPR
    see shared path restoration
SRLG
    see shared-risk link groups

SRN
   see stochastic reward nets
SSL
   see secure sockets layer
stateful firewalls, 28
state space models, 173, 174
static decision making intrusion response
     systems, 379–80, 381–6, 412
   characteristics, 381
stochastic game theory
   attacker behavior, 223–31, 242
   DNS service, 237–8
   one possible attack action, 231–2
   two possible attack actions, 233–5
stochastic modeling
   DNS service, 236–7
   security evaluation, 10, 216–21, 242
stochastic Petri nets (SPN), 174, 177–9
stochastic reward nets (SRN), 179
   survivability model, 200–3
stop forwarding attacks, 427, 431
straddling spans, 100
stream ciphers, 30
strictly omissive asymmetric faults, 117
striping scheme
   see decimation $(1, n, n)$ scheme
stub release, 98
subject profiles, 67
substitution attacks, 426, 427
survivability network analysis (SNA)
     methods, 114, 121–3
survivable critical (SC) services, 417–18, 438
   bandwidth protection, 420–3
survivable network design
   techniques, 82, 102–5
   traffic restoration, 86–91, 469
   typical architecture, 84–6
survivable rings, 93–4
   types, 94–5
   p–cycles, 99–101
survival by defense enabling, 400–1
switching node attacks, 309–10
symbolic algorithms, 248–50
   performance, 269, 271
symbolic hierarchical automated reliability
     and performance evaluator (SHARPE),
     179
symmetric faults, 117, 119
symptom-fault causality graphs, 490
symptom-intrusion causality graphs, 490
system survivability, 4, 7, 171–2
   applications, 139–41
   definition, 113–15

design, 120–1
   impact of fault models, 118–19, 141
   large distributed systems, 128–33
system-wide policies
   GAA-API frameworks, 383
system workload, 358, 361

T

3GPP
   see third-generation partnership project
TCP
   see transmission control protocols
TCP SYN flood attacks, 23–4
   detection, 507
   detection using HiFIND, 512–518
   existing detection schemes, 511–12
   HiFIND vs. other existing IDSs, 516–17
technical prevention techniques, 83
third-generation partnership project (3GPP)
   security mechanisms, 464
threshold random walk (TRW), 509–10
   HiFIND, 516–17
threshold schemes, 126–7
ticket(s), 44
ticket-granting tickets, 45
topological vulnerability analysis, 11, 280
   techniques, 283–4
topping attacks, 310
TP
   see transformation procedures
TR
   see trunk reservation
traffic analysis attacks, 308
traffic engineering
   network robustness, 419–23, 446
traffic management, 82–3, 87–8
   recovery techniques, 91–102
   service restoration, 88, 89–90
transactions, 56–7
transformation procedures (TP), 57
   certification rules, 57–8
transient data level errors, 359
transient faults, 116
transmission control protocols (TCP), 20, 23
transmissive asymmetric faults, 117
transmissive symmetric faults, 117
transport layer protocols, 20
transport layer security (TLS)
   see secure sockets layer
transshipment approaches, 102
Trojan horse, 54–5, 118, 161–3, 308

trunk reservation (TR), 421
trust, 255
    notion, 65–6, 156
trusted path functionality, 42
trust negotiation, 65–6
trust tickets, 68
trustworthiness
    domain name service, 236–40, 241
    evaluation, 10, 209, 210–11
Trust-X, 67, 68
    negotiation modes, 69
TRW
    see threshold random walk
two-original attack flow diagnosable
        networks
    sparse monitoring and routing, 342–5

U

UDI
    see unconstrained data items
UDP
    see user datagram protocols
unconstrained data items (UDI), 57
unidirectional path-switched rings (UPSR),
        94
UNN
    see upstream neighbor nodes
UPSR
    see unidirectional path-switched rings
upstream neighbor nodes (UNN), 315
user(s), 72
user-centric identity management
        frameworks, 73–4
user datagram protocols (UDP), 20
user identification, 40–1

V

verifiers, 131
vertical scans (Vscan), 513
    detection, 513–16
    detection validation, 518
VeryIDX project, 76
virtual cards, 74
virtualized networking
    enabling framework, 435–45
virtual network analysis simulators (VNAS),
        444–5
virtual private networks (VPN), 85
virtual trust routing and provisioning
        domains (VTRouP), 438–9

VNA
    see virtual network analysis simulators
voting approaches, 128–9
VPN
    see virtual private networks
Vscan
    see vertical scans
VTRouP
    see virtual trust routing and provisioning
        domains
vulnerability
    assessment, 36
    intrusion response systems, 410
    model checking, 273
    network-centric computing, 149–50
vulnerability-centric alert correlation, 11,
        280–2, 289–92
    empirical results, 298–300
vulnerability scanners, 36
    limitations, 279–80

W

WAN
    see wide area networks
wavelength division multiplexed (WDM)
        modes, 307
wavelength selective switches (WSS), 309
WDM modes
    see wavelength division multiplexed modes
WEP protocols
    see wired equivalent privacy protocols
wide area networks (WAN), 84, 85
Windows CE .Net
    error model, 359–61
    robustness evaluation, 351–2, 366–9
    robustness evaluation goals, 354
    workload, 361
wired equivalent privacy (WEP) protocols,
        32
wireless access networks (WAN)
    survivability, 190–1
wireless local area networks (WLAN), 459,
        461–2
    seamless operation between GPRS, 462–3
wireless network(s), 459, 461
    framework for comprehensive treatment
        of IA problems, 467–70, 471–2, 485
    hybrid architectures, 461–2
    IA, 459–60, 484–5
    interactions between IA components, 460,
        470, 472–5

security, 13, 460
security, current approaches, 463–5
survivability, 13, 460
survivability, current approaches, 465–6
wireless sensor networks (WSN), 459, 463
current security approaches, 464–5
current survivability approaches, 466
information assurance, 460
key management in heterogeneous
networks, 476–84
WLAN
see wireless local area networks
workers, 131
worm attacks, 24–5
WSN
see wireless sensor networks

WSS
see wavelength selective switches

X

XACML
see extensible access control markup
language
X-GTRBAC, 69–70
X-TNL, 68

Z

zero-day exploits, 25
zero-knowledge proof protocols, 76
Zotob virus, 161

Printed and bound by CPI Group (UK) Ltd, Croydon, CR0 4YY

03/10/2024

01040313-0005